SCOTCH: THE FORMATIVE YEARS

By the same author

Scotch Made Easy
published by Hutchinson

House of Sanderson
published by Sanderson

SCOTCH:
THE FORMATIVE YEARS

Ross Wilson

Constable London

First published 1970
by Constable & Company Ltd
10 Orange Street, London WC2
© *by Ross Wilson 1970*
SBN 09 456970 3
Printed in Great Britain by
Cox &Wyman Ltd, London, Fakenham and Reading

Contents

Contents

Illustrations

Foreword

FOR NEARLY two decades I have worked journalistically alongside Ross Wilson and I have admired him for his dedication to any task undertaken, his expertise, and the scholarship with which commissions are performed. His editors appreciate the promptness with which copy is delivered to them, and the skill by which the job of work has been completed.

Therefore when he suggested to me the writing of a series of articles which form the basis of this book, I can honestly say that I know of no other man who could, or would, have undertaken this monumental task; or whom I would have encouraged to do the work. The research which covered many years, and the task of writing it, have been a labour of love for this man, who is so dedicated to the success story of the Scotch whisky industry.

The final result, I hope, will be as satisfying to those people all over the world who will read the book, as it was to me reading the chapters as they appeared. I can only compare that satisfaction to me to the lovely feeling I get on my palate after drinking a drop or two of a fine old Scotch malt whisky.

The industry as it is presently constituted has not a long history, but what a colourful one it is from the numbers of interesting and adventurous individuals it has engendered! What a source of revenue it has been to the hard-pressed economy of this country, and I don't mean in the number of pounds sterling it has earned! I want to emphasise the incalculable openings it has made for British trade overseas, and the vast amount of hard and soft currencies accruing therefrom.

Out of the welter of interesting facts which Ross Wilson has assembled in this book, the references to the origin of blending will appeal to all those like myself, who have wanted to know who it was that started the blending of Scotch whisky commercially. The point is settled by him, I think, once and for all, in his account of the pioneers, two world-famed firms still operating today. Trade members will also be much interested in the story told about forestalling (anticipating increases in excise duties) and the action taken by successive Governments to restrict clearances from bond prior to a budget.

I may be wrong, but I think this book is, and will be a long time, the only authoritative book on the fascinating way that Scotch whisky has grown to be the drink of the world today, ousting brandy as the favourite drink of the Briton.

Hector King. Editor of *The Wine and Spirit Trade Record* for twenty-one years.

I

The storm brews

SCOTCH WHISKY achieved its world fame and acceptance through the skill and acumen of the blenders. The distillers certainly did their share; they produced superlative spirits. There lay part of the disadvantage: none of the hundred or more of them was able to produce year after year a consistently uniform beverage in sufficient quantity to make a world-wide appeal for itself alone. That was where the blenders stepped in: they blended, or mixed, the spirits of many distilleries to market in increasing amounts a beverage of consistent and uniform quality, a quality adjusted to appeal to the palates and pockets of their customers.

Their road to success was not unattended with difficulties. They were, above all, blenders, though some of them became in due course distillers, if only to ensure some of their supplies and to gain the advantage of so describing themselves. But the question was asked whether they were blending whiskies, or whether they were mixing whisky with silent, or neutral spirits.

For, basically, they were mixing spirits obtained by two different methods of distillation: on the one hand, unquestioned whisky obtained via the traditional pot still as had been in use for generations; on the other, spirit yielded from the then newfangled patent still.

No one could quarrel with the pot still; its name alone describes it and it was the historic birthplace of whisky. It is, in effect, a copper pot over a fire, a pot which is first filled with a weak alcoholic liquid, the wash, and the alcoholic element has then to be separated by distillation. At the end of one such operation, the distillate undergoes the same process again to yield the heart of the matter. Even so, only the middle runnings of this second distillation are accepted to graduate as the beverage whisky. So it had always been; there could be no argument.

But in the case of the rival patent still – its name alone would betray its modernity – the finished spirit was, and is, achieved by means of an interchange of heat in two columns in one continuous operation. Put wash in at one end and out comes drinkable spirit at the other. It was originally patented by Aeneas Coffey, one time Inspector-General of Excise in Ireland and later of the Dock Distillery in Dublin, in 1831, to begin work in late 1832. Coffey transferred to London and the first still of his patent to be set up in Scotland was established at Port Dundas, near Glasgow, around 1840. It was called the patent still simply as the easiest way of describing the newcomer. After teething troubles at Port Dundas and elsewhere, its use spread rapidly in the industrial Lowlands of Scotland. In time, and with the aid particularly of Gladstone, who as Chancellor of the Exchequer amended the Excise laws and regulations, the idea was conceived and practised of mixing, or blending, spirits from the patent still with whisky from old-fashioned pot stills.

This mixing began about 1860 or soon after, but details need not distract us beyond two points: first, patent still spirit, produced at about 165 to 168 degrees proof on the British scale of measurement as against 125 for pot still whisky was of much lighter and less pronounced character and flavour than the pot still spirit, lacking as it did so much of the fusel oil and higher alcohols to be found in the pot still product; secondly, it was much more up-to-date and cheaper to make than the traditional whisky.

There was the rub: was it entitled to the name whisky? Or was it just a cheap neutral spirit, silent in more ways than one – about its ancestry, for instance? One thing was indisputable: the success of the blenders. By the nineties they had conquered the English market and were beginning a world campaign. Then the whole thing came to a head.

As the social revolution of that closing decade of the century opened, the House of Commons appointed, in 1890, and reappointed in 1891 a select committee on British and Foreign Spirits. It was set up to consider 'whether, on grounds of public health, it is desirable that certain classes of spirits, British and foreign, should be kept in bond for a definite period before they are allowed to pass into consumption, and to inquire into the system of blending British and foreign spirits in or out of bond, and into the propriety of applying the Sale of Food and Drugs Acts and the Merchandise Marks Act to the case of British and foreign spirits and mixtures of British and foreign spirits, and also into the sale of ether as an intoxicant'.

It was like the warning breeze before the storm, before a gale which was to sweep the main protagonists into the police court and finally before a royal commission. It was only then, some twenty years after this early first probing, that the matter was settled whether blending, as applied to whisky, was a real blending of whiskies or the counterfeit admixture of neutral spirits, unable to be called whisky, to the only spirit entitled to that name, the product, that is, of the traditional pot still. In short, pot still spirit is whisky; what is patent still spirit?

Some of the select committee's findings deserve quoting. For instance: 'There is no exact legal definition of spirits going by popular names, such as whiskey [the spelling then, consistently], brandy, rum or silent spirits. Some witnesses desire to define whiskey as the spirit made in pot stills, and would deny that name to spirits made in patent stills, even though the proportion of malt and grain used in the production might be the same in both. Some of the distillers from malt desired that their whiskey should be called "malt whiskey" though the general name "whiskey" might be extended to those who mix malt with grain. On the other hand, certain distillers in Belfast and Scotland urged that spirits distilled in patent stills from malt and grain were entitled to be considered as whiskey; that they are used sometimes as such directly, and are now largely employed in blending pot still whiskey. They gave evidence that there was increased demand for whiskey of a milder kind, and that blends of pot still and patent still whiskey were in large demand by the consumers, who thus obtained a cheaper and milder whiskey containing a smaller quantity of fusel oil and other by-products.'

Again: 'Your Committee do not attempt a legal definition of whiskey . . . Whiskey is certainly a spirit consisting of alcohol and water, with a small quantity of by-products coming from malt or grain, which give to it a peculiar taste and aroma. It may be diluted with a certain quantity of water without ceasing to be whiskey, and it may be diluted with spirits containing little of the by-products to suit the pocket and palate of customers, and it still goes by the popular

3

name of whiskey. Your Committee are unable to restrict the use of the name as long as the spirits added are pure and contain no noxious ingredients.'

Their findings seemed to bless and encourage the spread of the new whisky blends, and that was just where the trouble lay. They were accepted as going 'by the popular name of whiskey', but no watertight legal definition was attempted. None had been asked for; it was outside their terms of reference. They were not invited to suggest or recommend any definition, though one could expect findings arising from an exhaustive inquiry to include, as a matter of expedient wisdom, things other than the legalistically interpreted minimum.

The committee were, happily, most explicit on blending itself. They reported: 'The blending or mixing of different kinds of spirits, chiefly whiskey, has now become a large trade. From thirteen to fourteen million gallons are operated upon in warehouses in this way. It is stated that public taste requires a whiskey of less marked characteristics than formerly, and to gratify this desire various blends are made, either by the mixture of pot still products, or by the addition of silent spirits from the patent stills. In the latter case, cheapness is often the purpose of the blend, but it is also stated that it incorporates the mixture of several whiskies more efficiently. The blends, even when made from old spirits of various kinds, are frequently kept in bond for a considerable time, although, in other cases, they enter into consumption soon after the mixture, according to the requirements or convenience of the dealers . . . Some witnesses were of opinion that patent still spirits should not be allowed to be blended with pot still products, but they admitted that this restriction could only be applied in bond, as the mixture could be made after payment of duties, and could not be detected by any chemical means. On the other hand, the Scottish and Belfast distillers, who make both pot still and patent still spirits, state that a large industry would be destroyed if any restrictions of this nature were put on their trade.'

The committee, then did not define whisky; it did not recommend the discontinuance of blending pot and patent still spirits. In effect, they cleared the practice and gave the go-ahead to the patent stills, a clearance the patent stills acted upon so as to reach a production peak by the end of the century. In fact, British blended whisky consumption has never again reached the figure it did then, in 1900.

In fact, the committee gave classic expression to the ethos of the period, the early dusk of the Victorian age of dominance: 'Your Committee do not recommend any increased restrictions on blending spirits. The trade has now assumed large proportions, and it is the object of blending to meet the tastes and wants of the public, both in regard to quality and price. The addition of patent still spirits, even when it contains a very small amount of by-products, may be viewed rather as a dilution than adulteration, and, as in the case of the addition of water, is a legal act within the limits of strength regulating the sale of spirits.'

Similarly, in the matter of compulsory bonding, the enforcement, that is, of a minimum age below which the spirits could not be sold for domestic consumption – a matter of which much will be heard in the years ahead – the committee found: 'Our general conclusion from the evidence submitted to us is, that compulsory bonding of all spirits for a certain period is unnecessary and would harass trade.' They later went on: 'The conclusion of your Committee is that as the public show a marked preference for old spirits, which the trade find more profitable, and as the practice has arisen of blending whiskeys with patent spirits, to fit them for earlier consumption, it is not desirable to pass any compulsory law in regard to age, especially as the general feeling of the trade is that such an obligation would harass commerce, and be an unfair burden on particular classes of spirits.'

They then turned their attention to the Food and Drugs Acts and the Merchandise Marks Act, the very stuff of the police court prosecutions in the next decade. The committee cleared the liquor trade: 'Your Committee are unable to recommend any further provisions as regard adulterations, because they have not found that the spirits of commerce are adulterated with any material noxious to health. Under Section 6 of the first Food and Drugs Act, a sale is illegal if the purchaser be prejudiced by buying "any article of food or any drug which is not of the nature, substance, and quality demanded by the purchaser". Under this section a vendor selling as malt whiskey spirits containing none of the by-products of malt, or of malt and grain, could be detected in the present state of chemical knowledge, if the malt spirit had been made in a pot still. So far the present law applies. But your Committee are unable to recommend any standard of purity and impurity which could guide such conviction, because spirits when made in the same distillery, and still more when made in different distilleries, show considerable variations in the amount of the by-products which give the character to spirits.' There the matter seemed to rest. Scotch whisky went on booming as never before. In 1887, the pot stills of Scotland produced 7,385,000 proof gallons of their undoubted whisky from malt alone, and the rival patent stills made 9,396,000 similar gallons of their whisky, or silent spirit, from malt and grain. Ten years later, in 1897, the pots made 13,979,000 gallons from malt only, and the patents 17,300,000 from malt and grain. In the financial year 1898–9 Scotland produced no less than 35,769,000 gallons of spirit and in the distilling year of the same date there were at work no fewer than 161 distilleries.

Then came, too, the biggest crash ever in Scotch whisky, the Pattison failure, as everyone tried 'to be in whiskey' and get quick and enormous returns. Then came a revived taxman's interest, setting the tone for the rest of the century, as Hicks Beach, the Tory Chancellor of the Exchequer, imposed in 1900, in the middle of the South African War, a war tax of an extra sixpence a gallon. The tax seems trifling by today's standards, but it should be remembered, first, that money then had at least ten times the value it bears today and Hicks Beach was, secondly, breaking a Tory tradition by taxing spirits at all. When he increased the duty by sixpence the proof gallon making the total eleven shillings a gallon, at which point it stayed until the Lloyd George war budget of 1909 – the war on want – it was described as a war emergency measure of taxation. We are now sufficiently accustomed to war emergency measures to feel no surprise that Asquith a few years later, as Liberal minister, said that the need for that emergency measure had not lessened. In the event, it marked the turning-point in domestic sales of Scotch whisky: they have never recovered since. The decline in British consumption led to additional efforts being put into the already existing export trade in Scotch whisky, small as those exports were then as compared with the mighty volume they present today.

Unbeknown to most participants, the spectre of the 1890–1 select committee was hovering in the wings of the stage. To encourage its re-entry on the boards was the world-wide campaign in the first years of the century for purity in food and drink. One climax, for instance, which has left a permanent mark was to be seen in the United States of America and the Chicago meat-packing scandals. In Britain, we can select, out of many such occasions, the brandy prosecutions as the most relevant to our inquiry and related directly to it.

The phylloxera scourge in France had ruined many vineyards there while impairing others, destroying the vines themselves. This had gone on for years, as men fought back at the disease. Wine output fell and with it brandy production. What an opportunity, thought many, particularly on the Continent, to come to the relief and comfort of brandy drinkers with silent spirit from the patent still – flavoured, either with a dash of true brandy or with essence of sorts, to resemble the true brandy. The British market was flooded with these counterfeits, these frauds.

Of course it was a fraud. It was an offence under the Food and Drugs Acts, possibly, and under the Merchandise Marks Act, certainly. It was giving the purchaser an article 'not of the nature, substance, and quality demanded'. He asked for brandy and was getting a mixture of brandy and silent spirit, or silent spirit and other substances, the silent spirit itself made as a rule from anything but wine.

The country witnessed a wave of prosecutions under that Section 6 of the Sale of Food and Drugs Act, 1875, noted above. Outstanding amongst them, and used as a test case everywhere, was that of Wilson *v.* Wilson & McPhee heard in the Sheriff Court of Lanarkshire at Hamilton in 1903. The Sheriff found the charge proven and the appeal on questions of law was dismissed.

The Sheriff's judgment gives a clear view of the issue: 'The only question is,' he said, 'was the liquor which was thus supplied brandy, or to use the words of the statute, was it of the nature, substance, and quality of brandy? If it was, the respondents are not guilty: if it was not, they are. The burden of proving that the liquor is not brandy lies upon the prosecution. They attempt to discharge this burden by establishing two propositions: (1) That brandy is a distillation of wine: (2) that the liquor sold was not such a distillation – was, in short, not grape spirit, and therefore was not brandy. I think the prosecution have established both propositions.

'As to the first proposition: The witnesses for the prosecution are all agreed that brandy is a grape spirit – a distillation of wine. The skilled witnesses for the defence were both, I think, driven to admit it.

'As to the second proposition,' he went on, 'viz., that the liquor in

7

question was not a grape spirit, Dr Clark testified distinctly that it was not. He got a sample of analysis, and the respondents admit the correctness of it . . . He adds that the the taste and smell showed that foreign spirit (that is, spirit other than grape spirit) was present, probably raw grain or beet spirit. Mr Gemmell, the respondent's chemist, testified that no chemical analysis will disclose the origin of the spirit present, and that the presence or absence of ethers depends entirely on the method of distillation, and is of no importance. I think that to rely entirely upon the small proportion of ethers present would hardly be safe. But the small proportion of ethers is, I think, a very important element in the case.'

Finally, he observed: 'If, then, the analysis showed too little of the ether element in the grape spirit, and far too much for grain spirit, and if the taste and smell indicated whiskey or grain spirit as much as brandy, I think it is safe to infer that the liquor was not pure grape spirit, but it contains a considerable quantity of foreign spirit as an addition.'

Similar prosecutions came thick and fast. One more instance we must notice. In March 1904, the Borough Council of Islington, London, brought nine summonses against various traders in the borough for selling as brandy an article 'not of the nature, substance, and quality demanded', an article containing varying amounts of spirit not derived from the grape. One case was taken as a test case, and the accused was charged, as above, and with, specifically, selling as brandy a spirit containing sixty per cent of spirit not derived from the grape. In fact, one of the defence witnesses agreed that the 'brandy' in the case contained grain spirit.

The magistrate, Mr E. Snow Fordham, of whom much will shortly be heard, said, in referring to the medical evidence, that it would seem desirable for the legislature to fix a standard for brandy, defining what brandy is and the proportion of ethers it must contain. He did not venture further on that score, because the presence of grain, or patent still, spirit in the 'brandy' was admitted by the defence. Coming closer to the problem, for so it was emerging, of the patent still, the defence claimed that silent spirit having its origin in the grape when blended with spirit distilled from wine was properly brandy. Mr Fordham would have none of it. He did not think that if a spirit obtained by distilling wine had been so highly rectified as to have lost the properties

peculiar to brandy it was still spirit of wine so as to fulfil the definition
of brandy. He finally did not have to rule on that matter, as the presence
of grain spirit was admitted.

In short, the Islington Borough Council won, and the trade associations concerned decided not to appeal. As a prominent shipper of
genuine brandy observed at the time: 'The only practicable course open
to the trade associations is to realise the fact that brandy has not yet
become a generic term, and that it is necessary to advise the trade that a
blend of grape spirit with other spirit should be sold as such. This has
now been done and labels of various descriptions are now being used
very freely, too freely, in fact, for those proprietors who are willing to
guarantee their product as genuine brandy.'

The *Islington Gazette* warned after the Fordham decision, 'It was
clear that "Fine Old Pale Brandy" under trial was not brandy, and, in
the interests of foolish public, the sooner goods are sold for what they
are the better.'

The *Lancet*, which was most prominent in the campaign for pure
food and drink, was much more informed and decisive. Noting that
public houses in North London were displaying, after the Fordham
decision, a notice stating: 'All spirit sold in this establishment as Brandy
is of the same superior quality as heretofore, but the percentage of pure
grape spirit is not guaranteed', the journal went on: 'Brandy is spirit
distilled from the fermented juice of the grape . . . There can be no
disguising the fact that of recent years a large section of the spirit trade
has adopted a method of business which has hoodwinked the public.
Spirituous liquors, chiefly brandy and whisky, have been placed upon
the market which were not accurately described by the labels upon the
bottles. We have pointed out again and again that the terms "Brandy"
and "Whisky" had specified meanings, these terms being used to
distinguish in the former case a spirit derived exclusively from wine
and in the latter case a spirit derived from barley malt. We have been
assured that the attenuation of genuine Brandy or Whisky with a
spirit made from grain, potatoes or other materials was the result of the
demand made by the public in favour of a spirit of negative rather than
positive characteristics. It suited certain sections of the Trade to say this,
while all the time they knew perfectly well that their real object was to
put upon the market a cheaper spirit and to gain a wider margin of
profit upon it. Whatever else may be said, such trading is not honest

dealing with the public, apart altogether from the question of whether this or that spirit is more wholesome than the other . . . For the purpose of a beverage, pure spirit is inadmissible because it is flavourless. Further, it is idle to contend that Brandy and Whisky are esteemed because they are merely alcohol . . . It is perfectly clear that when a person asks for a Brandy and gets more or less plain spirit he is not receiving an "article of the nature, substance, and quality demanded", and is obviously prejudiced . . . We hope that the issue of the case will do much to check the almost unbounded substitution which is being practised by the spirit trade. We cannot regard this decision in the slightest degree as a menace to the interest of the Trade. They have only to deal fairly with the public by disclosing in accurate terms the nature of the article which they offer for sale. According to the view that the public exhibit a preference for mixtures or substitutes the Trade ought not to lose by revealing the fact that the article is not a pure unblended spirit. Candour should put money in their purse on their own showing . . . The value of analysis was discredited by the Trade previous to the Islington prosecution case. It is an interesting sequel to the case that they now find that they must protect themselves against the further operations of analysis by disclosing to the purchaser the nature of the so-called Brandy in such unmistakable terms as are contained in the above notice.'

That was typical of the state of feeling when brandy was 'cleaned up'. The pattern of events is emerging: Whisky's turn next, but when and where? In Islington in the following year was to be the answer, but before then parliamentary action intervened.

In March 1904, The Sale of Whisky Bill, promoted by Sir Herbert Maxwell, Bt., M.P. for Wigtown, Kenyan Slaney, Arthur Balfour, and J. E. Gordon, was ordered by the House of Commons to be printed. They stated that the object of the Bill was to secure to purchasers of whisky a clear statement whether it was a whisky made from barley malt alone, or was in part made from unmalted grain. Or, as described by Mr William Ross, managing director of the Distillers Company Limited, the preponderant group of patent still distillers in Scotland: 'The essence of said Bill was to draw a sharp line of distinction between whisky made in a pot still and that made in a patent still – inferentially to the detriment of the latter.'

Thus the Bill said: 'In this Act – The expression "Malt Whisky" means spirits manufactured from barley malt, with the addition only of yeast and water, and distilled in a pot still.' Again: 'The expression "Grain Whisky" means any spirits of the kind sold as whisky other than "Malt Whisky". Every cask or vessel sent out – including even in bottle – was to be distinctly marked or labelled by the proprietor of the whisky with the like mark or label as the cask or vessel from which it is transferred.' That is, it was to be marked 'Malt Whisky' or 'Grain Whisky', as the case might be, even to the stage when sold on draught from an urn, or cask, and the like, in a public house, and with this important rider: 'Provided that where malt whisky is blended or mixed with spirits other than malt whisky, the vessels containing the blend or mixture shall be marked or labelled "Grain Whisky" and not "Malt Whisky".' Penalties for transgression were, of course, provided.

The Bill did not get beyond its first reading, but did prompt a pamphlet from the D.C.L. Some of it calls for quotation here. Thus: 'Until nearly the middle of the last century, whisky, as then known, was entirely made through the pot still, and was made either from malted barley, or partly from malt and partly from unmalted grain. This class of whisky is still produced, and the process has undergone practically no improvement during all these years. In 1833 [*sic*] a new still was invented by Coffey, which not only was much more economical to work, but in the process of distillation extracted a large part of the fusel oil and other impurities found in pot still whisky. The new still which ultimately became known as the "Patent Still", rapidly came into use, and largely took the place of the old-fashioned pot still – more especially in the Lowlands of Scotland. The patent still, being so much more rapid in its action, was able to produce a greatly increased output, and hence the working expenses and on-cost charges are very much lighter than in the pot still distilleries, where the quantity produced is necessarily small. The average quantity made in a pot still distillery in Scotland is not more than 2,000 to 3,000 gallons per week, while there are patent still distilleries which produce as much as 50,000 to 60,000 gallons in the same time. The opponents of patent still or grain whisky are wont to assert that the lower price of this article is due to the cheaper materials from which it is made, but it requires little practical knowledge to discern the great saving entailed in working costs when the output from a single distillery can be increased more than twenty-fold. The position of the distillery has also much to do with the cost of the article produced. In the North of Scotland, where the majority of the pot still distilleries are situated, the high rates of carriage for coals and other material all tend to add to the cost of the whisky, without enhancing its true value. We think we have said enough to prove that the difference in price between pot still and patent still whiskies is largely accounted for by circumstances entirely un-connected with the raw materials from which they are respectively produced.'

After a brief résumé of the successful development of the blending of the two types of spirit, to the elimination of others, the pamphlet goes on: 'In conclusion, the claim is made for Scotch grain whisky that it has supplied, and is supplying a much-felt want for a lighter form of stimu-lant than is available in the heavy malt whiskies; that it has increased the sale of these malt whiskies by the skilful manner in which it is blended therewith; and that, as the whisky of commerce is now undoubtedly a blend of malt and grain whiskies, nothing should be done to interfere with the name which it has justly earned for itself, viz., "Scotch whisky". If it is desired to have a more distinctive title for pure Highland malt whisky, there is nothing to hinder such a whisky being so described, and thereby distinguish it from its more popular competitor, which will be quite content with its present sobriquet – "Scotch Whisky".'

Battle was being prepared. Another member of Parliament, Mr Denis Kilbride, engaged in a regular campaign as to blended spirits, and question followed question in rapid succession in the House. A few only can be recorded here, but they are typical of a not insignificant attitude in the Commons and of a spasmodic element in the country at large. One blend made in Scotland, it was alleged, for instance, amounted to 2,500 gallons in all, of which 2,000 gallons were English spirit and 500 gallons were raw grain spirit less than one year old. 'No knowledge,' was the ministerial reply, with the grudging avowal that if the facts were as alleged, it would be an offence against the Merchan-dise Marks Act. Another parliamentary question asserted that grain and foreign spirits were mixed with malt whisky and then were labelled as 'Pure Malt Whisky' – and that this was done in warehouses under government supervision. Could it, would it, be prevented, it was asked. Chancellor of the Exchequer Austen Chamberlain said that any measures against such alleged acts would only be 'futile' and would 'only result in postponing the application of the description until after the goods had passed out of bond, and would afford no real protection to the public'. Another member asked the President of the Board of Trade whether the Government proposed to take action as regards the sale of whisky described as Scotch, Malt and Highland whisky, but which was really the product either of German spirit, or of maize, rice and molasses. The only reply granted him was that action could be taken if a breach of the Merchandise Marks Act were proved. In the summer, Kilbride took the whole matter up again in a Bill – which like the earlier one got nowhere – with four main provisions: compulsory bonding for at least three years; pot whisky to be sold for what it is; patent still spirit to be sold as such; and a blend of pot and patent still spirits to bear on the casks and bottles a statement of the component parts. Kilbride himself described the Bill as being 'for the protection of the public and of the pot still industry in both Ireland and Scotland from the fraudulent practices which obtain in the blending trade owing to lax Government regulation whereby patent still spirit made from foreign materials by the agency of sulphuric acid is allowed to be sold as genuine Irish or Scotch whisky'.

Certainly there were cases of the use of sulphuric acid to bring about the necessary conversion in the cereal used, generally in that case maize, but the habit had to be abandoned just about that time after revelations of the danger involved. And the *Lancet* summed up: 'The point is that the terms whisky, brandy, rum and gin have a special meaning and indicate practically the source of the spirit, and certain representatives of the spirit trade must be brought to understand that this meaning cannot be stretched to include a spirit produced from any material. If the basis of all alcoholic beverages is to be plain alcohol, patent or silent spirit, then these differentiating terms may as well drop out of usage. The practice of attenuating genuine spirits with cheap silent spirit has been growing enormously during recent years, and it is time that some effective control over the practice should be instituted.'

That was in late 1904. With the brandy decision behind them, and with the temper of the times as thus expressed, Islington Borough Council pounced on a dozen whisky vendors in 1905 and charged them with selling as whisky 'articles not of the nature, substance, and quality demanded'. They were charged with selling blends of pot still whisky and silent, or patent still spirit as whisky to the prejudice of the customer. Two cases were selected as test cases and came before the same magistrate, Fordham, in the same North London Police Court as had the brandy cases of 1904 in which the defendants were found guilty and no appeals were lodged.

2

The storm breaks

THE STORM we have seen long threatening whisky broke at Islington in November 1905, when two summonses were heard at the North London Police Court before the stipendiary magistrate, none other than Fordham of the brandy cases of the preceding year. In all, twelve summonses were issued and two were chosen as test cases. Found guilty, the rest would have followed suit. The charges were that the accused had contravened the now famous Section 6 of the Sale of Food and Drugs Act, 1875, in selling articles 'not of the nature, substance, and quality demanded'.

The Islington Borough Council chose out of the twelve the most flagrant cases they could find. Nobody blamed them for that; it was generally accepted, the normal routine. The two defendants were: licensed victualler Thomas Samuel Wells, of 66 Hazelville Road, Hornsey Rise, and off-licensee James Davidge, of 327 Hornsey Road, both within the borough of Islington.

As the case so quickly followed the brandy cases, the Off-Licences Association, which had fought and lost those cases at a cost of £1,000, could not afford the whisky cases. So the secretary, Mr Arthur J. Giles, well aware of the serious nature of the charges, addressed a circular letter to the principal members of the trade inviting them to join in the defence.

As a result, a conference took place at the Edinburgh offices of the D.C.L. where the whole position was discussed. The Glasgow Whole-sale Dealers' Association was represented by Mr F. J. Stevenson and Mr

George Ferguson; the Edinburgh and Leith Wholesale Dealers' Association by Mr James Mackinlay; the Scotch Grain Distillers by Mr William Ross and Mr William Sanderson. Ross's connection with the grain spirit we have already noticed; Sanderson was not only the founder of a Leith wine and spirit firm, owning a Highland pot still distillery, but was also one of the founders and managing director of the North British Distillery, a patent still distillery set up at Edinburgh by the blenders in the eighties of the previous century.

According to the memoirs of Ross, 'It was felt that the case was simply another attempt of certain pot still distillers to gain a supremacy over their patent still confrères by means of the Court – a supremacy which they had hitherto failed to effect by legislation or otherwise . . .' The Edinburgh meeting decided to take up the defence of the cases referred to. In view of the possibility of having to put up a big fight, Ross proposed that the whole grain distilling and blending trades should be approached to guarantee a fund of £5,000 to defray costs, but his proposal was not adopted, and so lightly did some of the delegates to the meeting regard the matter that £100 was suggested as ample to cover all expenses. Thus it came about that the grain distillers agreed to defray all the costs before the Police Court, on the understanding that, should the cases have to be appealed, the rest of the trade would then be invited to contribute. 'The decision had this advantage,' continues Ross, 'that it left the conduct of the case in fewer hands, unhampered by the necessity of consulting a larger body. The Scotch, Irish, and some of the provincial English patent still distillers thereupon agreed to be responsible for the costs of the action, and the arrangements for the conduct of the case were left largely in the hands of the D.C.L.'

The case, which attracted a galaxy of legal and scientific talent, opened before Fordham on 6 November; the hearing of evidence went on until 12 February following, and judgment was given a fortnight later, on the 26th. The defendants were found guilty – contrary to general expectation – and fined £1 each. Notice of appeal was given at once.

Mr J. Fletcher Moulton, K.C., soon afterwards Lord Moulton, led for the defence, supported by two other counsel and instructed by a prominent firm of London solicitors. Islington was represented by Mr A. M. Bramall, solicitor to the council. Moulton's opening speech for the defence lasted two hours and a quarter and was most vigorous. He quickly got to what he considered the heart of the matter, bringing in Dr F. L. Teed, public analyst to the council: 'Dr Teed deliberately sat down in the latter months of the year 1905 to decide what the English people shall call whisky, and then he sets up his precious standard on an article that was called whisky before he was born. (Laughter.) If he had told any member of the British public thirty years ago that unless whisky had a coefficient of 384 it was not whisky, the man would have looked round to see if there was any safe method of escape from a lunatic. Fancy a man sitting down and saying what whisky is to be.' To which the magistrate replied: 'Dr Teed is a chemist.'

The point at issue was that to be whisky it had to contain 384 parts of 'impurities' per 100,000 parts of absolute alcohol, and Teed's analyses had shown that both the Scotch and Irish whiskies involved in the case were mostly new silent, or patent still spirits, lacking the by-products obtained in pot still distillation. Wells was concerned with the Irish whiskey charge, Davidge with the Scotch whisky one.

Fordham's decision was, in effect, that patent still spirit is not whisky, and that the selling of a blend of that spirit and pot still whisky as whisky is a breach of the 'nature, substance, and quality' Section noticed. In short, a blend is not whisky; it is a fraud on the public.

In more detail, the decision itself was of this order: The 'Irish whiskey' from Wells was sold to an agent for the Inspector of Nuisances of the Islington council who asked for 'A pint of Irish whiskey' and was given a plain bottle filled with a fluid, which cost him 2s. 4d.; he asked for a bottle of Scotch whisky from Davidge and was given a bottle marked 'Fine Old Scotch Whisky' at the price of 2s. 6d. On analysis, they were both found to be ninety per cent grain spirit, and this was borne out by documentary investigation. This latter also showed that Wells' spirit was only one month old when it came into his cellar and was sold within six months. Davidge's 'Fine Old Scotch Whisky' consisted ninety per cent of spirit made in June 1904, or perhaps a year before. Fordham commented: 'Now having found that the fluids sold by the defendants were spirits produced in a patent still from a mash consisting of maize, to which a dash of pot still had been added, I find that Wells' sample is not Irish whisky, and Davidge's sample is not Scotch, as was demanded by the purchasers.'

17

He went on: 'Irish and Scotch whisky is one thing and patent still spirit with a little whisky added is another . . . But when a purchaser asks for and pays for whisky it should be given to him by the seller, or at any rate the purchaser should know what he is getting. Certainly if he is not getting what he asks for he is prejudiced. I find that both Wells and Davidge have infringed the law, and I must fix and order penalties in each of these two summonses.'

His closing remarks were even more alarming: 'Patent still spirit, made largely from maize, has been sold as whisky in a largely increasing manner for years, and the resulting product has been taken by an unsuspecting public to the benefit of the wholesale dealers and retailers, and the so-called blenders have dared to concoct and place upon the market raw, new patent spirit with a mere dash of Irish or Scotch whisky in it as Irish or Scotch . . . In my opinion the blenders who supplied the defendants should be the people to suffer, but at the same time in my judgment it was careless on the part of the defendants to sell it as they had done, and since they only are before me, they must pay the penalty of the law . . . I shall only impose a nominal fine of 20s., and £100 costs each; or in the alternative, two months' imprisonment in each division.'

On the subject of whisky, Fordham ruled specifically that: 'Whisky should consist of spirit distilled in a pot still, derived from malted barley, mixed or not with unmalted barley and wheat, or either of them.' Clearly, it was a triumph for the pot still distillers, and a defeat for the patent still distillers, and the blenders. On the latter, however, it should be remarked that it was the action of the brewers in supplying their tied houses with cheap spirit that was the cause of the whole débâcle, according to the leading spirit men and journals of the day. Fordham in effect touched on this sore: 'Although I believe that patent-still spirit alone is not whisky' – and nothing could be more affirmative than that – 'there is evidence before me that when it is mixed with a considerable proportion of pot still spirit, or whisky derived from malted barley, such mixture has long been sold to and accepted by the public in immense and increasing quantities as whisky. Indeed, many of the most largely advertised and popular makes of potable spirits are of this character, and contain, I have reason to believe, a very considerable proportion of pot still whisky . . . Irish whisky and Scotch whisky are just as much definite articles as Bourbon or Canadian whisky . . . and I must hold that by Irish or Scotch whisky is now meant a spirit obtained in the same methods by the aid of the form of still known as the pot still. The product of the patent still cannot in itself be either Scotch whisky or Irish whisky, although made in Ireland or Scotland.'

After that, there was no other course open to the patent still distillers and the blenders but to appeal. Before considering that appeal, let us pause a moment to catch echoes of the times. One leading spokesman for the blended whisky trade said in London: 'If the public accepts them in increasing quantities as whisky, it is not easy to see how the sale of them is to the prejudice of the purchaser. The public buys such blends because it likes them, finds them palatable, and less bilious than the pot still spirit. After all, the important question is not whether "whisky" is derived philologically from "usquebaugh", but what the purchaser expects when he asks for whisky. Reduced to its logical conclusion, Mr Fordham's decision amounts to this – that all whisky must be made in the most primitive fashion that can be discovered from ancient archives. All the improvements effected by science during the last hundred years must be discarded. One way out would be the fixing of a standard and the making of an attempt to come to some agreement on these lines with the authorities.'

That common-sense point of view was expressed also in a leader by *The Times* on the subject of the Fordham decision. 'In fact,' said the leader, 'nobody drinks whisky unless he takes very particular care to see that it comes from a distillery which sticks to the pot still – and he cannot be sure he has got the genuine article even then . . . that comparatively modern invention the patent still, according to Mr Fordham, cannot make whisky at all . . . a provokingly progressive world . . . But Mr Fordham has no doubt whatever on the subject . . . In the process of distillation, alcohol is extracted from the fermented wort, and that alcohol is absolutely the same whether it comes from barley, wheat, rye, potatoes, maize, rice, or sugar. But along with the alcohol other things are produced in smaller quantity. They are of various character, but they are collectively called "fusel oil" . . . In a very small quantity they do no great harm, and supply the flavour to the beverage. While alcohol is the same whatever its source, the fusel oil varies in composition with the source. Hence the difference between whisky and rum, and the difference between one whisky and another. Now in the primitive pot still, which has been used for thousands of years, the alcohol and the fusel oil come over together. The mixture is absolutely un-drinkable, and successive distillations have to be resorted to in order to get rid of the greater part of the fusel oil. On the other hand, the patent still separates the alcohol and the fusel oil as completely as can be desired at one operation. It is possible to get from the single distillation alcohol perfectly free of flavouring matters, and also free of all but two per cent of water. The alcohol is then perfectly neutral or "silent", and it does not matter in the very smallest degree whence the sugar came out of which the fermentation has produced the spirit. To give it the flavour desired by the public when they ask for gin, or for whisky, or for a particular type of whisky, is merely a question of putting in the appropriate material. That can be done in the case of whisky by leaving some fusel oil in the distillate, or by putting back a definite quantity of what has just been taken out, or by using a definite quantity of some high-flavoured whisky from a pot still. In the last case, it is important that the pot still whisky should be old, because it is age that develops the flavour due to the fusel oil. But it is of no consequence whether the plain alcohol was made ten years ago or the same morning, because alcohol is alcohol from start to finish and does not change by keeping. But it is the simplest thing in the world to put as much flavouring into the patent still whisky as there is in the other. It is not done because the public taste favours mild whisky instead of the highly-flavoured whisky in vogue twenty years ago. It is very difficult and expensive for the pot still people to get theirs mild enough, hence we presume the motive power of the attempt to get theirs declared the only liquor that may be sold as whisky at all . . . If the public want mild whisky they will get it, even if they should have to relinquish the romantic notion that it is descended from usquebaugh. It is rather a droll notion that a liquor which pleases the public is to be put under a ban because it is not made exactly as liquor was made by our rude forefathers in an apparatus of unknown antiquity. The patent still whisky is pure alcohol *plus* the kind and amount of flavour that the public like. The pot still whisky is not so much to the public taste and, if anything, it is less wholesome.'

Being wise after the event, it is possible to read very much into the fact that *The Times* leader quoted referred to 'patent still whisky', in contradistinction to Fordham who had ruled that that is just what it was not.

A brief glance at a few opinions voiced in Scotland must suffice. One leading blender thought there should be a maximum imposed of fifty per cent grain, or patent still whisky in a blend; another thought there should be a minimum age of four years imposed before it was released to the public. He went on: 'The tied-house trade has been the cause of the deterioration of whisky. Blenders and merchants had no desire to sell the "cheap stuff", but were compelled to meet the demands of the brewers who thought that anything was good enough in the way of spirits. New grain spirit is preferable to new malt, but it should not be labelled "Fine Old Malt Whisky".' Another big Glasgow blender agreed: 'The decision will be the means of the public getting better whisky, because the brewers will for their tied houses now buy better quality than what they have hitherto been buying.' A director of another leading firm in Scotland was not so sure: 'Mr Fordham leaves us all pretty much at sea. He also referred to the newness of the whisky in question, and on that point I am sure every respectable house in Scotland agrees with him, for no doubt he here touched the spot.'

Westminster also was not silent. Archibald Williamson introduced his Sale of Whisky Bill because of the Fordham decision with the express object of securing to purchasers a clear statement whether the whisky was made in a pot still from malt or from malt and corn, or was made in part – a blend, that is – in a patent still from unmalted grain. So there was seen yet again the same proposals as before that 'all whisky shall, from the time of leaving the distillery till sold to the consumer, be described by a mark or label on the cask or bottle as "whisky" or "blend of whisky and patent still spirit", as the case may be. Provision is made for similar information being given to persons purchasing whisky on draught.' This time Williamson was supported by Sutherland, Cathcart Wason, Bilson, and Harmood-Banner. The Bill got nowhere.

The County Council of Aberdeen forwarded a request which ultimately arrived on the table of the Local Government Board that steps should be taken 'for the fixing of an official standard of whisky', even should this need legislation. In this they were reverting to Dr Teed's 384 parts, and the proposition that patent still spirit in a blend should not exceed fifty per cent. The *Lancet,* a consistent advocate of pure malt, or pot still whisky, even quoted 'a man of scientific pursuits' that the Board of Inland Revenue encouraged patent still spirit as that beverage led to a greater thirst, by means of which greater quantities were drunk and more revenue accrued to the Board!

On the other hand, Sir Henry Burdett's *The Hospital* came out in direct support of the blends: 'The bottled Scotch whiskies are incomparably superior to the bulk or draught whiskies. As a class they are fair value for money, and not a single one presents any objectionable feature of quality . . . Speaking generally, in our opinion, whisky has earned its reputation as a hygienic beverage, and the article supplied to the public is as a rule of good quality. The only exception to this appears to be the increase in the sale of draught whisky of imperfectly aged spirits.'

Stage two of the whisky drama opened at the only possible Court of Appeal, Quarter Sessions, at Clerkenwell, London, on 28 May 1906, before W. R. McConnell, K.C., and a full bench of lay magistrates. The Court sat for seven sittings, and concluded its deliberations on 25 June following, when the chairman announced that no decision could be given as the Bench was equally divided. The appellants, the former defendants, could only apply for a fresh hearing before a second bench of magistrates at Quarter Sessions. Neither side was satisfied: the North London decision, Fordham's, was still the only legal finding, but it was robbed of a large part of its force as it had not been confirmed, in fact only half-assented to on appeal. The D.C.L. took immediately a bold, and premeditated, step: they advertised the day after McConnell's decision pure Cambus, or patent still whisky from Cambus patent still distillery on sale to the public per bottle.

To revert to the beginning of the Clerkenwell appeal. Islington was now represented by two K.C.'s and a junior, while the appellants, the former defendants, were represented by Mr A. J. Walter and Mr R. O. B. Lane. Opening for Islington, the respondents, Mr W. R. Bousfield, set the tone: 'The object of the patent still therefore is to produce a spirit that is silent as to its origin . . . What I do say is that you cannot buy a portion of patent still spirit and mix it with Scotch whisky and then call the mixture "Fine Old Scotch Whisky".' And Mr Montague Lush wound up for them on 25 June with: 'The sole question at issue is, have these two defendants committed an offence against the Food and Drugs Act? If you mix a foreign ingredient with the article demanded, you are supplying the purchaser with a different article to that asked for. The whole case depends whether members of the trade are to be allowed to conceal from the public, facts that the public ought to know, and facts that are very material. They had no wish to stop the sale of patent still spirit, and they had made no attack on the industry as has been alleged, but the prosecution asked that the public should know what they were buying, and should have their choice.'

In short, it was not two, or even twelve, North London retailers who were on trial: it was the patent still, its product, and the whole practice of blending while calling the resultant article 'Scotch whisky'. Was the name to be restricted to the pot still product, as Fordham ruled? Or, could it be extended to cover the patent still product also? Quarter Sessions could not decide; would they get any further next time?

Again a leading London exponent of the whisky trade went on record: 'We do not think that the distillers of patent still whisky have any reason to be down-hearted as a consequence of the failure of the Clerkenwell justices to arrive at unanimity. It is a distinct step forward to get magistrates divided in opinion. There seem to be weighty reasons to believe the Islington Borough Council are egged on by less disinterested persons . . . Undoubtedly a stronger case was made out at Clerkenwell for grain whisky than was placed before Mr Fordham. The export trade, now amounting to seven million gallons annually, has been built up on blended whiskies, just as the home trade has been. In the face of this universal appreciation of blends, it is absolute folly to set up malt whisky as the only genuine article. It is altogether too late in the day. And in extensively advertising Cambus as Scotch whisky, the D.C.L. have bearded the lion in his den, for according to Mr Fordham nothing is entitled to be called Scotch whisky which is not made from malt in a pot still. Will Dr Teed and his friends go for the D.C.L., and if not, why not. Other local authorities are not likely to emulate Islington.'

Ross of the D.C.L., came out with a broadside on the naming of whisky in late July, on the eve of a deputation to John Burns, the president of the Local Government Board, writing: 'We ourselves do not think the public care in the slightest how whisky is made, or the composition of the materials so long as they are assured that the materials are thoroughly sound and that the whisky is well matured and agreeable to the palate . . . Knowing the well-known antipathy of the average whisky drinker to a pure pot still whisky, we however welcome the suggestion to call each product by a distinctive name, and while preserving the name "whisky" as a generic term we are prepared to qualify this in such a way as to make it impossible for the public to be deceived in what they buy.' After instancing his own company's Cambus patent still whisky, and speaking of Irish pot stills and the composition of the basic cereals used at those distilleries, he went on: 'The correct description of their product should therefore be "Pot still Irish grain whisky" but for convenience may be abbreviated into "Irish pot still whisky". The Scotch pot still makers on the other hand should discriminate whether their product is Highland, Lowland, Islay or Campbeltown Malt whisky as distinguished from patent malt whisky. The suggested distinctions above described would prevent the various qualities *when sold as single whiskies* from being confounded with each other. Blends of pot still and patent still whiskies *when both are made in Scotland* should be described as blended Scotch whiskies, and blends of pot and patent whiskies *when both are made in Ireland* as blended Irish whiskies.'

On the last day of that month, a deputation consisting of Sir Robert Usher, as chairman, Dr Alex Cowie, as vice-chairman, and as chairman of the Central Malt Distillers' Association, Mr W. Rusk, as chairman of the West, South and East of Scotland Malt Distillers' Association, Mr W. H. Ross, managing director of the D.C.L., Mr Alexander Walker, of Messrs John Walker & Sons, and a member of the North of Scotland Malt Distillers' Association, Mr W. H. Seaman, of Messrs W. P. Lowrie & Co., Mr F. J. Stevenson, of Messrs Gilmour Thomson & Co. Ltd, Mr H. L. Garrett, of Messrs Dunville & Co. Ltd, of Belfast, and Mr James Andrew, law agent and secretary, waited upon John Burns, as president of the Local Government Board, the first Labour member of Parliament to reach the Cabinet. Seaman and Stevenson were representing in main the Glasgow and West of Scotland Wholesale Wine and Spirit Dealers' Association. The deputation was introduced by Mr George Younger, M.P., and Sir Robert, as chairman, explained their object which was to urge an inter-departmental committee or commission to ascertain the views of the trade, hear evidence and report as to the course to be followed. Mr Burns on his part promised the usual politician's 'consideration'.

Pending anything decisive from Westminster – actually, the executive was hoping the judiciary would give a decision on appeal before any action on their part was essential – applications were made for the appeal from Clerkenwell to be heard. McConnell wrote that he thought there should this time be an entirely fresh Bench, and the appeals were for ever being postponed. Several interviews with Burns took place, all equally without result.

So the D.C.L. prefaced the opening of the distilling season that year, 1906, with a letter from Ross, as managing director of the company, which ran: 'A new feature this season will be the offering to the public through the Trade of pure "Cambus" Scotch grain whisky put up in bottle and guaranteed by ourselves as having been stored in wood for over seven years. The attempts recently made to cast aspersions on the fair name of grain whisky have led us to adopt this course. We argue that if the public can have an opportunity of judging for themselves as to the merits of grain whisky, it will materially assist blenders in combating the arguments of the "Pure Malt" advocates that in using grain whisky their only object is economy, and to make a larger profit. We are amongst the largest makers of pure Malt and pot still whiskies in the United Kingdom, and did the demand warrant it we could produce, without any increase of our present plant, treble the quantity we are now doing, with greatly enhanced profit to ourselves. Our duty, however, is to produce the quality demanded by the public, and the favourable reception accorded to "Cambus" since it was placed before the public as a self whisky, amply confirms our belief that the taste is year by year growing more in the direction of a lighter and less flavoured beverage.'

That move and the initial 'Cambus' introduction to the home market had, of course, to be preceded by close and intimate talks with the blenders, as some of them suspiciously regarded it as a prelude to the D.C.L. entry on the home trade retail market given over to blends. Thus the careful phraseology of the letter. For much as the interested parties in the defence of blended whiskies and patent still spirit might suspect each other in way of business, they, together with the bulk of the pot still distillers, were only too willing to combine to achieve the freeing of blended Scotch whisky and the legitimation of patent still spirit. Some – a few – pot still distillers resented the advent of blended whiskies, but in the main they all combined together, realising that each had much to gain, and to lose.

Later that month, October, came another surprise for the trade. On the 29th there came before Fordham at the North London Police Court a case in which two summonses had been issued against a Mr Alfred Aylett Moore, of Virginia Waters, Surrey, and 15 Somerset Street, Portman Square, both granted on the complaint of William Walter Ward, one of the Islington Borough Council inspectors under the Food and Drugs Act. The first summons charged that 'on 12th July, 1906, by your agent at 637, Holloway Road, did sell . . . a pint of alcoholic spirit with false trade description, viz., "Old Scotch Whisky". The said spirit was not "old" and was not "Scotch whisky", inasmuch as the greater part of it was not made or produced in Scotland, and was not made from the materials (viz., malted barley) or by the processes (viz., pot still distillation) from or by which Scotch whisky is and should be made.' The second summons charged Moore with having in his possession for sale the spirit to which a false trade description had been applied.

Mr A. M. Bramall once more represented the council, saying that his 'feeling all along had been that the proceedings should be against other persons, and that Mr Moore might free himself if he would only give information which might be used hereafter against the persons who sold him the spirit'. The information was given, and the summonses by leave withdrawn. But what occasioned the surprise and concern was the fact that the summonses were issued at all, as there was then a tacit understanding that no further cases would be pursued until the pending ones were settled.

As the months dragged by no dates were fixed for the appeals and Burns remained unconvinced of the need for a commission or committee of inquiry; Williamson produced in the spring of 1907 his Sale of Whisky Bill calling for the labelling or marking of all whisky as 'whisky' or 'blend of whisky and patent still spirit'. This time the explanation was made that 'under the existing law the Inland Revenue are furnished with returns of the materials used in each distillation, and they have, by means of the permits or certificates required on the removal of spirits and the stock books required to be kept by rectifiers, dealers, and retailers, the information necessary for tracing the whisky till it reaches the retailer'. Williamson, by the way, was M.P. for Elgin and Nairn, the heart of the pot still territory-in-chief. The pot still distillers, or most of them, were willing to agree to blending provided that fifty per cent or more was pot still whisky and this would be entitled to be called 'whisky'; any blend with less than fifty per cent pot still in it should be called 'a blend'.

Altogether, everyone was becoming more than a little bored with the whole business and willing to compromise. Everyone, that is, except the die-hards. Islington especially was fed up: the council had now spent £2,446 on 'the pot *v.* patent controversy' and, as the local paper remarked: 'Litigation is costly and Islington has now a bitter pill to swallow.' The whisky cases had been adjourned yet again, this time pending a decision by John Burns as to a commission of inquiry or a departmental committee.

Then the borough gained a new council 'less disposed to throw away their constituents' money in a wild-goose chase than were their predecessors', as was said, So, on 26 June 1907, Burns received a deputation representing both Islington Borough Council and the malt and grain distillers and others. As Ross later recorded of the interview: 'The President responded in a friendly spirit, and eventually, in July 1907, he obtained the consent of the Government to the appointment of a Royal Commission.' After that, having avoided the issue, Clerkenwell announced on 9 July, that the Wells and Davidge appeals should be formally respited from time to time.

The following month, August, Ross, of the D.C.L., felt obliged to release another broadside, this time against Dr Harris, the medical officer of health in Islington, who had broadcast his opinions concerning the differences between pot and patent still whiskies. Among the many points made by Ross, this one is of particular interest: 'It is time this fallacy of the difference in cost between the two qualities of whisky was fully exposed,' he wrote. 'I don't mean to compare the higher grade qualities of either class, which because of some special virtue in style or character command a special price, but I will take an ordinary pot still whisky made either wholly from malt or from a mixed mash of malted and unmalted grain, and of its selling price (which is perhaps the surest guide to its cost) with the selling price of an ordinary patent still whisky made also from malted and unmalted grain. The difference in price is no more than 7d. to 8d. per proof gallon, or at reduced bottle strength a little more than 1d. per bottle. Is Dr Harris aware of the fact

that patent still whisky pays the same rate of duty as pot still whisky –
viz., 11s. per proof gallon, and has to bear the same cost for storage,
casks, etc., the only difference being this small advantage in cost of, say,
1d. per bottle? With his knowledge, would he have us believe that for
this paltry consideration, and no other, the publican would run the
risk of supplying his customer with an inferior article? The reason, I
doubt not, must be found in another direction.

'Dr Harris next says that pot still whisky is *kept* three years before
using, at a cost of 6d. per gallon per annum, while patent still is
generally used at once, thereby saving this extra cost. On whose authority
does he make such a wild statement? Not only is there no law to compel
pot still whisky from being used under three years, but, as a matter of
common knowledge, much of it goes into consumption long before
that period expires. I agree that it would be well if a compulsory age
limit for this spirit were adopted, and I think most of the pot still
distillers would welcome it; but while the present law remains the
temptation to use new "pot" is just as great as it is to use new "patent",
while the evils resulting therefrom are immeasurably greater. As
regards the sweeping statement that patent still whisky is "generally
used at once" – that is, when new – I can best answer this by stating that
there is at present lying in bond in Scotland at least fifty million gallons
of patent still whisky, and that of the withdrawals of this whisky
nearly fifty per cent *exceed* three years' age.

'Dr Harris states that pot still whisky greatly improves on keeping,
while with patent there is little or no improvement; hence there is no
object in keeping it. As regards the "pot" I agree; but my remarks
under the second head are sufficiently to condemn what he says
about "patent". Not only does patent improve by keeping, but long
prices are paid by blenders for well matured patent still whisky –
prices in some cases higher than paid for the same age of pot still
whisky.

'Dr Harris here deals with the chemical constituents of whisky. All I
have to say is that every essential element contained in pot still whisky
is also contained in patent, although in some cases in a smaller degree.
Therein the patent-still distiller considers he has effected an improvement, and has produced an article more in accordance with public
taste.

'Pot still whisky (Dr Harris states) is made entirely from barley malt in Scotland, and from a mixture of malt, oats, rye, and wheat in Ireland. I would add to this, "and sometimes maize", after which I don't propose to quarrel with his definition. Patent still whisky, he says, is generally made from maize, "but is sometimes distilled from potatoes, or even sawdust". I don't think anyone would desire to call a spirit made from the two last-named substances by the name of "whisky". Neither substance, as far as I am aware, has ever been employed in the United Kingdom, and where potatoes are used for the production of spirit, as they are in Germany, the spirit is sold for industrial purposes. In no case where patent still whisky is made either in Scotland or Ireland for home consumption, is maize alone employed. I can speak for my own company, and I can also speak with equal confidence for all the other Scottish and Irish patent still distillers, that a minimum of twenty-five per cent of malt forms part of every mash, and this percentage increases in some instances to fifty per cent, while other ingredients employed beside maize are barley, rye and oats. It was held by Mr Fordham in the decision which he gave last year on the whisky question that Irish whisky is produced from a mash consisting of seventy-five per cent malted barley, and the balance of unmalted cereals. I venture to say that if the decision were upheld, not twenty-five per cent, possibly not ten per cent of the pot still whisky made in Ireland today would conform to that standard, or my information is greatly at fault.

'While I do not agree that pot still whisky is only made in Scotland and Ireland, I will so far cordially agree with Dr Harris that Scottish whisky can only be made in Scotland and Irish whisky in Ireland. Whisky can be and is produced in other countries, but they cannot legitimately be classed either as Scottish or Irish whisky. I take these terms to mean purely geographical classifications.

'All that Dr Harris says under these two heads may be taken as in favour of the patent still, if we exclude his conclusions that only pure alcohol can be produced by its use. It can certainly be nothing but a great advance on the time-honoured pot still, to find another still which can do its work more efficiently in much less time, and at such reduced cost. In every other business improvements in machinery and appliances have taken place, having for their object the cheapening of production or improvement in quality of the article produced. Dr Harris would have us believe that the science of distilling is to be the exception to this rule, and that it is to be considered a heinous sin if we move a step in advance of our grandfathers' notions.'

It is of interest, but by no means surprising, that in the documents by Ross we have quoted, he almost exactly forecast the findings of the royal commission appointed by John Burns in 1908 to inquire into 'Whiskey and Other Potable Spirits', the 'What is whisky?' inquiry as it became known popularly.

3

The whisky inquiry

THE YEAR 1908 opened with echoes of the brandy cases: on the first of January came into force the French law, delimiting the Cognac region, home of the world's best brandy. As a leading London firm said in their circular: 'Such a law should have been passed a long time ago, and the quantity of rubbish that has been forwarded with the assurance that it was "pure grape", and containing the full quantity of ethers (added) would not have come to our shores. The effect of this new arrangement has been an immediate rise in the value of all genuine Cognac Brandies, and the market in Cognac at present is in a great state of excitement in consequence.'

The Scotch whisky market was soon afterwards put in an equally great state of excitement with Burns's announcement of a royal commission to investigate and report on whisky and other potable spirits. On the eve of that announcement occurred at Liverpool another 'whisky case': a charge similar to the Islington one was laid there concerning the sale of a bottle of whisky labelled 'Pure Malt Pot still' which was found by the public analyst to be of equal parts of malt, or pot still spirit and grain, or patent still spirit. The case was found proved, and a fine of 20s., plus costs, was imposed.

On the question of names, it is of some little importance to quote the opinion of a distiller-blender who remarked: 'It is interesting to observe the changes that have taken place in the naming of whisky in the last thirty or forty years. At the time when I entered the trade all whisky was invoiced as "fine malt aqua", but the term "aqua" was gradually replaced by "whisky". Some years later, the term "fine malt whisky" was changed to "fine Scotch whisky" – applied to both malt and grain whiskies. It was thought to be more honest to use the word "Scotch" than the old-fashioned term "malt".'

Burns did not bother himself about such fine points, but announced on 17 February 1908 the appointment of the commission, their names and their terms of reference. As he himself said, he felt 'that the better course was to refer the whole question to impartial men, none of whom were in any way committed to trade views or nominated by the trade, but who would take evidence as to the trade interests concerned, and consider not only those interests, but also those of the consumer and of the public health in relation to the matter'.

His wisdom was justified by the event, however little approbation he received at the time. The commission was headed by Lord James of Hereford, a distinguished and ageing Liberal lawyer, with whom no fault could be found. Next to him was appointed Laurence Guillemard, deputy chairman of the Board of Inland Revenue, the government department most closely concerned with the financial aspect of the questions at issue. The remaining six had all considerable repute as physicists or scientists. That was just the point attacked, in alliance with the absence of trade representation. The issue is not worth detailing at this time, but the actual membership must be recorded.

The six were: Mr W. E. Adeney, Doctor of Science, Fellow of the Chemical Society, Curator of the Royal University of Ireland; Mr J. R. Bradford, Doctor of Medicine, Doctor of Science, Fellow of the Royal Society, Professor of Medicine at the University College Hospital; Mr H. T. Brown, Doctor of Laws, Fellow of the Royal Society, and accepted by the trade as 'the distinguished brewers' chemist'; Dr G. S. Buchanan, Doctor of Medicine, Inspector of Foods to the Local Government Board of England; Mr J. Y. Buchanan, Master of Arts, Fellow of the Royal Society, and a well-known Scottish chemist and physicist; Mr A. R. Cushny, Doctor of Medicine, Master in Surgery, Fellow of the Royal Society, and Professor of Pharmacology at University College. The Buchanans were not related and had no connection with the well-known Scotch whisky firm founded by another of the same name.

Burns's general approach was that two members should represent the Board of Inland Revenue and the Local Government Board, that one should be nominated by the Secretary for Scotland and one by the Irish Local Government Board, and that there should be three other members with such attainments as would enable them to form a sound judgment on the various scientific matters referred to them.

The terms of reference were to inquire and report:

'1. Whether, in the general interest of the consumer, or in the interest of public health, or otherwise, it is desirable:

(a) To place restrictions upon the materials or the processes which may be used in the manufacture or preparation in the United Kingdom of Scotch whiskey, Irish whiskey, or any spirit to which the term whiskey may be applied as a trade description;

(b) To require declarations to be made as to the materials, processes of manufacture or preparation, or age of any such spirit;

(c) To require a minimum period during which such spirit should be matured in bond; and

(d) To extend any requirements of the kind mentioned in the two subdivisions immediately preceding to any such spirit imported into the United Kingdom.

'2. By what means, if it should be found desirable that any such restrictions, declarations or period should be prescribed, a uniform practice in this respect may be satisfactorily secured: and to make the like inquiry and report as regards other kinds of potable spirits which are manufactured in or imported into the United Kingdom.'

To anticipate their sittings, the commission are to be commended on the speed with which they acted. They began their sittings on 2 March after their appointment and, as Ross recalled: 'Recognising that some of the questions to be reported upon by the Commission were of serious importance to certain sections of the whisky trade, and in order to relieve the existing tension as early as possible, the Commission, after hearing all the evidence they could obtain bearing upon these points, very considerably and also very wisely issued an interim report on 24 June, 1908, in which they set forth the following conclusions which they had arrived at . . .'

The interim report must wait; suffice it to say that it cleared the patent still. To avoid confusion, the evidence and findings spell the word as 'whiskey', whatever its geographical origin.

Burns's announcement met, as noted, a mixed reception. An Irish member of Parliament asked, for instance, a week after Burns's declaration: 'Why is this Commission composed mainly of Englishmen, seeing that whisky is manufactured in Ireland and Scotland, and that Englishmen know nothing about whisky except the consumption of it?' 'Laughter,' records Hansard.

In Leith, the ancient wine and spirit port of Scotland and still a great nerve centre of the whisky trade, there was a general dissatisfaction with the composition of the commission, increased opposition to further possible restrictions in connection with blending whisky, and, a profound attitude, a willingness to accept a minimum maturing period of, say, two years. One most prominent Leither summed it up: 'The announcement of the appointment of a royal commission has come very unexpectedly. It is some considerable time since the president of the Local Government Board was approached on the subject of appointing a commission or committee, and the first we have heard of it is the announcement in today's newspapers. A royal commission on whisky at the present time is, in my opinion, absolutely unnecessary, but for the fact that the trade could not sit down under the decision of Mr Fordham as to the term whisky being applied only to distillation from pot stills. The delay is very much to be regretted. The discussion that has arisen on account of this Islington case, and the agitation in the London papers some three years ago as to the merits of Malt versus Grain whisky has been very detrimental to the Scottish whisky trade. As for the royal commission, I should say that its conception is not likely to be entirely acceptable to the trade, owing to the fact that there seems to be an absence of practical men who could suggest questions likely to bring out the fullest information from the witnesses. One officer of the Board of Inland Revenue, three Fellows of the Royal Society, two members of the Local Government Board, a Fellow of the Chemical Society, are, in my opinion, utterly unable to deal with a question involving the interests of such a vast and important trade. With regard to the reference that has been made to the Commission, I consider that the suggestions therein contained would result in great interference with the trade, and that they are quite uncalled for, with the exception of enforcing a minimum time for having spirits detained in bond. The questions proposed to be reopened were dealt with in the report of the British and Foreign Spirits Committee, who were appointed in July 1890, and reported in May 1891. That committee did not recommend any increased restrictions on blending spirits. They stated the addition of patent still spirit, even when it contains a very small amount of by-products, may be viewed rather as a dilution than an adulteration, and, as in the case of the addition of water, is a legal act within the limits of strength regulating the sale of spirits. They also came to the conclusion that the compulsory bonding of all spirits was unnecessary and would harass trade.'

A patent still distiller put the case for many when he said: 'As to grain whisky, it has been made and sold as such for over half a century. In fact, the distilling industry would not have grown to such an extent but for the blending of grain and malt whiskies. The chief demand by the public is for a blend, and no matter what may be decided by the commission it is my impression that the general public will have their way.'

The case even had its repercussions in the United States of America, where *Bonfort's Circular* commented: 'Whisky has given quite as much trouble to the Scotch whisky distillers over there as our own whisky question has to us here, and which unfortunately has been aired in the public press during the past year, has had something to do with the curtailing of Scotch whisky.'

A blender in Scotland was willing to forecast that 'he did not think much would result from the royal commission he thought the majority of people in the Trade would appreciate and help forward the idea of putting on a restriction as regards the age at which whisky can be sent out for consumption'.

The view of many Highland distillers was well put by one in particular, who said: 'The terms of reference are excellent. Those who drew them up knew exactly what they were about. The Highland distillers could never single-handed have spread their business to the far-off limits of other countries – they would have had to be content with what they could do at home. The big combinations of the south opened up markets all over the world; and in the wake of making grain whisky, on whose behalf these extensions were primarily carried out, the Highland distillers have been able to carry their own malt whisky, and thus their business has been extended without either trouble or expense so far as they are concerned. For this they have in a large measure to thank the blenders, and have no right to complain if the latter dominate the markets.'

The Highland distillers' minority opinion was put rather bitterly by one from near Elgin, who wrote: 'It was assumed that this commission has been appointed mainly, if not expressly, for the purpose of dealing with the question in the interests of the blenders and other dealers . . . The buyers alone will have the consideration of the commission. For them, something is going to be done at last, and for them alone.'

Such was the atmosphere of acrimony, contempt and suspicion in which the commission began its sitting on 2 March 1908, at the Westminster Palace Hotel, in Victoria Street, London, with, as first witness, Mr (later Sir) Arthur John Tedder, Chief Inspector of Excise. (He was the father of the later Marshal of the Royal Air Force Lord Tedder.) Mr Tedder's evidence that first day was mostly statistical, concerning the number of distilleries at work in each kingdom, their output, even their production of yeast, an important (and profitable) by-product of grain distilling which helped turn the scales a few years later in time of war. As he then said: 'Yeast making in patent still distilleries is now a very important industry.' Some of them sent out from 20 to 40 tons a week at prices from £30 to £40 a ton. His account of the operation of both pot and patent stills was very full and was accepted without dispute by those who followed. His attitude was the correct, impartial presentation of evidence in the best Civil Service manner, but was such as to create a predisposition towards the patent still in the minds of both commission and public.

Some of that evidence merits quotation. On blending, the heart of the matter, he said, to cite a contemporary journal: 'There was a very large trade in bottled blended spirits. By blended spirits he meant spirits from different distilleries. The object of blending was to obtain a particular flavour for a particular class of customer, and this is what the blenders would tell them. There was of course a difference of price so far as the blended spirits were concerned, but there was an art in the blending to get a particular flavour. The tendency in blending was to reduce the cost, because each spirit comprising the blend would have a different monetary value . . . There were two classes of blends – blends of pot still spirits made from different distilleries, and blends of pot still and patent still spirits. The latter class of blend largely preponderated. Where pot still spirits were blended, very often spirits produced from quite a large number of distilleries would be mixed so as to give a proper flavour. The proportion of pot still to patent still

36

spirits in the blending varied very much. When the blending took place the mark "blended" appeared on the casks, but the proportions were never given. In other words, the Excise officer had no indication of what the blend consisted, although he did actually know in many cases. In some cases he had quoted the blender might blend at two warehouses, and send the blend to a third warehouse and blend these two blends with some others. By the time they arrived at the third warehouse the identity of the blend would be entirely lost.'

Again: 'The export trade in British spirits was very important now. The quantity exported last year was 7,341,077 proof gallons, and the business seemed to be on the increase. A good proportion of the quantity exported consisted of good blends of spirit.'

The chairman intervened, asking: 'You told us that blending varied very much, the presence of pot still whisky being small in some cases and large in others. Are those blended whiskies sold at a uniform price?' – 'No.'

'Then what regulates the price?' – 'The initial cost of the spirit.'

'Then if a larger proportion of pot still is given, and a smaller proportion of patent still, the price is high?' – 'Yes. Age would also apply.'

'Do you think that if a member of the public got a bottle of whisky containing eighty per cent of pot still and another of six per cent he could tell the difference?' – 'I believe a whisky drinker could. He would do so by the flavour and aroma.'

Dr Brown: 'What is the distinctive character of pot still and patent still whisky which you regard as being essentially different in character?' – 'Well, I do not think there is any question about this distinction. I should have no difficulty in saying which was which.'

Chairman: 'Then there is a uniform flavour of pot still whisky?' – 'No. Each distillery produces whisky of a distinctive flavour. There is a pot still flavour in all of them and yet they may all differ.' 'I always understood that there is a difference between Irish and Scotch whisky from the fact that the Scotch whisky malt is prepared over peat, and Irish over coal, and that the flavour of the peat permeated the Scotch whisky?' – 'That is so.'

'How would you describe the difference between pot and patent still whisky?' – 'I am afraid we are now getting into touch with metaphysics.' (Laughter.)

'In the patent stills is maize a considerable ingredient?' – 'Yes. I think it would run as high as seventy-five per cent. Maize is of value to the distiller because of the large proportion of starch it contains.'

'Then that is one of the reasons why patent still spirit is cheaper – because maize is cheaper than malt?' – 'Yes.'

'Are these qualities beneficial to the consumer'? – 'That I cannot say.'

Mr A. M. Bramall, solicitor to Islington Borough Council, gave evidence the next day. Saying that 'the crux of the whole thing is to get a definition of whisky', he recalled how their attention was directed to certain sales of whisky and fifteen samples were bought 'haphazard' and 'only one was found to be genuine whisky'. The chairman had to intervene at this point: 'You must not say that, because it is still a question what is genuine.' Bramall, unperturbed, continued: 'In two cases the adulteration was so pronounced that proceedings were determined upon, and summonses were issued in two cases, which were to be taken as test cases.'

Bramall gave details – exhaustive details – of the composition and prices of the spirits and their constituents, and again crossed swords with the chairman, who said: 'According to you, the article contained ninety per cent of patent still whiskey?' – 'Patent still spirit.' To which the chairman had the grace to reply, 'I will accept your amendment. Do you say that is whiskey or not?' – 'We say it is not.'

His opposition to the patent still emerges most clearly in these extracts from Bramall's evidence: 'Indeed, the product of any patent still could not be termed whiskey, and a purchaser asking for whiskey would certainly expect the product of the pot still, and would know the difference between it and that of the patent still.' Again: 'By the term silent spirit is meant that it does not indicate what it is made from. It is a neutral spirit because nothing can distinguish it from any other kind of pure spirit. If the by-products are eliminated, it is reduced to pure spirit.'

And again: 'Travellers go round the public houses and persuade their owners to buy these things under the name of Scotch and Irish whiskey because they are cheap. Then they are retailed as Scotch and Irish whiskey, the sellers having no idea of how they are produced . . . The customer ought to know exactly what he is getting. Then there is the question of price. Purchasers are getting what they think is a genuine spirit, and are paying almost as much as if they were actually getting it.'

Bramall's picture of the pot still distillers does not quite accord with other evidence on the subject. He said: 'I was astounded when in Scotland to find the state of fear that the pot still distillers are in. They came to see me by night. They were afraid to come in the day-time.' 'Of whom were they afraid?' – 'The blenders.'

In the evidence given by Mr A. J. Walter, K.C., formerly counsel for the defence, it was stated that 'the blend produced by that was not a mere dilution, but was an essential feature to bring out the respective flavours of the pot and the patent . . . The primary object of the distillers is to protest against any decision that the addition or use of patent still spirit in blends would cause this to be termed a process of adulteration. They say that their blends are certainly Scotch whiskey because there are kinds of Scotch whiskey. Patent still spirit alone is Scotch whiskey.'

Among the press of witnesses, the evidence of the managing director of the wine and spirit department of the Army & Navy Stores, London, has its amusing side: 'The Army & Navy Stores,' he was reported as saying, 'did not sell, and during his management of the department had not sold blends of patent still whiskey as whiskey until quite recently when, in order to test the public taste, which they had been informed preferred a blend of grain and malt, he put two blends of grain and malt on the list. They were told that the public demanded it, and in order to prove the case to his own satisfaction he made two blends and described them on the labels, and the result had been an absolute failure.' His 'Mark A' was sixty-five per cent pot and thirty-five per cent patent; 'Mark B' was seventy per cent pot and thirty per cent patent. He likewise had no success with 'Cambus'.

Dr F. L. Teed, public analyst for Islington, as for the City of London and the borough of Camberwell, a 'pot only' advocate, curiously cited Mr William Sanderson, a distiller and blender, one of the founders of the large blenders' co-operative patent still distillery at Edinburgh, itself responsible about this time for something like one-third of the grain whisky output of Scotland, as saying: 'You cannot sell pot still unless you make it purposely for drinking by itself. The ordinary pot still whiskey is made for blending.' An illuminating remark, especially when cited by the 'pot only' faction. Teed was a vital witness for his side, and he proposed the following definition of whisky: 'Scotch whiskey means the spirit distilled in Scotland from the fermented wort derived from barley malt in a pot still. Irish whiskey means the spirit distilled in Ireland from the pot still from the fermented wort derived from malt or malt and barley, with or without the addition of oats, wheat, rye, or any of them, cereals indigenous to Ireland.' That ruled out the patent still spirit, and blending.

The next important witness was Dr Philip Schidrowitz, of Switzerland originally, who had been retained by the defence as a consulting and analytical chemist at the Islington trials, but was not there called. His testimony ranged from the chemical to etymological and historical. For instance: 'The whole question amounted to this,' he was reported as saying; 'they had a patent still spirit, and some people said it was right to call that whiskey and others said it was not. Under these circumstances, it would be a very retrograde step to make any restrictions on processes or apparatus, because after all, it was purely a manufacturing operation . . . Patent still whiskey had always been openly manufactured under the Excise . . . He did not think they would ever get a type of spirit which would go as whiskey from molasses, and at present he would object to such a spirit being called whiskey. His view of the matter was this: the Coffey still was never designed to produce a whisky of the pot still type, but if the distillers were put to it they could alter the still to produce something analogous to the pot still whiskey.'

One interesting snippet of his evidence: 'He knew of the case of a distillery where the whiskey produced was not that which was desired. A lot of experiments were made, and finally a couple of feet more cut off the length of the head, and an entirely different whiskey was made.'

Similarly, his analysis of the four generally accepted pot still geographical divisions of distilling Scotland has its appeal still: 'Taking the Islays first, they are a most highly peated whiskey. They show a very high type of flavour, and yet very fine and round quality when they mature. The Highland malts, taking the Speyside whiskies, are not so big as the Islays, and they show an ethereal flavour, rather than a peaty. Taking the north-country whiskies, they don't show the ethereal flavour quite as much. The Lowland malts are, on the whole, rather small in flavour and not quite as fine, although there are some very fine Lowland malts. And then, finally, there are the Campbeltowns, which are not quite so fine a quality as similar whiskies elsewhere; but I don't wish it to be understood that there are no fine Campbeltown whiskies.'

As for the grain, or patent still whiskies: 'The grain whiskies are of a very much lighter quality but are, in my opinion, distinctly potable spirits and most decidedly Scotch whiskies.'

That classification was later adopted, in the main, by the commission itself and persists today, but what must have commended him to many lies in the interchange:

'Do you recommend that everything should remain exactly as it is, without anything being done to inform the public?' – 'I don't see the slightest reason for altering things.'

'Your policy is rather conservative?' – 'No, I think it is very liberal.'

(A couple of years before, the Liberal party had trounced the Conservative party at a general election.)

His proposed definition of whisky was: 'A spirit distilled in Scotland from cereal grains.'

It was not until the tenth day, 6 April, that they reached the key witness of Ross, of the D.C.L. Mr William Sanderson, as a founder and managing director of the blenders' grain distillery the other leading patent still distiller of Scotland, was prevented by ill health from giving evidence; he died in the following month. Much of Ross's introductory evidence was statistical in nature, but points of interest emerge. Thus he considered the first patent, or Coffey still to be erected in Scotland was at Port Dundas, now within the D.C.L., in about 1840. The earliest reference to the use of maize at distilleries – Cambus and Cameronbridge – now in the company occur about 1864 or 1865, and he 'understood' it was first used in 1859. As to the vexed question of blending: 'Before 1860 the very little blending carried on had to be done after the spirits had paid duty. Irish whiskey at this time was predominant in the market, chiefly on account of its uniformity in style, whereas in Scotland, even amongst pot still whiskies, they were vastly dissimilar. When a man asked for Scotch whiskey or spirits, he never knew whether he would get the high-flavoured North Country, Islay or Campbeltown whiskey, or the less flavoured Lowland malt whiskey, or the pure grain whiskey (patent still). This was the blender's opportunity, and he soon began to mix the various grades of Scotch whiskey together, and produced a fairly uniform type of whiskey, with none of the pronounced flavours of any of the individual parts. The public at once took to this new style of whiskey, which they preferred to the stronger flavoured Irish pot still whiskey to which they had been accustomed. The popularity of Scotch whiskey in England was due entirely to blended whiskey, which was much better suited to those living a sedentary life.'

Further detailed evidence led to the quotation of the prices of different makes of whisky, Ross concluding: 'To sum up, the actual difference in cost between patent still and pot still whiskey, so far as the materials and the processes are concerned, is at most sixpence per proof gallon.' Further elucidation brought these gems: 'The cost of delivery of the whiskey and the agent's commission accounted for a considerable sum in the case of the Highland malt whiskies, but did not apply so much to Lowland malts or Irish whiskey. Patent stills were usually run all the year round, and with the large turnover their working charges were kept fairly low and a smaller profit sufficed. In the case of the pot still distilleries, very many of them were closed down six months in the year – some more, some less. As regarded the small Scotch malt distilleries, this shutting down was not so serious, as the plant was usually small and very few men were kept on during the stoppage.'

This observation was of prime importance: 'The Scotch malt distilleries have benefited by the growth of blended whiskies, and have participated to some extent with the patent still distilleries in the increase which has taken place . . . On the other hand, both patent and pot whiskey were often described simply as spirits or aqua. Up to two or three years ago the Cambus distillery always described their whiskey as aqua. I know of no case of any Highland distillery describing the product as Scotch whiskey, even at the present day.'

As for definitions, he had this to say: 'If blended, it should be sold as blended Scotch whiskey. I define Scotch whiskey as a spirit distilled in Scotland from grain, either wholly malted or partly malted and partly unmalted, but with at least a sufficiency of malt to carry through the complete conversion of the mash. Whiskey made in Ireland in the same way I would call Irish whiskey, and that made in England, in the same way, I would call English whiskey.'

On the then current position of the D.C.L. he remarked: 'As well as being distillers we blend for export only, and require a certain quality of higher class full-flavoured pot still whiskey to blend with our patent.'

The chairman closed his examination by summarising Ross's evidence as follows: 'He believed that the taste of the public had been changing in favour of a milder spirit. The name of whiskey had been built up very largely owing to the product of the patent still and the blenders, and he thought it would be most unfair to take away the goodwill represented by the name "whiskey" from a product from which the goodwill had been built up, and to give it to a product which was not appreciated so much by the public. The name "whiskey" was a trade mark, and it would be very hard indeed to take it away from patent whiskey or blended whiskey, and give to another product.'

Dr A. E. Harris, the medical officer of health for Islington, gave in his evidence some revealing sidelights on the glamorised Edwardian era. 'There were frequent complaints,' he is reported as saying, 'that the whiskey sold to labouring classes in London was poison, and caused much drunkenness.' Just about that time it came to his knowledge that so-called whiskey was being offered to publicans in Islington at tenpence a gallon. He was also informed by one of his inspectors that some time previous to this he was present in a public house when a traveller called on the landlord, and offered him a German spirit at tenpence a gallon, and certain chemical colouring matter or flavourings to be added to the spirit so that he might sell it either as Scotch or Irish whiskey as required. (The landlord in question kicked out the traveller, with threats.)

An elaboration of his analysis of the fifteen haphazard samples led to the following cross-examination: 'Two of these samples you had reason to believe were made in London?' – 'Yes.'

'You had no reason to suppose that there was anything especially objectionable in the fact that they were made in London?' – 'No, except that we asked for Scotch whiskey, and did not think that it was Scotch whiskey that was made in London.'

Dr Harris here caused considerable amusement – disbelief in some quarters – by his story of a Scotch whisky labelled 'N.S.S.', the initials standing for N—'s Special Scotch. Some sixty per cent of it was made in London, and the locals where it was sold had dubbed its initials as meaning 'Never saw Scotland'.

The doctor's own earnestness in the matter was vouchsafed by his declaring: 'I need not say that this question of the effect of grain spirit on the public health has given me very great anxiety, and I looked into it very carefully before the prosecutions. I find that lunacy from alcohol had certainly increased during the preceding fifteen years, but I thought it was unwise, indeed absolutely impossible, to draw any inference from that fact.'

After the Easter recess, the malt, or pot still distillers and blenders – many combined the two roles – began their appearances. One leading light was Mr John Macdonald, senior partner in the Ben Nevis distilleries of Fort William, who had also served as chairman of the Malt Distillers' Association. He put the case neatly: 'If it were not for the Highland malt, Scotch whiskey would be practically non-existent and but for the toning down by Lowland grain whiskey it would not have obtained its world-wide popularity. I have always found that our self-whiskey did not sell so well in the south as in the north . . . I sell to blenders and not direct to the public.' His definition ran: 'I define Scotch whiskey as spirit distilled in Scotland from cereals, the conversion being by malt and not by acid.' He thus avoided, by the use of the word 'cereals', the disputed use of maize at the patent still distilleries, and his reference to acid for conversion of the starch of the cereals to fermentable sugar is a glance at the earlier attempted use of sulphuric acid to effect that conversion. The attempt was abandoned after suspected poisoning had resulted.

Macdonald went on: 'I do not like to say what cereals might be used . . . but I do strongly object to new grain whiskey being sold as Scotch whiskey, and probably defined as the finest Scotch whiskey, but I think that, where practicable, Scotch whiskey should always contain some percentage of malt.'

His reading of recent events was this: 'The trouble came in when cheap whiskey was wanted. There is a certain class of traders who ask for a certain class of whiskey, regardless of price or quality. I would very much like to see cheap whiskey stopped altogether, but I do not see how it can be done.'

Alexander Walker, one of the managing directors of John Walker & Sons Ltd, was next. He spoke for the firm as owning two Highland distilleries with interests in others, both pot and patent, but, he emphasised, his opinions were purely his own. Thus, he stressed, any definition should be obliged to keep the words 'from cereals only with a proportion of not less than thirty per cent malted barley in the mash'. He felt the commission should fix a minimum of fifty per cent malt whiskey in any blend, and when asked why not twenty per cent or thereabouts, replied: 'Because in that case the whiskey holds less of the characteristics which I hold to be necessary to entitle it to the term "Scotch whiskey". I would not allow spirit to be sold as whiskey if it contained less than fifty per cent of malt, unless notification was given of the fact.' As for pure unblended patent still spirit, 'It is sold to the very lowest class trade,' he averred.

His evaluation of blending may be of interest: 'Blending had come into existence because it was practically impossible to sell a single whiskey, owing to its enormous variation in quality week by week and year by year. The blender was able to draw on so many sources that he was able to produce a palatable whiskey. By using malts alone, as they had endeavoured to do, they could not prevent discoloration, and the public would not stand it. Immediately a pot still whiskey was mixed with water – especially water containing a small proportion of lime – they got discoloration. Besides that, there was the question of over-flavour, which the public would not stand.' He, too, favoured a minimum age: 'In his opinion, all spirits sold for consumption should be matured in wood two years.'

Mr R. B. G. Greig, of Wright & Greig, Glasgow, spoke as vice-chairman of the Glasgow and West of Scotland Wholesale Wine and Spirit Dealers' Association, and gave a not uncommon view: 'The association which I represent is of opinion that if it can be proved that new whiskey is injurious, and would be less injurious if kept in bond for two years, then by all means keep it in bond for that period. Personally, however, from my own experience I know that many people prefer their whiskey new – they would not thank you for an old whiskey.'

Mr R. Brown, also of Glasgow, a blender, took a similar attitude, and on the question of compulsory bonding remarked: 'As to that, if it can be proved that it would be in favour of public health – of which I am not at all sure proof is possible – I would be prepared to acquiesce in an enactment that no whiskey should be cleared from bond for consumption under two years.'

Mr W. C. Teacher, of the firm Teacher's, of Glasgow, Highland malt whisky distillers and wholesale dealers in Scotch whisky and other spirits, was more emphatic on the subject. 'In my experience,' he said, 'I have never come upon any evidence of unwholesomeness in malt whiskey or grain whiskey, either new or old; but I have always found that individuals have personal tastes, generally resulting in their habitually consuming the same class or style of whiskey, and finding fault with any which is different, even though actually of higher value.'

As to the declaration on the label of the proportion of grain and malt whiskies in the blend, he thought it 'rather misleading than otherwise. I don't think it would be any guide to the consumer, he would not be a bit the wiser as to the whiskey he was getting . . . In regard to age, I have seen no evidence of new whiskey being less wholesome than old, and although there is comparatively little Scotch whiskey consumed new now, it is well known that long ago – say, fifty years ago – matured whiskey was practically unknown. From my own experience, I can say that twenty-five years ago a great deal of Scotch whiskey was consumed new. It would be against the interests of the public to impose compulsory ageing, because at equal prices it would not be possible to give the same alcoholic strength with two-year-old whiskey as with newer whiskey. Compulsory ageing would, moreover, give an unfair advantage to English gin as against Scotch whiskey in the cheaper class of English trade, as I do not suppose it would be found advisable to impose compulsory ageing upon gin, which has always been consumed new, and, from its nature, would not be improved by ageing. Since the royal commission in 1891 [*sic*], the average age of Scotch whiskey has greatly increased. The trader's business is to join in competition with his co-traders, and suit his wares to the public taste. It was the blender and not the distiller who had succeeded in this, and made Scotch whiskey known all over the English-speaking world. Any restrictions placed upon the blenders would hinder them in their business, besides unwarrantably throwing doubt upon the wholesomeness of Scotch whiskey as presently offered for consumption.'

James Mackinlay, who had been head of the Leith firm of Chas Mackinlay & Co., distillers and wholesale blenders, since 1867, was of the opinion, in regard to minimum age limit, 'that this might be a great hardship to the trade.' At the same time, he would not object to it, and he believed it was the feeling of the trade generally that some such limit should be extended to all spirits made in Great Britain, and also to all imported spirits. In his opinion, two years' notice should be given as stocks of whisky were not that large.

Others, too, were undecided on the whole question of age, and were, generally, against any limitation of the amount of grain whisky – that form of address was generally accepted by this stage – in the blend. But the pot still distillers' case came to the limelight on the sixteenth day with the evidence of Dr A. M. Cowie, owner of Mortlach Highland malt distillery and there as representing the North of Scotland Malt Distillers' Association. That association, he said, included forty-two out of about eighty distilleries in the district. After a long historical summary, he continued, according to a trustworthy report: 'With the trade, and also with the public to a certain extent, his view was that blended whisky was held to be a beneficial trade. He did not think there was any difference between the effect of a blended whisky or a pure malt whisky or a grain whisky, provided it was the same strength . . . Anything that interfered with the blending of these different whiskies would be injurious both to the trade and the public.' That was the opinion of his association. He thought there should be no classification of 'British Plain Spirit', but he wished to retain the name 'Highland malt whisky', and with a distinct permit granted by the Excise. There would be a different permit for blended whisky . . . In reply to further questions, Dr Cowie said there was no antagonism between the malt distillers and the grain distillers, so long as the grain distillers' product was kept in proper proportions. His association suggested the Scotch whisky of commerce should be fifty per cent of malt and fifty per cent of grain. Scotch whisky was originally all pot still, and the Scotch whisky that should be sold should be the characteristic article. That was in the interests of the consuming public, so that they should get value for money. There was nothing injurious in the cheaper whiskies, provided they had age. It was fair and just that there should be knowledge conveyed to the public. Patent still whisky cheapened the price to the merchant, the merchant was informed of the percentage of the blend. He thought there were blends coming to as low as 1s. 10d., or to any price up to 15s. – that was in bond – and he believed there were even cheaper ones than that.

On the question of minimum age, Dr Cowie was reported as saying that 'he considered that it would be to the advantage of the whole trade if spirit was aged. It would not make very much difference to the malt distillers, because their product was not used under an average of about five or six years old. Malt whiskey when new was quite pleasant – sweet. After six months or so it got a peculiar sort of nasty flavour and smell. Then it went through a process of refining, and came out a fine

47

old Scotch whiskey.' Any such legislation should apply the same to patent still spirit, said Dr Cowie.

He went on to define Scotch whisky 'as a spirit made in Scotland, which contains a mixture of malt and grain whiskies in such proportions that the whiskey has the characteristics which belong to Scotch whiskey . . . I quite acknowledge,' he said, 'my position is not a logical one, but that has come to be the whiskey of commerce, and the blenders say they are the men who make it . . . I do not think that the better class of drinker needs protection at all, but I think myself that the poor man wants protection. A blend with fifty per cent of malt and the rest grain is what you would say would come into the category of the better class drinker. The man we are thinking of is the man who gets five per cent of malt and ninety-five per cent of grain.'

On the seventeenth day appeared Colonel George Smith Grant, the sole partner of George & J. G. Smith, of the Glenlivet Highland malt distillery – perhaps the most famous and respected of all such distilleries in Scotland – who gave evidence not only for himself but also as president of the North of Scotland Malt Distillers' Association. He, too, favoured a fifty-fifty blend to 'be called Scotch whiskey'. He likewise had no objection to blending – 'if the proportion is right'.

Would he favour a minimum age? 'Yes,' was his reply. 'I consider that all whiskey or patent still spirit would mature and mellow and become more palatable by being kept at least two years in bond.'

Saying that he would exclude steam-heated pot still spirit from the definition of Scotch whisky, he was then asked: 'You would like to see the old-fashioned form stereotyped?' His reply: 'I do not think they can improve the old-fashioned form.'

'And what is the minimum age at which you consider your whiskey fit to be consumed as a self-whiskey?' – 'I should say about eight years, and going on for twelve.'

He was not entirely uncritical of blending, as the Press reported him: 'The tendency in blending,' he said, 'has been to use more and more of the cheaper article, the patent still whisky, and less and less malt whisky. And without indicating to the public that it was patent still whisky, or a blend of malt and patent still whisky.'

'Are those blends of bad quality,' he was asked, 'simply bad in quality because they contain a large quantity of grain spirit?' – 'That is it.'

One other nice distinction he drew: 'All malts are not the same. There are good and better malts.'

Many other witnesses, of course, were called and examined besides those few presented in brief here: they were drawn not only from all sections of the trade, but extensively also from Ireland. For Irish whiskies, especially the blends emanating chiefly from Belfast, were as much under investigation as Scotch whisky blends. Medical and scientific witnesses were also invited to present their side of the case and testify as to the medicinal properties of whisky, its chemical structure and therapeutic value.

The first phase of the inquiry was complete.

4

The 1909 report

ON 24 JUNE 1908 the commission made an interim report on their findings to date and in the following month it was made public. After restating their terms of reference, they declared:

'We have held twenty-two sittings and examined seventy-four witnesses. Certain of the Commissioners have visited distilleries in Scotland and Ireland, and have thereby gained much valuable information.

'Whilst the labours of the Commissioners are by no means terminated, we have arrived at certain conclusions, which we now humbly submit to Your Majesty as follows:

'1. That no restrictions should be placed upon the processes of, or apparatus used in, the distillation of any spirit to which the term "whiskey" may be applied as a trade description.

'2. That the term "whiskey" having been recognised in the past as applicable to a potable spirit manufactured from (1) malt, or (2) malt and unmalted barley or other cereals, the application of the term "whiskey" should not be denied to the product manufactured from such materials.

'We reserve for further consideration the question of the advisability or otherwise of attaching special significance to particular designations such as "Scotch Whiskey", "Irish Whiskey", "Grain Whiskey", and "Malt Whiskey"; of placing restrictions upon the use of such designations as trade descriptions; or of requiring such designations to be used in connection with the sale of whiskey.'

In short, the patent still had won; those buying what turned out to be blends, at Islington, had been given articles 'of the nature, substance, and quality demanded'.

The Times made it the subject of the first leader on 17 July, saying that the commission 'has wisely issued an interim report giving their conclusions upon the most important of the questions submitted to them. The effect will be to put an end to much of the confusion and uncertainty that has reigned in the whisky trade for the last two years.'

Further *Times* comment was: 'These findings dispose of the attempts that have been made in the interest of certain whisky producers to have the term "whisky" restricted to their own particular sort of whisky, and further to have it declared that no whisky made in any apparatus but theirs, shall be legally saleable under that name. It was always an audacious contention . . . In April this year the appeals were withdrawn by consent in view of the appointment of the Royal Commission. In the meantime every man has been drinking the whisky he prefers, or the whisky he can get, with that serene indifference which the public has always shown to the questions that agitate rival manufacturers and traders. But the trade at large has been put to quite gratuitous annoyance and uncertainty which the publication of this interim report will go far to terminate . . .

'If Scotch whisky is not to be whisky made in Scotland, then the name can have no meaning for the public, nor can science offer any means of determining whether a given sample was made in Scotland or not. If Scotch whisky is to be whisky of a particular character, the difficulty is equally great, because no two Scotch whiskies are identical. It is, of course, the same with Irish . . .

'As a matter of fact, the public chiefly drink blends, and a blender, trying to make a popular beverage, does not care one straw what is the origin of any liquor that serves his purpose as a component . . . They drink whisky because they like it, and when they find a whisky that suits their palates there is an end of the matter . . .

'In fact, there is no public interest at stake in this long, drawn-out controversy. The whole thing is a mystification got up in the supposed interests of certain manufacturers and traders. The public have found their own safeguard against bad whisky. That safeguard lies in the taste for mild whisky as against the highly-flavoured whisky once in vogue. To catch the public taste, whisky has to contain only very minute quantities of fusel oil, and whether that is eliminated by one process or another makes not the slightest difference. A strict classification, such as is practically impossible, would probably have effects very different from those desired by the promoters of the Islington prosecutions. It would put pot still whisky out in the cold, because the public will no longer drink it, unless by costly methods it is deprived of most of its special character.'

The commission went on to investigate rum, gin and brandy, together with related matters, holding their final sitting on 17 May 1909, with Tedder making a reappearance to recapitulate his evidence and explain points raised in his memoranda. The commission had 37 sittings, examined 116 witnesses, and visited distilleries in France as well as in Scotland and Ireland. Their final report was published on 9 August 1909. Their most important inquiry had, in effect, been settled by the interim report, and the final one by way of contrast fell somewhat flat.

At the annual general meeting of the D.C.L. in Edinburgh, on 16 July 1909, the chairman, Mr W. D. Graham Menzies, remarked: 'As to the Royal Commission, it was only a few days after our last annual meeting that they very wisely and considerately issued an interim report – although the inquiry was by no means finished – making it known that neither in respect of materials or distilling apparatus did they propose to recommend that any restriction should be placed beyond what had hitherto been employed in producing the article commonly known as "whisky". This decision was regarded by the Trade as setting at rest all doubt as to the legitimate use of grain whisky, either by itself or in blends, and gave rise to a renewed demand for the company's products. This, combined with considerable sales of old whisky, has been reflected in the profits for the past year, and enabled us to meet you today with what I am sure you will consider a very satisfactory report.'

After discussing the gross profit, he turned to the future – 'We are still awaiting the final report of the Royal Commission already referred to; but I think, after the broadminded way in which they dealt with that part of the inquiry already reported on, we need not have much anxiety as to their decision on the remaining points.'

The real heart of the final report in so far as it concerned whisky did nothing to disturb that chairman. It has now passed, with slight necessary additions and alterations into the statute law of the land. The core of the report was:

'Our general conclusion, therefore, on this part of our inquiry is that "whiskey" is a spirit obtained by distillation from a mash of cereal grains saccharified by the diastase of malt: that "Scotch whiskey" is whiskey, as above defined, distilled in Scotland; and that "Irish whiskey" is whiskey, as above defined, distilled in Ireland.'

While the report was hailed in many quarters, it was equally hated in some others, and of no more than passing interest to most people. As *The Times* leader commented: 'It does not arrive at any startlingly novel conclusion. The Commissioners find, indeed, that there is little or nothing to be added to the report of the Select Committee on British and Foreign Spirits appointed by the House of Commons in 1890 . . . The whole question of placing restrictions upon the materials and processes used in the making of whisky was set at rest by the Playfair Committee for many years . . .

'The public never had any real interest in the trade quarrel which found expression in the Islington trials. It was simply a squabble between people who make whisky in old-fashioned pot stills, and other people who make it in the more modern and efficient patent still . . . What the public wants is a wholesome spirit having the flavour it prefers, and it gets such a spirit from blenders who mix all sorts of pot still and patent still whisky in order to maintain brands of uniform character . . . A good deal of nonsense is talked about mysterious ingredients when it is just alcohol, no more and no less, that is doing mischief. The only thing pretty generally allowed is that liquor that suits a man's taste is by that very fact better for him than liquor that he does not like.'

Again, a most prominent personage in the City of London observed: 'These opinions were largely forestalled by the interim report, which, while it explains the comparative flatness with which the final report has fallen, does not in any way encourage the ideas put about in many quarters that the report is of a negative character. On the contrary, it establishes the position of patent still whisky in a most definite manner, and it is this very definiteness that some of our pot still friends find so very exasperating . . . It may seem like adding insult to injury to be told that new patent has just as much right to be called whisky as old pot, but the day for complaining has gone by. The public have shown their preference for a blend, exchequer exigencies have compelled cheapness, and the Commission has laid down its data.'

Ross, managing director of the D.C.L., the company which had been the most active in the whole concourse of events leading to the final report, gave a very wise and far-sighted opinion on the report, one well worth preserving. 'To say that this report is "eminently satisfactory and sensible",' he wrote, 'is only to repeat what nine-tenths of the Trade have been expressing in the same or similar terms during the past few weeks. I say this commission has not sat in vain.' Pointing out that the patent still and its materials had now been 'cleared', he went on: 'Let us hope that these slanderous statements against patent still whisky which have hitherto done duty, will now cease – otherwise the author and the newspaper publishing the same may have cause to regret their indiscretion. The further pronouncement that Scotch whisky must be made in Scotland, and Irish whisky in Ireland, only follows the lines of common sense, while the attempt which was made to put a restriction upon the type of still to be used has met with the ridicule it richly deserved.'

On the question which had been debated before the commission about the minimum age at which spirits might be released for public consumption he had this piece of wisdom to offer: 'The question of whether an age limit should be imposed upon all spirits before being allowed to be removed from bond was one of more difficulty, as the trade were more evenly divided on the subject . . . As soon as the commissioners had made up their minds that there was nothing deleterious to health in new spirits, the whole argument for compulsory bonding was knocked on the head. Most people, if given the choice, would prefer old whisky to new, but that is not a sufficient reason for imposing a restriction upon the Trade which has already more restrictions laid upon it than any other industry. Every one will in the same way admit that old wine is superior to new, and yet it is only the public demand which compels it to be matured. Why should whisky be placed in any other category? Doctors tell us that stale bread is better for us than new, but the man is still to be born who would be outrageous enough to say that no bread must be eaten until it is a day old . . .

'My answer is, if the public want an old whisky, and are prepared to pay for it, they will have no difficulty in getting it, but they cannot expect to get an old whisky at a new price. If the Select Committee of 1890 and 1891 saw no reason for recommending compulsory bonding of spirits then, there is even less reason now for recommending it when there is a superabundance of old whisky in the market ready waiting for purchasers. I have sufficient confidence in the members of the Trade to feel that they have no desire to foist new or immature spirits upon the public unless the public themselves demand it . . .

'The grain distillers have made no attempt to retaliate beyond defending themselves from the attacks; and now that they have fought and won, nothing will please them better than to work hand in hand with the pot still distillers for whatever is for the good of the whole Trade.'

Dr Teed in his quarterly report to the Islington Borough Council took a different view, writing that 'the members of the Commission were prejudiced against the views of the Borough Council from the outset; their reasoning being illogical, they have necessarily arrived at conclusions opposed to their own findings . . . The report of the Royal Commission is not law any more than the report of a Select Committee. I cannot imagine any responsible Minister of the Crown embodying these conclusions in a Bill before reading the report, and I am certain that no responsible Minister of the Crown will do so after reading it.'

Alas for Dr Teed! That is just what has been done!

Before going into the report itself, we may quote the later account given by Ross, many years after the event: 'In every particular, the report of the Royal Commission justified the attitude taken up by the grain distillers before the North London Police Court and the Clerkenwell Sessions, while it effectually condemned the decision arrived at by Mr Fordham at the first-named Court. The whole of the cost for defending the actions was borne by the grain distillers, and, although the inception of the trouble can never be excused, the brilliant victory obtained for grain whisky atoned for all the trouble and expense to which these distillers were put.'

The commission's analysis of the evidence, of the materials and processes, both pot and patent still, is masterly. In their historical

review of the matter as it concerned the patent still, the root cause of
the whole inquiry, they wrote: 'Most of the spirit produced by the
Scotch patent stills has been made from a mixed mash of malt and
unmalted grain. It is remarkable that when the patent stills were first
employed in Scotland, in the years 1830–1834, they were used for the
production of spirit from malt only. Since then they have been increasingly used for the manufacture of spirit from malt and unmalted grain.
Other materials, however, have at times been largely used in the Scotch
patent stills in the manufacture of spirits, but the evidence is silent as to
the extent of potable spirits so produced. Between 1850 and 1860 the
patent stills produced large quantities of spirit (3,860,643 proof gallons
in 1855) from malt, grain and molasses, sometimes from sugar also. In
1861, 1862, and 1863 these stills used molasses very largely . . . After
that date the use of molasses declined to some extent, but in 1872 the
production of spirit from molasses alone was again over 1,000,000
gallons. No other materials except malt, unmalted grain, and molasses
have ever been used on such a large scale in Scotland, but a small
quantity of spirit has been made at different times from sugar, potatoes,
rice, madder root, dates, currants, starch, locust beans, saccharum, and
malt extract. No evidence was placed before us as to the purposes for
which this spirit was employed. During the last eight years practically
no materials other than malt and unmalted grain have been used in
either pot or patent stills in Scotland.'

Their conclusion on this section of the inquiry was, therefore, this:
'It appears to us that whiskey as a commercial product is regarded both
by the manufacturers and by the public as a spirit made from no other
materials than malt and unmalted grain, and is as a matter of fact so
made at the present time; and we feel confident that the restriction of
the application of the term "whiskey" to a product manufactured
from malt and grain would meet with no opposition from any of the
traders in whiskey.'

They then moved on to consider the sort of grain which might be
used, with, in the case of Scotch whisky, maize particularly in mind.
They examined the matter at some length, and reported: 'Maize is now
very extensively used in the production of whiskey, both in Scotland
and Ireland, especially in the patent still process. Those who object to
its use in the manufacture of Scotch and Irish whiskey contend that
being an American cereal no spirit manufactured from it can properly

be called Irish or Scotch, that it is an inferior ingredient as compared with malted barley, and that it is only by employing the patent still process and thereby getting rid of the flavour that maize can be used at all. On the other hand it is maintained that maize began to be imported into this country in 1846 after the repeal of the Corn Laws, that during fifty years it has been "used as one of the constituents of the mash for the production of whiskey", and it is "being used at the present time in a pot still as one of the constituents of the mash for the preparation of pot still whiskey", and that, as it is and has been used "like other cereal grains because of the starchy matter contained therein", it is impossible to support the contention that it is a substance that should not be used for the preparation of whiskey. The objection to maize on the ground that it is of foreign growth must stand or fall as the objection to foreign barley.'

Their finding then came as no surprise: 'That the flavour obtained by the distillation of spirit from a mash of which maize is the principal constituent differs materially from the flavour obtained from a mash of malt or malt and unmalted barley is indisputable. But we see no valid reason for excluding the use of maize in the manufacture of whiskey. There is no evidence to show that maize is not a perfectly wholesome material, and that being so we cannot recommend the prohibition of an article from which is produced a very large proportion of the whiskey of commerce, by which we mean the spirit which is regarded by a large section of the trade and accepted by the public as whiskey.'

All whiskies were cleared on medical grounds, a matter which occupied several pages of the report. For instance: 'The evidence before us failed to establish that any particular variety of whiskey was specially deleterious. Statements were not uncommonly made that new spirits and the cheaper variety of spirits consumed, for instance, at fairs were specially liable to be deleterious and to cause some of the more severe symptoms associated with intoxication. This evidence generally amounted to little more than a mere statement . . . In some instances we were informed that it was the custom in certain distilleries for the workmen to consume new spirit, and that no specially deleterious effects had been observed to follow . . . The general tendency of the evidence on these matters was to show that any specially evil effects observed were rather to be attributed to the excessive quantity consumed, than to any specially deleterious substance.'

Not only, however, was patent still whisky cleared medically, whisky was found to be replacing brandy medicinally!

Now the whiskies so used were, of course, generally blends, which brought the commission to consider that section of their inquiry. They distinguished two particular classes of Scotch blends – mildly flavoured whiskies of particular characters and good quality, and, secondly, 'cheap, palatable Scotch whiskies'. In the first case, they reported that 'it is possible to produce Scotch whiskies of good quality, according to standard flavours and other characteristics, by blending together in proper proportions, spirits, well matured, from different distilleries, and that blenders exhibit their skill and experience in the various styles of whiskey, which they produce, and in the success with which they maintain uniformity in the flavour and quality belonging to the respective styles, from season to season.'

Of the second category, they had this to say: 'The principal object in this case is the production of cheap and palatable Scotch whiskies. It is necessary for pot still spirits to mature in wood in order that they should acquire a pleasant flavour. Patent still whiskies, on the other hand, although they are improved by keeping in wood, change to a less extent and mature more quickly, and it is stated that the blending of immature pot still with patent still whiskey has the effect of toning down the pungent, unpleasant taste of the former, and that the mixture then becomes "a palatable and not unwholesome spirit". Such a mixture would, if kept in wood, mature in a shorter time than the pot still whiskey would by itself. The proportion of pot still to patent still whiskey in these cheap blends is varied in accordance with the price to be paid for them. The cheapest blends may contain as little as ten per cent of the former, and even less.'

The commission reported, then: 'The blend, therefore, produces a more mildly flavoured and generally a cheaper article than the individual pot still whiskey. The market for blended whiskies is greater than that for the individual whiskies; so much so, that it would probably be safe to say that the majority of Englishmen who drink whiskey seldom drink anything but a blend. We are bound, therefore, to take into consideration the fact that any undue interference with the practice would not only destroy a flourishing industry, but would also prejudicially affect large numbers of the public.

'Finally,' they wrote in their consideration of the processes, 'we have received no evidence to show that the form of the still has any necessary relation to the wholesomeness of the spirit produced. For these reasons we are unable to recommend that the use of the word "whiskey" should be restricted to spirit manufactured by the pot still process.' With one or two asides, such, for example, as requiring a minimum quantity of malt in the blend, the commission were able to arrive at the general conclusion quoted earlier.

On the vexed and vexing question of compulsory bonding so that any spirit presented to the public for consumption must be of a minimum age, the commission found against the whole idea. We have already noticed some of the opinions of Mr Ross and others on the subject. As Mr Ross was to write later on the subject, 'all sections of the Scotch distilling trade expressed themselves as favourable to a certain age limit. The grain distillers were careful, however, to point out that in the case of their product this was not so much required in the interest of public health, as merely to give time to allow the whisky to develop a roundness and flavour.'

The trade wanted most a minimum legal age to be granted: the industry had been, in effect, over-producing since the turn of the century. Home consumption had been fluctuating, indeed, stationary; since 1900 it had fallen, and this fall in consumption had not only encouraged exports but had hit the pot still distillers in particular, who were less closely organised than the patent still distillers and whose product was generally left to mature much longer than the patent still one. In fact, some pot stills had closed down, and pot still whisky was, in many cases, selling at this time for little more, if any, than it had cost to lay down as early as 1898 and 1899.

But the commission had also to consider other spirits, such as home-made gin and imported brandy and rum. To their legal and exacting minds, no driving cause called for such state interference in industry and the obstacles seemed insurmountable or too trying by their own nature to be worth overcoming. They began off by quoting the 1890-1 committee that ' "compulsory bonding of all spirits for a certain period is unnecessary and would harass trade".' They noted the change in opinion of certain whisky spokesmen who had given evidence before them and commented: 'This partial change of opinion may possibly be accounted for by the fact that, as regards the whiskey trade generally, and certain sections of it in particular, both the stock of whiskey and the warehouse accommodation are now greater than in 1890–91.'

Nevertheless, the commission were adamant: 'It seems clear that a system of compulsory bonding would necessitate additional warehouse accommodation, and the provision of such accommodation would throw considerable expense upon some of the pot still distillers and the majority of the patent still distillers. In our opinion, the compulsory bonding of spirits for a prescribed length of time could only be justified if it were to establish that such a restriction of trade is necessary in the interest of public health . . . In our opinion the evidence is not sufficiently positive to justify us in holding that it is necessary for the protection of the public health to detain any spirits for a minimum period in bond. We may add that, apart from the fact that the price of spirits would have to be raised in order to cover the loss of interest consequent upon their detention in bond, the practical difficulties involved in any system of compulsory bonding would, in any case, make us hesitate to recommend such a restriction . . .

'If compulsory bonding is considered as a means of securing the maturity and flavour, as distinct from the wholesomeness, of spirits, it must be borne in mind that spirits of different character do not mature with equal rapidity. A very much longer period is required for the maturation of a heavy pot still malt whiskey, for example, than for a light patent still whiskey. Even in the case of spirits of the same character, differences in the conditions of storage, such as the nature and size of the vessel in which the spirit is kept, the relative humidity of the place in which it is stored, and the climatic conditions generally have a considerable effect in determining the rapidity of maturation. Whatever period might be fixed would inevitably be open to one of two objections; it would either impose an unnecessary burden on particular classes of spirits, or it would be too short for the maturing of other classes. The particular period most usually suggested, namely, two years, would, in our opinion, be open to both objections. For the above reasons we have come to the conclusion that it is not desirable to require a minimum period during which spirits should be matured in bond.'

Such was the reasoned opinion of learned and impartial men; within a few years, in the midst of a war and of personal and political animosities, it was overturned.

But by the time that final report was issued in the summer of 1909, the whole whisky and spirits trade was engaged on yet another deadly struggle, a politico-economic one. It is time to examine that fight for survival.

5

The 1909 budget

'MR EMMOTT, this is a war budget!' said David Lloyd George, Chancellor of the Exchequer, addressing the chairman of the Committee of Ways and Means, winding up his budget speech in the House of Commons on 29 April 1909. 'It is a budget for waging implacable warfare against poverty, and I cannot help hoping and believing that before this generation has passed away we shall have made a great advance towards the good time when poverty, with the wretchedness and squalor and human degradation which always follow in its camp, will be as remote from the people of this country as the wolves which once infested its forests.'

A war budget in two senses: against the demon poverty and against the menacing naval might of imperial Germany. More, a war budget conscribing the spirit industry of the country and, with pathological savagery, attempting to wreck it. The extremes of wealth and destitution, the malaise of the entire nation, the ardent reforming spirit of the years past need not delay us here. Let us admit them; no other course is open to the objective inquirer.

But the personal bitterness of the Chancellor calls for comment. A fervid Welsh nationalist and member of the Church of the Disciples of Christ, a hive-off from the Baptists, he was in constant demand as a youth and especially after he became a solicitor in 1884 at the age of twenty-one as a 'temperance' speaker. Returned as a Liberal party member of Parliament for Caernarvon Boroughs on 17 April 1890, his maiden speech was made the following 18 June – on a temperance issue.

Through the years which succeeded with their political and military vicissitudes, he retained his seat, despite such things as opposing the Boer War, and with the triumphal sweep back to power of the Liberals in January 1906 he became president of the Board of Trade. Through all those years, he pledged himself to a comprehensive programme which included justice for Ireland, religious equality in Wales, measures of land reform, direct local veto on the granting of licences for the sale of intoxicants, a free breakfast table (no duties on foreign food), a liberal extension of the principle of decentralisation, and other reforms. In fact, he made his first mark as a debater in the House in its two-year life after his accession thereto by joining in constantly in the debates of the Liquor Traffic Local Veto (Wales) Bill, as much as on the Elementary Education Bill.

His character, then, was not unknown, when he moved from the Board of Trade to the Treasury in 1908 on the resignation of Campbell-Bannerman and the accession of Asquith to the premiership. His main preoccupation that year was his budget in 1909: he visited Germany, Austria and Belgium to study social legislation; he seriously expressed the view to Mrs Masterman, whose husband was helping him with the novel and difficult land clauses, that 'all down history nine-tenths of mankind have been grinding corn for the remaining tenth and been paid with the husks and bidden to thank God they had the husk.'

But when Lloyd George introduced his budget that Thursday afternoon of 29 April 1909, the performance was a failure: the speech lasted four hours; it was read; it was diffuse; but it was nevertheless momentous. Even in the method of its anticipation it was revolutionary: it was preceded by a White Paper which told everything about the budget except how the additional money needed would be obtained. *The Times* forecast in its leader of budget day that it was generally expected that the 'taxation of licences was to be upon a scale so heroic that the wretched brewers, writhing under the scorpions of the Budget, would long for the whips of the Licensing Bill . . . though there is a general expectation that licence duties will be raised, Mr Lloyd George has probably discovered that the taxation of licences cannot be carried very far without defeating its own object.' The Licensing Bill referred to was the Liberal measure of 1908, which had passed the Commons and was rejected by the Upper House. The smart rankled to join forces with the personal vendetta Lloyd George was pursuing against the 'liquor traffic'. By throwing out the Liberal measures on education and licensing, the Conservative leaders restored the House of Lords to the forefront of politics, with results about to be noticed. For whisky was likewise in the forefront of the emerging battle.

That budget deserves attention at this point. On the then existing basis of taxation, he had to face a prospective deficit of £16 million. If expenditure could not be restricted, new revenue would have to be found. No more than any of his colleagues these days was Lloyd George willing to curb expenditure: in fact he was determined to increase it on the social side and it was perforce increased on the naval side by the force of external events. In rough outline, he proposed that for incomes exceeding £3,000 a year the rate was to be raised from 1s. to 1s. 2d.; in addition, there was a supertax imposed on all incomes over £5,000, leviable on the amount of their excess over £3,000; there were heavy increases in the death duties; an increase in the cost of liquor licences, with additional taxation on spirits and tobacco, were estimated to produce £6 million (and the duties would also help avenge the 1908 Licensing Bill defeat); and there were novel – and 'vindictive' – proposals for the valuation and taxation of land. These land taxes aroused great enthusiasm among Socialists. As Mr (later Viscount) Snowden crowed: 'There is no other way under heaven by which we can make the poor better off, except by making somebody poorer than they were ... This is not the last tribute which the idle-rich class of this country will be called upon to pay for dealing with the problem of poverty for which their riches are responsible.' (On this score there was, in brief, to be a new Domesday survey, with an exhaustive valuation, taking account of the value of the site covered, the site cleared, a tax on increased values, etc.)

In greater detail, in so far as Lloyd George's speech affected the matter of this inquiry, he then said, in his introductory passages, to begin with: 'There was, I will not say an alarming, but an encouraging, diminution in the consumption of alcoholic liquors during last year' – already his 'temperance' zeal is finding expression. 'This was partly due undoubtedly to the very bad trade from which we suffered. But the figures for the past few years justify me in assuming that it was also attributable to a very large extent to the steady growth in the habits of sobriety amongst the masses of the people ... I shall have to reckon upon a continuation of that steady growth in the habits of self-restraint among the people in the matter of indulgence in intoxicating liquors which is so gratifying to the social reformer and so discouraging to the revenue officer. And the Committee will bear in mind that a comparatively small decrease in the consumption of a certain class of very alcoholised liquor would account for a considerable drop in revenue. These elements taken together – forestalments and increased temperance – account for the considerable diminution which I anticipated in this branch of the revenue for the coming year.'

He acknowledged the general anticipation of the further taxation of licences and after a detour on the question of clubs, drinking clubs, for which he proposed a poundage on their drinks receipts, he went on to the licence structure itself which he intended to revise. 'But I propose to take the opportunity of revising the whole system of Excise licences – a system which is at present full of confusion and anomalies, both in law and practice – and to place it upon a simple and intelligible basis. These licences are divided into three main classes – (1) manufacturers' licences, (2) wholesale dealers' licences, (3) retailers' licences. Speaking generally, no licence of the first two classes requires a justices' licence, but, with a few minor exceptions, all the licences of the third class require such a licence . . . This does not, of course, mean that a further contribution to the Revenue by way of taxation cannot properly be required from the holders of the other classes of licences. Under the head of manufacturers' licences I propose to substitute for the present fixed duties, £1 and £10 10s., for brewers of beer for sale and distillers of spirits respectively, graduated scales of duty according to the amount produced . . . The distiller's licence will be £10 for any quantity not exceeding 50,000 proof gallons, with an additional £10 for every additional 25,000 proof gallons . . . I propose to increase the licence for rectifiers of spirits from £10 10s. to £15 15s.'

We need not pursue him into other licence details; suffice it to notice that since the reform of the distillery laws in 1824 which fixed the distillers's fee at £10 regardless of quantity, the only alteration until Lloyd George's budget had been the addition of 10s. to the £10 fee in 1840. Lloyd George went on to remark, quite accurately, about indirect taxation, 'The poorer people are, the heavier they are taxed.' But that did not prevent his then considering three other possible sources of revenue. 'Beer, spirits and tobacco,' was how he listed them. 'An increase in the beer duty sufficiently great to justify an addition to the retail price would produce a very large sum – larger, indeed, than I require for my present purposes, and would have, besides, in all probability, the effect of diverting the consumption of alcohol from beer to spirits, a change which would certainly not conduce to the social health of the country. (Hear, hear.) The incidence of a small duty, on the other hand, would, to a large extent, at any rate in the first instance, be upon the liquor trade, rather than upon the consumer; and I should not feel justified in imposing such a burden in a year when so considerable an additional contribution is being called for from that trade under the head of licensing duties.

'The case of spirits is, however, somewhat different. (Hear, hear.) I am aware that the small increase in the spirit duties which were made by Lord St Aldwyn during the South African War' – then Hicks Beach added 6*d*. per proof gallon to the duty of 10*s*. 6*d*. a proof gallon making it a total of 11*s*. where it had since stood – 'were disappointing in their financial results, and that any further increase would undoubtedly result in a considerably diminished consumption, which would, to a very large extent, at any rate, nullify the benefit to the Revenue which might otherwise be expected to accrue from it. It does not, however, follow from the result of this small experiment that we have reached the absolute limit of the profitable taxation of spirits, or that a substantial increase in the rates of duty would not, in spite of its effect upon consumption, produce an appreciable amount of revenue. I am disposed, at any rate, to try the experiment which, even if it ends – to take the most pessimistic view – in no larger revenue being raised from the higher rate upon a diminished consumption than by the existing rate upon the present consumption, will still, in my view, be conducive to the best interests of the nation. (Hear, hear.)

'It is perfectly true that the small duties imposed up to the present have not produced anything, and the reason for that is that the retailer found, probably by changes in the character of the whisky or other means, that he was able to get his money in another way, and the consumption decreased by a considerable amount. Therefore it is idle to put on anything except a fairly heavy tax.

'I propose, therefore, to raise the present duties of Customs and Excise by 3*s*. 9*d*. a gallon, or, approximately one-third – an amount which will, on the one hand, justify an increase in retail prices, and, on the other hand, assuming such an increase to be at the rate of one-halfpenny a glass upon each glass of spirits sold over the counter at a public house, will leave an ample margin for the publican to recoup himself for the loss of profit arising from decreased consumption and something over towards mitigating the pressure of the new licensing duties scale. (A laugh.) I do not expect to realise a very large amount from increased duty during the present financial year. This year there are exceptional circumstances. In the first place, the forestalments are remarkably heavy. It is not merely forestalment up to the end of the financial year, but it has been going on since, so that the wholesale dealers have in hand a sufficient stock of spirits to carry them on comfortably for a good many weeks ahead. Therefore, we shall not get much from this source for some weeks, probably for some months. That will make a very considerable hole in the yield. Not only that, but I have not the faintest doubt that the increased duty will have the effect of decreasing the consumption. It may drive a good many from spirits to try beer, and other expedients of that sort. (Laughter.) It will involve an appreciable increase of price on the commodity. Taking all these influences into consideration, I do not feel safe in counting upon receiving more than £1,600,000 additional revenue as the result of the change in 1909–10.'

A diabolically clever presentation of a devilish scheme of taxation: Lloyd George had certainly heard of the rule the Romans acted upon about dividing and ruling. He hoped to drive a wedge between different sections of the trade: licence duties were up, so that licensees would concentrate on their own troubles; wine was not touched at all; beer only indirectly; spirits were savaged. Yet it had been widely forecast on the very eve of the budget that Champagne, as the drink of the idle rich would be a prime taxation victim! All spirits were to bear this heavier taxation burden, heavier by about one-third, and domestic distillers and rectifiers were to be put at even a worse disadvantage as against their rivals. They were, in short, to be subjected to a productivity tax – and when the Scotch whisky industry was later to become a major foreign currency earner a 'Productivity Year', so called, saw no lightening of this Lloyd George imposition of 1909 by which increased productivity was penalised. 'A mad world, my masters . . .'

Austen Chamberlain made the Opposition reply and criticised the Chancellor for 'shadowing forth in this vague language vast projects that were little capable of immediate or early realisation', for making of the budget 'an electoral manifesto'. But Chamberlain, as reported in *The Times*, also 'noticed in the licensing proposals a welcome change in the attitude of the government from that which they adopted at the time of the Licensing Bill. They had now become aware that the growth of drinking clubs was a serious matter . . . But it was not primarily to promote temperance, which had been making steady progress for the last ten years. His colleagues had advocated these duties as a punishment for opposing his Licensing Bill . . . He would not say that this taxation had been imposed vindictively, but that it had been imposed with the hope that its effect would destroy a good number of licences . . . would put many licences out of existence and taxation which produced such an effect became spoliation . . . In increasing the tax on spirits the right honourable gentleman had manufactured a new Irish grievance, but it was a matter for congratulations that the proceedings of the Government in relation to the Trade on this occasion had extended to all parts of the United Kingdom and that they in England were not to be legislated for by Scottish and Irish members, without being able to mete out to them the measure which they accorded to the people of this country.'

Chamberlain was more on the spot than he realised with his reference to 'a new Irish grievance', for when the Irish later held the balance in Parliament, they withdrew their opposition to the increased tax on whisky in consideration of the promise of Home Rule for Ireland. Without that promise the Irish members would have voted against the budget, and so would have brought down the Government.

The Times devoted a leader a day for several days, in their first leader on 30 April remarking: 'An increase in the spirit duties from which £1,600,000 is expected will tend to strengthen the movement in the direction of temperance, and £1,900,000 to be got out of tobacco will probably be regarded in many quarters as making for righteousness; while the £2,600,000 to be squeezed out of licences upon principles of a somewhat austerely virtuous kind will positively rejoice the teetotal people . . . Taxes on motor-cars and upon spirits of all kinds used for driving them are not liked by motorists, but will perhaps be accepted without much opposition in view of the application of most of the money to the improvement of the roads . . .'

Returning to the same subject on Saturday, 1 May, *The Times* wrote: 'It must be admitted that some of his proposals meet with general approval . . . and the taxation of liquor consumed in "clubs" does something to remedy an injustice to other more open retailers of liquor . . . The gravest feature of this Budget is that by his use in time of peace of such heavy increases in the income-tax, the death duties, and the spirit and tobacco duties, Mr Lloyd George has weakened resources of which the country would seriously feel the want in the unhappy event of our being involved in war.'

The leader on the budget debate in their issue of Monday, 3 May, scarified Lloyd George himself, and on Tuesday the 4th *The Times* leader resumed once more the effect on the trade: 'The impost can be met only by a general rise in the prices charged for beer and spirits; and as that will be combined with a similar increase in the price of tobacco, the result will not be pleasing to hunters for popularity and votes. Mr Balfour points out that the new licence duties are in fact a tax and will operate as such; while no corresponding Customs duty is placed upon foreign beer and spirits. The ultimate results flowing from this arrangement will throw a pleasing light upon free trade finance *in extremis*.'

On Wednesday 6 May they returned to the charge with 'We presume that the brewers will not fail to raise their prices so as to meet the new imposts, and in that case the taxes will fall upon the consumers, chiefly non-propertied. Or, if they simply abandon licences costing more than they can earn, and distribute their beer by other methods, again the success of the Budget is far from conspicuous.' The Government having lost the elections at both Stratford and Sheffield, *The Times* made the editorial comment on Thursday, 6 May: 'It is becoming pretty clear that his taxes upon licences and liquor are not going to fall upon the shoulders he intended to bear them; and that apart from brewers and distillers, whom he might perhaps defy, he has failed to reckon with his Nationalist allies. Mr Asquith, in defending the Budget yesterday, somewhat oddly pointed out that the revenue from beer and spirits is a rapidly falling one, a circumstance hitherto regarded as prohibitive of increased imposts . . . Mr Snowden yesterday put the whole situation in a nutshell when he defended the Budget on the ground that it takes from the rich to give to the poor.'

The leader for Friday, 7 May, was devoted to 'German Finance and German Taxation' – an obvious reference to the Germanic origin of the social welfare and other schemes copied by the Chancellor – while that for Saturday the 8th commented on the Primrose League annual meeting at the Albert Hall and the address there made by Balfour in which he said: 'I will give you another very singular example of the ignorance of the Government as to the principles underlying their own proposals. You know that there is a new duty called the licence duty, which is in reality a tax placed upon the manufacture of beer . . . It was pointed out by many persons, by myself among others, with the aid of concrete cases, how enormous was the burden which this tax put upon a particular class of manufacturers. What was the reply of the Government? It was given by the Prime Minister on Wednesday and by the Chancellor of the Exchequer in an interview published today . . . The answer was this: 'You have no right, you the critics of this proposal have no right, to describe this tax as a burden upon a particular class of manufacturers, because, of course, they will throw it upon the consumer." . . . the whole argument of the Chancellor of the Exchequer in his Budget speech . . . It now turns out that, in spite of that declaration of the Chancellor of the Exchequer, they think that the licence duty on brewers is not a tax on the brewer, but on the consumer.'

The Times editorial comment we can take as fair and considered; impartial in the sense of considering first the national well-being and the rightness of the matter being debated. With Balfour we are moving towards the political wrangle attitude, a wrangling to be excelled in by Lloyd George, as in his Limehouse speech on 30 July, to an audience of 4,000 poor folk in east London, when he talked of the rapacity of parasitic landowners, living on the unearned increase in land value. 'Who created these increments?' he asked. 'Who made that golden swamp? Was it the landlord? Was it his energy? His brains? . . . It is rather hard that an old workman should have to find his way to the gates of the tomb bleeding and footsore, through the brambles and thorns of poverty. We cut a new path for him, an easier one, a pleasanter one, through fields of waving corn.'

If Lloyd George was making it an occasion for a demagogic harangue, the trade was no less backward in presenting its case, at first with the assurance of reason and justice, later with the hard spirit aroused by its opponents and their distorted approach to the subject.

On Thursday, 6 May, the trade held their mighty protest meeting at the Cannon Street Hotel. A few fragments must suffice. Here is the president of the meeting, Mr Richard F. Nicholson, of J. & W. Nicholson: 'If the duties had been imposed for the benefit of the Navy only, nobody could have objected to it, because they all wanted to see a strong navy for the protection of their country, but the imposts were designed to smother the trade as effectually as the pillows smothered the little princes in the Tower many years ago. A tax on income or profit is justifiable . . . but the sort of taxes put forward now are nothing more nor less than cutting away slices of capital, and I can only call it blackmail . . . the grossest folly imaginable.' Then came Mr Gordon Clark, of Matthew Clark & Sons, to propose 'That this mass meeting of the wholesale wine, spirit and distilling trades hereby records its emphatic protest against the increase of duties on spirits already so heavily taxed, which will have the effect of injuring an industry already greatly depressed.'

Clark's oration deserves quoting extensively; it strikes the keynote of the day as lived by the trade, and the violence of the passions then engendered by Lloyd George and his 'People's Budget'. Here's for Clark: 'You are all of one mind, are you not? (Hear, hear.) . . . It makes one, gentlemen, boil over with indignation when we consider them [the budget proposals] . . . We who have to live in a northern climate cannot do without spirits, and it is an iniquitous thing for the Chancellor of the Exchequer to say that we can get on better without it . . . The great point I wish to make is that the overburdening of this trade is not done for fiscal purposes only. The Chancellor of the Exchequer does not want the money for the country, but he wants to kill, or at all events to cripple a trade opposed to him. (Applause.) . . . what Mr Balfour said on the morrow of the Budget, when he pointed out that there was no justification for such heavy taxation on the Trade. According to the remarks made by the Chancellor of the Exchequer in the course of his Budget speech, it was quite apparent that he did not care twopence if he killed the Trade. His words amounted to this: "If I get nothing out of it I do not mind the money, as that is a mere matter of detail. I have only put it down at £1,500,000, I do not care for that, but I will have their blood . . . a cartoon depicting Lloyd George as a pole-cat that does not kill for food. (A voice: it is a Welshman!) Yes, you are right, it comes from the Welsh mountains. It does not kill for food alone, but it kills for the love of the killing . . . It will not leave the hen-roost until it has spilt every drop of blood to be found there, and this, gentlemen, this human pole-cat; not content with that; he sets light to the hen-roost by his precious Budget proposals. It seems to me that for every £1 the Government have budgeted for, they are going to do £10 worth of damage to the Trade . . . The effects of it are going to be less trade and worse quality . . . Mr Lloyd George might think that the British workman will not spend as much as he did before, but such will not prove to be the case.

'He will probably get the same quantity of spirits, but it will not be of such good quality. The philanthropic argument will not wash. It seems to me that the reason these taxes are being put upon the Trade is because behind the Chancellor of the Exchequer is the Cabinet, and behind the Cabinet is a spectre, the figure of the teetotal party. That I fancy is the true reason that this tax is to be put upon the Trade. The Chancellor of the Exchequer could have raised the necessary money that he requires in a far easier manner, but he has made these imposts with diabolical ingenuity . . . It is an unjust tax, which bears harshly upon an overburdened Trade.'

James Stevenson, of John Walker & Sons Ltd, seconded the resolution. His speech was brilliant. Here are some excerpts: 'I am glad to see that the Trade intends to hang together; it is better to do that than be hung separately. It has been said of this Budget that it increases births, decreases deaths, and makes living in between intolerable . . . Last year it was the Licensing Bill, now it is the Budget which has been conceived in malignance and born in spite . . . It has been said that the people who frequent public houses have no minds, and the people who frequent clubs have no souls, but the members of the present government have neither minds nor souls. The present proposals in the Budget seem to be quite Bismarckian. Germany looms largely in the public eye at the present moment, but if we go to that country for precept we should also go there for example . . . It seems to me that the present Chancellor of the Exchequer thinks he is going to abolish thirst entirely. (Laughter.) He must well know that the 3s. 9d. per gallon on spirits will bring him in a figure far beyond his estimate of its yield . . . It is more like a policy of strangulation of the Trade. Total abstinence of the individual and prohibition for the State . . . The blustering, humbugging interference of a temperance minority. (Applause.)'

The resolution was put and carried with acclamation. Then a resolution was put, and carried, protesting against the increased licences. The third resolution was proposed by Mr Andrew Jameson, D.L., of John Jameson & Sons Ltd, Dublin: 'That a copy of the foregoing resolutions be forwarded to the Chancellor of the Exchequer with a request that he will receive a small deputation of members of the Trade in order to discuss more fully the grievances complained of.'

Mr Jameson, in part: 'You may take it for granted that all branches of the Trade in Ireland are in harmony with you . . . that there is no single branch of our trade that has not been got at, and gone for, to the best of the ability of the Chancellor of the Exchequer . . . We have few industries in Ireland at present, as our former industries have been taken away from us, but we have two industries left which we have managed to keep, and that is distilling and brewing. The country is very largely an agricultural one, and the importance of these trades to the agriculture of Ireland is enormous. This Bill hitting straight at the very vitality of our Trade will be a serious and heavy blow to our country. So well is this known that you will see for once an absolute union of Nationalists and Unionists in opposition to the governing party of this country.'

The resolution was seconded by John McDonald, of McDonald & Sons, head of trade defence in Scotland where, he said, there was extreme concern about the whisky duty and an agreement was in force to raise bar prices with notices in the bars: 'The prices are raised by the Chancellor of the Exchequer.'

The closing resolution was proposed by Mr H. Armstrong, of N. P. Sandiford, Son & Armstrong Ltd, 'That this meeting pledges itself in conjunction with the National Trade Defence Association to take all possible steps to resist the unjust proposals of the Budget.' This was seconded by Mr Robert Clarke, of Lewis Clarke & Co., Worcs., representing the Midland Wholesale Wine & Spirit Association. The National Trade Defence Association had, incidentally, fought the 1908 Licensing Bill.

Before passing to a closer examination of the reactions of the Scotch whisky industry itself, it is worth pausing to consider the reactions, as printed, of the member of Parliament, Mr H. C. Lea, proprietor of the influential *Wine and Spirit Trade Record*, a monthly journal regarded as authoritative in its field. He himself wrote the leader, 'Vindictive', for his issue of 8 May: 'We doubt whether Mr Lloyd George's best friends would hesitate to call his Budget vindictive. He is punishing the Trade for the House of Lords rejecting his Licensing Bill. He doesn't quite admit that, but he is candid enough to admit that his endeavours are calculated to lead to a lessened consumption of spirits. He might have added that he is crippling the beer trade and paralysing the licensed trade generally ... A declining trade is not usually regarded as a suitable subject for bleeding operations, and certainly no one could have imagined that an attempt would be made to crush the trade out of existence altogether. This is where we think Mr Lloyd George is fundamentally wrong. He is using the Budget for carrying out his own political ideas, and incorporating with it the material for a whole sheaf of Acts of Parliament. Admittedly the idea of the State in taxing alcoholic liquors is to force the consumers of certain so-called luxuries to contribute more heavily to the national revenue, not as a punishment for consuming such luxuries, but for the reason that by consuming them the consumers are supposed to show themselves to be members of the classes whose superfluity of wealth is the proper subject of taxation.

'But Mr Lloyd George's scheme is obviously and very largely intended as a punitive measure, directed against the trade which supplies the beverages. The extra 3s. 9d. on spirits can, and we hope will, be passed on entirely to the public. If the trade is strong and united there will be no difficulty about this, but it will not succeed in doing so by putting only 6s. a dozen on cased whisky instead of 6s. 6d. or 7s. The increased licences are an altogether different matter, and can in many cases be no more charged to the public than can extra expenditure in rent or rates ... Without the slightest possibility of getting a penny of it back, and with a lessened consumption in prospect, he (a typical London wholesaler) has to face an increase in his licence duties of about one hundred and eighty per cent!

'If we turn to the retail trade the prospect is even worse. Introducing the assessment basis into his licensing scheme, Mr Lloyd George lays down a scale of charges which must inevitably lead to the ruination of large numbers of holders of free houses, and deprive the proprietors of tied houses of any opportunity of earning dividends for their ordinary shareholders ... As one of our correspondents says, he seems not only determined on robbing the hen-roost, but throttling the hen as well. Seriously, though, we regard the licence question as the most difficult one of the lot, and the one upon which the trade should concentrate most of its attention. The extra tax on spirits can, and should, as we have said, be passed on to the public, but the proposed scale of licences would be idiotic if it were not so iniquitous, and it seems scarcely credible that the way in which it works can have been anticipated by the author of this surprising Budget. If it has been, we can only conceive that he does not mind raising the ire of one, and a comparatively small, section of the electorate – the traders in alcoholic beverages. Possibly he will find before he has finished that he has arrayed against him the great majority of the consumers of alcoholic beverages – something between four-fifths and nine-tenths of the entire electorate.

'At the tax on output – both of spirits and beer – we were not altogether surprised, and yet the present seems scarcely a fitting time for the innovation. The Chancellor has hit the distiller on the head with a crushing duty, and then jumped on him with an additional impost. In years long since gone by revenue was raised on *pro rata* licence duties, but gradually those duties were merged into the Spirit or Beer duty, as the case may be. The re-establishment today of a *pro rata* licence duty is a breach of faith and a reactionary proceeding, for which there is little or no justification. And why should it be applied only to the brewing and distilling trades? Why not to boot-making or to motor-car building? The one is no more a monopoly than the other.

'We hold, and always have held, that what is wanted in this country is an improvement in the tone of the public house. This Budget will do nothing towards this end. On the contrary, it will, by its excessive licences, squeeze out of existence the better-class houses, and encourage the slum drinking-dens where there is very often a big turnover and small rateable value. The 14s. 9d. duty will inevitably lead to the sale of newer and commoner spirit, be it foreign or home-made. Certainly the Highland distiller does not stand to be benefited. Both he and the grain distiller will regard with envy the wine shipper who has escaped on this occasion, and we shall not be surprised if Mr Lloyd George's attention is forcibly drawn to the fact that where a gill of Port, strength 60 u.p., pays duty to the amount of only $1\frac{4}{32}d.$, a gill of whisky and water of the same strength pays $2\frac{7}{32}d.$, or nearly twice as much . . .

'Wine is given a preference, too, as regards wholesale licences, there being an increase to £15 15s. for Spirits and £10 10s. for Beer. True, the Spirit dealer's additional 3-gn. bottle licence is to go, and all other retail licences, and in their stead there is to be brand-new retailer's licences based on annual value with amounts that stagger . . . Separate retail licences for Spirits, Wine and Beer! For licensing purposes Wine is no better than Beer. Spirits are four-fold worse. The Chancellor evidently means the Trade to work for him . . .

'What is to be done? For our own part, we believe the Lords will not throw out the Budget, and they cannot amend it. Neither do we believe that there is the slightest chance of getting the Government to reduce the new impost on Spirits. In regard to licences we are more optimistic. We question whether Mr Lloyd George has gauged the full effect of his tariffs – wholesale and retail, on and off – and we should not be surprised if he were persuaded to make them more reasonable.'

Mr Lea also quoted elsewhere in the same issue startling facts from Lloyd George's pre-budget White Paper which demonstrated the decline in spirit consumption in the United Kingdom in the preceding decade. In the financial year 1899–1900, there were consumed in the United Kingdom 1·98 proof gallons of spirits per head of population. In 1900–1 this fell to 1·10; in the following year to 1·01; in the year 1902–3 it rose slightly to 1·03; then it dropped below the one, never to rise again: in 1903–4 it was 0·99; then 0·93; for the period 1905–7 it stayed at 0·91, falling in 1907–8 to 0·90, and further to 0·87 proof gallons per head of population in the year preceding the budget, 1908–9.

6

Scotch reaction

THE SCOTS were as quick into battle as ever their forebears were against the foe across the borders. Pride of time and place goes to William Ross, then managing director of the D.C.L., and the greatest statesman of the distilling industry. His immediate reaction deserves quoting in full, and runs: 'My opinion is that the Budget proposals affecting our trade are an unwarrantable attack upon an industry already too heavily taxed.

'Whisky already pays nearly five times as much duty as beer, relatively to the absolute alcohol which each contains. The increased duty of 3s. 9d. per gallon will increase that ratio to almost seven to one.

'Scotland being essentially a whisky drinking country will have to bear the brunt of this heavy tax – her proportion working out at £642,000 more than it should be if her population only were to regulate the tax.

'The absence of any increase in the wine duties is a further source of grievance to the distiller.

'The alteration in the distiller's licence duty from £10 10s. to one regulated by the quantity of spirit produced, is altogether unjust, and is an attempt to burn the candle at both ends. This will mean that a distillery producing 2,000,000 gallons annually will have to pay a licence duty of £790 in place of the former licence of £10 10s. As this is a tax which cannot be placed upon the foreigner, it is a direct handicap to the British distiller who produces spirit for manufacturing purposes in competition with the foreigner, and also to the distiller who has to compete against continental makers in the manufacture and sale of yeast.

'The whole proposals merit the severest condemnation, and it is to be hoped that the trade will use their utmost endeavours to prevent the Finance Bill from passing.'

And, be it remembered, that since Gladstone's Midlothian campaign, with its accompaniment of 'Sweet Williams' Scotland had been the great bastion of the Liberal party!

A few other judgments and reactions are worth quoting at this stage as demonstrating trade feelings and attitudes in the period before the formation of group statements. Thus J. G. Thomson & Co. Ltd, of Leith, the premier royal and ancient wine and spirit centre of Scotland, who declared: 'We consider that the increase in the duty on spirits of 3s. 9d. per proof gallon will have a disastrous effect upon the Scotch whisky trade. We think it will have the effect of lowering qualities, which is quite against the interests of temperance. It will undoubtedly reduce the consumption of whisky; but this again will not have any effect on temperance, as we think it will be the moderate and legitimate consumer who will be forced to deny himself, and not the small minority who abuse the use of drink, and who are the enemies equally of the trade and the community.

'We also consider that the heavy increase in licensing duties will cause the utter ruin of many hardworking and respectable traders, who are conducting their business entirely to the satisfaction of the local authorities.'

Again in Leith, the old-established firm of Charles Mackinlay & Co. issued their judgment: 'We consider it, as regards our trade, very unfair to Scotland and Ireland. The Chancellor estimates that the increase of duty on whisky will yield him an extra £1,500,000, whereas, supposing the consumption were remaining the same as at 31 March 1908 – by no means a high-water mark of consumption – the increased duty would bring in over £6,000,000. Apparently, therefore, he anticipates a very large shrinkage in the consumption of whisky, thereby inflicting serious injury upon one of the largest and most important industries in Scotland . . .

'It is impossible to estimate the effect of this heavy charge (licences) upon the retail trade, which has not for some time been in a prosperous condition . . .

'Distillers of fine malt are up in arms; the fear is that cheaper qualities may be substituted for the finest makes of Scotch whisky, and their output, which has for the last ten years been nothing like the previous decade, will still further be curtailed. Farmers and dairymen are also interested in this phase of the question, and dearer milk, caused by a short supply of draff – almost entirely used by cowfeeders in the north – will be a result the Chancellor did not look for.

'Altogether we consider the Budget, as regards our trade, a vindictive one, and bears out the threats held out by various members of the present government when the Licensing Bill was thrown out last year.'

A prominent east of Scotland firm summarised what they considered the main questions raised by Lloyd George's vicious attack on the trade:

'1. Unjust to the whisky trade as compared to the wine and beer producers.

'2. Unjust to Scotland with the large number of distilleries as compared with England.

'3. Involves a larger capital to carry on the business and will probably infer a restricted amount of business. With a restricted consumption the retailer has, besides, a higher licence duty to pay.

'4. The use of inferior quality and newer spirits.

'5. The smaller grocers (whose business has been much cut into by Co-op. stores, and who have been enabled to make a decent living through their liquid turnover) will in many cases be ruined.

'6. Distillers have no monopoly as anyone can start a distillery on payment of licence to inland revenue.

'7. Why should there not be a corresponding tax to reach teetotallers who get rid of about one-quarter of their fair share of the country's expenditure?'

A prominent distiller near Elgin, the whisky capital of the Highlands, made a most relevant point: 'The cost of whisky production is about 2s. 6d. per gallon. To increase the existing tax from 11s. to 14s. 9d. is unjust . . . when it is remembered that beer has been left untouched.'

And an equally prominent Glasgow merchant in wines and spirits made a most practical observation when he said: 'There is only one remedy available, one which the wholesale merchant must introduce, one which will lead to a great deal of friction between old friends; he must insist on prepayment of duty . . . And does the Chancellor imagine that illicit distilling is a thing of the past? If he does, he has revived it.'

But no call at Glasgow would be complete without the acute remarks of Mr P. J. Mackie, of Mackie & Co., Distillers, Ltd. A fire-belcher of his day, if ever there was one, he declared: 'The Chancellor of the Exchequer has carried out his threat to "rob the hen-roosts". The Budget is framed with a view to catch votes at the next general election. It is vindictive, oppressive to our trade, and is an attempt to pay off an old score by the Liberal party. We turned the Liberals out when Mr Childers put 2s. on the duty, and this may be done again . . .

'The whole framing of the Budget is that of a faddist and a crank and not a statesman. But what can one expect of a Welsh country solicitor being placed, without any commercial training, as Chancellor of the Exchequer in a large country like this? I might as well bring into my business and place at the head of it a bootmaker or shoemaker or country solicitor, and any man will know how incompetent he would be for the job.

'If he wanted to raise money and also to put a stop to a terrible curse, which causes more unhappiness than all the liquors put together . . . let him legalise betting through the medium of the totalisator . . . and make it absolutely prohibitive to conduct betting outside this agency as at present.'

With chaos and paralysis striking the trade, the Finance Bill was published on 28 May, and, as Mr Lea remarked, 'The Radical Shylock seemed to wish to hit the distiller, the wholesale merchant, the blender and the retailer in the most obnoxious manner. After the first surprise was over, the fiery cross was sent around. There was a great mustering of councils and committees, of societies and associations, and there is not a branch of the licensing industry but what has met to protest in most emphatic manner.'

Some of those protests as affecting Scotch whisky must now be considered. First, the petition of the grain distillers of Scotland: (1) The duty on spirits is already excessive and out of all proportion to the duties charged on other alcoholic liquors. To increase the duty by 3s. 9d. per proof gallon will make the breach still wider, and result in placing an enormous additional tax upon one class of consumers while letting another class entirely free. (2) As Scotland is essentially a whisky-drinking country, while England takes alcohol more largely in the form of beer, it follows that the additional tax will fall unequally on the two countries. A close calculation shows that per head of population Scotland will pay about 5*s.* 5½*d.*, while England will only pay 2*s.* 4½*d.*, or, in other words, Scotland will pay of this additional tax over £642,000 more than its fair proportion.'

It is not difficult to see there the master-mind of Ross of the D.C.L., whose first reaction has already been cited.

Distillers and farmers of Ross-shire met at Dingwall on 19 May and passed a resolution urging the Chancellor of the Exchequer to reconsider his proposals in view of the serious effect the whisky tax would have on the distillery and agricultural interests of the North, in respect both of the decreased demand for barley and the increased price of distillery by-products.

The distillers north of a line through Perth met in secret conclave in Elgin on the 7th of the same month after which the secretary reported: '(1) That this meeting, comprising all distillers, north of Perth, of whisky made solely from malted barley, strongly protests against this industry being selected to be unfairly penalised beyond others by the imposition of the extra whisky duty of 3*s.* 9*d.* per gallon on a declining trade suffering severely from many years of depression, and decides that deputations be appointed and representations made to the Chancellor of the Exchequer and the Prime Minister and other Members of Parliament, that this unjust and oppressive tax be departed from, as otherwise the distilling industry in Scotland, north of Perth, will be ruined; and this meeting is of opinion that the Chancellor of the Exchequer cannot realise how injurious this impost must prove to the north of Scotland, in which malt distilling from home-grown barley is the predominant industry – an industry which, although free to use other less costly raw materials, has always strictly adhered to the use of solely malted barley.'

The Campbeltown Distillers' Association made in its protest a point which recurred frequently through the disputes of the time when it commented on the Budget's increasing 'the sale of cheap wine fortified with German new potable spirit to the detriment of the working classes.' And the Gartloch Distillery Co., in a letter of protest to the member of Parliament for north-west Lanark, drew attention to a most vital matter to be raised in the world war looming ahead: 'We have no foreign markets,' they wrote, 'and have the keenest struggle to retain the home market for our principal product and by-product – namely, whisky and yeast – against foreign traders. The competition from Belgium, Holland, Germany and Denmark is very keen . . . Within the last twenty-five years the British distillers have built up a new industry for this country. Prior thereto, practically all the yeast used in Britain was imported from abroad, but the Scottish distillers, after many years of strenuous competition which still continues, are now manufacturing about £500,000 worth of yeast per annum . . . A distillery is essentially a factory.'

The opinion of John Grant, Dufftown, was made known about the time of the Elgin meeting when he listed the bad effects the Bill would have on the trade as well as giving an accurate picture of the industry at the time. It cannot be bettered. He methodically made thirteen points and cited facts and figures in support.

'1. Pure Highland Malt Whisky, the product of barley cereal, almost exclusively home-grown, is manufactured chiefly in the counties of Scotland and north of and including Perthshire.

'2. These distilleries, many of them of great age, are ninety-six in number. The distillation of pure Highland malt whisky is one of the very few important industries of that part of Scotland.

'3. The capital invested in these distilleries is enormous. A safe calculation places the cost price of buildings, plant and machinery alone of these distilleries at £2,500,000. The working capital in carrying them on is very great.

'4. During the last year these distilleries produced upwards of 7,000,000 gallons of whisky of the highest quality in the market, at prime cost of upwards of £1,000,000.

'5. Pure Highland malt, the cream of whiskies, reaches its finest quality only with age; and distillers have built, at very great expense, extensive warehouses at their distilleries, in which at present the enormous quantity of 45,000,000 gallons or thereby of whisky is lying maturing. This great quantity represents a money value of £10,000,000 quite apart from duty.

'6. For many years the tendency has been to use malt whiskies of increasing age, and consequently of superior quality. More capital, therefore, had been required to carry stocks, which are held by distillers and spirit merchants, and are largely financed by Scottish banks. The work of financing these stocks, in face of a declining consumption, has yearly become more onerous and difficult.

'7. The effect of the 3s. 9d. extra duty on these pure malt distillers will be disastrous. The extra duty will lead to the consumption of the cheaper and inferior raw-grain whisky, manufactured from foreign barley, maize, etc., costing to produce 1s. to 1s. 6d. as compared with 2s. 6d. to 3s. to produce pure Highland malts made from home barley. It will also entail a reduction in average age of whisky consumed by the public. Before the Budget one-third of Scotch whisky used was pure malt. Now it will be very much less. The increased duty on 7,000,000 gallons manufactured last year north of Perth works out at £1,312,500; and in view of the Chancellor of the Exchequer's Budget estimate, and his statement in the House, that, assuming the output of British and Irish distilleries remained the same, the annual produce of the extra 3s. 9d. duty would produce £9,207,970, the Government authorities admittedly and correctly anticipate a vastly reduced consumption of whisky.

'8. Another effect of the increased duty is the largely augmented capital which will be required by the distiller and wholesale spirit merchant in carrying on their business on the present scale. The distiller and spirit merchant in marketing whisky to the retail trade pay duty at once, and the trade terms are three months' credit, which is often extended, making an average of four months. It will, therefore, take one-third more capital to finance the Excise duty alone, and one-fourth more capital than at present to manufacture the whisky and pay duty on it. This, in view of the enormous capital at present invested in pure Highland malt whisky, and the difficulty in financing it, will inevitably end in blotting out many of the smaller distilleries and spirit merchants.

'9. In the history of Excise duties heretofore, any increase in the spirit duty has generally been concurrent with an increase in the Excise duty on beer. Whisky is the national drink of Scotland and Ireland. Beer is the national drink of England. Prior to this Budget, the inequality of treatment in taxing the alcohol in these drinks was unjust to Scotland and Ireland – the beer drinker getting the same quantity of alcohol in beer four times cheaper than the whisky drinker gets the same quantity of alcohol in whisky. The Chancellor of the Exchequer's failure to put on an equivalent duty has accentuated this national injustice.

'A gallon of spirits at proof is 14s. 9d. duty.

'Thirty-six gallons of beer at 1055° is 8s. duty. (This includes the additional duty of 3d. from the new rate for brewer's licence.)

'Beer as sold, if brewed about standard gravity, contains from eight to nine per cent proof spirit. A barrel of beer is therefore equivalent, at least, to 2·88 gallons of spirits from an alcoholic point of view. The duty on 2·88 gallons as spirits at 14s. 9d. is £2 2s. 6d. The duty on 2·88 gallons as beer is 8s. The duty on spirits or whisky is therefore now 5·31 times that on beer. Yet the Chancellor of the Exchequer hopes to induce sobriety by driving people from drinking whisky to drinking beer, which is taxed fully five times less than what whisky is taxed from an alcoholic point of view.

'10. The extra duty of 3s. 9d. on whisky is not adjusted in amount, so that it can be fairly carried on and placed on the consumer. The retail trader, in adding 1d. to the portion of whisky sold by him, nets 5s. per gallon. If he added ½d. on the same portion he could not recoup himself for the extra duty. This was specially noted by the Chancellor of the Exchequer, who invited the retailer to pay the extra licence duties imposed by the Budget out of his gain from whisky. This is again inequitable, and gives another unfair advantage to beer.

'11. The admitted great reduction of the output and consumption of whisky, if the increased duty of 3s. 9d. is continued, will very adversely affect farming, banking, railways, and many other allied and dependent industries in the north of Scotland. To produce the 7,000,000 gallons of pure Highland malt whisky made last year upwards of 3,200,000 bushels of barley were used, at an approximate payment to farmers of the north of Scotland of £500,000. To produce the barley required for the northern distilleries 100,000 acres of land are annually under crop. The northern malt distiller *alone* gives a much higher price for home-grown barley than for foreign barley; and always uses home-grown barley when it can be got, foreign barley not being so suitable for pure malt whisky distillation. The foreign barley used last year only amounted to 24,000 bushels. It will thus be seen that a material reduction of the output of pure Highland malt whisky will adversely affect the farmers of the north of Scotland.

'12. Draff or wet grains, the remains of the barley after the brewing process, is a very valuable by-product of distilleries. It is used for cattle-feeding, and is the most important feeding substance for dairy cows, as it has large milk-producing qualities. Last year 3,200,000 bushels of draff were produced and sold to farmers and dairymen in the north at a very cheap rate. The effect of the increased Excise duty will be to restrict the output of draff very much, and to increase the price of this valuable feeding material.

'13. Banking and railway interests in the north will be much injured. Reference has been made before to the difficulty already felt in financing the large stocks of pure Highland malt whisky, and the increasing difficulties in face of the larger duty.

'The two northern railways have during many years largely benefited by the distilling trade in the north of Scotland in carrying coal, draff, whisky, yeast, etc., and a safe computation puts the railway rates for a year, incident to the carrying of the ninety-six Highland distilleries, at £150,000.

'Many other allied and dependent industries will be seriously affected by the increased Excise duty, particularly so in Banffshire and Moray-shire, which have forty-two distilleries; and a great restriction in the employment of working men will ensue.'

That is not only a reasoned argument of the pot still distillers' case, but a most valuable exposition of their industry itself at the time. For, it should be remembered, that the final report of the royal commission inquiring 'What Is Whisky?' had not then been issued, though enough had emerged in the interim report of the previous year to show which way the wind was blowing.

The pot versus patent fight then appeared in new guise, in fresh armour suited to the fight. So the secretary, Mr James McConachie, reported to shareholders of a leading Highland malt distillery, Craigel-lachie-Glenlivet, with blending affiliations: 'It looks as if this Budget were framed to crush an old enemy, and to satisfy private animosity against political opponents. It is a cunning device to pit the brewers against the distillers and thus break the unanimity of the trade . . . Unless the spirit duty is altered the demoralising influence that will ensue will be so far spread that it will be throwing the march of progress back for years.'

And about the same time, May–June 1909, Mr P. J. Mackie, of Glasgow, whose firm also controlled that Highland malt distillery, put forward in a letter to Lloyd George a proposal which was tantamount to a continuation of the pot versus patent fight. Mackie wrote, in part: 'The proposed large increase in duty is already tending to the sale of new and cheap quality grain whisky. This is a regrettable incident. While if the duty were charged according to age it would promote the sale of matured and high-class spirits, and thus remove many of the objectionable features consequent on new drink. Starting with an increase of duty of 3*s*. 9*d*. on spirits under six months of age (as no one admits using new spirits no one could object to this increase):

Under two years of age 2*s*. 6*d*. extra duty would be charged.

Under three years of age 2*s*. extra duty would be charged.

Under four years of age 1*s*. 6*d*. extra duty would be charged.

Under five years of age 1*s*. extra duty would be charged.

Over five years old the old duty of 11*s*. per gallon.

'Excepting brandy, most foreign spirits are imported new. The age would be required to be calculated from the date of landing here, though from our own possessions a certificate of age from the Customs House on the other side might be accepted. This also might be arranged with regard to brandy.

'The only objection to urge against this scheme is that of gin, which it has always been considered does not improve with age. It is the competition of cheap gin that is responsible for much of the cheap whisky that is now sold. It is this cheap liquor that does so much harm and causes so much drunkenness and degradation. But gin would not suffer any disability in submitting to the same scale of duty as whisky, as the equivalent prices between gin and other liquors would still be maintained; and as there are people who are now advertising Old Gin it would appear that it does improve with age like other spirits.

'I know of no departmental reasons why there should be any difficulty in ascertaining the average age of either blends or single whiskies, as they are all recorded in the Excise books, and there could therefore be no difficulty in averaging the age of blends.'

That scheme of graduated spirit duties, as it came to be called, really set the heaths ablaze. As Ross later recalled: 'The distillers immediately raised a protest (about the extra duty), and asked that a deputation be received by the Chancellor of the Exchequer, so that they might represent their views. By the unfortunate action of a section of the Trade, viz., the Highland Malt Distillers, the Trade became divided in their views, and, as had so often happened before, they did not present a united front – thus giving Mr Lloyd George an excuse for doing nothing in the matter. The Highland distillers suggested a graduated

A typical Highland malt pot still distillery

A malt whisky distillery on Islay, off the west coast of Scotland

scale of duties according to the age of the spirits cleared from bond, which was, of course, a direct attack upon the grain distillers, and led to separate deputations being received – each advocating their own particular views in place of insisting vigorously upon the remission of the whole advance.'

In retrospect it would seem that the battle over this graduated scheme became of more importance to the participants than the budget proposals themselves. In June a deputation representing the Scotch malt distillers and some agricultural societies waited upon the Chancellor suggesting just this graduated scale of duties outlined by Mackie. Lloyd George gave every appearance of being impressed with the idea but pointed out that he 'had not heard opposing interests . . . suggested the distillers should lay their heads together and submit a scheme showing how such a tax would work out.'

After the interview, the Highland malt distillers' deputation had an interview in a committee room at the House of Commons with Scottish members to whom they gave the figures they had just shown Lloyd George and which showed that the extra duty would throw out of work 700 to 800 distillery workmen with their dependants, rendering destitute over 5,000 people in the Highlands. The prospect had no apparent effect on the author of the 'People's Budget'. Even the forecast of a decrease in farming to the extent of over 1,600,000 bushels of barley fewer being harvested left him unmoved and unaffected.

One natural consequence was that early in July, another representative distillers' deputation had an interview with the Chancellor, this time protesting not only against the extra duty proposed on the whisky, and the distiller's licence fee increase, but also stating a case against the graduated duty proposal. The deputation was not only of Scottish distillers but included also representatives from England and Northern Ireland. Both pot and patent still distillers were in the party, along with those interested in the blending, distributing and rectifying trades. Indeed, they were able to boast that their combined output of 35 million gallons a year was equal to three-quarters of the total British production of potable spirit.

They stressed the 'extraordinary difference' of the relative taxation of the alcohol in beer, wine and spirits, but it was on the graduated scale of taxation that they concentrated. The interview was successfully 'leaked' by an interested correspondent, whose report brings out more than just the interview itself. 'With regard to the proposed scheme of graduation,' he was able to write, 'suggested by a small section of the Scottish distillers and obviously favoured by the Chancellor and a good many members of Parliament, who do not in the least understand the question, but simply support it because they are told that if adopted it must result in the average whisky being a good deal older than it has hitherto been – which is by no means the fact – this proposal should be thoroughly understood not only by the Trade, but by the public themselves, for it would probably have somewhat far-reaching effects and would impose restrictions on the former, whilst it would undoubtedly increase the cost of the beverage all round to the latter without conferring any very definite benefits on them in return.

'The Chancellor, of course, is satisfied because the compromise suggested means a permanent addition to the spirit duty of at least 2s. and probably an average addition of nearly 2s. 6d., and would enable him to pose as a public benefactor before those who do not understand the question, namely the public at large . . .

'The deputation very properly drew his attention to the fact that the graduation scheme would have the effect of compulsory bonding of all spirits for the whole period suggested – i.e., four years – without any notice being given to the Trade to prepare for such an innovation. Now the Royal Commission on Potable Spirits . . . has gone most minutely into this very question of the necessity for compulsory bonding or otherwise. If their finding is that in the interests of the health of the consumer, if from a hygienic point of view compulsory bonding is unnecessary, then graduation must be absolutely unnecessary also.

'If, on the other hand, the Royal Commission recommend a certain measure of compulsory bonding, then any scheme of graduation would be wrong because no spirits should be allowed to be consumed until the period of bonding considered necessary has elapsed. Indeed, if the Government adopted any scheme of graduation under such circumstances they would practically be compounding a felony, for they would be accepting a bribe in the form of a higher rate of duty for allowing such spirits to go into consumption. If, however, compulsory bonding is not considered necessary, then there is no reason why spirits of a particular age should be given an arbitrary fiscal preference over others, merely because a certain number of distillers have made far more spirit than they can sell, and think that by some such method they can put an artificial value on their own manufacture. Surely it is no part of the duty of a Government to create a market against the consumer for those who have over-produced and are over-stocked with old spirit.'

The approach and even the phrases employed all indicate that the author behind this biased 'leak' could have been none other than Ross, who was himself the guiding genius of the patent still distillers. But the mere fact that they took such biting strokes against the graduated scheme is itself an indication of their apprehension that it might easily come to pass. And as we shall see later, Lloyd George had a private penchant for compulsory bonding.

The inspired 'leak' went on: 'Another fatal objection to graduation, at least from the trade point of view, is that it does not in the least recognise the obvious difference in character between various makes of spirits . . . It is common knowledge that grain whisky and the lighter made Lowland malts become mellowed and matured and ready for consumption by the most exacting critic at a much earlier period than do the heavier Highland malts. Thus a term of bonding which may be necessary to bring the latter to perfection is neither necessary nor effective in the case of the former.'

Their 'revelations' on the interview then turn to give a most lively picture, for us, of the state of the market then, and the animosities rampant. The account went on: 'It is clear that this suggested scheme of graduation has been framed entirely in the interests of those traders who make a speciality of high-priced bottled spirits and who do not cater for the working man . . . They look to graduation merely as a means to reduce the duty, for they would not be affected by the restrictions imposed thereby as would the much larger and more important section who cater for the less expensive spirits sold over the counter, the cost of which would undoubtedly be raised to the extent of the added ninepence quite unnecessarily, for it does not require ageing to make it either wholesome or palatable.

'With regard to blends – in which form nine-tenths of all the whisky manufactured both in Scotland and Ireland is sold – compulsory bonding, and especially graduation, would be a very serious detriment, and, indeed, an injustice, for it has been conveyed more or less officially that the age of the blend would be that of the youngest constituent. This is obviously unfair to the trader who endeavours to give a good article by skilfully mixing together several different whiskies, each at its best,

and would be distinctly to the disadvantage of the public, who would
no longer get the very large proportion of well-matured spirits,
because the age of the youngest constituent would have to be raised in
order to escape the higher rate of duty, whilst the age of the older
constituents would have to be reduced in order to compensate for the
cost of the other alteration. Some distillers seem to be unable to see that
it is by blending, and by blending only, that whisky has become so
popular a beverage all over the world. No doubt it is the blender who
bulks large before the public eye, and the distiller who really produces
the article which enables the former to make his name is frequently
obscured and forgotten; but nevertheless, the latter should be careful
not to saw away the branch on which he is sitting, because nothing he
can do will ever induce the public again to drink unblended those pot
still whiskies which are only adapted for blending, and if they are not
consumed in a blend they will not be consumed at all. Nor should we
lose sight of the fact that graduation is after all only a temporary
expedient for relieving him of surplus stock.'

Lloyd George had then apparently been subjected to a long dissertation on the evidence given at the 'What Is Whisky?' commission on
the effects of maturing, the wholesomeness of immature spirit, the
palate appeal of the mature product. But the grain distillers were
obviously worried by the graduated duty scheme and all out to repress
it at birth. They summarised yet again their arguments on the subject,
saying: 'In the face of such evidence as this it is very hard to see why the
Government or the House of Commons should adopt the idea of a
graduation scheme which is:

'1. Not extensive enough to bring pot still whisky of the heavier
kinds to perfection from a palatable point of view.

'2. Too long for the lighter makes of pot still and grain whiskies to
attain the same objects.

'3. Absolutely unnecessary from a hygienic point of view.

'4. Not in any way asked for by the ordinary consumer, who has
long ago found out for himself where he can get an article he likes.

'5. Only asked for by a section of the trade who either have stocks
far too large for their requirements, and see in this scheme a chance of
artificially enhancing their value if only for the time being, or who at
any cost must have a reduction in the duty, and consider graduation the
only way.

'6. Of no benefit to the country from a revenue point of view.

'7. Contrary to the interests of the consumer of the less expensive spirits, as the price of these would be enhanced.'

After further time spent on the problem of gin, which needs no maturing, the anti-bonders, anti-graduated duty types, really went to town on a political keynote. The Liberals, who formed the government, of course, were ardent free-traders; they would have no tax on imports, especially on food imports. So the deputation 'leaked' this closing passage to their only too willing informer: 'The final claim for consideration put forward by the advocates of the Graduation Scheme and perhaps the wildest of all, though it is understood that this is the main reason which commends it to the Liberal members of the House of Commons (of all people in the world), is the interest of the British farmer in this matter. Now it is not so long since the whole country was covered with representations of large and small loaves, the former being the article produced by the present government, mainly at the expense of the British farmer. It is hardly conceivable that those members who shout so loudly about the rights of the consumer to buy in the cheapest market regardless of any effect the necessarily open door has on home industries or production, it is hardly conceivable that they seriously claim that whilst the importation of foreign cereals of all kinds should be encouraged so long as they are going to be made into bread, no matter what happens to the British farmer, who would be only too glad to grow the same cereals if he could get a living out of them, yet if these same cereals are to be made into whisky, the consumer must be forgotten and the British farmer protected at once!'

The cereal mainly used, of course, for grain, or patent still distillation was maize, generally imported from the United States of America. The anti-graduators held that it should be allowed in under Free Trade principles along with wheat and other cereals which had ruined the British farmer towards the close of the last century, and were still impoverishing him at the time of the deputation.

The closing paragraph of this barely disguised propaganda 'leak' is most noteworthy for revealing the depth of the chasm dividing the two sides in this civil war within the Scotch whisky industry. It concludes: 'The present Government – or perhaps the present Liberal majority – has advocated and, indeed, passed a good many measures very inconsistent with Liberal traditions, but it has not yet gone quite so far as the handful of Scotch pot still distillers, who are solely responsible for this whole extraordinary proposal, would have it go. Surely the Trade generally will unhesitatingly oppose the whole scheme, and will make it clear to the Chancellor of the Exchequer that whilst they are quite prepared to pay their share of the additional financial responsibilities of the Empire, they claim that if alcoholic beverages are to be subjected to further taxation, all forms of alcohol should bear their proper share of the burden, so that the retail price may be proportionately affected.'

In short, they were willing to give in to Lloyd George, with the face-saver about 'Empire' so long as they beat the 'graduators'.

Later, this same propaganda blast was issued, modified, as a circular by the Committee of Grain Distillers, incorporating the sections of the newly issued final report of the royal commission on whisky and other potable spirits as they referred to the health findings on there being no need for compulsory bonding. And instead of the government criticism implied in the closing paragraph of the above quoted 'leakage' they inserted this one: 'We may point out also that, besides the farmer, there are innumerable employees of all grades, including many working men, who depend largely, in many cases entirely, on the companies and firms which we represent. If our business is to be curtailed and crippled, we venture to think that their claims to sympathy are at least equally worthy the attention of Parliament as are those of the farmer who, after all, is invariably able to sell any cereal he can grow if it is fit for use.'

This circular was not issued until 5 October, and was called forth in reply to one from the North of Scotland Malt Distillers' Association addressed to Scottish M.P's, but given a wide external distribution. That letter contained much of the material and framework of the opinion given earlier of John Grant of Dufftown. But in their letter to the Chancellor they also now make the interesting point on wine: 'Ten and a half million gallons of foreign wines were consumed last year in this country and according to the respective alcoholic strengths the Excise duty upon these only averages 4s. to 7s. per gallon, as compared to 14s. 9d. upon whisky. This is giving an unjust preference to the foreigner, encouraging his industry to the detriment of the home manufacturer. The duty on whisky has been advanced from time to time, while the duty on wines is lower than it was fifty years ago.'

But the revelation which got the Grain Distillers' Committee was this one: 'A deputation from these North Country Malt Distillers had an interview with the Chancellor of the Exchequer on 15th June last, when he agreed to favourably consider the question of graduation of the duty on whisky according to its age, provided this could be carried out by the permanent officials, and asked the deputation to meet the permanent officials. Immediately thereafter the deputation had a meeting with the permanent officials, when, after discussion, these officials informed the deputation that there were no Excise difficulties in the way, and that if they had the instructions of the Chancellor of the Exchequer to carry out a scheme of graduation they could do so.'

The urgency of the question arose from the fact that on 24 September the whole increased duty was passed by the Commons, and Lloyd George pledged himself 'to reconsider this question of graduation before the Report stage of the Bill'. And some indication of the urgency is given by the fact that just as the Grain Distillers issued their circular immediately after the Malt Distillers had issued theirs, the latter had to come back immediately themselves with this brief one: 'With reference to the circular issued by the Grain Distillers to members of Parliament, the North of Scotland distillers have to state that their proposed scale of graduation simply places the retailer in a position to supply the public with matured whisky at the same price as the newly manufactured article. This graduation scheme would certainly induce the retailer to raise the standard of whisky supplied to the public, and public opinion is overwhelmingly in favour of the matured article. If the Royal Commission on potable spirits, in place of relying mainly on expert evidence, had taken sufficient evidence from publicans and the general public and of the police, of what takes place at fairs and markets, and in the slums of large cities, they would have obtained proof within personal cognisance of these witnesses that new spirit is injurious.

'There is no reason why the proposed graduation should benefit pure Malt whisky more than Grain. Malt distillers consider that graduation will raise the standard of the cheapest qualities retailed to the public, and safeguard the quality of whisky to the advantage of the consumer.

'Pure Malt Whisky, like pure French brandy, is distilled in a pot still, and certainly contains ingredients beneficial to health, and which, with age, produce the flavour and aroma characteristic of Highland Malt Whisky.

'The Grain distillers rely upon Grain and Malt Whisky being the same spirit, and plead the Report of the Royal Commission on potable spirits in support, but when dealing with Cognac Brandy the Commission said that it depended upon *the wine used and grown in a particular district and the skill of the stillman by distillation in pot stills*, and allowed it the special description of Cognac Brandy.

'The patent still is undoubtedly an efficient instrument for producing a neutral spirit and an industrial alcohol, but if the Grain distillers' argument, that graduation be propounded only on the basis of purity, be carried to its logical conclusion, then a still producing pure alcohol, no matter from what materials, would be superior to anything at present made in Great Britain.

'Graduation would neither decrease nor increase the price of whisky to the working man, it would simply tend to give him an old matured sound whisky in place of new spirit.'

But the circular of the Grain Distillers' Committee, signed by Ross, Edinburgh, Nicholson, London, and Sydney Greer, Belfast, drew a much more direct attack in a letter to the Chancellor from Peter Mackie, of Glasgow, whom we have met before. Rightly describing himself as the original proposer of the graduated scale idea he had been left with the impression, after two interviews at the Treasury with the Financial Secretary, that 'you recognised the advantage of a graduated scale of duty for age in the public interest, which you have so much at heart'. As the grain circular seemed to have some weight in influencing the Government, Mackie begged to reply to it.

'I shall be perfectly frank and explain my position,' he wrote, 'I am a malt distiller, but I am also a shareholder in the grain distillery company, so ably managed by Mr Ross, and am a believer in the use of grain whisky in its proper place. I am not, however, a member of the North of Scotland Malt Distillers' Association.'

So, to business: 'To the uninitiated the circular is totally misleading. It is drawn up by grain distillers, whose product is the cheapest class of spirits in the market, and, although chemically purer than malt, as they state, and which I quite admit, yet it is principally used when aged for blending with malt whisky, but when new constitutes the chief whisky for the cheapest and lowest-class trade in the poorest public houses. Alcohol is a degree purer than grain whisky, but that does not give it a superiority over malt whisky, as those grain distillers claim for their grain whisky. No one thinks of drinking pure alcohol.

'As regards the alleged purity of grain whisky as compared with malt

whisky – scientific authorities have established the fact that it is the so-
called impurities, i.e., the ethers and the higher alcohols and by-products
in the malt that are the valuable properties for medicinal purposes, but
it is necessary that they should be matured – so that those gentlemen's
comparison is totally misleading.' He then quoted from three medical
sources, the most to the point being the *Westminster Review*, 'one of the
organs of the Government', which had said: 'Whisky was used
generally, and especially in cases of typhoid fever and pneumonia, as a
stimulant to the heart, and other purposes, such as insomnia. We believe
that the by-products of whisky are the most potent factor in stimulating
the heart. The combination of the by-products with the alcohol is
what we want. Pure alcohol is useless, and is never prescribed.'

Mackie then gives us most interesting sidelights on the trade of the
day, incidental to arguing his case. He continues: 'The main principle
at stake is one of age, and it is on this question of age that the dishonest
merchant cheats the public. No one sells whisky as new. Old matured
whisky is expensive, therefore the opening to cut with cheap young
whiskies in the trade. Apart from the above quotations, the common
sense of the public will guide them to form an opinion adverse to the
three grain distillers, who seemingly think that the trade of the country
and the public good are to be subservient to their private interest.

'These gentlemen found their opposition to a graduation duty on the
Royal Commission and quote extracts from the same. Everyone knows
the value to be placed on evidence given before a Royal Commission.
The most of the evidence given was axe-grinding, and directed by the
pecuniary interests of the party called. Any person in the Trade could
see this.

'I do not quarrel with the decision of the Commission, except with
regard to the ageing of whisky. If carefully read, the report quoted by
these gentlemen merely says: "The evidence before us failed to
establish," etc., etc. In another paragraph: "In our opinion the evidence
is not sufficiently positive to justify us in holding that it is necessary for
the protection of public health to retain any blends for a minimum
period in bond." You will notice simply that the evidence was not
sufficiently positive, because there was no special attempt directed to
give evidence on that point, but that does not mean that evidence does
not exist . . .

'Those gentlemen further assert that a number of distillers have far more whisky than they can sell, and that by graduation they will relieve an over-stocked market. This is an insinuation unworthy of their ingenuity. For speculative purposes this may be so, but the legitimate whisky market is not over-stocked. Large stocks of whisky in bond are the best guarantee of the continuance of the supply of high-class whisky that the public can have.

'There is no whisky,' he thundered, 'either heavy or light, malt or grain, which could safely be used under two years of age, but, on the contrary, all whiskies would be greatly improved by maturing from three to ten years, so that a two-year limit would prove no injustice to any spirit, no matter how light or pure.'

The argument based on gin's not needing maturation, he dismissed by reference to Booth & Co. and their claim that it does improve with age, asking: 'Do these three gentlemen mean to say that Messrs Booth's advertisements are false and misleading?' And he was quickly back at the three writers of the circular letter again.

'Their other objection is that the graduated scheme,' he wrote, 'would stop all progress in the direction of producing a pure spirit other than by ageing. Hitherto all artificial methods of ageing have proved to be of no use, and I think they are likely to prove so, but it will be true enough to consider removing an age limit when such an innovation is discovered. I am glad to know that the three gentlemen in question are employing their talents in that direction.'

After that shot of sarcasm, Mackie resumed the argument: 'Another objection urged is that the scheme has been engineered in the interests of those traders who make a speciality of high-priced bottle spirits, and who do not cater for the working man. It is quite true that most vendors of high-classed as well as high-priced whisky support the graduated scheme.

'It is in the interests of the working men, many of whom are not judges of whisky, that they should be protected from the young, cheap, fiery whisky which is offered. Experience teaches that most of the riotous and obstreperous conduct of drunks comes from the young and fiery spirit which is sold, while the man who may overindulge in old matured whisky becomes sleepy and stupid but not in a fighting mood. In the protection of the working man, the graduated scheme is absolutely necessary, just as the Food and Drugs Act is.'

After asides about the desperate plight of farmers in Scotland unable to sell their barley to distilleries which had had to close down, Mackie produced his solution of the graduated scheme with the background to the reform: 'Lastly, there is no doubt that for the Scotch whisky trade, both Malt and Grain whisky are absolutely necessary for its proper development and to satisfy the public demands, and the proportions in the blends are purely a matter of price and taste, but the essentials are quality and age, and the more age the better, not only for the interests of the public but of the distillers if they would look far enough ahead. This is a matter which requires to be dealt with by common sense and not by theory. It must be patent to every reasonable man the advantage of a good scheme of duty for age. Australia has adopted a limit of two years, and is now asking a certificate of age by the authorities here before the whisky is shipped, and I am sorry to understand that the British authorities have refused to give this certificate, and are thus damaging British trade. I am writing entirely in the interests of the high-class whisky trade, and I am sure that the common sense of the public will admit the necessity of providing a graduated scheme of duty according to age, in order to encourage the sale of old and well-matured whisky.'

7

Whisky in the crisis

LET US leave the Scotch whisky industry for a moment and follow the course of events in Parliament. The first real shots on the whisky front were fired in the debate on the report stage of 24 May 1909, when Sir John Dewar, as he then was, the Liberal member for Inverness, the capital of the Highlands, opened up. Sir John said 'there had never been a budget in which such a large increase as 3s. 9d. had been proposed, and the Chancellor of the Exchequer was not in a position to estimate with accuracy the effect it would have upon the trade. Why had no tax been put upon other forms of alcohol?' he asked. 'Why not beer? (Cheers.) And wines? Wines which came from Hamburg contained a large amount of alcohol, yet they paid 4s. per proof gallon as against 14s. 9d. to be paid on spirits . . . The demand for spirits had been steadily diminishing for many years. This would penalise Scottish and Irish industries. The Chancellor of the Exchequer anticipated a reduction of something like eleven per cent in the demand. That meant that eleven per cent less would be exported, and eleven per cent less would be sold from Scottish distilleries. That would be a very serious thing to many districts in Scotland, particularly in Morayshire and Banffshire. The industry in Banffshire was very far from flourishing. In late years it had suffered severely, and this tax would put the finishing touch to many distilleries there.'

As for the supposition that the tax increase would promote temperance, he said 'he did not think that an additional charge of one penny per glass would prevent the intemperate drinker from getting all he wanted, and no consideration of the results to himself or his dependants would affect his consumption of alcohol'. On the more strictly financial side he remarked that 'the tax might deflect a certain amount of trade in spirits to beer and wine. If it did that, then it was very bad finance for the Exchequer, because alcohol in spirits paid seven times as much as alcohol in beer, and four times as much as alcohol in wine . . . At present,' he went on, 'England used thirty per cent more alcohol than Scotland, and paid forty per cent less in taxation. England at present paid 16s. 10d. per head per taxes on alcohol, while Scotland paid 22s., while the proposed new tax would make matters infinitely worse. (Cheers.)'

The Liberal member for Elgin and Nairn, the heart of Highland malt whisky, Mr Williamson, took it a stage further, and also provides us with accurate background on the period. He is reported as explaining that 'there were two classes of whisky distilleries in Scotland. First, there was the native spirit distilled from barley malt, and it had to be remembered that the number of that class of distillers was far greater than those which produced the raw grain whisky. The latter numbered only 10 or 12 to 120 of the former class, and there was no native industry required for the raw grain whisky, which was largely distilled from foreign maize. For some time there had been a grievance in Scotland as to the sale under the name of Scotch whisky of a blended article in which the percentage of real Scotch whisky had become comparatively small. They in Scotland feared that if the price of whisky was raised by the extra duty of 3s. 9d. per gallon, the tendency would be not only to reduce the consumption of whisky but to reduce the consumption of malt whisky and to use more of the raw grain article. This could not be for the good of the public. (Hear, hear.) The statement had often been made that if a man got drunk on good, sound, old malt whisky he might get pleasantly drunk, but if he fell over raw grain he would become mad drunk. (Loud laughter.) Whether that was the case or not, it was the widespread opinion of the people that it was better to use old and good, than new and bad whisky. (Cheers.) . . . The tendency of the proposed tax, however, would have a distinctly contrary effect . . . He would suggest to the Chancellor of the Exchequer that out of an admittedly mistaken policy he might retrieve a mistake by graduating the tax according to the age of the whisky. He should severely tax the new, strong, and harmful mixture and reduce the duty

according to the age of the whisky. The tendency would be to introduce more malt into the blend, and the practical effect of the graduation
would be to satisfy a larger number of distillers, farmers, labourers, and
shopkeepers, and go a long way to satisfy the general consumer. (Hear,
hear.)'

Replying, Lloyd George's underling at the Treasury, Hobhouse,
Liberal member for Bristol, said that 'the figure of 3s. 9d. had the
advantage that it provided a substantial increase of revenue and, he
thought, prevented the avoidance of the tax by the producer or the
consumer; and it did enable the trade to do, what it was legitimately
entitled to do, viz., to pass on to the consumer a very considerable part,
if not the whole, and even more than the whole, of the charge imposed.
The whole controversy that afternoon was really not as to the increase
of the duty proposed, but an internecine quarrel between two schools
of thought in the production of whisky and two systems of manufacture, one of which was modern and the other antiquated. One hon.
member described malt whisky as being the finest production of whisky
possible, but in view of the interim report of the Royal Commission on
whisky, he did not think it must be accepted there that taxation which
it was alleged was driving out one kind of whisky in preference to
another was really doing any harm from the point of view of health, at
all events to the whisky-consuming public. Taxation would not affect
the proportion in which malt whisky was consumed as compared with
raw grain spirit. Public taste during the last eight or ten years had been
in favour of malt spirits; and if this extra tax was thrown on the
consumer, as he believed it would be, he saw no reason to suppose that
the public taste would change.'

Austen Chamberlain, the Opposition shadow Chancellor, criticised
Lloyd George's estimate of £1·6 million from the new spirit tax. 'That
figure is ridiculous!' he exclaimed. 'The Chancellor of the Exchequer
should give us a detailed calculation by which he has arrived at his
estimates. The low estimate of the yield of the tax must be due to the
Chancellor of the Exchequer calculating on a tremendous reduction in
the consumption of whisky. The only explanation of the Chancellor of
the Exchequer's low estimate must be that he anticipates, like the hon.
members for Ireland and Scotland, that the Trade is to be so treated as
to kill a number of distilleries, and to destroy a number of industries
dependent upon them, and to grievously affect those directly or

indirectly concerned; and this is the Budget in regard to which it is
the proud boast of the President of the Board of Trade that it injures no
trade or industry. If they want to put down spirit drinking, as a social
evil, let them strike at it as such, and forbid it by law; but they have no
right to raise taxation to a point which make it impossible for a man to
carry on his business. If it be a fact, as it is alleged, that the pot still
industry can less bear heavy increased taxation than can the patent still,
they are striking that whisky which is most valuable to the agricultural-
ist.'

Lloyd George himself intervened at this point to say, according to a
contemporary report, 'Tobacco and whisky were luxuries. It was
perfectly fair that extra taxation should come out of the spare money
which people had to spend on luxuries rather than out of the essentials
of life. That was why the Government chose these two articles. He had
been challenged about the estimates. It was very different to forecast
what one would get out of a tax in the first year; a good deal depended
on conjecture, and in nothing more than in spirits. What were the
elements when one sought to estimate the revenue derived from spirits?
First, there were forestalments. There were considerable forestalments
before the end of the financial year; and still more considerable
forestalments during the month of April. Probably for the next few
weeks the spirit trade, speaking of it as a whole, need not withdraw
anything out of bond. During the first year the trade might be able to
reduce the contribution to the Revenue, although eventually the matter
righted itself because the consumer discovered what was going on. The
trade might keep down their stock, which would make an enormous
difference to the Revenue; there was the prospect of diminished
consumption, while the steady decrease in the use of spirits in this
century had to be reckoned with. There was also the question of
measure . . . People ordering whisky asked for a small or large 'tot' . . .
He understood that some restaurants were reducing their measures by
twenty per cent. If they did that he would not get his £1·6 million.
This was the first experiment in putting on a tax that drove the retailer
to put it on the consumer. He had done that deliberately because he did
not think it fair to embarrass the trade and make it very difficult for
them to pass it on to the consumer. Here they were able to do so, and
the retailer was enabled to provide, as he was doing, for his increased
licence duty out of whisky. By the increased charge the publicans

would make, even on a diminished consumption, an extra profit of £4 million a year. In addition, they were charging the full penny in respect of millions of gallons withdrawn from bond on which no increased taxation had been paid . . .'

Mr Balfour, leader of the Opposition, spoke next, saying 'he had heard about endowing the Trade, but never on the same scale as on which the Rt Hon. Gentleman was endowing it. He understood the Rt Hon. Gentleman was going to get £1·6 million for the Exchequer, and that the distillers were to get £4 million. Did any human being ever hear of taxation being defended on these grounds? (Cheers.) . . . The Rt Hon. Gentleman said he could not estimate more than £1·6 million this year because there was this way and that way of evading the tax. Then he would be making too much money next year. (Laughter.) Did the Rt Hon. Gentleman not see the extraordinary absurdity of putting on a gigantic tax because it would not be wanted? (Loud laughter and cheers.) The Rt Hon. Gentleman openly said he meant to drive the population of these islands who still drank whisky to drink beer.'

Lloyd George denied he had ever proposed the tax to drive whisky drinkers to beer, and when the House divided there were 243 'for' and 126 'against', a government majority of 117. On the resolution for the extra 3s. 9d. 243 votes for, 123 against, a government majority of 120.

On the debated estimate of consumption and clearances from bond, Hobhouse replied to Joyson Hicks that in 1908–9 there were 38,626,000 proof gallons of spirits duty paid and it was estimated that in 1909–10 there would be 29,700,000 gallons. As there were 5,100,000 gallons duty paid before 30 April at the old rate, that left 24,600,000 gallons to be cleared in the remainder of the financial year. Lloyd George elaborated: since 1 April there had been 4,250,000 gallons of home-made spirit cleared, and 847,000 gallons of imported spirit duty paid, giving a total of 5,097,000 gallons in April at the old rate.

On the basis of these figures, the chairman of the Wine & Spirit Association showed that 38,626,000 gallons duty paid at the old rate of 11s. per proof gallon yielded £21,244,300 whereas the estimated 29,700,000 gallons at the new rate of 14s. 9d. would yield only £21,903,750, an increase of only £659,450. Further, with the falling off of the total quantity consumed of 8,926,000 gallons, there would also be a falling away of labour connected with the production and distribution of potable spirits. The increased revenue to the Exchequer would be some £659,450; the annual turnover would be reduced by twenty-five per cent.

Similarly, at the annual general meeting of the D.C.L. on 16 July, the chairman, Graham Menzies, moving the adoption of the report, said: 'Gentlemen, after the rejection of the English Licensing Bill last session by the House of Lords, and after all the troublous times the trade has recently experienced, one naturally hoped for a period of rest, but the Extraordinary Proposals affecting the Liquor Trade as disclosed by the Budget, and so far unmodified, have caused the greatest alarm and distrust . . . The enormous increase in the spirit duty in times of peace greatly aggravates the existing inequality of taxation of alcoholic beverages between the three parts of the United Kingdom to the further detriment of the Scotch and Irish taxpayers . . . On the basis of the reduced consumption resulting from the great increase in the spirit duty (the Exchequer) will actually receive less revenue than from the old rate of duty . . . Gentlemen, if it were not for this dark cloud hanging over our trade, I think the position of the company would never have been stronger than now.'

As the summer wore on, the falsity and incorrectness of the Exchequer's forecast about receipts became glaringly apparent. Thanks to Sir John Dewar, the House, and so the nation and trade, were kept fully informed about clearances from bond and the duty payments received. The five months of April–August that year saw £6,480,000 received by the Exchequer as duty payments, as compared with £7,885,000 for the same months in 1908, and £8,396,000 in the corresponding period of 1907. So there had been a decrease of twenty-two and a half per cent in two years, and the 1909 figure was eight per cent down on that for 1908.

It became known that in the financial year 1908–9, there had been received as revenue from home-made spirits £17,420,000, and in the current financial year there was expected an increase of £1·2 million (a decrease from the earlier forecast of £1·6 million) making a total of £18,620,000. This would mean a total consumption of home-made spirits of 26,250,000 gallons (as against the former forecast of 29·7 million gallons) including the 4,250,000 gallons duty paid in April at the old rate of duty. No explanation was offered as to the decreased estimate, and again when it was further reduced, by estimate, to 24·4 million no comment was offered, no explanation of the discrepancy was vouchsafed.

In 1908–9 about 32 million gallons of home-made spirits were duty paid, including one million gallons in anticipation of a Budget rise. The actual consumption, then, was 31 million gallons. Taking it as a notional figure for 1909–10, there would then have to be deducted the one million gallons already cleared, and the 4·25 million cleared in April, leaving 25·75 million gallons for the rest of the year. But it was discovered that most areas of the country that summer were reporting drops in spirit consumption of twenty to thirty per cent in sales for consumption over the bar. More, the duty received in July 1909, was twenty-seven per cent less than in July 1908, though the impost per gallon was up by thirty-three per cent. One thing only could be expected: a very substantial permanent decrease in spirit drinking, and the conservative estimate was around twenty-two per cent.

Taking then the 25,750,000 gallons arrived at above, and taking off the twenty-two per cent, or 5,665,000 gallons, there was left a total of 20,085,000 gallons to give a total of estimated clearances for 1909–10 of 24,335,000 gallons. This would equal the Chancellor's revised estimate of 24,400,000 gallons. Taking his estimate, the Trade and its politicians argued, and deducting from it the April clearances of 4,250,000 which were duty paid at the old rate, of 11s. per proof gallon, there would remain for the Chancellor's new rate only 20,150,000 gallons. This would yield an estimated revenue of £14,860,125; add to this the April revenue received of £2,354,000 and the total revenue for the year would be £17,214,625. This would be *less* by £1,400,000 than the Chancellor's own estimate in the Budget and less than the preceding year's revenue by £200,000. Not unnaturally, the question was asked in the lobbies and committee rooms, Why not revert to the old rate?

That extra 3s. 9d. duty bestowed upon the Commons one of its longest sittings, partly as a result of the calculations just outlined, and drawn from documents of various members then alive. The extra 3s. 9d., Clause 61, was considered for the whole sitting which began on 23 September and did not conclude until 4.15 a.m. on the 24th. Sir William Bull moved that instead of 3s. 9d. the extra should be only 1s., saying that 'the fall directly the new duty came in force was very striking'. This was further elaborated by Sir John Dewar who described the extra as 'economically unsound' and continued that 'he was fully in favour of the taxation of luxuries, but whisky was, of all luxuries, the least able to bear extra taxation. (Hear, hear.) It was already taxed eight hundred per cent, or nine hundred per cent more than it cost. It bore a tax of 11s. duty, whilst it did not cost much more than a shilling a gallon . . . Whilst proof spirit in beer was taxed at 2s. 2d. a gallon, in spirits it was taxed at 14s. 9d. per gallon . . . The result of whisky becoming unpopular would be that the Chancellor of the Exchequer would probably get less from the 14s. 9d. tax this year than he got last year for the 11s. tax. Englishmen consumed 4·6 proof gallons per head of alcohol, and the Scotchmen 3·2 proof gallons per head. The Englishman's consumption was four parts beer and one part spirits, and the Scotchman's three parts beer and four parts spirits. The result was that the Englishman for his 4·6 proof gallons of alcohol paid 16s. to the revenue and the Scotchman for his 3·2 proof gallons paid 22s. to the revenue . . . while the Scotchman consumed less he contributed 5s. 2d. more to the revenue per proof gallon of alcohol consumed than the Englishman. The consumption of spirits in England was 22 million proof gallons, Scotland 7 million gallons, and Ireland 3,600,000 gallons, which showed that England consumed more than Scotland and Ireland together. The proportion of taxation was England 80, Scotland 11, and Ireland 9, and the result was that Ireland and Scotland contributed more than their share to the revenue, and England less than her fair share.'

On the other side of the problem, Sir John also said that 'the tax hit the Scottish manufacturer very seriously. It meant a reduction in Scotland of twenty-five per cent in the making of whisky, and would make a vast difference to the Highland distilleries in the districts of Banffshire, Inverness-shire and elsewhere.'

Lloyd George's underling Hobhouse replied as financial secretary to the Treasury. The reply was nonsense, and is largely quoted here as a record of what was officially said in justification and as a warning to politicians and their adherents. 'There were two quite clear and absolutely explained reasons,' he declared, 'why there had been a great falling off in the consumption of whisky, or at all events a decrease in the withdrawal from bond and a consequent falling in the revenue. One reason was that it was due to an anticipation which took place previous to the present financial year, and secondly an anticipation which took place on April 30th of this year. The result had been that there were undoubtedly forestalments resulting in a swelling of the revenue for last year, but depleting it for the present year . . . In addition to that . . . there was some considerable hope on the part of some of those who dealt in spirits that the duty imposed would not be permanent, and that owing to an electoral division the proposals may be nullified altogether. (Opposition cheers.) Both these anticipations were now past . . . There had been a great decrease in consumption . . . the decrease in consumption . . . was certainly not deplored by the Government and its supporters and although the tax was not put down with a view to morality yet if it led in that direction he did not think that any person could possibly raise any objection. (Hear, hear.) . . . Sir John Dewar had alluded to the fact that a sixty per cent tax upon whisky had failed to produce any revenue, and that that was an indication that the taxation of spirits had reached its highest point. The fault of putting on so small a tax was that it was quite possible to defeat the intention of the revenue by decreasing the strength of the whisky and at the same time increasing the quantity. It was for that very reason that the Rt Hon. Gentleman had decided to put on so high a tax. He believed it was justified, and that it would be impossible to evade the tax by the means he had mentioned.'

Of course this called for a blistering attack by Irish nationalist Mr T. Healy, of the party of which more will soon shortly be heard. As for Scotland, the theme was taken up by the Scottish member, Younger: 'After all, this is not a temperance measure. It is difficult to believe, but it is a Finance Bill. (Laughter.) . . . a perfectly ludicrous and monstrous tax . . . The people at Motherwell were most seriously attacked by this tax. They depended almost wholly on the distilling industry. It was not expected that a single gallon of whisky would be made there this winter, and there would be no employment for those 6,000 to 7,000 people, who had got a miserable winter to look forward to . . .'

As for Hobhouse's dissertation about reduced strength and the need for a high rate of taxation, Younger took the reasoned offensive: 'That would probably have been true enough before the tax was raised to 11s., but since then whisky had been sold in public houses at something so closely approaching to the minimum standard allowed by law, that it was impossible further to dilute it. (Opposition cheers.) Mr Hobhouse ought to have known that. It was perfectly well known to the Inland Revenue Authorities.'

The Chancellor of the Exchequer moved the closure to the accompaniment of cries of 'Oh!' from the Opposition, and upon a division the closure was carried by 112 to 95. On the amendment the Government had a majority of 18 – 94 for, 112 against. There was much savage criticism of Lloyd George's closure action: it had not been thought needful to put up a cabinet minister to state the case from the Government's point of view; it was 'an extraordinary thing' on Lloyd George's part to say that he did not intend to trouble about the Scottish and Irish case; the Chancellor of the Exchequer was taking the line 'I have my majority!' and that was tantamount to an insult to the House, and members were entitled to something better than the 'shambling statement' presented by Hobhouse.

The Government had a majority of 13 (97 for, 110 against) on the motion to report progress and Sir John Dewar then moved to add at the end of the clause of the Bill this amendment: 'Provided that, if the spirits be of an age of no less than five years, the duty shall be 2s. per proof gallon, and if the spirit be under five but over three years of age the duty shall be 2s. 9d. per proof gallon, the age of the spirits that have been blended or vatted being taken to be the age of the youngest spirit in the blend or vat.'

The amendment was offered to Lloyd George as an opportunity to make amends to Scotland for his sweeping disregard. Dewar, while adopting here Mackie's graduated scale, in effect, urged that the experiment was worth trying; it would result in no diminution of the revenue in any case.

Lloyd George took his opportunity. He pointed out that 'those engaged in the manufacture of whisky were very divided on this subject. Those who produced large quantities,' he said, 'are undoubtedly against it.' Since he had received a deputation on the subject, they had all received a copy of the report of the Whisky Commission and that 'did not encourage this notion'. Under the circumstances, he did not see his way to doing what was asked. 'Those engaged in grain distilling,' he went on, 'resented it very strongly on the ground that it would give an unfair preference to one branch of the trade against the other. I must confess that although I felt inclined to accept something on these lines at the outset, the Government could not decide between the two sections, and I cannot accept the amendment.'

Agreeing that there was such a division in the trade, Younger then

107

urged a two-year minimum: 'That would probably put grain and malt on the same level, and would tend to put an end to a great deal of drunkenness. There is no doubt that raw whisky is responsible for great violence.' Williamson naturally championed the graduation cause: 'New whisky is not so good for the consumer as the older whisky, and the proposal would, therefore, be good from the point of view of sobriety . . . Lord Peel's Commission reported unanimously that the effects of new raw whisky were deleterious in a high degree. There is no doubt that new whisky is bad for the consumer, and causes more maddening drunkenness.'

To the interjection by Mr Leif Jones that the member had failed to establish that new whisky was worse for the consumer than old whisky, another member cried out amid laughter: 'Try it and see!'

Austen Chamberlain was more serious on the subject. He considered that 'if it was desirable for the sake of health that whisky should be retained in bond, the question was a proper one for legislation, but not for a Finance Bill. The hon. member had failed to show that any hardship alleged in the trade in respect of the age of the whisky was in any way due to the tax. The duty had not to be paid when the spirit was distilled, but when it was taken out of bond. The pressure on whisky was not heightened by the time it was kept in bond. The Finance Bill was not a Bill to deal with the matter in question.'

Comedian-member Lupton 'convulsed' the House with this: 'After 200 years' experience with different kinds of whisky, I wish to point out that it is difficult to say what old whisky is like. If it be kept in bond two years,' he proceeded, 'it would be "all right", and then would be "very little better" unless it was kept in bond for 200 years. It is at the least regrettable to see the business of the nation conducted in such a spirit of ill-informed levity. Such members deserve to lose the confidence of their electors; unhappily the party machine is only too often too violent for the electors.'

Sir John Dewar at this stage wished to withdraw his amendment, but leave was refused. It was defeated: 70 for, 116 against, a government majority of 46. Lloyd George was then in a squabble, from which nothing really emerged, over his estimate of decreased consumption and the revenue resulting, with Austen Chamberlain claiming that 'they had brought the tax to an unproductive point and had increased it to an unparalleled extent at a time when consumption was falling. The Chancellor of the Exchequer,' he closed, 'was simply killing the goose which laid the golden egg.'

When the Committee of the House divided on the motion that the Clause stand the Government got a majority of 33: there were 117 for, and 84 against.

On 4 October, the House resumed the Committee stage of the Finance Bill and in considering the progressive distiller's licence duty, whisky again came into the foreground. Irishman T. Healy called it 'free trade run mad . . . are the Government,' he asked, 'after revenue or are they after revenge?'

Herbert Samuel, for the Government, said that there was already a duty of 11s. a gallon, which the Government were increasing by 3s. 9d., and to say that this additional one-tenth of a penny per gallon would ruin the distillers was absurd. He even went to the length of claiming that 'to some extent' the duty gave protection to the English distillers against foreign competition: 'When the corn tax was imposed by the late government an additional tax of 1d. per gallon was imposed on foreign distillers to counter-balance the extra charge which it was expected would be thrown on distillers in this country. When the corn tax was removed, the extra duty was retained.'

Belloc, ardent party man, asserted that 'in view of the enormous increase in the consumption of whisky in the last generation and of the position of the distillery companies, it could not be pretended that the impost was of a serious nature on a trade that was so wealthy, so well organised, and so able to support it.'

On this now forgotten subject of debate, the victorious proposal to increase the distiller's fee as he increased his output, had a Government majority of 35: the voting was 97 for Scott Dickson's amendment, and 133 against. Similarly, the amendment to reduce the new rectifier's licence fee was lost, with a Government majority of 42.

Samuel countered another amendment on the distiller's licence fee – this one proposed by Irishman Dillon would have replaced the progressive £10 fee by £1 – with the same old arguments, claiming that it was impossible to conceive that a duty of one-tenth of a penny per gallon was a serious consideration in the case of an industry which was already taxed 11s. and which under the Finance Bill would be taxed 14s. 9d. per gallon . . . The distillers would be called upon to pay only £16,000 in their manufacturers' licences, while the brewers would be called upon to pay £149,000.

Several members, notably Mooney, objected that even this one-tenth of a penny extra duty on the distiller might make the whole difference between profit and loss to the small distillers. Mr H. C. Lea pointed out that many distillers in the Lowlands of Scotland and in Belfast produced spirits of a very cheap quality. They had to compete in the neutral spirit markets with the cheap spirits made under bounty-fed conditions on the Continent, and the addition of one-tenth of a penny per gallon would be a great factor in the matter. The price was cut so fine, he added, that some distillers could not carry on business were it not for the sale of yeast, which was one of the by-products of the industry.

After a Belfast member's interjection favouring the increased distiller's fee, Belloc countered with an observation valueless in itself but most illustrative of lingering animosities roused first by the Boer War. Belloc asked the member 'whether he considers that this taxation is being levied because this country got into a financial mess through a Jewish war in South Africa?'

Likewise Gwynn said that 'every great liquor lord in Ireland is the enemy of the Nationalist party, from Lord Iveagh down'. So Samuel moved the closure, got it and in the voting on Dillon's amendment scored a Government majority of 76 : 98 for the amendment, 174 against it.

Another amendment, moved this time by Staveley-Hill, sought to reduce the £10 payment on quantities over the first 50,000 gallons by substituting 50,000 gallons in the place of 25,000 by which the progressive scale moved up. Samuel now found how valuable the tax was and said 'the Government could not consent to reduce the yield of this part of the tax by one-half.' Once more the amendment was lost, this time with a Government majority of 66, the voting being 96 for, 162 against. The Government were, for the time being, having everything their own way as the party members marshalled as ordered.

It was at this juncture that was published the annual report of the Inland Revenue for the year ending 31 March 1909, but containing previous years by way of background and comparison. Let us pause a while from the dust and dirt of parliamentary wrangling to see what had been happening that century.

First, how had Scotch whisky production been going? We have already heard much of a decline, and figures bear this out. In the financial year 1898–9, to start with there were made in Scotland 35·8 million gallons of spirits. That production fell year by year until in 1902–3 it was only 26 million gallons. It recovered slightly the following year, then began to slip again, year by year to 25·2 million gallons in 1904–5, then to 23·8 million, up to 24·8 million in 1906–7, and down to 22·2 million in 1907–8 and up again to 24·4 million in 1908–9.

Similarly the number of Scottish distilleries at work fluctuated, mostly in the overall downward direction. In the distilling year of 1897–8, there were at work 157, the next year it moved up to 161, before beginning the long downward trek: down to 159 in 1899–1900, to 156, to 152, to 149 in 1902–3, after which was a slight recovery the next year to 152 followed by 153, but in the years 1905–7 the figure stayed at 150 and in 1907–8 it fell to as low as 132.

Stocks in bond told the same story in other terms: the increase in stocks as consumption tailed off. On 31 March 1899 there were 103 million gallons in bond in Scotland and this quantity mounted steadily, as production went ahead in unco-ordinated manner until at the same date of 1905 there were 122 million gallons in bonded warehouse.

Production, then, had varied pretty wildly, generally in a lower direction; stocks had mounted in response and with the accompaniment of decreased consumption at home. This picture is not as explicit as that presented us today but the overall picture of spirit consumption in the United Kingdom shows that in 1898–9 35 million gallons of home-made spirits paid duty on passing to consumption and in 1899–1900 the peak was reached of 39·6 million gallons. Thereafter the general trend was downwards, however a slight improvement might be made in the period 1902–4. In 1908–9, the total figure was down to 33·4 million gallons.

Although direct Scotch whisky statistics are not available, it is possible to get at some idea of 'Scotch' home consumption by adding the quantity produced in any one year to the amount in stock at the end of the previous financial year, and from the total thus gained deducting the amount in stock at the end of the year under review. The quantity so obtained represents the removal from bond in Scotland in the last twelve months.

This method is not of perfect and unchallengeable accuracy, but gives as good an estimate as it is possible to arrive at. So in 1898–9, the 'Scotch' removals from bond were 22 million gallons and in the following year, 1899–1900, it moved up to 25 million gallons, where it stayed the next year also, slipping to 24·8 million in 1901–2, but recovering to 26 million gallons in 1903–4, before beginning another stationary course. Thus in 1908–9, there were probably only about 24 to 25 million gallons of 'Scotch' consumed. It may indeed have been even lower as the figure works out at roughly two-thirds the overall figure for home-made spirits consumed in any one year.

With that marking-time in spirit consumption overall, there had likewise been a drop in tax revenue from them. In 1898–9, the U.K. public paid £17,967,000 in duty on home-made spirits; for the next two years it was around the £20 million mark, then gradually dwindled, in the main to £17·5 million in 1908–9.

Scotch whisky was not then an export of any magnitude. Of home-made spirit in general, there were only 5 million gallons exported in 1898–9, but, significantly, as home demand wavered and halted, exports rose, however slightly: to 5·3 in 1899–1900, then to 5·8, to 6·3, to 6·4 back to 6·3 in 1903–4, then up again to 6·95 in 1904–5, to 7, to 7·3, to 7·9 and in 1908–9 they were 8·2 million gallons. Scotch whisky was not the only product in this; there were Irish whiskey and gin also to be remembered – but was probably about two-thirds of this total.

Enough detail has been presented, in any case, for it to be deduced that there was a decline in spirit drinking, and the producers were increasingly turning to export markets to compensate themselves. That is just what they did with particular ferocity after the 1909 budget. Asquith, in his 1906 budget speech, put it all down to the growth of temperance principles, and Lloyd George was later to harp on the same theme. But *The Times* had, as usual, some pertinent remarks to make on aspects of the problem. 'The value of the figures contained therein,' said the newspaper of the Inland Revenue Report on whisky production, 'have again been impaired by the failure to discriminate between pot still and patent still production of whisky, a distinction which would be of great value to traders, and would go far towards preventing those alternating periods of "boom" and depression to which the trade appears to be subject.'

Further: 'The decrease in the Scottish figures (of production) was largely due to the anxiety of the distillers, both pot still and patent still, to restrict the production as far as possible in view of the fact that the stocks exceeded the actual requirements of the trade, and that the consumption instead of being on the up grade was dwindling year by year.'

Little use could be made in the Commons of these facts and figures in so far as they affected the extra taxes on whisky, and the Finance Bill passed the Commons. What, asked the nation, would be its fate in the Upper House? How would it all affect the Trade, more particularly the spirit section of it? Mr H. C. Lea, wrote from his dual knowledge as a member of Parliament and an authority on wines and spirits: 'If the House of Lords refuses to pass the Finance Bill, the question immediately arises as to the legality of paying any of the spirit duties which are not imposed by statute. If duties can be charged by the House of Commons alone, what need is there for passing Finance Bills through the Lords? Law means to the taxpayer assent of Commons, Lords and King, and law is the only authority for taxation. Rejection of the Finance Bill would therefore result in a loss of millions sterling, and if the revenue authorities refused to refund and insisted on charging tea duty, spirit and tobacco surtaxes, wholesale litigation would immediately spring up.

'The irreparable loss of money to the Crown ensuing on rejection of the Bill suggests at once that some precautions will be taken to safeguard the interests of the Treasury in the event of the peers deciding to give the Finance Bill its knock-down blow. It is not so much the whisky and tobacco taxation that the Lords stick at as the land and licence taxation, and had these latter subjects been omitted, the surcharges on spirits and tobacco would long ago have passed the Second Chamber.'

After speculating on what might happen, Mr Lea went on: 'As money has already been collected from the spirit surtax, this and the other "collections" would doubtless be included. If the Commons refuse [to accept an emasculated Bill], then the Lords can wait until either the Commons comply or the King creates new peers to swamp the Opposition . . . The probability of having the oppressive surtax removed from spirits is very small if it exists at all. It will most likely continue to be charged under some Parliamentary device until, at least, next Budget night, and the best frame of mind is undoubtedly to expect no relief, but to work and wait for a favourable turn of the political wheel.'

A few more figures are relevant before we turn to consider Lloyd George's revealing remarks at the final stage of the Finance Bill in Committee. These were elicited by parliamentary question and reveal that already the spirit surtax was having its effect: in the period May to October 1908, the United Kingdom drank 17,484,000 gallons of spirits and paid £9,688,000 in duty on them; in the same months of 1909, they drank 9,012,000 gallons and paid duty of £6,620,000.

Attempts made yet again to reduce the excise and licence duties in that final stage failed again. Here are some of Lloyd George's gems from the occasion: 'The working classes, I assumed, would probably purchase a smaller quantity of spirits. Supposing a man says, I spend 2s. 6d. on drink; he would not spend more, therefore he would consume less. I made a rough calculation upon such information as I had how that would affect the consumption of whisky as a whole, but I find the change has gone far beyond that, and my information now is not merely that there are thousands of people who drink a percentage which is, in proportion to the increase, less, but some of them drop it altogether. Some of them are barely drinking half what they were before. Altogether a most extraordinary effect has been produced upon the habits of the people. I am not here to apologise for it.'

And again: 'I did think people would have been driven to articles of that kind [Hamburg Port] . . . People have not even been driven to consumption of beer. It is really almost unaccountable. People have not been driven from one form of alcohol to another, but they have been driven from alcohol altogether. The fact is very extraordinary, and has gone beyond anything I anticipated. We thought at first people might be driven from the stronger alcoholic liquors to the lighter alcoholic liquors, like beer, but beer is going down. As far as wine is concerned, there is no appreciable difference . . . Our anticipations now are that the consumption of spirits, both of foreign and home manufacture, will go down by something between twenty to twenty-five per cent. That means a smaller quantity of spirits will be consumed in this country during this year by eight or nine million gallons. A few extra gallons of Hamburg Port may be consumed, but they are infinitesimal compared with that enormous reduction. We are also drinking less beer; so the *improvement* all round is gigantic!'

On abiding exchequer principle: 'It is said that the Chancellor of the Exchequer's first consideration ought to be a financial one. That is not strictly accurate, however, so far as these taxes on alcoholic liquors are concerned . . . The history of the taxation of alcohol, they will find that every minister has used the weapon of finance for the purpose of counteracting excess in the drinking of some particular spirit. I think that was the way gin-drinking was destroyed in this country. Whenever it was found that there was excess in some particular form of alcoholic indulgence it was through the Chancellor of the Exchequer for the time being that legislation was introduced, and, what is more, legislation of that kind has always been more effective than purely restrictive legislation. I am told that Scotland only became a whisky drinking country within quite modern times, having formerly been a beer-drinking country, and that the change was the result of a tax.'

After Younger's interjection, 'It was really a claret-drinking country,' Lloyd George continued his revelations, not always historically accurate but illuminating in their correct sphere: 'The Scottish people were driven, I believe, from strong ale to stronger whisky, and they are now being driven by a tax on whisky to lighter beer – All the Chancellors of the Exchequer of the past have arranged their taxation on alcoholic liquor otherwise than merely with a view to revenue. Why do you charge Port wine and the more heavy alcoholic wines more than the lighter Clarets? It was done partially as a temperance measure. Mr Gladstone always claimed that as one of his objects. It is true there was a great deal about French wines; the matter was no doubt partly commercial.

'When whisky is charged 11s. on its alcohol and beer a smaller sum, it is recognised that it is better to encourage the drinking of the lighter alcoholic beverage in preference to whisky . . . Undoubtedly there is indication of a great improvement in the habits of the people . . . To a considerable extent the improvement has come to stay, and that so far as twenty per cent is concerned we are in favour of a permanent reduction in spirits – so long as we are not driven to the expedient of drinking Hamburg Port . . . but I do not think there is any danger of that.

'It has been said that only moderate drinkers have given up drinking whisky, but anyone who looks at the returns of arrests for drunkenness – Glasgow, for instance – will not agree with that, for these are not arrests of moderate drinkers, but of men who have "done themselves well". Arrests have gone down in numbers by something like thousands in Glasgow alone, and that shows that the whisky tax has been of infinite value in improving the habits of the people.

'I regret very much that there should be any men thrown out of work in the industries of barley-growing, malting and distilling. No doubt this will be a cause of temporary distress we must all regret, but at the same time we must take into account what is meant by the reduction of eight to nine million gallons in the consumption. Though a few hundred men get less work in barley-growing, malting or distilling, the increase will be of enormous comfort in the habits of hundreds of thousands of homes.'

The rot had begun. 'In view of the depression in the whisky trade and the uncertainty of business in the near future owing to the Budget,' Rosebank Lowland malt whisky distillery could not recommend a dividend be paid on the ordinary shares.

8

The budget battles on

IN THE event, the Upper House chucked out the Finance Bill. 'It amounted,' wrote Trevalyn, 'to a claim on the part of the Peers to force a General Election whenever they wished; for a Government unable to raise taxes must either resign or dissolve. If the Peers could throw out a Budget, any Parliament not to their liking could be dissolved at their will. The rejection of the Budget was also a violent breach with the custom of the Constitution.' So, the question was: 'Shall Peers or People Rule?'

Lloyd George was jubilant. 'We have got them at last!' he cried. And on 2 December 1909, Asquith, as Prime Minister, proposed the resolution that 'the action of the House of Lords in refusing to pass into law the financial provision made by this House for the service of the year is a breach of the Constitution, and a usurpation of the rights of the Commons.' It was carried by 349 votes to 134; Parliament was prorogued and dissolved on 10 January 1910.

Asquith set the tone of the forthcoming struggle in his speech of 10 December when he said: 'We are going to ask the country to give us authority to apply an effective remedy to these intolerable conditions. What is to be done will have to be done by Act of Parliament. The time for unwritten conventions has unhappily gone by.'

It made the technical question of paying the new surtax on whisky no simpler, and the Wine and Spirit Association held a special meeting after which was issued the following guidance to members: 'That, while entirely objecting to the surtax of 3s. 9d. per proof gallon, the

Committee feel, as there is every probability of the increased rate of duty being temporarily legalised by the new Parliament, the interests of the wholesale trade will be best studied by all merchants paying to H.M. Customs & Excise the increased duty of 3s. 9d., and charging their customers accordingly.'

Mr Ross, managing director of the D.C.L., felt it necessary to send a circular to employees of the company 'to put before you a few facts'. As he said, 'I have no intention to interfere with your politics. That must be left to yourself to decide, but I have quite a right to show you in which direction your interests as a distillery employee may be affected by the result of the next election.'

The increase in duty from 11s. to 14s. 9d. represented a thirty-three per cent increase, and he pointed out: 'No similar increase in taxation was proposed to be placed upon beer, or upon any of the foreign wines coming into this country.' Recalling the deputation, reported earlier as 'leaked' and later formulated in the circular of protest, he reminded his readers that it could all result in lower wages and lower profits. He was able to quote the May to October figures on spirit withdrawals we have noted above, with the fall in revenue at the higher rate of £3,022,000 and exhorted: 'Whatever justification Mr Lloyd George may have for ruining a perfectly legal and vastly important industry, it surely cannot be said that this is finance. To impose a tax upon a given article with a view to raising additional revenue is legitimate finance. To tax an industry beyond a point which it can bear, with the result that less rather than more revenue is obtained, belongs to another category, and is one which surely the second Chamber have a perfectly legitimate right to interfere in.

'As the Prime Minister has said that if the present Government is again returned to power, the Budget will be reintroduced line for line with all its objectionable features as far as our industry is concerned, it is well to consider what this would really mean for our Company. It is estimated that if the higher duty be retained it will cause a permanent reduction in the consumption, and consequently in the manufacture of spirits in the United Kingdom of about twenty-five per cent, or say 10,000,000 gallons.

'The Company . . . produces almost one-third of all the spirits made in the United Kingdom, so that if we have to stand our *pro rata* share in the reduction, that will mean a permanent drop of fully 3,000,000

Copper pot stills at a Highland distillery

Barley being turned on the malting floor

gallons. This means the produce of two average-sized distilleries, and it matters not whether we have to shut down two distilleries altogether or keep the whole going at a reduced rate . . .

'We hear a great deal about taxing "unearned increment" but what about "decrement" thus brought about solely through Government action?'

On the question of beer versus whisky taxation, Ross had this to add to what he had already said: 'It is unfair to tax whisky without taxing beer. It is fair to add that it is proposed to tax certain brewers in another way. There can be no doubt also that, had the Government not been afraid of the effect which a rise in the price of beer would have had on the English working man's vote, this unequal taxation would not have been proposed. They no doubt thought that Scotland was safe, and therefore Scotland has to bear the heavy load. Truly a curious way to show their gratitude!

'Not content with taxing the whisky far beyond its relative proportion, Mr Lloyd George must needs impose a further burden of £15,000 upon the distillers of the United Kingdom for the privilege of working here, while his regard for the foreigner is again shown by no countervailing duty upon that favoured individual.'

We need not venture into the details of the constitutional struggle which resulted in the Parliament Act nor the protracted party and regal negotiations in which, for instance, in December 1909, King Edward VII told Asquith that much as he regretted the action of the House of Lords he disliked the Government's remedy as 'tantamount to the destruction of the House of Lords'. So when Asquith and the Liberals went to the country in the general election of January 1910 he knew that victory would not carry out the new Parliament Bill but only the old Budget. The result of that election was that the Liberals lost 100 seats, but kept, with the Irish, a majority of well over a hundred.

This was just where Irish whiskey came into the tangled web: the Irish now held the balance in the Commons and they hated the budget because of the increased whisky duty, which they regarded, rightly, as a body blow at one of their few remaining industries. The position was this: the Liberals held now 274 seats; the Conservatives and Unionists 273; the Labour party was reduced to 41 seats, and the Nationalists with 82 seats held the balance. Thus an agreement had to be entered into, otherwise the Irish by voting against the budget would have brought the Government down, by which they would only forgo their opposition to the Finance Bill in so far as it affected the spirits duty if they were assured the Government would forge ahead with the Parliament Bill, limiting the powers of the (unionist) House of Lords, and then produce a Home Rule for Ireland Bill which would get through under the terms of the new Parliament Act, as it would be by then. So the Home Rule question, which had been simmering if not boiling over for a generation, now exploded with whisky. If there had not been the excessive spirits duties imposed by a Welsh fanatic and megalomaniac the whole of that sorry story would have been averted. It was to carry through his spirits punishment that Lloyd George managed to persuade his colleagues to make this under-cover deal with the Nationalists. No doubt that question of Home Rule would have to be settled sometime, if only in the interests of abstract justice, but the predominant part played in the whole issue by whisky must not be overlooked.

In fact, as Mr Lea reminded those interested at the time of the election, no Scottish member voted against the 3*s*. 9*d*. extra in the 1909 session and similarly no Irish member voted for it. A neat commentary on many things. It was, in fact, only when the Irish had got assurances that the Home Rule Bill would immediately follow the Parliament Act that they at last consented to vote for the Finance Bill which was sent to the Lords and passed at once.

The timetable was that on 21 February 1910, the King opened the new Parliament with a suggestion of so defining relations between the Houses as to secure undivided authority on Finance Bills and a pre-dominance in legislation to the Lower House; on 29 March, Asquith, as prime minister, moved his notorious three resolutions: the first defining money bills, the second declaring that if any Bill passed the Commons in three successive sessions and was three times rejected by the Lords it should become law, subject to a time factor of two years, and the third limiting the life of Parliament to five years. These were finally carried on 14 April and a Bill based on them was that same night introduced by Asquith. The King returned from Biarritz on 27 April; the budget was reintroduced and passed substantially unamended through the Commons and became law on 29 April, just a year after it had first been presented by Lloyd George. The King, who had feared for the whole hereditary principle, died shortly afterwards on 6 May.

The later convolutions of that peers versus people struggle need not delay us here. But that budget now safely passed had marked a turning-point in the trade, a turning-point to a new road which has never since been forsaken. Mr John L. Anderson, writing an account of the House of Dewar some twenty years later, was able to speak of that tumultuous year, 1909, this way: 'On 1st April [1909] an epoch-making event occurred in the amalgamation of the Customs and Excise Departments. The fusion had had a long and painful course of incubation, but it was apparent to all that such union was bound to come and the longer it was delayed the more difficult would it be to bring about its consummation. To signalise this great Departmental Union, the Government thought fit to saddle the Trade with an extra 3s. 9d. of Spirit Duty, raising it to 14s. 9d. per proof gallon. From that date, the Home Trade began to slacken under the heavy burden, and there has been a continual, if irregular, decline ever since.'

Customs and Excise were not, incidentally, the only amalgamation of that year: there had for some years past been a number of smaller ones, and in that year negotiations, which came to nothing at the time, opened between Buchanan, Dewar and Walker for unification. It was to eventuate later, as we shall see in time.

As for the home trade the chairman of the D.C.L. put it succinctly in his annual statement in July 1912. 'It is a somewhat unfortunate characteristic of our Trade that they have spasmodic fits of depression or else of nervous excitement. For some reason or other the market has now come to take the view that there is a shortage in the stock of grain whisky, having regard to the increasing consumption of this article, and, while in some respects it is very pleasant to know that the whole of our production for the last half of 1912 has already been sold, the situation has its disquieting features. I cannot help taking this opportunity of sounding a note of warning to the Trade. It is only three years since we thought [in 1909] we had overcome the evil effects due to the super-abundance of stocks caused by the over-production of spirits eight or nine years before. Then came the Budget of 1909, which appeared to knock the bottom out of the whisky trade. The available stocks in distillers' warehouses jumped up nearly one and a half million gallons between 31st March, 1909, and 31st March, 1910. We, in common with other grain distillers, then considered the time had come for still further curtailing the production, with the result that the quantity produced between the half-year ending 30th September, 1910, was the smallest for many years and the stocks in distillers' warehouses by 31st March, 1911, had fallen by more than the previous increase. This was caused not only by the short production but by a revival in demand, which appears to have continued ever since. The stocks are now virtually what they were previous to the 1909 Budget, and if production is maintained at the present high rate for the remainder of the present year, we ought to have accumulated sufficient stocks to supply all probable requirements. If we thought more whisky was required we would gladly make provision for even a larger make, but we have no wish to repeat the mistake which was made twelve years ago and led to such over-production as made it unprofitable for ordinary buyers to hold a stock.'

So the entire distress of the whisky trade cannot be laid at the door of taxation. Taxation was unnecessarily severe, but, as is shown by the unchallengeable statement just quoted, the trade had also itself to blame for much of its trouble. It was generally agreed in trade circles, that in the boom at the beginning of the century prudence was largely thrown to the winds, manufacturing facilities were enormously augmented with the resultant over-production and its consequent incubus, so that many ten-year-old whiskies were selling at little more than they cost to make, and strong rumours were afoot of a giant combine to takeover pot still production.

The malt and pot still whiskies, were suffering a further hardship: light-bodied whiskies, with more grain whisky in them, were becoming more popular than a quarter of a century earlier and the enlarged use of grain whisky also reduced costs as it sold for less than pot still whisky. With this habit, the pot still stocks stayed high, and their reduction to negligible dimensions became more remote than ever. A compulsory age limit, it was agreed, might have helped but even this was not universally conceded. The position was that grain whisky production was in a few hands; malt whisky lay in many scattered units, each with true Scottish independence, and they were unable to come to a common understanding on the question of the regulation of production. Such an approach was anathema to them. One result which might have been foreseen is reported here by Mackie, 'The outlook is more than even gloomy. Some distilleries are threatened with extinction; already many are shut down and men are paid off.'

One immediate tightening of the grip on the grain spirit industry, on the other hand, was the purchase of Hammersmith distillery, London, by the D.C.L. and some of the central control of the patent still distillers of Scotland over-production may be seen from figures issued by the Excise. These show that in Scotland distilleries making yeast with patent stills also at work produced 6·8 million gallons in the distilling year 1906–7, some 6·9 million the next year, and 7·7 million in 1908–9. Those patent still distilleries not making yeast produced 3·9 million gallons in the opening year of the series, 3·8 million in the following year, and 4·1 million gallons in 1908–9. No pot stills were engaged in the manufacture of yeast, though a few distilleries listed as having both pot and patent stills made a fairly constant amount of spirit, directed, in the main, of course, to a standard production of yeast and a few distilleries combined both pot and patent without the complication of yeast-making; these also showed little variation, and the output was not significant in any case. But the production figures for pot still distilleries tell another story. Thus in 1906–7, they made 10·5 million gallons; in 1907–8, they produced 8·2 million gallons, and 1908–9 some 9·8 million gallons. The tables give overall production figures for Scotland of 25·2 million gallons in the first year considered, 22·0 million in the next and 25·5 million gallons in 1908–9. It thus becomes evident that when the budget blow was aimed, production, warily in the case of the patent stills and less cautiously in the case of pots, was getting back on its feet again.

But home market consumption gave the gloomy picture already described: in the first quarter of 1908, consumption in the United Kingdom of home-made spirits amounted to some 7·7 million gallons; in the first quarter, a pre-budget quarter, of 1909, there were some 8·3 million gallons, and in the opening three months of 1910 only some 4·3 million gallons. There would, then, seem some relevance in the remarks of Sir Thomas Dewar at the annual banquet of the Off Licences Association in April 1910, where he said: 'The Government is in retreat like Napoleon from Moscow – not in a cloud of glory, but with their illusions moulted, their wings clipped, and their claws filed . . . The extra duty has been paid without comment, and for that you will neither be covered with glory or medals or anything else. Politics have neither shame, remorse, gratitude, or good will; or, as an American once told me, it is the long arm, the glad hand, and a swift kick in the pants. Gentlemen, this incomprehensible red flag burglar's Budget is not a finance Bill' – it was on the eve of its final passage – 'but brigandage against a particular class of the community . . . Taxation is a fine art; and around it swings that sublime thing we call statesmanship. Taxpayers should be chloroformed into paying and unconscious of doing it. Tax too severely and too conspicuously and your subjects will rebel as they have done. It is almost incredible that we are paying £10,000 a week interest for money which the Government will not accept . . . When your trade is reduced nearly thirty per cent and your licences in some cases increased a few hundred per cent.'

At just about the same date as his budget was making its final progress through the House of Commons, Lloyd George was offering his own curious explanation of what had been happening in home consumption. He then said: 'The main loss in Customs and Excise is on spirits . . . There is a considerable diminution due to the fact that there were heavy forestalments. In March this [1910] year 1,600,000 gallons were withdrawn from bond, and last year [1909] 4,255,000 gallons were cleared. This is not due to the diminution in the drinking of spirits altogether, or anything like it. It is due largely to the fact that there were considerable clearances in March in anticipation of the Budget. Then we come to April. The Budget had been introduced on April 29th, and the clearances in April were 5,130,000 as compared with 3,175,000 the previous year [1908]. There were 2,000,000 gallons of forestalments. But that does not entirely account for the diminution – in fact I am certain it does not . . . Undoubtedly the traders engaged in this business have been trading on the lowest possible reserve of stock . . . so that a good many of them really lived from hand to mouth. But there is no doubt that they reduced their stocks. The revenue from spirits suffered very largely also from political uncertainty. No one knew quite what was going to happen, and no one knew whether the Budget was to be thrown out, while in some quarters there were sanguine anticipations that the country might not ratify the action of the late Parliament . . . There is yet a third cause which accounts for the diminution, and that is the very striking decrease in the consumption of whisky. (Hear, hear.) The decrease has been due to a large extent to the imposition of this additional duty. I think that the additional charge put on the consumer by the retail traders was in some cases one half-penny and in some cases a penny.' (That extra would be per nip, not, of course, per bottle!)

Later he went on to elucidate in greater detail. In the April preceding the budget's introduction some 5,130,000 gallons of spirit had been cleared from bond; in May only some 660,000 gallons and in June 956,000 gallons. The figure rose gradually until November when the figure was 2,246,000 gallons. 'Up to that period,' he continued, 'the trade had been living upon its forestalments, and even upon short stocks and upon the reserves. Then we come to Christmas. Christmas always makes a difference in the withdrawal of spirits from bond. It is undoubtedly the best time for the Customs and Excise. At Christmas the figure rose to 4,293,000 gallons. That is the month when the Budget was thrown out. The figure was almost double in the course of a single month . . .

'There were two reasons. First of all, the Christmas trade is much heavier in spirits in the month of December than in any other month of the year . . . I think the main reason was that the trade knew fairly well that whatever party came in they would not take the 3s. 9d. duty off until the end of the financial year . . . They cleared out of bond, there-fore, a sufficient quantity of spirits to enable them to trade in an easy and comfortable way for the next three or four months . . . But then the Revenue suffered in the next three months of January, February and March, during which the figure went down again steadily from four million gallons to 1,900,000 gallons. Then it declined from 1,900,000 to 1,600,000 gallons and in March by another 1,600,000 gallons. So that in the last three months, compared with the corresponding three months of the preceding year, only five million gallons were drawn out of bond, whereas in the corresponding period of last year ten million gallons were drawn out of bond . . . Nine million gallons without forestalments as compared with five million this year . . . During the last three months traders have been trading again on short stocks. The Revenue has suffered, and that is why I fear today we are £2,800,000 down in respect of whisky.'

At this point Austen Chamberlain as the Opposition's shadow chancellor of the exchequer rose to say that 'as a matter of fact, the Government have not got what they expected, and the Trade has suffered tremendous loss and injury which is not confined to those actually engaged in distilling, but has extended to all those who were

dependent on distilling in subsidiary trades or in agriculture. (Cheers.)
Can you have,' he asked, 'a greater condemnation for a tax than that it
should have been ruinous to trade, have thrown vast numbers of people
out of work, have destroyed agricultural prosperity in certain districts,
and have done all this for the sake of a revenue which the Treasury have
not got? (Cheers.) The Chancellor of the Exchequer estimated in
May that he was going to get £1,600,000. In November his hopes
had fallen to £800,000. He has got nothing. (Cheers.) . . . The Rt Hon.
Gentleman has taught the Trade a lesson they will be slow to unlearn,
and that he will find them trade in future on less stock than ever
before . . .

'He may go on to temperance platforms and pose as a great promoter
of temperance by means of his 3s. 9d., but that is an accidental accretion
of virtue. (Laughter.) The object of the Chancellor of the Exchequer
is to get revenue, and his failure will not, I believe, be limited to this
year.'

At the third reading on 27 April, with Bonar Law declaiming: 'This
is not a Finance Bill, but a penal code', it was revealed that the quantity
of spirits duty paid in the financial year 1908–9 was 38,939,000 gallons
and in 1909–10 it was 25,993,000 gallons. Further, this latter figure
included 6,774,000 gallons cleared at the old rates, viz., 5,144,000
gallons before the duty was raised on 30 April 1909, and 1,630,000
gallons between 3 December 1909, and 1 April 1910.

On the passing of the budget, Mr John McDonald, chairman of
Long John's Ben Nevis distillery, told the Scottish Licensed Trade
Defence Association: 'The extra duty has crippled the only industry the
Highlands possess. In laying their case before the Chancellor, the
distillers calculated upon a fifteen per cent reduction, but it has been
nearly thirty per cent. And besides the great loss of capital involved, it
means that in labour 1,600 to 1,800 fewer men are required; or, with
their dependants, in all 10,000 are without employment in the Highlands.'

Peter Mackie, as only to be expected, took it up most vigorously, and
wrote for the *Empire*: 'Never in the history of our country has such a
remarkable Finance Act been passed as the Budget of 1909; referred
back for the decision of the people by the House of Lords, it has now
been passed by the Commons with the aid of Mr Redmond's Irish
votes.

'Originally the main object of the Budget was to kill Tariff Reform, which has been making great strides of late . . . I mean the binding of the various parts of the Empire by a reciprocal tariff, by which they will have a preference in a self-contained market, the same as other markets have . . .

'The first objection is it is a heavy burden on the working man; the second, it is vindictive, and an attempt to penalise the Trade for the Lords' rejection of the Licensing Bill. It is thus morally tacking on licensing reform to a Finance Bill – although denied by the Government.'

As for the duty now of 14s. 9d. per gallon, Mackie said that the average, original price was in the region of 2s. 10d. But as the tax was 'not bringing in the revenue expected, he should have at once asked powers to reduce the duty to the former rate . . . The whisky tax has resulted in a great reduction of revenue, and a great loss of legitimate industry . . . Foreign wine touts come here and sell wine without a licence; indeed, our whole system is protection for the foreigner, while encouraging consumption against ourselves . . . Is a country lawyer a suitable person to be the Chancellor of the Exchequer of a large Empire?' he asked in conclusion, repeating his earlier jibe.

In fact, it became a slogan of the wine and spirit trade at this time: 'Keep your stocks of spirits low and your stock of wines high.' And the trade has never got back to the same largess of duty-paid spirit stocks it held before that disastrous budget of 1909.

Other significant results of that budget included the pinch felt by many of the higher-class Highland malt whiskies, as the advance in the art of blending permitted the use of less costly malt whiskies than would have been considered before the beginning of the century. Some of the Highland distillers were themselves trying to capture a share in the export trade, but, as it turned out, with little success.

Further, the blenders were increasingly making their bargains without the intervention of the middle-man, a factor which meant a saving for the blenders. Of this line of action, one result was that there remained in the hands of both distillers and brokers large stocks of such plethoric makes as those of 1895, 1897 and 1898. The chances of their being used by blenders were most remote: their prices were too high; stocks of younger, and so cheaper whiskies suitable for the blenders were large enough for them to disregard them. It was even widely suggested that blenders, brokers and distillers should discuss putting all the old stocks into a vat and drawing off from that to clear the backlog.

Another budget hung over the land, that for 1910–11. Lloyd George was still Chancellor. This time, in June, he said of his needs, in so far as they affected the trade: 'The biggest drop of all is in respect of the licensing duties . . . Undoubtedly last year we lost a good deal of revenue under the head of spirits. I have no doubt a great deal was due to the effect of the extra duty of 3*s*. 9*d*. – (Hear, hear.) Our estimate was completely wrong – it was wrong by millions . . . There were three causes of depression – two temporary, and one, I hope, permanent. (Hear, hear.) The first temporary cause was the forestalments in March and April in anticipation of a possible increase of the spirit duty. It was very well justified. (Laughter.) Taking these forestalments on the 14*s*. 9*d*. basis, it amounts to £1,400,000 new revenue. Then, of course, there was the fact that the 3*s*. 9*d*. was not charged at all in respect of April . . .

'The second temporary cause? Depletion of reserves. The Trade drew largely on its cellars . . . they will go on with very short stocks, and still conduct their business quite efficiently. Probably the lesson they have learnt they will take advantage of in the future. I think it is very likely that they will not restock their cellars to the same extent, and will not keep the same reserves . . .

'Now I come to far and away the most important and substantial cause of the diminution, and that is diminished consumption. What is it that accounted for that? . . . A variety of causes. Curiously enough, they are partly political. (Laughter.) The Conservative was so angry about his whisky being put up by a Radical Government that he declined to buy it. (Laughter.) The extraordinary thing was that the Radical was equally angry with the publican for putting the price at a figure which he thought was more than justified, so he would not drink it. (Laughter.)

'But I am sure a good many of those who have discovered that they are so much better off under the diminished consumption have decided to make it permanent. (Hear, hear.) But the true cause was this. The consumer undoubtedly found he could not pay the extra price, and therefore he put down the price . . . The Trade is, however, still divided about it. There are two parties. There is the party who puts up the price, and there is the party, a growing party, with whom is the future I believe, who puts down the measure. (Laughter.)

'They discovered that they could not do business by selling at a higher price, so now they are resorting to the other expedient of selling at the old price but supplying a smaller quantity. (An hon. mem. – "Lloyd George's.") The old measure was something like a quarter of a gill. Now they have put it down to one-fifth. And they have done it rather cleverly, so I am assured. They use a measure which externally is exactly like the old one, but it has a raised bottom. (Laughter.) That is very good for the publican, because it enables him to pay this extra duty and make a little profit, and it pleases the customer. I do not think he is at all conscious that he is drinking less, and there is nothing that gives greater satisfaction to a man than to feel that as he is growing older he is able to drink exactly the same number of glasses and carry it better. (Laughter.)' (The usual price of a glass before the budget was 3*d.* in the ordinary man's public house; the addition in price varied at either ½*d.* or 1*d.*)

'At any rate,' went on Lloyd George, 'between one cause and another, there has been an enormous diminution in the quantity of spirits consumed in this country. Comparing 1908–9 with this year, there will be a drop of ten million gallons in the consumption. (Cheers.) I have to consider this from two points of view. As Chancellor of the Exchequer I have, first of all, to consider the effect on the revenue; but I do not think a Chancellor of the Exchequer is bound merely to consider that . . .

'There is an idea that we have lost money by it. We have not. There was a steady, continuous diminution in the quantity of spirits consumed in this country. There was a drop of five per cent between 1907 and 1908, taking the true revenue of 1908. If you assume for a moment we had not touched the whisky duty, but kept it at 11*s.*, and that the diminution, which had been steady and continuous for years, at an average rate of about three per cent, had gone on at the same rate in 1909 and 1910 what would have happened? If you put the revenue at 11*s.* on that basis, and compare it with the revenue of the diminished consumption at 14*s.* 9*d.*, we are at least half a million to the good. It has, therefore, been a substantial gain to the revenue and not a loss. (Hear, hear.)

'It has been a distinct gain to the community. (Cheers.) The results have been perfectly startling . . . Taking the whisky-drinking parts of the country, those parts where whisky is a beverage and not beer, from the moment the tax was put up drunkenness dropped down, and a very long drop. The effect seemed to have been instantaneous . . .' (On figures for Scotland) 'there is a drop of thirty-three per cent in the convictions for drunkenness. (Cheers.) The same thing applies to Ireland . . . The same thing applies to England . . .

'And it is bound to react on other branches of the revenue. (Hear, hear.) You are increasing the consuming and the purchasing power of the people. Ten million gallons of highly alcoholised liquor withdrawn from consumption! It is difficult to measure the benefits in improved health, in increased efficiency, in the comfort and happiness of the homes of the people which have been affected by it. (Cheers.) . . .

'I say that if any Chancellor of the Exchequer, in the face of these facts, in response to any appeal from any interest, were to alter a tax which had such beneficial results, he would be guilty of a crime against society. (Cheers.) Therefore, we must adhere to this whisky duty, which, financially, and from the highest point of view, I consider to have been an unqualified success. (Cheers.)

'I estimate that this year will be an increase in Customs – I am dealing now purely with spirits – that there will be an increase in the amount to be derived from the revenue by the spirit duty of something like £1,800,000. That will be due very largely to the fact that the forestalments have been eliminated; and, in addition to that, we reckon that a good quantity of spirits will be withdrawn from bond to correspond to the quantity that was consumed out of reserves last year.

'The total income from Customs this year I put at £30,095,000. That is an increase of £1,355,000 on the Budget estimate of last year. I expect an increase from spirits of £268,000 . . . Wine, I expect, will be down by £48,000 . . . Now I come to Excise. Here I expect an increase of £1,088,000 on the net receipts of last year. The extraordinary fact about the diminution of whisky is that people do not seem to have been driven to the consumption of either beer or wine, or any other forms of alcohol. (Cheers.) There has been a diminution all round. Spirits I put up by £1,555,000 . . . The total from Excise I put at £34,270,000.'

From the distilling industry came an equally authoritative voice, as the chairman of the D.C.L., Graham Menzies, addressed shareholders on 18 July in Edinburgh. Thanks to 'the exceptionally adverse influences which have affected our business during the past year', profits were down by £6,000, he reported, and, 'Of this deficiency, half is accounted for by the new manufacturing tax, which had to be allowed for, and has since been paid from October 1st last . . . An increased burden to the company of from £5,000 to £6,000 per annum, is grossly unjust and indefensible.

'Most people expect the Government to encourage by every means in its power the home manufacturer who gives employment, and who earns money upon which income and other taxes are paid. In this case, however, we have a Government which deliberately taxes the home manufacturer because he trades in this country with British capital and employs British labour. The foreign manufacturers of a similar spirit have no such tax to pay, and, in competition with the British distiller, benefits to that extent. It is no excuse to say that this tax equals a rate per gallon which is too small to impose a countervailing duty upon the foreign distiller. This argument could and should be met by removing this manufacturers' tax altogether from the home distiller and placing both on the same footing . . .

'It may be necessary very soon to close down one or more distilleries permanently . . . An increase in the spirit stocks, as while the directors have reduced the production considerably, the effect of the increased spirit duty has been such as for the time being to almost paralyse the industry . . . It is very evident that the Chancellor of the Exchequer has succeeded in dealing a most severe blow to an industry already overburdened with taxation without in any way benefiting the Revenue. The directors are taking every means in their power to keep down the production of spirits to what the probable consumption will warrant, and with that in view an unusually large number of the Company's distilleries have been shut down this summer . . . causing a considerable number of workmen to be thrown out of employment.'

As for rumours of a new grain distillery, Graham Menzies said that 'there does not seem to be much encouragement for competitors'. He gave the sidelight that they could only earn about seven per cent on the total capital employed. As for Hammersmith distillery, it was that company which approached the D.C.L. asking to be taken over. The dividend was kept at ten per cent, tax free, the twelfth year at this level.

A Highland malt pot still distillery, Glenlossie-Glenlivet, announcing at the same time, was able to declare no dividend at all. Another, Benrinnes-Glenlivet, once more announced no dividend on the Ordinary: there had been none since 1905, and the distillery was floated in the boom year 1896. Linkwood-Glenlivet was nearly the same: no dividend on the ordinary for the past year, though they had declared two per cent the year before. But a Perthshire distillery poster summed it up:

What the Radical Government does for Scotland.
This malt distillery (using Home-grown barley) is *Closed Down* on account of Lloyd George's *Extortionate Whisky Tax which is driving Consumers on to Cheap Spirits made from Foreign Grain and Other Things.*

Aldour, Pitlochry.

P. Mackenzie & Co.
Distillers Ltd.

Another odd suggestion to help overcome the new tax on whisky deserves passing attention: the idea that the bottled variety should be further reduced in strength, thus lowering the tax element in the price. The official figure of alcoholic strength was 25 degrees under proof, or a quarter of water, in effect. Some thought that low enough in content: the bottled product earlier that century used often to be put up at 10, 12 or 14, sometimes 16 or 18 degrees under proof, the latter being regarded as extremely low. Most public house trade was carried on by the publican buying the spirit in bulk at 100 degrees proof or more and reducing it himself to bar strength; this practice was only ousted during the coming war as the bottled product marched to final victory. By the time of the 1909 budget and the disturbances it was causing were beginning to settle down, strengths of 20 and 24 degrees under proof were common. The result was, sections argued, the customer received less in alcoholic strength yet had to pay more for it.

'It would be suicidal to lower the standard of strength still further,' it was argued. 'The number of sales with a smaller margin must be increased, rather than standing out for a bigger margin off fewer customers. Total abstinence created in the latter fashion is likely to be more permanent than the kind boomed by the teetotal organisations. Good value will help the trade to regain temporarily lost ground, but cheap and inferior goods can only have the reverse effect. If the strength of bottled whisky were further cut down, less malt and grain whiskies would be required, and thus the weight of the stocks upon the industry would be made more burdensome than ever, while the production of new whisky would also be interfered with. Then there is the further matter of the export trade, the case of Canada, for instance, where no imported duty allowance is made for any lower strength than 15 degrees under proof, the saving grace of high quality.'

The new distilling season opened in October 1910, and opening prices for the new makes displayed there was practically no interest in them. Stocks were too big for blenders to bother with new makes. Should they wish to mature their purchases for years, it would mean locking up unnecessary money for too long: there was plenty of well-matured spirit available. There was no change in grain whisky prices, a few reductions in malt whiskies, but in the main little varied from October 1909.

The annual report of Customs and Excise was published just about then, the report, that is, for the financial year April 1909 to March 1910. It was the first such joint annual report. It revealed that the budget estimates for the year were £30,740,000 from Customs, £36,110,000 from Excise, making a total of £66,850,000. Amounts actually paid into the Exchequer were: Customs, £30,348,000; Excise, £31,032,000, giving a total of £61,380,000. The realised deficit was, then, £5,470,000. But the payments included a considerable sum realised by the reduction of balances, following on the amalgamation of the Customs and Excise departments. The actual net receipts were, Customs £30,122,583, Excise £30,541,917, to give a total of £60,664,500. The actual deficit on receipts was therefore £6,185,500. It was pointed out, also, that these receipts included amounts which, at the end of the financial year, were technically deposits, on account of the duties on tea and motor spirit, and the additional duties on spirits and tobacco, which were not legally enforceable until the Finance Bill for the year became law. But the deposits on account of those duties which were withheld by merchants until the passing of the Bill must also be included to show the real revenue. Thus the Customs spirit duties amounted to £39,000, the Excise spirits duties to £280,000, and these, together with similar amounts from tea and tobacco, amend the year's revenue to become £30,269,000 from Customs, £30,822,000 from Excise to give a total of £61,091,000. This is £5,759,000 less than the estimates.

But the Excise estimate also requires adjustment to arrive at a true picture, because the new licensing duties proposed by the Finance Bill did not come into operation at all during the financial year. The budget estimate for the yield of the increased Liquor Licence duties was £2,600,000, an estimate reduced on 29 October to £2,100,000 in consequence of concessions made in the Committee stage of the Bill's progress. So from the budget estimate of £36,110,000 it is necessary to deduct the duties not levied of £2,860,000 and we get the true estimate of £33,250,000.

The pattern which now emerges is a Customs estimate of £30,740,000, an Excise estimate of £33,250,000 to give a total of £63,990,000; receipts from Customs of £30,269,000 and from Excise of £30,822,000 to total £61,091,000; deficits of £471,000 on Customs, of £2,428,000 on Excise, in all £2,899,000. This deficit was due almost entirely to spirits. Broken down and examined afresh from another angle it emerges again, with the true estimate for spirits at £21,055,000, the receipts outstanding and including deposits at £18,177,000, and the resultant deficit of £2,878,000. Other heads contributed a difference of £21,000 in deficit of receipts below estimate.

Disregarding duties levied on imported spirits, chiefly rum and brandy, and turning to home-made spirits, chiefly whisky and gin, this is the picture. In 1908–9, home-made spirits yielded £17,456,000 in duty with imported adding another £3,961,000 to give a total of £21,417,000. But this figure included as much as, probably, £500,000 of receipts from home-made and £195,000 from imported spirits forestalled in March 1909, on the eve of the budget. This lowers the actual as against the seeming consumption in that year, 1908–9. In view of this and declining consumption which had prevailed for some years, the estimated receipts for 1909–10, if the duty had not been altered, would have been about £2,000,000 less than the actual receipts of 1908–9. On 30 April 1909 the duty was raised on home-made spirits to 14s. 9d. and on imported in proportion. Now there had been further forestalments in April leading up to the budget, but the additional duties were expected to produce in 1909–10 £1,200,000 on home-made and £400,000 on imported spirits. The estimates were £17,200,000 on home-made, and £3,855, 000 on imported, the total being £21,055,000. So the estimated total was £362,000 less than the actual receipts of 1908–9.

Those actual receipts in 1909–10 were, on the old rates on home-made spirits £2,337,000 and on imported £484,000, a total of £2,821,000; on the new rates on home-made £12,228,000 and on imported £2,809,000, a total of £15,037,000. These figures give totals of £14,565,000 on home-made, £3,293,000 on imported, a grand total of £17,858,000.

But some amounts on spirits cleared in 1909–10 were not collected until the 1909–10 Finance Act became law in April 1910, so the revenue was really £14,845,000 on home-made and £3,332,000 on imported spirits, giving a grand total of £18,177,000. Now this total was £3,240,000 less than the receipts of 1908–9, and £2,878,000 less than the budget estimate. That is to say, the increase in the duties which was estimated to result in a gain of £1,600,000 actually resulted in a loss of £1,278,000.

This deficit was due, no doubt, to a heavy fall in consumption but also to a great reduction in duty-paid stocks. So the clearances of the year are far from representing the true consumption – that cannot be stated exactly – and tables of intake are to that extent misleading. They reveal, however, that home-made spirits yielded in duty some £20,124,000 in the year 1900–1; this became £18,136,000 in 1904–5 and thereafter dropped without intermission to £17,456,000 in 1908–9 and to £14,565,000 in 1909–10.

Expressed in another fashion, these official figures showed that 1900–1 saw 0·89 gallons of home-made spirit consumed per head of population in the United Kingdom; in 1908–9 this fell to 0·72 gallons, and in 1909–10 to 0·48 gallons. That method of computation is, notoriously, inexact, but it does present in vivid form a trend.

It is revealed again in the Government tables of production, showing this time that in 1900–1 there were 36,704,000 gallons of home-made spirit retained for consumption, as we have noticed earlier; by 1904–5, this had fallen to 33,158,000 gallons; in 1908–9 to 32,051,000 gallons and in 1909–10 to 21,446,000 gallons.

Scotland was, of course, the major spirit producer out of the United Kingdom countries and in 1900–1 Scotland made 30,196,000 gallons. In 1904–5 this figure became 25,185,000 gallons and dwindled thereafter to become 24,408,000 in the year 1908–9. In 1909–10 it crept further down to 22,309,000 gallons. Similarly, the century at its beginning saw 159 distilleries at work there; in 1904–5 there were 153, after a few years of fluctuation. A couple of years at 150 and in the distilling year of 1907–8 there were only 132. Certainly in a similar year 1908–9, in the middle of which came the budget, there were 142 at work, but that does not necessarily imply that they were all at work full blast all the time. They may, many of them, simply have worked for a few weeks.

The picture of home-made spirits in bond also presents a confusing image in the case of Scotland, where all but negligible amounts of Scotch whisky would be stored. Thus in the financial year 1900–1 there were 114,853,000 gallons registered as being in bond there. This mounted the next few years to become 121,778,000 in 1904–5, after which there was some slight reduction to 114,188,000 in the pre-budget year of 1908–9. With a decreased consumption following the budget, it mounted again to become 115,880,000 in the year reported on by Customs and Excise, 1909–10. A significant aside lies in the fact that where detections of illicit distillations generally numbered one or two in these years they amounted to four in 1909–10 in the case of Scotland.

It has generally been thought that the 1909 budget brought about a change in the nature of the Scotch whisky industry to make it more and more an exporting industry. It did nothing of the sort. The industry had been exporting in some quantity since the early nineties. Before that date exports were, admittedly, small, but they had begun growing, with Australia as the main market, since the middle of that decade.

In fact, from Australia, New Zealand, South Africa and Canada came reports early in the century that they were being flooded with numerous brands of unknown whiskies as well as the recently established blends. The former had fancy names, were the products of firms with no existence, had a very illusory quality and the brands were generally shipped on consignment with no chance of their establishing a permanent trade. Many of the receiving firms had up to a dozen agencies and one result of this flooding in was to depress prices of the regular brands. These fly-by-night brands were generally put up to auction as the consignors pressed for payment and they were sold for the price of the bottles and cases. The Australian government, partly in reaction to this type of trade, introduced a minimum age of two years, to be proved by government certificate, and some of the proprietors of this cheap whisky could not as a consequence be traced.

It may be worth noting that even then there was a trade in bulk whiskies, shipped in cask, to the United States. In the first years of the century around the 50–60,000 gallon mark of bulk whiskies were shipped into New York as against a constantly rising quantity of bottled whisky from Scotland. Thus in 1899 only some 67,000 cases of bottled 'Scotch' were unloaded at New York, but in 1901 this had become 100,000 cases and with slight occasional variations this had crept to 160,000 cases by 1909.

The overall export picture as revealed by the Customs and Excise report we were considering shows that in 1900–1 there were exported some 5,774,000 gallons of spirit made in the United Kingdom. Not all of this was Scotch whisky, but that beverage predominated. For the next few years it hovered around just under the seven million mark and in 1905–6 it just passed that level, and moved up to just under eight million gallons in 1907–8 and in the two following years, from 1908–10, it passed the eight million gallon a year mark. Thus it is rubbish to say that it was because of the Lloyd George budget that Scotch whisky began exporting; it is more than rubbish, it is a downright lie, but politics being what they are . . .

Mr H. C. Lea, M.P., had to issue a warning on the subject of exports about this time, and his testimony goes further to disprove the political lie. 'The export market,' he said, 'is one of the most valuable assets of the whisky trade; and, in view of the depression in the home trade, the overseas market is bound to increase in importance. The dumping upon export markets of brands of whisky bearing highly imaginative Scotch or Irish names, and of a type of quality calculated to do harm to the legitimate brands is bound to do immeasurable harm to the legitimate trade. On the other hand, there are the subsidiary brands of the well-established firms to be met with alongside the regular brands sent out by the same firms with the intention of meeting the needs of a cheaper class of trade. They do not compare very favourably with the regular brands . . .

'The remedy seems to be an extension of the age principle of Australia to other export markets. But it is useless to blink the fact that there is too little cohesion, and an excess of competition in the whisky trade . . . Then there is the consignment abomination, an abomination which is as old as the export trade itself, and the general impression is that dearly bought experience has done much to stamp out the evil . . .

'With the home trade demoralised, the export trade is assuming a

more important aspect than ever, but wild plunging and taking abnormal risks will aggravate the evils rather than relieve them.'

Another competent observer remarked at about the same time, that
'it is the blenders who have brought the export whisky trade to its
present highly satisfactory position. They know how to handle the
overseas markets, not merely so far as placing upon them whiskies
entirely suitable for their various needs, but also in the matter of pushing
those brands. Year by year the export whisky market becomes increasingly difficult to cultivate. Expenses grow instead of decreasing,
and competition becomes keener. New firms trying to make headway
for their brands find their progress barred unless they are prepared to
incur a lavish introductory expenditure, with only problematical
results. The shrinkage of the demand in the home country will, in all
probability, cause keener competition in the export market. That the
export trade is one of the best assets of the trade, there is not the
slightest doubt.'

The budget had, as we have noted in passing, an effect of some
magnitude on the bottled whisky trade. Much of the public house trade
was done by selling in bulk at around proof strength to the publican
who then reduced its strength. Some publicans were adopting the
already reduced spirit in bottles, and the 1909 budget hastened that
trade's progress. It was calculated after that budget that there could be
little doubt but that the future of the whisky trade rested with the sale
over the counter to take away rather than with the sale by the glass over
the bar. It will depend, it was argued, very largely on the quantity sold
in bottle either by the wine merchant or the grocer. Not much
progress was expected from the public house trade. The total output was
bound to be considerably reduced because of the smaller measure given.
The proprietors of some of London's West End bars expected their
barmen to get twenty-five sixpenny nips out of a four-shilling bottle of
whisky, and, it was assumed, the customer was bound to feel some
resentment, while the distiller and the merchant were scarcely being
fairly dealt with. The customer would, it was argued, show his feelings
by going off whisky altogether or by buying his own bottle and
taking it home with him. Once he began that habit, it would persist and,
it was thus asserted, 'it is for this reason that the firms who cater for the
bottled trade are able to speak quite optimistically as to the future of that
branch'.

In this connection it should be noticed that in May 1911 was introduced the new Customs and Excise regulations forbidding the use of
such phrases as 'Bottled in Bond', 'Bottled in Customs (or Excise)
Warehouses', or any other such form of words implying official
countenance, guarantee of correctness, and the like. While virtually the
same as the old paragraph of the Customs and Excise Warehousing
Code, it was warmly welcomed in the older established sections of the
wine and spirit trade as putting a stop to labels and such which implied
that the trader concerned was a licensed distiller, when, in fact, he was
nothing of the sort.

Also in that month – May 1911 – Lloyd George made yet another
budget speech and harked back to his one of 1909. He ranted: 'Last
year proved that a good deal of the exceptional fall in 1909' – he was
not now arguing there had been no fall – 'was due to what I call
"cellarage" – the very fact that they were clearing out their cellars to the
very lowest keg rather than take any more spirits out of bond until
they were quite sure what was going to happen to the 14s. 9d. duty.
Last year they replenished those stocks, but not altogether . . . They will
never fill up their stocks to what they used to be before that date, and
therefore, although they have not really replenished their depleted
stocks and put them in the position they were prior to 1909, I believe they
are restocking and they have done as much restocking as they are likely
to do . . .

'What is the actual fact? Instead of the quantity being 35 million
gallons this year it would be 29 million. But instead of a revenue of
£19,600,000 we shall have a revenue of £21,400,000. There will,
therefore, be a decrease in the quantity of spirits consumed by the
country of 6,600,000 gallons with an increase in the revenue of
£1,800,000 . . . There will be £21,400,000 for spirits, £12,662,000 for
beer . . . Wine £1,100,000, there again there is a slight reduction due
very largely to events in France.'

At the same time, *The Times* accorded fresh and newsworthy
prominence to the renewed activities of a proposed syndicate – resultant
from the 1909 budget along with the depressed sales both before and
after it – to corner all the old malt whiskies. There had been much
unobtrusive buying up of malt whiskies of 1900 and the years following,
but in fact their stocks had cost them more than they were worth on the
market at the time of writing. The blenders were, in fact, on to a very

good thing: they were able to buy better whiskies cheaper than ever. The syndicate might have been able so to corner the market that they could then have rectified the prices in an upwards direction. It came to nothing in that form, though, as we shall see, other amalgamations were also afoot.

The syndicate resulted in this manner: up to 1898, the year of the failure of Pattisons Ltd, there had been a boom in Scotch whisky and the banks had lent on stocks; then came the failure and the depression of the industry down to the Great War. After the Lloyd George budget it was possible to buy Highland malts of 1897, 1898 and 1899 at little more than cost. Of course this was a serious matter for the distillers, but a boon for the blenders: they need hold no stocks but could buy at rock bottom prices as the need arose. Then by the close of 1910, there were signs of depletion of those old stocks and there was a slight rise in prices. The intention seems to have been that with a capital of £500,000 they should buy up and hold the whisky for prices which would work out at an average of about 5s. 6d. per gallon, or about 1s. 6d., above the current level of values. The members were thought to be all large holders of old Highland malt whiskies and they hoped to control the remainder of the makes dating from 1896 to 1899. It was to be a struggle of endurance between the blenders and the holders, frequently Highland distillers.

It did not eventuate: production was back to the 1894–5 level and a competent estimate of Scotch whisky production and stocks put the former for malt whisky at 7,742,000 gallons in 1910 and for grain whisky at 14,567,000 gallons, while with stocks at 115,890,000 gallons in 1909–10 they were only 1,702,000 gallons up on the previous year, having been up by as much as 7,557,000 gallons in 1896–7 over the previous year and in 1897–8 up by 12,586,000 gallons over the preceding twelve months. In effect, only grain whisky was in excess at the time the syndicate foundered.

The *Glasgow Herald* summed it up early in 1911: 'There is no market for anything like the full production of which the existing distilleries in Scotland are capable, and that a number will be compelled to cease operations permanently, while most of the others will have to curtail their output by at least one-third seems certain.'

9

Early Scotch exports

THAT 'LIBERAL' budget of 1909-10, then, left the whole of the Scotch whisky industry reeling, a catastrophe from which it had barely recovered when the world was plunged into war in the summer of 1914. The years between the budget blow and the crash of war in Europe were spent in a realignment of forces and trends existing within the industry since its rise to pre-eminence, to its position as more than the purveyor of a local beverage in the far north of the British Isles. But the overall effects of that budget, whose importance cannot be over-stressed, were to give fresh emphasis to trends long at work. Primarily, the budget may be viewed as reasserting the financial element in the industry. That is, it is true, the case for all industries everywhere subject to increased and seemingly overpowering taxation. Only the mighty and major can persist when the taxation machine sets to work to pulverise any industry. Finance then is foremost, while all other factors assume a minor role, a very minor role which is theirs. What has previously been felt, toyed with, accepted spasmodically, then becomes of prime importance.

The exact working out of this principle will be seen in due course, but it had particularly in the Scotch whisky case two major offshoots. These were, first, the acceleration of the trend towards amalgamation, and, secondly, the fresh importance accorded to exports. To take the former, the renewed drive to amalgamation, now to become the predominant chord in the Scotch symphony. Amalgamations had always occurred; it is simply that following the 1909-10 budget they came thick and fast.

Moreover, the Scotch whisky industry was by no means alone or singular in the spate of amalgamations which moved to a peak before World War I, when came a fresh outbreak of the principle. To take but a few of the many instances, and only outstanding ones at that, the amalgamation of Customs and Excise in 1909 itself; the idea in the first decade of the century of one big union, representing the workers of all industrial groups and in fundamental opposition to the capitalist state the merging in 1913 of three of the four manual railway workers' unions to form the National Union of Railwaymen; the earlier organisation, in 1910, of the National Transport Workers' Federation; the initiation of the moves which culminated just after the war in leaving the five great joint-stock banks in a predominant position; the same moves which brought about, post-war, United Dairies Ltd; the preliminary mergers which finally resulted in 1926 with four firms amalgamating to form the Imperial Chemical Industries. In general, then, it may be said that it was not only individual firms but also whole industries and trades which experienced a modification of their internal relationships and this had repercussions on the activities and competitive position of small as well as large firms.

The Scotch whisky industry was only one among many industries in the United Kingdom, and was subject as much as others to prevailing economic climates and conditions. It was, in effect, the supersession of free competition by combination, and this was as true then of the producing as of the labouring and distributing sections of the country. Indeed, as true internationally as nationally.

It will be recalled that the D.C.L. was the early and classic example of amalgamation in the Scotch whisky industry when six grain spirit distillers combined in 1877, to be joined a few years later by the major independent grain distiller. The D.C.L. did not stop at that original junction. As Lord Forteviot, formerly Sir John Dewar, said at the Edinburgh dinner celebrating, in 1927, the jubilee of the company's formation: 'This company has been a series of amalgamations. Its birth was the result of an amalgamation, and the company has gone on amalgamating ever since . . . We have closed down something like twenty distilleries within the last twenty years without very much hardship to anybody. That could not have been done without amalgamation. They would have been closed down, no doubt, but somebody would have suffered severely.' There is a major aspect of the nationwide movement to amalgamation, and the clear exposure of the supremacy of the financial element in all considerations henceforth taken in this as in all British industries.

To trace through the persistence of that amalgamating instinct which came so strongly to the fore in the early years of this century as the industry felt a recession on the home front. As early as 1902, with the threat of over-production of grain whisky the D.C.L. acquired the Loch Katrine distillery, Adelphi, Glasgow, and the Ardgowan distillery, Greenock, the latter being fully amalgamated in 1907. Three other distilleries were then offered the D.C.L. – and declined. Then Dundas-hill distillery was taken over – and closed down – as was Drumcaldie distillery near Cameron Bridge. The Irish grain distillers amalgamated to form the United Distilleries Ltd and after complex negotiations there was an exchange of shares between them and the D.C.L. In 1907 came the important acquisition by the D.C.L. of the Vauxhall distillery at Liverpool of Archibald Walker & Co., whose Adelphi distillery had been acquired five years earlier. This led on then to an agreement with industrial distillers culminating in the Industrial Spirit Supply Co. Ltd. Then in 1910 came the acquisition by the D.C.L. of Hammersmith distillery, which gave the company a preponderating influence over industrial spirit. The following year there came about the adoption of an interest, later consolidated, in the liqueur distillers of Bloomsbury, Humphrey Taylor & Co. Ltd. A few months and the D.C.L. consolidated its Irish interests and the interests, in effect, of the whole distilling world in Great Britain, by acquiring Dundalk distillery, in August 1911. Then in 1913 was formed the Distillers Finance Corporation to acquire a half-interest in the United Distilleries Ltd, in which, as noted above, the D.C.L. had an interest, and in various blending concerns. Later, after the passage of the Immature Spirits Act, the D.F.C. came cap in hand to the D.C.L. to be taken over; terms were arranged; a hitch developed; the fusion took place seven years later. Truly, as Bryce has remarked, 'In history, nothing is isolated.'

But outstanding was the amalgamation of five Lowland malt distilleries, known as Scottish Malt Distillers Ltd, and essentially the product of the recession emphasised and underlined by the 1909 budget. Times were bad for many distillers, and the long-established firm of A. & J. Dawson Ltd, of St Magdalene distillery, Linlithgow, was obliged to put itself in the hands of a liquidator. A proposal was made to the D.C.L. to purchase; it was not welcomed; eventually an arrangement was worked out by which – and the amalgamating instinct is predominant here – Mr J. A. Ramage Dawson, managing director of the old company, took up the whole of the preference shares, while the ordinary shares were subscribed for by the D.C.L. Mr Dawson, John Walker & Sons, and others of less note.

In the case of another threatened failure, the combination element emerges quite clearly: whisky merchants James Ainslie & Co., of Leith Walk, got their affairs very involved, and it was found that among their assets was a half-interest in the Clynelish distillery, Brora, Sutherland, the other half being held by Mr John Risk, then late of Bankier distillery, Stirlingshire. Mr Risk bought Ainslie's share of the distillery and offered this to the D.C.L. A share arrangement was organised and the D.C.L. subscribed for one-half of the shares and Risk the other.

Now the D.C.L. acquisition of an interest in St Magdalene, Linlithgow, speeded up the tentative moves that had been made for fusing some Lowland malt distilleries that had been in financial disarray, what with falling home demand, and a plethora of mature stocks of whisky selling for little above the making price. Confidence was lacking in the industry, closures threatened, the lack of capital was now a serious matter, and the only combine with any capital or confidence was the D.C.L. The banks had burned their fingers over Pattison and colleagues; the budget and the wavering home market did nothing to restore confidence or hope. But the D.C.L. move on St Magdalene was taken as a practical vote of confidence in the industry's, in Lowland malt whisky's future. There were rumours of a London-based syndicate buying up a number of Highland malt distilleries and of the same sort of thing happening in the Lowlands. Major James Gray, of Leith and of Glenkinchie Lowland malt distillery, had been trying for years to organise a grouping together of all the Lowland malt plants, but when the St Magdalene deal took place only five members emerged for the new amalgamation. These five were: St Magdalene, of Linlithgow; Glenkinchie, of Pencaitland; Rosebank, of Falkirk; Grange, of Burntisland; and Clydesdale, at Wishaw.

In that fateful July before the outbreak of war in 1914, it was announced on behalf of the new company, the Scottish Malt Distillers Ltd, that 'It is anticipated that the amalgamation will result in considerable economies. The cost of manufacturing will be reduced by concentrating production, as far as possible, at certain distilleries. Raw materials will also be obtained at a lower cost through the large quantities bought. In addition, there will be the substantial advantage of the experience at all the distilleries being placed at the disposal of each individual concern, while there should be a saving of administrative costs. At the same time, it is intended to preserve the various staffs intact as far as possible, at least for the present, but no doubt in due time considerable economies will be effected through the concentration of administrative work.' The new company was registered on 1 August 1914, just before the outbreak of the holocaust which, curiously, was in 1915 to be of tremendous assistance to it. The chairman of the amalgamation was none other than Ross, managing director of the D.C.L.

Meanwhile, the old-established whisky export business of Daniel Crawford & Son Ltd, of Glasgow, an old customer of the D.C.L., was offered to them – and taken over. To round off the period, in November 1915, the Coleburn-Glenlivet Highland malt distillery was secured by the D.C.L. and it was intimated that John Walker & Sons Ltd. had agreed to take a half-share in the venture. Later, it was arranged that this distillery should be merged into the Clynelish Distillery Co. Ltd, referred to above, that company increasing its capital by £10,000 to be subscribed for by Walker, who thus got a one third interest therein, the other two-thirds being held by Mr John Risk and the D.C.L. Wise after the event, we can see these part-ownerships of the D.C.L. and John Walker as foreshadowings of the big amalgamation of 1925.

But those amalgamations of the war years, except in so far as being closely linked with the pre-war years, must wait their turn. The conditions of wartime in Britain brought about by their very nature a fresh spate of amalgamations, with a slightly different flavour from those preceding the war. Similarly, only brief notice can be vouched the D.C.L. amalgamation of yeast interests, climaxing first in 1899 with the formation of United Yeast and later expanded in the pre-war years.

To turn to some of the leading distilling and blending firms of the time we find the same principle of amalgamation at work long before the budget, yet accelerated by it to reach frenzy pitch. These firms began acquiring distilleries of their own in the 1880s, a trend which was accelerated again further in the 1890s and the first whisky boom, as they endeavoured to ensure their supplies and to reduce costs. But that amalgamating movement only reached its peak in this century and was given a fresh impetus by the 1909 budget. Take, for instance, the firm of James Buchanan & Co. Ltd. In 1906 Buchanan acquired control of the firm with whom they had long had dealings, W. P. Lowrie & Co., of Glasgow, a control which was increased in succeeding years. The following year, 1907, Buchanan acquired a controlling interest in the North British Bottle Manufacturing Co., whose works were at Shettleston, Glasgow. There, in 1908, Peter Latta introduced U.S. manufacturing advances he had brought back from the United States, then the world-leader in glass bottle making. About the same time, Buchanan added to his distillery interest – Glentauchers and Bankier – by acquiring Convalmore. In 1907 his company also acquired its own case-works and on the eve of the 1909 Budget began talks with Dewar and Walker about amalgamating. These did not mature at that stage, but their outcome will be seen in 1915 and 1925. 'In history, nothing is isolated.'

About 1894, the firm of John Haig & Co. Ltd, newly floated as a limited company, began negotiations for amalgamation with Haig & Haig, founded by Mr J. A. Haig, brother of Mr H. V. Haig, of Haig's. But after a year's working arrangement, the temporary amalgamation was not proceeded with. Again in 1912–13 negotiations for an amalgamation of the two Haig firms were pursued, but again they failed at the last moment. Certainly, John Haig had amalgamated as early as 1882 – with Davis Smith & Co., of Leith – but the Haig saga is comparatively free of the amalgamation trait, bearing in mind that the wine and spirit, including whisky blending, business of Haig's was split off from the distilling firm when the latter amalgamated as a founder member of the D.C.L. in 1877. It was only in 1903 that Haig took over the Glen Cawdor distillery, by Nairn, it was only as World War I drew to its close in another spate of amalgamations that John Haig & Co. passed into D.C.L. control and it was only in 1923 that the long-deferred amalgamation with Haig & Haig was completed.

After purchasing Cardow Highland malt whisky distillery in 1893, John Walker & Sons Ltd in 1899 formed an interest in Slater, Rodger & Co. Ltd, of Glasgow. Then in 1904 Mr (later Sir) Alexander Walker was added to the board, and as Slater, Rodger did a large amount of blending and bottling for Walker, negotiations were set afoot for

Walker to acquire a controlling interest, which they did by October 1911. We have briefly noticed the abortive negotiations to amalgamate with Buchanan and Dewar in 1909 and 1910. Then in the following year Walker took over the Glasgow wholesale wine and spirit business of Malcolm Ferguson & Co., just ahead of their controlling interest in Slater, Rodger. A complete purchase of the latter was effected in 1914. Then to ensure an adequate and cheap supply of bottles, Walker took first an interest in the bottle-making firm of John Lumb & Co. Ltd, of Castleford, Yorks, the firm being later taken over completely. We have already noticed their acquisition of an interest in St Magdalene distillery, and their close working with D.C.L. in that and other acquisitions. Again, in 1912, Walker took over Wm Wallace & Co., of Kilmarnock, together with the rights of their brand of whisky.

Such are but a few of the many amalgamations common, as noted earlier, to the whole of British industry in the last quarter of the last century and the pre-war years of this. Combination and amalgamation are, then, no new thing; they are no simply present phase, and the Scotch whisky industry has shown itself the creature of its times in exhibiting the same symptoms as the rest of British industry. As Henry Ford once put it: 'The age of the individual is past; the age of the combine is here.'

If this digression has been necessary to understand the workings of the Scotch whisky industry with particular reference to the 1909 budget and its effect of making the financial motive all powerful, the same is needed to understand that other major side-effect of the budget: the expansion of exports. Not that the budget created that exporting drive, since dominant in the industry; it only accelerated an overseas expansion already well in force before Lloyd George made his vicious 1909 onslaught on the industry and the drinkers of the country.

An examination of some records and routines will soon show the truth of this position, and the complete inaccuracy of politicians' – and others' – declarations that Scotch whisky only owes its export successes to the taxman. From its very inception, Scotch whisky was an export. For example, a newspaper article on the 1904 overseas sales expedition of Mr John Grant, of Wm Grant & Sons Ltd, puts it in handy perspective : 'Messrs Wm Grant & Sons do a large export trade with England, the United States and Canada.' A nice listing of export markets: England first, then across the Atlantic. For years England was regarded by Scotch whisky producers and blenders as an *export* market. Irish whiskey had long dominated the English market; it was only, roughly, in the last quarter of the century that Scotch whisky began a really serious rivalry, a rivalry which was now an ascendancy.

To revert to Grant's. By 1904, the home market was set on its slow but sure road to steady progress and John Grant gave up his school-mastering to seek overseas markets for the family firm's whisky. Remember, that the home market was not flourishing; sales for all were difficult as home consumption decreased overall year by year, and that home market recession can be taken as the second main cause for the increase in exports of Scotch whisky. However, John Grant set off for Canada and the United States where he opened agencies, whilst Charles Gordon, a son-in-law of the founder William Grant, made a fifteen-month tour of the East – India, Burma, Malaya, Hong Kong, China, the Philippines, Australia and Tasmania, and Ceylon. William Grant's son Edward was about to open up an export market in Brazil when he was unfortunately killed. That was the kind of drive displayed by all Scotch houses in their pursuit of sales: they had conquered the English market, thereafter there was none to withstand them.

To take some further instances to nail the lie that Scotch whisky owes its export achievements to the successive depredations of the taxman, let us glance for a moment at the actualities as seen by Slater, Rodger and Johnnie Walker. An old shipment book of Thomas H. Slater & Co., precursors of Slater, Rodger, shows that as early as April 1856 they were exporting whisky, wine, bottled ale and various provisions to Australia, India, South Africa, South America, the West Indies, Canada and the United States. In 1886 they opened a continental agency and by the end of that year were shipping to forty-five different foreign markets. By March 1888 that number had grown to seventy such markets; certificates were gained in the United States for cased whisky, and in the eighties and nineties certificates at exhibitions were likewise gained as far afield as Melbourne, Australia, and Jamaica.

Messrs John Walker & Sons Ltd show us the early and exploratory days of overseas sales of Scotch whisky. Alexander Walker, sen., son of the original John Walker, the firm's founder, gave particular attention to the export side of the business and about a century ago first joined in under the system of 'Adventure Merchant Business' whereby a group of merchants and manufacturers consigned their goods on board a vessel bound, probably, to one of the colonies. The owners of the vessel, through the captain or agent at port of destination, sold the various goods to the best possible advantage, retaining a percentage of the proceeds to cover freight and services. Now, Alexander Walker shipped a great many articles of general consumption and, continuing on these lines, he soon built up an overseas connection which formed the basis of the firm's later whisky export business, so that today it is probably the largest selling Scotch in the world.

By 1880, Walker had so far advanced in exports – to England – as to open their first London office. Alexander Walker, sen., died in 1889, and the next year his second son, John, left for Sydney, Australia, to open an office and keep in touch with the developing trade which had been established there. His health broke down and he later died there, but his work was reflected in the mighty expansion of Walker's trade to Australia. (That continent was a prime market for years: the strong Scottish element in the population provided a ready-made market for the beverage, and until World War II, Australia was the best overseas market for Scotch whisky.)

With the death of John Walker in Australia, so important was that market that Mr George P. Walker went there to reorganise and consolidate it, appointing a manager of the Sydney branch to control the Australian business, and another as agent for New Zealand. In 1897 agents were likewise appointed for South Africa, and year by year exports to overseas markets increased. At the time we are especially considering, they appointed agents in 1910 for a growing Paris and French market; in 1911 for Burma and the Federated Malay States; the Egyptian market was further developed at the same time – it was the hey-day of white dominance in these regions – and literally market after market abroad was explored and developed, largely by the wise and careful selection of agents resident in those markets.

In the case of what we today know of as White Horse Distillers, Ltd, their first full records are only available from 1883, but it is to be noted that even then there was a certain amount of cased whisky exported. Peter Mackie (later Sir) became the driving force shortly afterwards and as early as 1896 Mr G. W. Hope-Johnstone became a director and toured most of the overseas markets to appoint agents. Naturally, they secured awards at many exhibitions around the world, culminating with the Grand Prix at the Franco-British Exhibition in London, 1908.

Sir Peter later told of the outstanding progress both at home and – more important – abroad in the years preceding war in 1914 and attributed it all to the 'hard and long work of directors and staff'. Directors made repeated visits to all parts of the globe to secure advantageous agency agreements, and here it is pertinent to note that Sir Peter's only son – killed outside Jerusalem in 1917 – Captain J. Logan Mackie was only just completing a world tour for the firm's export trade when he heard of the outbreak of war and hastened home to join up.

Or take the instance of John Begg, Ltd, of Royal Lochnagar distillery, near Balmoral. To meet the demands of their blended whiskies, the firm established warehouses near the docks of the port of Aberdeen – the reason is obvious – and in 1906 such was the pressure of export demand from the world overseas that warehouses had to be set up in Glasgow. Aberdeen was becoming an inconvenient port for their export trade. And this was a decade before John Begg's amalgamation with the D.C.L. The general executive and sales management were in fact in Mark Lane and then Great Tower Street, London, the centre then as now of the wine and spirit business of the United Kingdom. One of the directors, who was also a trustee of the estate of the family firm, Mr Wm R. Reid, visited about this time, Europe, Canada, the United States, Australia, New Zealand, and so on, purely for the purpose of encouraging existing agents and of appointing others where there were none.

Similarly with the Leith firm of Wm Sanderson & Son Ltd, Mr W. M. Sanderson, the head of this family firm after the death of the founder, William, in 1908, made it his business to tour across Canada collecting business for this distilling-blending firm. In May 1912 – the date is most relevant – his younger brother and partner, Arthur Watson Sanderson, left Tilbury on a world-wide tour, returning only in February of the following year. In the course of the tour he arranged a branch office and firm for the family company at Perth, Western Australia – this state having at the time the highest spirit consumption in Australia – moved through all the capitals of all the states, went across to New Zealand where he visited both islands, passed via Australia again to Batavia through Java and went on to Singapore. After appointing agents wherever he could in South-East Asia, he moved on to Ceylon and from there to India, appointing agents on both coasts and to the north and south of the Indian peninsula, then in its hey-day of British rule. Returning via Egypt, agents were, of course, appointed for that land.

Again with James Buchanan, by 1889 their exports to the Continent brought them the Paris Exhibition Gold Medal in that year, and by 1895 – the firm was only some ten years old – had established their own export department: previously, the trade in the principal export markets had been conducted by London agents. Around this time Buchanan himself made a number of trips abroad, including to Europe, Canada, the United States, South America and New Zealand. The year 1902 saw the opening of branch offices in Paris and New York – their first such offices overseas. As post-budget intensity of the export drive mounted, William Morrison toured the United States for the company and advised on the appointment there of agents rather than their own branch office, which resulted, in due course, in the New York office being discontinued.

Similarly with the House of Dewar. In 1885 they set about an earnest onslaught on the English markets and by 1891 they had appointed agents for such far away markets as Australia and South Africa. This led to an event of prime importance in the firm's history: the two-year tour in which Mr T. R. Dewar – as he then was – visited twenty-six different countries appointing thirty-two first-class responsible agents and arranged for opening shipments on consignment to all the great commercial ports and cities of the two hemispheres. This, admits the firm, was 'the sure and solid foundation on which, ten years later' – well before Lloyd George's budget – 'Mr P. M. Dewar was to build the handsome and enduring superstructure of the Company's world-wide business.' Moving forward in time, in 1904 Dewar's were awarded a Gold Medal at the St Louis, U.S.A., exhibition which gave their U.S. trade 'a considerable fillip', for they were by then shipping in greatly increased quantities to all the leading states in the United States. In 1909 Mr John Dewar assumed the role of the company's worldwide traveller and setting out in the spring of 1910 he visited all the company's branches and agencies in the eastern and western hemispheres, the New York office even then being amongst the most important, as witnessed by the appointment of Mr W. J. Davies to manage it as early as the end of 1907. The first half of 1914 was jumpy both nationally and inter-nationally, yet it did not deter Mr P. M. Dewar from setting out on another business tour of the world, intending to visit India, the Far

East, the Antipodes, and to return by North America. How violently this was interrupted and how promptly and effectively Dewar responded is shown by the fact that in October 1914, their Johannesburg agents – of German personnel – had seen their premises set on fire and gutted by the mob. The agents themselves fled to Portuguese territory. Mr P. M. Dewar was in Sydney, Australia; he went at once to Johannesburg, where he arrived a month later, decided to set up a branch office, with staff from Scotland, and by New Year 1915 the office was fully functioning. Dewar's export efforts were brought even more closely into touch with the war when in May 1915, their London manager, Mr Alexander Campbell, who had been in the United States and Canada on a business tour for the company was lost in the sinking of the *Lusitania* as it returned to Great Britain.

By 1912, the House of Haig had agents practically all over the world, and held as distinctions warrants appointing them to supply whisky to King Edward VII and also to the King of Spain, while on the death of Edward VII, the royal warrant was renewed for his successor, as it was, of course, for many other whisky firms. In the years 1912–14 attempts were made to open up the American market and New York agents were appointed. Haig & Haig had a good business in the United States and this factor was taken into account in the 1912–13 negotiations – which fell through – for amalgamation, but the outbreak of war in 1914 and prohibition nipped their American exploits in the bud. Haig & Haig had given, in 1897, the exclusive rights to sell their 'Pinch' in the United States to Roosevelt and Schuyler, which rights were transferred later to Otto Schmidt Wine Co. Ltd. Later, also, this was rearranged for Roosevelt and Schuyler to sell 'Pinch' in the eastern states and for Schmidt to do likewise in the western states. By 1912–13, then, Haig & Haig had a particularly good business in the United States and it was only at the last minute that negotiations to amalgamate with the House of Haig – John Haig & Co. Ltd – failed. It was just about this time, on the eve of war, in fact, that John Haig began using the 'Gold Label Liqueur' for both home and export, and Mr Tom Wilkinson made two trips to the United States to promote American sales, appointing as agents James McCunn & Co., whose saga was only halted, as we have seen, by the war and prohibition.

The firm of J. & G. Stewart had been shipping their blend to Spain since early in the last century and in the 1880s Ebenezer Hughes, then in control, began the extension of the firm's business around the world. So successful was he that by the 1890s 'the name of Stewart became a household word' in Sweden, for instance. Their subsidiary firm of James Grey, Sons & Co. Ltd – the influence of early amalgamations again – did around the turn of the century a fine export business with Canada, South America and a few other countries, while Andrew Usher & Co., later to become a subsidiary of J. & G. Stewart, was able through its sales overseas – to Japan in particular – to give Edinburgh its Usher Hall. Space permits no further illustration than to draw attention to what the D.C.L. at this early stage did about exports. The D.C.L., it must be remembered, began life as a group of grain whisky distillers; their real interest and activity in the blending and bottling side only came about in World War I. But with the erection of the North British grain distillery, by blenders, with a productive capacity then of two to three million gallons a year, the D.C.L. looked about for other sources of income. Now from the formation of the company a small export trade had been done in blended whiskies for export in continuation of a connection which founder member Messrs John Stewart & Co., of Kirkliston distillery, had built up. They decided to develop it and after carrying on for years from Kirkliston built more suitable premises at South Queensferry, near Edinburgh. By 1891, the D.C.L. had appointed a 'round-the-world' traveller to develop their export trade, Mr J. Stuart Smith. They had for three years earlier employed another such traveller, but D.C.L. whisky was for him only one among several agencies. Their determination, then, to push exports led to this first-ever such world-traveller appointment and he set off at once to open up agencies abroad solely for the D.C.L.'s behalf. This was criticised within the trade, by some of the D.C.L.'s biggest customers among the blenders, but the D.C.L. and the blenders were thereby only pressed by the natural forces of competition to further export efforts. By July 1897 the company had decided to open a branch office in Melbourne, Australia, then the best overseas market for Scotch, and Stuart Smith was instructed to go there immediately to do so. He did, and also superintended the other Australasian agencies of the company.

A tribute to the company's export trade and to the very real work done by Stuart Smith is to be seen in the fact that when the export side was being treated afresh in the post-budget, pre-war years, Stuart Smith was recalled from retirement in 1912 and appointed to the board of the company to fill the place left vacant by the death of Mr George A. Drysdale, director.

But, as Ross, later chairman of the company, was to put it at the 1927 Jubilee dinner in London that 'although we have an export trade in blended whisky – of moderate dimensions – for over forty years, it was only during the war that we really entered this side of the Home Trade.'

Not all the amalgamations and export achievements of all the firms in the industry have here been elaborated at any length, but sufficient has been outlined to illustrate that these two strands of the industry's history do not owe their birth to the Lloyd George budget, or any other, however much they may have been accelerated by it. For the overriding effect of that budget was not only to depress home sales in such a manner that they have never recovered since, but to bring to the forefront the financial motive of the industry and its emphasis on concentration as found in any industry producing an over-taxed commodity.

10

Before the Great War

'IT WOULD be difficult to find a more trying or unsatisfactory period than that just closed,' wrote the *Wine and Spirit Trade Record* in January 1911. 'The greater part, if not the whole, of the responsibility for the dullness lies with the Chancellor of the Exchequer and his advisers. Prior to the introduction of the Budget of 1909, the industry has shown unmistakable signs of emerging from the heavy cloud of depression which had overshadowed it since the collapse of Pattisons Ltd, towards the end of 1898 ... The immediate effect was to cut down the consumption of home-made spirits by one-third.'

Yet from Edinburgh came the information that 'some of our very largest buyers seem to think that they had better look ahead a bit and bought, in December, more freely than they have done for a considerable time past. Whiskies of all ages and classes were wanted, but more particularly grains of 1906 to 1908, and Highland malts from 1903 to 1907 ... We saw one invoice for between £30,000 and £40,000, and we fancy that this will be a record deal, at any rate for a good many years ... One of our largest holders of old whisky sent out an invoice for over £10,000 for Old Malts ranging from 1896 to 1901.' But what he did not mention was that malt whiskies of twelve and thirteen years of age were changing hands at the original cost or little more. It meant a heavy loss to the bonders, but a great benefit to the consumer and to the blender.

And the *Glasgow Herald* was impelled to comment on these tumultuous years that the outlook of the industry 'is not encouraging', that it 'will have to resign itself to a materially reduced basis of consumption', and that there was 'no market for anything like the full production of which the existing distilleries in Scotland are capable, and that a number of these will be compelled to cease operations permanently, while most of the others will have to curtail their output by at least one-third'.

That was the mood of the times. Or, as Peter J. Mackie put it to Bristol licence holders: 'The Trade has been helpless even to defend their own rights, and we are now suffering a policy of revenge and being slowly bled to death by the swinging duties threatened by Mr Ure, which we are helpless to resist.' And he put it in this perspective: 'Today the consumption of home-made spirits for the United Kingdom is only 0·49 gallons per person, three bottles per person per annum, a fall of thirty per cent in five years.'

Lloyd George's budget in April 1911 evoked little interest in the trade and industry and, apart from the figures on home consumption the Chancellor then produced, his speech is of relevance in showing the lines on which the trade would roll in the future: 'Last year,' he said, 'proved that a good deal of the exceptional fall in 1909 was due to what I call "cellarage" – the fact that they were clearing out their cellars to the very lowest keg rather than take any more spirits out of bond until they were quite sure what was going to happen to the 14s. 9d. duty. Last year they replenished those stocks, but not altogether . . . They will never fill up their stocks to what they used to be before that date, and therefore, although they have not really replenished their depleted stocks and put them in the position they were in prior to 1909, I believe they are re-stocking and they have done as much re-stocking as they are likely to do . . . What is the actual fact? Instead of the quantity being 35 million gallons this year, it will be 29 million. But instead of a revenue of £19·6 million, we shall have a revenue of £21·4 million. There will, therefore, be a decrease in the quantity of spirits consumed by the country of 6·6 million gallons with an increase in the revenue of £1·8 million . . . There will be £21·4 million for spirits, £12,662,000 for beer . . . Wine £1·1 million, there again there is a slight reduction due very largely to events in France.'

Once more *The Times* gave news of the proposed syndicate to corner all the old malts, news allegedly based on the unobtrusive buying of Highland malts, of 1900 and less, as the stocks were just beginning to fetch more, due to the blenders improving their blends at no extra cost to themselves and the upward movement of the export trade over the previous two years. *The Times* reporting on the subject ran like this: there was a 'Scotch' boom until 1898 as the banks loaned on stocks; then came the bust, initiating a depression which had lasted until the time of writing: Highland malts of 1897-9 were selling at little more than the original cost, with this natural eventuality that blenders, able to get their raw material on unusually easy terms no longer needed to hold stocks; they could buy at rock bottom prices as the need arose. But latterly, wrote *The Times*, there had been some signs of depletion and prices had risen as certain big blending houses tried to continue the former method: since the beginning of 1911 the price had risen fourpence a gallon; holders were stiffening quotations; and this was possibly the work of the financial syndicate – the over-powering influence, as we have suggested, since the 1909 Budget, of that same financial factor – who were trying to hold the whisky acquired for prices which would work out at about 5s. 6d. per gallon, or 1s. 6d. more than they had paid for it. Members of the syndicate were, asserted *The Times*, all large holders of old Highland malts and it was believed that practically all the more important holders had agreed to join the syndicate. What was foreseen was a struggle of endurance between the syndicate and the big blending houses.

Attention was then diverted in this still distracting and turbulent year by the refusal of H.M. Customs and Excise to grant age certificates for whisky, despite the pressing of the Wine and Spirit Association and the developing exporters. Customs and Excise finally lost the day, but it was a long struggle, though overseas governments, spearheaded by the Australian Government, were insisting on them to qualify under their minimum age requirement, a requirement rejected to this date by the British Government, though toyed with by the industry in order to cope with ageing and non-selling stocks. The *Record* paid, in advance, its tribute to the later achievement of the Association and about summed up the then current situation, when it wrote: 'In any other country but ours, there would be no difficulty in the matter, but the Circumlocution Department is apparently just as great an obstacle to progress as it was in Dickens's time. If the Wine and Spirit Association can beat down its obstruction in this matter, it will have achieved something very like a miracle.' It did.

Then a probable rise in Highland malts came once more to the fore.

W. H. Chaplin & Co. Ltd recalled how they had written in 1898 that 'the building of new distilleries goes on apace, and it would seem likely that in a few years we may be suffering from a surfeit of stock'. It had been, they claimed, fulfilled – it has its warning note for today: 'The surfeit has continued to dominate and depress the market more or less ever since. Now, at last, however, the tide seems likely to turn; at any rate, the once enormous stocks have sufficiently shrunk to make buyers more anxious, and holders more firm. There is talk of a syndicate of distillers to control the remaining stocks, and so force up the quotations to more profitable figures, and rumour also speaks of an opposing syndicate of blenders to counter this movement.'

That note of dawning hope was given authoritative expression by the chairman of the D.C.L., Graham Menzies, when he moved the adoption of the report at the annual general meeting and said that though they had reduced the price of their spirit because of the cheaper grain price prevailing, that price was going up and so would that of their spirit. He rounded it off thus: 'There has undoubtedly been a more hopeful tone in the trade during the past year, due, no doubt, to the feeling that we know the worst, and any change is more likely to be for the better . . . has induced the trade generally to buy more largely than they have done for some years past – the consequence being that stocks which have lain dormant with us for many years have gradually moved off at prices which, although not perhaps very remunerative to holders who have had to cover rent and interest, nevertheless brought a considerable revenue to this company who had not these items to come against them. The increased profits from this source must therefore be looked upon as quite exceptional . . . I may just remark that we, in common with other grain distillers, are keeping a close watch upon the production and consumption, so that as far as it is possible to regulate it, there shall not be over-production on the one hand nor a shortage on the other.'

That autumn saw the victory of commonsense and the Wine and Spirit Association over Customs and Excise in the matter of age certificates for whisky exports to Australia in order to meet the needs of the Australian Act of 1906, the comment being: 'We are quite sure the concession is in the best interests of the whisky trade, for Australia was getting spirit which could not boast of being two years old.' But, at the same time, the echo of the other element in the industry: the sale for

£750 of Kingussie distillery, built and equipped at a cost of nearly £20,000 – so that it would be dismantled.

There followed the opening of the whisky season in October with barley fetching a high price and so limiting malt whisky production – 'a blessing in disguise' it was called, for in the previous year's short season when 10 million gallons less were made than in 1901–2, it had 'the very wholesome effect of enhancing the price of existing stocks'. Those stocks, with lessened production, were then nearly eight million gallons less than they had been ten years before, although home consumption was down by twenty per cent. So, despite the intensified export drives, there was no reason seen for feeling any anxiety as to the ability of the warehouses to supply all demands.

As to grain whisky, the distillers were scarcely able, after previous reductions in output and the healthier demand Graham Menzies had spoken of, were scarcely able, that is, to keep up with the current demand. The danger seen was the possible use of a greater proportion of grain whisky in the blends because of the advance in the price of malt whisky, but as there would probably be an increased figure all round – again, as in Menzies' statement – because of the extra cost of the raw material, the *status quo*, it was thought, might be maintained.

As the year drew to its close, the Customs and Excise report for 1910–11 at length appeared – it had been the complaint that the only effect of amalgamating those two branches of the revenue was to delay further their report – showing that only 0·56 gallons of home-made spirits had been retained *per capita* for consumption in the year, a recovery from the 0·48 of 1909–10, but well below the 0·81 of 1901–2; that 25·3 million gallons of home-made had been taxpaid in the year reported on as against 21·4 million in 1909–10; that the revenue from home-made had been £18,471,000, an increase of £3,626,000 over the preceding year; but that the number of distilleries at work in the distilling year 1909–10 had sunk to 124 as against 142 in 1908–9; that exports in the financial year 1910–11 were past the ten million gallon mark as against just over eight million in the previous year. Production at Scottish distilleries in the distilling year 1909–10 presented this pattern: dual pot and patent distilleries making yeast – 818,000 gallons; patent only making yeast – 7,527,000; dual pot and patent not making yeast – 1,655,000; patent only – 3,428,000; pot only – 6,676,000, a total of 20,105,000 gallons, a drop of some size when compared with the 25·5 million of the previous distilling year. Nevertheless, control and rationalisation in certain quarters had reduced stocks at 31 March 1911, to 112·2 million gallons, compared with 115·9 million a year before and 114·2 million on the eve of Lloyd George's disastrous budget. It must be remembered that in 1905 those stocks had been as high as 121·8 million gallons. Discipline had, then, achieved some reform by 1911, but, alas, it was to prove a most misleading strictness and reform in 1915, when the minimum age requirement received statutory force.

As the year closed with a serious fire at the Caledonian distillery, Edinburgh, with complaints that the two years' certificate fee should be less than the demanded five shillings, there came prognostications that the price of grain whisky was to be raised – currently sixpence a gallon less than it was in 1877 although maize was three to four shillings a quarter dearer, and at the same time rumours that the old pre-1909 Buchanan–Dewar–Walker merger ideas were in action once more, with the addition this time of their intent to erect or purchase a grain distillery of their own. The Highland distillers were in the unenviable position of not being able to increase their filling price yet making whisky which would cost fourpence to fivepence a gallon more to make than a year before. Some of the Campbeltown distilleries did raise their prices: another instance of the lack of combination among the pot still distillers *vis-à-vis* the grain producers.

Nevertheless, the *Record* summed up the year past as 'decidedly encouraging' and attributed it, at least in part, to 'really good and intelligent publicity', continuing: 'This campaign of advertisement may almost be held responsible for the undoubted change in our national beverage, for it must be remembered that fifty years ago the consumption of whisky was very small.' (Or, as Sir Thomas Dewar was to put it later in the year as vice-chairman of Pears' soap: 'The constant advertiser is the man that gets the trade.') A Highland correspondent wrote that 'the Scotch whisky trade in general has had an unusually prosperous year. A great deal of difficulty has been experienced, it is true, but the various obstacles have been overcome to a large extent, and distillers and blenders alike are now agreed that the business of 1911 proved far better in bulk and much more remunerative than they had anticipated.'

Exports of Scotch whisky for the calendar year 1911 had just passed the ten million gallons mark as compared to well under it in 1910, and

under eight million gallons in 1909, and home-made spirit consumption
for the same calendar years showed a recovery in 1911 to just short of
1909 after the drop of the intervening year.

Nevertheless, the industry was far from complacent or at ease: it was
distracted, indeed, as a brief glance at the year will show, distracted by
internal animosities, by endangered profits and livelihood and by the
possibility of further governmental interference against a backcloth of
the most serious labour disturbances the country had yet seen and the
greatest race to Armageddon among European nations that the world
had ever witnessed.

Reports of the syndicate being formed to buy up large quantities of
old whisky continued to flourish with the addition now of several
leading blenders – who were finding that with restricted makes in the
previous few years stocks were in danger of running short with prices
long. It was considered that by the short make of the current season
with high barley prices, the distilling business was being put 'on a more
stable basis' and that 'many whisky companies' shares are rising in
value in consequence of the all-round better conditions prevailing.'
Along that line of thought, of optimism, Messrs D. & J. McCallum
reported they were now exporting more of their 'Perfection' in one
week than in the whole of 1897; Peter Mackie said at the opening of
new 'White Horse' bonded warehouses in Glasgow, that 'ten years
ago it was only one and a half acres, and thirty-five years ago when I
joined the firm, it was not a tenth of the present size'.

But on the other side of the picture there was also the more gloomy
side. The budget that year had 'Nothing for Nobody' – 'Nobody in the
liquor trade,' it was said, 'expected anything, nor ever will expect
anything, from the present government, but income-tax payers deserved and would have been thankful for "a bit on account".' The
Scottish Local Option Bill – Temperance Reform (Scotland) – was read
for a second time in the House of Commons on April Fools' Day: 'The
old proposal to rob the Trade to please a set of fanatical so-called
temperance reformers.' Peter Mackie told the City of London Licensed
Victuallers' Protection Society that 'The Government which has done
its best to ruin your trade – in order to pay off old scores – is presided
over by two evil geniuses, Mr Asquith and Mr Lloyd George, who
have shown themselves absolutely untrustworthy and unbusinesslike
during their whole term of office. The latter has done more to ruin the

commercial morality of this country than any other Chancellor of the Exchequer.' A petition was put in for winding up A. & J. Dawson Ltd, Linlithgow, proprietors of St Magdalene Lowland malt distillery, for creditors, mainly the British Linen Bank and depositors. It was judged insolvent and a neutral liquidator appointed.

Yet, on the other hand, Sir John Dewar, M.P., chairman of John Dewar & Sons Ltd, told the annual general meeting that 'both in turnover and in profits new records were established'. The profits, in fact, were £30,000 more than in the previous year. The prospects, as he saw them 'were indeed most promising'; there was 'an enormous stock of old whisky'; their business had 'quite outgrown the present premises'.

The boom in grain whisky continued and although Highland malts still commanded top prices their position was being threatened by grain. It was even argued that there was an artificial boom in progress, with the aim of inflating prices and with the probable result of ending in another débâcle. Indeed, Edinburgh went so far as to complain of a certain amount of speculation – 'There is no question about it, that it has always been the rock on which Highland malts have come to grief.'

The D.C.L. maintained its dividend, and Ross, as managing director, had to come out with an admonition that the Company had 'a firm belief in altering prices as little as possible'. Later followed the D.C.L.'s annual meeting, always the highlight of the whisky year, and one from which we have already had occasion to quote the chairman, Graham Menzies, on the 'boom and bust' tendency of the industry, but which merits further quotation at this point: 'For some reason or other the market has now come to take the view that there is a shortage in the stock of grain whisky, having regard to the increasing consumption of this article, and, while in some respects it is very pleasant to know that the whole of our production for the last half of 1912 has already been sold, the situation has its disquieting features. I cannot help taking this opportunity of sounding a note of warning to the Trade. It is only three years since we thought we had overcome the evil effects due to the superabundance of stocks caused by the over-production of spirits eight or nine years before . . . We, in common with other grain distillers, then considered the time had come for still further curtailing the production . . . The stocks in distillers' warehouses by 31st March, 1911, had fallen by more than the previous increase . . . The stocks are now virtually what they were previous to the 1909 Budget, and if the production is maintained at the present high rate for the remainder of the present year, we ought to have accumulated sufficient stocks to supply all probable requirements. If we thought more whisky was required we would gladly make provision for an even larger make, but we have no wish to repeat the mistake which was made twelve years ago and led to such an over-production as made it unprofitable for ordinary buyers to hold a stock.' But a crisis of contemporary similarity blew up more fiercely on the home market – the 'price cutting' of proprietary whiskies as many tried to get what they could of the now diminished domestic market. At the conference representing almost every county in England, many organisations and firms, the chairman Mr W. T. Burrows spoke the mind of the meeting when he said they were there 'to put an end to a practice that perhaps had been allowed to exist too long, and which if not taken in hand at once would eventually be ruinous to all concerned. The time has now come,' he said, 'for some definite and drastic action.' He appealed to distillers and blenders in the hope that 'as a result of the meeting they would recognise that it was as much in their interests as in the interests of the retailers that cutting should be discontinued'.

The meeting was chiefly concerned with the cutting of prices of whisky and a scheme was adopted of tracing bottles by markings, though, as much of the domestic trade was in bulk whiskies still, the one adopted was not watertight. The Associations' delegates returned to the hall and were told the distillers and blenders favoured the scheme and 'with a view to putting it into force had decided to form an association of their own' – the Proprietors' Association. Some said, as did indeed, James Stevenson, of John Walker & Sons Ltd, that they would cease supplying the price-cutters. After the meeting the Associations' delegates held a further meeting and agreed to the idea of a standing joint committee to act with the new Proprietors' Association.

The month closed with the annual meeting of the Clydesdale Distillery Co. Ltd announcing its inability to pay any dividend and with a petition for the Glenmoray Distillery Co. Ltd to be wound up. The company, it was said, had ceased distilling in 1910 but still carried on business in London and Elgin and counsel for the company went on record that 'owing to the trade depression, the company considered it expedient not to distil during the past season. At least ten other distilleries in the same district followed the same course . . . at present there is no market for Highland distilleries . . . the market is over-stocked with Highland whisky, but owing to the reduced amount of distilling that has taken place during the last few years the market is improving.' Kingussie distillery was mentioned in evidence and its cost then put at £40,000 and its sale price at £1,600. Nevertheless, their lordships decided it would be premature to pronounce the winding up of the company with its distillery. It was in this setting that the long postponed charging rent at Highland distilleries was mooted – and had to be turned down. The blenders behind many of the distilleries took an entirely opposite view and the plan fell, for the time being, by the wayside.

On the subject of earnings, it is relevant to pause and consider a *Financial Times* survey which set out that despite several unfavourable factors the distilling industry had in the past year 'appreciably im-proved in earning capacity' and reported 'substantial gains in net profit'. There had been little cessation of competition and little proportion of the extra costs had been recovered from the consumers, though certain classes of whisky had found it possible to advance their rates.

Two companies emerge from the study as 'giants' – the D.C.L. and Dewar. Further, the net earnings for 1911–12 when contrasted with those of the previous year, 1910–11, reveal the confused state of the industry. First, the D.C.L.: net profit in 1911–12 was £225,500 as against £194,600 in the preceding year and in both years the ordinary dividend was ten per cent. John Dewar & Sons Ltd showed a profit risen to £169,700 as compared with £155,100 in the earlier year; the dividend was forty-two and a half per cent, an increase of five and a half per cent over the thirty-seven and a half per cent, of 1910–11. Bulloch Lade & Co. increased their net profit to £25,300 against £24,700 in the earlier year and their dividend to six and a quarter per cent against five per cent in 1910–11. Craigellachie-Glenlivet, possessing a Highland malt distillery, fell to £7,200 in 1911–12 from £7,400 the year before, but maintained a dividend of ten per cent each year. Dailuaine-Talisker, a merger itself of distilling interests and activities, showed the benefits of mergers: £12,900 net profit in 1911–12 compared with £6,300 the year before, and the dividend now five per cent against nil. Glenlossie-Glenlivet distillery company, however, showed a drop –

£3,300 net profit in 1910–11 with dividend of one and a half per cent and £2,700 and no dividend in 1911–12. The Lowland malt distillery company – a founder member of the merger which produced Scottish Malt Distillers Ltd – of Clydesdale showed a drop, from £2,400 to £1,700, with no dividend in either year. On the other hand, John Robertson & Son turned a £3,200 loss in 1910–11 into a profit of £300 in 1911–12, and neither year saw any dividend.

The Craigellachie-Glenlivet annual meeting, presided over by Peter Mackie, saw him in fine form, attacking the preposterous tax imposed by Lloyd George and the Scottish Temperance Bill and exclaiming: 'Our trade, unfortunately, is dominated by politics. We have a government of doctrinaires, fresh from the university, exploiting the country, in my opinion, for their own aggrandisement.'

In this setting began to emerge the first moves to an amalgamation of malt whisky distilleries. It had been mooted over and over again, especially, as it was said, that many in the Highlands might just as well be not working for all the profit they were showing. The Lowland malts were as badly off, as we have seen: Dawson's Linlithgow distillery, St Magdalene, was in liquidation; Clydesdale, at Wishaw, had made only a decreased profit, and still paid no dividend. Auchtertool distillery had made no whisky since May 1911; Rosebank paid no dividend; sixteen Lowland malt distillers meeting in Glasgow in October 1912 said they had to make an increase of twopence a gallon to meet increased costs and had limited the increase to that small amount as they feared for a diminishing market. Even so, they said, the increase would not fully meet the increased costs.

So there began the moves to amalgamate the Lowland malt distilleries. The D.C.L. was approached with the proposal that it buy Dawson's Linlithgow distillery and on second or third thoughts the D.C.L. acquired the Dawson company in November 1912, 'on the basis of the Company assuming all the liabilities and acquiring all the assets, and paying over in cash to the liquidator a sum of £14,000 which will enable him to pay the preference shareholders in the old company 10s. per £'. Steps were at once taken to form a new company under the same name with a nominal capital of £60,000 divided into 40,000 ordinary shares of £1 each and 20,000 preference of the same amount. The whole of the preference were taken up by Mr J. A. Ramage Dawson, managing director of the old company, while the ordinary shares were subscribed for by the D.C.L., Mr Dawson, John Walker & Sons Ltd, and a few others.

This Linlithgow purchase had several effects, the most immediate being a scramble among blenders to secure Lowland malts once it became known the D.C.L. was in it. This was because large quantities of Linlithgow were hanging fire on the market and being offered at a very moderate price and the blenders considered that as the whisky had now fallen to the D.C.L. it would not be thrown on the market to get what price it could. In consequence, prices of Lowland malts were made firmer all round. Then it set off again the idea of a Highland combine as talks proceeded to form a Lowland malt combine. Although the Lowland combine scheme was put to practically all the main Lowland malt distillers, after much haggling only five entered into the partnership. Valuations were the difficulty in forming the Lowland combine: the valuations of the properties, stocks and other assets were carried out by proper valuators and were then reduced to a figure which allowed the capital of the company to be fixed at £300,000 divided into 220,000 five per cent preference and 80,000 ordinary shares, both of £1 each. As was said at the time when the valuations were proceeding: 'It is understood that the valuations have again been closely scrutinised, and, as a result of discussion, further written down. The amount by which these valuations have been written down is a very large one, and it might almost seem as if the vendors were too generous in their concessions . . . The vendors will, in the end, get back whatever they may elect to part with in the meantime, as they are retaining in their own hands the ordinary shares.' This meant, of course, that there was no public issue, and had there been it would have met with a poor or even negligible response from the public and banks who had, in general, no confidence whatsoever in the Scotch whisky industry.

This amalgamation was made a little difficult not only by the valuations, but also by the fact that two of the distilleries, Rosebank and Clydesdale, were public companies and shareholders in these, in many instances, had got their shares on terms which made them loth to accept the new concern's shares, which represented a heavy decline. In the event they accepted shares on what the new company, registered on 1 August 1914 as Scottish Malt Distillers Ltd, as we have noticed above, described as 'on a scale which may be regarded as liberal in view of the present quotations'. Under the chairmanship of Ross members of the board consisted of one representative from each of the distilleries amalgamating: St Magdalene, Rosebank, Glenkinchie, Grange and Clydesdale.

That shareholders' problem resolved, as was also that of A. & J. Dawson – St Magdalene distillery – and the D.C.L. experiencing such a demand for new grain whisky they undertook the restoration of one of their distilleries. Port Dundas grain whisky distillery had been gutted in 1903 and out of action ever since. It was now fully restored in 1914, and the chairman told the annual general meeting of the D.C.L. in July that year: 'The demand for the company's products has been fully maintained during the past twelve months, and the same difficulty as we have had for two years past has been experienced in satisfying the requirements of our regular customers. It is, therefore, with a sense of relief that your directors are looking forward to the early resumption of work at Port Dundas distillery . . . the most fully equipped of any distillery in the United Kingdom.'

It came on stream at the end of that fateful July; the European Armageddon was unleashed in August; a disastrous fire put the D.C.L.'s Cambus grain distillery – of 'What Is Whisky?' inquiry fame – out of action in September – where it stayed until 1939. Indeed, it may be affirmed that it was only on the eve of war that the industry was making anything resembling a real recovery from the problems of the pre-1909 recession and of the budget of that year. The war was to bring further troubles, and once more the virulence of Lloyd George.

11

The minimum age

By the time of the outbreak of war in August 1914, Scotch whisky was about recovering its balance at home, primarily, and to a less urgent extent abroad. This sense of returning self-assurance and confidence was reinforced by the formation of Scottish Malt Distillers with the D.C.L. as members of the group. Yet that financial confidence had by no means fully returned. Even so notable a firm as John Dewar & Sons Ltd felt this distrust in certain quarters and the chairman, Sir John Dewar, Bt, M.P., was constrained to tell shareholders at the annual meeting in the March before the war that they had intended, the previous year, to issue additional capital, 'but the condition of the money market during the year had made a postponement desirable'. In short, the money market did not trust Scotch whisky. When the company was floated in 1897, Sir John said, their assets were £625,000 and at the time of meeting they were £2,116,912. In 1897 their profits were £52,837; the profits he was reporting were of the order of £203,029. The additional capital had been obtained, in short, by the means of loans from the directors and from the accumulation of reserves. As was commented shortly afterwards, in discussing the industry at home and abroad, 'It is confidence that is wanting on the part of the public to invest in whisky shares as they did fifteen or sixteen years ago, pretty much a case of "once bitten, twice shy", and the firm floating now would, we fear, find the public very shy.' Nevertheless, Ross, the managing director, standing in for the chairman, told the annual meeting of the D.C.L. that they had just finished 'the best year in the history of the company', one in which they had 'difficulty in satisfying the requirements of our regular customers'.

On the whole, however, 1914 – apart from the outbreak of war – presented 'a dismal record', one which was particularly exemplified in the case of the Highland distiller. Before the crops were reaped, occurred the beginning of 'the greatest war of all time' (to their date) with the result that raw material prices soared to heights which seemed to prohibit the possibility of beginning distilling operations. Prices, luckily, fell, but with Turkey's entry barley rose again in price. By the end of the year came two events of trade importance: the increasing of the beer duty to 23s. the barrel at the standard gravity of 1055, with others in proportion, and the beginning of distilling at between one-half and two-thirds of the distilleries, but with an output expected in most cases at a level below that which permitted the making of any profits. But, it was said, 'Like the big distributing houses, nothing seems to disturb the grain whisky distillers in the even tenor of their way. In this circumstance alone may be found ample justification for the degree of combination which is so conspicuously absent in the other branches of the Trade. Throughout war's excursions and alarms grain whisky has been able to live up to the [unrealistic] axiom "Business as usual", and although it may at present be doubtful what the new year holds in store for them, there is no reason to anticipate anything of the nature of a collapse. Indeed, it is just possible that the heavy additional duty which has been imposed on beer may turn out to the advantage of grain whisky, by diverting the consumptive demand to that commodity for a time at least.'

New whisky prices, it was noted, had remained unchanged throughout the year, yet there seemed little fear of anything approaching over-production – unfortunately, as the war years were to show – and although raw material prices had tended upwards at the end of the year this was offset by the fact that the grain distillers always bought well ahead and their now virtual monopoly of the home yeast market – to prove a most valuable bargaining point with Lloyd George and the prohibitionists in the years ahead – provided some measure of compensation. To confirm this reasoned attitude, in January 1915, the grain distillers issued an 'Important Announcement' that they were 'just as much interested as other sections of the Trade in avoiding those recurrent periods of glut and scarcity which in the past have been the cause of substantial losses to distillers, bonders, and holders alike'. They made no secret of their opinion during the past two years that production was being overdone and that grain whisky prices had been 'carried to an unduly high level'. The post-1909 shortage had been made good, and to such an extent that there was even the possibility of having to extend warehouse accommodation. To this accommodation shortage was now added that of casks and the new, wartime problem of ensuring continuity of supplies. The solution, they declared, was to average clearances for the previous two years, add a slight element for 'reasonable margin of expansion' and fix their total production at that level.

Into this arena stepped the Chancellor of the Exchequer, with his anti-trade obsession attuned to its highest rabble-rousing pitch of fervour. As he put it later in his *War Memoirs*: 'And as war work increased the earnings of the multitudes, those who drank, drank deeply, for they could afford the indulgence as they never did before. The evil was not confined to men – it spread to women . . . Liquor consumption had certainly gone up rapidly. Drunkenness was greatly on the increase, particularly in the industrial areas which we relied on for munitions.' Thus his rabble-rouser at Bangor on the last day of February 1915, the initiation of his prohibition dream went: 'I hear of workmen in armament works who refuse to work a full week's work for the nation's need,' he thundered. 'What is the reason? . . . Sometimes it is one thing, sometimes it is another, but let us be perfectly candid. It is mostly the lure of drink . . . Drink is doing more damage in the war than all the German submarines put together . . . We have got great powers to deal with drink, and we mean to use them.' One immediate result of that speech and mood was the establishment of the three years' minimum age for whisky on the home market.

Meantime, failures and suspensions increased in the whisky world: the trade was apprehensive of Government action which would seriously injure it; the bankers were reluctant to finance anything but the most necessary and immediate business; there was no encouragement to carry huge stocks of the raw material on slender security margins. A month after the Bangor speech Lloyd George met a shipbuilding employers' federation deputation who, he claimed, wanted prohibition for the war, and, in particular, the closing of public houses and clubs in areas where munitions were being produced.

The restrictions were imposed with increasing intensity by the

Central Control Board (Liquor Traffic) under the chairmanship of the 'upper class' drifter Lord d'Abernon, formerly Sir Edgar Vincent, who had been everything from a dragoman at Istanbul, to Guards officer, to a Conservative candidate at the close of the century, and then a Liberal candidate, as both of which he was rejected by the electorate. He was raised to the peerage as Baron d'Abernon of Esher, Surrey, from an old family seat of Stoke d'Abernon, in 1914, and became chairman of the Central Control Board in 1915. In that office he urged the heavy taxation of all alcoholic refreshments, both because he was convinced of alcohol's bad effects in the human body, and, agreeing with the taxation line we have already noticed as triumphant, because he argued that no loss would be caused to the revenue, as consumption did not decrease *pari passu* with the increase in taxation. (In 1920, Lloyd George selected him as the first ambassador to the new German Republic, a choice which caused both wide surprise and criticism.)

However, we are anticipating. From the shipbuilding conference, Lloyd George moved on to secure 'The King's Pledge' to abstain from alcohol – a pledge not shared by Lloyd George's fellow parliamentarians or the public. Instead, the Chancellor went through a series of unprecedented gyrations around the 'Drink Trade', or the 'Liquor Traffic', as he variously dubbed it.

Referring to the passing of the Immature Spirits Act, the great whisky event of the spring of 1915, Graham Menzies of the D.C.L., said that before it was proposed, 'various expedients were put forward by the Chancellor of the Exchequer for dealing with what was spoken of as the "Drink Question". We now know that much that was spoken and written about the slacking in the making of munitions having been due to excessive drinking was greatly exaggerated, and that while the fault was very largely due to lack of proper organisation . . . the liquor industry for the time being was made the proverbial scapegoat. The first proposal was to prohibit the sale of all alcoholic liquors during the war, then in kaleidoscopic review the scheme changed to prohibition of spirits only and then to a scheme for nationalisation of the whole liquor traffic. Afterwards an attempt was made to crush the industry by imposing double duties, only to be dropped later for a scheme of graduated duties which in turn was relinquished for the provisions contained in the Immature Spirits Act.'

In brief, then, the boasted three years' minimum age for such spirits as whisky, brandy and rum emerges from the shadows of bargaining under the stress of war to save the face of a defeated and incompetent Chancellor of the Exchequer with megalomaniac tendencies, on his move to the newly created Ministry of Munitions which he also marked by setting up the Central Control Board which attempted to change the pattern of Britain, free of parliamentary control and supervision with 'roamer' d'Abernon at the helm.

In March 1915 Lloyd George laid before the Cabinet proposals for total prohibition. Russia, he alleged, had prohibited vodka for the war and France absinthe, so, why not whisky? he said. 'His agile mind,' wrote Lord Beaverbrook, 'flew off at a tangent, and all through April he was more concerned with his scheme of State purchase of the liquor trade than with compelling Whitehall to give the Shell Committee full information on the needs of the Army. His energies became directed rather to seeing that the working man got less beer than to make certain that the soldier got more shells. The abolition of vodka in Russia went to the Chancellor's head, and he determined to carry State purchase and control in England in order to promote war efficiency.'

Or, as Lloyd George put it himself in his *Memoirs*: 'I was at this time giving very serious consideration to the idea of dealing with the Drink Traffic by buying out on behalf of the State all the private interests, and thus enabling the Government to obtain a perfectly free hand to carry through whatever measures were felt to be in the national interest, unhindered by the immensely powerful influence which the Trade has always been able to exert on politics in this country.' Plender gave him a rough estimate of the cost of brewery shares and brewery property including tied houses together with the value of all free public houses and other on-licences as being between £225,000,000 to £250,000,000. 'It will be observed,' notes Lloyd George, 'that this rough estimate did not include the value of distilleries.'

A significant point: his mood changed as much as the sky on a windy day, and while wishing once to prohibit spirits for the war, if not for ever, he also thought to prohibit spirits by taxing them out of existence. He later came to see reason, thanks to the arduous work of that whisky statesman, the late William Ross, then managing director of the D.C.L., and because of the indispensable part the whisky industry did towards winning the war, with the provision of alcohol for munitions, fuel oil for aeroplanes, yeast for the public, etc., a realm to be surveyed later.

That conversion was some way off, however, and in the meantime Lloyd George had set up a 'Liquor Trade Finance Committee' to advise the Government on the financial arrangements of the state purchases should it be decided to do so, to control the branches of the retail liquor trade not so purchased and to prohibit temporarily the retail trade in spirits.

Timing is now of importance. On 1 April 'The King's Pledge' was announced; on the 15th the Houses reassembled after the Easter recess and the Committee submitted a series of recommendations as to the extent and manner of effecting state purchase of 'the liquor interests'. The trade and the public were vaguely aware their drinking habits were about to be threatened and on the eve of Parliament's reassembly there was a wave of panic buying of whisky by the public and 'exceptionally large withdrawals' of whisky from bond. The rumours increased in volume and credibility and on the 15th was forecast 'State Control of the Liquor Industry'. Budget time was approaching and it was protested that he would 'certainly have to face a serious loss in revenue from the forms of liquor – whisky chiefly – against which the Cabinet has decided to take drastic measures'.

He was to submit the Government's proposals to the House of Commons on Wednesday, 28 April, although they were understood not to be fully adjusted, or prepared. *The Times* forecast five heads under which the Government intended to act: the prohibition of the sale of immature spirits; the encouragement of the brewing of lighter beers; special public house restrictions in munitions areas; reduced hours of sale generally; and compensation for interests affected. *The Thunderer* commented: 'The Cabinet have arrived at this moderate and common-sense policy after examining a great variety of temperance schemes, large and small . . . very serious consideration to two ambitious projects – the total prohibition of spirits and the expropriation of the whole of the licensed houses in the kingdom . . . Both have now been rejected for good.' Elsewhere the comment-leak was allowed, 'It is understood that there will be new regulations prohibiting the sale of fiery and immature spirits under a certain age . . . Good spirits and light beers are to be encouraged.'

That day, 29 April, Lloyd George announced his budget and, as it affected the trade, it proposed: to double the spirits duty; to impose a graduated surtax on beers with over seven per cent proof spirit, ranging from 12s. to 36s. per bulk barrel according to specific gravity; the duty on wines to be quadrupled, and that on sparkling wines to be raised to 15s. the gallon; the maximum dilution of spirits permitted by law to be increased from 25 to 35 degrees under proof; the Government to take powers over public houses, to control or close them in certain areas; and fair compensation in these cases to be paid.

The Times devoted its first leader to the proposals, saying they were on 'reasonable lines' and commenting on the double duty on spirits: 'The effect of raised prices is similar to that of lowered wages in times of depression. In the one case he has to pay more out of larger means; in the other he has less to pay with. Experience has repeatedly shown that high taxation on liquor, though imposed for revenue purposes, has this effect on drinking. Mr Lloyd George's own heavy Budget addition to the tax on spirits was an illustration. And spirits are unquestionably the most pernicious form of liquor . . .'

In his speech to the House on the 29th, Lloyd George, announcing the quadrupling of wine duties and the doubling of spirit duties, gloated on what he called facts: that spirit consumption was up in the past four or five months 'enormously'; the 3s. 9d. extra of 1909 had cut spirits consumption by something like twenty-five to thirty per cent and after it consumption was down something like seven to ten million gallons. 'That was the effect of a mere addition of 3s. 9d.', he was happy to say. 'If the addition of another 14s. 9d. will answer the same purpose, we shall have achieved very largely the purpose we had in view without prohibiting the sale of spirits in this country.' (Prohibition by taxation, in effect, which we have witnessed growing ever since Lloyd George's slashing attack on the spirits drinker.)

Curiously, *The Times* gave prominence on the same day as Lloyd George's proposals to a letter by Mr A. Stodart-Walker, of no connection to Johnnie Walker, accusing the brewers of immature whisky sales: 'Upon them lies the responsibility of supplying raw and immature spirit through the media of the public houses which they control. It is no defence against a charge that you supply poison to submit that you stock an elixir . . . High-class distillers have always had a complaint against the public house system.'

French wine interests protested against the new duties, but it was once more the Irish who saved the day – in so far as it could be saved –

for spirits. It was announced on 5 May that Lloyd George was prepared to modify the drink taxes 'because of widespread hostility. The liquor taxation proposals,' wrote *The Times*, 'of the Government are dead . . . for all practical purposes the national part of Mr Lloyd George's scheme has been killed by public opinion. The Irish Nationalist Party held a meeting at the House of Commons yesterday [4 May] and decided to oppose the new taxes by every constitutional means. This resolution was communicated to Mr Lloyd George, and it no doubt influenced him in deciding to meet deputations from "the trade" today with a view to framing proposals for the drink question.'

On the 5th Lloyd George met the distillers to consider an alternative to the scheme of doubling the duty, a last minute improvisation in any case. The new scheme was based on the principle Peter Mackie had earlier propounded and Lloyd George had rejected: that of discriminating against raw and immature whisky. The idea was canvassed that the Scottish distillers might agree to a surtax of 7s. 6d. on whisky under two years old, of 5s. under four years, and of 3s. 6d. under seven years, whisky beyond that age to be free of surcharge. The Trade in Scotland was tempted to agree to a surtax on a scale beginning with 5s. on whisky under two years old.

On the night of Friday, 7 May, a statement was issued by Lloyd George that a settlement had been arrived at on the question of spirits. The White Paper attempted to show and claimed that a good deal of mischief, especially in the northern yards, came from the drinking of raw, cheap spirits of a fiery quality. The Government therefore, it went on, proposed to substitute for their taxing proposals a complete prohibition of the sale of spirits under three years of age, to be accomplished by compulsorily bonding all spirits under that age. As accommodation problems were considered likely, an inquiry was to be instituted on that subject at once and in the meantime all spirits up to two years of age were to be compulsorily bonded and a surtax of 1s. was to be placed upon all spirits between two years and three years of age taken out of bond.

Arrangements, it was said, would be made for extending the same principle to all imported spirits. In order to meet the case of the gin distillers, rectifiers were to be allowed to receive spirits under two years of age for rectifying purposes at 16s. 9d. duty – 2s. more than the 1909 and existing whisky duty – of which 6d. would be refunded on certificate of rectification. As to beers, a scale was agreed with the brewers which would have had the effect of encouraging light beers, but the Irish representatives 'could not see their way to accept it, and as the Government is pledged not to press forward any controversial proposals, it had been decided not to proceed with the scale. The beer duties are, therefore, withdrawn without any modification. The wine duties were presented as a corollary to the increase in the spirit duties, and now that another arrangement is proposed in respect of spirits the wine duties will not be proceeded with.'

'Good Intentions' was the third leader of *The Times* on 10 May, which began as follows: 'The predominant feeling at the withdrawal of the proposed increase in the liquor duties is a sense of relief, not confined to any particular party or section of public opinion. No emphasis need be laid upon the fact that the principal influence which secured the withdrawal was that of the Irish members . . . equally effective opposition would certainly have been encountered from other quarters. The proposal failed because . . . the right way to deal with the liquor traffic in relation to the war is not by seeking to tax it out of existence.

'What remains from the wreckage of the Government plan is not impressive. No doubt a good deal of cheap and bad new whisky has been sold hitherto in England and Scotland. The prohibition of the consumption of whisky under three years of age simply means that the public will consume either better whisky or other immature spirits. As to whether the mature whisky now to be sold will be less injurious, there seems to be some difference of opinion. The Royal Commission on Whiskey and Potable Spirits reported that new whisky is not more injurious than mature whisky, and it is certainly not more alluring. Whatever else may result from the change, it seems unlikely that this particular step can of itself have any definite effect upon the prevalence of drunkenness. Mr Lloyd George, in short, has certainly not solved the liquor problem.'

The day's press was dominated by the sinking of the *Lusitania*: that tragedy should have banished his party schemes from Lloyd George's mind. It did nothing of the sort.

Lloyd George's own account of his crawl-down varies from that just outlined. He simply says: 'These proposals roused considerable opposition both in and out of the House of Commons. The Irish Party was particularly angry in view of the big brewing and distilling interests in that country. One by one I was compelled to abandon, *for the time being*, these proposed taxes, and could only retain one insignificant but quite useful little *restriction* in the shape of a *prohibition* on the sale of spirits less than three years old, the object being to *prohibit* the newer and more fiery spirit. Even around this, a fierce controversy arose between rival distilling interests – the "Pot versus Patent" fight – for manufacturers of pot still whisky made a practice of keeping their product several years to mature, whereas the output of the patent still was marketed straight away.

'But though I lost this opening round,' he boasted, 'I succeeded in subsequent years in carrying through the policy of high taxation of alcoholic beverages, dilution of spirits and the encouragement of lighter beers.'

Nevertheless, the fact remains, as expressed by Ross, of the D.C.L., writing some ten years after the passing of the Immature Spirits Act, that the measure 'was suggested to Mr Lloyd George and clutched at by him as the last straw to cover up the defeat of the other proposals. 'The effect,' went on Mr Ross, 'was a curious one. Those members of the Trade who had largely traded in young whisky were caught short of stocks as soon as it was made compulsory to keep spirits in bond for two years – extended to three years at the end of twelve months. Such firms, if they were to remain in business, had perforce to go into the market and buy old stocks at ever-increasing prices, while many of the fortunate possessors of old stocks took the opportunity of clearing out of business at values hitherto undreamed of.'

Or, as Ross put it at the fiftieth anniversary dinner in London of the company, 'Induced, no doubt, by the higher stock values then ruling, due to the passing of the Immature Spirits Act and to the closing down of all distilleries for potable purposes for a certain period of the war, over fifty firms on the blending and distributing side of the business cleared out of the Trade. Their valuable stocks were acquired by the firms that were left, and a large proportion thereof found its way into this company's hands, and into the hands of those with which we are now associated; if we had refused to take a hand in this market speculation, not only would our position have been immensely weakened by the loss of those fifty potential customers, but our position as against the bigger firms which remained would have been almost intolerable;

hence the policy which we have pursued and which today has resulted in bringing into the fold many otherwise conflicting interests.'

At the time, however, and whatever the criticism, the Act was not disliked in all whisky quarters. Many in the trade had urged some such measure for years, as we have seen, if only to clear redundant stocks stretching back fifteen or twenty years, and Graham Menzies expressed the opinion of the wiser elements in the trade at the annual meeting of the D.C.L. in the following July when he said: 'So far as this company is concerned, we have never opposed a measure of compulsory bonding, although your directors think that ample time ought to have been allowed for the members of the Trade to adapt themselves to the new conditions. A scheme having that in view was put before the Chancellor of the Exchequer by our managing director [Ross] and approved of by all but a small section of the Trade, but this was not adopted, and the Trade have consequently suffered great inconvenience and loss which otherwise would have been avoided.' Both Mr Menzies and the board, and Mr Ross writing later, thought and said 'there can be no doubt that this measure [of compulsory bonding] has been for the ultimate good of the Trade and of the public'.

Although common knowledge in the higher echelons of the whisky trade, it was years before the true origin of that three-year minimum age was revealed. Towards the end of 1920, Sir James Stevenson, as he then was, a great public servant and a managing director of John Walker & Sons Ltd, whose career and character are evaluated later, told a Trade audience: 'I am the real author of the Immature Restrictions Bill. It was I who suggested to the present Prime Minister when he was Chancellor of the Exchequer, that "All spirits should be kept in bond for three years." Mr Lloyd George has done many fine things for his country. To those of us who really know, his modesty is not one of his least virtues, but I can assure you in all truth and sincerity that by no means the least of his achievements was the placing on the Statute Book "That all spirits shall be kept in bond for three years" . . . far too little credit has been given to that enactment by the Control Board and other authorities who have blazoned forth the improvement in sobriety of the people as due to their absurd restrictions. There is no greater enemy of Pussyfootism than good liquor. Served under good conditions it will withstand all attacks.'

Tempers have cooled and wisdom prevailed since that introduction of the three-year minimum age for certain spirits, but on the eve of the budget in 1915 the *Record* felt compelled by the facts of situation to head its leader, 'The biggest crisis in the history of the Trade'. After the switch from the doubled spirits duty to the minimum age the May leader described the situation under the heading, 'Lloyd George Climbs Down', and, detailing the events in Parliament and the Cabinet, used the overall description, 'The Budget Fiasco'. By June, attention was diverted to 'Hardships under the New Act', instancing the most acute of the problems facing the trade: 'At present bonded warehouses throughout the country are well stocked with grain whisky, bonded to use in blends of ages under two years. Clearly, none of these stocks are now available, and if blends are to be proceeded with, as they must, grain spirit of over two or three years must be promptly purchased. Unfortunately, however, the stock of grain or patent still whisky available of the necessary age is extremely limited, and those who hold it, realising the dictating position they hold, not only demand vastly enhanced prices but pick and choose their customers to whom they sell. Indeed, so precarious is the position for the blending trade that very shortly the limited stock of aged grain about must become exhausted. In that event, blenders will be seriously placed, not only as to the maintenance of the character of blends but also as to price.'

It will be remembered that grain whisky production was more tightly controlled throughout the century than malt whisky and after the 1909 budget in particular grain whisky output had been deliberately restricted, only getting back into a more vigorous vein about 1912 and 1913. That extra output had been quickly taken up, so there was little three years old, or more, in the spring and summer of 1915 after the Immature Spirits Act came into force. Of course, it opened the door for many fine old malts to secure sales which had never been expected, and in that sense the public benefited by receiving in their blends an increased percentage of well matured Highland malts. But the switch over to an increased malt element in blends was to entail further complications the following year when the enforced dilution of whisky was evolving under the direction of that Lloyd George monster the Central Control Board (Liquor Traffic).

That benefit of duty paid withdrawals of previously disregarded malts had the further effect also of really putting on its feet the new Lowland malt whisky amalgamation, Scottish Malt Distillers. We have seen that D.C.L. intervention in bringing about that amalgamation had hardened the prices of Lowland malts, earlier a drug on the market. As Ross, chairman of Scottish Malts, told the second annual meeting in October that year, reporting a net profit of £31,132 14s. 5d., 'exceptional circumstances have been largely instrumental in bringing it about. I refer particularly to the passage of the Immature Spirits Act in May of this year which caught the market short of grain whisky stocks of the requisite age and threw a larger demand upon this company's production. This has naturally led to a much larger sale of old whiskies than would otherwise have been the case, and to that extent our reserves in the shape of old whisky held at low valuations have been encroached upon.'

As Graham Menzies pointed out, whiskies of the necessary age advanced by one hundred to one hundred and fifty per cent in a few weeks after the introduction of the Act. At the same time, demand for new grains to lay down in bond was suddenly increasing, increasing to such an extent that it was 'more than taxing' the distillers' abilities to make the spirit. Some brokers and blenders even went to the length of suggesting that the distillers were holding up the stock, so as to increase their price. From 1 June it was increased by fivepence a gallon, new, and while early 1915 grain whisky was being quoted at 3s. 6d. per gallon, three-year-old grains were fetching nearly 6s., and advancing without halt. That advance, of course, in all prices of all whiskies, continued without interruption throughout the war, a process still with us today, ever since the recovery from the post-Great War slumps and depressions.

But the real budget of 1915 came in the autumn, under the then new chancellor McKenna, Lloyd George having gone to the newly created Ministry of Munitions, and with McKenna came the fruition of Lloyd George's long complaints against pre-budget forestalments and the introduction of restrictions on them, challenged at the time but now woven into the law of the land.

12

1915 developments

EVEN BEFORE the distorting budget of 1909, Buchanan, Dewar and
Walker had been in consultation about amalgamating, in consequence
of the retarded condition of the home market and the growing export
one. Later, with the home market reeling from the disastrous budget –
an attitude it assumed for years afterwards – talks were resumed and in
March 1915 it was announced that James Buchanan & Co. Ltd and
John Dewar & Sons Ltd were to merge. 'An arrangement', it was said,
had been arrived at whereby they 'are to be brought into "close and
permanent association with each other".' As the *Record* said at the time,
it was 'one of the most notable features in the history of the Scotch
whisky trade', continuing: 'We must all hope it will be for the good of
the Trade as a whole, as well as of those who are more directly concerned. The rise of these gigantic concerns has been almost romantic in
character. It really seems only a few years ago that they were trading in
modest surroundings, the one firm in Queen Victoria Street, and the
other in Warwick Street, off Cockspur Street, And now there is a new
company to be formed with a capital of £5,000,000.' That is, a private
holding company, with a capital of £5,000,000, under the style of
Scotch Whisky Brands Ltd, had been formed to pool the profits and
exploit the resources of the two concerns under a joint directorate, to
take effect from 1 April 1915. The two companies were to maintain
separate existences, but, as was stated at the time, 'the association will
result in being so carried on as to utilise their respective resources and
organisations with the greatest advantage and economy in the interests

of both concerns'. The two companies, with their own subsidiary undertakings, claimed – and rightly – to hold the largest and most valuable stocks of maturing whisky in Scotland.

A glance at their previous story reveals the aptness of the *Record's* comment on the romantic character of their rise. Dewar then dated back about 100 years, but it was only in 1897 that the then present company was authorised with a capital of £600,000 in £10 shares, £250,000 being five per cent cumulative preference, and £350,000 being ordinary. All the ordinary shares were issued to the vendor company fully paid and all the preference were subscribed at a premium of £1 each. For the three years ended 31 January 1912, 1913 and 1914 the ordinary shares received forty-two and a half per cent. Buchanan was formed into a company in August 1903, after less than twenty years of James Buchanan's having set up for himself, with an authorised capital of £1,000,000 in £10 shares, equally divided into six per cent cumulative and ordinary. The subscribed and paid up capital was, at the time of the 1915 merger, £850,000, of which £490,000 was in ordinary and £360,000 in preference.

Sir Thomas Dewar, as he then was, the managing director, went on record as to the background of the merger: 'The two firms have been in friendly relations and reciprocated ideas for some years past,' he said, 'and the idea of an amalgamation originated a few months ago. Our reason for taking the new step is to protect ourselves against the heavy taxation which is now in force and that is to come. By amalgamating forces we shall be better able to take advantage of the large channels we have for the distribution of our goods. We shall be able to co-operate in many different ways to reduce expenses and lessen competition, and we shall have the largest stocks in existence of fine old whisky. The new arrangements will be to our mutual benefit and to the benefit of the public, because we shall be able to give the public exceptional value and thus keep for Scotch whisky the favour it now enjoys in all parts of the world. It is a financial amalgamation only, to enable us better to meet the high taxes and the high price of raw material. There will be no policy of interference with the policy of the firms and with the conditions under which they now work. Each will retain its own distinctive features and we shall keep all the members of our existing staffs. But there are so many things that we can do better together that the wisdom of the new arrangement appears to be quite apparent.

There will be no money subscribed but we shall be doing the Chancellor of the Exchequer some good, for stamp fees alone in connection with the registration of the company will amount to nearly £40,000.'

The distinctive feature of the merger was the size of the parties involved, not the fact of the merger itself. The D.C.L., it will be remembered, was the result of an amalgamation nearly forty years previous, but even their authorised capital was less at the time, under half the Buchanan-Dewar capital, and only £2,000,000, later halved. It was in fact symbolic of the times, which were now impinging on the major firms in the industry. Amalgamations were now moving beyond the realm of lesser firms being merged into larger; the marriage of the giants was on the horizon to be carried to its greatest conclusion ten years later with the Big Amalgamation when the D.C.L. amalgamated with Buchanan, Dewar and Walker after years of co-operation and sharing in ownership in different ventures.

With Buchanan-Dewar in mind, the success of the Lowland malt amalgamation increasingly evident, the summer of 1915 saw a revival of the attempt, spasmodic over the years, to amalgamate some of the more important Highland malt distilleries. In the middle of March there had died Thomas Mackenzie, managing director of Dailuaine-Talisker Distilleries Ltd. A glance at his career is relevant: his father founded Dailuaine distillery in 1851, and on his death his widow leased the distillery for a term of years to a Mr Fleming; with Scotch whisky about to make great strides on the English market, in 1879 Thomas Mackenzie became Fleming's partner and later continued as managing partner. As business increased, Mackenzie enlarged the distillery and its output until it became the largest Highland malt distillery in Scotland. During the boom of the 1890s he was the prime mover in building Imperial distillery and the large warehouses owned by Carron Warehouse Bonding Co. Ltd, formed in 1898 with a capital of £580,000. The group of distilleries taken over by the company included Dailuaine, Talisker and the Aberdeen grain distillery, burnt down just before the war and never rebuilt. He had no family, his wife was dead, and his own death speeded up this idea of a Highland malt amalgamation.

It had long been felt that there was much useless competition and overlapping amongst the Highland malt distilleries and the best thing to be done was to imitate Scottish Malt Distillers formed as we have seen, by an amalgamation of Lowland malt distilleries. One very real difficulty was to find anyone sufficiently neutral to take the lead, so the obvious man was picked: William Ross, managing director of the D.C.L. and the chairman of the Scottish Malt Distillers. He called a meeting of seven or eight leading Highland distillers; it broke up; with characteristic patience and perseverance, he called a second meeting. Intensive discussions and negotiations were pressed on with, but finally Ross had to admit defeat of his rationalising proposals. To round off the Dailuaine story, the result in one sense of the failure of the 1915 meetings, in the spring of 1916, the board of Dailuaine-Talisker Distilleries, one of the most important of the Highland distillers, approached Ross for advice. The result was that D.C.L., Dewar, Walker and the W. P. Lowrie subsidiary of Buchanan purchased the whole of the shares (a small minority only objecting) and the new board carried one representative from each of the four purchasing companies with Mr Ross as chairman. That same spring, to anticipate events, D.C.L. also purchased the whole share capital of John Hopkins & Co. Ltd, of London and Glasgow, and of John Begg, Ltd, of Glasgow, partly because of their valuable export connections, partly because of the shareholders' willingness to get out of the worrying whisky trade which had, to them, a most uncertain future. The age of dominating giants was a stage nearer.

To instance but a few of the spate of amalgamations and withdrawals then current, may be mentioned the acquisition in May 1915, of Saucel distillery, Paisley, by the D.C.L. There was a scarcity of bonded accommodation; the chairman of D.C.L., Graham Menzies, offered to buy Saucel, where the distillery was dismantled but where there were valuable maltings and bonds; so the property passed into D.C.L. hands on the 15th of the month, nicely timed for the introduction of the three-year minimum age rule. Later that year, in November, the Coleburn-Glenlivet distillery already mentioned in another connection, the property of John Robertson & Sons Ltd, of Dundee, was secured by the D.C.L. for £5,000, Walker taking a half-share in the venture. Later it was arranged that Coleburn should be merged with Clynelish Distillery Co. Ltd, outlined earlier, that company now increasing its capital by £10,000, to be subscribed by Walker (who thus got a one-third share in it) while the other two-thirds were held by Mr John Risk, mentioned above, and the D.C.L. With the addition the following spring of Hopkins's Tobermory distillery on the island of Mull, and of Begg's Lochnagar distillery, by Balmoral, the first glimmerings of order in the malt whisky distilling world were becoming evident, as was D.C.L.'s now important incursion into it, a world from which they had earlier, apart from Knockdhu, kept fairly apart, restricting themselves to grain whisky production, yeast and fusel oil. The essence of existence is continuity, the development of trends and events to their own inherent, logical conclusion; it was the genius of Ross to analyse the events, discern the underlying trends and so fashion the industry which we know today.

Indeed, the address presented to him in May 1932, at a representative gathering of leading members of the Scotch whisky industry best sums up his dominant influence in this direction. It records: 'Our gratitude for the eminently helpful services which you have ungrudgingly rendered to Trade over a long series of years during which, by the exercise of your diplomatic qualities and wise guidance, your impartial judgment and your calm, kindly and just influence, you successfully directed the handling of the many complex questions which, from time to time, assailed the industry.' Referring to the difficult years of World War I, when the Trade came so largely under the control of the Ministry of Food, the Spirits Trade Advisory Committee, the Ministry of Munitions, etc., the address went on: 'Your leadership was not only valuable during those fateful years but for long afterwards by reason of the revolutionary changes which arose as the aftermath of war.' In the absence of a physical memorial to him, his monument can best be seen in the flourishing state of the industry today.

Recalling those initial war years, Ross said: 'I recall that in the early days of the war, Mr Lloyd George had the idea that the whole distilling trade should be stopped. The Trade met in London . . . It was felt that the patent still distillers held the key to the position, as they had the strongest argument for being left unmolested, and it therefore fell to me at that time, as a member of that deputation, to put the views of the patent still distillers before Mr Lloyd George. At the end of my remarks I had the gratification of eliciting from Mr Lloyd George the statement that he had learned more about distilling and its ramifications than he had ever known before, and that it had altered entirely his view as to the position; therefore we were saved the feeling that we had to give in at that time. We had to face the circumstances later, but for a year or more we were left unmolested.'

Indeed, it may be said, in brief, that without the patent still distillers of Scotland, their provision of alcohol, acetone, and fusel oil for government and industrial use, and yeast for the feeding of the nation, Great Britain would have lost that war. Of course, they were not alone in winning it, but the fact must be emphasised that without the patent still distillers that war would have been lost by Britain. It may also be said with respect and gratitude that no other industry in the land gave so freely and plentifully of its members on the field of battle, never to return to their native shores. And it is especially in 1915 that the pages of the *Record* make the most doleful reading with page after page of deaths and casualties among men formerly in the Scotch whisky industry. If their toll diminished in the war's later years, it was only because they had been amongst the first to go, and were, in consequence, the first to fall.

In the maze of uncertainties confronting the whisky industry during 1915, with its three-year compulsory bonding after the kaleidoscopic changes of Lloyd George, with its intensive restrictions imposed on the sale of spirits by the ever-encroaching Liquor Control Board, the possibility of a steep increase in duty in the necessary autumn budget, one body at least, as well as the D.C.L. read the signs aright: the board of Craigellachie–Glenlivet distillery, who stated in their report that 'the present tendency of trade is all towards large combinations, and the directors have within the last two or three years made various attempts to amalgamate with some large concern, but without success'. It should be remembered that for years, since even before the 1909 budget, Highland malts had been in a state of uncertainty, of recession. Now Mr Peter Mackie was chairman of the distillery company and of Mackie & Co. Ltd, now White Horse Distillers Ltd. An approach was made to Mackie's; an 'advantageous offer' was received from them, and the distillery company was absorbed by an exchange of shares.

In September came the dreaded budget. The trade had feared the increased duties in the spring, and there had been large withdrawals in anticipation. The point about this budget – which, in fact, added nothing to spirit duties – was that it was preceded again by large forestalments, and, as phrased then, 'it was heralded by an entirely new restriction in the "forestalment" precaution taken by the Government'.

The idea was most novel: it had never been put into operation before; it is now part of the national pattern of life in Great Britain, and as such merits some little attention.

The practice so frequent today – so frequent as to qualify for 'normal' – of anticipating heavy duty increases in the budget by withdrawing heavily before the budget in what have come to be known as forestalments, with corresponding governmental restriction on those forestalments, originates in that disastrous and precedent-setting budget of 1909. Prior to that, within living memory, it had not been necessary. For instance, in 1860 Gladstone seemed – and was wrongly thought – to have wrecked the spirit trade. Instead, his duty of 10s. per gallon stayed adamant for a quarter of a century, the quarter that saw Scotch make its gigantic strides on the English market. When Childers tried to add 2s. to the duty in 1885, it was promptly removed in two swipes of 1s. each time. Goschen's 'whisky money' of an extra 6d. added in 1890 stayed, but when Harcourt tried to add another 6d. in 1894 it was taken off the following year after a snatch vote on cordite. Then Hicks Beach, the Tory tactician who took it off, had to replace it in the middle of the Boer War. It was absorbed by the trade and industry. The question of massive increases in duty and the avoidance of their impact did not arise. After the defeat of the Liberals' Licensing Bill in 1908, and with premonitions of Liberal revenge for that defeat and of Lloyd George's 'Socialistic' 1909 budget, the trade made heavy withdrawals in fear of a massive duty increase, which proved in the event to be even more massive than they had feared. There was no governmental effort to clamp down on withdrawals from bond, but the bitterness of being what he considered the victim of a Tory plot, and an unscrupulous ruse remained with him. During the year-long debates on the budget, it was often on Lloyd George's lips and in his venom.

Not only had he as Chancellor been tricked out of revenue, his 'temperance'-inspired campaign to reform man's social state had been delayed by the distillers' Tory guile. He would take steps. Lloyd George spotted the forestalments in his original budget speech on 29 April 1909. 'I do not expect to realise a very large amount from increased duty during the present financial year. This year there are exceptional circumstances. In the first place, the forestalments are exceptionally heavy. It is not merely forestalment up to the end of the financial year, but it has been going on since, so that the wholesale dealers have in hand a sufficient stock of spirits to carry them on comfortably for a good many weeks ahead. Therefore, we shall not get much from this source for some weeks, probably for some months. That will make a very considerable hole in the yield.'

He reverted to this grievance in the debate on the Report Stage on 23 May. 'What were the elements when one sought to estimate the revenue derived from spirits?' he asked. 'First, there were the forestalments. There were considerable forestalments before the end of the financial year; and still more considerable forestalments during the month of April. Probably for the next few weeks the spirit trade, speaking of it as a whole, need not withdraw anything out of bond. During the first year, the trade might be able to reduce the contribution to the Revenue, although eventually the matter righted itself because the consumer discovered what was going on. The trade might keep down their stock, which would make an enormous difference to the Revenue.'

The forestalling figures obscured the picture of what had really happened to whisky consumption under the new duty. And in the Finance Bill debate of 23 September 1909, Hobhouse, Lloyd George's understudy at the Treasury, said that 'there were two quite clear and absolutely explained reasons why there had been a great falling off in the consumption of whisky, or at all events a decrease in the withdrawal from bond and a consequent falling in the Revenue. One reason was that it was due to anticipation which took place previous to the present financial year, and secondly an anticipation which took place on 30 April this year. The result had been there were undoubtedly forestalments resulting in a swelling of the Revenue for last year, but depleting it for the present year. (Hobhouse was Financial Secretary to the Treasury.)

Enough has been recalled to bring out the point of Lloyd George's animosity to forestalments. The next move lay in March 1910, when Customs and Excise issued an order to suspend opening of bonds beyond the legal hours, of 4 or 5 p.m., on budget days, a practice we have grown so accustomed to these days that it would have been taken as natural and not requiring an order. The order was, of course, made on the instructions of Inland Revenue.

Then in presenting his budget on 19 April 1910, Lloyd George took up the theme of forestalments once more, saying: 'The main loss in Customs and Excise is on spirits . . . There is a considerable diminution due to the fact that there were heavy forestalments. In March this year 1,600,000 gallons were withdrawn from bond, and last year 4,255,000 gallons was cleared. This is not due to the diminution in the drinking of spirits altogether, or anything like it. It is due largely to the fact that there were considerable clearances in March in anticipation of the budget. Then we come to April. The budget had been introduced on April 29th, and the clearances in April were 5,130,000 as compared with 3,175,000 the previous year. There were 3,000,000 gallons of forestalments.'

No increase in whisky duty had been anticipated that budget so clearances were, as Lloyd George gave them above, of a normal pattern and the Customs and Excise order precluded any last minute rush. But speaking on the budget on 30 June, Lloyd George said that there would be an increase in Customs – 'I am dealing now purely with spirits' – a revenue of 'something like £1,800,000. That will be due very largely to the fact that the forestalments have been eliminated.' His third budget, in May 1911, was regarded with little or no interest in so far as the trade was concerned: they had not then encountered the years in which we live where every budget can bring an increase in duties on alcoholic beverages. Thus forestalments and their restriction by government did not arise. The same sort of opinion prevailed around the 1912 budget: 'Nobody in the liquor trade expected anything, nor ever will expect anything, from the present government,' said *The Record*.

Again, any forestalments before the April 1913 budget were negligible. Lloyd George thought – and boasted in his budget oration – he had given the demon drink a deadly wound in his 1909 budget brawl: 'One of the most successful taxes ever imposed on the community,' he exclaimed.

His next spring budget was taken in its stride, but the autumn budget with its massive increase in the duty on beer led to heavy forestalments in the panic atmosphere of Lloyd George's kaleidoscopic plans for the trade before the budget of April 1915, the budget which began by doubling the taxes on spirits and ended with the compulsory bonding for whisky, as related above. Both Lloyd George and his henchmen were determined that such forestalments, recalling the rush of March and April 1909, must never again be allowed to happen. The spring budget was a poor one in every way, and an autumn one was an obvious necessity, if only to straighten out the muddle Lloyd George had thrown the national finances in during his period as chancellor. McKenna was now Chancellor of the Exchequer. In the best Lloyd George vein and frame of mind, he wanted 'resolute' action against the trade.

The trade, aware of the great enmity shown it by the Liberal Party, and relying little on the coalition government, took instant action in traditional manner. Forestalling was heavy, or, rather, attempted to be. There had been heavily increased clearances from bond in the spring, and to avoid a repetition McKenna issued instructions, which he himself admitted were illegal, with the aim of preventing unusually large withdrawals from bond in anticipation of the budget in September. These instructions, limiting withdrawals – at the most to the daily average of the last three months, and then to the daily average of the last six or twelve months – were a source of considerable anger and impatience, to wholesale houses in particular.

As the *Wine & Spirit Trade Record* observed at the time: 'The Budget was heralded by an entirely new restriction in the "forestalment" precaution taken by the Government.' The very idea was 'novel'; it had never been operated before. Worse, the quantities allowed as 'forestalment' clearances were based on three months' deliveries that showed an abnormally low average. The irony of this first use of government restriction of pre-budget clearances was that where it might have been an immediate misfortune to the trade, it turned out the very reverse, immediately: it had the good result that there was no unnatural dislocation of stocks; there was no increase in spirit duties.

Although Lloyd George had left the Treasury, he had left behind, in one of his unpredictable moods, the axiom that 'the taxable capacity of spirits has reached its limit', a view by no means shared by his follower Lord d'Abernon at the Central Control Board (Liquor Traffic). In any case, McKenna did not increase the duties that budget and the trade could, in a sense, be pleased with him for restricting them from overloading their stocks with duty-paid spirits.

But he by no means met with the gratitude of the trade: his restrictionist order had completely disorganised the trade as it coincided with the pre-budget rush and the question of its legality was raised extensively. At the same time, the very fact that limitations had been imposed increased the rush of the trade to make duty-paid withdrawals – it was taken as a sure sign of a coming increase. It was also seen as raising an important question as affecting future budgets: if the Government were to retain the right of restricting clearances for pre-budget times, the only thing to do was to accelerate clearances well ahead of Budgets and make them larger than previously. It was 'wholly indefensible', it was argued, to impose limitations of this kind on withdrawals when there was no intention to increase the duty. It was bad enough to disorganise the trade for three or four years by duty alterations, but for it to be made 'an annual affair is intolerable'. The 'intolerable' times are now with us.

McKenna clarified and legalised his position in – as he admitted, illegally – imposing restrictions on duty-paid withdrawals for the home market in advance of his budget by means of inserting retrospective legislation in the Finance Act. To quote Section 15 of the Finance (No. 2) Act, 1915: '(1) During the continuance of the present war and for a period of twelve months thereafter, the Treasury may by order authorise the Commissioners of Customs and Excise, during any period named in the order not exceeding three months, to refuse to allow the delivery of any goods or commodities for home use from ship's side or warehouse on payment of duty in any cases where deliveries are demanded of amounts exceeding the deliveries which appear to be reasonable deliveries in the circumstances. (2) Any refusal of the Commissioners of Customs and Excise within one month before the 21st day of September, nineteen hundred and fifteen, to allow the delivery of goods or commodities is hereby confirmed, and shall be ruled as if an order of the Treasury had been in force under this section.'

There was also a clause on the effect of contracts consequent on the section just quoted, clearing the person disabled by the government limitation from any actions, proceedings, etc., for failure to perform the contract.

It has been said that the first victims of any war are truth and liberty. The major portion of truth has been regained in Great Britain after the two main wars she has been engaged in during this century, but the predominant part of the pre-1914 liberty is still a prisoner-of-war, in Government hands. That attempt, of doubtful legality, in September 1915, further to restrict the freedom of the trade and trader has so far succeeded and been perpetuated as now to figure, in revised wording, of course, in the current Customs and Excise Act 1952.

Already, at that time, the *Record* could see its continuance beyond the war, and may be quoted here as representing the authoritative voice of the trade: 'No doubt the novelty and doubtful legality of the imposition affected that fairness which the experience then gained will secure, and we look forward to a wider and more common sense average of deliveries henceforward. In a realisation of this hope, the Trade will find no fault with the object of legislation, and will doubtless see that pre-Budget clearances shall represent full requirements not only for current orders but for the replenishment of normal stocks. Should stock-taking close to Budget-date reveal any shortage of normal, such should be made up well before Budget-eve to avoid disappointment through probable rush of deliveries.'

The Customs and Excise Report, 1915–16, published in June 1917, noted a surplus over the September estimates in the matter of spirits, and remarked: 'A considerable part of this surplus, however, was due to forestalments, i.e. clearances made not for current consumption but in anticipation of increases in rates of duty. Clause 15 of the Finance (No. 2) Act, 1915, gave the Board power (under Treasury authority) to check this practice by refusing to allow deliveries of dutiable goods in excess of amounts which appear to the Board to be reasonable. This power was exercised (in advance of legislation) as regards all dutiable spirits before the Budget of September, 1915, with the result that about £1,000,000 was saved to the revenue. Before the Budget of April, 1916, deliveries of . . . (non-Trade commodities) . . . were restricted, but no action was taken with regard to wines and spirits.'

At last, Lloyd George had had his revenge on the forestalments of 1909, and currently memorialises it on the Statute Book in the form of another restriction on the (allegedly) freedom-loving British by allowing them at certain times of the year only to withdraw their own goods from bonded warehouses in quantities bureaucrats think 'reasonable'. Is it reasonable that the power to limit what a man or firm does with its own goods should be so curtailed, limited, restricted, in a reputedly free land? And that 1952 Customs and Excise Act reached the Statute Book under a Tory Government!

13

The 1917 strength reduction

LLOYD GEORGE boasted that although he lost 'the opening round' in his campaign against 'the drink traffic' by his budget proposals of 1915, which were abandoned and compensated for by the 'one insignificant but quite useful little restriction in the shape of a prohibition on the sale of spirits less than three years old', he had 'succeeded in subsequent years in carrying through the policy of high taxation of alcoholic beverages, dilution of spirits and the encouragement of lighter beers. In this campaign,' he continued,' I was able to utilise the aid of the Food Controller, under whose care the supplies of grain required for brewing and distilling had been placed. Not only was the total amount brewed and distilled restricted, but the release of such grain as was allowed was made conditional upon a proportion of the beer being of a light character, and the spirits being considerably diluted . . . The compulsory dilution of spirits and the elimination of the heavier beers had an especially beneficial effect, for they reduced the quantity of alcohol content of the beverages imbibed by a high percentage. The weekly average of convictions for drunkenness in England and Wales, which in 1913 were 3,482, had by the first part of 1917 fallen to 929.'

It is time now to look at that process of enforced dilution which finally became effective early in 1917, a dilution now standard and usual in this country but the product, the bitterly resisted product, of Lloyd George's anti-drink campaign and the exigencies of war. Truly this year was a formative one for the structure and standing of the whisky industry as well as of the nature of its product. As the

Record was later to say of the year when so much happened: 'The year 1917 will long be remembered in the Scotch whisky trade. Without a doubt it has been the most sensational twelve months ever experienced. The prohibition of distillation, the restriction of clearances, and, above all, the remarkable advance in prices have combined to make it the reddest of red-letter years.'

On that question of prices, the year opened with whiskies at 20s. a gallon and closed with their touching 80s., a fact which, as will be seen, induced rigorous governmental intervention and taught a lesson the industry remembered and acted upon in World War II. But that allegedly speculatory advance in prices was soon overtaken, in 1917, by the introduction of an Order of the Central Control Board (Liquor Traffic) – the addition of 'Liquor Traffic' was deliberately intended to smear the trade with the odium of the white slave and drug traffics – which Order prohibited the sales in areas scheduled as 'controlled' areas of spirits of a higher strength than 30 u.p. As most of Britain – never Ireland – was becoming a scheduled area, it resulted in the nation's adopting 30 u.p. as the standard strength of spirits, and is still with us today.

Nothing happens in a vacuum, and to see how this anti-freedom compulsive Order came about, it is necessary to turn back the pages of history even into the last century. The Central Control Board began its phase of restrictions by, for instance, prohibiting a man from buying a drink and doing what he liked with it, such as giving it to a companion, his wife, or even by way of business sample, moved on to a multiplicity of restrictive practices, including, in areas the board scheduled, the sale, as a minimum for off-licence sales, of the reputed quart of spirits, a restriction with us for a generation. It issued an Order, effective 11 October 1915, as follows: 'The sale of whisky, brandy and rum, reduced to a number of degrees under proof which falls between 25 and 35, and of gin reduced to a number of degrees under proof which falls between 35 and 45, is hereby permitted, and accordingly, in determining whether an offence has been committed under the Sale of Food and Drugs Act by selling to the purchaser, brandy, whisky, rum, or gin, not adulterated otherwise than by the admixture of water, it shall be a good defence to prove that such admixture has not reduced the spirit more than 35 degrees under proof in the case of whisky, brandy, or rum, or 45 degrees under proof in the case of gin.' Every licensee and secretary of a club was to keep a copy of the Order 'permanently affixed in some conspicuous place'; the teetotallers of the Central Control Board, backed by Lloyd George, were determined to wreck the trade.

The Order was, in effect, a non-parliamentary amendment to Section 6 of the Food and Drug Amendment Act, 1879, which fixed the minimum permissible strength at 25 u.p. Its further effect was to offer a strong temptation to make up the increased cost of whisky and other spirits resulting from the Immature Spirits Act while diminishing the sales of whisky through the operation of permitting it to be weakened to the utmost permitted. It was seen as foreshadowing the extinction of spirits as a beverage, the very objective of the board and its backers.

Indeed, ever since the Lloyd George budget of 1909 adding 3s. 9d. to the duty on a proof gallon, there had been a gradual process of reducing the strengths at which spirits were sold retail with consumers complaining unavailingly that they were getting less and less value for money. The greater proportion of whisky deliveries before the 1909 budget were made in bulk at around proof strength; bottle trade was still only making its way. And earlier in the century whisky was usually broken down, by the publican and the off-licensee, in many cases, to about 10 or 15 u.p. Gradually the strength dropped – the proof strength whisky was made to provide more drinks without diminution in price – to about 17 or 20 u.p. and after 1910, with the securing of the 1909 duty, the 25 u.p. limit was more and more approached. Moreover, the practice had been growing up of reducing below that permitted level of 25 u.p. and displaying a notice 'warning' customers of the diluted strength. Now, with the October 1915 Order, appeared the last straw, it was said, in the legalisation of 35 u.p. The trade had no wish, had even a disinclination, to reduce whisky to the lowest legal limit, or even appreciably. This was particularly the case with the better grade whiskies, but with the commoner types sold at bars the reduced limit was seen to be the profit-maker, and thus the chief factor in depreciating whisky as a popular beverage.

'In other words, what the consumer gains in improved quality through the operation of the Immature Spirits Act,' commented the *Record*, 'he loses by the imposition of extra dilution . . . just such an imposition as must in time react on consumption. Far better, in our opinion, more honourable and eventually the wiser policy, to maintain the quality and strength or either diminish the quantity or raise the price.' Some few vendors did the latter, but too many in the trade ascribed to the new Order an emergency character, forgetting that repeal of a hardship on the licensed trade is so uncommon as to be discounted.

There the matter remained for some months: the trade was too busy coping with increasing costs and prices, with amalgamations real or rumoured, with the deaths of the older generation and deaths in France, with the attempt to secure some grain whisky as the demands of the governmental and industrial users mounted, with the spread of the reputed quart, with the octopus growth of the Central Control Board and its unconstitutional powers, and the hundred-and-one other things of direct day-to-day concern, the near-impossibility blenders were experiencing in finding whisky, particularly grain whisky which qualified under the Immature Spirits Act, while brokers were ceasing business through lack of activity.

With the approach of the 1916 spring budget, forstalments once more came to the fore but with no official enforcement of daily averages no alteration in duties was expected nor brought about. (Among other tax changes in the Budget was one of 4*d*. a gallon on cider and perry and a tax on mineral waters.) Instead came further action by the Central Control Board on the vexed question of compulsory dilution beyond that authorised by Act of Parliament. The board had extended, as noted above, the dilution limit to spirits sold in munition areas to 35 u.p. without any notification to the purchaser that the article sold was 'to his prejudice'. To give some semblance of propriety the board then sought to cover up in an 'expert' report showing, it was alleged, that no hardship would result from the dilution proposal. The Government chemist was instructed to carry out breakdown experiments on seven samples of whisky – two from 'eminent distillers', the others, presumably, from common or garden sources. It was not stated what types of whiskies they were, or, if blends, what were the constituents in type or proportion. The results were as might be imagined: the affirmation of the daily knowledge of the whisky trade that 'practically every self whisky, and particularly every malt whisky, becomes opalescent or cloudy when reduced even to the old limit of 25 under proof – that the defect was inherent in the whisky, that it was got rid of with extreme difficulty, and in some cases not at all, and that it increased with increase of dilution.'

The Immature Spirits Act, with its insistence on the three years minimum age here played its part. Grain whisky distilling in the years following the 1909 budget up to the war had been only about equal to an average of use, and it was generally taken up and used soon after manufacture. With the Immature Spirits Act, and a scarcity of eligible grain about – its price rose above that of older malts – increasing recourse had to be made to more fully matured malts in greater proportion. Had the previous proportion of grain whiskies been in the blends the same degree of opalescence would not have been encountered; it was the governmental insistence on the minimum age with the use of more and better malts in the blends which made only more acute the difficulties of this, as it seemed, excessive dilution. When the blends averaged about 15 to 22 u.p., the problem of opalescence hardly arose, but with this lower strength limit, and the absence of enough fully matured grains, the problem seemed insoluble. Had there been a full quantity of grain to call on to allow the lower strength without opalescence the further danger would have arisen that the whisky would have lost its distinctive character. On the other hand, repeated filtering or subsidence of the whisky after the extra dilution was, first, too costly and slow a process, too elaborate and too wasteful, and secondly, the very process to rob the whiskies of their true characters, similar, in effect, to a rectification. This much may be said in favour of these efforts to reduce the retail legal strengths: with reduced distillation, particularly of grain whisky, the increased dilution would stretch the stocks further, would allow the production of more retail bottles and casks from a fixed proof gallonage.

But worse, the Central Control Board had permitted dilution down to 50 u.p. in munition areas, though, first, the proprietors of the leading brands refused to take advantage of the 'concession' and after some formal correspondence between Sir Thomas Dewar, as he then was, and Lord d'Abernon of the Central Control Board, representatives of the spirit trade met a Central Control Board committee on 1 May 1916. The trade deputation consisted of members of the Wine and Spirit Brands Association, to give birth to the Whisky Association the following year, 1917, members of the Wine and Spirit Association and of the London and County Wine Merchants. Unfortunately, the Irish representatives were 'unavoidably absent'. Meanwhile, a dozen or so leading members of the Wine and Spirit Brands Association made reduction experiments to 25, 28, 30, and 35 u.p. and satisfied themselves that 'the successive filtrations necessary to secure bright spirit have the result of very materially destroying the characteristic flavours upon which the reputation of the several brands has been built up'.

To quote from the memorial originally presented by the Wine and Spirits Brands Association, bearing in mind the trade's adamant refusal to go below that hitherto legal minimum of 25 u.p. and moves in 1967 to go down to 35 u.p., or lower, the memorialists, after referring to the board's suggestion that whisky currently sold at 20 u.p. should be reduced to 'a very low strength', proceed: 'Your memorialists venture to remind the Board that compulsory dilution to a degree that would rob high-class brands of their distinctive characteristics, and practically reduce all brands to one common level of mediocrity, would obviously be to the advantage of those whose aim is cheapness rather than quality.' They then submitted that if compulsory reduction to too low a strength were accomplished a new method of drinking would arise – 'without any further dilution, very much after the established practice in which American cocktails are now consumed in the United States, or Gin and Bitters in this country'. Then with the usual 'upright' drinking here would come 'quick' drinking followed by 'excessive' drinking. Secondly, 'as many munitions areas workers now buy a bottle of whisky, because of restricted hours, with a reduction in strength, two bottles instead of one would very likely be bought'.

They then moved on to the fact that excessive dilution is detrimental to quality and that it is 'exceedingly difficult' to keep bright high-class brands containing a considerable percentage of malt whisky. They stated, admirably, the position then obtaining: 'Although it has been permissible for a long time past to bottle whiskies as low as 25 u.p. (without any notification on the label) a general concensus of opinion has established that about 20 u.p. is as far as it is wise to go with high-class brands; and, in dealing with this point, it should also be observed that it is only in recent years – and after much experiment and investigation – that it has been found feasible to go even as far as 20 u.p.'

They acknowledged the shortage of matured stocks available and the demands of the Ministry of Munitions and industry on the distilleries, thus reinforcing their plea that they would 'be disposed – were it practicable – to welcome reduction in strength from the point of view of assisting them to maintain adequate stocks' in order to avoid 'a whisky famine'.

On the matter of the suggested filtration – some methods being admitted as more drastic than others – to remove opalescence, that, it was agreed, could be achieved with the inevitable result of 'the extraction to a greater or less degree of the essential oils, etc., that are characteristic of fine whisky. Filtration is, in practical effect, a modified form of rectification.' To that must be added the varieties of whisky – some are more amenable than others – and of the waters available, for instance, distilled or hard water. Moreover, they stressed that it takes years to establish a proprietary brand, that its establishment implies technical knowledge, business organisation, capital investment, etc., with the goodwill asset thereafter built up – which goodwill 'would be entirely destroyed if proprietary whiskies were to be so reduced as to lose their individual characteristics and qualities'.

In addition, the dilution would have an adverse effect on Highland malt distillers, whose whisky, adverse to excessive dilution, would be increasingly discarded or – 'some of the oldest and finest distilleries in the world would only be able to survive by sacrificing their old-established reputations for making whiskies of pre-eminent merit, and by substituting therefore a completely different type of whisky', which would only become available after years of waiting.

Attention was also drawn to 'existing stocks of whisky at 20 u.p. now held by blenders, the distributing trade, and off and on licensees' which it would take 'a considerable time' to clear. All of which, they concluded, added up to their being unable to endorse reduction beyond the strictly limited degree and, 'in their opinion, the utmost dilution that it would be possible to make in high-grade proprietary brands would be 24 u.p. Should such a strength be acceptable to your Board, your memorialists would consent to adopt it generally throughout Great Britain; but they cannot see their way to go beyond this figure for their general home trading requirements.' (Export requirements also came into the argument there: overseas markets, of which examples were supplied, insisted that whisky to be called whisky must retain the essential characteristics that would be lost by excessive dilution.) They closed with the regret that whiskies below 25 u.p. did not now have to conform with the law and state the strength on the label.

All of which compelled the *non sequitur*: 'Apart from the facts that the public will not only resent being served with "whisky and water" from a bottle without any notice on the label, but will also regard such a practice as almost in the nature of a fraud on purchasers, your memorialists have a very strong conviction that the implied permission to tamper with the contents of a bottle of proprietary whisky is calculated to encourage practices which, in the public interest, it is most desirable to suppress. Your memorialists, therefore, respectfully suggest that where whisky is reduced below 25 u.p., the fact should, as in the past, be made evident to the consumer.' In brief, the industry was usurping the role, against the governmental body, of consumer protector.

Some small measure of success attended the memorial and the deputation. The 'Dilution of Spirits' article in the Orders was revoked, and instead 25 u.p. was made compulsory, the only permissible strength, except for whisky, and other spirits, bottled before 6 June 1916, while it was made permissive only for munition areas. The Board's object had been to make 50 u.p. compulsory in these areas, while the trade had achieved its object of preserving the individuality of brands. By compromising at 25 u.p., which would then become general and not in restricted areas only, the owners of proprietary whiskies were able to preserve the characteristics of their brands.

A circular of Bowen and McKechnie put it in perspective. Pointing out that the Central Control Board had issued an Order restricting the strength at which spirits might be sold to 25 u.p., they continue: 'Their power, however, only extends to those areas which they have scheduled as "munition" and therefore in other parts of the country this Order is not effective. Gradually, however, further districts are being scheduled, and the probability we think is that by degrees the whole country will be subject to the Board. It would be manifestly impossible for the wholesale trade to bottle the same article at different strengths for munition and non-munition areas respectively, so we have arranged that all the various qualities of spirits we supply shall conform to the Board's orders. The strength of 25 u.p. as arranged is, however, probably only temporary, for the Board desire a further compulsory reduction to 30 u.p. and this . . . is likely to operate from January 1st next.'

It did. And as to the extension of the scheduled areas, even the predominantly rural areas of Kent, Sussex and Surrey were brought into the areas where regulations prevailed before the summer of 1916 was out, and the sale of spirits was prohibited, for example, in the Motherwell region – of Scotland! As enforced dilution to 25 u.p. continued, withdrawals from bond for the home market showed a marked decrease, the clearances being, of course, expressed in terms of proof gallons. The number of scheduled areas, where the Central Control Board ruled supreme and tyrannically, kept increasing and the Wine and Spirit Association felt compelled to issue a long table of the Control restrictions – spirits could only be sold, in the London area as elsewhere, between 12 noon and 2.30 p.m. from Mondays to Fridays, for instance – and reported the notice that 'the on and off sale or supply or introduction into an area of whisky, brandy, rum, or gin unless reduced to 25 degrees u.p. is prohibited,' apart from those bottled as noted above. But, the sale of whisky, brandy, rum and gin at 50 u.p. without its being stated on the label was permitted, as agreed earlier.

The trade continued, however, to be incensed by the Central Control Board's intention to reduce the compulsory strength from 25 to 30 u.p. in scheduled areas from 1 January 1917. As the *Record* said as 1916 drew to a close: 'Distillers of malt whisky will suffer peculiarly, inasmuch as the increased dilution hits at their product to a more serious degree than it does grain or neutral spirit, on which, in effect, it confers a premium comparatively.' That question we have already examined sufficiently exhaustively, yet despite the arguments of the trade deputations in May of the year and the findings of the Board's official analytical nominee supported by his chemical experiments, the 25 u.p. limit got only a temporary confirmation and it was announced that from New Year's Day the compulsory limit would be 30 u.p. with 50 u.p. as permissive.

Of course the trade did not take it lying down: it had public opinion behind it; a deputation waited on d'Abernon; the feeling grew that prohibitionist propaganda rather than national necessities inspired the Board's action. James Robertson, chairman of The Highland Distilleries Co. Ltd, said in his annual report to the company that the 30 u.p. proposal was 'detrimental' to the company which produced 'only high-class malt whisky'. The dilution to that strength would, he said, result in 'a whisky milky and turbid' and anything like 'drastic filtration' would 'eliminate a great part of the flavours that were essential to the individual whiskies; in other words, they approached a neutral spirit . . . The company, along with other malt distillers, are protesting against this new Order.' As was said of the year ahead, 1917, 'The most serious battles in defence of our Trade are yet to be fought.'

The General Committee of the Wine and Spirit Association, meeting early in January that year, could only regret that the Central Control Board 'were not taking any steps so as to render legal in *non-scheduled areas* the sale of spirits which had been diluted below the requirements of the Sale of Food and Drugs Acts in accordance with the Board's Order for sale in *scheduled areas*'. Mr A. B. J. Norris, of the Wine and Spirit Association, found it necessary to say: 'Subscribers should bear in mind, however, that they are open to prosecution in *non-scheduled areas* where spirits have to meet the requirements of the Sale of Food and Drugs Act, viz.: brandy, whisky or rum, may not be diluted to more than 25 degrees u.p. – and they should accordingly take steps to notify intending purchasers, either by a label or a clear notice that the spirits have been diluted.'

In the upshot, the new Order of the Central Control Board came into force on 1 February 1917, making compulsory the reduction to 30 u.p. of whisky, brandy, rum and gin, except that bottled before 6 June 1916, and allowing 25 u.p. if bottled before 1 January preceding, while permitting reduction to 50 u.p. The only legal consolation they could give the trade – which proved of little use against ardent local officials – was that in determining if there had been an offence against the Food and Drugs Act and selling to the prejudice of the purchaser, that it would be 'a good defence to prove that such admixture had not reduced the spirit more than 50 u.p.', Not only, then, was the whisky industry faced with bottling at two separate strengths for home, but in addition at a separate strength again for overseas. Curiously, though, it not only meant an extra burden for the blenders, but, in effect, that the elimination was carried a stage further of bulk supplies to the home trade. Many firms under the stress, as, for instance, James Buchanan & Co. Ltd, abandoned the supply to the home market of anything else but bottled whisky. Mr J. P. Lowrie, who had died in the previous summer of 1916, had said when the enlargements to Buchanan's Washington Street, Glasgow, warehouses with bottling lines were being opened in 1907, that he hoped the increasing orders being received for bottled whisky did not mean that the bottled trade was going to develop and that the demand for bulk whisky would still continue! Pity poor Lowrie, one of the first in Scotland to introduce blending of malt and grain whiskies on any practical scale, did not die before his time; his passing marked the end of an age.

To revert to the difference between the scheduled and non-scheduled areas and the legal entanglement resulting from the two different legal standards of strength resulting. The trade compelled the solicitor to the Central Control Board and the legal adviser to the Local Government Board to get together and agree that if a disclosure notice were to be exhibited on the premises that would be sufficient and there was no need to print it on the label. This notice was drafted: 'In order to meet the requirements of the Sale of Food and Drugs Act and to comply with the Order of the Central Control Board (Liquor Traffic) dated 1st January, 1917, compelling reduction of strength, notice is hereby given that all spirits sold in this establishment are now sold as Diluted Spirits.'

A further problem arose of licensees serving across the bar 25 u.p. whiskies, drawn from their existing stocks, and it was only with great difficulty and against solid resistance of the Board that finally some concession was made in this case.

Nevertheless, prosecutions outside the scheduled areas continued apace, as witness what Messrs W. H. Chaplin had to say: 'The scandal is that outside munition areas "Food and Drugs Act" prosecutions for selling spirits under the stipulated strength without printing it on the bottle still go on. It is almost inconceivable . . . that government agents should still be at large instituting fatuous and time-wasting prosecutions for doing the very thing which in munition areas it is so fervently desired should be done.'

Again, the *Record* summed it up: 'To prosecute licence-holders in non-munition areas for selling at less than 25 u.p. and to insist in other areas on 30 u.p., is, of course, the limit of foolishness. Even the authorities are beginning to realise this, and probably we shall hear no more of such prosecutions.'

It remains to say that wisdom of a sort was allowed to prevail and the trade settled down to supplying the whole of the domestic market – with the exception of Ireland which was never 'controlled' or touched by the Central Control Board – with whisky at the reduced, diluted strength of 30 u.p. The blenders and bottlers adjusted themselves so ably that by the time scheduled areas came to an end with the war well over, and with three successive budget increases in duty, in 1918, 1919 and 1920, with the onset of the busting of the post-war boom, the trade found it only too necessary in order to preserve any sales on the domestic market to maintain the war-enforced diluted strength of 30 u.p. still with us today in general, and now generally described as 70 degrees proof.

14

Great War achievements

IT WAS during the First World War that the Scotch whisky industry first assumed national status, was summoned from the near-disrepute in which it had lingered, and manifested itself as a food provider for the nation, a most vital supplier of war materials, and an indispensable part of the national economy which helped quell industrial unrest at home. It has ever since retained that position as a respected and fundamental element of the nation and its economy. Before 1914, it was distrusted as a parasitic element of the community largely responsible for the undoubted social and moral evils of the times. Half-way through the war, responsible opinion realised how wrong it had been in the assessment, and the industry emerged into a position of international respect, symbolised by the ennoblement of many of its leaders.

What did it do to achieve this? First, it provided the yeast with which to make the people's and the Forces' bread. Second, it provided the militant nation in arms with an indispensable munition of war, the spirit needed for explosives together with such necessary aids as fusel oil for protecting the nation's aircraft, as alcohol for anaesthetics, as feeding stuffs for the cattle in a sea-besieged island imperilled by the submarine menace intent on starving Great Britain into surrender. In fact, such an indispensable part of the nation did the industry become that the Government intervened to control whisky prices and keep them within the reach of all lest there be an outbreak of industrial unrest and violence, a lesson recalled by the industry itself in World War II and an attitude jettisoned by governments since which no longer care or wish to see the people contented and happy with a modicum of their native spirit.

First of all, yeast. It will be remembered that with the establishment of the North British grain distillery in 1885 the D.C.L. intensified their efforts in the direction of yeast production with the assistance of Dr W. S. Squire, a consulting chemist. At the 1886 exhibition in Edinburgh it obtained a special prize, caught on and before long not only Cameronbridge, but Port Dundas, Carsebridge and Glenlochil patent still distilleries were equipped for yeast-making. Lucky for Britain that they were.

At this time the company sold its yeast, baker's yeast, of course, through dealers, and beginning 1899 the distributing side was consolidated into the United Yeast Co. Ltd. The distilleries went ahead producing yeast, as well as the spirit, of course, and before the royal commission of 1908–9, Arthur Tedder, then Chief Inspector of Excise, gave evidence that some of the distilleries sent out between 20 and 40 tons of yeast a week, at anything from £30 to £40 a ton, adding that 'yeast making in patent still distilleries is now a very important industry'. How that grew, necessarily, during the war is exemplified by these figures: in 1913–14, eight patent still distilleries in Scotland made 10·7 million gallons of spirit; in 1916–17, seven made 13·8 million gallons. Naturally, there was an ever greater output of yeast. There had to be. Before that war there had been intense competition from German, Belgian and French yeast, and the yeast distillers tried in vain to have Excise regulations amended to allow them to compete in less restricted fashion. They got nowhere until the outbreak of Armageddon, when unnecessary restrictions and regulations were swept away at once to liberate them and their process. Yeast from those three markets ceased with the outbreak of war, and the trickle which came in from Holland, and less still from Denmark, was curtailed and prohibited in 1916.

In short, without the yeast from Scotland's distilleries there would have been no bread, or very little, for the nation after 1914. As Ross, then managing director of the D.C.L. put it at the company's first annual meeting after the holocaust: 'As yeast production, which forms a necessary ferment for bread making, this trade at one time was almost entirely in the hands of the foreign distillers. About thirty years ago, however, the British distillers took up the manufacture with the result that at the outbreak of war, the home-producer held about two-thirds of the whole trade in this country. [This fits with the rise in spirit-plus-yeast production from 10·7 million on the eve of war and 13·8 million in mid-war.] The three major suppliers were cut off; shipping difficulties and shortages presented themselves in the cases of Holland and Denmark, and not only the home market but also the British Forces on the Continent had to be supplied. The time was 1916. The Restriction of Imports Department,' continued Ross, 'therefore approached the British distillers to ascertain if they would undertake to supply the whole requirements of this country for yeast, as well as keep up the supplies to the British Expeditionary Force in France. If so, they were very anxious to prohibit the imports of foreign yeast altogether. The British distillers advised caution in this respect as their plant was then taxed to its utmost extent, and they did not wish to see a shortage of yeast in this country. They, however, agreed to extend their plant at considerable capital outlay to enable them to meet the whole requirements – after which the importations from the Continent absolutely ceased. From then on, until now, the first consideration has been given to our armies in France, but after that, without a break, we have been able to meet the whole requirements for yeast in this country. In all these arrangements you will see that the patent still distillers had throughout the war given the Government the fullest support which it was possible to do, and this has been acknowledged more than once by various departmental officials.' That latter phrase has a sting in it: officials acknowledged the debt; the politicians never, whether by written or spoken word. Instead, all they did was to multiply the excise duty by nearly fivefold in three budgets, from 14s. 9d. to 72s. 6d.

As that fine public figure, who killed himself in devotion to the public welfare, Sir James Stevenson, of John Walker & Sons Ltd, put it in late 1919: 'The Government in the spring of 1915 had decided on the total prohibition of spirits in war. They did not realise that without distillation there would be no bread for the people, no fusel oil for dope for aeroplanes, no anaesthetic for the wounded – no possibility of expansion of our output of propellants for our guns.' And working to his subject he declaimed: 'Is it not realised that if the distilling trade had not been properly organised we must have lost the war?'

(He then made the interesting observation that it then took 25 million gallons of spirits a year to yield the necessary yeast for the country's bread.)

Stevenson's not-so-rhetorical question still cries aloud for an answer. His implication was most exact; he was not a man to waste time nor to make mistakes. And agreeing with his implication – that without the distillers the war would have been lost – we must carry it a stage further: the patriotic and successful co-operation of the distillers, in yeast as in other matters, hinged on one man, William Ross, born at Carluke, Lanarkshire, in 1862, who entered the service of the D.C.L. in 1878, a year after its formation and twelve days after the collapse of the City of Glasgow Bank with which he had begun his employment. In 1897 he became general manager and secretary, a post which had to be split up in the boom year of 1900 when he joined the board as managing director. Thereafter, as we have noticed during the 'What Is Whisky?' case and commission and in the times of the Lloyd George 1909 budget, he became the moving, ever-active genius of the spirit world. The industry as we know it today, is of his fashioning and is his great memorial.

In fact, it was solely his perspicuity which brought the patent still distillers to the service of the Government less than a year after the war began. For all of which he received the O.B.E.

To revert to Stevenson, it took some 45 million gallons of British high-strength spirit to produce the propellants used in World War I and to cater for other British and Allied war services. The mention of Stevenson recalls at once the fact that he was himself a gift from the Scotch whisky industry to the people and government of Britain of the day and was a most vital person in leading the conduct of the war to victory. After a brief spell with W. P. Lowrie & Co., he became connected with John Walker & Sons Ltd, of Kilmarnock, his home town, moving ultimately to London and becoming joint managing director. On the outbreak of war, Stevenson placed his services entirely at the disposal of the Government – on a strictly honorary basis – and in June 1915, of Lloyd George, Minister of Munitions, becoming director of Area Organisation within that Ministry.

His description of his methods, with a sidelight on how that war was almost lost, bears repetition, in his own words: 'The first thing I did was to call for a map. I might as well have called for the moon. But, nothing daunted, I went out and bought one, for the price of which the Government still owe me, I divided the map into ten areas, the limits of which (with a few exceptions) followed county boundaries, and proceeded on the ordinary commercial lines of decentralisation . . . Curiously enough, one county was left out – Hereford – with the remark: "We will leave that to the Board of Agriculture!" But in that neglected county the greatest shell filling factory in the Kingdom was later built . . .'

Stevenson then began as director of Area Organisation and held the post until 1917 when he became vice-chairman of the Ministry of Munitions Advisory Committee and was made a baronet. He then held other prominent governmental positions and was raised to the peerage in 1924. He died in 1926 and Mr Winston Churchill, as he then was, sent to the press an appreciation of him of which I reproduce the parts relevant to our inquiries: 'It is now ten years almost to a day since James Stevenson in the crisis of war entered the public service as an unpaid volunteer. During the whole of that time he has been constantly employed by every Government which has been in power upon tasks of high importance and difficulty. He rose rapidly under Mr Lloyd George to a commanding position in the vast organisation which developed at the Ministry of Munitions. Among all the ablest business men, striving under wartime pressure to do their utmost for the country, he was always first or among the first . . . Not only did his special department for the supply of guns and shells far exceed all previous records or expectations during the period of his control, but in the general work of the Munitions Council and in the adjustment of difficulties inseparable from the strain of wartime administration, he showed the qualities of a business statesman and leader of men. My own obligations to him are measureless . . . It is the language of bald truth to say that in ten years' public service for honour alone he wore out and consumed the whole exceptional strength of his mind and body. Barely fifty he had exhausted in the service of the State the vital forces by which an easier and less disinterested career might have been carried to a long old age. He ranks with the good soldiers who die of the injuries and strains they received when giving all that was in them to the national cause.'

Such was the spirit of Scotland – and of Scotch: Stevenson personified all that was best in the industry in its national endeavour in war, an endeavour which raised it for the first time to a position of a national institution and character.

Another personality we must first notice as we get down to the part played by the industry in winning that war, W. H. Rattenbury. In 1915 he offered his services to the Ministry of Munitions and was appointed a buying assistant in the Propellants branch of the Explosives Department. When the question of supplies of alcohol became vital, he was placed in charge of the alcohol section. He then submitted a memorandum to the Minister – Lloyd George – in connection with the formation of an Advisory Committee on Alcohol Supplies for War Purposes, which, incidentally, came to be regarded as the text-book on the supply of alcohol.

The result was the appointment of a committee, all the members – with one notable exception – being Rattenbury's nominees. They merit listing, and the contribution of the British distilling industry is at once apparent. They were: Col. Sir Frederic Nathan, Director of Propellant Supplies; Sir Arthur J. Tedder, a commissioner of Customs and Excise, the same Tedder as gave vital evidence at the 1908-9 Commission; F. Gosling, of the Board of Trade; S. C. Bayne, representing the Irish Patent Still Distillers; Andrew Jameson, for the Irish Pot Still Distillers; Richard F. Nicholson, for the English Patent Still Distillers; James Robertson, for the Scotch Pot Still Distillers; W. H. Ross, for the Scotch Patent Still Distillers; T. Shelley, for the Methylators and Rectifiers; and Alexander Walker, for the blenders and merchants. Walker is the exception mentioned earlier: his name was added at Stevenson's suggestion, it being a firm secret that Lloyd George was in close touch with him and received from him advice and assistance on many difficult questions. The Committee later declared that the alcohol used for war purposes totalled more than 92 million proof gallons; there was never a shortage, and that about half of that spirit came from the British distillers with Scotland in the van.

Archibald Walker here deserves mention: the eldest son of Archibald Walker of Loch Katrine and other distilleries, he had to assume full responsibility when young because of the death of his father, and when Loch Katrine was merged into the D.C.L. in 1902 he joined the board. During the war he was entrusted to superintend the introduction of acetone manufacture into British distilleries as well as the manufacture of alcohol from potatoes at Ardgowan distillery, Scotland.

Let us now examine more precisely the part undertaken by the Scotch distillers. It will be recalled that early in the war Lloyd George had the crazy idea of stopping distillation. The trade met in London to consider the position and appointed a committee to discuss the matter with him. It was rightly felt that the patent still distillers held the key to the position as they had the strongest argument for being left unmolested. It fell to Ross to put the patent still distillers' case to Lloyd George. Frequently, indeed, Ross had to act without consultation with the recognised trade bodies – time was the essence of the matter – and he often had to travel twice, sometimes thrice a week between Edinburgh and London. In fact, Ross's brilliant intervention saved the day for the distillers and elicited the tribute from Lloyd George that after Ross's explanation of distilling and its ramifications he had learnt more than he had either known or thought possible.

In September 1915 the Explosives Supply Branch estimated that the production of alcohol – to be supplied by the 27 grain distilleries at 66 over proof or more – would be 'ample for all probable requirements'. By November, complaints were pouring in from industry and government munitions plants of a shortage of spirit. This was partly Lloyd George's own fault: his Immature Spirits (Restriction) Act was resulting in a boom in bondings to meet the three-year demand of the Act. The patent still distillers, via Ross and London associates, agreed to do everything possible to assist the Government, although many of them had never supplied spirit previously for industrial purposes. News came to Ross when the large munitions works at Gretna were under consideration and the Government proposed erecting a distillery to make their own alcohol.

On behalf of the patent still distillers, Ross approached the Ministry of Munitions, through Major Bagot, then principal officer of the Propellants Branch, and Lord Moulton with the offer to supply any percentage of the patent stills' manufacture which the Government needed from the output of practically the whole of the U.K. patent stills. Not only that, Ross arranged to give the Ministry the benefit of the D.C.L.'s distributing agency – the Industrial Spirit Supply Co. – through which all spirits required by the Government were to be invoiced and settlements effected. This, of course, saved a considerable outlay, and that no charge of profiteering could, or should, be made, the distillers agreed that the profit chargeable on all alcohol supplied should be on a strictly pre-war basis, and government accountants were invited to inspect accounts and agree at the end of each three months what the price should be for the ensuing quarter. Ross recalled, post-war, that Sir Frederic Nathan one day told him that, despite his own, Nathan's, assurances that the distillers were not overcharging, 'there were some others in the Ministry' who thought the books should be checked. Nathan then asked for a governmental accountant to go over the books. He was, of course, welcomed to do so, and in, for instance, the case of the D.C.L. books he did so. Let Ross resume the table: 'The accountant came to me and said that he could justify the figures charged, but thought there was something amiss. He thought there had been omitted certain items which would justify the distillers in charging 1½*d.* per gallon more. On the matter being put to me by Sir Frederic Nathan, I suggested that the distillers should make the Government a present of 1½*d.* per gallon for the last six months ... That was agreed to, and no further question was raised as to the prices charged by the distillers.'

At first, following the distillers' proposal to help save the country, it was only necessary to supply about twenty-five per cent of their production. But early in 1916, two other difficulties arose: the shortage of tonnage for importing grain, and the difficulty of obtaining acetone from America. Now acetone was essential in the preparation of high explosives, yet in the United States at that time British firms were competing with each other and with agents of the Allies to buy acetone there. 'Prices were being forced up,' wrote Lloyd George. 'American contractors were selling their output twice over and defaulting on their contracts. They even went to the length of insisting upon an advance in price upon their existing contracts with the British Government, and in the case of their default it proved impossible to recover damages from them.'

As our old friend cordite, which brought down the Liberal Government in 1895 and led to Harcourt's additional sixpence per proof gallon on spirits being taken off by motion of Hicks Beach, which sixpence Hicks Beach had to restore in his April 1900 budget to meet the cost of cordite for the South African War then in progress, as cordite, then, is so intertwined with acetone which in turn is deeply involved in the distilling industry's part in World War I when it assumed something of a national stature, that product merits a little examination.

This smokeless propellant of cordite was first devised by the Ordnance Committee in 1891, with a Dewar intervening, and was later developed and perfected. But what was essential for its production was acetone, as a solvent, or gelatinising material. In pre-war, even into wartime conditions some of the acetone was lost, early in the war, a considerable proportion. Now, acetone was little manufactured in Britain – some had been made in the Forest of Dean – and resulted from the destructive distillation of wood, sugar, cellulose, etc. So it was always present in crude wood spirit, from which the greater portion could be recovered by fractional distillation. Obviously, a case for action by the patent still distillers. 'The matter is urgent,' wrote Lloyd George, 'for without acetone there can be no cordite for our cartridges, for either rifles or big guns.'

The matter complicates with the intervention of C. P. Scott, of the *Manchester Guardian*, who introduced to Lloyd George the Manchester University chemist Weizmann. Born somewhere near the Vistula, Weizmann was devoted to the Allied cause and 'the one thing he really cared about was Zionism, and he believed that in the victory of the Allies alone was there any hope for his people'. At Lloyd George's request, he solved the problem of producing acetone in a few weeks: 'After a prolonged study of the microflora existing on maize and other cereals,' wrote Lloyd George on the subject, 'also of those occurring in the soil, he had succeeded in isolating an organism capable of transforming the starch of cereals, particularly that of maize, into a mixture of acetone butyl alcohol ... he had secured a culture which would enable us to get our acetone from maize. Now maize contains about two-thirds of its weight in starch, and our sources of supply were very wide; so that this discovery enabled us to produce very considerable quantities of the vital chemical.'

Associated with Weizmann's solution of the problem may be mentioned the Balfour Declaration on Palestine and the fact that as the patent still distillers used mainly maize as their basic cereal for distillation, they were a 'natural' to make this chemical, without which – as admitted by Lloyd George, erstwhile enemy of the distillers – the war could not be won. The patent still distillers thus not only entrenched their stake as a nationally recognised element of the lifeblood of the nation, but now, in a very real sense, moved on to the international stage in the company of statesmen and as part-originators and witnesses of events in Palestine and the Middle East today.

The patent still distillers, after the Weizmann announcement, proffered their assistance and six of the largest distilleries in the United Kingdom were handed over by the owners for conversion to acetone production without a penny of compensation being paid, while, as will be seen, the others were made to give an ever-increasing proportion of their make to Government purposes. Those six handed over were: the North British, Caledonian and Ardgowan distilleries in Scotland; and Three Mills, Wandsworth and Hammersmith distilleries in England. Ireland, we notice, was omitted: the year was 1916 in any case. The Advisory Committee on Alcohol Supplies was also formed about the time of the acetone adventure. In fact, only two of these six got to the production stage: Ardgowan, under the direction of Archibald Walker mentioned above, produced it on a commercial scale, and Three Mills, owned by J. & W. Nicholson, produced it on an experimental scale. The others had been chosen because of their size and ease of conversion, but the entry of the United States into the war changed the whole picture: it was cheaper to import acetone from there than to make it in Britain, so the distilleries were told to drop it, and became silent. (Ardgowan began making alcohol from potatoes, of which there was a glut, but as governmental deliveries were spasmodic and irregular that too was dropped.)

The distilleries, as noted, were added to those silent at the time. Early in 1916, with the growing submarine menace, there was some difficulty in importing sufficient grain to keep the distilleries going, and in May 1916 an Order-in-Council prohibited the use of materials for the manufacture of spirit except where a permit had been obtained from the Ministry of Munitions. This immediately brought the pot stills of Scotland (and Ireland) under the virtual control of the Ministry together with the grain distilleries, although war alcohol was only to be got from the latter. The distilling season was then approaching its end, and for the 1916–17 season it was agreed, under governmental compulsion, that the Scotch pots should only be allowed to make seventy per cent of the average output of each individual distillery for the preceding five years. Ultimately, this was an incentive to amalgamation, since 1909 such a feature of the industry: a group of pot still distilleries was able to concentrate production at the chosen plant or plants of the group.

By the end of the year, the needs of the Government and industry for spirit from the patent stills increased most impressively: the twenty-five per cent of output had crawled up the ladder in the year to fifty and then to sixty per cent, and at the end of the year the patent still distillers and the Advisory Committee on Alcohol Supplies agreed that the figure should be advanced to one hundred per cent. These were the black days of the end of 1916 when panic was general, and the proposal was even made that the Government should commandeer all the stocks of whisky in the country in order to provide what was thought would be necessary for munitions requirements. This, it was pointed out, most vigorously, was being most uneconomic and it was promised that supplies could be provided in another way. One means of so providing was the unassisted extension and expansion of existing distilleries. This also saved, such was the panic prevailing, and only conquered by the force of character of Ross, the conversion of the breweries into distilleries, one of the unnecessary proposals then made.

Luckily, another technical revolution then occurred: it was discovered that alcohol which had been once used for solvent purposes in the production of munitions, could be used again and again without diminishing the quantity. The existing distilleries could provide all that was needed and still have some over. Ross suggested that the surplus should be retained by the distillers for their potable spirit customers: they were so fearful that there might be a shortage that they would not immediately agree to this distillers' proposal, but eventually Ross arranged that the spirits which had hitherto, in the war, been bonded at 65 over proof should be reduced to 11 over proof so that in time, if they were not required for munitions, they would be available for the trade.

By the end of 1917 the distilleries were closed down, but for those producing yeast and those engaged on spirit production for industrial and munitions purposes. As far as possible the yeast producers had to be kept at work and their spirit was chiefly used for the industrial, etc., ends. The Temperance Movement, particularly the Strength of Britain Movement, which later came to a sticky end, took great advantage of what they alleged was misuse of vital foodstuffs in time of national peril with the nation, under the U-boat campaign, almost isolated and being forced to adopt food rationing. The trade, again largely under the guidance and inspiration of Ross, defeated the slanders, proved their case, and the Strength of Britain Movement foundered in its own squalor. By the end of 1917, overseas allies and dominions – America and Canada, for instance – were first restricting and then prohibiting the import of whisky, and the shadows of the black night of complete prohibition in both countries were falling. At home, withdrawals of potable spirits had to be restricted to fifty per cent of 1916 withdrawals, and what with this limitation, the cut-backs in production, the potable demands of the Government for the forces, an apparent national prosperity, indeed, boom, whisky prices once more advanced. The speculator made his appearance; old-established firms began to withdraw from the industry, and the process of amalgamation once more reintroduced itself.

In December of that year came the biggest absorption to date the industry had witnessed: the acquisition by the D.C.L. of the famous old house of J. & G. Stewart. As the *Record* observed at the time: 'The deal is one of the biggest ever put through in the whisky trade.' The company held large stocks: little short of 8,000 butts, with a value in the neighbourhood of £2,300,000. And, 'with whispers of other deals of a similar nature,' the *Record* went on, 'what all this portends it is difficult to forecast, but obviously these developments are of far-reaching importance to the Trade as a whole. The tendency to concentrate the diminishing stocks in a few hands must be fraught with incalculable consequences to the smaller houses. This is all the more obvious in face of the ever-tightening control of officialdom, whether through the media of the Central Control Board or the Food Controller. All the same, we cannot help feeling that the big interests who are increasing their stake in the Trade so substantially know what they are doing, and that they will use their giant's strength in no tyrannical fashion.'

It is of interest to record what Ross himself wrote of the Stewart acquisition, especially as it underlines the export ambitions of the industry stretching back beyond the century: 'When the stocks of whisky were purchased from this firm in 1917,' he wrote, 'the intention had been to utilise these stocks for supplementing the requirements of the Company's growing export business. The Advisory Committee set up by the Commissioners of Customs and Excise had, however, compelled all firms doing business during 1916 to continue to supply their regular customers on the basis of fifty per cent of the quantities taken by them during that year. So it came about that, against its own inclinations, the Company was forced to enter into the home business for blended whisky, and having conformed to such a policy, it was decided to perpetuate the trade so far as possible.' Yet another revolution, and yet another major facet of the industry's present structure and character was thus brought into being under the combined impulse of war, economics and government policy.

Before leaving the period considered under this aspect of wartime, it is of interest to record a few facts: the distillers went on record concerning the 'uniform courtesy and tact in all the dealings with the distillers of Sir Frederic Nathan, who was in charge of the Propellant Supplies Branch of the Explosives Department, and none the less by Mr W. H. Rattenbury, his able assistant in that department. The fact that no less than 45,000,000 to 50,000,000 gallons of proof alcohol passed through their hands during these war years is testimony not only to the volume of work committed to their charge, but to the great service rendered by the patent still distillers to the country during this trying period.'

Nevertheless, in the spring of 1918 the Government more than doubled the duty on whisky, and introduced a form of price control which further penalised the trade.

15

The Scotch Whisky Association

BUT BEFORE we turn to consider those three punitive budgets which resumed the theme set by Hicks Beach in 1900, given fuller orchestration by Lloyd George in 1909 and now fully extended under his direction and motivation, we must, first, notice the emergence of an association which over the years and the appearance of the Scotch whisky industry on the national stage in a new status role was later to give rise to that respected body we know today as the Scotch Whisky Association.

That Association can trade its descent back, ultimately, to the price-cutting war which followed the 1909 budget as customers resisted the inevitable increase in the price of a bottle of whisky. We have witnessed the same consumer resistance since recent budgets with price-cutting as their corollaries.

Around the turn of the century 'free competition' in many products was given way in the face of nationwide brands and controlled prices. Much the same sort of thing was happening before that 1909 budget to the leading whisky brands, and such competition as persisted expressed itself more in the offering of varying qualities at equally and correspondingly varying prices. Many preferred to deal in bulk whisky, but the cased product was making its way increasingly. As it did so rough uniformities for categories of 'Scotch' emerged. Then came the Lloyd George bombshell as he tried to achieve prohibition by taxation, a trend still to be found at Westminster.

With a shrinking home market there was a scramble to get what trade in whisky was going. All the years of this century up to the outbreak of World War I saw a decline in the real value of money and this but added to the difficulties of selling whisky in an atmosphere of frequent unemployment and now an unheard of budget duty increase. In presenting his April 1913 budget, Lloyd George was able to boast: 'The effect of the heavy additional duties imposed in 1909 became more and more manifest last year than it had been in the previous year . . . The four years preceding the Budget of 1909, and they included one year of great trade depression, 1908, but the consumption of spirits in this country only fell from forty million to thirty-nine million gallons . . . The four years since the Budget of 1909, you will observe that there has been a fall of eight million gallons in the consumption of spirits in this country, but whilst there has been this drop in consumption the revenue has benefited to the extent of an additional two million pounds. So that it is satisfactory in both ways, in the increased revenue and in the lesser consumption of alcoholic spirits. Taking the whole four years together, the consumption of alcoholic spirits is down by 28,750,000 gallons, and the revenue has profited by £5,000,000. I think it may be said that in more than one respect this is one of the most successful taxes ever imposed on the community.' That was the atmosphere of officialdom and its associates, just the climate for rigorous price-cutting.

The Wine Trade Club took up the matter early in the price-cutting phase and in January 1910, just as it was becoming really painful, held a meeting of members to consider the question, 'Are fixed selling prices desirable?' The chairman, André Simon, incidentally, was of the opinion that fixed prices were 'a mistake'; the 'system could not produce good'. The meeting was undecided; price-cutting went ahead full steam, particularly of whisky. The trade itself was more than puzzled how to re-popularise whisky, commenting: 'Is Scotch whisky as a beverage going? . . . Ever since Mr Austen Chamberlain's Budget, whisky has been going back . . . Knocking off the 3s. 9d. will not restore Scotch whisky to the position it was making for itself four or five years back' (the date is 1910). 'And it is idle to talk of waves of sobriety. Its greatest strength is in sober people . . . We are become an effete people, groaning and burdensome to ourselves, through dieting and hypochondria . . .'

In April of that year, 1910, Sir Thomas Dewar, as he then was, told the annual banquet of the Off-Licences Association: 'Politics has neither shame, remorse, gratitude, or goodwill; or, as an American once told me, it is the long arm, the glad hand, and a swift kick in the pants. Gentlemen, this incomprehensible red flag burglar's budget is not a finance Bill, but brigandage against a particular class of the community . . . when your trade is reduced nearly thirty per cent and your licences in some cases increased a few hundred per cent.'

Among the solutions propounded for the falling sales at that time was a reduction in the strength of the whisky. One trade personality deplored the proposal in these words: 'I can recall the time when bottled Scotch was put up at 10, 12 and 14 u.p., 16 or 18 u.p. being regarded as extremely low figures . . . Today, however, 20 to 24 u.p. are common enough figures of strength nowadays, and it has to be borne in mind that while the customer receives less in alcoholic strength he pays more for his whisky. One fourth water is quite enough . . . but of all the miserable concoctions which can be put before the public, an over-watered whisky tops the list . . . It would be suicidal to lower the standard of strength still further . . . The number of sales with a smaller margin must be increased, rather than standing out for a bigger margin off fewer customers.'

As the year drew to its close, with Christmas sales ahead, the prophesy was made that 'the future of the whisky trade rests with the sale over the counter rather than with the sale over the bar . . . It will depend very largely on the quantity sold in bottle either by the wine merchant or the grocer . . . While the proprietors of some West End bars expect the barmaid to get twenty-five sixpenny nips out of a four-shilling bottle of whisky the customer is certain to feel some resentment, and the distiller and merchant are scarcely being dealt fairly by. The customer shows his feeling in the matter by going off whisky altogether or by buying his own bottle and taking it home with him. If he once does the latter, he will probably continue doing so, and it is for this reason that the firms who cater for the bottled trade are able to speak quite optimistically as to the future of that branch.'

This proposition was borne out, as instanced by Mr H. E. King, managing director of Seager, Evans & Co. Ltd, in March 1914, addressing students at the Sir John Cass Institute on 'Retail Management of Wines and Spirits.' The mere fact that the lecture had to be on such a subject and under such a title is sufficient indication of the even then faltering state of the home market. 'My advice to you,' said King, 'is to take pride in your own special whisky. It is owing to the fact that in the past inferior whisky was given by the licensed victualler to the customer that the proprietary brands have come into vogue. I am acquainted personally with a few successful publicans who set their faces against proprietary whiskies, and pride themselves on their own special whisky, with the result that their trade has increased . . . In the olden days, publicans were noted for their own specialities, but at the present time they supply their customers, more often than not, with some advertised brand.' The shape of the then future was emerging fast.

It was the uneven quality of their own blends, reduced by themselves, sold in the tied houses which stimulated people to ask for a particular brand by a well-advertised name. The proprietary brands had come to stay: the only assurance of value for increased price. The quality of the draught whisky was still leaving much to be desired in many tied houses; the publican pushed his own brand because of the bigger profit, but such was the competitive state of the home market that the man in the street knew he had only to name the brand he wanted to get it. (There were, of course, cases of adulteration, refilling, substitution, etc., of the proprietaries, which only increased the vigilance and determination of the leading blenders to get together.)

There had been formed in 1904 an Anti-Cutting Association, and with that in mind occurred a decisive meeting at Bakers' Hall, in July 1912, on the price-cutting of those imperilled proprietary whiskies. Areas, organisations, associations and firms all gathered there to debate the problem. Almost every county in England was represented as well as the City of London. As the chairman of the meeting told them, they had gathered there 'to put an end to a practice that perhaps has been allowed to exist too long and which if not taken in hand at once will eventually be ruinous to all concerned. The time has now come,' he went on, 'for some definite and drastic action. Distillers and blenders will recognise as a result of the meeting that it is as much in their interests as it is in the interests of the retailers that price cutting should be discontinued.'

There was propounded a scheme to fix prices and trace the bottles by their marks. Association delegates withdrew for a time, and on their return to the Hall were told that the distillers and blenders favoured the scheme and with a view to enforcing it had decided to form an association of their own, the Proprietors' Association. The question then arose about merchants' own brands. That remained unsolved; only persuasion was mooted, but led by James Stevenson, most blenders agreed to cease supplying the price-cutters. Over the years, this proved moderately successful, though never completely, and its partial success was ensured by associations' delegates endorsing the idea of a joint standing committee to act with the new Proprietors' Association.

There would seem to have been little room for price-cutting. At the Brewers' Exhibition held that summer, blended whiskies were entered in three classes, at strengths from 17 u.p. to 25 u.p., according as they retailed at 42s., 48s., or 54s. per dozen bottles. Generally, however, it was found, to quote from a trade circular of the time, price-cutting 'sleeps but never ends'; that it did nothing to increase consumption but much to decrease profits; that the existing anti-cutting association had had to be supported by a newly-formed special association of the distillers and blenders co-operating with the merchants of the trade as represented by a standing joint committee. For instance, in October the representatives of the associations met at the Cannon Street, London, Hotel and passed two resolutions: first, that the Wine and Spirit Brands Association be approved of, and secondly, that blended whisky proprietors should be asked to fix wholesale prices immediately after fixing retail prices. They met again that afternoon with the Proprietors and the Wine and Spirits Brands Association was established with Mr J. King Stewart as secretary, a name of which we shall hear much in the course of the story. He shortly published a list of 'protected' whisky brands and as necessary, from time to time, issued 'Stop Supplies' lists of dealers found price-cutting brands on the 'protected' list.

The home trade was recovering slowly, very slowly, and early in 1913 the forecast was made that 'if the export trade increases at the rate it has been doing during the past twelve months, it will not be long before it overtakes home consumption'. Partly, of course, then, because home trade was so faltering. We have already noticed Lloyd George's remarks at the time of the budget in 1913, and shortly after it there was issued a Customs House statement which read, on spirits, in part: 'In true consumption (i.e., as against retained for consumption) there is believed to have been a fall of over twenty per cent in 1909–10, a slight recovery in 1910–11, a considerable rise (about three and a half per cent) in 1911–12, and a smaller rise (about one and a half per cent) in 1912–13. At the time when the duty was altered, consumption had been falling for about ten years, at an average rate of over two per cent per annum. It is believed that if no change had been made in the duty, the fall would have continued into 1909–10, but would have almost ceased in 1909–10 and that in 1911–12 and in 1912–13 there would have been a rise, as there has been under existing conditions, since this rise appears to have been due to general causes.' This theme was echoed by Mr W. D. Graham Menzies, chairman of the D.C.L., later that year in the annual report, when he said: 'I cannot claim the past year as a record one for profits, although with the exception of the previous year it is the best we have had since the formation of the company.'

By the beginning of 1914, *The Times* was able to comment that practically all the distilleries were working to capacity, 'this being the second year in succession that the production has been largely increased'. The additional comment was then pronounced: 'It might be inferred that the trade is threatened by another glut of supplies, but so far the larger output seems to be justified by the shortage of medium ages, which a previous glut and consequent reaction brought about.'

Such was the background against which the Wine and Spirits Brands Association went about its strictly delimited work of retaining prices on the home market. There had been a Scotch whisky exporters committee set up before the 1909 Budget, mainly concerned with the American decision under President Taft as to what was whisky, but luckily the primary conclusion arrived at was negatived and blended Scotch whisky was able to pursue its penetration of the market without any but normal trade and economic hindrance. But it must here be stressed that such export problems or the attitudes of overseas countries were not the concern of the Wine and Spirit Brands Association, unlike its ultimate successor, the Scotch Whisky Association of today.

Then came the war, just after Graham Menzies announced at the annual meeting through the person of the managing director of the D.C.L., William Ross, that they had just had the best year in the history of the company and 'difficulty in satisfying the requirements of our regular customers'. Some of the experiences of the industry during that war have already been noted, but the first major impact was no doubt Lloyd George's vicious budget of the spring of 1915 when he proposed to double the rate of duty on spirits and finally settled for

a three-year minimum age in the case of whisky. The scope of operations for some body representing the industry was widening. There
followed, as recounted in the previous chapter, the entrance of the
distillers into the sphere of national armament, international politics
and the national food supply. Lloyd George's own demagogic threats
on drink, by which he meant spirits really, the demand to ban whisky
as Russia had banned vodka and France absinthe, his proposal to
nationalise the distilling industry and the setting up of a financial
committee to examine the cost as regards Scotland, all pointed to the
need for a body directly representative of the industry, faced, as it was,
with new experiences and a novel setting, and the new grouping of
ownership emerging. In this scene and Europe a blood-bath, Asquith
and advisers tottering before the machinations of Lloyd George; the
annual meeting in March of the Anti-Cutting Association may be
passed over as may the restricted and defensive day-to-day operations
of the Wine and Spirits Brands Association. In fact, with a new
national prosperity there was little real need for a whisky association to
protect prices on the home front.

Already prices were about to rise; there was no question now of
price cutting. Drucker Brothers reported in the middle of the year, for
instance, that 'already the cheapest consumable whisky has doubled in
value'. W. H. Chaplin & Co. Ltd stated that 'so greatly are the Scotch
and Irish markets disturbed that we find it impossible to fix quotations
this month for whiskies, either in bond or at distilleries'. These are but
typical of many, and one Edinburgh correspondent noted that 'English
buyers have made special journeys north, and not always with the
degree of success anticipated', to which a Highland correspondent
added 'Highland distillers are obtaining advances varying from 8*d.* to
1*s.* per gallon, while the more popular bondings are being disposed of
at an advance of 1*s.* 2*d.* per gallon.'

There ensued the autumn 1915 budget with its illegal restriction on
clearances, since made legal and with us for ever after, the increased
interfering activities of the Central Control Board (Liquor Traffic), the
proliferating activity of the teetotallers, always with us, be it remembered, the threats of over-dilution of whisky, and by the end of the
year it was decided to increase the prices of whiskies of proprietary
brands, the increase being of the order of three shillings a dozen bottles,
or threepence a bottle. The Wine and Spirits Brands Association was

given thereby a new lease of life. The wonder was that it had not come earlier: many blenders had not large stocks to draw on and lived off the market. In Scotland, no whisky with a three-year age was selling for less than 6s. a gallon, many were priced 6s. 6d., some 7s., and it was becoming difficult to see how any blended whisky could sell at less than 7s. or 8s. a gallon.

Barley, rye and maize prices were up; labour and other charges increased and early in 1916 the leading whisky proprietary brand owners met at the invitation of the Wine and Spirit Brands Association to increase the minimum price of their goods by threepence a bottle. As the *Record* commented following their announcement in February, 'Their joint action will be convincing to retailers and public alike, but in the old days of jealousy, suspicion, and mutual recrimination and misunderstanding, there would have been a kind of internecine warfare which would have had the baneful effect of over-clouding the good faith of everyone of the firms engaged.' Thus, indeed, began to emerge a feature and characteristic of the trade today, until destroyed by the abolition of resale price maintenance and the destruction of 'restrictive' trading agreements of the last decade. Nevertheless, with 'tap' whiskies still then available there was nothing like uniformity of prices.

No longer any need to stop price-cutting, as when founded, the Wine and Spirit Brands Association found new activities in the new and changed circumstances. The Central Control Board was insistent on the reduction of the strength of whisky retailed. From February 1916, d'Abernon's Central Control Board had permitted dilution of whisky down to 50 u.p. (with the intention of wrecking the whisky trade), but d'Abernon and colleagues maintained that the 'beneficial effect' of that permission was marred by the consistent and all-round refusal of the proprietors of the leading brands to 'take advantage' of the option. There was some formal correspondence between Sir Thomas Dewar (as he then was) and d'Abernon with the result that the latter arranged for representatives of the spirit trade to meet a committee of the Central Control Board. Meantime, a dozen or more of the leading members of the Wine and Spirits Brands Association made reduction experiments to 25, 28, 30 and 35 u.p., and satisfied themselves that the successive filtrations necessary to secure bright spirit had the result of very materially destroying the characteristic flavours upon which the reputation of the several brands had been built. We have already detailed later developments in that field, and it is mentioned here as exemplifying the changing nature of the activities of the erstwhile price-protection role of the Wine and Spirit Brands Association.

Then in May of the year came a further interference with the life of the industry: apart from the grain distilleries as making yeast and industrial spirit, already virtually controlled by the Ministry of Munitions, no distilling could be carried out but by permission and before long it was decreed that production for the forthcoming distilling year should be restricted to seventy per cent of the average of the previous five years.

By the beginning of 1917, such was the national importance of the distilling industry, led by Scotland, that the Minister of Munitions appointed the Advisory Committee on Alcohol Supplies, under Nathan. The role of the industry was changing fast. As was said that March: 'Great as have been the trials of the Trade in the past, it may safely be said that they bear no comparison to the trials of the present.' Then came the Order of the Food Controller, Lord Davenport, restricting taxpaid clearances of wines and spirits from bond for home consumption to fifty per cent of 1916.

On 23 May 1917 came the long delayed and equally long needed move. At the annual meeting of the Wine and Spirits Brands Association, the great majority of the membership of which consisted of the Scotch and Irish distillers and blenders, it was resolved the association change its name to the Whisky Association, which aimed 'at the creation of a strong, centralised, homogeneous body in London, the seat of the Government, which will be capable of adequately voicing the opinions and defending the interests of all Scotch and Irish whisky distillers, blenders and exporters'. It was further added that the elimination of the word 'brands' from the title meant they need not limit themselves to the protection of the interests of proprietary brand owners – their scope and function had been stretched far beyond that modest aim – but they did not intend abandoning the suppression of any price-cutting of same.

Sir Alexander Walker, K.B.E., giving evidence to a royal commission in 1930, on behalf of the Whisky Association, summed up, in response to a question put by the chairman, Lord Amulree, the object of the Association by saying: 'It is a trade union. It is really to correlate the enormous number of points that arise in the Trade in the matter of its regulation and also it acts as a central body in dealing with foreign governments. As a matter of fact, even the Inland Revenue asked us to form an association in order that we might be a unit in discussing points with them. There are a large number of points in which it is necessary to have a unified body to deal with.' (The emergence of the monumental state and society.)

But henceforth it was to be limited to the whisky trade, Scotch and Irish, only. The president was, not unnaturally a Dewar, Lord Forteviot, as he was by then, with vice-presidents, as then named: Mr James Buchanan, Mr Andrew Jameson, Mr P. J. Mackie, Sir John Nutting, Bt, Sir Thomas Power, Mr William Ross, Sir Robert Usher, and Mr G. P. Walker. The council consisted of, with their firms' names in brackets: Mr Robert Brown (Robert Brown Ltd), Mr Peter Dewar (John Dewar & Sons Ltd), Mr H. L. Garrett (Dunville & Co.), Mr Samuel Greenlees (Greenlees Brothers), Capt. R. B. G. Greig (Wright & Greig), Mr W. Harrison (James Buchanan & Co. Ltd), Mr Alfred Moore (James Watson & Co. Ltd), Mr Robert Montgomery (McConnell's Distillery Ltd), Mr J. Stuart Smith (the D.C.L.), Mr J. Stevenson (John Walker & Sons Ltd), Mr E. Ludlow Thorne (R. Thorne & Sons Ltd), Mr D. Landale Wilson (Andrew Usher & Co.). Mr R. Montgomery was to be chairman of the Council, and the secretary was Mr J. King Stewart.

The membership was in two sections: home trade, and export, the fee being five guineas per section; members could belong to one or both. All distillers, blenders and exporters of Scotch and Irish whisky were invited to join because 'There is little doubt but that, in the times which lie immediately ahead, the Trade will require all the vigour and ability resident within its ranks to defend itself from encroachment which, as all legislation pertaining to the liquor trade has shown in the past, is not apt to be tinged with too much consideration for, or even an elementary sense of justice to, the Trade.' Under the auspices of the old association was launched the Whisky Exporters Association, and this became now the Export Section of the Whisky Association, under the immediate chairmanship of Mr P. M. Dewar.

We cannot here detail the day-to-day functions and activities of the association and/or its export section. But before it had been long in existence and with the black days of 1917 enveloping the country, imperilled by the mounting submarine menace and the slaughter-house of the Western Front, to the accompaniment of the Russian revolution, distilling, except as for yeast and industrial spirit, was prohibited for the impending season. The industry was learning fast the lessons which remained in the forefront of its mind when World War II descended upon us.

To revert to 1917, whisky prices were soaring and a conference was held between the deputy to the Food Controller, Mr G. Walter Roffey and the Council of the Whisky Association towards the close of the year. Lord Rhondda, the Food Controller, wished to control prices – as 'the representatives of the working classes had been protesting violently against bar prices', an anomalous situation in a sense with d'Abernon trying to eliminate bars and drinks while the Food Controller had to restrict their prices because of the very real danger of industrial unrest and strikes! As the *Record* then noted: 'The Government are disposed to treat it [the whisky trade] with much more respect than was formerly the case and to realise that it forms an essential part of the national fabric. The very fact that the Government are determined to fix a retail price for whisky is evidence of their dependency on the trade.'

First step, and auctions of whisky were banned. The fifty per cent of 1916 deliveries at home was continued. A formal Order, after an initial verbatim one, was issued, as a blow against the speculator, prohibiting the sale of whisky at an auction unless authorised by the Food Controller and with additional restrictions in detail. The responsible sections of the trade welcomed it. As Graham Menzies, chairman of the D.C.L., had said at the annual meeting in 1916: 'This company is not in business for today only . . . Our policy has been to conserve the future and act in the best interests of the whole trade.' That profound and wise principle was accepted and enforced by the Whisky Association, which had as a vice-president, Ross, then managing director of the same company as Menzies.

The Order for fixing whisky prices lay in a state of suspension until the 1918 budget, and we can examine it more closely when considering the three vicious budgets of 1918, 1919 and 1920. About the same time, in March 1918, the General Committee of the Wine and Spirit Association held a special meeting with delegates of the Whisky Association and other trade associations because of the Central Control

Board's suggestion that dilution of spirits to 36 u.p. be compulsory and permitting up to 42 u.p., in place of 50 u.p. It was recorded at the time: 'Strong disapproval of the Order was expressed by those present, and a draft memorandum was read embodying the views of The Whisky Association to the effect that the Trade could not accept responsibility for carrying out the proposed dilution order, and it was arranged that the same, after certain amendments to be approved by the respective chairman of the Wine and Spirit Association and The Whisky Association, should be laid before the Central Control Board (Liquor Traffic) on the following day by the chairmen and secretaries of the two last-named associations.'

What with increased duty resulting from the 1918 budget, and Government-controlled prices of whisky, the shut-down on potable distillation, and the many other lesser factors noticed by the way, as well as the major wartime role played by Scottish distillation, it came as no surprise that at a meeting of Scottish members of the Whisky Association held in Dowell's Rooms, Edinburgh, on 20 June, it was resolved unanimously to form a Scottish branch of 'that powerful organisation' the Whisky Association, and non-members were invited to join. Unity is strength, be it remembered.

A General Purposes Committee representing all sections of the trade and consisting of nine members was agreed and for immediate action on a specific problem a deputation of four was selected to wait on the Food Controller or his representative with reference to control of prices. At the general meeting of the Scottish Branch on the same spot 29 July the personnel structure was announced. The chairman was to be that notable figure, now awarded the O.B.E., Mr William Ross, managing director of the D.C.L., and the other members of the General Purposes Committee of the Scottish Branch were to be (firm in brackets): Mr James Robertson (Robertson & Baxter Ltd), Mr R. Brown (R. Brown & Co.), Mr A. J. Cameron (John Dewar & Sons Ltd), Mr R. I. Cameron (Elgin), Mr Thomas Herd (James Watson & Co. Ltd), Mr Andrew H. Holm [Mackie & Co. (Distillers) Ltd], Mr F. J. Usher (Andrew Usher & Co. Ltd), Mr James Watson (Charles Mackinlay & Co.), Mr Thomas W. Kennedy and Mr G. M. Thomson. Mr J. King Stewart remained secretary of the Whisky Association and Mr Andrew Wishart, W.S., was secretary of the branch.

In closing, it may be remarked that the Scottish Branch very promptly issued recommendations on invoicing, discounting, etc., under the control price Order in force and it remains only to remark that not only was William Ross, O.B.E., a vice-president of the Whisky Association from its inception and chairman of the Scottish Branch from its formation, but in 1922 he was unanimously elected chairman of the London Council so as to co-ordinate the work of the two centres.

On 15 May 1942 the Whisky Association was dissolved, in terms of its constitution, and its functions were taken over by the Scotch Whisky Association. The latter association, still, happily, with us, came into being as a result of a meeting held in Glasgow on 17 April 1942. The chief reason for the dissolution was the fact that the constitution of the Association was no longer in accordance with the method of carrying on its affairs and contained no provision for alteration. Such alteration could only have been made by obtaining the written consent of every member.

On formation, the objects of the Scotch Whisky Association were defined as: '(a) to protect and promote the interests of the Scotch whisky trade generally both at home and abroad and to do all such things and to take all such measures as may be conducive or incidental to the attainment of such objects; (b) to protect the interests of owners of proprietary brands of Scotch whisky by taking such steps as the Association may think fit to regulate prices, both wholesale and retail, and to prevent such proprietary brands being sold either wholesale or retail at prices above those fixed by the Association.'

No doubt in the stress of war and the industry's participation in armament and food supplies, together with the inevitable concomitants of war on a global scale as was witnessed in World War I, some such association as the Whisky Association would have come into being, but, as reflected in (b) above, dimly, the origins of the association lie in the whisky price-cutting consequent upon ten years of declining sales and the Lloyd George budget of the year 1909.

16

Wartime developments

THAT NOTHING in history is isolated is axiomatic, and those three penal budgets of 1918, 1919 and 1920 were but the fruit of the preceding years, and a further example of the steady encroachment this country has witnessed this century of the Executive on the freedom of the individual. We must, then, turn to look more closely at the whisky saga of the years before the taxman resumed his onslaught, an attack mildly begun in war by Hicks Beach in 1900, resumed in strength when Lloyd George declared another sort of war in 1909 and brought to a fresh peak as the European conflict neared its bloody solution in 1918. They were, further, years in which the Scotch whisky industry learned, and learned the hard way, to adapt itself to a rapidly changing world, a world in which the Executive fixed quotas and maximum prices, lessons, again, which the industry acted upon of its own accord in the second world butchery. The lesson had been learned, and the industry had the wisdom to act ahead of the Government.

Ross, managing director of the D.C.L., put it all in perspective in an address at the annual general meeting of the company in July 1920, when seconding the chairman's report. Reverting to the Lloyd George increase of 1909, he said that they had 'protested most strongly against that increase as likely to have an injurious effect upon the industry. That their fears were justified is proved by the fact that the consumption for the United Kingdom dropped by no less than ten million gallons. It is true that as the years went on this loss was partially recovered until in 1916 the consumption had reached to within three million gallons of what it was prior to 1909. In the following year, the Government found it necessary to restrict the clearances to fifty per cent of the previous year's quantity and a further drop of ten million gallons took place, to be followed by a still further reduction in 1918 of eight million gallons. This brought the home consumption of home-made spirits to the low water mark of 10,300,000 gallons. In that year Mr Bonar Law increased the duty from 14s. 9d. to 30s. per proof gallon, but as the quantity restrictions were partially removed before the end of the financial year, the home consumption of spirits slightly increased to 11,800,000 gallons. This seems to have emboldened Mr Chamberlain to try a further increase, this time of 20s., bringing the duty of 50s. per gallon, and with a further easement of clearances the home consumption went up to 17,800,000 gallons. So far, the results had justified the two last increases from a revenue point of view, but when Mr Chamberlain again returned to the docile cow for a further augmentation this year of 22s. 6d. per gallon, raising the duty to the enormous rate of 72s. 6d. per gallon, it was time for the Trade to protest . . . The price of whisky to the public has been controlled for the last four years . . . The Trade was fairly well protected when the control price was first put on, the margin then allowed had been twice cut into through the Trade having been prevented from passing on to the public the whole increase in duty placed on spirits on the last two occasions.'

As Ross allowed, it did not affect their position as distillers 'directly' but the company's customers it did 'affect very seriously'. There had been a deputation to the Chancellor, whose attitude was summed up by Ross in these words: 'As the larger whisky companies seemed to be very prosperous and making lots of money they could well afford to contribute more to the Exchequer. It was in vain that we pointed out that these profits were largely being made out of stocks acquired previous to the war, and that after paying all the Imperial taxes now being exacted in the shape of Excess Profits Duty, Income Tax and Corporation Tax, there was not sufficient left to replace the original stocks at the greatly enhanced cost of new whisky.'

As was elucidated, immediately after that third budget duty increase, 'Once again the Trade is compelled to bear a portion of the extra duty – a high-handed act on the part of the Chancellor which is as unjust as it is unconstitutional. The object appears to be that of squeezing out the smaller houses in the Trade with a view to State Purchase of the bigger ones later on. Raising revenue is apparently a secondary consideration.' It was recalled that when, in 1885, under a Gladstone administration, a two shilling increase in spirit duty was proposed – from ten to twelve shillings per proof gallon – 'it was enough to enable the Trade to bring down his government'. But in 1920 – and still today? – there was a lack of combination in the trade and it was on this that 'the Government,' it was said, 'seem to bank, and we fear they will bank successfully until the brewer and the distiller; the on-licence holder and the off-licence holder; the importer, the distributor and the retailer make a united effort to defend the interests of the Trade.'

Let us now revert to those formative years in such detail as is here possible. Just before the war, the industry began making a delayed recovery from the 1909 budget and the international and industrial unrest of the period. As Ross, managing director of the D.C.L., was able to state on behalf of the chairman, who was ill, at the annual general meeting in July 1914, he was reporting on 'the best year in the history of the company', one in which they had 'difficulty in satisfying the requirements of our regular customers', adding, 'As a matter of fact, we had to go into the market ourselves to secure sufficient stocks of old whisky to meet the requirements of our export business'.

But with the beginning of 1915, war was already making itself felt: the prices of raw materials were soaring to heights 'which seemed to prohibit the possibility of beginning distilling operations'. Luckily prices fell, then Turkey entered the war and barley rose again in price. By the end of the year, a half to two-thirds of the distillers had begun work, but in the vast majority of cases output, it was thought, would be below a level permitting profit. It looked like being the smallest output for a quarter of a century, an event not disliked by all, who saw a chance of getting rid of old stocks.

There followed, in due course, the budget attempt of the spring of 1915 to double the tax on spirits, and the compromise of allowing Lloyd George instead to bring in a three-year minimum age for whisky and certain other spirits. One result was to send prices, prices of usable whisky, soaring, particularly of grain whisky, the production of which had been, in general, little more than the equivalent of consumption.

As was noted on the advance in prices: 'When we mention that grain whisky of early 1915 is quoted at 3s. 6d., and that three-year-old grains fetch from 5s. 6d. to 5s. 9d., some idea can be formed of the astonishing strides prices have made during the past two months. Yet it is not likely that the grain distillers, who from the 1st July raised their price by 5*d.* per gallon, will make in excess of requirements; indeed, the enhanced cost of raw materials may compel them to make less. In view of all this, it is difficult to understand why the brand proprietors decided upon not raising their prices at a time when the distributors and the public were fully prepared for a rise because of the increased cost of labour, freight, bottles, etc.'

Malt whisky prices then began rising also, and, as we noted earlier, the three-year minimum, despite its year's grace to two-year-old blends, served to make a shortage of suitable singles and blends with the natural consequence that their prices rose. By the time the war had been a year in progress, it was claimed that 'any tendency towards a reduction in consumption should be welcomed by blenders who had to buy on the open market'. With three-year-old grains at 6*s.* and malts of the same age at 5*s.*, and 'with the loss in ullage and the cost of blending, how', it was asked, 'is it possible for any firm paying these prices to sell at the minimum of 6*s.* per bulk gallon?' Prices did not halt on their way up, whatever the well-meaning comment. Moreover, that governmental and industrial usage of spirits distilled, above all in Scotland, exacerbated increasingly the demand for new grains to lay down. Another reason for prices to rise. Buyers began to panic.

With the new season of 1915–16, many distillers were not able to fix prices because of the situation in the barley market, but as a rule Highland malts were up by one shilling a gallon, and the same went for Lowlands, with the proviso that these prices were based on a 45*s.* quotation for barley on the Elgin market: an increase of 1*s.* 6*d.* in barley, and whisky would be advanced 1*d.* a gallon. For firm orders, as, for instance, in the case of Scottish Malt Distillers Ltd, threepence a gallon was added to the quotation. Government demands, as we have seen, began to increase, and the price of grain doubled, partly in consequence.

Without detailing all the price rises and increased costs, suffice it to say that by the end of the year it was decided to increase the prices of proprietary brands by 3*s.* a dozen, or 3*d.* a bottle. It was wondered it had not come earlier: with the bulk of blends getting 6*s.* 6*d.* a gallon, and some even 7*s.*, with three-year-old grain at 6*s.* 6*d.*, it was difficult to see how blended whisky could sell at less than 7*s.* or 8*s.* per gallon.

The proposed solution was that 'blenders are enabled to sell at 6s. per gallon, or a little more, only by having recourse to their stocks of single whiskies which were purchased at a very much lower figure than that now ruling'.

The new year, 1916, saw grain whisky filling prices advanced by what amounted to 5d. a gallon, and with other adjustments in grain whisky transactions. Prices of casks, bottles, fuel, labour and other necessities as well as the barley and maize went up yet again and another increase of threepence a bottle was recommended to proprietary brand owners by the Wine and Spirit Brands Association.

Anyway, panic again set in with rumours that the government intended to take over all distilleries, both pot and patent still, a panic hardly assuaged by (the then) Sir Thomas Dewar's remark to a reporter that whisky might soon rise to ten shillings a bottle. (It just about did by the end of the war.) There came, too, to add to the whisky crisis developing, restrictions on grain imports, and on imports of certain other spirits. Certainly all this time the Central Control Board (Liquor Traffic) was making the whisky go further by enforced dilution, an enforced dilution to be fixed early the following year, 1917, at 30 u.p., with most of the country then adhering to this strength.

In May 1916 came an Order in Council restricting production of spirits to those only who had been granted a permit. The time limit for its enforcement was later adjusted on negotiation – to allow the distilleries to use up their stocks of barley, now standing at around 65s. the quarter – but the writing was on the wall: State control of the industry. As Messrs W. H. Chaplin & Co. Ltd remarked: 'The underlying motive may be traced to the enemies of our Trade . . . The "permit" will be granted to grain distillers, but only so that they may be able to make for the Government with liberty to buy back what is not wanted. Malt distilleries will probably be brought to a standstill . . . With all these restrictions and prohibitions, whisky threatens to become quite a curiosity . . . It seems inevitable, therefore, that prices will be forced up still higher and higher.'

That prophecy was borne out by Graham Menzies at the annual meeting in July 1916 of the D.C.L., when he said: 'I would not have it supposed that we have been exacting an undue toll out of our customers. Prices have had to be raised, of course – raised in proportion to the advance in the cost of raw materials, wages, etc., but had we wished to exact the full advance obtainable for our various products, we might easily have doubled our profits.'

The facts of production and consumption about this time may be observed from comparing figures of stock in bond in Scotland in March 1909 when it was 114,188,443 gallons with March 1916 when the figure was only 106,730,173 gallons. As a Highland correspondent observed about this time: 'Meantime, bondings are gradually going into fewer and fewer hands. Big concerns are buying them up, and amalgamations are being effected that will tend still further in this direction. Undoubtedly a serious time awaits many distillers, especially those connected with the smaller concerns, and the new season is bound to be a critical one.'

It was indeed. After protracted negotiations, distillers in Scotland were able to make seventy per cent of the average of the last five years' production of pot still whisky. The Scotch distillers had had, luckily, a good year in 1914 and the five years' average enabled them to bring in that year's output. The agreement did not include the grain distillers – they were engaged almost exclusively on spirit for war purposes and the D.C.L. could supply the trade from only one of their distilleries while the whole output of the others went to the Government. Thus Mr John Archer, chairman of Bulloch Lade & Co. Ltd, reported a 'successful year' for the one past, but 'anxious times ahead'. And as Ross reported the following year, as chairman of Scottish Malt Distillers Ltd, the 1916–17 season had been cast in a role severely against the company: some of the basis years in their case had been very small ones and included years before the company was formed. It had only been formed because of the intense depression of Lowland malt distilling. In their case, they gave a further example of the benefits of amalgamation: they had concentrated production at three distilleries only, but even so, their production in the season reviewed had been only fifty-seven per cent of the previous one. Profits, however, had not suffered, which showed a further benefit of amalgamation.

But, indicative of the rising prices, was the fact that in the late summer of 1916 three-year-old (and older) blends were selling at 13s. 6d. a gallon on average. And with the depleted stocks, rising prices and curtailed production was emerging another feature of the industry constant since then: blenders began to concentrate on the higher-class branches of the trade; the cheaper blends were going to the wall and ceasing to be. By the end of the year whiskies averaged about 8*s*. 6*d*. the gallon, or double what they had been a twelve-month before. And at the annual general meeting of Scottish Malt Distillers Ltd, held late in that year, Ross was able to report that the balance sheet was 'satisfactory' due to 'the abnormal advance which has taken place in the price of old whiskies, fair stocks of which the company fortunately possessed. We also had the advantage of a very large output of new whisky, produced from barley bought at a moderate price.' Mr James Robertson, chairman of The Highland Distilleries Co. Ltd, was also able to report about the same time that the past year, that ending in 1916, was more satisfactory than they had been for some years... '(they) benefited by small sales of old whisky at market prices. With stocks held by the company, and the ready market they were likely to meet when matured, he was hopeful they might be able to maintain the dividend at something like its present level.'

By December, whisky was fetching 20*s*. a gallon, and it was said that 'further advances will not astonish'. The Central Control Board was doing its best by way of restrictions and dilution to cut back consumption, but prices went on merrily rising and the industry moved, in 1917, into a period of unprecedented boom with speculators active at forcing up prices again. As was said of the year, 'The year 1917 will long be remembered in the Scotch whisky trade. Without a doubt it has been the most sensational twelve months ever experienced. The prohibition of distillation, the restriction of clearances, and, above all, the remarkable advance in prices, have combined to make it the reddest of red-letter years.'

At the beginning of the year three-year-olds were costing 20*s*. a gallon: by its end they were touching 80*s*. Speculation caused part of the rise, but it was mainly due to the smaller blenders living from hand to mouth and holders hanging on to stocks in the anticipation of further increases in price while the bigger blending houses themselves went on to the market, partly to meet their own needs and partly to insure for the future. These 'big houses' realised early on that in the circumstances prices, to begin with, were below intrinsic values and they were only too happy to seize any opportunity of buying parcels of appreciable bulk.

By the year's end a gallon of Highland malt bonded in November 1913 was fetching 80*s*., and three-year malt and grains close on 70*s*.

Prices simply knew no bounds, it was said. Or, as *The Times* put it in review of the year past, 'the year showed a marked advance in prices... far beyond anything anticipated twelve months ago, bonded whiskies sold in the public sale-room realising prices which show a premium of more than two thousand per cent over the filling price of three years ago.' The result was government interference to fix prices, a matter to which we shall return to examine in detail.

Leaving aside a recounting of the monthly advances in prices, it is sufficient to note that at the beginning of 1917 a bottle of Scotch cost 6s. in general. By March, the leading brand owners – the Whisky Association was about to be born out of the Wine and Spirit Brands Association – agreed to raise prices by 6s. a dozen, or 6d. a bottle. And from 1 April, home clearances were restricted to fifty per cent of 1916 withdrawals for the home market. This had been forecast in February when Lloyd George said: 'We must guard against driving the population from beer to spirits. That would be a serious disaster. Above all, whilst we are cutting down the barrels that can be brewed in this country, we must have a corresponding restriction on the placing of spirits on the market.'

Imports of wines and spirits were to be cut back – food stocks were at their lowest ever, and the German submarine menace was threatening the nation's life – and Lloyd George proposed that beer production should be limited to 10 million barrels for the year. Lord Devonport, the Food Controller, ordered that wines and spirits clearances should be reduced to fifty per cent of the calendar year 1916 withdrawals. It was in this setting that the Whisky Association, as noted earlier, was brought to fruition and the chairman of W. P. Lowrie & Co. Ltd found just the words at the annual general meeting: 'The Trade is passing through the most anxious crisis in its whole history... problems undreamt of in the piping times of peace ... I am glad to say that the foresight of the Board in the providing of and conserving of stocks ensures a continuance of the business for many years ahead.' Prices kept on rising; firms withdrew from the struggle, sold their stocks or were amalgamated; the Government threats of state purchase assumed new proportions.

Lloyd George told a Scottish delegation that 'State purchase and prohibition are not rival propositions. State purchase might possibly be the most direct route to prohibition.' His wife told Judge Neil, of

Chicago, 'I think ultimately the women voters will secure the abolition of public houses and the liquor traffic.' Lord Milner told the House of Lords: 'On the road we are at present travelling, we shall arrive, I hope and believe, at a system of control of the liquor traffic which, being introduced under the necessities of war – and I think it could be introduced only under that pressure – will be able to be continued and developed on the same lines when the war is over.' Lloyd George was more specific to the U.K. Alliance and the Strength of Britain Movement: 'If nothing were done, now, to acquire complete control over the Trade, I fear that when demobilisation comes there will be an irresistible demand to put the Trade back practically where it was before.' In the House, the Chancellor of the Exchequer hedged on the issue, saying only that 'the subject will not be settled till the House has had an opportunity of considering it, but it must be dealt with and considered by the Government before'. (The Wine Trade Club had their own debate: 'That this meeting hereby protests against any attempt of the Government to convert the Wine and Spirit Trade into a State monopoly. Such an act would be contrary to the best interests of the public, and would be in direct opposition to all the principles upon which the British Trade is founded.' They appreciated the galloping threat by the Executive to freedom.)

A memo of the Central Control Board to the Government was then published as a White Paper in which it was reiterated that 'the successful prosecution of the war is still being hampered by excessive consumption of intoxicating liquor . . . The Board are of the opinion that the time has now come when comprehensive measures, beyond their present powers, are necessary in order to carry to completion the work of restriction and control which the Board were established to discharge . . . There are three possible policies: (*a*) More stringent restriction; (*b*) Prohibition; and (*c*) Direct and complete control by the State of the manufacture and sale of intoxicating liquor throughout Great Britain.' Signed by Lord d'Abernon, they wanted more power.

The price race went on unheeding. At an auction that summer Dailuaine Malt Whisky fetched 38*s*. and 39*s*. the gallon; 1914 Glen Grant fetched 37*s*. 6*d*. and 40*s*.; John Jameson 41*s*.; Oban 22*s*.; John Power 33*s*. for the 1915 make and 38*s*. for the 1914 make. Summer 1914 prices by way of comparison ranged from 3*s*. 1*d*. to 5*s*. 11*d*. at extremes.

As the summer passed, it was noted that 'all previous records have been left far behind', the reasons being not only the element of specu-lation but, as a fundamental cause, the three years' minimum age and the cutting of supplies by the (necessary) embargo on production. In addition, the big distributing houses were buyers rather than sellers and there was a new class of consumers because of increased wages in wartime. It was expected – and came about – that some prices would touch 100*s*. a gallon by the year's end.

The Food Controller stepped in: because of the sensational prices fetched at auction by whisky and demanded over the counter by some retailers. His deputy, Mr G. Walter Roffey, met the Council of the Whisky Association. The age of freedom was ending: an article was ceasing to be what it would fetch, but what bureaucracy said it must fetch. An artificial atmosphere was being created, an artificial world later, by the Chancellor of the Exchequer, laid at the door of the industry in increasing its taxation. The Food Controller, Lord Rhonda, hoped to control prices for a reason which will seem unbelievable in the over-taxed whisky world of today: representatives of the working class 'had been violently protesting against bar prices'; his department was receiving hundreds of letters daily on the subject of dearer whisky at lower strength; the Food Control Department explicitly attributed a great deal of industrial unrest to the 'high prices of liquid refreshment'. At the conference the trade was asked to suggest 'practicable methods of enforcing maximum retail prices per bottle of whisky at "on" and "off" licensed establishments and per measure at public houses, strength as well as quantity to be considered in this connection'.

The usual points were made: the Immature Spirits Act had auto-matically enhanced the price of all usable whiskies; no distillation of potable spirits was being carried out; the restriction on clearances meant there had to be a greater price for the lesser quantities handled; an article is worth what it will fetch; the proprietors of the bigger brands had enhanced the prices of whiskies by buying up what they could, and the Central Control Board was responsible for the weaker strength.

For, although the Government now treated the whisky industry on a national level, it had been forced for the distilling season 1917–18 to prohibit potable spirit distilling completely, which again added to the market price of stocks as the resumption of distilling, in the dark days of the end of 1917 and the early months of 1918, could not be foreseen with any accuracy.

And as was remarked at the time, in January 1918, 'Government are disposed to treat it (the whisky industry) with more respect than was formerly the case and to realise that it forms an essential part of the national fabric. The very fact that the Government are determined to fix a retail price for the whisky is evidence of their dependency on the Trade.'

The first governmental action was to forbid whisky auctions, except under conditions, an Order made for the purpose of driving outsiders from the market. In this sense it was welcomed by the established trade, and a 'prominent distiller' went so far as to say that it 'can be regarded with equanimity'. It was aimed, in effect, at the speculator, and as such was accepted gladly by all responsible sections of the trade.

For the price of a bottle, at the reduced strength of 70 degrees proof, had now reached Dewar's forecast of ten shillings, and this, with its reduced strength, caused the fear to spread that it was 'calculated to do the Trade permanent injury', while the whisky trade itself, in the absence of any increase of duty, was being 'widely accused of profit-eering'.

The trade could not come up with any suggestions, as requested by the Food Controller, above, and speculation as to the outcome was rife. It was guessed that the maximum price of three-year-old in bond would be fixed at 25s. a gallon for the broker and 30s. for the blender, with retail prices fixed at 7s. 6d., 8s. 6d., and 9s. 6d. the bottle, the whole-sale prices, per case, being 60s., 68s., and 72s. By fixing the 30s. per proof gallon for a blend, it was said, the commodity would be virtually standardised and the blender will know what he can afford to pay for his material, which should, in turn, control the prices of singles.

Further to the interests of the home consumer, exports were forbidden and it took all of King Stewart's efforts, as secretary of the Whisky Association, to allow the passage of any whiskies at all under licence from the War Trade Department. Moreover, the feeling was growing in that last eve of spring of the war that the budget would impose additional duties on spirits, and if the government-fixed prices were delayed the rumour would gain in credibility. The price-fixing order remained in a state of suspension and the fears of the industry multiplied. It was realised that it would be ridiculous for the Food Controller to fix whisky prices and have to alter them in a few months because of the action of the Chancellor of the Exchequer.

But the equally ridiculous anomaly was also emerging more clearly that while the Central Control Board was wishing to curtail, if not prohibit, spirits, and other drinks, the Food Controller was acting to allow their wider circulation. The Armed Forces had long been calling on whisky for the troops – generally whisky for Officers and N.C.O.'s, rum for other ranks – and the farce was completed on publication of a report by eight 'eminent medical men' who had been appointed by the Central Control Board 'to consider the conditions affecting the physiological action of alcohol, and more particularly the effects on health and efficiency'. The main and general conclusion reached, to the chagrin of the Control Board, was that 'There can be no doubt that alcohol is a food in the sense of a fuel that the body can use'.

But more of an augur of the impending storm was a notice issued by the Ministry of Food which stated: 'Owners of registered and proprietary brands of whisky who are not registered in the Wine and Spirit Trade Diary, 1918, are requested to forward their addresses with particulars of their brands to the Ministry of Food (Brewing Section) ... not later than February 21st.' In addition, Roffey asked for gross and net invoice prices at which on 30 November previous (or the nearest prior date) registered or proprietary brands of whisky were being offered or sold.

17

Post-war budgets (i)

WITH DUTY-PAID clearances from bond of Scotch whisky for the home market restricted to fifty per cent of the calendar-year clearances, and although those clearances were put on a government-enforced quota basis to existing trade customers, the obvious corollary had perforce to ensue; government control of their price. In all, a lesson well learned by the Whisky Association and adopted quickly by it, and continued by the Scotch Whisky Association after the outbreak of World War II. Better, it was reasoned, in the light of World War I experiences, to act as an industry than suffer the intervention of bureaucracy. Thus even before the end of the 'phoney', there was issued, at the beginning of 1940, notice of a home-rationing scheme to operate from 1 March 1940, limiting quotas to the establishments concerned to eighty per cent of purchases in the year ending 29 February 1940. That same rationing scheme was carried on by the Association until the post-war government intervened (quite unnecessarily) and it was only from 1 January 1954 when the Government agreement limiting releases for the home market ceased to operate, that members of the Scotch Whisky Association were left free to decide their own distribution patterns for themselves. In short, it was a self-control learned from the pains of government control in World War I.

The other element of government control, price-fixing, originating from World War I, was also adopted by the Association, and first found expression early in 1944 on the part of the Scotch Whisky Association when the council recommended to members that they should incorporate on their invoices a condition of sale to the effect that the bottled whisky was sold on the condition that it would not be resold except in and from the bottle provided and exactly as supplied and at prices fixed by the Scotch Whisky Association. Further, it was pointed out that it was an offence against the by-laws of the Association to sell, etc., any proprietary brand at prices above those fixed by the Association, contravention of which condition could result in the offender's being placed on a stop list and receiving no further supplies from members of the Association.

Action was prompt. In July that year was published the first stop list from the Association, a list redolent, in one sense of the then far-distant origin of the Scotch Whisky Association from the Wine and Spirit Brands Association and its formation to maintain fixed prices in the year before World War I. For the stop list announcement read, in part, 'For the purpose of carrying into effect its policy of securing and preserving adherence to and compliance with the fixed selling prices, wholesale and retail conditions of sale of proprietary brands of Scotch whisky, The Scotch Whisky Association issues, pursuant to its By-laws the subjoined Stop List.' The wine and spirit merchant was of Leicester, and the only difference of the Association from its origins was that in the forties it was trying to prevent over-charging to the customer; pre-1914, it was trying to prevent price-cutting.

The reference in the recommendation of the council of the Association to the bottle is also another echo of World War I. Soon after the 1915 passing of the Immature Spirits Act, the larger blending and distributing houses ceased to supply bulk whisky to their trade customers in order to retain their stocks for their bonded goods, a conserving of whisky which accentuated the then growing shortage to which reference has already been made. Then with the restriction of releases, and supplies to customers from 1 April 1917 of fifty per cent of the 1916 releases purchases, bottled whisky made yet another advance: in order to tie retailers, the trade considered, to the distributors, who took advantage of the 1917 position to strengthen their proprietary brands, supplies were, as a rule, though not quite entirely, refused in bulk and limited only to bottled whiskies. The trade, especially in Scotland, held – vociferously – that it was 'absolutely contrary to the spirit of the regulations', but contrary or not, the bottled product was completing its victory, was here to stay.

An adjective the then Chancellor of the Exchequer was quick to seize on best described the situation of the whisky industry in 1917 – 'artificial'. Artificial because there was government-enforced restriction and direction of releases from bond, but no control of prices. That soon came about, and in a manner and to a degree never forgotten by the industry. Distilling itself, except for war and yeast purposes, was then forbidden, and the general situation thus heightened in its artificiality. A syndicate of some of the biggest houses was buying up single whiskies on a large scale, although in no immediate need of further supplies themselves – and it is of further significance and a note of things to come that these large blenders, distributors, etc., should combine in a syndicate to do so.

A pre-budget restriction, 1918, came into force: an Excise order limiting clearances from bond of whisky for the fortnight preceding the introduction of the Budget to a 'daily average', or $\frac{1}{154}$ part of the quantity permitted under the previous authority to withdraw and for the six months ending 30 September. It was forecast that the most drastic addition to be expected would make the base figure for spirits taxation 30s. the proof gallon, and thereby get pre-war revenue from a fifty per cent consumption. The forecast was remarkably accurate: that is just what the budget did, raised the duty from 14s. 9d. to 30s. the proof gallon. Yet it was observed: 'It can safely be said that the Trade never before regarded an increased tariff on spirits with such imperturbability; and naturally so long as the man-in-the-street is willing, even glad, to pay 10s. a bottle for whisky 30 under proof.'

It was a bad April that year, as bad on the home front to many as it undoubtedly was to others on the Western Front and on the Atlantic. Bonar Law – 'The Unknown Prime Minister' as he was known as later – introduced the budget on the 22nd and immediately afterwards there came the Government-fixed prices, with the trade absorbing part of the increased duty.

First Bonar Law, the Canadian of Scots extraction orphaned back to Scotland. Warming to his proposals, he said: 'The House will not be surprised to learn that I propose to get additional revenue out of the spirit and beer trade. The trade, as everyone knows, is in a position which is entirely artificial. On the one hand, the commodity is so scarce and the desire for it is so great – I know in some quarters they do not desire it – but the desire is so great that sellers, if left to themselves, could obtain practically any price. It is, therefore, a monopoly. On the other hand, the condition is artificial because prices are regulated by the Food Controller. As regards spirits, the present duty is 14s. 9d. I propose to make that duty 30s., or an addition of 15s. 3d. per proof gallon.' (How dominated by Lloyd George – and yet the instrument of his 1922 overthrow.) 'That will bring in during the present year £10,500,000, and in the full year £11,150,000. I have, in coming to this decision, not only examined the figures most carefully, but I have consulted many of those connected with the industry, whose advice is worth having, and I have no doubt whatever that the trade, at the prices fixed by the Food Controller, which will be announced to-morrow, can pay the additional duty and still make reasonable profits.'

The 'most important event of the year' was how Graham Menzies, chairman, described it at the annual meeting in the following July of the D.C.L., voicing the general feeling of the industry when he said: 'Regarded merely as a necessity for raising additional revenue in war-time the Trade has shouldered this enormous burden without a grudge, but they do so in full belief that when taxation comes to be revised they will receive equal consideration with other taxpayers in a lightening of the burden.' (We are still waiting.)

But in the House on 22 April, Sir J. D. Rees said he 'thought that the tax upon beer and spirits was excessive. The Revolution in Russia and the evils which had followed in its train, and are still multiplying, were due, he believed, quite as much . . . to the prohibition of the spirit traffic, which was far more instrumental in producing the Russian Revolution, as to the faults of the Romanoffs, who were not half so bad as was generally supposed.' Colonel W. Thorne said 'he knew that in this case what the Chancellor was aiming at was to make the brewers and the distillers pay, but they would find means of passing it on to the consumer'.

When the House considered the budget resolutions in Report on 1 May, Bonar Law returned to his *motif* of the 22nd, saying that 'the whole Trade was in an absolutely artificial condition, and . . . he was told by those who were good judges that a further increase in price would have led to industrial unrest. With regard to the margin of profit, the conditions were so vague and so difficult to adjust that whatever figure was fixed upon, it ran the risk of being unfavourable to one section or the other. The whole matter had been gone into

The peat fire for drying the malted barley

The dried and ground malt is mashed

carefully, and they had come to the conclusion that the duty as fixed was fair to everyone concerned and not least to the Treasury.' Later he quoted 'representatives of the Trade' as being of the opinion that the duty was 'not unfair', but – 'they said he was going to the extreme limit', and Bonar Law himself 'would not have been surprised had there been a good deal of opposition on the part of the brewers'.

The *Wine and Spirit Trade Record* was not wholehearted in its judgment of the budget and the Government's fixed prices, which had not been considered so carefully as claimed: they had shortly to be quite recast. 'It could, of course, be argued,' remarked the *Record* leader, 'that there is no adequate reason why the duty should not be put at 30s. *as a war measure*.' And it was a first principle that the duty was always passed on, but 'to expect, as the new Price Order does, that one-third of the extra spirit duty should be borne by the Trade is a departure which must be resented to the utmost, not only by the spirit trade, but by every other which handles a dutiable commodity. Because if it is whisky today, it may be tobacco tomorrow.'

The retail trade was satisfied with the prices fixed but the rest of the trade was far from it. It was considered that the wholesale price in bond of 20s. less fifteen per cent per regauge proof gallon for three-year-old whisky was altogether inadequate and inequitable. (That figure was doomed: the press bureau initially sent out the figure of 29s.) This spelt the end to the small blender, and as to the broker – it seemed just another nail in the coffin. The price-fixing also held this danger to the larger houses: they would be left in sole possession of the field and the risk of their being taken over by the Government on unsatisfactory terms was all the more increased.

In brief, four prices were fixed, depending on category and strength of the whisky, the prices being 8s., 8s. 6d., 9s. and 9s. 6d. per bottle of 70 degrees proof. The prices for the four bottled categories were laid down throughout the industry and prices were also fixed for bulk supplies. The price was also fixed for the bar sale, per gill, quartern or noggin and for any other part of licensed premises than the public bar. We need not here pursue the details of this misguided plan, described, for instance, by Wm Longmore & Co. Ltd as 'an amazing production . . . drafted by someone with only a very meagre knowledge of trade conditions . . . The situation would really be laughable were it not so serious.'

Though Peter Mackie was a little kinder: 'The scheme of categories drawn up by Mr Roffey's Department is quite a good one, and we hope he will stick to it, and, although prices are low and not all that might be desired, yet he gives the public a choice of different qualities at reasonable prices. To revert to a flat rate would be the greatest folly, especially as if the prices were fixed on the level of the lower quality brands and a flat rate was carried into effect on this basis, the high class brands would require to lower their quality to sell on the level of the low class brands. The Trade should level up, not down, and we hope Mr Roffey will not listen to any such proposal.'

Others were as vocal, but it is unnecessary to quote them here. By the end of May, the trade was prepared to see the four categories wiped out, and replaced by a price verging on the former 9s. 6d. a bottle limit. By the end of June the meeting had been held in Edinburgh and the decision taken to form a Scottish branch of the Whisky Association and Ross, who was later chosen as chairman, received the O.B.E. for the magnificent job – worthy of much more than the distinction granted – he did as leader of the distillers in ensuring the British victory. The whisky brokers addressed a lengthy and closely reasoned letter to the Food Controller pointing out the deficiencies of the Spirits (Prices and Description) Order, 1918, fixing prices and establishing categories and grades.

By mid-August a new Spirit Prices Order was issued, and without going too closely into details suffice it to say that a bottle of whisky at 30 u.p. was to retail at 9s. the bottle, or reputed quart. Proportionate prices were fixed for smaller sizes and weaker strengths as well as for location of sale. Bulk was to sell at 50s. per gallon. Sales to licensed traders were fixed at 100s. per case, or 47s. 6d. per gallon, with the 30 u.p. rule in each instance. Sales in bond were at 20s. per regauge proof gallon less a discount of a minimum of fifteen per cent, and duty paid sales at 42s. per gallon of 30 u.p. less a minimum discount of twelve and a half per cent. Bottled sold in bond at 30 u.p. could not exceed 45s. per case less a discount minimum of 6s. per case and duty paid not exceeding 87s. 6d. per case less a discount minimum of 6s. per case.

The discussion in the trade continued, the Whisky Association council issued recommendations on invoicing and discounts and on this momentous matter, as follows:

'Sale of only one and the leading brand.

'That all companies and firms should sell one brand only and that the leading one, at 87s. 6d. per case and at no lesser price.

'It is considered that the only safe procedure for distillers and blenders to adopt is to charge the maximum prices named in the Order for bulk or case, otherwise unfair discrimination will be set up as between a trader who is accustomed to buy direct from a distiller or blender and one who buys through a wholesale house.' It was recommended that all other discounts should be abolished and there should be cash payment within seven days.

The Prices Order dealt, of course, with other spirits and led to confusion and disagreement in their connection, but a general spirits recommendation of the Manchester Brewers' Central Association is worth noticing: 'You are recommended,' it ran, 'only to serve out of bottles.' In short, bury bulk spirits. And the *Record* picked on a point buried in the fine text of the Order which it had interpreted for readers: 'This Order defines for the first time a wholesale sale as more than two gallons and a retail sale as any sale other than a wholesale one, i.e. two gallons or less.'

Omitting detailed consideration here of all the criticisms and queries arising from the Order, it will be enough to give the judgment of that industry's premier statesman, William Ross, who wrote on the Order: 'I give credit' to the Food Controller and assistants, 'for having done their best to remove many of the hardships and difficulties of the original Order . . . The most serious blot which remains is the price of 20s. per regauge proof gallon fixed as a maximum for spirits of all ages and all qualities . . . Pointed out again and again that the price was inadequate to cover some of the finer and older grades of whisky . . . One has to remember that whisky is a commodity not at present being produced, and, therefore, something more than mere interest and actual expenses is required to cover the shrinkage in value of goodwill and the high percentage exacted for income tax and excess profits duty . . . The authorities concerned either cannot or will not see the difference between this commodity – whisky – the manufacture of which has been absolutely stopped for the time being, and other commodities which, however restricted, are still being produced.'

'It is difficult to excuse the absolute unfairness,' went on Ross later, 'of including single whiskies in an Order at a fixed price per regauge proof gallon. It is only little over three years since Mr Lloyd

George brought in the Immature Spirits Bill which was to protect the public from the alleged evil effects of immature whisky. Most reputable firms even before the passing of this Act were in the habit of supplying the public with much older whisky than this. Now it seems this attempt to please the public has all been a mistake, and the firms who have prided themselves on giving the oldest whisky are to be compelled to realise a lower price than those who supply an article only just over the required three years' standard. Verily this war has opened our eyes to many things, but the vagaries of government departments are as obscure as ever!'

As to single whiskies, Ross wrote: 'I suggested that these whiskies should at least be allowed to be sold at the original instead of the regauge proof gallon, and proposed that if a maximum price for blended whiskies was retained at 20s. per regauge proof gallon, the price of single whiskies might be fixed at 18s. per original proof gallon. The difference of 2s. per gallon would be sufficient to cover the loss by evaporation during the first five years, while any further loss beyond that period should be borne by the buyer, who would get increased value in the age of the whisky for the small loss in quantity he would be asked to bear . . . This modest suggestion was turned down, with the result that many of the oldest parcels of single whiskies will be held up "for the duration", or until we revert to the normal position governed by the natural law of supply and demand.'

As a provincial firm put it in a mood of bitterness at the rapidly changing world in which whisky now moved: 'The intention seems to be to try and eliminate the wholesale distributor by the proprietors of the advertised whiskies, and to fix the bulk with no discrimination between a three-year-old and a ten-year-old or older, which is simply putting a premium on cheapness.'

One other result was simply to bring the whisky trade within the Trade to a standstill. There was created a deadlock felt more keenly as time went on, and resolved, in the main, as firms withdrew from the industry by amalgamation as the favourite technique of getting out while they could.

What also resulted from the fixed maximum prices was that these became the normal: there were none below them. Categories of whisky disappeared, as recommended by the Whisky Association, the biggest blenders reduced their operations to one brand a piece, they further declined to give a retailer the discount reserved for the wholesaler – 'perfectly reasonable' was the verdict – and registered clubs were included, for the first time, in the category of licensed traders. This was considered 'most objectionable' from the trade point of view, and interpreted as a vote-catching expedient to the numerous political clubs.

It was the passing of an era for Scotch whisky and the commencement of a new age. A death in the October of the year epitomised it all, that of Sir Oliver Riddell, born in 1844, knighted in 1904, and who passed the sixtieth anniversary of his service with Andrew Usher & Co. just before his death. 'He was one of the first, if not *the* first, Scotchmen,' it was written, 'to introduce blended Scotch whisky into England.' And before long that firm was to be absorbed into the rapidly growing D.C.L. as budget-inspired amalgamations proceeded apace.

By the end of the year, the war had ended, but no end was in sight of the Central Control Board restrictions imposed on the trade and nation. The distillers, still prohibited from distilling, asked to be allowed to resume 'as soon as the food supply of the country is assured'. The consumers and the trade, it was claimed, had 'the right alike to demand that the alcoholic strength of the various beverages be restored to the pre-war standard'.

'All restrictions on the selling prices of wholesalers, if not on the price to the consumer should be removed as early as possible,' it was said. 'So long as the ultimate maximum selling price is fixed, all the other gradations may be left to find their own level. The removal of the maximum selling price to the consumer is a more difficult proposition. The present retail maximum selling price is quite high enough. Little ultimate benefit will be derived from profiteering, and no world-wide demand is likely to be built up on an article of inferior quality at an exorbitant price.'

Lloyd George in the Khaki Election again tried to smear the trade by writing in his election manifesto of the 'Traffic in Drink' and Lord d'Abernon returned to the attack at the head of the prohibitionists with a paper on 'Rival Theories of the Causes of Drunkenness'. American whiskey began appearing on the British market, despite trade difficulties placed in its way by government departments. Quite unexpectedly, in February 1919, the fifty per cent of 1916 releases for the home market was raised by half, making them seventy-five per cent of the 1916 total. Some distilling, at pot still distilleries, was allowed again – under licence from the Ministry of Food, a fantastically detailed regulation which provoked the cry from Bowmore distillery that 'We would be glad to know whether we can utilise the malt as made, into the natural spirit product of our distillery at Bowmore, when, and how we please.' The Ministry withdrew and in any case there was little inclination to start up.

The lesson was not lost on the new Chancellor of that season, what with the scarcity of labour, the high price of materials, from coal, transport and wood to cereals. As it was put, succinctly, 'A distiller might invest £10,000 this season, and the same the next, but the price he would get for his whisky when it was three years old is "wrapt in mystery".'

To revert to that measure of 'liberalisation' of the home drinker's ration. It was quickly taken up, despite the increased price resulting from the budget increase of 1918. The Customs and Excise Report, not published until August 1920 for the financial year 1918–19, revealed that some 15·6 million proof gallons of spirits were consumed in that year, against the anticipated – and planned – 14 million, and there was a surplus of nearly £3 million because of those increased clearances from late February on and because of the demobilisation spending spree as much as the curious piece of governmental book-keeping by which the Ministry of Munitions had to pay duty on over 1 million proof gallons because of failing to satisfy the revenue requirements governing the use of duty-free spirit. (The spirit was to be used for making poison gas.)

But the increase in spirit receipts was mainly because of 'the large increase in duties'. An ominous way of thinking in official circles, and well examined before publication of the report. It is a useful point at which to examine the ten-year figures. In the calendar year 1910 nearly 25·4 million proof gallons of home-made spirits were taxpaid in the United Kingdom; that fell to just over 24 million the following year, hovered around the 25 million mark for two years, passed the 26 million mark in 1913, only to slip back to 25 million in 1914. The next year, despite the minimum age requirement, with its one-year grace to younger, two-year-old, spirit, the figure moved well past the 28 million mark, only to slip back, what with the war intensifying and the growing shortage of matured spirit, to 22·6 million gallons in 1916. Then came the part-1917 restriction and consumption fell to little over

13 million gallons. In 1918, with the full fifty per cent restriction for the whole of the twelve months it was just under 11·5 million gallons.

But the figures of Excise receipts on home-made spirits reveal another side to it all. In the year ending 31 March 1910, the first full year of Lloyd George's 14s. 9d. duty, they amounted to £14·6 million, were over the £18 million mark for three years and in 1913–14 reached £19·5 million, to become £20 million and £21 million in the two following years. They slumped in 1916–17 with the fifty per cent restriction on clearances, and the financial year only produced £7·1 million in home-made spirits' receipts. Then came in Bonar Law's budget the more-than-doubling of the duty to 30s. and the slight enlargement on clearances we have noticed, so that by the end of the year on 31 March 1919 they amounted to £18·7 million.

The lesson was not lost on the new Chancellor of the Exchequer, a Liberal Unionist. Notice the word Liberal, with its Lloyd George connotations. He was Austen Chamberlain, secretary of state for India from 1915 to July 1917 when he resigned following the revelations of mismanagement of the 'Mespot' campaign. He entered the War Cabinet early in 1918 and later became Chancellor, presenting in all three budgets – from 1919 to 1921 – which truly betrayed Lloyd George's dominating influence, at least as regards 'the drink traffic' and prohibition by taxation. Indeed, so close was his adherence to Lloyd George and so much dissatisfaction did it arouse that the October 1922 meeting at the Carlton Club was held that ousted him and colleagues of his opinion.

Then came the now customary restrictions on clearances prior to the budget, not, this time, restricting to 'daily averages' but allowing only one-sixth of the total permitted under control for the six months beginning 1 April. The budget was presented on the 30th of the month.

The Chamberlain speech on the occasion might have been a Lloyd George one. 'New taxation,' he remarked. 'I come first to spirits . . . It was found necessary to restrict the delivery of spirits from bond, as from the 1st April, 1917, to a limit not exceeding fifty per cent of the deliveries in 1916. Owing to a variety of causes, including the restriction just referred to, the increased duty on spirits, the operation of the Immature Spirits Act, and, I am afraid I must add, some withholding of stock, the supply of spirits fell short of the demand and the prices rose to an extent which led the Food Controller, in consultation with my predecessor, in the spring of last year, to limit them by imposing a maximum scale of prices which was announced by Budget Day, and provided for a substantial increase in duty. Two changes affecting the position have since occurred. In the first place, the scale of prices was revised in August so as to afford relief to a section of the Trade which had bought their stocks at somewhat inflated prices, and had not then had an opportunity of disposing of them. The quantities allowed to be delivered from bond were increased as from 24th February last from fifty per cent to seventy-five per cent of the quantities delivered in 1916, bringing the authorised clearance up to 21·4 million gallons a year.

'Both of these changes have further increased the profits of the Trade and they are now in the aggregate more than my predecessor estimated, and more than I think reasonable. And the Committee will not be surprised to know that I propose to ask that, at any rate, part of these profits should be diverted to the Exchequer by a further increase in spirit duty from 30s. to 50s. per proof gallon. This increase will involve some readjustment of Trade prices to prevent the burden falling unequally on different sections of the Trade. The scale consequently is being revised so as to distribute the additional duty as equitably as possible throughout. The alteration will only affect the consumer in a few cases, such as the price of spirits sold to him in bottle, or in jar or cask. Owing to the great rise in the cost of bottling and the prices fixed for the bottle and the glass respectively, the sale of spirits by glass has been much more remunerative than the sale by bottle, and I think that some of the difficulties complained of in the early part of the year during the epidemic of influenza in reference to the obtaining of spirits were due to this cause. The increase will produce an additional revenue of £21,650,000 in the full year on the present authorised amount of clearance.'

The main alterations, in the fixed prices based on a bottle at 30 u.p., were that the maximum price per bottle for 'off' consumption was raised to 10s. 6d. and the price per jar to 58s. per gallon. On any other sale to private customers the maximum prices remained unaltered. As regards traders' prices, the special schedule affecting sales of small quantities to licensed traders was abolished and in the schedule governing sales to licensed traders the maximum price of bulk spirits sold in bond was 15s. per regauge proof gallon less a minimum discount of fifteen per cent; when sold duty paid was 52s. per gallon, less a minimum discount of ten per cent; as regards spirits sold in bottle, the maximum price for its bond sale was 32s. per case, and when sold duty paid 103s. per case, both prices subject to a minimum discount of 6s. per case. The precise details of all the schedules need not detain us here.

The *Record* expressed the more rational and less violent reactions of the trade: 'When the duty was doubled in 1918 a most unconstitutional act was committed by its being made impossible for the Trade to transfer the additional burden to the shoulders of the public. Now the same enormity is being repeated in an accentuated form, the only transferable part of the latest increase being the 1s. 6d. added to the retail price of "reputed quarts" . . . It was Mr Austen Chamberlain's intention to make the Trade bear the whole of the additional impost, and it was at the last moment that he consented to mulct the buyer of a bottle in an extra eighteen-pence . . . No other trade has ever been dealt with on the lines now adopted for the second time in regard to our Trade . . . Strong protests are being made by the representatives of every section – distiller, blender, distributor and retailer.'

The Whisky Association issued a manifesto beginning, 'The simple solution of the whisky trouble is to free the controls. Let competition regain its pre-war sway, and the questions of price and quality will soon be settled in the interests of the public.' Of which we will hear more later. The wine and spirit deputation, the greatest of its kind ever seen, waited upon the Chancellor on 13 May. That met with stubborn opposition only, and a reading of the verbatim note reveals the enemy within our midst with whom we have annually to struggle.

18

Post-war budgets (ii)

First, the Whisky Association's manifesto following Austen Chamberlain's 1919 budget when he raised the duty on whisky from 30s. to 50s. the proof gallon and the continuance of the system by which the trade was unable to pass on the increase to the consuming public.

After asserting, as we have seen, that the solution lay in the abolition of control and the restoration of pre-war competition, the manifesto went on to a brief résumé of the outstanding trials of the war years: reduction in strength, curtailment of releases, restriction and prohibition of distillation. On the reduction in strength, the manifesto sums up: 'We want to emphasise the point that we distillers have from the very beginning resisted all attempts of the Government to water the whisky that is sold to the public. We have stood for decent whisky all the time. We are not responsible for the short supply, neither can we be called to account for spurious whisky. We tried our utmost to prevent both.'

Then to the all-important question of price: 'The distillers have no qualms of conscience on the question of price. It is not they who are the profiteers. The proposed Government price is 103s. per case. Of that the Government itself immediately takes 70s. for duty – very nearly two-thirds. Who is profiteering here? The case and bottles, corks, capsules, labels, and other incidentals cost 10s. at present prices, and another 2s. goes on delivery leaving 21s. or 1s. 9d. per bottle. If we supply through a middleman it is necessary to allow him 6s. per case, or 6d. per bottle, which further reduces the amount remaining for the distiller to 1*s*. 3*d*. per bottle. For this he has to supply one-sixth of a gallon of whisky, pay his establishment expenses, make a profit, and replace his stocks, which now cost about three times his pre-war price.' What they feared might result was the penetration of the market by whisky of 'the lowest quality' – the present day quality keynote was by then in the ascendant.

That quality note was resumed with the observation that while some of the public were paying anything from 20*s*. to 23*s*. for 'small whiskies', the distillers and distributors wanted only a few pence more per bottle – 'to enable them to give the best quality. If that is profiteering,' continues the manifesto, 'we have yet to learn the meaning of the word.' For this was the dilemma: 'The volume of our trade has been restricted by government intervention, whilst our establishment charges have increased in addition to the costs of production.'

We have mentioned that certain other spirits were controlled by the same Orders, and the manifesto now turns to them: 'The same price is fixed for Gin and Rum as for the finest Whisky. Gin is consumed new. A gin distiller can turn his money over perhaps seven times in a year. A whisky distiller or dealer is not allowed to turn it over more than once in three years and in practice it works out more nearly once in seven years.'

Then back to the abandoned differentiation of four qualities made in 1918, then abandoned in favour of one quality, and one price: 'The authorities now intend to make all whisky the same price, the lowest quality the same as the best. This may mean that the lowest quality whisky may get the market, and that the public will ultimately be driven to undesirable substitutes . . . We say deliberately that a Government duty of 50*s*. per proof gallon of the alcohol contained in whisky is a tax calculated to kill the trade in whisky. It is almost incredible, but it is true, that Port Wine, which is fortified by spirit, comes into this country at a duty per proof gallon of its constituent alcohol of 7*s*. 4*d*. Why,' they ask, 'this discrimination against alcohol in whisky?'

The statistical problem was dealt with: 'The shortage is very largely accounted for by the fact that distillation was stopped for two years by the Government and that the whisky which is now being distilled must be kept in bond for a minimum of three years under the provisions of the Immature Spirits Act. It is entirely untrue to suggest that the export

Scotch: the formative years

trade is being favoured, so far as supplies are concerned, at the expense of the home trade. Under the old Order we were asked to supply fifty per cent of the 1916 supply. The figures show that the home trade has received its full quantity under that Order, whilst the export trade obtained in 1918 only thirty-two and a quarter per cent of the allocation to which it is entitled.'

It closed with an appeal for freedom: 'The demand of the whisky trade is the same as that now being made by all other trades which have suffered from Government "controls" during the war. Let those controls be removed and competition restored, and the public will have no cause to complain of price or quality, or, in the long run, of quantity either.'

Second, that deputation from sections of the trade to the Chancellor in the middle of the not-so-merry month of May 1919. Austen Chamberlain was supported by a fine pack of henchmen, to wit, H. A. L. Fisher, C. A. M'Curdy – parliamentary secretary to the Ministry of Food – three from H.M. Customs and Excise – Sir Laurence Guillemard, Sir William Gallagher and Mr O'Brien, while private secretary R. P. M. Gower was in attendance. The deputation was most representative; it was headed by Mr Walter A. Sandeman, chairman of the Wine and Spirit Association; Mr R. Harford, deputy chairman of the same Association, was also present, and the others were: Messrs R. Montgomery, chairman of the Whisky Association; A. P. Threlfall, chairman of the United Provincial Wholesale Wine and Spirit Association; W. H. Ross and W. Williamson, of the D.C.L. and Haig & Haig Ltd, respectively, and representing the whisky distillers; R. F. Nicholson, for the Rectifiers' Association; Chas H. Lamb, for rum; P. McKechnie, chairman of the Off-Licence Association; W. Harrison, as representing the Whisky Association; Augustus Day, for the Wine Merchants' Union; A. B. J. Norris, secretary of the Wine and Spirit Association, and J. King Stewart, secretary of the Whisky Association.

The mind and approach of the Chancellor became immediately clear, and Chamberlain's bearing throughout illustrates, first, how the Chamberlain family made their commercial success in Birmingham, secondly, why the era he personifies is still distrusted, if not hated in certain quarters, still today. Above all, for our present purposes, an examination of the working of the conference and of the 'mind of the

258

Chancellor' can be of value even at this space in time. An old saying, but true: Know your enemy – and never before or since has the progress of such an encounter as this been made fully public.

Mr Sandeman began by introducing the team and immediately got down to the real purpose of the deputation: the discussion of 'this proposed taxation and duty. It is really, barring a small amount which the Trade is allowed to pass on to the customer, a direct tax on the Trade, and I presume you intended it to be so'.

Chamberlain's riposte was brief and to the point: 'That, of course, was the intention in this case.'

A protest was made at this and a review was made of the 'enormous increase' proposed of 20s. in addition to the previous year's addition of 15s. 3d. Mr Harford gave a long and detailed review: as to the allegation of booming times, they were not so for the time just ahead and were gradually ending. Then the great increase in capital needed for the duty change – 'which must cripple a very large number of traders'. Pre-war, the duty on a puncheon of rum, for instance, was £84; at time of deputation it was £370. Thirdly, it was unfair to the spirit trade to be singled out for this 'exceedingly heavy taxation', adding: 'We believe it is quite an innovation in the finances of this country that any trade should have to bear a large proportion of the duty without being able to pass it on to the consumer.'

There followed a long and detailed review of the period, from which a few enlightening instances only are culled here: trade profits had recently been higher than pre-war, largely because of maturing stocks which were being used up and of which, with interrupting to distilling, there would be no replacement for a long time. They had all had to buy at high market prices and as to excess profits, the state already took eighty per cent in excess profits duty. Wages were up; prices were up: pot still whisky was now fetching 10s. 6d. a gallon on filling new; then the cash would have to be locked up for a minimum of three years (five to six for a high-class whisky) making the gallon worth 15s. at the end. Which all meant they could not afford to sell at the fixed price less fifteen per cent, except at heavy loss. New grain whisky was comparatively cheaper, but thousands of gallons had, because of shortages, to be bought at prices similar to pot still whisky. To Chamberlain, who wished to reduce the price from 10s. 6d. a bottle to 9s., Harford replied: 'We have a grievance in regard to the incidence of the duty that we cannot pass it on.' To which Sandeman added: 'The argument, I think, is that the duty as a whole is too high.'

After further indecisive threshing, the chairman of the Whisky Association, Montgomery, introducing himself as a 'poor Irish distiller', asked leave to call upon Mr W. H. Ross, chairman of the Scottish Branch, and managing director of the D.C.L. – the biggest whisky concern in the country if not in the world. Ross handed in a copy of the speech, and a few salient points, indicating the trend of the trade under the stress of war and heavy taxation, the changing nature and struggle of it, are all there is space for here. Pre-war stocks often gave an inadequate return and during the war supplies were sent out 'from carefully husbanded stocks'. There was a profit, yes, but – 'Are they to receive no consideration for the risks they originally took, for interest on the money they have embarked on this stock, and for the fact that these stocks when sold have to be *replaced* by others at fully three times the original cost? . . . Neither in assessing him (the merchant) for income-tax nor in the amount claimed for excess profits duty was this factor allowed for by the Inland Revenue, and hence it was quite impossible for most firms to make adequate provision for this contingency.' This was particularly applicable to the smaller firms who relied on buying singles on the market for their blends, and, went on Ross: 'The passing of the Immature Spirits Act led to a number of these smaller firms to see the unwisdom of trusting to the open market for their supplies of whisky . . . Even before the present budget and revised control prices came into force they found it difficult to make ends meet.'

'Was it,' he asked, 'the Government's intention to run 'em out of business?' To which he replied: 'We hear sometimes that the Trade is fast becoming the monopoly of a few large firms. Sir, I would have you believe that this is far from being the case, but if anything will encourage such a condition it will arise through the operation of this kind of budget and the Controlled Prices Order, which the larger houses in the interest of their smaller brethren now ask you to amend.'

The plea was succeeded by a long and detailed comparison on the taxation of alcohol in spirits and in wine (which brought no concurrence from Chamberlain, but sowed the seeds for his 1920 budget when he dared recast the wine duties which had not been changed since 1899).

We cannot here pursue all members' speeches in detail, but may note that when Nicholson (Gin Rectifiers), protesting that the rectifiers did not want the high prices, said that '10s. 6d. for a bottle of spirits is a fraud', Chamberlain butted in to exclaim, 'I have a strong objection to it myself,' adding a moment later, 'But I reluctantly gave way to other people and agreed that 1s. 6d. should be given to the Trade.' A revealing aside. And when Sandeman introduced Mr W. Harrison of the Whisky Association, the Chancellor said that he was 'sorry', wished no more deputations and that 'unfortunately the trades concerned, or the various bodies concerned in these trades, cannot be got together at one moment or in one deputation'. Nevertheless, Harrison set about endorsing everything Ross had said, gave most interesting and valuable sidelights on the trade of James Buchanan and W. P. Lowrie, rising to this conclusion that with small firms pressed, 'you may be faced eventually with a condition of affairs when you will get no whisky for the consumers we had in 1916'. Chamberlain immediately revealed his own approach and character by interjecting the question whether this latter point meant 'the suggestion or the argument that the price must always be fixed, not at all to the average of the trade, what a good business under reasonable conditions can do, but to the pace of the lamest horse in the trade?'

Harrison persevered, and said that on 1918's price, 'the big firms gained, but you on your side took it eventually in another way from us . . . The position is exactly as it was last year, even a little worse, because the stocks are not there'.

At which Chamberlain asked would they like control abolished altogether? To which all agreed, 'Yes.' Chamberlain, 'Assuming that you cannot have that for the time' did they favour prohibition of credit sales? To which Harrison said they scarcely existed in the wholesale trade: the retailer paid in seven days; there was no lock-up of capital there, the lock-up of capital was in the stocks.

In his reply to the deputation, Chamberlain began by sneering at the 'splendid isolation . . . of the industry' and reminded them that 'on beer also the tax has been heavily increased'. Then as to excess company tax, it had been 'reduced to half of what it was, the extra profits duty, and that is something to set against any new burden on whisky . . . You had your increased sales of whisky some time ago,' he went on, 'without any corresponding increase of the duty. [Must the two gang thegither?] Now whatever duty you could afford to pay when the sales were on the lower level you can afford to pay an increased duty when you have increased sales.'

To which Montgomery replied, 'No; we are exhausting our stocks.' Chamberlain: 'Do you mean to tell me that a business cannot make increased profits when it has an increased turnover?' Montgomery: 'No; we do not want an increased turnover.' Chamberlain: 'There I believe you; I think that is the truth.' Montgomery: 'If we could brew every month and sell every month we could do it.' Chamberlain: 'You say you do not want an increased turnover.' Montgomery: 'We want it if we can afford it.' Chamberlain: 'That really is rather a crucial observation. I have heard a great deal from you people today about people being unable to get spirits, and I am puzzled why they cannot get them, and then you come and tell me that you do not want an increased turnover. I think, perhaps, that explains why people cannot get spirits.'

To Montgomery's attempted explanation that they were using up their capital, Chamberlain made a long oration, here cut: 'I have some figures here, and it amazes me if it does not pay you. You have gone on steadily getting better and better years, from 1911 and 1912 onwards. Last year was not quite so good as the year before, but it was much better than any of the years immediately before the war . . . If you want me really to look into this matter further you must give me something to go upon, not broad general statements that you cannot do this or you might not be able to do that in the future, or that your replacement of stocks, coupled with your anticipation that presently the working man is not going to earn such big wages, and will not be able to pay so much, will ruin you in the years to come. Show me what profits you have been making, and how they have been destroyed by the tax, and then I shall have something concrete to go on, because at the present time all the information I have shows that you have a very handsome margin of profit left after the new taxation . . . As Chancellor of the Exchequer I want the biggest revenue I can get. It has always been the policy in this country to get out of alcohol . . . the largest revenue possible without stifling the Trade.' Illuminating.

After more broad dissertation, Chamberlain went on: 'I did not fix the figure of the tax arbitrarily. I did not fix it with the belief that you could not pay it. I fixed it with the belief that you could pay it and still get a handsome profit. If you put it to me that the distribution of the sum which you are allowed to take from the consumer amongst the different branches of the Trade, is not skilfully arranged, if you amongst yourselves as traders can come to some agreement on that point, I think the Food Controller would have no trouble in recognising your agreement in his scale . . . I should like to get more money out of wine. The only reason why I do not do it is because people do not buy wine. [Nearly 20 million gallons were drunk in 1919.] There are really two reasons: one is, I should have a European's hornet's nest about my ears, and the other is that wines do not respond to an increase in duty.' (In line with the politician's deception, his next budget made a slashing attack on wine, including an ill-fated *ad valorem* duty on sparkling wines, another attack on war-devastated Reims.)

Curtailing Chamberlain's eloquence, the last passage merits reproduction, and consideration by those in charge in our trade: 'I am not responsible for the control of the liquor Trade as the Chancellor of the Exchequer,' said Chamberlain. 'I am responsible with my colleagues for any control which the Government maintains . . . But when you are dealing with me, as Chancellor of the Exchequer, you must understand that this control is not imposed at the request of the Chancellor as a revenue measure . . . The control of the Trade is decided by the Government, and I, as Chancellor of the Exchequer, in fixing taxes apportion my taxes to the measures of control upon which the Goverment have decided; that is to say, that there being such and such an output and no more allowance by the Government, and such and such a price to be charged to the consumer and no more, I apportion my tax, as it were, between those two fixed points. But I am not imposing control as a revenue measure.'

Acting on the meeting thus summarily dismissed by Chamberlain, the Minister of Food convened a meeting of the Spirits Trade Advisory Committee on 27 May when all sections were represented; they fully discussed the bearing of the new taxation on their particular branches but arrived at no decision. They met again on 2 June, and again there was no result.

As Harrison put it at the June annual meeting of W. P. Lowrie & Co. Ltd, of which he was chairman, the consumer was 'not made to carry the whole 20s.' of the extra duty, and 'a proportion had to be borne by the distiller and blender' which all meant that 'whilst the larger firms might be able to bear it . . . it would hit very hardly the great majority of firms which had not been accustomed in pre-war time to carry large stocks, but had bought on the market to meet their actual requirements . . . The position of the whisky trade today is naturally much altered from that of pre-war days'. The shadows of the approaching amalgamations are growing shorter as they come nearer to hand.

Likewise a brief quote from the speech of the chairman of the D.C.L., Graham Menzies, at the annual meeting in July. After recalling some of the wartime efforts of the company, Menzies continued: 'In other words, the Government contemptuously kick from beneath their feet the ladder which has placed them in a position of safety.' The same theme was renewed by Ross in seconding the report when he also gave an outline of some his remarks at the May visitation to Chamberlain.

In December that year came the removal of all restrictions on clearances from bond for the home market, though the price structure and the 30 u.p. regulation remained. The Scottish branch of the Whisky Association met on 25 November, a week after the Food Controller's announcement of the ending of restrictions and issued a statement, also adopted at the London end, on the matter, allied with an appeal to patriotism in view of the mounting imports of American and Canadian whiskies. After analysing the position, the statement commented that the public must therefore accept less whisky than in 1916 – stocks would not allow more – as they were 'strongly opposed, in the interest of the general community, to any reduction in the age below the present limit of three years, and they [the committee] also regard it as essential to provide a better-class whisky for a different clientele at an average age of about seven years'. The committee also recommended those able 'to release as much as they can in order to make good the deficiency of those who are short of stocks'. The then current shortage of supplies, they noted, was 'more keenly felt amongst that class of the community who are accustomed to acquire their supplies in bottle . . . we recommend members who are prepared to release additional supplies to see that the class referred to is reasonably catered for at the controlled price of 10s. 6d. per bottle'.

Charles R. Adam, of Edinburgh, thought the Government's freeing of withdrawals would not have 'much effect in producing more whisky for public consumption. . . Candidly speaking, I consider the Government's section a mere dodge to throw the onus of the present shortage on to the shoulders of the Trade to save their own skins'.

Buchanan-Dewar displayed another facet of the industry's developing form, in line with what Ross said at the May meeting with Chamberlain, by issuing on 1 December a prospectus offering 1·5 million seven and a half per cent cumulative preference shares of £1 each at par as part of an issue of 2½ million, the remaining million the directors having agreed to purchase. It is noted that the profits for the half-year ending with September that year, 1919, were 'substantially in excess of those for the corresponding period of the previous year'.

Disregarding at this juncture the progress of the trade, the amalgamations, the voluntary liquidations, rising costs and increasing production and consumption, we must now come to Chamberlain's budget speech on 19 April. As Ross put it at the annual meeting of the Whisky Association in 1921, they did not approach him before the 1920 budget – his experiences at the May, 1919, meeting were no doubt decisive. Mr Ross's words at the annual meeting of the Association in 1921 bear the closest scrutiny and consideration as enunciating a policy of action: 'One of the primary duties of the Association in the near future,' he said, 'will be to try and have the duty reduced by the same steps as it has been increased. We are not likely ever again to see it down to the level of 11s. per gallon, but we could get it by easy stages in the direction of reduction until the duty arrives at a more reasonable figure than that at which it at present stands. Even if we can get a reduction to 50s. per gallon that will enable a decrease to be made in the retail price per bottle. If we can reduce the bottle price to even 10s. that will be a great step towards placing whisky on the popular platform it has hitherto enjoyed, as it is unlikely that the Trade can be maintained on its present basis at the existing rate of duty ... Not to indulge in a full dress deputation to the Chancellor of the Exchequer, but we should more appropriately address ourselves to converting the permanent officials of the Customs and Excise to the reasonableness of the request, and approach the Chancellor when his officials have been converted.'

The lessons of experience ... and from one of the great statesmen of the industry, if not the greatest. His words cannot be dismissed, and there is reason to believe that they have not been entirely disregarded since he uttered them.

But to revert to Chamberlain in April 1920, presenting his budget.

On spirits he had this to say, in full Lloyd George vein: 'At the time of my last Budget the delivery of spirits for Home consumption was still subject to restrictions. In November all restrictions upon supply were removed. The Trade is now free to clear to the full extent of the demand. Owing to a variety of causes, the cost of the manufacture of spirits, in which I include the cost of replacement of stock, has risen within the last year . . .

'Nevertheless, the removal of all restrictions on supply, coupled with the permitted scale of prices, leaves a margin of profit to the Trade which is still more than reasonable, and I propose now to appropriate a further share of that profit to the Exchequer. But the amount which I could obtain from this source is insufficient under the present circumstances. On this occasion I must ask the consumer, as well as the Trade, to contribute. With their combined help, which I am sure they will readily give, I propose to increase the duty by 22*s*. 6*d*. to 72*s*. 6*d*. a proof gallon. Prices will be adjusted accordingly, the retail price being raised by 2½*d*. per gill in public bars, and by 2*s*. per bottle. I estimate the increased duty will yield in the current year £23,500,000 of revenue, and in a full year £24,500,000.'

He then went on to attack beer, and, as forecast above, wine, untouched since 1899, and including an *ad valorem* extra duty on sparkling wines of fifty per cent, soon reduced to thirty-three and a half per cent, and done away with before the year was out. Later, Chamberlain himself admitted 'the immense increase in the spirits and beer duties', and that there had been 'a certain diversion of drinking from spirits and beer to wine'.

The Whisky Association organised a deputation including representatives of all sections of the trade interested in the sale of spirits to the Chancellor on 29 April. Chamberlain asked the sections in the delegation to confer with his official advisers 'to whom he gave permission to show the figures upon which his additional tax was based, and which figures, unless shown to be incorrect, left him no alternative but to believe that the Trade as a whole could bear the additional impost and could supply the needs of the public and still be left with a profit'. Nothing came of it. On the next day, another Spirits (Prices and Description) Order came into force, fixing prices on the basis of 30 u.p. and applying to whisky, British brandy, rum and British gin. In brief, sales to licensed traders for their trade fixed prices of 16*s*. 8*d*. in bulk in bond and per regauge proof gallon, less a discount of a minimum of fifteen per cent; duty paid, 66s. per gallon 30 u.p., less discount of a minimum of eight per cent; in bottle in bond, 36s. per case less discount of 6s. per case; duty paid, 137s. 6d. per case less the same discount. Off-sales, 12s. 6d. per reputed quart; in bulk 70s. per gallon. On sales and other price details need not detain us.

The *Record* comment in the leader was to the point: 'Everybody admits that the Chancellor of the Exchequer has a difficult task in making ends meet, but he would find things much easier if he were to cut down his expenses by reducing the number of Cuthberts and Gerties who spend most of their time in creating work for one another to do.' (Times do not change!) Then, 'From the Trade point of view, the two principal flaws in the Budget are the *ad valorem* duty on Champagne and the impossibility of passing on the whole of the increased spirit duty to the consumer.' And again, later, 'Once again the Trade is compelled to bear a portion of the extra duty – a high-handed act on the part of the Chancellor which is as unjust as it is unconstitutional. The object appears to be that of squeezing out the smaller houses in the Trade with a view to State purchase of the bigger ones later on. Raising revenue is apparently a secondary consideration.'

Some small consolation was offered the whisky industry in the royal birthday honours: P. J. Mackie and J. H. Stewart were made baronets, while Sir Alexander Walker was created K.B.E. Graham Menzies, chairman of the D.C.L., found the trade's outlook 'rather obscure' at the annual meeting in July, except that 'the need for fresh capital' was very clear. Ross, seconding the Chairman's report, said that with the 1918 and 1919 increases and the easing of withdrawals, the results had justified them from a revenue point of view, but – 'When Mr Chamberlain again returned to the docile cow for a further augmentation this year of 22s. 6d. per gallon . . . it was time for the Trade to protest . . . the price of whisky to the public has been controlled for the last four years . . . the Trade was fairly well protected when the control price was first put on, the margin then allowed has been twice cut into through the Trade having been prevented from passing on to the public the whole increase in duty placed on spirits on the last two occasions . . . As the larger whisky companies seemed to be very prosperous and making lots of money they could well afford to contribute more to the Exchequer,' was the explanation given by the Chancellor, said Ross, who continued, 'It was in vain that we pointed out that these profits were largely being made out of stocks acquired previous to the war and that after paying all the Imperial taxes now being exacted . . . there was not sufficient left to replace the original stocks at the greatly enhanced cost of new whisky.' He closed by observing that 'ready cash requires replenishing' and the capital was to be raised from £2·5 million to £4 million.

An equally important development of the increased taxation of whisky, one most actively with us today, was emphasised in his address at the annual meeting in 1921 by the Chairman of the Whisky Association, Mr Montgomery, when he said: 'Although it was generally assumed that the Trade would revert to the pre-war strength of 20 u.p., it was impossible for them to do so, because the public could not be induced to pay more than 12s. 6d. per bottle, and even that sum most reluctantly, and a higher strength could only be supplied at a correspondingly higher price. The first step in reverting to pre-war strength must necessarily be for the Government to abate something of the savage duty at present imposed . . . There was a disposition on the part of the retail Trade to claim a return to credit principles, but it was obviously impossible to pay cash in advance to the Government to the extent of more than four times the value of their product, give credit and at the same time good value . . . It was not sound policy to pay 72s. 6d. of duty per gallon except on whisky of the finest grade.'

This latter principle has ever since dominated the industry, and is one of the battle scars which is by no means a disfigurement.

19

Scotch exports progress

SCOTCH WHISKY, as we have already seen, has been an export since the days it first left its home in the Highlands and Islands, teamed up with its Lowland kinsman and crossed the border to conquer the English market. Impelled by its own power of penetration it proceeded to percolate into the markets of the world, under the impetus, as previously noted, of those most skilled of modern salesmen, the Scots.

At the beginning of this century something around five million proof gallons were shipped abroad. Pressed by the recession in the home market, those overseas sales had risen by the time of the royal commission on Potable Spirits – the 'What Is Whisky?' inquiry of 1908–9 – to some seven million and a half. That advance was steady up to the outbreak of the World War I in 1914, and although we have examined already some of that advance and the movement even of the previous century, a few outstanding points in general deserve recording.

On the eve of that movement upwards to seven million and a half, and aided, in the event, by the Australian fixture of a compulsory minimum age, Scotch sales in the Antipodes made such advances in 1907 that the *Record* felt impelled to comment that 'Australia is still going strong and has beaten the 1906 total by about 90,000 proof gallons, with, as was to be expected, a satisfactory rise in value. In 1908 we should see this magnificent market for Scotch Whisky well over the two million gallons total, while there is no doubt that the standard of value will be correspondingly maintained. Recent legislation will make certain upon this score, and whatever temporary difficulties may arise there can be little doubt as to the ultimate satisfaction which will follow upon the institution of an age limit for whisky.' That age limit was two years, and just as the age limit introduced into the United Kingdom, in 1915, assured the quality role and place of Scotch on the home market, so that enforced age limit in overseas markets has been of paramount importance in ensuring the established niche of Scotch whisky today in the markets of the world, a point to which frequent reference will hereafter be made.

Also coming into prominence of a sort was the American market, and late in 1909, it was observed that: 'For the last few years the U.S. market has been receiving a large measure of attention from the exporters of British and Irish whisky. That success has attended their efforts is a matter for much satisfaction, for a twofold reason. First, the exacting nature of the requirements of American consumers of whisky, and second, the very large extent of protection afforded the manufacturers of the native product ... Last year the million gallon mark was exceeded, and the present year, unless something very unforeseen happens, will show a still further advance ... In the United States there is a highly paradoxical position of the apparent advance of Prohibition on the one hand, and over against this is the paternal solicitude displayed by the Federal authorities for the native distilling industry, as well as the whole-hearted manner in which they lay a firm hand upon the revenue from imported liquors ... Altogether it may be said that the present position of whisky in the United States is full of interest and encouragement to Scotch and Irish exporters.' Every facet of that quotation will necessitate examination in due course.

But something 'very unforeseen' was on the verge of happening in that market while the *Record* was writing. With Britain in the midst of a 'What Is Whisky?' inquiry, the United States did the same. President Theodore Roosevelt appointed a commission of inquiry, and prominent Scottish exporters immediately set up their own Scottish Whisky Exporters' Association. This was well before, for instance, the 1909 Lloyd George budget, and is but one more example of the pioneering spirit of export in the Scotch whisky trade well before that budget: that budget did nothing, I repeat nothing, to introduce the export element into the trade. Frederick Reid Sanderson, then head of Robertson, Sanderson & Co. Ltd, whose brand 'Mountain Dew' was probably the outstanding Scotch then sold in America, was one of the first in

Scotland, in 1908, to see the danger and relevance of Roosevelt's commission, especially as some Scotch whisky shipments were seized. In reply to his urgent messages to New York the importing firm replied: 'The firms on this side seem rather indifferent just now, but when the proper time comes will doubtless stand together . . . The fact that you may have to label your goods "Compound" would certainly reflect upon your product . . . Your remark in regard to the composition of your whisky are noted, and we also realise that "All Malt" whiskies must taste pretty bad.' (The blender *made* the success of Scotch as much overseas as at home.) 'The verdict of the Royal Commission does not carry the same influence here as in Great Britain, but it will no doubt be of considerable assistance to us. What you say in regard to what happened while Dr Wiley was in Cognac and Bordeaux, we have read with considerable interest, as we have often wondered why there are some apparent discriminations in favour of the French products and producers; for instance, the French shippers have permission to blend together several ages of their product and ship same here under a simple "Cognac" label; while if the whisky blenders put together two straight whiskies, they are compelled to call it a "Blend"; we fail to see the difference. You will note that at the present time Dr Wiley has apparently gone crazy over the colouring matter, so we are preparing for another troublesome period in regard to this. This party had several of our shipments held up before on this account and as they were all of lots shipped direct to customers, you can imagine the trouble we had.'

The saga, in effect, of how Scotch won its West! By March the following year, 1909, came word from New York of a further hitch: 'The Commission appointed by President Roosevelt to determine the question "What is Whisky?" rendered a report not in accordance with the ideas of Dr Wiley and Attorney-General Bonaparte, and favourable to the blenders. The President would not accept the report and conditions remain as before, this fact being evidently what frightened everyone into the belief that seizures were to be made at once . . . Dr Wiley told him that the only thing that prevented seizures being made was the diplomatic arrangements between your Government and our Government.' (The U.K. Government was even thus early on being goaded into action by the whisky exporters!) 'Mr Hamilton then had an interview with Mr Young of the British Embassy, and Mr Young assured him that there was no immediate prospect of the diplomatic arrangements being altered, and that the mere change of our President and Secretary of State did not in any way alter conditions, as the arrangement was between Governments and not between individuals.'

To be brief: it was only in January 1910 that the annual general meeting of the Exporters' Association was informed in Glasgow by Mr J. G. Dawson, chairman, of the upshot of the incident when he reported that President Taft's decision had come to hand on 'What is the meaning of the term "Whisky" under the Pure Food Act.' Mr Dawson was able to tell the gathering that the President had decided that spirit made from cereals was 'Whisky' while that made from molasses was 'Rum', and that there was no objection to colouring. The President had also decided that the general public was entitled to know whether it was buying 'straight' or other whisky, and in this connection had 'remitted to the Secretary of the Treasury and the Commissioners of Internal Revenue to prepare the proper regulation under the Internal Revenue law for "labels" and the "branding" of packages'.

Consumer protection, whichever side of the Atlantic may be considered, is no new thing. Incidentally, right up to prohibition of spirit imports, Scotch was imported in bulk as well as in bottle, with bottle imports always well in the lead and until the 1917 emergency of America entering the World War I, the bottles were taxed per proof strength content, not at 100 proof whatever the content.

So much, for the present, for that particular market. We have already noticed the insistence on matured quality as contributing to Scotch whisky's lasting world success. It was not always the case that such quality prevailed. In the year just mentioned, 1910, attention was drawn to 'Black Spots' in the whisky export trade: 'The export market is one of the most valuable assets of the whisky trade and, in view of the depression in the home trade, the overseas market is bound to increase in importance.' An importance met today, when it takes some four-fifths of world consumption!

With that theme of insistence on quality as the key to success went thunder against 'the dumping upon export markets of brands of whisky bearing highly imaginative Scotch or Irish names, and of a type of quality calculated to do harm to the legitimate brands ... the subsidiary brands of the well-established firms to be met with alongside the regular brands sent out by the same firms ... for the needs of a cheaper class of trade . . . they do not compare very favourably with the regular brands . . . The Remedy seems to be an extension of the age principle of Australia to other export markets . . . It is useless to blink the fact that there is too little cohesion, and an excess of competition in the whisky trade . . . The consignment, as old as the export trade itself, and the general impression is that dearly bought experience has done much to stamp out the evil . . . The export trade needs calm and careful consideration. With the home trade demoralised, the export trade is assuming a more important aspect than ever, but wild plunging and taking abnormal risks will aggravate the evils rather than relieve them.' That advice was soon learnt, but in a more difficult school than was envisaged in that golden sunset of Edwardian England.

The Lloyd George budget finally passed into law, the King died, the arms race went on apace from the first Armageddon of the century, but glancing at its own trade, the *Record* was able to close the year on a note of congratulation – to the blenders: 'It is the blenders who have brought the export whisky trade to its present highly satisfactory position. They know how to handle the overseas markets, not merely so far as placing upon them whiskies entirely suitable for their various needs, but also in the matter of pushing those brands. Year by year the export whisky market becomes increasingly difficult to cultivate. Expenses grow instead of decreasing, and competition becomes keener. New firms trying to make headway for their brands find their progress barred unless they are prepared to incur a lavish introductory expenditure, with only problematical results. The shrinkage of demand in the home country will, in all probability, cause keener competition in the export market. The export trade is one of the best assets of the trade, there is not the slightest doubt.'

But enough has already been instanced to prove that that trade did not expand of itself. Enough to say that in 1912 and 1913 both, more than ten million proof gallons of British and Irish spirits, of which the great bulk was whisky, were shipped abroad. That is, in each of those years the export gallonage was double that of the beginning of the century. It is a trait which Scotch whisky has not lost, but, luckily for all, has retained to the present day. Messrs D. & J. McCallum, for instance, reported in 1912 that they were exporting more of their 'Perfection' whisky in one week than they did in the whole of 1897. But so troubled by the home market, the goings-on of Lloyd George, the industrial unrest at home, the gathering war clouds for those who could read aright, that exports gained little prominence in what company reports were published, and, be it remembered, many of what are now prominent firms in the whisky industry were still private companies. Nevertheless *Bonfort's Circular*, published in New York, was able to declare that 1913 had seen broken all records for the import of Scotch and Irish whiskies into New York – 206,000 cases of whisky imported bottled, and 65,000 American gallons imported in wood. Altogether, said the *Circular*, there were then an hundred brands of Scotch whisky on the U.S. market. At the same time D. & J. McCallum announced their record shipment to their Canadian agents – 5,000 cases in one individual shipment.

Those overall shipments of British and Irish spirits for the two years are of a particular interest: the 10,194,009 proof gallons shipped in 1912 were valued at £4,240,625 and 1913's 10,089,937 proof gallons were worth £4,187,979. We shall have occasion later to note the steady increase in the value of whisky exported, the value, that is, per proof gallon.

As the same sort of position is quite possible today with the operation of the 1966 Government's export rebate scheme, it is not out of place to consider the complications produced in the American market by the allowance of threepence per proof gallon granted by the British Government on all British spirits shipped abroad. In this pre-war boom on the American market, the U.S. Treasury, jealous of the interests of Americans, imposed a countervailing duty of nine cents – then 4½d. – per gallon on all Scotch and Irish whiskies imported into the United States because, it was said, of the refusal by Great Britain to abolish the 'bounty' of threepence per gallon granted the British exporters. It was estimated that the trade would amount to about $2,500,000 a year, or £500,000. The official American explanation given at the time was: 'Great Britain has been paying an export bounty of threepence per gallon to exporters for many years past. The fact was not discovered until recently by the Treasury Department and negotiations for the removal of the bounty have failed.'

The U.S. Treasury regulation was not then brought into force because of the British Foreign Office, who explained, at the instance of the Whisky Exporters' Association, that it was not a bounty, i.e. a subsidy, but of compensatory nature because of Excise restrictions.

(That threepence was, for more firms than we care to mention, the largest single element in their profit on overseas sales.)

Just before the outbreak of war in 1914 the matter came once more to a head: it was decided in Washington, partly because of the very success of 1913 Scotch and Irish whisky imports, to impose the counter-vailing duty. The Wine and Spirit Association conferred urgently with the Whisky Exporters' Association and further action was taken on the lines that the 'export allowance' was never a 'bounty' and was officially disowned as such. The help even of Lloyd George was here enlisted, and the reply given by him – not written by him, of course: the permanent officials are, fundamentally, the most important element, as Ross was later to tell the trade – was as follows: 'No bounty is paid on the export of British spirits from this country. An allowance of three-pence per gallon is granted on British plain spirits on exportation as an equivalent to the British distiller for the cost to him of the requirements and restrictions imposed by the revenue laws and regulations in con-nection with his plant and method of manufacture. A further allowance of twopence (i.e. fivepence in all) is granted on British compounds in consideration of the loss due to the manufacture being required by law to be carried on with duty-paid spirits on premises distinct from those of a distiller. These allowances are granted in order to put the British distiller on an equality with the foreign distiller, who is not hampered to the same degree by the revenue laws of his country.'

In that last July before the European blood-bath, the chairman of the D.C.L., Graham Menzies, was ill and unable to take the chair at the annual meeting in Edinburgh. His place was taken by the managing director, Ross, who was able to report 'the best year in the history of the company', one in which they had 'difficulty in satisfying the require-ments of our regular customers'. For the first time, the export note crept in: 'As a matter of fact,' said Ross, 'we have had to go into the market ourselves to secure sufficient stocks of old whisky to meet the requirements of our export business.' A most significant and revealing passage: two words to be noticed in particular, with a wealth of ramifications – 'old' before whisky, and 'export' before business.

Shortly before the 1915 budget of the spring – the autumn one saw the unconstitutional introduction of restrictions on withdrawals – the *Record* commented on the 'remarkable clearances' and also that the export trade in British and Irish spirits was doing 'remarkably well considering the difficulties and the enemy'. There were, of course, no sales to Germany, but that loss had been more than made up elsewhere.

That spring budget of 1915 brought about James Stevenson's face-saver for Lloyd George after the failure of his attempt to double the duty on spirits and quadruple that on wines, the face-saver of the three years' minimum age of certain spirits, chiefly whisky and brandy. Incidentally the United States accepted and insisted on the British certificate of age in August 1916, when the American government, under Section II of its Food and Drugs Act, 1906, the one that caused the earlier analytical bother we have spoken of above, decided that all spirits exported from Britain to the United States must confirm to the requirements of the Immature Spirits (Restriction) Act, 1915, as to compulsory bonding. This was, of course, resumed after the repeal of prohibition.

A sidelight on the American and other markets in relation to Scotch at the time is recorded in an interview with a trade personality who had recently been to the United States. He reported the American as saying, 'My dear fellow, when your people come out to the States, they *will* have their Scotch or Irish whisky, as it may be, but when our people come over there, they are quite content to have your whisky and do not think of asking for American.' The Briton went on: 'I expressed the opinion that that was a great compliment to our whiskies, but observation shows it to be true. The fact is that we are sending to the principal colonial and foreign markets a very high class of whisky, and I believe the trade will go on growing in spite of analysts and standards.' That is, the more practical and day-to-day emergence of the insistence on quality earlier ruled for both home and export markets. Its value is obvious and needs no underlining.

Though the war was beginning to play havoc with whisky, as with other exports, by the end of June that year, things were not too bad: in June that year were exported 732,663 gallons of British and Irish spirits, as compared with 942,879 in the corresponding month of the previous year, making a total for the first six months of 1915 of 4,167,713 gallons, as against 5,376,556 in the first half of the preceding year. The day had not arisen when whisky exports must take precedence of all sorts of things, and in any case a drop of about half a million gallons in the 1915 decrease could be attributed to the absence of business with Germany.

At the annual general meeting of the D.C.L. that July the Chairman made no reference to the export section of the trade, though in the meeting of the following year, which dealt with much of 1915, he reported the acquisition of two large exporting houses: John Begg Ltd and John Hopkins & Co. Ltd. As Ross put it in his history of the company: 'On 3rd March, 1916, the purchases of the whole share capital of the two businesses of John Hopkins & Co. Ltd., London and Glasgow, and of John Begg Ltd, Glasgow, were confirmed by the company. Both of these concerns possessed valuable export connections, which the Company resolved to continue under their respective names and brands. Messrs Hopkins also brought over as part of their assets the Tobermory distillery in the Island of Mull, while Mr Begg's trustees possessed a lease of the Royal Lochnagar distillery, of which the limited company reaped the benefit until Whitsunday, 1923, when it passed into the hands of the present lessees.' (It has since reverted to Begg.)

As the new season approached at the end of that summer of 1915, as the export trade was once more recovering and growing and as the home market was in confusion following Lloyd George's spring face-saver of compulsory bonding, four problems in the industry began to define themselves: the increased cost of raw material, the increased cost of freight and handling, the uncertainties of transport and distillery staff, and, ominous, the colonial governments' increasing tendency to restrict the consumption of alcoholic beverages as the world-wide trend to 'prohibition' mounted. A fresh hindrance, in effect, to the pre-war growth of whisky exports. Indeed, as the year drew to an end, what with the restrictions also being placed on the home market by the Central Control Board (Liquor Traffic), firms were not finding that overseas markets were offering the compensation for home restrictions. The American market, where the prohibition forces were gathering strength, it was found, 'was not proving a responsive market to whisky shippers'. What could only be described as 'the unprecedented excess of exports' had, however, to make headway against the first paralysing effects of war. Yet despite the hesitancy of the American market, a market 'never particularly remunerative or easily-developed market for Scotch whisky shippers', many were 'convinced from personal experience on the spot that it has great possibilities – possibilities which will probably be greater than ever as a result of the war'.

The reason then given was 'the fabulous gains' being made by the

United States out of the war: American participation was not then envisaged, nor the personal introduction of American servicemen to Scotch whisky and British gin on their home grounds.

During that same year of 1915 came to a head the 'absolutely ridiculous' suggestion that 'large quantities of Scotch whisky were reaching the enemy', but a rumour credited in high Whitehall places which led to restrictions on the export of Scotch. Truly the beverage was assuming not only a national status, as exemplified by government insistence that adequate quantities at controlled prices were to be made available but that none must be allowed to reach our opponents! It was even suggested that Scotch whisky reaching the Central Powers was being used for munition purposes, a reflection of the increasingly important role the Scotch patent still distilleries were playing in the quest for victory.

In short, the more Scotland's distilleries did for victory the more suspect became the beverage Scotch. On 10 May 1916 came an Order in Council giving the Minister of Munitions – Lloyd George – the power to control spirits production and to prohibit it under licence, a nice reflection of that common attitude, still with us, of officialdom which can think of nothing but prohibition or restriction. Then in the following July came a royal proclamation, amending an Order of July, prohibiting certain exports of spirits. The excuse made for this drastic step was the necessity, induced by the 'evidence' of increasing quantities of spirits, chiefly rum, going to neutral countries contiguous to the enemy and so reaching the enemy, thus the necessity of stopping these 'loopholes'.

Whisky was also accused of so assisting the enemy. It was claimed that there had been a 'striking' increase in whisky exports to Scandinavia, an increase which was continuing, to the Netherlands, and so to Germany. An effective rebuttal was made by Mr James Watson, of Leith, who explained, for instance, that shipments to Germany in 1914 were of industrial spirit, well before war was thought of, at the rate of 1s. 9¼d. per gallon, and to the Netherlands at 1s. 8d. per gallon, while exports to Scandinavia were of purely potable spirits. Exports to Sweden in 1913 were at the rate of 7s. 9d. the gallon; and in 1914 at 8s. the gallon. And any increase in 1915, he went on, in value was due more to the effect of the Immature Spirits (Restriction) Act of 1915, which had raised the value of spirits all round. Ross, of the D.C.L., completed

The spirit safe

Blending vats

the rebuttal, pointing out that most German spirit production was from potatoes, of which there had been a poor harvest there in 1910 and 1914; that Germany and Holland compounded spirits for trade with the west coast of Africa, and that there was no need to elaborate on Mr Watson's exposition of the Scandinavian set-up, except to add that those countries' usual imports of brandy and wines from France and Germany had been cut off and interfered with by hostilities.

On 26 July 1916 was issued another Order in Council amending the royal proclamation of the previous May to the extent of adding to the list of export prohibitions and restrictions 'potable spirits of a strength of less than 43 degrees above proof' as prohibited to all foreign countries in Europe and on the Mediterranean and Black Seas, other than France, Russia (except through the Baltic ports), Italy, Spain and Portugal. The effect was to stop the export of Scotch whisky and other dutiable spirits to all neutral as well as enemy ports in Europe. It had no effect, however, on such trade with British colonies, allied countries, or countries outside Europe, such as the United States and other parts of the American continent.

The restriction was also one outcome of the restricted output of the controlled distilleries and the import restrictions on distilling materials – the German submarine menace was already stepping up – and the object of the restriction on exports was obviously to confine the output to the smallest proportion absolutely necessary for home consumption. Of course the Government's decision in the matter was a serious blow not only to exporters, but to distillers and holders of spirit stocks, for in the face of diminished home trade, the chief hope of keeping the trade in whisky going during war conditions was increasingly the export business. It was recognised that the principal markets, the colonies – dominion status had not then arrived – and the American markets, were exempted from the prohibition, but its application to Scandinavian and other European markets hit badly those firms which had long and sedulously cultivated the very ones outlawed.

On 8 October 1917 a royal proclamation prohibited the export of all goods, with minor exceptions, to Sweden, Norway, Denmark and the Netherlands, and in the last year of the war, as the Allies fought back the last German push, came on 22 January 1918 an Order in Council prohibiting the export of wine and 'potable spirits of a strength of less than 43 degrees o.p.' to all destinations. Stocks were, in any case, meagre, but many had been confining their trade almost solely to exports.

It was a case for strong action at once by the Whisky Association. Mr J. King Stewart, the energetic secretary of the association, at once took the necessary action, so that goods for shipment to Canada if presented on or before the 31st of that January would be permitted. For other destinations previously permitted and now prohibited, he established a routine of applying for an export licence, and in fact it was virtually settled before long that each trader established to the satisfaction of the War Trade Department received a general licence for a stipulated period. At the end of that period, it was further adjusted, the renewal would occur without hindrance. The establishment of the Whisky Association in the previous year, under stress of events, was already proving its worth, while on the horizon looming up could be seen the birth of the Scottish Branch later to devour its parent.

So much for official restriction and control. It was not limited to the United Kingdom, of course. We have already mentioned colonial government restraint on whisky imports. Shortage of shipping accommodation and expensive freight rates and insurance added their burden.

British exports of spirits thus fell, understandably hovered, that last calendar year of the war, 1917. In 1915 they slipped back to 8,912,750 gallons, to the value of £3,724,168; in 1916 they surged forward to 9,563,718 gallons, to the value of £5,132,990, but in 1917 they fell back – the submarine menace was at its height – to 5,755,633 gallons worth £4,601,604. One reason for that decrease was the American prohibition of spirit imports.

By the U.S. Treasury Decision Circular (T.D. 37.315), of 20 August, based on Section 15 of the Act approved on the 10th of that month, was ruled that on thirty days after the passage of the Act no spirits were to be imported – or made and the Customs were ordered to refuse entry to any distilled spirits arriving there after midnight on 9 September 1917. So seemed brought to a close by 'the great American experiment' one of the bravest ventures of the Scotch distiller and blender. In the event, it was anything but.

Before leaving the period, it is of interest to note export prices in the last phase of the war. In January 1918 there were exported to the limited markets available 267,801 gallons of British and Irish spirits, of the value of £275,260, or, a trifle over £1 per proof gallon. In January

1916 the 788,569 gallons shipped abroad averaged 9s. the gallon. In January 1914 837,749 gallons exported worked out at less than 7s 6d. the gallon, although this latter month cited included 124,492 gallons of plain spirit for Germany, valued at less than 2s. per gallon. Small wonder, then, that the business-like blender was confirmed in his high regard of the export market: he has held it ever since.

Events of the following months that year, 1918, were to confirm him in that business estimate with the rigid control of prices throughout the trade in line with the controlled releases permitted for the home market. The home market became, in effect, an unwanted hanger-on, denuding valuable stocks at bureaucratic prices out of line with reality.

One happy note to terminate this section: where other markets were feeling the squeeze of the world-wide prohibition market, from the Australian market, at that time the leading world market for Scotch came heart-rending reports that the trade in the cities there 'viewed with much concern the growing diminution in existing stocks of whisky and the increasing difficulty experienced in obtaining further supplies from Great Britain'. Stocks in local stores and in bond were so low that several leading trade figures 'cabled direct to distillers in Scotland, seeking exclusive shipments'. Their efforts were only partially successful, for distillers were able to quote only for small quantities, and then at enhanced prices, amounting in several instances to about sixty per cent over the rates ruling prior to the war – the date is mid-1916 – and even then intervened inseparable shipping difficulties. The difficulty in securing shipment and the delays in transit contributed to the general shortage – blenders were only too willing to oblige, if possible – and it was feared that 'It is only a matter of months before stocks will be exhausted . . . Probably the price of bottled whisky, now 6s 6d., will also be increased by about fifty per cent.'

At home, the shadows of budget day shortened. Its major whisky effect was – to its surprise – to confirm the exporting nature of the industry.

20

Scotch marches on

THE AMERICAN disaster of the prohibition of spirituous imports might
have destroyed men of lesser breed. Only a year before that prohibition
Bonfort's Circular had been so impressed by the imports that it went on
record: 'Scotch and Irish whiskies continue to be the most extensively
advertised articles in the wine and spirit trade.' (Shades of Tommy
Dewar and his aphorism, 'It's the constant advertiser that gets
the trade.') 'There are a great many distilleries of Scotland and Ireland
represented in this country, and it is not uncommon to find as many as
seventy different brands listed by some of our large retail distributors.
During the past few years the receipts in bulk have increased, due to the
efforts of certain Scotch distillers to send their whiskies to importers
here, who, in turn, bottle them under their own brands.

'Owing to the restrictions placed upon Scotch and Irish whiskies by
the British Government, it has been necessary for distillers to raise their
prices. A number of brands of Scotch whiskies are now put up in non-
refillable bottles. While the majority of these bottles may be refilled,
they have, nevertheless, had a tendency to increase the sales and to decrease, at least in a degree, the pernicious habit of refilling bottles.'

A Glasgow correspondent noted the same facts about the American
market shortly afterwards: shipments to that market were 'very
heavy', the non-refillable bottle had made its appearance, and despite
the price rise, 'friends abroad are quite alive to the position, as they are
buying very freely at considerably enhanced prices'.

The same theme was resumed shortly later by Mr Charles Laird, chairman of Messrs John Robertson & Son Ltd, Dundee, at the annual general meeting who said that 'the accounts were pleasanter reading than they had been accustomed to for a number of years . . . The passing of the Immature Spirits Act in May 1915 put an end to the demand for cheap-class goods, a class of trade which never appealed to them, and which never did show a profit. They immediately experienced a demand for good class whiskies, and, as the stocks they held were held for this better class of business, they had done fairly well'.

An Edinburgh correspondent took up then the theme of export prices. 'The export houses,' he wrote, 'are well occupied, and find their efforts to expand business well rewarded.' They suffered a certain amount of maritime inconvenience because of the unavoidable irregularity of shipping, but despite their need to enhance prices – in some cases by as much 'as cent for cent', orders had by no means fallen off. Most colonial markets, he reported, had nevertheless increased their orders, and it was his experience that American buyers were 'inclined to haggle over prices'. Part of the reason, it was argued later, of increased orders from importers the world over lay in the irregularity of shipping and the tendency of prices to advance: it was safer, they thought abroad, to carry large stocks against further price rises. One result was to place prices of whisky exported in bulk – and one of the trade's very real problems was a cask shortage for that purpose – 'practically on a level with those in the home market'.

But despite that American prohibition of imports of spirits, the possibility of its being adopted in Canada, the boom in exports went ahead. This new-found extra zeal for exports as the salvation of the Scotch whisky industry, faced with declining sales and restricted consumption at home and in some foreign markets, is best summarised by the action of the D.C.L., then becoming accepted as the most important single element in the industry in Scotland. It was in 1917 that the D.C.L. bought the old-established firm of Messrs J. & G. Stewart Ltd, one of the biggest deals ever put through in the Scotch whisky trade. The company held much stock – all but yeast and munitions distilling was prohibited, remember – probably in the region of 8,000 butts, worth something like £2,300,000. The *Record*'s comment bears repetition: 'What all this portends it is difficult to forecast, but obviously these developments are of far-reaching importance to the Trade as a whole. The tendency to concentrate the diminishing stocks in a few hands must be fraught with incalculable consequences to the smaller houses. This is all the more obvious in the face of the ever-tightening control of officialdom, whether through the media of the Central Control Board (Liquor Traffic) or the Food Controller.'

William Ross gave it its correct slant in his history of the company, where he wrote: 'When the stocks of whisky were purchased from this firm in 1917, the intention had been to utilise these stocks for supplementing the requirements of the Company's *growing* (our italics) export business. The Advisory Committee set up by the Commissioners of Customs and Excise had, however, compelled all firms doing business during 1916 to continue to supply their regular customers on the basis of fifty per cent of the quantities taken by them in that year. So it came about that, against its own inclinations, the Company was forced to enter into the home business for blended whisky, and having conformed to such a policy, it was decided to perpetuate this trade so far as possible and to form a new Company under the same name of J. & G. Stewart, Ltd, which was registered on the 8th August, 1919, with a nominal capital of £50,000 entirely owned by the D.C.L.'

Truly were these years nothing less than troublous – and formative!

Or as the same statesman of the industry put it at the Golden Jubilee festivities of the D.C.L., when he was commenting on their wartime entry into the home trade, an entry brought about partly by accident, he said, and partly on account of their determination to preserve their position in the trade. 'Induced, no doubt, by the higher stock values then ruling, due to the passing of the Immature Spirits Act and to the closing down of all distilleries for potable purposes for a certain period of the war, over fifty firms on the Blending and Distributing side of the business cleared out of the Trade. Their valuable stocks were acquired by the firms that were left, and a large proportion thereof found its way into this company's hands . . . Hence the policy which we pursued and which today has resulted in bringing into the fold many otherwise conflicting interests. I regard this consummation as one of the best things which could have happened for the whole Trade.'

That was, then, one result of governmental increasing control over the home trade, a result which has affected the whole nature and structure of that trade, and one which came about, ultimately, because of an intensity of interest in the export trade of Scotch.

The whole business of that concentration on exports was put in convenient perspective by Mr C. H. Marshall, of James Watson & Co. Ltd, of Dundee, when presiding as chairman at the half-yearly meeting of the Scottish Licensed Trade Defence Association at Glasgow towards the close of 1918. 'The export trade,' he told his audience, 'had always been recognised by the blenders as a very important department of their trade long before the war, in many instances more profitable than the home trade. In the export trade, however, it was necessary to compete with distillers who were producing home spirits of the country to which Scotch whisky was being exported. Accordingly, the prices of Scotch whisky exported since the passing of the Immature Spirits Act had not increased in the same ratio as prices in the home trade. The export connection which the large blending houses built up previous to the war had cost them enormous sums of money, and they naturally desired to retain this connection after the war as far as possible, even though it should cost them financial sacrifices in the meantime. The Government would also naturally encourage export at present, as any goods exported contributed to the balance of exchange in favour of this country.'

Marshall was ahead of his time by more than two decades, for it was not until World War II that Scotch was accepted both sides of the Atlantic as the British resource which kept, or greatly helped to keep the balance. But that same theme of Scotch exports was taken up by Mr William Harrison, chairman of the Buchanan subsidiary W. P. Lowrie & Co. Ltd, at the company's annual meeting in June 1918. It was his hope that 'the Government would permit at the earliest possible moment the resumption of distillation in order *to safeguard the world-wide trade in Scotch whisky*, which had cost so much to acquire'. (Author's italics.)

Meantime, between earlier speakers and Harrison, there had fallen the budget, increasing – more than doubling – the tax on Scotch, and fixing a schedule of prices for blender to retailer to the public. The Food Controller and the Chancellor were insisting the public got the quantity and the price of the whisky they wanted, while the taxman took his enlarged pickings, at the same time as Lord d'Abernon and his Liquor Traffic Control Board tried might and main to prevent their having any. Enough has already been said on the set-up in this and previous passages. But the controls, so foreign to Britain, hitherto the freest nation in Europe if not the world, and since embedded in a passion for state control, the controls could not make compulsory purchases from distillers, speculators and other holders of their stocks. It could insist on those in the home trade honouring their fifty per cent releases to regular retail customers, but that was all.

Others holding blends and singles were free to do what they liked with them. With fixed regauge proof gallon prices, those who had no obligation to the home market just did not sell them at the controlled price. There were plenty of other applicants willing to pay the price asked and indeed some holders saw such a wonderful thing in it that they sold completely for the export market, where no price control was capable of being imposed by the British.

A glance at those exports. In 1916, as we have seen, there were exported 9,563,718 gallons of British and Irish spirits, a figure which became 5,753,631 gallons in the ensuing year, only to plummet in that last desperate year of the war to 2,936,969 gallons. The whisky was just not there. Home demands had to be met, there was a shortage of shipping, and holders were slow in releasing their stocks. Australia, that then premier market, took 2,460,000 gallons in the earliest of these years, falling, purely by war circumstances, to 1,386,000 the following year and to only 798,000 in 1918. The United States presents an even sadder picture: 1,240,000 proof gallons in 1916, 736,000 gallons in 1917 and as low as 1,666 gallons in 1918.

In March of 1919 home clearances were increased to seventy-five per cent of the base year, 1916, a pre-budget move in anticipation of another whacking increase in duty by Austen Chamberlain, to 50s. the proof gallon. The public, still then in the money, were delighted. There were some half-hearted attempts to strike off the fetters that had been bound around the trade and industry during the war, but these were more apparent than real. The fifty per cent increase on home clearances bringing them to seventy-five per cent of 1916 only began formally from 1 April and highly coloured stories began to circulate of the 'huge quantities' of whisky shipped to overseas markets, while the home market was kept short. Fables, baseless fables.

All along the home consumer had been getting his government-permitted fifty per cent and no matter what quantity was being shipped it had no direct effect on home supplies. Even the quantity that could be cleared for abroad was still – despite the advent of peace – strictly limited by the War Trade Department, and even the colonies and

British dependencies were put on half-rations. In point of fact, they were getting even less: only a fraction over one-third of pre-war shipments.

Then became clear a dichotomy in the Scotch trade: many firms were not anxious to ship abroad, as they expected to have for years ahead a ready market at home for all the whisky they – the firms – could obtain; but there were others, particularly the now major distributing houses, whose interests were already becoming mainly to be found overseas. As the *Record* commented, 'It would be a very short-sighted policy for the Trade to allow their overseas markets, built up as the result of years of patient endeavour and very great expense, to be usurped by alcoholic beverages from other sources. It may be confidently anticipated that in course of time the whisky trade will resume the full volume of its activities, and that, with an adequate production and reconstituted stocks, it will again be in a position to supply the demand in any part of the world. Besides those selfish and ill-informed critics at home are ignoring entirely the claims of consumers in our possessions abroad. Surely our kinsmen across the seas, many of whom made such tremendous sacrifices to help us in the day of our dire need, are entitled to be considered as well as the consumer at home. We have no desire to make invidious comparisons, but are strongly of opinion that the colonies who fought and bled for us are entitled to as much consideration as the profiteering workman at home, who, it may be, while of fighting age and capacity, was protected by his occupation.' In contrast, let us recall the World War II and its aftermath, how the Whisky Association introduced home control and rationing for releases in the first winter of the war and there was no freedom of rationing standard brands on the home market until the spring of 1959 – some fourteen years after the end of hostilities in Europe. Even at that measure of freedom from quotas and rationing, many de luxe brands were still often in short supply – often unobtainable, that is – and it is only under the staggering slamming of the taxman that some freedom of choice of brand may be said to prevail. The trade and industry has moved far from those narrowly selfish days of the World War I armistice period.

But in those easier times, after the four years of hell on earth, the quest for whisky and plenty of it went on unabated. Certainly, it reflects well the esteem in which the beverage was held, but it also

reflects a considerable degree of selfishness and lack of proper information and education by the trade of the public. The fables of exports
depriving the home-trade drinker of his Scotch reached Parliamentary
level. Sir Arthur Fell, in search of public esteem, asked in February
1919, 'Is it fair that spirits should be exported in large quantities when
old people in this country cannot get any?' Shouts of 'Hear, hear', of
course. The influenza epidemic was also a good excuse, and it was
alleged in the House that medical certificates could not be met, were
not being met for the whisky to which it was thought they gave
entitlement. To Colonel A. Ashley's addition 'Why is there any
restriction in taking whisky out of bond?' Mr Roberts, replying for
the War Cabinet, could only, weakly, say, 'That is a matter of policy
and not for me to determine.' (An hon. member: 'Is the hon.
gentleman aware that whisky is now being sold at Christie's as a
curiosity?')

But the abiding, underlying sting was that of resentment at alleged
exports robbing the thirsty and the 'sick' at home. The point really was
that about only twenty per cent of stocks of singles was controlled by
brokers, holders for the trade and distillers, while the other eighty per
cent was held by blenders – 'particularly the four great distributing
houses whose ramifications are world-wide', wrote an acknowledged
expert. 'The proportion controlled, directly or indirectly, by the big
distributing houses is believed to have been substantially increased
during the war,' he continued, 'by the acquisition of stocks of firms
desirous of realising at the big prices which were obtainable before the
maximum prices were imposed. These stocks were in some cases
acquired at prices substantially in excess of the controlled prices now
obtaining (the date is the spring of 1919), 'but it is said that this does not
materially concern these big blenders because they have ample stocks
of very much cheaper whisky with which to average. In any case, these
firms, having a great outlet for duty-paid whisky, obtain prices which
more than cover the highest prices they paid for single whiskies.' And
among those 'great outlets' must be numbered, of course, the export
outlet, where, again, no price control prevailed. The shape of things to
come was emerging rapidly.

The Whisky Association passed resolutions at members' meetings
pledging they would do their utmost to supply the extra fifty per cent,
but, as remarked then, 'This is at best a pious hope, and does nothing to

improve the supplies of whisky.' The only remedy seen was 'nothing short of the removal of control of prices of single whiskies'.

But Canada contributed its assistance to the British drinker, quite apart from the supplies of Canadian rye which had been flooding the country since the end of the war. In February 1919 the Canadian Consolidated Prohibition Order was issued, incorporating the Order of December 1917, prohibiting the import of alcoholic beverages, the prohibition on and after 1 April 1918 of the transport of liquor into any part of Canada, and prohibiting the manufacture of intoxicating liquor in Canada, at a date to be fixed. Another market seemed to be out of the running. Would whisky, some asked, be restricted to the United Kingdom – if the prohibitionists allowed it even there? The Whisky Association issued a manifesto towards the summer, opening with the heart-stirring words, 'The simple solution of the whisky trouble is to free the controls. Let competition regain its pre-war sway, and the questions of price and quality will soon be settled in the interests of the public.' That came shortly after Austen Chamberlain had fulfilled his pledge to Lloyd George to increase the whisky tax – making it nearly double, 50s. in place of 30s. the proof gallon.

As far as the export trade went, it only came in at the end of the manifesto, which contented itself with saying, 'It is entirely untrue to suggest that the export trade is being favoured, so far as supplies are concerned, at the expense of the home trade. Under the old Order we were asked to supply fifty per cent of the 1916 supply. The figures show that the home trade has received its full quantity under that Order, whilst the export trade obtained in 1918 only thirty-two and a quarter per cent of the allocation to which it is entitled. The demand of the whisky trade is the same as that now being made by all other trades which have suffered from government "controls" during the war. Let these controls be removed and competition restored, and the public will have no cause to complain of price, of quality, or, in the long run, of quantity either.'

All of which bears out, in addition, the theory which interprets World War I and its aftermath as a dress rehearsal for World War II.

In any case, Scotch was partially freed by the end of the year as far as quantity of releases for the home market was concerned: the governmental price structure remained as did the 30 u.p. dilution rule. This was accompanied, incidentally, with an appeal to the Great

British Public by the Whisky Association to see that the whiskies on sale were genuine Scotch, not American or Canadian whiskies masquerading in some little force, what with prohibition 'over there', the end of the war and enforced shortages on the British market. For Scotch and the war had seen great changes in the U.S. market: in 1914, American imports of alcoholic beverages were valued at five times the export of the same; in the fiscal year ending with June 1919 exports from the United States were six times, and in the eight months ending with August, nineteen times the value of imports. There were parliamentary questions concerning the admixture of American whisky with Scotch, but the subject is too complex for the investigation here it would require. Suffice it to say, that post-war Scotch experienced considerable and not always honest competition on its home ground from transatlantic whiskies and moving ahead somewhat, to 1921, we may note in connection with this mighty market, that 'the outward cargo of trans-Atlantic steamers is mainly Scotch whisky. This is excellent testimony both to the quality of the British article and the effort of the spirit Trade to re-establish British credit abroad . . . A marked contrast to the condition of other industries. Unfortunately, it is not uncommon for a British liner to sail with nothing in her holds but whisky and ballast, while vessels flying the Stars and Stripes coming laden to the load-line return without a pennyworth of freight'. Already then Scotch whisky was entering the role it has displayed so brilliantly ever since: as the great export of the British Isles.

Reviewing the year 1919, *The Times* observed on Scotch whisky that 'the export demand continues abnormally good, the shipments going to nearly all parts of the world. Even prohibition countries such as Canada and the United States are drawing on the Scottish trade for large quantities of whisky, the Canadian supplies going through what is termed the Department of the Prohibition Commissioners'. Although this is not the place to elaborate upon the devices by which Scotch managed to assuage the prohibition-famished Americans, we may mention and applaud the extraordinary outbreak of ill-health in the United States necessitating Scotch whisky as a form of medical treatment.

Meanwhile, the D.C.L. had continued on its acquiring way, and after the sale of their Edinburgh distillery to Scottish Malt Distillers in 1919. Messrs Andrew Usher & Co. Ltd began the disposals of their bonded stocks, part of which came to the D.C.L. through a third party and the remainder directly to them. The point of export interest is that it was carried through on behalf of J. & G. Stewart Ltd, whom the D.C.L. acquired in 1917 for the sake of developing their export trade, although diverted by government order that time into entering the home market as blenders. This acquisition of Usher, then, must be seen in conjunction with that of Stewart and as a part of the export drive of the industry which assumed fresh proportions and impetus after the war.

Nevertheless, the 'outlook for the Trade (was) rather obscure' the chairman, Graham Menzies, told the annual meeting of the D.C.L. in 1920. 'There will be need for the greatest caution on the part of the distillers in order to prevent a serious over-production,' said Menzies. 'The closing down of certain markets such as America, the competition from American, Canadian and other spirits in this country and in other parts of the world', all contributed to this obscurity. On the other hand, Haig & Haig advertised broadcast that 'the Government has so mismanaged control that it is not worth while selling fine whisky in the Home Market. That is why a lot of Haig & Haig is being exported instead of being sold at home'.

Messrs Southard & Co. Ltd about summed up the position towards the end of 1920 when they wrote that it was becoming 'more and more difficult to obtain supplies of available whisky, and the situation will be accentuated during the coming months. The export trade, being particularly good, makes the position more difficult. We doubt if orders for new bondings are being given as freely as distillers would like, but we imagine that shortness of capital is responsible for this to a large extent. That 1920 make will be required no one doubts, but at the present control prices it requires some pluck and optimism to buy young whiskies'.

Or as an Edinburgh correspondent put it around the same time: 'The one section of the Scotch whisky trade that is booming is the export . . . Export prices are not controlled, and he is able to dispose (i.e. the holder of singles) of many parcels acquired at prices which make it impossible to sell in the home market at the controlled price. So keen is the demand from most of the overseas markets that exporters could sell much more whisky than they have available. The big exporting houses are keenly on the alert for parcels of matured whiskies – even though the age falls short of the three years required for the home trade – and attempts have been made in more than one direction to buy out firms with fair stocks. It is said that one firm which holds half a million pounds' worth of whisky recently declined a very tempting offer by one of the biggest exporting concerns in the country . . . Mr James C. Calder, of Leith, has acquired the business of Messrs Donald Fisher Ltd, Howden Street, Edinburgh, who are known to carry very substantial stocks of whisky.'

The home market was, in any case, relaxing its pressure of demand by this time. The post-war boom burst about August 1920; a bad winter followed, with more thrown out of work, and it became common knowledge that 'the working men and lower middle classes, with the cost of living at its present level, cannot afford the present prices for whisky'. A theme of the times which has persisted to today as a fundamental of whisky sales. It did at least stop further depredations of the public's pocket in the ensuing budget which saw no further increase of the tax on whisky.

The United States does not appear in the Board of Trade returns as published around this time as a destination of Scotch whisky, but there was then and is today no doubt that a considerable proportion of the Scotch whisky being shipped in increasing quantities found its way to the United States. The British Government was even then adopting one of its cults it has never since relinquished, an anxiety to promote the export of Scotch to the United States in order to help the foreign exchange balance, a cult which rewarded it more than handsomely in the next world conflict and its succeeding years.

One of the unexpected side-effects of prohibition in that mighty market, and one to which insufficient attention has hitherto been paid was the establishment of Scotch whisky as the premier imported spirit in America. By one of those quirks of fate that constitute the irony of history, Scotch whisky indeed owes a very great debt of gratitude to the great experiment, prohibition in the United States. The evidence is legion, but this passage from the *Saturday Evening Post* must suffice: 'First off, the most apparent effect of the prohibition law, or lack of effect of it, is that it has not abolished the liquor traffic, but that it has changed the liquor traffic . . . It has brought about an organised liquor traffic, clandestine but effective as to both distribution and profit . . . The greater part of the foundation on which all this crookedness rests in the medicinal use of whisky . . . and a nation that has developed enough sickness in eight months to require 18 million gallons, or there-about, of whisky to alleviate its suffering may be depended on to remain sick indefinitely.'

After remarking that Scotch whisky entered the United States from Canada, and other contiguous territories, and by 'rum runners', the journal continued: 'Scotch whisky is dealt in mostly, because Scotch is harder to get now than rye or Bourbon. The stream of rye and Bourbon coming out of the bonded warehouses has depressed the price of these liquors, but Scotch continues at its high price, cheaper in the seaport towns, where it can be secured for about $110 a case of known brands, to $130 to $200 in the west, where it comes in from Canada . . . The smuggler gets all he can, and what he gets depends on the acuteness of the needs of the consumer. However, any person in want of Scotch or Canadian rye by judiciously shoppping round can get a bottom price at almost any time, because it isn't coming in by the gallon, but by hundreds of barrels.' (The Canadian wartime prohibition expired 1 January 1920.)

The further point of interest lies in Scotch's being 'harder to get', a key not to be disregarded in understanding Scotch whisky's resounding success since the difficult days of World War II and its aftermath years of shortage.

That is, in the years immediately following World War I, Scotch whisky not only resumed its role as an export formulated before that war and continued under difficulties during it, but aided by the depressed state of the home market, where prices were still controlled by the Government, it so changed its character as to be primarily an exporting industry. The home market was henceforth an appendage, an appendage to be cared for to some extent, but what primarily mattered were the overseas markets. Where before World War I, the home market was *the* Scotch market, with a burgeoning interest abroad, once the war was over, the overseas markets assumed priority. The home market was relegated to second place. And what finally clinched and settled that attitude was the clumsy attempt by the British Government to interfere in industry and fix prices throughout. Further, in that new emphasis on overseas sales, prohibition in the United States may be said to have given a new importance to that market, as it itself gave a new acclaim to Scotch, an acclaim based, finally, on shortage and difficulty.

Agreed, that in view of the wide disparity between export and home trade prices, competition among shippers quickened in the closing months of 1920 and the opening ones of 1921 with the result that the quantity-freed home market saw a lot of the whisky it had been expecting diverted from it. As *The Times* put it: 'One of the outstanding features of the trade throughout the year [1920] has been the extraordinary activity displayed in the export of Scotch whisky to foreign countries and the British Dominions. The demands made on exporters have been almost overwhelming, and in view of home requirements the manufacturers and wholesale firms have been unable to fulfil all the orders which have come to them from abroad. This is shown by the fact that in the majority of cases export licences have only been utilised up to about fifty to sixty per cent of the total amounts for which they were granted. From the commercial point of view, this trade is one of considerable importance because in several of the export markets from seventy to one hundred per cent higher prices can be obtained than in the home trade. Every case of whisky sold for home consumption, therefore, may be regarded as representing a loss to wholesale firms in view of the prices that could be obtained for export. But in spite of this fact, the quantities of whisky for which duty was paid during the year for consumption in this country have exceeded those of previous years and we have averaged fully seventy-five per cent of 1916 clearances from bond.' That seventy-five per cent of 1916 clearances was, of course, not only a ceiling, but also compulsory until 19 November 1919, and had 1920 not been without its own troubles plus the export demands home consumption should have exceeded not only the seventy-five per cent of 1916, but 1916 itself. In the calendar year 1913 some 20,164,352 proof gallons of home-made spirits were retained for consumption in the United Kingdom; in 1919 the figure was 16,092,468 gallons and in 1920 it rose only to 16,698,656 gallons.

Another feature of that export trade, a feature still with us, was what an Edinburgh correspondent described as follows: 'A very regrettable development of this competition has been the shipment of whisky with little or no age to commend it. New firms, with little in the way of stocks of matured whiskies, have barged into this the most remunerative branch of the Trade, and one also hears of individuals who seem to have become the possessors of voluminous export licences without having the stocks of matured whisky to back them. The reckless shipment of practically new whisky is bound to do the legitimate trade in the matured article incalculable harm, and yet it is a practice difficult to stop without invoking fresh restrictions, of which we have more than enough already. Complaint is also being made that in some cases the purchasers of going businesses with stocks of whisky are not supplying the old customers of the acquired businesses with the proportion of spirit they had been in the habit of getting, but are disposing of as much as possible in overseas markets.'

In short, the export market was supreme; the home market hardly mattered to many. But the interest must centre on that export of new or immature whisky. Early on the real industry set its faith in quality, in age, in excellence. The great proprietary brands owned their success at home, in the first instance, to the unsatisfactory quality supplied by the majority of publicans and those who controlled them, and the same great brands carried that lesson in their minds as they widened their field of operations to make them global.

On this export of immature spirits, it is of present use to recall that when Lloyd George brought in the three-year minimum in 1915 the then small Labour Party voted solidly for it as a measure protective of jobs in Scotland. We have experienced after World War II the same frantic endeavour to cash in by shipping new whisky, an export still opposed, fruitlessly, by the Scotch Whisky Association. As early as 1921, colonial governments were showing 'an increasing disposition' to bar the import of immature spirits – in which field Australia was foremost soon after becoming a federation – and the Whisky Association had to 'petition' the Board of Customs and Excise to issue a general order instructing officers to grant an age certificate when required for any overseas market.

However, that year of 1921 saw the beginning of the tapering off of whisky exports as the world began to get over its post-war boom years. The transformation had by then, however, been effected. Scotch whisky was henceforth to be primarily an exporting industry. Exports were not back to their pre-war volume, but the effort to surpass it was now dominant. In fact, 1913, the last year of peace, when 10,090,000 gallons of British and Irish spirits were shipped abroad compared with 3,302,000 in 1919, the first year of peace. The boom of 1920 saw that more than doubled to 7,328,000 gallons. Scotch whisky had taken on a fresh role in the world.

21

Post-war exports

IN LESS than two years from the signing of the Armistice in November 1918, the post-war inflationary boom was over. Reduced wages unemployment and smaller earnings were to be, increasingly, the rule of the day. With price control still in force, an unheard-of rate of duty – 72s. 6d. against the pre-war 14s. 9d. the proof gallon – and the prevailing economic conditions and unrest, the home market future for Scotch looked black. It was, however, but a further incentive to concentrate on the markets of the world.

But the United States had officially begun the era of prohibition at midnight on 16–17 January 1920, and other countries – Finland, for example – had either adopted it outright or were imposing increasingly tight restrictions on spirits. Not that official prohibition of alcoholic beverages was always that effective, and as Lord Forteviot was able to tell the annual meeting of shareholders in Buchanan-Dewar Ltd in May 1921, prohibition in the various countries where it has been imposed 'had no effect upon the sales or profits of the concern. Both at home and abroad the demand has been larger than ever'. In the spring of that same year, Mr John Arthur Dewar, a nephew of Lord Dewar, set out on a fifteen-month overseas tour in the best Dewar vein of personally drumming up sales and business for the firm in every market open. During the trip he visited all the leading countries in Africa, the Orient, and Australasia, returning by way of Canada and the United States.

As the year wore on there did even seem some prospects of a revival in export: Americans must have 'medicine', it was suggested, in the more palatable forms and not all Canadians had as yet signed the total abstinence pledge. But the 'improvement', it was considered, was associated solely with the economic demand possible under universally heavy taxation and world-wide unemployment, the aftermath of an artificial prosperity.

But when the returns were in, it was with the depressing news of a tapering off of overseas demand, a decline of one million and a quarter gallons from the previous year, and one fairly well spread over the leading markets, while the falling away from the 1913 peak was in the neighbourhood of four million proof gallons. Overseas reports indicated that 'the huge increases made in the various spirit duties were generally blamed for the heavy falling off in demand. In some markets . . . there were signs of a recovery . . . India is said to hold out the best prospects'. They were, of course, the days of British rule there. Even so, the landed price of Scotch in export markets was in the region of 28s. 6d. per proof gallon, a drop from the year before when it was around 32s. the gallon, or very nearly double the controlled price, before duty, on the home market. In this setting was pronounced on the now usual age and quality theme, 'The shippers who use young whiskies are not likely to stay the course long.'

That the theme was correct was proved by its reiteration by Lord Woolavington at the Buchanan-Dewar annual meeting in May 1922, when he said that 'the world-wide reputation enjoyed by the brands of the associated companies of Buchanan-Dewar Ltd have been acquired by the constant maintenance of a very high standard of quality, whisky of great age only being used in these brands, and the recognition of which is materially evidenced by the continually increased demand, both in the home and export markets'. Adequate stocks, he added, were the solution: the combined firms' stocks amounted to 23 million proof gallons.

But whatever the solution to overseas sales, they were, as noted, in the event well down. Taking 1913 as the best comparison – 1914 was too interrupted by war – we find that exports then were just over the ten million gallon mark for British and Irish spirits, of which Scotch whisky formed the bulk. The exigencies of war brought them to as low as under three million in 1918. The following year saw them move up less than half a million, and in the boom year of 1920, as the bubble was about to burst, they more than doubled to reach a year-end total of

7,328,000. But in 1921 the keynote of almost a double decade was struck: they fell, to just over six million gallons.

One possibly bright spot and gleam of hope was discerned by *The Times*, in reviewing 1921, which remarked that 'during the year, considerable quantities were sent to the United States. Shipments to this quarter showed no great diminution on those of the previous year, the American Government continuing to import spirits under licence for medical purposes. An increase in the export of whisky to certain parts of Canada is reported,' added the newspaper significantly.

The decline in exports, however, continued into 1922 when it was recorded that well under six million proof gallons had been shipped abroad, or 5,701,000. As was then observed, 'Within a few years, world-wide prosperity has given way to the direst depression . . . and the legacies of the war (apart from irreparable losses in manhood) are mainly unemployment and prohibitive restrictions upon trade in intoxicating liquors . . . Stocks of grain whiskies have been held in the hope of improved demands from overseas; the value of these deteriorate as newer spirits mature. Money has been lost heavily in falling markets in many commodities, and it is unlikely that whisky will prove an exception.' The forecast was correct.

The United States was not included in the export list for the year reviewed, but an unusual line was spotted and further details asked. The line was this: other countries, 1920, 2,014,000 gallons; 1921, 1,910,000; 1922, 2,043,000.

The Board of Trade did as requested and dissected the 'other countries' and introduced a new heading into the table of British West Indies Islands (including Bahamas) and British Guiana to which were exported in January 1923 alone no less than 121,790 gallons, as compared with 26,914 in the same month of the previous year and 35,052 in January 1921.

Baldwin, as Chancellor of the Exchequer, gave further illuminating details in a written reply on the exports of British and Irish spirits to certain countries from 1918 to 1922 inclusive. These showed Canada rising from 149,000 gallons in 1918 to a peak of 1,702,000 in 1920 and falling by about equal amounts to 803,000 in 1922. The British West Indies recorded 21,000 gallons in 1918, rose to 107,000 in 1920 and took 91,000 in 1922. The Bahamas did much better: beginning at 944 gallons in 1918 they mounted first steadily then by leaps and bounds to

386,000. The Bermudas fared a little less well, but still appreciably: from 958 gallons in 1918 to just over 41,000 in 1922.

Further investigation of quantities shipped per port and per destination revealed that while the United States imported from British ports an 'infinitesimal quantity' of British spirits – some 3,000 gallons from London, Liverpool and Glasgow combined as against a 1913 figure of 544,000 from Glasgow alone – St Pierre and Miquelon, the tiny French islands off the south coast of Newfoundland – took what was described as 'quite a respectable quantity for an island population of 6,000 people', the quantity being 83,000 gallons from Glasgow, 24,000 from Liverpool, 1,318 from London, 4,555 from Cardiff, 3,000 from Milford and 2,702 from Plymouth.

Now there was no secret that cargoes might, and did, reach prohibition America though the port of destination on the Customs books was St Pierre. The then abounding prosperity of St Pierre and Miquelon was attributed quite openly to its location as a base for bootleggers. From time to time H.M. Customs in Great Britain called for certificates of landing for the whisky exported, particularly when the cargo had been plundered before the ship was away. They regularly withheld the discharge of the bond and payment of the export allowance until a duly authenticated certification of foreign customs was received.

A rumour began circulating in the trade that British Customs and Excise, with a view to checking whisky exports to the United States, were demanding payment of full duty if there was any doubt as to the destination, or, alternatively, certificates of landing at the port to which goods were consigned. Some ships with whisky cargoes had actually got into difficulties, returned to the British port and the captains prosecuted crew members for broaching the cargo.

Actually there was no new regulation being enforced and there was no novelty in the action of calling for certificates of landing as concerned whisky shipped from such ports as Glasgow. The Spirits Act, 1880, then operative, gave full authority for the action and it is possible that the rumour was begun by the Customs authorities themselves in view of what they knew of American officialdom's concern.

An arranged question was asked of the Prime Minister in the House of Commons whether any representations had been received from the U.S. Government as to 'the extensive smuggling of spirituous liquor from Nassau, Bahamas, and other West Indian ports into the United

Scotch: the formative years

States' and 'whether it was proposed to take any steps to prevent owners of British shipping abetting breaches of the law of a friendly state'. Mr McNeill, replying for the Prime Minister, said: 'Representations have been made by the U.S. Government with reference to the export of liquor from West Indian ports which appears subsequently to be introduced into the United States by small craft putting off from the U.S. coast and manned by U.S. citizens. It is very difficult for His Majesty's Government to interfere with the legitimate export of any article from British territory, especially as the action of H.M. Government alone would merely drive the trade into other channels. H.M. Government would, however, deplore any complicity of British subjects in infringements of the United States, and I am considering, in consultation with the other departments concerned, whether any action can be taken in the sense desired by the U.S. Government.'

Washington complained further, and Mr Ormsby-Gore similarly went further than McNeill and frankly stated 'that business would go to one of the more convenient islands belonging to another nation'. It was common knowledge that much whisky was cleared for ports to be used as bases for the rum-runners, bootleggers, etc. There were clear grounds – in the early months of 1923, for instance – that much of cargoes recently dispatched would not actually be landed at the port specified in the shipping notices, as the commercial part of several transactions was completed on shipment. Again, many of the ships used were foreign vessels and their owners were thus in no way subject to British authority once they got beyond the three-mile limit.

In fact, the requirement of a certificate of landing went back to the times when Scotch whisky exported to England had to be sent by sea on drawback of the duty, the English duty being collected on landing, and it was only in 1832 that Customs agreed to consider goods lost on the voyage as satisfactorily accounted for. Then, the overseas trade in spirits was of little consequence, but as it grew the provision was found useful for protection of British Customs, if only to penalise the re-landing of goods ostensibly shipped to foreign ports – in this case, say, St Pierre or Nassau.

For a short time, the merchants of the free port of Hamburg bottled Scotch shipped from the United Kingdom merely for the profits in labour, corks and cases. But they soon found a much more profitable line: they bottled the silent spirits for which Hamburg was famous

300

after impregnating them with some Scotch and other flavours of German compounding, similar to those evidenced at the Islington trials in
1905–6. They, too, found their way into the transatlantic market and
with memories of the American-aided defeat of 1918 they were not
favourable to any diplomatic approaches from Washington. The only
doubt about the whole matter felt in British circles was that if Washington made fresh approaches to London with the charge that sales of
Scotch were made in British ports to people who took delivery on ships
that did not intend to fulfil the requirements of the British exportation
laws, such complications would arise as would force the British Government to make an example of someone.

In any case, the commissioners of H.M. Customs did not cancel the
bonds of a number of shipments for which they demanded certificates
of landing. A notorious bootlegging ship left the Clyde with a cargo to
smuggle into the United States; the prohibition officials, by intercepting
the letter of a Scottish member of the crew, knew all the plans, details,
etc., but were powerless in the event. The most that could be done was
to get a decision from the U.S. Supreme Court to prohibit the carrying
of intoxicating liquors into American territorial waters by any ship,
American or foreign, though it is, of course, the law in most nations as
it was then, that spirits must be carried as part of the ship's equipment.

There was even a rather ironic proposal made to install a distillery, or
at least a floating liquor store, just outside the American three-mile
limit! There was, it was claimed, nothing exceptional in the way of
vessels needed to carry a plant and material sufficient to make 5,000
proof gallons a week; there would be no embargo on Sunday work;
there would be no Excise restrictions; only the worst storm imaginable
might interfere with mashing of pot still distillation!

We cannot here pursue the daily or even yearly comings and goings
of the bootleggers and their suppliers and methods, though two points
may be recalled: one outstanding Scotch distiller lost heavily by way of
unpaid debts owed him by smugglers, and committed suicide before
being declared bankrupt. Secondly, Lord Stevenson drew a moral at
the annual general meeting of John Walker & Sons Ltd in July 1925,
by observing, in seconding the chairman's report, that the firm did not
indulge in bootlegging: 'Its profits are not dependent upon dealings
with bootleggers, and its connections stretch out from every village
and hamlet in the United Kingdom to the Dominions, Colonies,

Protectorates and Mandated Territories, as well as to foreign countries.'

The *Record* about this time summed up pretty accurately the whole smuggling procedure and long-term effects: 'With American whisky out of the way and an ever-increasing demand for good Scotch brands, there must be a greatly increased business, seeing that prior to Prohibition the amount of Scotch whisky consumed in the States in comparison to American was, we believe, somewhere in the region of five per cent.

'Apparently, "bootlegging" has got a long life in front of it, and notwithstanding the recent representations to the British Government for assistance over the 12-mile area' – shortly to be explained – 'we are convinced that no serious effort is being made to stop it, and we do not make this assertion without reason. Whilst on this subject which has been of considerable importance during the year, it may be of interest to the Trade generally to know that fines have recently been inflicted by H.M. Customs on certain whisky houses for non-production of landing certificates of whisky exported. Now it is very questionable in the first place whether the Government could possibly enforce these fines, as, after all is said and done, the sole purpose of an export bond is to guarantee against any possibility of spirits once exported finding their way back into this country without payment of duty, and not in any way to assist Prohibition in a foreign country. The result is that all ships loaded with whisky for this business proceed to a Continental port for their landing certificates before setting out for the U.S. coast. The result is that when a ship reaches, say, Hamburg, the clever German takes the opportunity of putting on board a few thousand cases of German "Scotch Whisky", among these being certain well-known brands cleverly imitated in every way except the contents.

'As the United States are asking for Scotch whisky surely it is better for them to get the genuine goods than the filthy spirit provided in Germany. There is also the question of shipping, and now that the 12-mile area is practically agreed to, it will be far better for the "bootlegger" to charter his ship from some Continental country and thus enable him still to work just outside the three-mile limit.'

(An important judgment was obtained, for instance, by Mackie & Co. Ltd – 'White Horse' – in the court at Mainz against a person there selling an imitation Scotch, 'Black & White Horse Whisky', a cruel combination of two famous brand names. The man in question lost the case, was fined 1,500 marks for every case of infringement, to which had to be added compensation for damages and Mackie's costs.)

Canada had meantime dropped out of the Scotch race in great measure. Early in 1923 the Board of Trade received a formal memorandum on the state of the liquor trade there: (1) Sale over the bar was abolished throughout the Dominion; (2) Seven of the nine Provinces 'by a large majority of the vote of the people have, as provinces, voted against the sale of liquor for beverage purposes. The other two provinces, viz., Quebec and British Columbia, have placed the sale of liquor under Government control'; (3) In the Province of Ontario delivery of native wine by the case to the home and its consumption was permitted; (4) In the other prohibition provinces, no liquor was allowed to be sold when of a greater strength than 2½ per cent S.P.; (5) By a vote of seven of these prohibition provinces taken by the Federal Government – Alberta, Manitoba, New Brunswick, Nova Scotia, Ontario, Saskatchewan and Prince Edward Island – legislation was enacted 'prohibiting the importation into these provinces of spirituous liquor for beverage purposes'.

On the American eastern seaboard things soon reached fever-pitch, battle stations, indeed, in 1925, and the story of the Battle of Rum Row must suffice for present purposes. It was a naval blockade in reverse, a blockade conducted by the U.S. Coast-guard, engaged on, in effect, a cops-and-robbers mission. The busy waters of Rum Row extended from the southern shore of New Jersey, through Long Island Sound, around Cape Cod and up as far as Canada. Rum Row certainly witnessed action stations in May 1925, and Rear Admiral Frederick C. Billard was the busiest flag officer in the United States.

The admiral assembled a fleet of 60 vessels, 40 to 60 feet long, off Staten Island. All were equipped with machine-guns, some with small cannon. Their mission: 'Drive the rum-runners and the smugglers from our shores.' The American Government had extended its territorial waters to a distance of 12 miles from the shore in its efforts to crush the smugglers, and only beyond that limit were alcoholic beverage cargoes untouchable.

By mid-May Billard spotted 30 good-sized ships riding at anchor off New York harbour. They were all suspected of carrying liquor and they were anything from 18 to 35 miles off-shore. Billard expanded his fleet to 400 vessels and issued the order, 'Shoot to kill!' Still the illegal goods got through. In New York, drinkers had the widest choice of imported brands, all the best.

A blockade of a hundred miles was set up, running from Cape Cod to Cape May, New Jersey. Scotch was later found to have been unloaded at Fisher's Island in Long Island Sound, and carried in small boats to New London – the site of the Coast-guard Academy. Many of the coast-guard crews were suspected of being traitors, or friendly to the 'enemy'; some were even thought to be in the employ of the liquor barons.

Next the admiral ordered seaplanes into action to patrol the sea-lanes and keep watch on the anchored rum-runners. At least two picket boats were placed in the vicinity of each liquor transport. The commanding officer and ten crew members of one guard craft were arrested for smuggling. Mysterious visitors and telephone callers began threatening wives and families of coast-guardsmen. A petty officer was shot and killed from ambush on Block Island. Two of his uniformed companions were seriously injured by gun blasts.

From his battle H.Q., Billard announced the enemy was being driven from the sea. Partly right: denied food and water, the ships moved north and unloaded on Upper New England shores. At the same time, thousands of cases of Scotch were being unloaded at Halifax, Nova Scotia – and the northern parts of Maine, U.S.A., experienced such an outburst of truck activity as had never been experienced before.

Then there was talk of ordering the U.S. Navy to assist the coastguard in the blockade that had failed to 'sweep the rum fleet from the sea'. That action was never taken, but it was a recurrent proposition from time to time as officials and politicians felt themselves goaded into some semblance of action. It was the Great Depression of late 1929 and the world mass unemployment of the following years that did more to restrict and curtail Scotch imports – legal and illegal – into the United States before sense prevailed and repeal took place.

A little before that repeal, in November 1930, Sir Alexander Walker was giving evidence before a royal commission on Licensing (England and Wales). How that subject of inquiry came to embrace the sale of Scotch to prohibition America is only dimly to be comprehended. But during his interrogation after his formal statement on behalf of the Whisky Association, Sir Alexander was cross-examined by the Rev. Henry Carter. I reproduce the passage in full.

'37,468. Rev. Henry Carter: Have you noticed any large increase in the volume you export to any given country of recent years? – Canada and the countries adjacent to the United States have, of course, increased in the quantity they have imported.

'37,469. When spirits are shipped from this country are you able to know to what country they are going? – 'We do not know, because the order goes to our agent, but we get very close information of what happens to the goods after the agent gets them.'

'37,470. Would the spirits exported to the British West Indies in large quantities of recent years be ordered from the distillery for that purpose, or at what point is the buying done?' – 'Ordered for what purpose?'

'37,471. A very considerable quantity of spirits reaches the British West Indies and other countries contiguous to the United States?' – 'That is so.'

'37,472. I put the question in this way. From whom are those spirits bought in this country?' – 'They are bought from the distillers.'

'37,473. Would the distillers be aware that the spirits were going to countries contiguous to the United States?' – 'We never know. We may get the inquiry and afterwards all the business may be done through the agent, who again may sell to another island in the West Indies. There is a great deal of what one may call intermediary business done there, and it is difficult to trace through the number of hands which it ultimately goes through, and where it ultimately goes to. We have a very strong suspicion where a good deal of it goes. We know, of course, that in particular areas, say, Canada, the Government dispensaries are selling these goods in their area and they go straight across the border.'

'37,474. Take a case which is perhaps a little clearer. Take St Pierre and Miquelon on the Gulf of St Lawrence; obviously the population there does not want all the spirits that get there?' – 'I agree.'

'37,475. The assumption is that it goes southward?' – 'Yes. I have not got the data or anything in connection with the ultimate destination of the goods. I am only speaking very generally. I do not know whether that falls within the compass of our reference here or not.'

'37,476. I was hinging my questions on your Appendix V, which gives the export figures. I will only ask one more question. Assuming there is knowledge within the Scotch whisky trade that the clearance of spirits for a country contiguous to the United States means that those spirits will really get to the United States – that is the anticipation – how do the Scotch whisky distillers regard that?' – You spoke, for instance, of St Pierre and Miquelon. Some goods may be ordered by a totally different party, say, a Belgian, a Frenchman, or otherwise, for consignment. He pays for the goods and he gives a consignment to St Pierre or Miquelon. We get paid for them probably in this country in cash. The question of destination follows afterwards. The man buys the goods in France, Belgium, Canada, or elsewhere. The question of destination does not interest us as long as we do not have the goods entering an agency area.'

'37,477. Let me put it in this way. Could you, if you would, as whisky distillers, stop a large proportion of the export of liquors to the United States?' – 'Certainly not.'

After that brilliant exposition, we must revert to the American scene. The American administration had admitted a partial defeat in 1922 when in the Tariff Act of that year they bowed to the belief that Scotch whisky, like certain other alcoholic beverages, possessed a medicinal character; it could be imported, under licence, and on payment of a duty of five dollars an American gallon. In the event, such imports were negligible, but it provided background to the urgent American requests of the ensuing years to obtain stringent British action to prevent rum-running. A concession, it was argued, had been made on the American side, and a comparable concession was expected to be forthcoming from the other side, the exporters. But in addition to the 'medicinal' duty of five dollars a gallon, the whisky, gin, brandy, etc., had also to pay the U.S. Excise tax. The 1922 Tariff Act duty of five dollars was then carried on in the 1930 Tariff Act without change and was effective at the time of repeal.

At this point it becomes necessary to retrace our steps to American entry into World War I. As noted earlier, Scotch imports into the United States before that war were of two kinds, in bulk and in bottle, the latter predominating. Then the imports were charged a duty according to proof strength and that duty was taken to include also the excise duty, the internal revenue tax on distilled spirits.

At the time of the American war entry – 1917 – the duty on Scotch was $2.60 per U.S. gallon, and there was no additional excise. The duty on domestic spirits was $1.10, which left a protective tariff on imports of $1.50 per gallon. In the Revenue Act of 1917, concerned with raising money for the prosecution of the war, a provision was inserted that the tariffs provided for alcoholic beverages of all types and kinds should be in addition to the internal revenue tax paid by American domestic spirits. It had this effect, a permanent one which is one of the banes of the industry to this day (1969) and has resulted in the soaring growth of shipments of Scotch in bulk at American proof strength to be reduced in strength and bottled there to the danger of the continued existence of bottled exports of whisky from Scotland to the United States: it brought imported spirits under the rule of American domestic legislation on spirit taxation.

In 1868, at the end of the American Civil War, the Federal Government, in order to prevent the substitution of water for whiskies stored in distillers' bonded warehouses, changed the basic taxing law on a proof gallon basis when the spirit was withdrawn from bond, by adding that the tax should be paid on the wine – i.e. liquid – gallon when below proof. Thus, it was thought, if someone managed to substitute water for whisky, there would be no loss of revenue for the Government, since if the whisky were below proof strength it would still pay the full proof strength internal revenue tax. Importers were not affected then by the law: they paid the tariff rates only.

But under the 1917 wartime Act, and beginning with 1918, all potable spirits entering the United States in bottles at below proof strength paid on the basis of 100 American proof strength, whether they were or not – and most bottled spirits are not: Scotch imported in bottle into the United States is generally 86·8 proof on the American scale, or 75 degrees Sikes, the British scale. It is one of the lesser tragedies of the Scotch whisky industry that during the prohibition years no one paid any attention to this hangover of World War I, as there were virtually no legal imports, and the tariff being based on a 'medicinal' fiction the 1917 change was ignored.

With repeal of prohibition, there were many much more pressing matters to deal with, as will be seen, and the taxpayment of bottled imports at 100 proof rate was laid aside for the time being. But what it has meant in Scotch whisky's post-repeal development in the United States is that bulk whisky imports are still growing at a startling rate.

That rapid growth of Scotch in the American market was originally delayed by the depressing circumstances of all nations between repeal

307

on 5 December 1933, and the subsequent war, which in turn was followed by an acute shortage of matured whisky. But the upward bound of bulk Scotch whisky shipments began properly in 1960, when supplies were fairly free and the bulk Scotch whisky imports tax paid in the United States just passed the million gallon mark. At the end of 1969 they reached well over the thirteen million gallons mark. Obviously, the 1917 decision and change in law has made and continues to make a terrific impact on the whole structure of the Scotch whisky industry, even to the extent of encouraging American ownership in Scotland itself.

The American Government recognised this concealed form of discrimination in 1951 when an attempt was made to eliminate the bottled spirits disadvantage in an Administration measure to modify the administrative provisions of the Tariff Act, 1930. It came to nothing; maybe there are too many and too deeply entrenched interests concerned.

The late Mr W. Reid, then chairman of the Scotch Whisky Association, gave it its correct assessment in a private speech delivered to members of the National Association of Alcoholic Beverage Importers, Inc., in New York, in June 1960. He then said: 'Our greatest mutual problem in the United States at present arises from the wine gallon basis of assessment. There is nothing illegal in anyone exporting in bulk from the United Kingdom or anyone importing in bulk from the United Kingdom. There is nothing unethical in it either. I have no criticism of anyone who does so. Indeed, so long as imports in bulk remain at the present percentage I have little comment to make. On the other hand, the percentage has been increasing and the indications are that it will continue to increase. Frankly, I regard that position with some concern . . . From our point of view, if this thing is carried to its logical – or illogical – limit, all bottling of Scotch whisky will take place in the United States . . . I view with alarm the thought of a substantial proportion of our process of production being removed from Scotland, from our own works, and the final form of our product, as presented to the purchaser, being taken out of our hands . . . What I am sure of, however, is that any substantial increase of Scotch bottlings in the United States will react against the standings and the prestige of Scotch whisky in the eyes of the American public. I go so far as to suggest that it might even reverse the astonishing but nevertheless solid and steady progress which Scotch whisky has made in the U.S. market over the past decade . . .

'What we can do, however, we have done and are doing. We have succeeded in persuading our Government, at the highest level short of the Prime Minister, to make representations to your State Department and Treasury Department.' In 1969 nothing had emerged, though the matter was listed to be discussed at the Kennedy Round of tariff negotiations.

But Mr Harry Lourie, who was executive vice-president of the Importers' Association for twenty-seven years, from its foundation early after repeal to his retirement in April 1961, and so one of the real architects of that Association and of American wine and spirit imports as a result, said to members of the Association in a farewell speech in March 1961: 'It has been the view of the Association that every importer, as well as every foreign producer or exporter, has the right to decide whether the spirits brought to the United States should be bottled in the country of origin, or should be bottled in the United States after taxpayment. The position of the Association has been that the internal revenue tax on spirits bottled in the country of origin and then exported to the United States should be based on the alcoholic content of the product, thus resulting in the internal revenue tax being identical, whether the product was bottled abroad or bottled in the United States. I urge that the Association maintain the position it adopted so many years ago that no discrimination should exist in the collection of the internal revenue taxes on imported distilled spirits whether bottled abroad or bottled in the United States.'

Now we must examine just how those architects of the American market, responsible for about half the world shipments of Scotch whisky, dealt in detail – and successfully – with repeal of prohibition and the problems which have never been absent since.

Scotch and repeal

SUPPORT FOR the repeal of prohibition was one of the two main planks in his election campaign by which Mr Franklin Delano Roosevelt won his first election as president of the United States. As Mr Harry L. Lourie, shortly to become the executive vice-president of the reorganised National Association of Alcoholic Beverage Importers, Inc., of Washington, told a World Trade Conference, early in 1960: 'In 1933, we were in the depths of a depression which had shaken the very foundations of our nation's economy. We had millions of unemployed; bankruptcies and foreclosures were the order of the day. Repeal of Prohibition and the restoration of a legal industry meant employment not only in the producing and distributing trades, but also in our international trade. It was of tremendous importance in the real estate business, in the hotel and restaurant trade, and, of course, it offered increased tax receipts for Federal, State and local governments.'

The main issue at Roosevelt's election was a reduction in the Federal Government's expenditure, and it is of importance here to recall that the new Secretary of State, Cordell Hull, was a fervent Wilsonian, and thus a believer in low tariffs and in international co-operation. These facts were to have a profound effect on Scotch exports to the United States.

The probability – almost, the assurance – of repeal of the Eighteenth Amendment, an amendment to the American constitution which initiated what President Hoover had called 'the noble experiment', was taken for granted throughout 1933 as was evidenced by the number of

American applications to Scotch whisky distillers and blenders for agencies of their brands in the United States. Some Americans went so far as to offer to buy Scottish firms outright and be both their own producers, exporters and importers. Some of that invasion from the North American continent we have already glanced at, particularly in its Canadian form.

Many of the pre-prohibition American importers had passed out of existence, and few of any seeming importance remained. The difficulty for Scotland was in establishing the financial status and distributive ability of the majority of the applicants. Many Scotch firms sent out their own men to investigate and check on the spot. The D.C.L., for instance, dispatched a deputation of ten: four left in mid-October 1933, to do the preparatory work, and the remaining six on 21 October, all ten being greatly helped by one of the company's Canadian officials, Mr Archibald Kelly. Moreover, the D.C.L. had long-standing relations – we have glanced at a few of them – with different firms in the United States interested in the alcohol, yeast and solvents industries. Most of that D.C.L. delegation returned early in December 1933, and on the 5th of that month the repeal of prohibition was announced.

President Roosevelt entrusted to Mr Joseph, Jr, the task of reconstituting the distilling, brewing and wine-producing industries and, of course, the import trade in these beverages. Codes of fair practice were promulgated for all these branches of the industry, including the wholesale distributing branch, and the alcoholic beverage industry began its long years of endeavour to overcome the evils resulting from prohibition. The importers decided that their principal task – internally – was the restoration of public confidence in the industry and their products, both of which had been badly smeared and disfigured by the evils of bootlegging, gangsterism and other side effects of the prohibition experiment.

As Mr Harry Lourie told a meeting of the Scotch Whisky Association in Edinburgh in February 1960: 'The original basic programme for future work which my group adopted shortly after it was organised on 12 January, 1934, included important items, such as the establishment of rules and regulations governing labels, age statements, advertising, entry for consumption in the United States, etc. These dealt primarily with matters which had to be taken care of, so that the importation of Scotch whisky, as well as other wines and spirits, could be established on an every-day basis, with a minimum of clashes with governmental authority.'

As Lourie will be to the fore in the ensuing pages in the cause of Scotch whisky, it is advantageous to present him more personally at this juncture. After his retirement, Her Majesty the Queen forwarded to him the O.B.E., together with four other Americans, 'in recognition of their services to British interests in the United States and to the furtherance of Anglo-American friendship'. The award and presentation were made at the British Embassy in Washington and Lourie treasures the warrant signed by the Queen. (In the following October, the Spanish Government made him a Knight of the Order of Civil Merit of Spain.)

It may also be of interest to recall that in January 1961, the year of his retirement, Lourie was awarded an 'Edgar' for 'The best Overall Contribution to the Industry by an Individual, 1934–61.' To quote only part of the 'citation': 'Harry Lourie is known in many cities of Europe as a true prophet. In Edinburgh, the members of the Scotch Whisky Association regard him with affection, respect, and trust. He has prophesied for them and his predictions have come true . . . The National Association of Alcoholic Beverage Importers . . . is the product of Harry Lourie's brilliant mind . . . The N.A.A.B.I. is the shadow of Harry Lourie. Since Repeal, when he began work as the importers' executive secretary in Washington, he has conducted the association's home office affairs in such a way that it set an example for trade associations in every industry.'

Similarly, the late Mr W. Reid, in making his farewell to Lourie and speaking as chairman of the Scotch Whisky Association, said in New York in March the same year: 'It is not possible for me to think of new things and further words to say about Harry Lourie. I personally have known Harry for many years. I have always admired him for his perception, his clear and analytical mind, his determination, his energy and good humour. My views regarding Mr Lourie's qualities are shared by the Council and, indeed, by all the members of the Scotch Whisky Association who have certainly not been the least to benefit from his service and achievements.' (It was on the same occasion, complimenting the Scotch importers on their successful promotional work, that Reid took up the root theme of Scotch whisky's success as we have earlier traced it, by assuring his audience that 'we shall give you the greatest support which is within our power, that is, to continue to ship to you whisky of the highest quality'.)

To revert to the importers' and Mr Lourie's work following repeal. To cover the anticipated demand for foreign wines and spirits in the United States, a marketing agreement was made under which quotas were set up for each country, and these quotas were divided, in accordance with the rules adopted by Mr Choate, among the various import houses who had received permits from him and were subject to the rules of the Importers' Code Authority. In other words, there was to be no free market and imports were to be decided by the bureaucrats. The announcement of quotas allotments to various countries aroused a storm of protest because of the impossibility of such quotas being fair to all concerned. It is a matter of record that one of the first steps taken by the new Importers' Association and Lourie with the Code Authority was to have the quotas eliminated root and branch. So the Scotch whisky industry achieved freedom of choice in the United States with respect to the products to be imported and distributed there: it has proved a godsend to Great Britain as a whole as well as to the Scotch industry, firms, the Americans and the importers themselves.

Then there was the repetition of the 'What is Whisky?' argument. There was a group in the United States which was positive that the Coffey or patent still produced a neutral spirit as known and ruled in the United States. This belief was so widespread that even American Excise officials believed it as a fact. This was all because Coffey had tried to devise a still which would, in effect, make neutral spirits as they are known in the United States, which means virtually pure alcohol of 190 proof or more, on the American scale of determination. Luckily, Coffey did not succeed in his aim, but the Scottish pot still distillers' antipathetic description of Coffey still spirits as 'silent spirits' was taken up in official and American distilling circles as meaning that Scotch grain whisky was a neutral spirit, incapable of being described as 'whisky' under American law.

Because of this widespread misunderstanding – deliberate or not, it is better not to inquire too closely – it took twenty-five years of work by Lourie and associates to persuade the U.S. Government that 'Scotch Type Whisky' should not be permitted in America. Speaking at U.S. Government hearings as early as 1934, Lourie protested strongly against the proposal that the labelling regulations should include a provision for 'Scotch Type Whisky' made in the United States. It was only in April 1958 that the American Government announced the adoption of an amendment to the regulations eliminating the standard for 'Scotch Type Whisky', to be effective 3 April 1961. Involved in the background to that amendment was a complete chemical study of authentic samples of grain and malt whiskies sent to the United States by H.M. Customs and Excise officials and analysed by American grain whiskies as known in the United States.

It was a fortunate coincidence that in the British Finance Act earlier in the years in which repeal became effective, 1933, there was provided a legal definition of Scotch whisky, a definition based on the royal commission of 1908–9 report, with which we began, plus the 1915 minimum age requirement – 'Spirits described as Scotch whisky shall not be deemed to correspond to that description unless they have been obtained by distillation in Scotland from a mash of cereal grains saccharified by the diastase of malt and have been matured in a bonded warehouse in casks for a period of at least three years.' That definition was reproduced almost exactly in the Customs and Excise Consolidation Act, 1952, and had again to be quoted in a defensive role in the 1958 American investigation of the U.S. Tariff Act with respect to whisky. On grain whisky, the Scotch Whisky Association memorandum had to go to the great length, in preserving that status accorded earlier and referred to by Lourie above, of giving distillation proof strengths, saying, 'There is only one distillation in this process (the Patent or Coffey still) and the whisky is taken continuously off the still at 165 degrees to 165·8 degrees British proof (equivalent to 188·4 degrees to 189·3 degrees U.S. proof).' And again, 'No other distilled spirits are added during ageing and no spirits distilled at over 166·4 degrees British proof (equivalent to 190 degrees U.S. proof) are ever used in Scotch whiskies.' The 190 degrees U.S. proof or over would have disqualified Scotch grain whisky as whisky: it would have classified the spirits not as whisky but as 'Neutral Spirits'.

That 1934 acceptance of blended Scotches as containing all whiskies, and no neutral spirits was of great value to the industry – and its product's acceptance – particularly as regards labelling. The importers worked out a plan accepted by the U.S. Government late in 1934 which

has persisted since. We need not here follow the details of that procedure, except to remark that it soon convinced the American consumer
that the goods he was buying, unlike prohibition days, were honestly
labelled and described. Without that confidence in the truthfulness and
accuracy of the label, Scotch would never have achieved its current
standing and acceptance in the States.

Meantime, the first Scotch to be landed in New York since repeal
had arrived there: King William IV, then marketed by Messrs Ainslie
& Heilbron (Distillers) Ltd. It arrived in New York on the *Cameronia*
with as many other brands as the ship could hold, and luckily was the
most fortunately stowed as to compose the first slingful out of the hold
with a woman piper in Highland dress balanced on it – a Scots lassie,
Miss Ruth Vollmer.

But opinion in Scotland did not all see repeal as the salvation of the
industry: there was always the oppressive home duty that was killing
the industry and trade of Scotch whisky on the home front in a period
of severe economic distress. With the world depression added to the
high spirit duty, there were at work – often not fully – in Scotland in
1933 only 15 distilleries where at the beginning of the century they had
numbered 150 – ten times as many!

As an Edinburgh correspondent put it at the time: 'The papers have
painted a truthfully sombre picture of the Speyside area, where
distilleries have been closed down and their employees have been
thrown out of work. What was once a prosperous area is now faced
with ruin, but when they say that the demand from the United States
may sweep away this depression they are speaking about something of
which they have no sound knowledge. Not only that, but they may be
giving the Government totally erroneous ideas of the situation. The Government is never keen to reduce taxation and would be only too pleased
to grasp at any excuse for not having to do so . . . Judging from the
trade that was done in Scotch whisky in the United States before
Prohibition, the quantity which will be required would certainly not
even absorb the stocks at present in bonded warehouses – which, it
must be remembered, amount to fifteen years' consumption at the
present rate – far less enable the distillers to relight their fires again and
dispose of their full production.'

Similarly, Major Alexander J. Wrightson, a director of Highland
Distilleries Ltd, a member of the Scotch Whisky Association: 'It is not

fair to buoy up the hopes of distillery workers and farmers in the north by exaggerating the effects of America's changed policy when the only hope of real improvement lies in the reduction of the whisky duty in this country. In 1913 the exports of Scotch whisky to America amounted to only 895,026 gallons. The total exports to the world amounted to ten million gallons . . . Apart from this, American has not been entirely without Scotch whisky, even during Prohibition, in consequence of the bootleggers. It is, of course, impossible to give figures concerning bootlegging, but . . . it is doubtful whether the additional quantity of whisky required by the United States will be very considerable . . . It is our own excessive duty that has been to some extent responsible for the falling off in the world export trade . . . Foreign countries, seeing that Britain was increasing the duty followed suit, and thus sent up the price of whisky, with a consequent large decrease in consumption and the closing of distilleries in Scotland.'

Or, as the then managing director of the D.C.L., Mr Thomas Herd, put it in a New Year's message to the staff: 'In the public mind the fact that we have resumed the production of malt whisky seems to be associated with the repeal of prohibition in America, but I would remind the staffs that the continuance of the increased employment which we have thus been able to provide depends upon the increase of consumption throughout the whole world, and more particularly at home, where the demand has suffered most.'

It was to just that, the duty, that the American importers turned their attention. They had got rid of the import quota proposals. Now it was the turn of the duty. That must be got rid of, too. As stated above, during prohibition, the Tariff Acts of 1922 and 1930 treated all alcoholic beverages as medicines. So when prohibition was repealed, the importers were faced with a tariff of $5.00 per gallon, plus the internal revenue excise duty. By 1 January 1936 they had halved the five dollars tariff.

It came about this way. Under the urging of Cordell Hull, with his ideals of international co-operation and low tariffs, Congress adopted the Trade Agreement Act. During those early years of the first Roosevelt administration, the international and domestic scene kept changing with startling rapidity, but the Importers' Association took an immediate interest in the Trade Agreement Act and its working. They presented evidence in the important negotiations between the

United States and the United Kingdom, between the United States and Canada, and other countries.

The State Department announced the first trade agreement with Canada of 18 November 1935, and included whisky in the list of products, giving as reason for the concession: 'During the period of prohibition in the United States, large quantities of whisky of American type (rye and bourbon) were manufactured in Canada. With the end of the prohibition period, Canadian distillers were left with great stocks . . . The shortage of properly aged whiskey in the United States since repeal of the prohibition amendment has created a demand for this Canadian supply. The fifty per cent reduction in the heretofore high duty of $5.00 per gallon applies also to Scotch, Irish and all other whiskey aged four years or more in wood.'

That is, there was then a fifty per cent cut in the tariff, and where Mr John A. Dewar had written from Perth, Scotland, that 'The American orders, so far, have not yet realised expectations', Scotch exports to the United States at once began, from 1 January 1936 when the reduction became effective, to show a remarkable increase.

To summarise, the tariff rates have continued to lower: after World War II, the importers got the rate on Scotch whisky down to $1.50, later to $1.27 and it stood in 1967 after further reductions at $1·02 per gallon. The tariff reduction obtained before the war was immediately passed on to the consumer, so that by the outbreak of the war in 1939, some 4,784,000 proof gallons of Scotch were shipped to the States.

This has not met with the approval of all American whiskey distillers. In February 1956, for instance, the Kentucky Distillers' Association had read to the House of Representatives their memorandum on the matter in which they outlined duty reductions to that date and commented, 'By 1939 there were ample supplies of aged domestic whiskies available, and there have been ever since. Nevertheless, whisky has been included as an item of import concession in each renewal of the trade agreement with Canada and the United Kingdom . . . The alcoholic beverage industry is a tremendously important factor in the economy of our country . . . If for no other reason than that of the revenue which it produces, our Government should be vitally interested in the economic health of the American distilling industry, which at present is far from good . . . The industry's domestic market is a contracting one . . . While the present total consumption of distilled spirits is less than it was in

1942, it becomes interesting to note the amazing progress which imported distilled spirits have made during the same period. Imports of distilled spirits have more than doubled during this period . . . Thus we see that during this twelve-year period, two forces have been at work, to the detriment of the American dollar. The exorbitant rate of excise taxation . . . and a considerable portion of what was the domestic market has been captured by whiskies of foreign origin, the importation of which has become increasingly easy under our liberal laws and regulations and successive tariff reductions.'

They returned to the attack in September the same year, making a statement before the sub-committee on Customs, Tariffs and Reciprocal Trade Agreements of the Committee of Ways and Means, with particular attention to the Token Import Plan in force in the United Kingdom limiting the import into Great Britain of American whiskies to $1,900 per annum. Warned, the Scotch Whisky Association were able to reply, in a memorandum of January 1958, to the investigation then being pursued into whisky in relation to the U.S. Tariff Act. 'Since the war,' it read, 'and until 1956 the American distiller was at a disadvantage compared with the Scotch distiller in competing in the U.K. market in that owing to British currency difficulties, imports of American whiskey were restricted to a small quota. Following repeated representations by the Scotch Whisky Association at the very highest government level this restriction was removed last year (i.e. 1957) and American whiskey has since been able to enter the United Kingdom free of quota.' That decision of the British Government was a most important and timely one: without it sales of Scotch to and in the United States might well have been imperilled.

As imperilled as on the eve of war, and its outbreak in 1939, after the importers had done the background work of tariff reduction, labelling, definition, free imports, etc., with their own government. Immediately after the outbreak of war in September 1939 the U.S. Congress had before it an embargo act which would have prevented American flag-vessels from entering the ports of any of the belligerents. The big problem was to move to the United States as quickly as possible a substantial volume of foreign wines and spirits and to have this movement on U.S. flag-ships to avoid the heavy war risk insurance rates which had gone into effect for the flag-vessels of the countries which had gone to war.

Scotch and repeal

The Freight Committee of the American Alcoholic Beverage Importers' Association made an arrangement whereby the United States Lines agreed to put seven vessels under its charter into Glasgow, Scotland, in October 1939. One vessel was seized by the Germans on the way over. The other six made the round trip successfully and brought back to the United States in the same month, October, the then unbelievable quantity of 875,000 cases of Scotch whisky – for which the N.A.A.B.I. members paid on the spot. (To get gallonage, multiply the number of cases by two!)

The Scotch Whisky Association, with World War I experience in mind, introduced home-market rationing early in 1940 and began its closer attention to export markets. These, of course, had never been neglected, especially since the home-market crisis of 1920, but were henceforth to receive even more concentration, especially the dollar market of the United States. Thus in 1940 itself, over 11 million British proof gallons were exported to world markets, including nearly 7 million to the United States.

With the continuance of the war and its increasing severity, the cessation of distillation in Scotland, the alarming decrease in stocks in the warehouses in Scotland, the difficulties of shipping, and the like, exports to the United States – as elsewhere – necessarily thereafter dropped year by year: it was a case of dragging out the stocks, making them last. As with increased scarcity of Scotch on the home market, what happened was, in effect, an enhancement of its intrinsic value on the American market. The all-time low was reached in 1945 when only just over two million British proof gallons were shipped to the United States.

In 1947, the British Government, as a condition of making a limited quantity of cereals available for distillation in Scotland, ruled that the industry there adopt a certain pattern in respect of its sales. In effect, a further cut in the home-market ration, and a division in export markets between 'soft' and 'hard' currency markets, the United States being included in the latter as one to which exports must be stepped up. So 1947 saw nearly four million proof gallons shipped to the United States. There was a tariff reduction there beginning 1 January 1948, and what with that and the extra exporters' efforts, the total sent the United States that year reached 4,649,000 gallons, passing the five million figure in 1949 and has gone on climbing ever since.

This has not been accomplished without opposition, as hinted at above with reference to the Kentucky Distillers' Association. Mr Harry Lourie summed it up when addressing a World Trade Conference, in 1960, in New Orleans: 'The large and important market created by importers in the United States for items such as Scotch and Canadian whiskies, Cognac, foreign table wines of all types and kinds, and various foreign specialities, is the result of careful planning and careful studying of market possibilities in the United States. The market has been created despite the ceaseless efforts to hamper the trade by local interests who favour the surrounding of the United States with a tariff wall which they hope will prevent all imports, or at least reduce them to a mere trickle . . . The widening of markets, the developing of opportunities, the establishing of brand names, the ceaseless work to have tariffs reduced, the maintenance of a constant watch to prevent ocean freight rates becoming destructive, are exemplified in the growth shown during the years since Repeal.'

We have already cited some of that growth; suffice it now to point out that in 1969 alone the total exports of Scotch whisky amounted to nearly 53 million British proof gallons, valued at over £167 million, of which total nearly 26 million gallons, priced at £81,108,000 went to the United States.

Lourie made an interesting point on that growth in America when he wrote, about the time of the twenty-fifth anniversary of the formation of the Importers' Association that 'In the last twenty-five years, there has been spent in the United States for advertising the leading brands of Scotch whisky an enormous amount of money, probably in excess of $50,000,000. That money, although it was directed towards brand advertising for relatively few number of brands, also helped in expanding the overall market for Scotch whisky. The result is that a substantial percentage of the entire business is concentrated in a relatively few numbers of brands. The public knows those brands and despite the fact that in every market unadvertised Scotch whisky is available at lower prices, the sale of the advertised brands keeps growing.'

Shades of the late Lord (Tommy) Dewar and his 'It's the constant advertiser who gets the business!'

We cannot do better than to close with a quotation from the U.S. Tariff Commission's report of March 1958:

'The consumer's choice between a domestic and an imported whisky is determined primarily by personal taste preference. This is particularly true of the choice between Scotch whisky and American-type whiskies, both of which have distinctive flavours. The flavours of these whiskies differ more than do the flavours of Canadian whisky and some American-type whiskies, particularly American spirit blends. Recognising this fact, six of the seven largest producers of American-type whiskies distribute Scotch and/or Canadian whiskies in the United States in addition to their own domestic products.'

And as a footnote to the above quotation said: 'Many producers of Bourbon state that Scotch and Bourbon do not compete with each other, except indirectly, because of the great difference in flavour.' Nevertheless, there may be discerned of late an attitude on the part of Bourbon whiskey producers which is more aggressive to Scotch than previously.

23

The troublesome twenties

BETWEEN THE world blood-baths of this century lie two decades of violent and revolutionary change, of revolution and fundamental economic change, of a slough of human hope, of despair, such as survivors of the period hope never to experience again. Boom and depression, culminating in the Great Depression, succeeded each other rapidly; World War I was prolonged in local warfares and into government by – ineffective – international government; strikes and unemployment, rising to a crescendo with the miners' and the general strike of 1926 in Great Britain, adorned the twenties. This country reverted to the gold standard and was forced off it in the world economic crisis, Mussolini seized power in Rome, Hitler in Germany, Japan went to war in Manchuria, Italy in Abyssinia, war preparations and the American war debt bedevilled the international financial world and helped vastly to destroy production and distribution. Obviously Scotch whisky could not be unaffected.

At home, the post-war boom broke in August 1920 less than two years after the Armistice. There were in effect three major economic cycles in the twenty-year period. First, the great burst of activity immediately following the Armistice as the world replenished its stocks in lands fit for heroes. This was complete by the end of 1920 and there was an equally rapid plunge into the first depression, a depression which went exceptionally deep. Towards the end of 1922 began emerging a slight recovery, a recovery which went on haltingly and fumblingly until 1929. Industrial and commercial activity declined again, for instance, in the early months of 1925, and the coal and general strikes of 1926 brought about another reversal. The following year saw some activity, activity bent on making up the arrears.

Then came the New York stock exchange collapse of 1929 and the Great Depression. The nadir of that depression was reached about the beginning of 1933 and the world vainly struggled to right itself until 1937 when the recession that began later that year was halted only by the preparations for another war.

Such is the background to Scotch whisky's valiant attempts at exports during those fateful years. It is to the lasting credit of the men and the industry that there was achieved as much as there was. But the fundamental fact remains that exports of British spirits which in the two years of 1913 and 1914 reached the ten million gallons mark never saw that level again before the outbreak of World War II. In 1913–14, for instance, British spirits were exported to the volume of 10,406,626 proof gallons; in 1938–9, the figure was 8,955,000 gallons, of which Scotch whisky comprised 7,702,000 gallons, the distinction being made that year for the first time. And except for a slight upsurge, due entirely to the American market, in 1937–8, even that figure just cited had never been reached between the wars. That is, the export achievement of 1913–14 had never been bettered and was only passed in the first year of World War II by the action of the American importers, as related above.

During those inter-war years, exports fluctuated wildly year by year, though without ever resuming their pre-war volume. In 1918–19, mostly, of course, a war year, they sank as low as 2,794,411 gallons, nearly doubled the following year and in 1920–1 reached the high of 7,668,767 gallons, to dwindle to just over five million for the next couple of years. They then zoomed up, in accord with those three cycles mentioned earlier, to nearly eight million gallons, passing it, just, in 1924–5 only to melt away to the six and seven million gallon mark again. The year 1929–30 seems at first to have been extremely successful in having passed the eight million mark in the midst of the onset of the Great Depression, but this is a misinterpretation of the figures which that year included a lot of industrial spirits sent to the Continent. Thereafter they hovered around the five million mark in the starving thirties only recovering, as noted, as war preparations enlivened the economies of the world. Indeed, but for that war, there might well have been another 1929–32 with all the misery, suffering and revolution that spell entailed.

Giving evidence before a royal commission in 1930 on behalf of the Scotch Whisky Association, the late Sir Alexander Walker, K.B.E., was asked by the chairman, Lord Amulree, to explain these wild variations, and his reply gives some little insight into the difficulties that Scotch whisky industry and trade had then to face. 'There are very large variations,' said Sir Alexander, 'due to the possible chance of a duty rising in any particular country. You sometimes get two or three countries where there are such expectations, and measures are taken to forestall it, and there is very heavy buying. You also get variations in the spirit consumption largely due to the monetary value in this country *vis-à-vis* the country of receipt. But it is very difficult to account for the variations. After all, we would not consider it as more than a normal trade variation between 7,000,000 and 6,000,000 gallons . . . As I tell you, you get these variations when there is exceptional possibility of a country imposing a high duty. Where you get expectations of that kind you find they import heavily in the year before, or a few months before. We have, I think, seen cases where in two or three countries at one time there has been suddenly an extraordinary demand, and when we ask the reason for it we are told that it is in anticipation of a possible rise in duty.'

All of which expert evidence gives indisputable testimony not only to Sir Alexander's own brilliance but to the apparently insuperable nature of the obstacles whisky exporters had to overcome in those inter-war years as the ruling financial classes destroyed the ordinary man's belief in their ability to guide and master the world's economy. The enduring importance of the Great Depression cannot be disregarded in viewing the history of the Scotch whisky industry: with some three million unemployed in this country, over thirteen million in the United States and about half that number in Germany – to take but a few random samples – there could, obviously, be little sale for Scotch whisky, at home or abroad. It is significant of the times that for the greater part of the thirties exports of Scotch whisky were about level with those at the beginning of the century, and in the worst year, 1933, only fifteen distilleries were at work in Scotland, or one-tenth of the number open when the century dawned.

Protection and governmental planning became the order of the day the world over, and the additional fundamental factor, as regards the Scotch whisky industry, which emerged was the transition of the pre-war primary producing countries, such as Canada and Australia, to secondary industries together with this protective planning. First, there came a spell of close imperial unity, a dream which had haunted the Conservatives since the inception of the century and which had been revived by the Dominions' support in the recent bloody conflict. If the world was going protectionist, it was argued with some skill and success, let the Empire go protectionist, a movement which was to culminate in the Ottawa Conference of 1933 and the Imperial Preference tariffs. Even before then there had been a revival in some measure of imperial preference in so far as British import tariffs were concerned, and it may justly be claimed that during the twenties the leading British Dominions constituted the main overseas markets for Scotch.

It was this mood of imperial protectionism and the predominantly British markets overseas for Scotch whisky after World War I – the United States were, officially, prohibitionist and most American imports of Scotch came from neighbouring territories – which led to the British Empire Exhibition at Wembley in 1924 and 1925 under the leadership of Sir James Stevenson, managing director of John Walker & Sons Ltd, raised to the peerage on the eve of the exhibition as Lord Stevenson of Holmbury. But already by then the more important of these countries had advanced, under the impetus of the war to the secondary producing stage, a transition which had a profound effect on the Scotch whisky industry, leading it to become a distilling industry around the world. For in that move towards industrialisation, the Dominions concerned introduced intensely protective duties for their new industries, including distilling, and further pleaded the example of the British Government's extortionate rate of taxation of potable spirits.

Even in 1921 that slump in Scotch whisky imports abroad was noticeable and those in close touch with the markets blamed the heavy increases which had been made in the spirit duty in those markets, although as a rule it was not so steep and penalising as the British home rate of duty. The only hope extended within the trade was that as these overseas outlets, then lately expanded under the influence of controlled prices, at home, were too valuable to be lightly surrendered and that the slump would only prove temporary as 'the consumer has the happy knack of becoming reconciled to even doubling or trebling the price he was wont to pay.'

The pernicious influence of the British Government in increasing the spirit duty at home and so encouraging its being copied abroad was shortly given classic expression in the Memorial on the spirit duty presented by the Scotch Whisky Association in March 1922, to the Chancellor of the Exchequer, Sir Robert Horne. After recounting the punitive effects on the industry and the home consumer, the Memorial moved on, in Point 2 to the effect of those high duty rates on Empire countries. Said the Memorial: 'Encouraged by the precedent at home, the Colonial Governments have been asking to increase their revenue by raising the duty on spirits. The result has been similarly disastrous, the total exports of British and Irish spirits for the past year showing a decline of 1,260,000 proof gallons as compared with the preceding year, and of no less than four million proof gallons as compared with 1913, when they touched high-water mark. While these exports do not contribute directly to the revenue the importance of the overseas markets to both distillers and blenders can hardly be overrated, as they provide an outlet for large quantities of spirits at generally remunerative prices, and eventually make substantial contributions to the Exchequer in the form of Income Tax, Corporation Duty and other taxes. The importance of encouraging these exports from an economic point of view needs no elaboration at our hands, while any action taken by this country calculated to encourage Colonial Governments to exclude our goods is to be deplored.'

The petition by the Highland Distillers, without going into this overseas problem in the same measure, was able to substantiate the effect on overseas sales by affirming the usefulness of the distilling industry to the agriculture of Scotland. Similarly, the Memorandum of the D.C.L. and the U.D.L. associated itself with that of the Scotch Whisky Association, while not neglecting, of course, other aspects of the problem.

Again, in the following March of 1923, the Scotch Whisky Association Memorandum to the Chancellor of the Exchequer, Mr Stanley Baldwin, went over the same ground of the overseas markets but extending the sphere of influence further and not just confining it to colonial governments. 'Encouraged by the British precedent,' it declared, 'overseas Governments, both Colonial and Foreign, have been

The troublesome twenties

seeking to increase their Revenue by raising the Duty on spirits. The
result has been similarly disastrous, the total exports of British and
Irish spirits for the past year showing a decline of 369,496 proof gallons
as compared with the preceding year, which follows upon a decline of
1,260,000 proof gallons in the preceding year. When comparison is
made with the high-water mark touched in 1913 the decline amounts to
no less than 4,384,421 proof gallons. While these exports do not
contribute directly to the Revenue of this country,' the Memorandum
continued on the lines of the previous submission, it underlined the
urgency of the matter in its closing sentence which reads: '... any action
taken by this country calculated to encourage Colonial or Foreign
Governments to shut out British goods by means of prohibitory duties
is to be deplored.'

As Sir Alexander Walker put it in the case of the foreign governments just referred to when giving evidence and being cross-examined
at the royal commission already quoted: 'France raised its duty enormously because whisky is a British product and because it is consumed
by the British in France . . . The duty has been vastly intensified. In
Germany they have raised it also for the same reason, because it is
consumed by British and Americans travelling in Germany. They have
raised the duty to nearly three times what it was. I am only giving you
indications of what every other country is doing. If you take our own
country of Australia where the traditions are the same as our own, look
at the enormous difference in the duty between our own goods exported
there and their goods imported here. Take Canada, which is also our
own flesh and blood with the same tradition; they do not worry about
tradition when it comes to a question of helping their own people.'

Or as Sir Alexander succinctly phrased it in his formal statement:
'The Commission will be well aware of the tariff imposed on British
spirits in foreign and Empire Dominions giving in most cases an
enormous advantage to their own production. I would also draw the
Commission's attention to the high and oppressive duty imposed on
British spirits specially as a war measure and continued since with the
effect as shown . . . and which has had the result of raising the duties all
over the world on the plea that if we can impose it in the United
Kingdom on our own product, why should they not follow our
example. At the same time, they do not impose the same increased duty
on their own production.'

327

After these few masterly excerpts of the wisdom, the truth and fact, of the matter, uttered and written so long ago, no one can dispute particularly in the light of recent events – 1969 – that nothing is thicker than the hide and skull of the politician and bureaucrat.

Then the Scotch whisky industry was suddenly moved on to the international stage, a position it has held since. Early in 1922 among the then usual crops of rumours of takeovers and amalgamations, came the startling suggestion – some said, fact – that American interests were actively contemplating a combination which would embrace the leading firms in all sections of the Scotch whisky trade. On the face of it, it seemed wildly improbable, not only because of the colossal finance that would be involved but because of the world-wide influence and power of the prohibition movement. It was thought that American experience of the dangers besetting the trade in their own country would make them chary, to say the least, of taking similar risks in a foreign land. Then as the story was thought 'too tall to swallow', the trade fell back on a more prosaic version that a big combination of distilling interests was in contemplation with the D.C.L. as the nucleus. After the Buchanan-Dewar annual statement, with its announcement of a stock of 23 million gallons of whisky, a proprietorial interest in eleven malt whisky distilleries and a dividend of twenty-five per cent, free of income-tax, as well as a huge allocation to reserve, it was thought that Buchanan-Dewar Ltd and American interests would combine in the D.C.L.

Such an international linkage was not entirely unexpected: at the time of the Pattison crash at the close of the last century, American interests had attempted to buy their way into the Scotch whisky industry by purchasing some of the assets of the bankrupt brothers, but the D.C.L. had prevented such an entry, buying not only bonded warehouses in Leith, which they wanted, in any case, but also a particular brand name and the stocks which went with it. Moreover, during World War I, particularly in view of their munitions spirit production and their venture into acetone, the D.C.L. had formed transatlantic links, reinforced after the American entry into the war.

Shortly before the annual meeting in July 1922 the D.C.L. 'caused quite a sensation' with the announcement that it had signed a provisional agreement to purchase the ordinary shares of the Distillers Finance Corporation for approximately £3 million, the reason lying in the somewhat complex conditions obtaining in the yeast and industrial spirit industries.

Seconding the Chairman's statement at the annual meeting, Ross, as managing director, put the whole matter, including the American deal rumours in perspective and the clear. 'In these matters,' he said, 'the Stock Exchange usually knows a great deal more of what is going on than what mere directors know, and we have got the credit in turn of having been bought up by an American syndicate for £12 million; of having bought up one or other or all of the important blending businesses of this country . . . There has been no offer by, nor yet any negotiations with the large Scotch blending firms to acquire their interests, nor has there been any offer of £12 million or any other sum by an American syndicate to buy up this company. It is true that such a suggestion was thrown out – not for any given sum, but in the nature of a proposal. The whole idea, however, of a syndicate emanating from a country which prides itself upon being a "dry" country seeking to control the whisky industry of this country appeared so ludicrous that it was turned down without serious thought.'

But the mere fact that such rumours persisted on the stock exchanges of both Great Britain and America is itself evidence of the world-wide position now occupied by this sometime farming sideline which had developed through the persecutions of the tax-gatherer and by means of the native skill of the Scot. 'It is but fair to say that the American proposals had as their origin,' Ross went on, 'a desire to put an end to the rival yeast productions of the world and if, therefore, some scheme can be formulated dealing with this position of the industry only and safeguarding our interests as distillers we shall be quite prepared to consider such when presented. Growing out of these proposals and with the desire to consolidate still further the production of spirit in this country, your directors have had under consideration during the past month proposals to acquire the remaining shares in the United Distilleries Ltd, of Belfast, of which we already own practically the one-half. The other half of these shares which carry with them control of that company are held by the Distillers' Finance Corporation Ltd which also owns or controls various other important blending and distributing business in the North of Ireland, Glasgow and London.'

The American interest was Fleischmann. We have seen how the

distilling industry in Scotland (and Ireland), by the provision of yeast for both the civil and military population of Great Britain, had saved this country and its forces from starvation during the war, and had earlier fought off the inroads of Continental yeast-makers. Now at the time Ross was speaking of a considerable quantity of foreign yeast was again making its way into this country, especially from Dutch and Belgian sources said to be under U.S. control. It was this which once more put the Scotch whisky industry in the international limelight. In that distilling year of 1921–2, in no way exceptional in this regard, eight patent still distilleries in Scotland making yeast also made 9,735,066 proof gallons of spirit, while the usual two patent still distilleries not making yeast made only about half that amount of spirit, or 4,472,939 gallons. The pot still distilleries did not, of course, make yeast and in that year 119 of them made 11,788,464 gallons. These were the usual proportions prevailing after the Armistice. In brief, whisky and yeast were inseparable, and any American intrusion into the profitability of whisky-making was to be fought tooth-and-nail.

As Ross explained later in his history of the D.C.L., the fact that the Irish interests, the U.D.L., 'had formed in conjunction with the Fleischmann Co. of New York, a company called the International Yeast Co., whose object was to compete with the D.C.L. in the yeast market, made it necessary for one more effort to be made to put an end to the dual interest, and to combine both concerns in one company. This necessity was all the greater inasmuch as the spirit trade in Ireland had practically collapsed and had forced the Irish company to look for an outlet in the industrial spirit market to the detriment of the D.C.L. interests.'

Luckily in that International Yeast Co., the Irish firm had retained a fifty-two per cent interest, while Fleischmann had to be content with forty-eight per cent. By acquiring the Ordinary shares of the D.F.C., accomplished by the end of 1922, which controlled fifty per cent of the U.D.L., the D.C.L. became possessed of the fifty-two per cent in the International Yeast Co.

Remembering that whisky and yeast were indissolubly linked, especially after the William Ross-inspired formation at the end of the previous century of the United Yeast Co. Ltd, let Ross resume the story of this phase of whisky's appearing on a major international scene such as had never previously been envisaged in times of peace: 'Thereafter ensued a long series of discussions with the Fleischmann Co., in which the latter endeavoured to improve their position in the British market, while the D.C.L. consistently opposed this endeavour. Many proposals were put forward, including one for merging the whole of the yeast trade not only in this country but in America and the Continent as well, and when this was proved to be impracticable, the suggestion was made by the Fleischmann Co. that the International Yeast Co. should acquire one or other of the Company's English yeast factories . . . This proposal was resolutely turned down by the D.C.L. Directors.'

The death of Mr Julius Fleischmann, president of that company, eased matters which had been approaching boiling point and the D.C.L. acquired the Fleischmann shares in the International Yeast Co. and entered into an agreement with Fleischmann for twenty-five years whereby neither was to encroach on the other's territory for that length of time and the two companies would mutually exchange all improvements in processes. Such was, then, the international stature of the Scotch whisky industry as embodied in the D.C.L. and the person of William Ross who became chairman of the Whisky Association in the middle of this year, 1922, an appointment which saw somewhat of a change in the policy of that Association.

Price-cutting was once more becoming rife at home, and, as alleged at the mid-year meeting of the Association, even abroad. As the *Record* phrased it in a leader on the Association and its new chairman, 'Not only at home, where the higher duty and reduced purchasing power of the consumer were combining to restrict business, but in overseas markets as well an ever-contracting demand was being experienced, with the result that there became apparent a tendency on the part of some firms to break away and sell below the Association prices, even although this may have involved a reduction in quality.'

Now it was that insistence on quality from the dawn of the century as noted earlier that had helped put Scotch whisky on the world markets and led to its pre-war high of 10 million gallons. It was this continued insistence on quality in the chaotic markets of the inter-war years which kept the best brands to the fore.

This was made explicit at the annual meeting in London in May 1922, by Lord Woolavington – the former James Buchanan – when he told the meeting of shareholders in Buchanan-Dewar Ltd: 'The world-wide reputation enjoyed by the brands of the associated companies . . . has been acquired by the consistent maintenance of a very high standard of quality, whisky of great age only being used in these brands, and the recognition of which is materially evidenced by the continually increased demand, both in the home and export markets. The essential factor to ensure the maintenance of a consistent quality of superior excellence is the holding of adequate stocks . . . For two years distillation was stopped by the Government . . . At that time we held, as we still hold, the largest stock of Scotch whisky in Scotland . . . We own, or are interested in, eleven distilleries in Scotland, all producing malt whisky . . . the combined firms have in stock over 23 million gallons of Scotch whisky.'

There lies the secret: while overall sales of Scotch whisky were falling and fluctuating violently on both the home and overseas fronts, the larger firms, as exemplified by Buchanan-Dewar, were increasing their proportion of the world markets. The structure of the industry as it is today, and as it has been known for the past generation or more, was rapidly in these years of stress taking shape and becoming concrete. As the Edinburgh correspondent in the centre of whisky's capital, put it that summer during the 'silent season': 'The big distributors with a world-wide connection are finding their sales wonderfully well maintained and there is some reason to believe that the rank and file of the proprietary brand owners are not so happily situated . . . The more difficult to sell, the greater need there is for advertising,' he wrote, putting his finger on one of the causes of major world esteem; 'all publicity is well worth while. Exporters are now taking a more hopeful view of the outlook.'

But later that summer he had to report that while some sections of the export trade were 'suffering from the shortage in the supplies of fine old matured whiskies', the consumption 'in the colonies, as elsewhere, has been adversely affected by the greatly increased Customs duties on spirits, and by the less general prosperity, with the result that there are well-known and reputable firms in the export trade who could handle more business than they are getting'. The cure of those inter-war years: the wildly fluctuating bouts of employment and unemployment, of prosperity and poverty, of excessive taxation on spirits and of protective tariff barriers the world around.

Indeed, the whisky industry was then at a serious disadvantage with a gloomy outlook for the future: it was saddled with expensive stocks laid down in the artificial period of prosperity that followed the Armistice, and the considerable inflations resulting from wartime restrictions and the important liquidations that had attracted new financial interests when business looked rosy in the first two post-war years. Even compulsory bonding and a fixed minimum age played its part: although it had improved the quality of the whisky offered the public, it was a buttress of inflated values. And during those inter-war years there was more often than not no room for inflated values out of scale with the position.

Nevertheless, Lord Dewar was able to tell shareholders of Buchanan-Dewar Ltd the following year, 1923, that 'the business of the companies are in a very sound progressive condition, the demand, both for home and export, yearly increasing. Buchanan-Dewar Ltd, through its subsidiary companies, is in a very strong, and, in fact, an exceptionally strong position as regards stocks, which guaranteed to consumers at home and abroad a maintenance of a high standard of quality, for which the subsidiary firms have always had a high reputation'.

In the summer of that year came preliminary notice of a major export move, this time by the D.C.L. As Ross told the annual meeting in Edinburgh they were about to carry out an important organisational change. The company had been in the export trade of blended whiskies since the eighties of the last century, but had never pursued it vigorously until the war, when, as remarked earlier, in order to retain business following the 1915 Stevenson-inspired minimum age the company had begun its acquisition of blending firms.

As Ross said, at the 1923 annual general meeting, about the number of interests combined under the wing of the D.C.L.: 'In large measure these various subsidiary companies are engaged in the blending and distributing of potable whisky which is a brand of the business which, previous to the war, we did not touch unless for export markets. This branch of our business, however, has now grown so important that your directors consider it could be better organised under a separate company. It is therefore proposed, while retaining the individuality of the various brands of whisky, to transfer the shares of the subsidiary companies to one holding company, whose shares, on the other hand, would be held by the D.C.L., instead of the present arrangement . . . In this way it is hoped to co-ordinate the policy of the various companies in a manner hardly possible under existing conditions.'

There was, accordingly, registered in Edinburgh on 25 January 1924, as a private company with a nominal capital of £1 million, the Distillers Agency Ltd 'to acquire the blending, export and other business carried on by The Distillers Company Limited at South Queensferry, Linlithgowshire, and the distilling, malting and other business at Knockdhu distillery, Banffshire.'

As Ross put it in his history: '. . . . arrangements were made for forming a new subsidiary company called the Distilleries Agency Ltd, to take over the export branch of the D.C.L. and thus segregate that section of the company's business from the actual manufacturing. The assets taken over by the new company included the distillery at Knockdhu, which had originally been built as a support to the company's export trade. The capital was fixed at £1,000,000, the shares in which are all held by the D.C.L., who otherwise continued their financial support.'

Thus arose a new milestone in the export activities and world conquests of Scotch whisky, an event the full significance of which was only appreciated a few years later.

24

Imperial expansion

ALTHOUGH WORLD trade made a slight recovery in 1923 and 1924, the emphasis in all trade was on protection, and the empire tried to weld closer the links which had seen it through the Great War to fight the battle of world markets. The first result was the 1924 Empire Exhibition at Wembley, repeated in 1925, under the leadership of Sir James Stevenson, managing director of John Walker & Sons Ltd. It was a natural and most happy choice: the Scots had peopled, won and invigorated the second British Empire which arose in a fit of absent-mindedness after the American Revolution, and no pioneers of British international and Empire trade could rival the distillers of Scotland.

How empire-minded the Scotch whisky industry was at this stage is amply evidenced by a few figures. The six largest overseas customers for Scotch whisky in the year before the exhibition, as for many years before and after, were the colonies, in this order: Australia, with imports in 1923 of 1,217,000 gallons; Canada with 820,531; Bahamas, 581,164; New Zealand, 470,477; British India, 439,080; and South Africa, with 259,806. In that year, Scotch exports earned a total of close on £10 million, but the gallonage, although about one million and a half better than in the previous year, was still nearly three million below the pre-war figure.

With Sir James Stevenson raised to the peerage in the Wembley honours, and with his wide contacts in the whisky industry allied with his own driving, forceful personality and his belief in empire, the Scotch whisky firms presented themselves in force at the exhibition in the Palace of Industry. About forty-odd were represented there in specially constructed central premises, modelled as a fifteenth-century baronial castle with a spiked portcullis, over which was the motto 'Alba Gu Brath' – 'Scotland for Ever', the famous battle-cry shouted by the Gordon Highlanders at Waterloo as they charged the French, clinging to the stirrups of the Royal Scots Greys and together routed a French force ten times their number.

How strong were those export, especially empire sales was instanced shortly after the opening of the Wembley exhibition when Lord (Tommy) Dewar presided at the ninth annual general meeting of Buchanan-Dewar Ltd, and told shareholders that 'Last year has been in every respect the best year we have ever had . . . (the sales of both companies) . . . show both in the home trade and in the export trade a remarkable increase, amounting last year to more than £2,000,000 over the previous year's sales.' The pattern of the export trade was rapidly emerging, and the firm's 'continued expansion' constituted 'a record year, six important distilleries having been acquired, which acquisitions,' it was noted, 'have enormously strengthened the company's trading position, while the dividend paid shows an increase . . .' 'During the year,' said Lord Dewar, 'a year in which they increased the issued ordinary capital to £4 million by the issue of one bonus share in respect of each ordinary share previously issued, they had also purchased several very large stocks of old whisky from companies which had retired from the business, so strengthening their position in dealing with the largely increased demands for their brands, particularly overseas.'

Similarly John Walker & Sons Ltd, who in March the year before had made an offer of debenture and preference shares, were able to report that 'the sales for the period under review, both at home and abroad, have been the largest in the history of the business'. And at the annual meeting in July of the D.C.L., Ross, the managing director, told shareholders that as regards the scheme remarked upon the previous year for a holding company possessed of the shares of the subsidiary companies in the blending trade, it transpired on further consideration 'that this would involve considerable expense, out of all proportion to the benefits sought to be obtained, and the scheme in its original form was consequently abandoned. It was, however, deemed advisable,' he continued, 'to separate the export blending business carried on at South

Queensferry from the strictly manufacturing portion of the company's business. A new company, which is called the Distillers' Agency Ltd, has been formed with a paid-up capital of £1 million, and embraces not only the blending business already referred to, but also the Highland distillery at Knockdhu, Banffshire, hitherto carried on in connection with that business . . . Our various subsidiary blending companies, including the Agency, will still be retained as individual units and be separately managed . . .' But it underlines the growth and inportance of the whisky industry, particularly on the export side that when, in 1880, some D.C.L. shares were offered to the public the issued capital of the company was £650,000: in 1924, the paid-up capital of the export subsidiary was £1,000,000.

But the dream of imperial free trade was doomed. By the end of the year *The Times* Australian correspondent reported that the tariff revision in favour of Australian goods was likely in the near future to be applied to Scotch whisky. The following year was dominated by news of the big amalgamation – to be reviewed in due course – but early on that year came news from that other prominent colonial market, Canada, which was, along with the Australian duty increase, to mark another phase in the development of the Scotch whisky industry into an international distilling body.

In anticipation of further commerce with the United States, Canadian whisky interests were making optimistic efforts to interest British capital in the idea of producing grain spirits of a similar character to those distilled in Great Britain. The promoters of the scheme could claim to have obtained an important concession from the Canadian Government, which in itself was an extremely valuable asset. There was some criticism of the scheme; it was pointed out that there is a vast difference between prospectus profits calculated by men who fancy whisky can be obtained from agricultural refuse by mould ferments, and the sound finance of practical men. There was nothing, it was added, to prevent Canadian capitalists from purchasing British brains and adopting British processes. It was theoretically easy to distil in any part of Canada, but it was imperative to study every detail in Scotland from malting to the warehouse. A further *Times* correspondent report from Australia indicated another line in which the D.C.L. – fundamentally whisky producers – was to branch out: the distillation of power alcohol in Australia from cassava and other starch-bearing crops.

That development we cannot here pursue in detail. Suffice it to remark that it was but another instance of the inter-empire spread of distillation by companies based in Great Britain, the assumption of yet another international role by the Scottish distiller.

It is of passing interest to note that there had even been rumours before the budget that the Chancellor of the Exchequer, Mr Winston Churchill, intended to impose an export duty on spirits in the 1925 budget, but in keeping with the times the budget did mark another advance of imperial preference, a preference granted the colonies in their exports to Great Britain, but rarely repaid by similar concessions, as we shall shortly see. But the rumours of that export tax were taken so seriously that Ross, presiding at the July annual general meeting of the D.C.L. as chairman for the first time, had to take lengthy notice of it. 'Previous to the last budget,' he said, 'rumours were current that an export tax was to be placed upon spirits. We did not treat the suggestion seriously, as we could not conceive that the Government would ever so far forget themselves as to place a handicap upon any commodity which formed a staple industry of this country. An export tax might be justifiable in the case of some commodity which is scarce, or where its free export was drawing upon the capital reserves of the country, but neither of these conditions apply to the spirits trade today, and, therefore, it is the duty of the Government to encourage, rather than hinder, the export of goods manufactured in this country.'

It was the ill-fated year of the return to the gold standard with the pound at pre-war parity, and knowing there is no smoke without fire, it may reasonably be concluded that such an ill-considered tax was contemplated. In itself, it is in a retrograde sense a testimony to the value of the exports of Scotch whisky, and yet in 1924–5 British spirit exports, at just over eight million gallons, were slightly down on the previous year.

As indicative of the difficulties then surrounding the whole of international trade, difficulties which did not spare the Scotch whisky industry, it should be noted that the summer of 1925 saw an increasing export of single malt whisky to Canada to blend there with Canadian grain spirits. While in those 'dull times' almost any business was considered acceptable, the *Record* said, 'there is every possibility of Canadian distillers turning their attention to the manufacture of malt spirits. In fact, no secret has been made of the efforts of certain

Canadian importers to obtain information of distilling practices, and sooner or later they may offer a sufficient inducement to attract experienced workers to Canada. Whether they will succeed,' concluded the *Record*, 'in producing the typical Scotch flavour is, of course, another proposition.'

Now the Canadian Government had imposed a preferential duty on Canadian-made spirits which resulted in Scotch being penalised by an extra duty, in excess of the local spirits' duty, of one dollar a gallon. In Australia, the locally-made whisky was enjoying a protective duty which made Scotch pay 9s. a gallon more. Home trade was in the doldrums; profits had to be made somewhere; the D.C.L. secured rights of various processes with particular reference to industrial alcohol. By the end of 1926, Ross told shareholders in July the following year, they were 'approached by local interests both in Canada and Australia to join them in acquiring and building distilleries in each of these parts of our Empire. It was not so much a question of financing such ventures as the local interests were prepared to put up all the money if necessary. What they desired was the experience which they felt we could supply. Deputations were appointed to visit both countries, with the result that, acting on their advice, the directors have acquired a fifty per cent interest in a new distillery situated near Montreal, in the Province of Quebec, which is already in operation. They have also agreed to build a distillery in co-operation with the chief whisky buyers in Australia – the site chosen being near Geelong, in the State of Victoria. The object in both these cases is to take advantage of the preferential treatment given by the respective governments to the domestic product as compared with the imported whisky and gin. The directors have strongly impressed upon their associates in these ventures that they can never hope to make Scotch whisky in either Canada or Australia, and believe that there will still be a demand for the Scotch-made article from those to whom price is no consideration . . . If there is to be a change-over from a Scotch to a locally-made article, then the company must be prepared to meet it.'

In short, the British taxman's evil activities had come home to roost: the 72s. 6d. duty per proof gallon on whisky had been imitated, as remarked above, overseas; the world was in the throes of a protective tariff malady; an overseas substitute was, in consequence of the British Chancellor of the Exchequer's high duty rate, in course of replacing

Scotch whisky, and so reducing employment in Scotland, as well as British foreign earnings.

At that same D.C.L. meeting, Sir James Calder, who had gone to both Australia and Canada, recounted first the power alcohol producing plant in Queensland, Australia, and then went on to speak of the potable alcohol plant near Geelong, Victoria. The 9s. duty differential on Scotch, he said, made 'a big difference in the price to the consumer of whisky, and there are always a number of people not sufficiently well off to be prepared to pay the extra price demanded for the better article . . . It is wise to provide a good local article in conjunction with the wine merchants of Australia, who are very anxious that we should support them. I do not myself think that this local article will affect the consumption of Scotch whisky to any large extent, but if it is going to supplant Scotch whisky, the company may as well supply it.' Sir James Calder also told how he returned through Canada and said of the distillery near Montreal in which the company had taken an interest that 'It is a first-class distillery and is making a very good whisky.' And on the sale of the group's own Scotch whiskies he was able to report that 'Everywhere I went . . . I found the brands of the company not only the leading brands, but in many cases the only brands.' This he described as 'very satisfactory', adding the truism that 'after all it is on the public demand that our results depend.'

Ross's history of the company details at some length the course of events in both the Australian and Canadian developments. On the Australian potable spirits distillery he told how the proposal emanated from 'some of the largest wholesale spirit merchants in Melbourne . . . The essence of their report was that the Federal Government of Australia was apparently determined to foster home industries at the expense of all imported products, including even those from the home country, and, as an instance, the preference on local-made spirits was now 9s. per gallon as compared with the duty on spirits coming from the United Kingdom. As a result, the aforesaid merchants were of opinion that the tendency would be for the sale of locally-made spirits to grow, and conversely the sale of imported spirits to diminish. They had, therefore, agreed amongst themselves to erect a distillery in or near Melbourne, and their desire was that The Distillers Company should join them in the venture. The point was a difficult one to decide, as for the D.C.L. to meet the wishes of the Melbourne merchants might merely hasten the injury which they suggested was in prospect for our existing export trade. On the other hand, by refusing to participate in the new venture, we might throw the business into other hands and entail a loss both ways. The Board wisely decided to send out a deputation to collect the views of the local representatives and, if so agreed, to confer with the other interests as to a possible site and plan for the new distillery.

'The deputation comprised Sir James Calder, and Mr Peter M. Dewar, who had the assistance of Mr J. Stuart Smith and Mr A. Vyvyan Board, both of whom were already on the spot. After fully weighing up the whole situation and obtaining the unanimous approval of the local representatives of our associated companies, the deputation cabled their approval of the proposal and received authority to look for a site, which was ultimately obtained at Corio Bay, Geelong . . . A company was in due course formed with the title of the Distillers' Corporation (Pty) Ltd, and a capital of £250,000, of which the D.C.L. agreed to subscribe fifty-one per cent, with the right to nominate the chairman.'

Associated with the Australian development, and the Scotch whisky industry striding the imperial world, was the Canadian proposal. As Ross recalled, 'Messrs Bronfman arrived from Montreal with an offer to sell a half-interest in a new distillery erected by them near Montreal. Unlike the Australian proposition, which covered the manufacture of both malt and grain whiskies to be locally made and afterwards blended in imitation of the Scotch product, the Messrs Bronfman proposed to import the malt whiskies from Scotland and blend these with the locally-made grain spirits, and thereafter to sell the product as a Scotch style of Canadian whisky. A deputation, consisting of the Chairman [Ross], Mr Herd, and Mr Nicolson, was appointed to visit Montreal and report upon the whole matter. These gentlemen, having carefully considered the situation, agreed to recommend that the company enter into such an arrangement, and an agreement was eventually drawn up for the distillery and its whole other assets and liabilities being transferred to a new company called the Distillers Corporation, Ltd, with a capital of 25,000 shares of 100 dollars each to be held in equal parts by the D.C.L. and the Bronfman interests. Part of the arrangement was that the D.C.L. or its associated companies should license certain brands to the new company, so that these could be operated in Canada under its name. With this object in view it was resolved to incorporate a second company in Canada under the title of the Distillers Company of Canada, Ltd, which would act as the Holding Company for the Company's share interest in the Distillers Corporation, and would also be the medium through which the licences above referred to would be granted.'

Taking into account other activities of the D.C.L. than its whisky ones, it is of interest to note that today overseas companies listed in the annual report are: D.C.L. (Holdings) Australia (Pty) Ltd; Destilaria Gordon Limitada (Brazil); Distillers Company (Canada) Ltd; Distillers Company Ltd (Delaware, U.S.A.); Distillers Company (New Zealand) Ltd; Gordon's de Venezuela C.A.; Gordon's Dry Gin Co. Ltd (Delaware, U.S.A.); Gordon's Dry Gin Co. (South Africa) (Pty) Ltd; Tanqueray Gordon & Co. de Mexico, S.A.; Tolley, Scott & Tolley Ltd (Australia); and United Distillers (Pty) Ltd (Australia). In three of the foregoing the D.C.L. does not hold all the shares, but in each of these cases the shares held constitute eighty per cent or more of the total. But the D.C.L. was not the only Scotch whisky firm possessed with the imperial idea of setting up distilleries in Australia and Canada.

Messrs W. & A. Gilbey who had begun as wine merchants after returning from the Crimean War and who had opened their own London gin distillery in 1872, had, naturally, had an interest in Scotch and Irish whiskies. As Scotch whisky came to the fore in the eighties of the last century, they had purchased their first Highland malt whisky distillery, Glen Spey, near Rothes. A few years later, as Scotch approached its peak boom of home consumption, in 1895 they bought Strathmill Highland distillery, near Keith, in Banffshire. Early this century, in 1904, they had added to their distillery possessions the Highland malt distillery Knockando, on Strathspey. Incidentally, it was only in 1905 that W. & A. Gilbey began blending their malt whiskies with grain whisky, a matter on which Mr. Alfred Gilbey gave exhaustive evidence at the 1908–9 royal commission of inquiry into whisky and other potable spirits.

The firm had many overseas interests and properties, particularly to do with their wine and brandy activities, and as Mr Alec Waugh summarised in the centenary history of the firm, *Merchants of Wine*. 'Later, as a corollary to their development of overseas distilleries, they established their own plants in Canada and Australia for the production of local whiskies. Slightly different methods were employed and no attempt was made to imitate the bouquet or taste of Scotch. Each brand stood on its own feet and was destined for a particular market, in the country of its origin.'

We have seen something of the Australian trend in favour of local production and manufacture, and it coincides perfectly with D.C.L. action in the matter that as Australian-made gin had become such a dangerous rival to Gilbey's because of the preferential-protective tariff Geoffrey and Alec Gold, partners in the firm, toured Australia in 1927 to examine conditions on the spot. To quote Mr Alec Gold's own account of the matter: 'After exhaustive inquiry of all agents . . . they cabled a recommendation that as a first step Gilbeys Gin should be shipped at a high strength, first in bottle then in drums, to be rebottled in Australia, so effecting a considerable saving in duty and enabling the price to the consumer to be brought down to meet local competition. A site for a bottling establishment was purchased in West Melbourne.' That was in 1927, when their total investment in Australia was £25,000; at the time of the firm's centenary, in 1957, the investment was of the order of one million Australian pounds.

For late in the thirties, Messrs Alec Gold and Derek Gilbey decided that in addition to distilling gin in Australia they must become their own spirit producers and ultimately another site near Melbourne was settled on where they erected a spirit distillery which came on stream in 1937. After the 1939–45 war, pre-war plans to undertake whisky distilling in Australia were carried through and two projects were undertaken: the production and storage of Australian whisky at Moorabbin, suburb of Melbourne, and the acquisition of the old-established distillery of Milne & Co., in South Australia, producing and holding stocks of whisky and gin.

When the two Golds returned from Australia in 1927, they made the passage via Canada and visited Toronto where it was put to them and agreed that a distillery would need to be established before long. As Mr Alec Waugh puts it in the centenary history already referred to, 'In Canada, too, local competition soon forced the house to install a distillery in Toronto. As the first partners had travelled over Europe, forming direct relations with wine-growers and shippers, so the third generation travelled throughout the Empire making the business global, enlarging the number of their agencies, setting up distilleries in the New World.'

With the Canadian preferential tariff protecting the domestic product, then, the two Golds visited Toronto again in 1932 and the Gilbey spirit and gin distillery began there in 1933. It was only after the war that Gilbey managed to begin whisky production in Canada: permission was obtained from the Bank of England, with the support of the Board of Trade, for the remittance of dollars to Canada and the retention of profits there for the erection of a warehouse – at first consisting only of a basement and ground floor – and the necessary equipment to enable whisky production to begin. A suitable blend was found and large quantities laid aside to mature; as the storage space was filled up, further storeys were added to the warehouse. As Mr Alec Gold recalls, 'When supplies of matured whisky were available a modest start was made to place one brand on the market, and other brands were gradually introduced in different price brackets, all of which have proved a success. In view of the prospects of the future prosperity of Canada, extension of the distilling capacity has recently been effected,' he added in February 1957.

Mr Waugh, after noting the post-repeal of prohibition moves of the firm, just as the D.C.L. also made major gin moves in the period, writes in summary fashion as follows: 'The export trade is, in a sense, the more interesting because it is new. Gilbey's activities are now world-wide: they have established plants in Canada, Australia, South Africa and the United States, and the shelves contain many items that are not available in the United Kingdom. There are, for example, three different kinds of rye whisky: Golden Velvet, Black Velvet and Golden Special, that are only sold in Canada. For the Australian market also there are three different kinds of Australian whisky: Castle Malt, Gauntlet and Bond 7 – the last a very fine liqueur.'

We cannot here follow the progress of every year's shipments of Scotch whisky to every market and enough has been described to portray the framework in which the industry struggled before the last war, and its manifold reactions in the changing situation. During the thirties of this century overall British spirits exports, as we have noted earlier, dwindled with the Great Depression, recovered a little in the armament-prompted boom just before the war, were materially assisted by repeal in the United States and by the immediate reaction of the American importers following the outbreak of hostilities. Later, during that war, what with the cessation of distilling under the conditions of war and the need to stretch stocks for as long as possible, together with the natural wartime shipping restrictions, exports of Scotch once more diminished – except for the Canadian market, which was never rationed.

In both 1945 and 1946 under five million gallons of Scotch were all that could be spared for the palates of the overseas world while the home market was reduced to about one-half of the pre-war year consumption. But, it should be noticed, the industry began its own export drive in 1945-6, well in advance of the Government-inspired one. The industry had been an exporting one since its earliest days, when it exported first from the Highlands to the Lowlands, to England across the border, and then to the empire.

Now the reversal of roles in the two world wars of this century should be noted. In World War I, the Government intervened to ensure supplies for the home market and in 1917 insisted that that market should receive fifty per cent of its 1916 supplies, a proportion later raised to seventy-five per cent and with a fixed maximum price structure. We have already had occasion to observe the industry's own fixing, and insisting on maximum prices of its own volition in World War II to preserve the interests of the home drinker.

They had learnt, in effect, the hard way that it is best in such times to anticipate official intervention by reasonable action on the part of the industry itself. Where the Scotch Whisky Association, then, itself introduced rationing early in 1940 and stepped in to help the foreign exchange position by selling abroad all that could be spared, it was only in the spring of 1947 that the official government export drive began with unfortunate results on the whisky industry. The industry's contribution during the 'cash and carry' period of the war was in itself spectacular and just as splendid were its efforts in the years after the conflict.

But officialdom must have its way, and from the spring of 1947 until the end of 1953 an arrangement had to be made annually between the Ministry of Food, the Board of Trade and the Scotch Whisky Association setting an export objective for Scotch whisky and the allocation for the home market. The bureaucratic blackmail was the threat to withhold the raw materials, the cereals, necessary for distilling. Over the period of this enforced agreement, exports exceeded the obligatory target, that target being for the last year of the agreement some 11 million gallons for export (and 2,750,000 for home!). In that year, 1953, the actual quantity exported was in fact 13,202,464 proof gallons. It was, then, only since the beginning of 1954 that firms were freed of imposed export quotas, and such has been the nature of the industry in the last generation that it was only about the spring of 1959 that the home market became free of quotas, or rations, imposed by the blending firms themselves as they pursued, successfully and profitably, world markets with the necessary high quality and well matured blends of whiskies.

Today those overseas markets are consuming over 167 million proof gallons of Scotch whisky as compared with some 9 million in 1939, just under the 1913 figure of 10 million gallons, and today's exports, some half of which are drunk in the United States, return some £120 million or more to Great Britain. With the home market once more shrinking, as it did through the twenties and thirties, assuming a minor role beside foreign markets, it is time to consider it in more detail.

25

Scotch survives the twenties

THE HOME market for Scotch whisky in the inter-war years suffered all the wavering vicissitudes of the British economy. Even with the upward fillip of the economy, under the somewhat inept rearmament programme towards the end of that period, home consumption of Scotch was less than 7 million proof gallons in the last complete financial year before the outbreak of war. Exactly how diminished that total was will be seen in due course. But as a, strictly speaking, non-essential product, on a par with food and clothing, the home market Scotch consumption was bound by its own very nature to feel more acutely the strains and stresses of the British economy during those most formative of years, the two decades between the termination of one war and the first shots of the next.

The twenty-year period may be sub-divided into three main periods, each of which is reflected in the adventures of the industry. Soon after the Armistice of 1918 there began, not unnaturally, a great burst of activity of the nature of a boom, as the nation and its leaders thought they could resume the world as it was pre-war, and as customers replenished, in a bout of inflation, their depleted stocks. That miniature boom reached its height in the summer of 1920 and was matched by an equally steep dive into a depression, with the whisky industry bearing its inflation-level rate of excise duty. That descent into depression lasted until well into 1922, when an intermittent recovery began, a recovery of the economy which encountered repeated checks as politicians and financiers lost their way in the 'brave new world' of the post-war years: the early months of 1925 saw a decline in industrial activity, and the general strike and the protracted coal strike of 1926 brought about another savage reversal. In 1927 there was a brief stimulus as arrears were attempted to be made up, but towards the end of 1929, encouraged by the Wall Street collapse of October that year, all activity again turned downwards and the depression grew rapidly worse and world-wide. Never in the history of man had there been such a wide fluctuation in such a short time. The bottom of the depression was reached in 1933 – with some three million out of work in Great Britain –¹ and a sluggish upwards movement set in until 1937, the best year of the thirties, after which another recession, staved off only by war, set in again.

The year 1913, a boom year for Scotch at home as it began to recover from the Lloyd George budget increase of 1909 and abroad as world prosperity stimulated exports, was also a peak productive year for British and world manufacturing. That level was not reached again until 1923, and it has been calculated that if the pre-war trends had continued, the British and European manufacturing output achieved in 1929 would have been attained in 1921. With the loss, that is, of eight years' growth of capital output, the economy as a whole was bound to suffer, Scotch whisky particularly.

In the vagaries of international finance, in an atmosphere of post-war inflation, the pound's purchasing power fell faster than that of the dollar, and as the American price level began to drop rapidly in 1920 the reductions needed in British prices were formidable. Credit restrictions, which in turn bit deeply into Scotch whisky productive and distributive abilities, were the order of the day and continued even into the slump of 1921 and 1922, when every rational consideration would have suggested just the opposite measures. Gradually and unevenly, the pound and the British economy recovered their wavering stability, and in May 1925 the most disastrous step of the return to the gold standard at a pre-war parity with the dollar was embarked on.

Stability, the sort of pre-war stability that was sought for by the pre-war men in charge still, had barely returned when the 1929 depression broke to hurl down what had been painfully and doubtfully restored. World trade collapsed; international lending ceased. Of course it all had the consequence of bringing on a sterling crisis in mid-1931 and in the two months from mid-July there was an external drain of over £200 million from the London money market. No more convincing evidence of the inadequacy of the previous policy could have been forthcoming, and drastic measures had to be initiated. In September that year the gold standard was suddenly abandoned. This was unavoidable, for Britain, though solvent, as an international banker did not have the abnormally high liquid reserves needed in 1931 and was unable to continue borrowing them as it had done earlier in that summer. At least that flight from the gold standard depreciated the value of sterling and so helped exports by lowering prices on world markets for British goods, but the depreciation of the dollar in 1933-4 about wiped out any British advantage. It was beginning to dawn on the powers that be, at the cost of almost untold human suffering as unemployment stalked the land and hunger-marchers strode to Westminster, as the bulk of the nation downed tools in the first-ever general strike, as fortunes collapsed and suicides mounted, that fresh measures were needed to control and manage the economy of the nation.

How could Scotch whisky hope to resume its pre-war sales when crippled by an inflationary duty rate and with unemployment such as the country had never known before? In 1920 there were roughly nine hundred thousand registered as unemployed; in 1922 the figure had had another million to it to make a total of 1·9 million. It gradually fell back to 1·2 million in 1926 only to leap up to 1·4 million in 1927, falling away again to 1·2 million in 1929. From then on, the picture rapidly darkened: to 1·9 million again in 1931, to 2·7 million in both 1932 and 1933, improving only to 2·2 million in 1934, and becoming – still high – 1·5 million in 1937, after which the signs of depression set in again with an increase to 1·8 million in 1938. Such figures, obviously were not irrelevant to Scotch whisky production and consumption. The wonder is not that Scotch sales dropped so severely at home in those years between two of the bloodiest – and most expensive – wars ever fought by Great Britain, but that there were any sales outside the gilded cages of the well-to-do.

As John Boyd Orr reminded us in his 'Food, Health and Income', in the early 1930s, some fifty per cent of the British nation were living on less than twenty shillings per head per week, or less than eight shillings spent on food for each person each week. One person in ten had a total income of less than ten shillings per week, of which four shillings went on food, while there were persons attempting to continue on as little as two shillings a week. The Scots in this category could add porridge to their menus, but in the main the less than ten shillings a week classification had to live on potatoes, bread, margarine, cheap jam and tea.

It is in this framework that we must now turn to consider how the Scotch whisky industry survived, some of the measures it was driven to take and how the present pattern of its structure was forced upon it.

When Austen Chamberlain raised the excise duty on Scotch whisky in his 1920 budget to the then unheard figure of 72s. 6d. the gallon, the country was booming. No one minded paying the new – controlled – price, a price in which the Treasury shared to the extent of 8s. 5½d., of the total of 12s. 6d. of a bottle at the wartime strength of 70 degrees Sikes. This left the entire trade and industry the magnificent sum of 4s. 0½d. to meet all costs and leave profit margins to all who handled it. When Bonar Law was Chancellor he had taunted the industry with living in an artificial world with demand and supply controlled by the Government and with the price fixed by the same power. Until September 1919 the home market was restricted to fifty per cent of its 1916 deliveries, a percentage which increased that month to seventy-five per cent and in the December following all restrictions were removed from clearances from bond. Even so, the great majority of the retail trade received only about seventy-five per cent of their 1916 purchases, simply because of the shortage of supplies of matured whiskies suitable for consumption.

A strong feeling prevailed among the leading blenders and distillers that they needed to conserve existing stocks – the same principle as they were to act upon in World War II – and would have to do so for a few years ahead until the distilleries had had time to put into stock enough spirits to make up the shortage in the amounts then maturing. When Chamberlain increased the duty in the following April, the trade murmured, as we have seen: but the consuming public went on spending, reassured by the Government price-freeze of Scotch. As Ross, managing director of the D.C.L., told the annual meeting that July, 'So far the results had justified the two last increases from the Revenue point of view, but when Mr Chamberlain again returned to the docile cow for a further augmentation this year, raising the duty to the enormous rate of 72s. 6d. per gallon, it was time for the Trade to protest . . . The price of whisky to the public has been controlled for the last four years . . . The Trade was fairly well protected when the control price was first put on, the margin then allowed having been twice cut into through the Trade having been prevented from passing on to the public the whole increase in duty placed on spirits on the last two occasions.'

A few figures to illustrate what was happening: in the financial year 1913–14 there were retained for consumption in the United Kingdom 26,795,000 gallons of home-made spirit; under restrictions, this fell to 10,325,000 gallons in 1917–18; edged upwards to 17,826,000 gallons in 1919–20, and what with Chamberlain's increased excise and the depression beginning about August 1920 it fell in the following financial year to 15,463,000 gallons, a drop of more than two million gallons in a year. It was to fall by another million in each of the next two years, depression years, as we have seen, to 14,546,000 gallons in 1921–2, and to 13,864,000 gallons in 1922–3. Nevertheless, in 1920 and into 1921 the most pressing need of the trade was the securing of matured whisky, a requirement made the more difficult by the immediate post-war intrusion of speculators into the market, and the cessation of distilling towards the end of the war. This need became so urgent, as we shall see in due course, that it was responsible for refashioning the entire structure of the industry. A large proportion of existing stocks was held by the big distributors – more popularly today called the big blenders – who would not sell on any terms to the wholesale trade, least of all to their competitors. Some of the distributors, indeed, were so prepared to buy stocks, particularly ahead of rivals, as to induce many to get the quick profit and leave the whisky trade altogether.

As *The Times* put it: 'The most active purchasers have been among the most powerful interests in the Trade, who, while possessed of big stocks, still see that these may prove inadequate, and in any case appreciate better than any the extent of the shortage, present and prospective. The hand of those Big Interests may not always be clearly apparent, but it is generally there, and there is no disguising the fact that the control of the Scotch whisky industry is rapidly passing into that self-same hand.'

Early in 1921, the depression having only been in course a few months, came an ominous disturbance from the Highlands, a strike of distillery workers, a Scottish reflection of the malaise affecting the entire British labour structure in the years between the wars. In the event it was 'amicably overcome'. The union maintained that tun-room men, under-brewers, mashmen, stillmen, drum-men, and firemen were entitled to overtime rates, and that the Highland Malt Distillers' Association had broken the original agreement by drawing up a new one, and refusing to pay overtime rates. The original application by the men was for a minimum wage averaging £3 10s. for a forty-eight-hour week; the employers offered a minimum wage of £3 per week for a fifty-three-hour week and special rates for different grades of workers; they also offered to pay at the rate of time plus a quarter for overtime which was accepted by the men. The new scheme was drawn up and it was with regard to overtime that the trouble arose. The men's representatives were quickly on the scene; terms were agreed, and the result was that distillery workers became 'the best-paid class of workmen in the Highlands'.

But however willingly and well the distillery workers worked, the fate of Scotch whisky was decided in the cities of the land, above all in Westminster. The Government proposed – it was still a Lloyd George administration – in July 1921 to permit the sale of whisky at its pre-war strength provided the Licensing Bill got the royal assent. It will be remembered that the retail strength of whisky had been compulsorily reduced to 30 u.p., or 70 proof, as is more commonly said today, as a 'war measure'. This permitted reversion of strength to its pre-war level was not regarded in the trade as exactly a concession. It aroused little enthusiasm among blenders and bottlers. They realised that the existing controlled price, in a period of recession, was the maximum that could fairly be asked of the consumer, or that he was likely to pay. Pre-war strength, it was agreed, would be attractive to some, but those who preferred a stronger spirit used to purchase it by the gallon jar and it was thought that they would revert to it as soon as it became available again. In fact, there was no prospect of any immediate change from the 30 u.p. – it is with us still, in the main – and it was agreed that until the Government reduced the rate of tax on whisky there was no inducement to compete with a stronger blend.

The Scotch Whisky Association met late in July at Bakers' Hall, London, to discuss the matter of reversion to pre-war strength. As the chairman of the council of the Association, Mr R. Montgomery, put it: 'Although it is generally assumed that the Trade will revert to the pre-war strength of twenty under proof, it is impossible to do so, because the public cannot be induced to pay more than 12s. 6d. per bottle, and even that most reluctantly, and a higher strength can only be supplied at a correspondingly higher price. The first step in reverting to pre-war strength must necessarily be for the Government to abate something of the savage duty at present imposed. The Bill provides that whisky may be sold as low as 35 u.p. without notification to the public. We regard that as a retrograde movement . . . Control by the Ministry of Food will no doubt be removed at no distant date, with the consequence that the Trade will be left free to fix its own prices and sale conditions. The scale of discounts to the wholesale dealer has formed the subject of much anxious consideration in conjunction with the Ministry of Food officials, and I think the discounts as set forth in the Spirits Order are fair to all concerned. There is a disposition on the part of the retail trade to claim a return to credit principles, but it is obviously impossible to pay cash in advance to the Government to the extent of more than four times the value of our product, give credit and at the same time good value . . . It is not sound policy to pay 72s. 6d. of duty per gallon except on whisky of the finest grade.'

William Ross, of the D.C.L., regarded it as unfortunate that the association had not been able to stem the rising tide of duty which had taken place year after year and one of the primary duties of the association in the near future would be to have the duty reduced: they were never likely to see it 11s. per proof gallon again, but if they could get back to the 50s. which prevailed before Chamberlain's latest addition they would then be able to effect a cut in the retail price per bottle, preferably to 10s. the bottle.

As Graham Menzies, chairman of the D.C.L., put it at the company's annual meeting that same July: 'The consumption of liquor in this country is being rapidly killed except amongst those customers who can afford to pay the present prices and those who while not able to afford it are yet willing to spend their last sixpence to get what they want, no matter at what cost. Between these two sections lie the great mass of the population who can neither afford to pay the present exorbitant prices nor who desire to drink to excess, but yet feel the want of their usual stimulant. Do the Government really think that they are studying the best interests of the country by compelling abstinence of liquor through high duties and diverting into other channels the money which but for these high duties would be used for the legitimate enjoyment and sustenance of the body? Last Budget we refrained from pressing our demands that the duties on the liquor trade should be reduced to a reasonable basis, as we felt that the Chancellor of the Exchequer was in a difficult position, but when we see how doles are given here and there to placate certain interests and money is still being squandered in needless extravagance, I think the time has arrived when the whole Trade should unite with the moderate opinion of the country in demanding next year that these exorbitant duties shall cease, and that the legitimate trade of the country shall not be strangled by excessive taxation.'

On the first of September that year, 1921, the Central Control Board (Liquor Traffic) ended. The trade was free. The new Licensing Act came into force on the same date. The 30 u.p. rule was ended, officially. Questions of selling price came to the fore with a leap, and, indeed, assertions were made that the Control Board had been got rid of only 'to make for an even more autocratic body originating in the Trade itself, which will impose restrictions on the retailers more irksome than those devised by the Control Board'. The 72s. 6d. duty, it was agreed within the trade, precluded any possibility of reducing the price below 12s. 6d. the bottle, and further in line with the remarks of the Scotch Whisky Association, it was also agreed that while it would be possible for consumers to get a stronger whisky at a proportionately higher price, it seemed the best policy for the trade to stick to the 30 u.p. at a uniform price rather than open the door to consumer complaints of trade 'profiteering'.

Thus the trade circular of Bowen & McKechnie: 'With the removal of control over whisky, a certain amount of friction may arise, for it will not be possible to reduce quotations for fine matured qualities, which will continue scarce for some considerable time. In our opinion, though the profit of 1s. ½d. on a bottle at 12s. 6d. is clearly insufficient for the 'off' trade, there remains the question whether it would not be more judicious to maintain that figure, rather than perhaps antagonise consumers by seeking a higher profit.'

But with the all-round depression, unemployment, falling wages, general commercial and industrial stagnation, everything had combined to reduce the demand for Scotch very considerably, as we have seen in the foregoing figures. So widespread was the decline in economic health that a Highlands correspondent wrote that 'the distillers forced last year to raise wages abnormally have now decided to allow each individual company to make their own terms and recommend a reduction of seven shillings per week'. Later meetings of distilleries and workmen arrived at amounts fairly close to those wages we have quoted above: 68s. per week for stillmen, for instance, with overtime and night rates; washmen at 72s. per week plus 1s. night extra, and so on.

But with the freeing of the trade from the Central Control Board a host of problems, particularly of prices and discounts, had to be settled promptly. A general meeting was called in Edinburgh in mid-October of the Scottish branch of the Whisky Association, with Mr Ross in the chair. As de-control came so quickly, without warning, he said, the London and Edinburgh executive bodies had to do what they thought best. Personally, he would have suggested that before coming to any finding that they would have done well to have had conferences with their brewing friends on the one hand and with the retail interests on the other, in order to find out whether it was possible to come to some common agreement on such vexed questions as discounts, inter-trade prices, and the prices to be charged to the public. 'It was regretted,' he went on, 'that a few of the members had found it necessary to disregard the temporary recommendations of the executive and had thereby made the position more difficult. He had no wish to rub this in – it was perhaps inevitable during the period following de-control – but he did hope that as a result of that meeting they would see a new-born zeal to obey the rulings of those entrusted with executive powers. (Hear, hear.) It must be admitted by everyone that the Whisky Association had done yeoman service on behalf of its members during and since the war. (Hear, hear.) Surely the ground they had gained by this friendly co-operation was not to be thrown away at the first indication of competition! None of them wished to see conditions drift back to the position which had obtained seven years ago – (Hear, hear) – and yet unless they held together, that was where they were drifting.'

The first item on the agenda was the retail price. The reason for fixing that was that without fixing it there would have been an increase in the price to the public, a consequent fall in demand – 'which had already gone down very materially,' said Mr Ross – and public dissatisfaction. 'He knew it had been said that their action was simply perpetuating the control under Government auspices,' said reports. 'But he thought they were pretty well agreed – certainly the Executive were – that such control was necessary for a little time until the neutral competition could again come into play.'

Item No. 2 was the inter-trade minimum price. On this Ross said that 'it seemed to them it would be a pity if the whole of the duty-paid trade were brought into the classification of in-bond Trade. Rather than that should be done they thought it would be possible to preserve the balance by reducing the margin of profit between the one price and the other, and so they came to the decision to reduce the duty-paid price from 94*s*. 3*d*. to 92*s*. That apparently did not satisfy some of the members, and with their approval that day would strongly recommend that the duty-paid price should be reduced to 91*s*., leaving a difference between the in-bond and duty-paid price of 1*s*. 10*d*. per gallon.'

In the ensuing discussion, Sir Alexander Walker supported the recommendation of the Council and the General Purposes Committee to the price of the minimum of 91*s*. He thought that 16*s*. 8*d*. plus the duty would be the ultimate figure at which ninety per cent of the trade would be done. They had to be very guarded and move very cautiously in attempting to get any excessive profits and he felt that 2*s*. 10*d*. was an excessive profit for the services and loss due to the clearances in duty-paid stores. As Sir Alexander had to say later when revisions in all directions were being proposed: 'It is really in sympathy with the smaller men and to get loyalty and to ensure loyalty that I support the recommendation of the committee that 91*s*. should be adopted.'

After the vote, Ross, as chairman, was able to remark: 'There is no doubt about the majority. Had there been any close decision I would have deferred to the other side, but here the indication seems to be very much in favour of the 91*s*., and I think I can safely declare that proposal as carried. Now, can we depend,' he asked, 'upon the general members following the guidance and recommendation of its council and committee, because that is the crucial point, and one which means either the continuance or abandonment of the Association.'

A discussion followed and each member gave an undertaking to adhere to the result above. Then arose the item of cash terms. The phrase itself was open to misunderstanding: the London Council wanted it set forth that it meant payment on receipt of invoice; in Scotland it often meant cash within seven days as stated on the invoice. Here the Londoners said they would regard it as cash if they got it within seven days, but it might easily mean fourteen days or longer.

Ross summed up in these words: 'Now the understanding here is that seven days is the general interpretation of cash terms and if it is found that a customer wilfully neglects to pay in that period or within a day or two afterwards he should be put on a *pro forma* list and pay in advance.' By general acclamation it was so agreed.

The 'Wholesale or quantity discounts' item led to the meeting's agreeing with the Council's recommendation 'to retain the present system, certainly until a more satisfactory one could be devised'. A matter to meet much difficulty and recrimination later, as will be seen.

A brief eavesdropping on the luncheon that followed is worth while. Lord Forteviot, after appraising the work and value of the Association, went on to say that 'The Whisky Association is not only a Trade protection society in the ordinary acceptance of the term. No trade needed more vigilant protection than the whisky trade, but, in addition, its members desired the Trade to be carried on in harmony with public opinion . . . The Whisky Association was, with the very best results, consulted from time to time during the period of control, and it was ready and willing to confer with the government or any agency which sought to remove abuses or improve the conditions under which the Trade was carried on.'

Sir Peter Mackie reminded members that 'they should never lose sight of the fact that the Trade had to deal with a third party – the public – who were the Trade's best friends. The Trade should look carefully after the interests of the public and give them value. Then, in time of trouble, as, for instance, during the prohibition campaign, the public would stand by the Trade. The Trade should also try to eliminate the objectionable element within itself, as they all suffered from it.'

Mr James Robertson predicted 'trying times to come . . . He did not think honest competition need interfere with their good relationship.' Mr A. N. Heilbron 'vehemently attacked the practice of selling as Scotch whisky anything other than the produce of Scottish distilleries. He said they had in Scotland redundant distilleries for which they should try to find employment. Scotch whisky should be a spirit such as did them credit, with the requisite age and quality.' (Mr Heilbron was not himself a distiller.) Mr H. Earnshaw stressed 'the need for hard propaganda work on the part of every section of the Trade . . . He proceeded to refer to the prejudice caused by the sale of American whiskey as

Scotch whisky, which, he said, had cost them thousands of votes at the recent polls.'

Nevertheless, it was an open secret that 'considerable activity' continued to prevail in the Whisky Association. Price cutting and other breaches of the (apparently) unanimous findings of the Association were giving a good deal of dissatisfaction. So insistent became the complaints that a full meeting of the Association had to be held again in Edinburgh, at which it soon came out that in some quarters there was a strong feeling that members should be given more latitude in such matters as prices and discounts. The result was that it was remitted to the committee to draw up a more simple and less restricted agreement than that just outlined. As was noted at the time: 'The Whisky Association is feeling the draught of dull times. Competition has again become exceedingly keen in the whisky trade, and certain traders seem to be unable to suffer even a slight temporary disadvantage for the sake of ultimate gain of substantial character. The complaints now being made as to the more or less open breach of the various provisions adopted by the members of the Association are more bitter than ever, and it is becoming a moot point whether the regulation of prices and discounts can be persisted in . . . A feeling in some quarters that the Association should revert to its original conception of a defensive organisation pure and simple, giving the members an entirely free hand as to prices, etc. The reckless cutting of prices in a declining market can, of course, only lead to chaos and heavy loss all round, but it is better that the important organisation which has been built up should be retained for defensive purposes than that it should be allowed to disappear . . . The Trade will be urgently in need of all the organised effort of a defensive character it can command.'

In short by means of the Association the whisky trade was falling in line with vast segments of British industry of the time organising itself to fix prices, output, terms of sale and the like throughout the industry as a whole. The same process was also to be seen both at large and, as will be noted later, in the whisky industry itself in the amalgamation of every sector of the trade so as to form an overpowering body. Had some of the 1920 leaders of the industry as they struggled out of the morass left by World War I had their way, there would undoubtedly have been erected in Scotland, if not in Great Britain as a whole, a simple monolith of spirit production and distribution.

In short, some of the industry was accepting the fact that competition had returned to stay, some wished not to be forced back to it, particularly as it prevailed before the war, when, as Lord (Tommy) Dewar put it in characteristic phrase, 'Competition is the life of trade – but the death of profits.' In any event, what with the higher duty and reduced purchasing power at home combining to restrict business, there became apparent a tendency on the part of some firms to break away from the Whisky Association's recommended structure and sell below Association prices. So the whole matter had to be brought up at a Scottish branch meeting in Edinburgh, when Mr Ross had now succeeded Mr Montgomery as chairman of the parent association as well. A questionnaire was circulated to members in the light of which it was possible to arrive at a unanimous decision on all vital points. The most important changes were: the abrogation of the former resolution limiting the flat rate of discount of 6s. per case to big buyers for resale only and the substitution of a new scale of discounts graduated from 1s. to 5s. per case according to quantity, and allowable to all buyers whether for resale or otherwise; prices for home and export were left untouched, as were also the discounts on whiskies sold in bulk either in bond or duty paid; the abandonment of labels on proprietary whiskies restricting the selling prices to 12s. 6d. and 6s. 6d.; some minor alterations in the allowances on returned empties, the allowances having grown up during the war as a result of timber and other shortages. It was felt in 'influential quarters' that any attempt to raise prices under the then existing conditions would only have a detrimental effect on the already declining consumption.

When the new regulations became effective on 1 June 1922 they created a storm, particularly among distributors who urged that 'the new discounts are out of all proportion to the amount of capital involved and the high prices of freight, labour, etc.' It had to be considered whether the average blender could possibly sell below the terms fixed by the Association. 'It is all very well to instance the case of probably the biggest blenders of proprietary whiskies being able to pay a dividend of twenty-five per cent, free of income-tax,' it was said, 'and carrying hundreds of thousands to reserve. That was only possible because the company held huge stocks of single whiskies bought at pre-war prices. How many blenders are in that position, and what would be their plight today if the big blenders cited had taken advantage of their exceptional position to reduce the price of the finished article to a level which showed only a modest margin of profit on cost price? . . . The only other way in which the distributors' margin of profit could be increased is by raising the price to the consumer and that, in the best Trade opinion, would be a serious blunder under existing circumstances. It is to be hoped, however, that those who do not find the new regulations all that they could desire will keep in mind the benefits which every member of the Trade has, directly or indirectly, derived from the work of the Whisky Association. In these trying times it is essential that the Trade should have an organisation sufficiently powerful and sufficiently flexible to permit of ready action being taken on every question, no matter how important, as it arises. This it has in the Whisky Association, and it is a matter for congratulation that it has been found possible to maintain the Association unimpaired.'

Plenty lay ahead for the Association as the industry continued to strive to adjust itself to the new peacetime conditions of decreasing sales, tougher competition, and the national economic wanderlust.

26

Domestic developments

Now THE Scotch Whisky Association's old scale of discounts, which
were allowable to those who bought for resale, was a source of practically continuous irritation. It was widely infringed in the letter as well
as in the spirit; it was a relief to the great bulk of the trade when it was
decided to return to what was considered the more simple method of
granting discounts graduated according to quantity. Except for big
brand owners with pre-war stocks no section of the whisky trade
enjoyed the profit margin it was felt it should get, and the only way to
raise that aggregate profit margin was to raise the price to the consumer.
But there the slump in consumption following the 1920 duty increase
and parlous state of the British economy was enough warning of itself
as to what could be expected after any such price rise. The retailer who
bought at 137s. 6d. and sold at 150s. a case, or 12s. 6d. a bottle, maintained that a gross profit of eight and one-third per cent on turnover
was quite inadequate in view of working costs. But it was also argued
that it was unfair to work out the profit as a percentage on the duty-
paid turnover as it was open to all distributors to buy in-bond and to
clear spirit as required. On that basis it was held that the profit ratio was
larger than pre-war. The proprietary brand owners indulged in lavish
advertising – 'The constant advertiser gets the trade,' said Lord
(Tommy) Dewar – and so created a universal demand which, in turn,
meant the retailer could turn his stock over more frequently so making
a substantially larger profit on the same capital.

We cannot here pause to consider in detail all the ramifications of the arguments for and against, but we may notice, as indicative of the state of trade, that wholesalers themselves were often giving up part of their wholesale discount to customers in order to attract business. The proprietary brand owners looked at this askance, as it seemed to argue that they must themselves be paying the wholesaler too much.

In this setting, the Scotch Whisky Association met and discussed the situation with other trade bodies, after which it issued a circular modifying the new scale of discounts to the extent of increasing the allowances on 100-case and 50-case lots by 1s. per case. It left the allowances on smaller lots unchanged. What the Council and General Purposes Committee of the Association had to take into account were not the exceptionally well-bought stocks of the 'big three' – Buchanan, Dewar and Walker – but the conditions as they affected the average member of the Association. In brief it meant that 100-case lots carried a discount of 6s. per case and 50-case lots of 5s., though it must be admitted that some member firms gave as much as 8s. a case to wholesalers for resale. What was happening was that as the market shrank and as supplies of 'available' whisky increased, competition – not unnaturally – increased in like manner.

All that summer the discussion, controversy, if you like, went on and even the circular just referred to did not settle the matter. It was held in some quarters that the circular was 'not entirely free from ambiguity', and apart from higher discounts than those listed, some firms found business so difficult to get that they offered the maximum allowance of 6s. the case on any quantity, however small. The 'big three' did not accept the new and increased discounts – of 6s. and 5s. as stated – but adhered to the original policy of allowing 1s. per case less than the trade generally on the larger quantities, and making the minimum quantity subject to discount one of 12 cases. Their structure was, accordingly: 5s. per case on 100-case lots; 4s. per case on 50-case lots; 2s. on 25-case and 1s. per case on 12-case lots. The principle underlying it all was that the customer accustomed to taking 100- or 50-case lots of any of the 'big three' could hardly be expected to take similar quantities of another brand, and yet might wish to stock it, provided he bought on the same terms as from the 'big three'.

On returns, it is of historical interest to notice that returned empties, non-returnable cases, sent free, gained 6d. each, and returnable cases gained the allowance above the invoice price of 1s. each. Bottles gained 1s. 6d. per dozen, these being accepted as a rule and carried forward. The blenders also tried to meet the distributors by allowing the full rate of discount per specified lots, though the delivery might be taken in smaller lots. Thus a customer who had bought a 50-case lot might have it delivered, within six months, in lots as small as six cases a time.

It was argued that such a diversity of practice showed such a lack of unanimity in the Association as amounted to chaos and it would be better to scrap this attempted price-control. But the most glaring contraventions were mostly by the smaller firms who just had to get business at any cost and had little to lose by sacrificing quality to expediency. The larger firms were punctilious in observing the regulations because they were only too well aware that shortage of supplies and the very high prices of fully matured single whiskies made them necessary. As the *Record* propounded at the time, words still relevant today: 'No section of the Scotch whisky trade is likely to benefit in the end from unbridled price-cutting . . . With the heavy decline in consumption, the time is approaching when whisky will again be in over-supply . . . The various sections of the whisky trade should endeavour to compose their differences amicably . . . No single section of the whisky trade can do without the other sections, and the sound common sense of traders, no less than economic pressure, tends all in good time to equalise both the opportunities and rewards of the different sections.'

With the ending of resale price maintenance in Britain in 1964 and successive duty increases on whisky, a similar situation arose in the matter of price cutting, after years of there being no possibility of that, and the National Federation of Off-Licence Holders' Associations of England and Wales reported in May 1966 on pre-war days as follows: 'Off-licensed retailers in business before the war will recall that in those days, the official wholesale price of whisky was 137s. 6d. a dozen bottles.' (As given above.) 'Very few retailers paid this price. In 1939, tenants of brewery companies, although tied for beer, were free to purchase their wines and spirits on the open market. As a result, the accepted wholesale price for whisky by the market houses was not 137s. 6d. but 132s. 6d. a dozen. In some cases competition which then existed resulted in retailers being able to obtain their supplies at even less than 132s. 6d. a dozen. During the war years, shortage of supplies brought to an end the ability of retailers to obtain supplies at competitive and advantageous prices.' This is not the occasion to enter into the tortuous by-ways of the matter currently under dispute, but it is enough to note that the whisky trade is back where it was forty years ago with the added difficulty that a parliamentary act now forbids such attempted regulation as was then undertaken by the Whisky Association in the mere effort to impose reason on the law of the jungle.

Year by year home consumption continued to fall, despite the annual appeal to the Chancellor of the Exchequer – whose response varied in phraseology each year but never in content, which was a firm 'No' – despite the frantically active promotional ideas and advertising practised, despite, in effect, every attempt of a dying industry to save its life. The 1923–4 figure was 13,781,000 proof gallons, only a little below the previous year, but it fell to only just over the 13 million the next year and under it in the subsequent twelve months, 1925–6. In the following period it was even lower, only a little more than 11 million, made a recovery of roughly one million in 1927–8 but continued to slip the two years following, bringing it to just over 11 million in 1929–30. The decline continued throughout the 1930s, dropping, first, to little over 10 million at the beginning, to under the 9 million gallon mark in 1931–2, only halting the decline in 1935–6 and mounting to 9·3 million in 1936–7, the best year of the thirties for whisky as for British industry as a whole, but still woefully below even the depths of the twenties. It is of particular interest to observe that for the year 1938–9, the first for which official figures of home consumption of Scotch whisky were published, the latter's total for the year was 6·9 million gallons, whereas the comparable figure for home-made spirits as a whole was 9·2 million. It can be assumed that a similar proportion persisted throughout the earlier years to which reference has been made when particular Scotch figures themselves were not made available.

Year by year, then, the decline went on. We cannot follow each in detail, but one notable element needs attention: if the overall consumption fell into a decline, that by no means indicated a fall in the sales or output of every individual firm. Far from it; it was a case of the big getting bigger, the small getting still smaller, by comparison if not in fact. The well-informed consumer drank only whisky of the best quality available: he considered that as the price he paid was two-thirds taxation, this duty element was the same whatever the quality. The outstanding feature then was the public's insistent demand for certain proprietary blends which had attained a wide degree of popularity and retained it by persistent advertising and adherence to quality standards. Soon after the war, a large quantity of American and foreign spirits had been sold in the country; the public came to realise it, and consequently demanded the best proprietary blends. The day of the bottled proprietary brand was now here in unquestioned brilliance. Gone for ever the days of the bulk supplies before the war to the publican who reduced the strength to 'around 80 proof': with taxation as it was, the customer had to be sure of the best; he had to know exactly what he was getting.

So Lord Woolavington, chairman of Buchanan-Dewar Ltd, the first major amalgamation of our period, told the annual meeting in May 1922, that 'the world-wide reputation enjoyed by the brands of the associated companies' had been gained by the consistent maintenance of 'a very high standard of quality, whisky of great age only being used in these brands, and the recognition of which is materially evidenced by the continually increased demand, both in the home and export markets. The essential factor to ensure the maintenance of a consistent quality of superior excellence is the holding of adequate stocks . . . At that time we held, as we still hold, the largest stock of Scotch whisky in Scotland . . . Our distilleries have been working at full pressure since distillation has been resumed . . . We own, or are interested in, eleven distilleries in Scotland, all producing malt whisky . . . The combined firms had in stock over 23 million gallons of Scotch whisky.' It is no surprise that the same dividend was declared: twenty-five per cent free of tax.

The following March, John Walker & Sons Ltd went public: the lists opened at 9.30 a.m. and closed at 10.30 a.m., over £13 million being offered, or nearly four times as much as the amount asked for. At the Buchanan-Dewar annual meeting the following May 1923, with Lord (Tommy) Dewar as chairman, it was again reported that 'the businesses of the companies were in a very sound progressive condition, the demand, both for home and export, yearly increasing. Buchanan-Dewar, through its subsidiary companies, was in a very strong, and, in fact, an exceptionally strong position as regards stocks, which guaranteed to consumers at home and abroad a maintenance of a high standard of quality.' Later that year Buchanan-Dewar made an offer to the public and reported rising profits from 1919–20 to 1922–3, in the latter year of £2,302,079, declaring assets and liabilities at 31 March 1923 as £10,188,716 and £3,527,686 respectively. Stocks were then also declared as in excess of 29 million gallons.

When John Walker & Sons Ltd reported in 1924, on the company's operations for its seventeen months to the end of May, it was declared that the average annual profit for the eight years ending 31 May 1922 was £688,300 before tax, and the accounts for the period reported upon showed a profit of £1,130,000, being at the rate of £797,600 for the year. Which meant, as pointed out, 'the prospectus average has been agreeably exceeded'. Moreover, 'the company's liquid assets are heavily in excess of its current liabilities, and its trading results afford very gratifying evidence of its stability and profit-earning capacity . . . The sales for the period under review, both at home and abroad, have been the largest in the history of the business.'

Enough has been revealed to display the fact that if the industry as a whole was undergoing difficult times, not every member of it was, except maybe in the sense that they might have done even better but for the distressed times in which they were operating! As an Edinburgh correspondent put it – on more than one occasion – the public considered 'the prudent thing to do is to buy the brands which have a name and reputation behind them . . . the big distributors with a world-wide connection are finding their sales wonderfully well maintained, though there is some reason to believe that the rank and file of the proprietary brand owners are not so happily situated.'

Interesting that at the D.C.L. annual meeting in 1922, the chairman, Graham Menzies, took some pride and pleasure in reporting that whereas a year before he had recorded a drop in profits below the exceptional year of 1919–20, he was now able to chronicle a recovery to the extent of almost exactly half, 'all the more remarkable as it is coincident with a curtailment in our production by no less than 2·6 million gallons of whisky during the twelve months'. He never again had occasion to refer to any drop in profits. But, as we have seen, it was a case neither of profits growing all round for everyone, or losses all round mounting for all. As Graham Menzies told the annual meeting of the D.C.L. the following year, 1923, they had joined in the presentation of a case to the Chancellor before his budget for a spirit duty reduction 'not so much in the interests of the large firms in the trade who were fortunate in possessing stocks of whisky bought and paid for before the war, but in the interests of the smaller, although still important, firms who in many cases were obliged to buy their supplies of old whisky on the market at high prices with which to carry on their businesses, or do as so many had been forced to do – liquidate their wholly inadequate stocks and go out of business altogether . . . With duty at 72s. 6d. per gallon, the capital required to finance a good going business tends to drive the Trade more and more into the hands of the few who can command the extra capital . . . As in the case of all articles which are taxed beyond the ability of the consumer to pay, the Revenue was undoubtedly suffering . . . the present position constitutes an undoubted Scottish grievance.' The way ahead was emerging: the small independent man or business was in the course of disappearing into the larger unit, a process we shall investigate in its details later.

Moving ahead to July 1925, when Ross made his first annual report to shareholders in the D.C.L., as chairman of the newly much-enlarged company, that after paying a steady ten per cent free of tax for twenty-three years 'there is now less reason for us to be so ultra conservative in our distribution as we have been in the past, and I hope it will be possible, therefore, to at least maintain the new rate of dividend in the years to come. After all, this twenty per cent, which we are now going to divide for the first time, has only been attained after years of toil and by careful handling of the finance. Like a provident parent we have been careful to husband our resources and put back into the business, each year, sums of varying amount, which in their turn have borne fruit.'

He went on to cover many subjects and aspects of the industry, particularly the increased duty on whisky. The duty of 11s. a proof gallon prevailing at the beginning of 1909, he pointed out was now 72s. 6d. a gallon, or practically 8s. 6d. a bottle out of the standard price of 12s. 6d. Against this he posed the pre-war picture where the whole cost of the bottle of whisky, including duty was not more than 4s. 'Can it be wondered,' he asked, 'that the home consumption of whisky has fallen from 32,050,000 gallons in 1908–9 to 13,039,000 for the year ending 31st March 1925?' He saw a stimulation of agriculture – then in the doldrums – by reducing the penal tax on whisky 'and so permitting the gradual recovery of the distilling industry . . . There is likely to be a drastic reduction in the distillers' requirements of home barley for the next few years,' he continued, 'if the present over-production of whisky is to be tackled as it should be.'

The following year he again had reason to return to the subject of the spirit duty and its effects on home consumption, for although it was not mentioned by Ross, it has since been established that the pound had by comparison with the value of a Treasury note of 1920 so risen in real value that the 72*s*. 6*d*. duty imposed that year was approximately £7: and the general return to earth after the artificial prosperity of 1920 had forced an all-round reduction of the taxation of every commodity except spirits and a few trifles. But to revert to Ross on that occasion in July 1926, he recorded that 'the present exorbitant rate of duty is gradually but surely bleeding the whisky trade to death. Year by year consumption in this country is decreasing . . .' The financial year ending with March 1926 had seen 'a fresh low record – if we exclude the two years 1918 and 1919 when control was in operation – of 12,074,000 gallons. This compares with a relative figure of about 28 million gallons in 1916 . . . Little satisfaction to the Chancellor of the Exchequer, to the distilling industry and its allied trades, or to the large mass of the public who desire to indulge in the moderate use of whisky . . . Hitherto, our request for a reduction in the duty has been met by refusal unless we could guarantee that there would be no loss of revenue occasioned thereby.' Such a pledge could never, of course, be given, a fact the scheming politicians of Westminster well knew when making the proposition.

The fiftieth annual meeting of the company, in 1927, saw a return to the charge of the 'repressive whisky duty' and Ross exclaimed, 'When one considers the state of trade during the past twelve months one can only marvel that our profits have been so well maintained.' The coal strike alone had added £50,000 to their coal bill for the year; the greater unemployment and stagnation of industry had 'the inevitable result of decreased business'. A passage of importance still: 'The conservative management of this company in the past was never more justified than in the crisis we have just passed through,' expatiated Ross. 'While I consider that it is the bounden duty of every company to so provide for such contingencies, it is difficult to anticipate what the Government may do either in the direction of legislation or taxation. If anyone had predicted that the repressive duty placed upon spirits in 1920 would have survived such a long period without remission of any kind his prediction would have been received with incredulity – and yet such has been the case.'

What with the Government taking two-thirds of the price of a bottle, leaving only one-third for the junior partners led him on to this comment: 'Little wonder the farmer is crying out for protection, but what he requires is protection not against foreign imports but protection against the Government, who, by their action in sustaining this high duty, are reducing the area of barley cultivation year by year.' The further shrinkage in home consumption of Scotch of 1,336,000 gallons was paralleled, said Ross, by a drop of whisky production in Scotland from 26 million gallons in 1926 to 16·5 million in 1927, a decrease of virtually 10 million gallons in a year.

So the tale of diminishing production and consumption went on from year to year, with the annual appeals to successive Chancellors of the Exchequer meeting a stony response. In November 1930, as the country and nation teetered towards bankruptcy, Sir Alexander Walker gave evidence on behalf of the Scotch Whisky Association to another royal commission, this time on licensing in England and Wales. The chairman of the commission, Lord Amulree, presided.

About 8 million gallons of malt whisky and 12 million of grain were produced, said Sir Alexander, in Scotland in the last year, a little more than the 'record low' of 1926–7 but well below the 28 million produced in 1913–14, as was brought out in the tables he entered. On the question of stock, he explained that Scotch whisky stocks at 31 March 1930 were 137,247,906 gallons; the removals for that year were 17,095,065, 'or, say, over seven years' stock. That is to say,' he went on, 'that the average age of bottled brands of Scotch whisky when they reach the public is over seven years and is of higher quality and greater age than it has ever been in former times.'

Explaining the division of the retail price of 12s. 6d. the bottle into 8s. 5½d. duty and 4s. ½d. for the 'junior partners', he gave evidence that that latter amount 'has to carry the cost of whisky, ullage, maturation, insurance, transport, bottles, cases, etc., and carriage on returned empties and the profit to distiller, wholesaler, and retailer'.

Sir Alexander gave a résumé of the changing social habits as they had affected whisky-drinking, part of which was as follows: 'I can well recollect during the late eighties and nineties that the habits of the people of my town and district had much need of reform . . . While earnings had increased, their standards of living had remained very stationary, i.e. they had learned how to make money but not yet how to spend it wisely.' (This is in line with increased earnings and the rise in the true value of money we have already noted as assisting the whisky boom of the nineties) '. . . Small wonder then, if with surplus earnings in their pockets, the people found liquor – and sometimes to excess – the only escape from boredom and the mechanical uniformity of their tasks. During my whole lifetime in the trade I have never ceased to urge that temperance must come from the education of the public to a wider culture and interest in nature, arts and sports, and I am glad to think that this has come about. The change in the last fifty years is marvellous and it may be argued that entertainment is now the first necessity and work the secondary. At any rate, the inordinate consumption of alcohol for the sheer delight of intoxication has practically ceased.

'I notice that some of the witnesses attribute this to the regulation of the Government, both during and since the war, and these officials are naturally obsessed with their own regulations. If the Commissioners, however, will examine the figures from 1900 onwards showing the consumption of spirit per head, they will note that the fall from 1·17 proof gallons in 1900 to 0·67 proof gallons in 1913 is a fairly uniform curve showing a reduction of 0·50 proof gallons per head in thirteen years or 0·038 proof gallons per annum. There is no doubt in my mind that the consumption at 0·67 gallons per head would have remained more stationary but for the heavy rise of duty, which cut off the supply to more moderate incomes.

'Since 1913 the fall has been 0·38 gallons in sixteen years, or ·024 gallons per annum. That is to say, that before there was any severe alteration in the duty, dilution regulations or shorter hours of sale, the steady fall in consumption of spirit was at an even greater rate per annum per head than since such changes. I am sure the Commission will appreciate the distinction between temperance with liberty and temperance by police . . . Any legislation in advance of public opinion must fail and I cannot see any indication of public opinion desiring further legislation in restricting facilities to the trade.'

A brief glance at the complex tables provided by Sir Alexander will put us in the picture as to what had been the trends up to the time of his evidence. First, the distilleries at work in Scotland in the distilling year ended 30 September: in the 1913 year, 127, rising to 133 the next year; fluctuating with the war to reach their lowest point in 1917–18 when only eight – only yeast and munitions spirit were made – were operating; reaching 134 in the 1920–1 season and thereafter declining to 84 in the 1926–7 season. A slight recovery was noticed in the 1928–9 season, a recovery hit on the head by the Wall Street crash and the world depression that ensued and entailed the British financial crisis of 1931 with its continuing disasters, so that in 1932–3 there were only 15 distilleries at (intermittent) work in Scotland. That latter figure was one-tenth of the distilleries operating in Scotland in the boom year of 1900–1 when 156 were registered as being at work. That, maybe better than anything, underlines and highlights both the nadir reached by the whisky industry in the years of national disaster in the thirties.

Sir Alexander's next table was of spirit production in Scotland for the financial years beginning 1912–13, when the total output was 24 million gallons, rising the next year to 28 million, falling, as already noted, to 14·8 million in 1917–18 and to 13·2 million the following year when production was forbidden and prevented for potable spirit as such, with a late permission. In 1919–20, it leapt to 22·5 million gallons, and with the boom just breaking nevertheless reached 29·3 million in the year ended 31 March 1921. Thereafter it dropped at once to 24·6 million gallons; was in the 27 million region for three years; slipped back to 26 million and plunged to 16 million in 1926–7. By 1930 it was hovering around the 20 million mark.

But, moving on from Sir Alexander's evidence, in 1930–1, it drooped to little more than 15 million gallons, the next year began its rapid slither down the perilous slope of extinction and recorded only 9 million, and in the crisis year of 1932–3 managed to produce only 5,926,000 gallons. We may remind ourselves that in the boom year of 1900–1, Scotland produced 30,196,000 gallons – and there was no minimum age requirement for whisky then.

The third table presented by Sir Alexander Walker analysed stock, distillation and removal figures for Scotland between 1912–13 and 1929–30. The first of these years showed stock at 110·7 million gallons, distillation at 24·1 million and removals at 24·6 million, giving a difference between distillation and removal of minus half a million gallons. The next two years saw stock, production and removals all mount, with plus differences in the last column. There came then four years, from 1915–16 to 1918–19, when stock fell, production first rose then decreased, as we have noted in the course of the story, while removals at first rose steeply and later fell as heavily. In the first of these four years, removals were 34·3 million gallons, as against 25·7 million for the preceding year, but by the last of these four the figure had fallen, under Government control, to 19·5 million. All these years saw less distilled than removed, and the minus difference in 1917–18 was as much as 13 million. Potable distillation was that year not permitted.

After the brief boomlet following the war stock climbed steadily, from just over 100 million gallons in 1921–2 to 137 million when Sir Alexander presented his evidence. Distillation was much more varied: it reached, as noted above, 29 million in 1920–1, its best figure until 1937–8, and moved erratically as already recorded. The result of declining removals, removals which were persistently less until almost the outbreak of war in 1939, was that the difference between them and production became an excess of the latter over the former of the order of 9,692,000 gallons in 1920–1, was back to 9,274,000 gallons in excess output for 1922–3, rambled around the plus figures of 6 or 7 million gallons and removals were only below – by 1,338,449 gallons – production in 1926–7, when not only national economic forces took their toll but also the vigorous action of Ross reduced output. Thereafter was a gradual increase of distillation over removals up to World War II, on the eve of which the industry was deliberately and of intent stock-piling in view of the imminent disastrous years of tragedy ahead.

Sir Alexander also provided among his tables, which moved far beyond Scotland and the United Kingdom as a whole, figures of home-made spirits retained for consumption in each of the three kingdoms and the consequent United Kingdom total. England, we notice, had fallen from 16·9 million gallons in 1912–13, despite an early war years' rise, to just over 8 million in 1929–30. Consumption was halved. The same was true of Scotland: 5·7 million in the first of these years, an early war increase, an equally rapid drop later, a mini-boom just after the war – though even then consumption in Scotland at around 3 million gallons was only half the 6 million of early war – and a con-tinuous decline to just over 2 million in the closing year. That is, Scotland's consumption of Scotch whisky and other home-made spirits, had fallen with war, taxation, and national mismanagement of the country's finances from 5·7 million to 2·1 million. The Irish figure is not as clear, because of the setting up of the Irish Free State, and the inclusion of Northern Ireland figures in the England table, but overall, a decline from 2·6 million in the opening year of the table results in the drop of the millions element to give for 1929–30 a total of only 635,243 gallons.

Thus the United Kingdom total column opens with 26,285,991 gallons, of which we can take something over two-thirds as being of Scotch whisky, as being retained for consumption, a decline as noted earlier from the 1900 boom total. The figure wavered, and in 1915–16 reached its highest ever since: 28,949,493 gallons. Government control and restriction of releases led, as we have seen, to its fall to 10 million gallons in 1917–18, its gradual recovery after the war and the steady decrease experienced – beyond Sir Alexander's tables – almost up to the war.

In a partisan cross-examination by a tendentious commission, Sir Alexander made a lengthy, lucid and valid case for the taxation of all alcoholic beverages per degree of proof spirit contained within them, a case he argued in his brief supported by photographs of the comparative sizes of bottles illustrating the duties they paid. As remarked, the commission was tendentious; he got nowhere.

Questioned by Mr B. T. Hall, who asked him: 'Pre-war the tax was 14s. 9d. per gallon and the general strength was only 22 under proof, I make it that the tax on the bottle of whisky was somewhere about 1s. 10d., with 1s. 8d. for the distiller, making 3s. 6d. in all. That is, 1s. 8d. has now grown to 4s. [the 4s. ½d. referred to above for junior partners] between two and three times as much. Can you say which of these items warrants that increase?' Sir Alexander replied: 'Is there anything which has not advanced by at least one hundred per cent? I notice that almost everything has grown, certainly in the labour factors, and in the salary factors, by very nearly three times.'

The argument degenerated, under Mr Hall's probing, attempting to discredit the industry into the classification as profiteers, into an obtuse disbelief of the facts on the part of the commission, leading up to Sir Alexander's reminder: 'It emerges, however, that a great many businesses have gone out of business within the last few years because they could not make a profit . . . Let us assume a distiller doing a home business in spirits alone; I think it is an extremely difficult thing for a very large number of houses to make five per cent on their capital . . . Many very well-known firms have discussed with me the possibility of selling their businesses, and on going into their profit and loss accounts I find that the value of their stock if realised and invested in Government security, would yield them a slightly higher profit than they are getting now on their business. That is where they are doing a home trade only.'

Mr Hall: 'They do not realise, but they still go on?' – Sir Alexander Walker: 'It is not a question that they do not realise. The point is that they cannot find a buyer at the moment. The business does not look sufficiently rosy to tempt the buyer.'

A Mr A. Sherwell took up the profit theme again in his turn, asking Sir Alexander how 'in regard to the great decline in the consumption of spirits in recent years' he would 'explain the very high profits that have been earned by the distillers of Scotland?' To which Sir Alexander replied that 'there has been an enormous variety of other businesses which you have to add to distilling. You forget that we are the biggest yeast producers by a long way, and we are the biggest malt extract producers by a long way. We have very large financial interests in Canadian distilleries, and we have also large interests, as you know, in Australian distilleries. Our interests are not confined to potable alcohol. I suppose you are taking the Distillers' Company . . . I have given you instances of other firms who are prepared to sell their business on the basis of the market price of the goods, and on which they will make a higher profit by so doing than they are making in business.'

Such was the state of Scotch and Scotland as the nation and industry entered the troublous thirties – it paid better to get out of Scotch.

27

Through war and taxation

BEFORE VENTURING further into the slough of despond which was the
whisky market of the thirties, we must attend, if only briefly, to the
whisky/barley situation of the troubled twenties. As early as the spring
of 1922 the alert Whisky Association was raising the problem of
depressed British agriculture in its efforts to have the restrictive spirits
duty reduced. In their memorial to the Chancellor of the Exchequer of
that year, the Association claimed that 'This submission is made not
only on the ground that the existing duty bears harshly on the Whisky
Trade as a whole, and on every section and individual thereof, but also
because it involves serious losses to many allied trades, handicaps and
restricts British agriculture, directly causes unrest and discontent
among the working classes, and is resulting in loss of revenue to the
State.'

In the course of propounding their case, the memorialists went on:
'Among the interests which will suffer directly from the curtailment of
the Whisky Trade, agriculture takes a foremost place. Very large
quantities of home-grown barley are used by the distillers, who
generally pay the top prices of the market, and so encourage a high
standard of quality in the barley grown. In the North of Scotland
particularly, it is safe to say that large areas would be allowed to go out
of cultivation were it not for the outlet for the crops provided by the
distilleries. The benefit to the farmer by no means ends there, as the
barley used in distillation returns to him in the form of valuable feeding
stuffs. If these feeding stuffs were not available, large quantities of other

and more costly cereals would be required, resulting in a substantial increase in the cost of various farm products to the consumer.'

The petition of the North of Scotland Malt Distillers Association, pleading the case of ninety-one distilleries north of Perth, took up the same theme, pointing out that more than half the barley crop of Scotland went to the making of Scotch malt whisky, so that the interests of the Scottish farmers were allied with those of the distilleries. The distillers paid the highest price for the barley; they gave the farmer a market on his own doorstep; with rail rates as they then were, the north country barley could otherwise only be used for feeding purposes. This, in turn, would mean that its cultivation would not be profitable and would be abandoned. The farmer depended on his barley crop for a 'quick cash return'. In addition, the by-products of the malt, the draff, culms, and burnt ale, represented about twenty-eight per cent of the food value of the barley, and this twenty-eight per cent formed the principal feed for dairy cows where there were distilleries. In the average distilling year at the time, the by-products of the distillery provided nutriment sufficient for 5,400 cows and to produce 4 million gallons of milk. The by-products were sold to the farmer at a low price and any curtailment of them 'must seriously affect the milk supply' of the nation.

The same arguments were used in anticipation of the following year's budget, but with no more success, unhappily. Instead, the Chancellor, quite unfairly, granted an abatement of the beer duty. And it was just at this juncture that barley entered the throes of Whitehall and Westminster. It was proposed to impose a duty of 10s. per quarter on all foreign barley used for distilling and brewing in order to assist British agriculture. In effect, this would have been a further tax on spirits. In 1902 the 1s. per quarter corn duty had raised £2,346,796 in the year, maize bearing only half the duty as it was said to be a staple article of food of the Irish poor. The duty was repealed after only one year of life. So any introduction of a barley duty in 1922 would indeed have been revolutionary.

The Scotch malt distiller did not use solely home-grown barley, and the effectiveness of the duty might have been, as it was, argued from that standpoint. The distiller valued foreign barley because it was invariably ripe and dry. That is, it was properly sun-dried and not withered in the kiln, and as a rule it was lighter in oils. Moreover, it was procurable in large quantities, as against the dribbling in of much English and Scottish barley which arrived intermittently in odd sacks, and not invariably dry. The foreign barleys were also appreciated in the distilleries for the size of their husk, which was invaluable for promoting the drainage of the mash tun.

At this point it is relevant to look at barley imports on the eve of the war. Russia was the largest single supplier of barley to the United Kingdom in 1913, the quantity coming from Russia that year amounting to 6,105,000 cwt, the United States coming next with 4,438,100 cwt. British India was third with a contribution of 3,619,400 cwt, and the others, in descending order, were: Canada, 2,561,800 cwt; Asiatic Turkey, 2,232,300 cwt; Romania, 1,388,800 cwt, and many other countries with six-figure and less amounts. The total foreign barley imported that year was 16,277,648 cwt, and the total colonial 6,211,600 cwt, making a grand total of 22,439,248 cwt. This was in excess of both the preceding and following years, but significantly above the poor import year of 1910, when all spirits were suffering both consumption and production losses as a result of the Lloyd George budget of 1909–10.

The proposal got nowhere; it was put aside as some slight measure of prosperity returned for the moment. The first Labour Government took office and the feeling of unrest once more pervaded the commercial world, only dispelled with the speedy return of the Conservative party. That party has always been the ally of the agricultural interest, and it is of more than passing interest that towards the end of 1924 there was a meeting at Elgin of the Moray branch of the Scottish Farmers' Union at which it was suggested, with full support, that whisky bottles should be labelled to show whether they contained, or not, the products of home-grown and foreign barley. The use of imported barley in whisky distilling was held to be 'an injustice' to the Scottish farmer. And the question was once more, as so often before, raised: 'Why should not the growing of barley, a species of grain that varies so much, be done for the use of malt whisky distillers by a more scientific system than the happy-go-lucky method that now so frequently obtains?' (I am quoting a contemporary of the Elgin meeting; in the last few years that Elgin suggestion has been acted upon by distillers, in aid of the Scottish farmer.)

A Highland correspondent took the matter up and it was established that much of the Danish and Danish Island barley imported into

377

Scotland did not grow in Denmark, but had been shipped there for sale and in order to masquerade as Danish. He also established that large quantities of Karachi barley were being used in pot still distilleries, describing it as follows: 'A thin barley but cheap, and is giving good extract at the mash tuns and a superior fermentation. The bulk of distillers are now using it, and it is looked upon as the best value in the markets today. Reports from all quarters recommend it.'

There followed the Churchill budget, variously described at the time as 'a rich man's budget' and as 'a piece of patchwork', but without relief for the spirits duty and without mention of the barley tax. That a duty on barley imports, even with imperial preference, was very much in the wind, as was the idea of taxing whisky exports, can be seen from the fact that Ross, the new chairman of the D.C.L., in his annual statement to shareholders that July felt bound to discourse on it. The Scottish conference on Agricultural Policy had then recently favoured a duty on imported foreign barley as a remedy for the very real distress being suffered by Scottish farmers. But as Ross pointed out, any such duty on malting barley would increase the cost of whisky and beer. If this increased cost was passed on to the consumer, there would be a further shrinkage in the already diminishing whisky market. His advice to the farmers, therefore, was to apply pressure on the Government 'to reduce the present monstrous duty on whisky, and so recover part of that market which they had lost for their barley through the greatly diminished consumption' of whisky. Distilleries were being closed down, and agriculture was enduring the double loss of smaller markets and fewer sources for by-products, as outlined above.

Even so, the proposed duty of 10s. per quarter on barley imports was revived, this in the midst of a decision of representative distillers to curtail their malt whisky production in the 1925–6 season, and so also match not only declining demand but the closure of some grain whisky distilleries. In truth, it was as much the Tory coquetting with the idea as the farmers themselves, and the distillers had once more to take time off to roll out their arguments for foreign barley – its ripeness, its sun-dried qualities, its delivery by shiploads, its cleanliness, its large proportion of husk, etc. – and in criticism of home-grown barley: its availability in small quantities, the fact that when fairly ripe it was seldom screened or graded, the constant need to kiln it before storage, the 'invariably excessive' proportion of back-liers (non-starters) if the season was at all bad. It can be summed up this way: the distillery and the farm were not nearly so closely associated as they had been a generation previous. Good quality English barley was too valuable in breweries for the distillers then to look to Yorkshire or the southern parts of England for supplies, and the additional of 10s. to the price of an imported quarter of foreign barley, it was calculated, would mean an extra 1s. 1d. a bushel, with the result that malt whisky distillers would have to increase their prices by sevenpence the proof gallon. The additional cost to grain whisky, which uses mostly maize in its production, would be in the region of twopence the proof gallon. However, that valiant spokesman for his electorate, Robert Boothby, the Unionist Member of Parliament for East Aberdeenshire, was in no mood to let the grievances and requests of his constituents go unvoiced, and he asked the Chancellor of the Exchequer about the use of foreign barley in the north of Scotland to make Scotch whisky and 'whether, in view of the difficulties with which Scottish farmers were contending, he would consider the advisability of imposing a Customs duty on barley imported into this country for distilling purposes'. The Financial Secretary to the Treasury took the easy way out: he was 'unable to anticipate a Budget statement'. Boothby then called for the Government to 'Prohibit the importation altogether'. Before long there was the General Strike, and the idea of a tax on imported barley was shelved among the proposals in limbo which are always useful to drag out when politics slacken.

But as late as 1935 the Scottish Chamber of Agriculture petitioned the Import Duties Advisory Committee to recommend a tax of 10s. per quarter on barley imports in place of the ten per cent *ad valorem* duty imposed in the financial crisis of the thirties. In this narrative we may discern the background and motives which have led to the endowment of Scottish agricultural research and the insistence of many, notably the D.C.L., on the use of home-grown barley to the normal exclusion of imported varieties. The reply of Sir Alexander Walker, at the 1930 royal commission, may aptly serve to close this section of our inquiry: 'In our case we manufacture all the raw material ourselves except the barley,' he told Mr Gerald France, J.P.

The very year after Sir Alexander gave his evidence to the royal commission saw also another changing facet of the whisky industry in

Scotland emerge. In 1931 there came to Scotland an American by the name of Mr Duncan G. Thomas who, sensing prohibition was about to end in the United States acquired, Littlemill malt whisky distillery situated at Bowling-by-Glasgow. It had been closed for eighteen months in the general depression then prevailing in the industry, indeed, in the whole of the British Isles. In 1967 it was producing some 400,000 gallons a year, and in September 1966 was opened a million pound malt distillery plus bonds, storage and bottling and other facilities, sponsored by Mr Thomas and American associates. True, his interests were not, initially, directed to the home market, but that precursor of the current American invasion set the tone of what has since grown increasingly in Scotland: the direct investment in plant and production of their own whiskies by Canadian and American interests.

The Canadian distilling firm of Hiram Walker-Gooderham & Worts Ltd made their first venture into the Scotch whisky trade in 1930 when they purchased a sixty per cent interest in the Stirling Bonding Co. Ltd and, Messrs Jas. & Geo. Stodart Ltd, blenders and exporters. It was, however, not until 1936, with prohibition in the United States well repealed that the minority interests in these two companies were secured, and in that same year Messrs Geo. Ballantine & Son Ltd was added along with the two Highland malt whisky distilleries, Glen Burgie and Milton Duff. Their greatest incursion was, however, the building of a grain whisky distillery at Dumbarton, down the Clyde, on the west side of Scotland, a distillery then proclaimed as 'the largest in the British Isles'. This was formally opened in September 1938, just as the 1937 financial improvement was about to give way to the recession only avoided by the outbreak of war in the following year, 1939. At the opening, that chairman, Mr Harry C. Hatch put the whole enterprise in perspective and indicated the lines of development of the industry which have since come amply to pass: 'The great whisky distillery,' said Mr Hatch, speaking at Dumbarton, 'has been rendered possible and an advisable undertaking . . . only as a result of the reception given by the United States to the Scotch whisky shipped to that market by the blending and exporting firms here'. That is, the home market was no reason at all for its inception: the home market could not even support what distilleries there were. 'This plant is the creation of Scotland itself,' however, he continued, 'It is the demand actually established and still growing for a Scottish product to which it owes its inception!'

But since their Ballantine acquisition in particular they had become 'increasingly conscious of the scarcity of grain whisky in Scotland. In fact, there were times when we could not secure from the then available sources sufficient for our estimated requirements . . .' He then found it somewhat necessary to enlarge on what he admitted might be taken not as 'a note of confidence' but as 'belligerence' by adding that 'The competition we bring to these Isles will be a competition based upon quality, efficiency and service.' Mentioning the D.C.L., the greatest grain whisky distillers in Scotland, Mr Hatch hoped that company would not 'regard our operations here as anything other than a development which corrects a situation in the industry which in the long run we believe could not have been for its ultimate benefit'.

Continuing that same empire theme we have already noted in inter-war exports of Scotch whisky, Mr Hatch confessed to 'thoughts of Empire' when they built the distillery, saying that 'Our investment in Scotland amounts to £3 million sterling – half of which was placed in Great Britain' and that 'this issue represented the largest industrial financing for a Canadian company carried out in the London market since the war. In other words, British investors are partners with us in this enterprise to the extent of that large total. Their interests are our interests; and our interests are theirs,' he declaimed in fine rhetorical style, giving Scotch yet another role in the tale of empire. 'It is the contribution this plant will make to the industrial equipment of the Motherland in the event that war should come. We all hope earnestly that no such eventuality will arise; but if it does, we have here the most efficient plant of its kind which modern science can devise, ready with its industrial and technical resources available for His Majesty.' The formal opening was done by Lord Nigel Douglas Hamilton who summed up the then position of the whisky industry in these words: 'It is not a fancy trade, but a stable, well-organised industry.'

Hiram Walker have since made further acquisitions in Scotland, and have been followed by those other Canadian distilling interests we have noticed as being concerned with the inter-empire trade of Scotch earlier, and deeply committed to the American market. At the same time, since that initial Thomas and Hiram Walker incursion, other leading American distilling interests have established themselves in

Scotland, such as Barton, Publicker, Seagram and Schenley, with activities covering the production of malt and grain whiskies, add the blending and bottling of whiskies for consumer level. Today upwards of a third of the industry may be said to be in transatlantic hands.

Now in 1936 and 1937 there were faint signs of recovery in the whisky industry, though, as noticed, home consumption had not even got back to the 1929 level and exports had still not attained the grade of the 10 million gallons shipped abroad before World War I. In line with this brief recovery and with the dangers of another world war in mind the industry set about increasing its output and stock-piling in the event of the conflagration that was to come. So at the beginning of the year before the war, in 1938, the D.C.L. formally reopened its Cambus grain whisky distillery. This distillery was one of the original six which formed the company in 1877; it had been burnt down just before World War I. That war precluded its rebuilding for four years and the chaotic times of the industry in the post-war years again deferred its reconstruction. At the beginning of 1937 the slightly improved conditions and the threat of war made the D.C.L. hasten its reconstruction so that it was acclaimed as 'the most modern distillery of its kind in the world'.

In short, after a double decade of turmoil and uncertainty, the whisky industry hoped times were returning to normality, a hope soon to be shattered. The decade opened with panic and the worst depression of British history; it closed with another world conflict. In February, 1931, Snowden, the Labour Chancellor of the Exchequer, stated: 'I say, with all the seriousness I can command, that the national position is grave; that drastic and disagreeable measures will have to be taken if the Budget equilibrium is to be maintained and industrial recovery is to be made.' His April budget did not face up to the 'disagreeable' facts; it was frankly dishonest. At the end of July came the bombshell of the May report, forecasting a budget deficiency of £120 million, which could be made good only by new taxation, or economies, or both. Great Britain was manifestly heading for bankruptcy. A serious financial crisis occurred. On 11 August, the Bank of England borrowed £50 million from the Banks of France and the United States. Prime Minister MacDonald called a meeting with bankers and the Cabinet that same day and the next consulted leaders of the Opposition. On 19

August the Cabinet sat for eleven and a half hours, agreeing on drastic economies and on the 20th the Government proposals were put to certain Labour leaders, and the General Council of the Trades Union Congress, who refused to accept them. On the 22nd the King interrupted his Scottish holiday, personally took charge, called in the leaders of the three parties and on the 24th MacDonald resigned. He was then entrusted with a National Government by the King. The supplementary budget of 10 September revealed an appalling financial situation economically, but the budget was balanced and the first phase of the crisis was over. The following year, 1932, Chamberlain effected a fiscal revolution comparable in its comprehensiveness with Peel's fiscal reforms of 1841–6. But the unemployment problem remained. It is no surprise in this context that no taxation relief was given to whisky. The surprise is that no burden was added to its excise taxation. The only interpretation is that the point of diminishing returns had been approached; extra duty would, obviously, have meant lesser and lesser revenue.

Perhaps the handiest exemplification of the sluggishness of the home market for whisky can be seen in the fact that when in November 1930, Sir Alexander Walker was giving his evidence to the royal commission he stated the life of the 137,247,906 gallons of whisky in stock to be seven years at the then rate of consumption. In September 1932 that life at the then prevailing rate had risen to fifteen years. At the annual meeting held that month in Elgin of the Scottish Pot Still Malt Distillers Association it was recommended to members that distilling should be stopped for one year. It was further proposed, by Mr James Robertson, of Highland Distilleries, Glasgow, and seconded by Mr A. Horsfall, of Scottish Malt Distillers Ltd, the D.C.L. subsidiary, that 'This meeting of the pot malt distillers of Scotland resolves to close all pot malt distilleries in Scotland for this coming season in consequence of the high rate of duty.' The two dissentients only asked time to consider it. Workmen at distilleries had been going on the dole since 1927, and Major Alexander J. Wrightson, of Highland Distilleries Ltd, Glasgow, said at the time of the Elgin meeting, 'One salient fact must be recognised, and that is that unless there is a substantial reduction in the duty at home, there is not much hope for the distillery worker, the farmer, or anybody else.'

The industry, like the nation, descended into the maelstrom. At the final meeting of the D.C.L., in July 1935, at which he presided as chairman, Ross told of the 'grievous disappointment' of no reduction in the whisky duty, saying that the Chancellor repeated what he had said the previous year: 'That he was convinced the duty was too high and should receive consideration at the earliest date.' Which drew from Ross the remark that 'it left us in pretty much the same mood as the love-sick maiden found herself in when her swain kept putting off naming the happy day'.

However, in the ensuing years before the war, as the industry stock-piled under the influence of threat and economic improvement, production mounted slightly, as we have seen, so that in the distilling year October 1938 to September 1939 some 37·8 million gallons of whisky were made in Scotland as against 36·3 million the previous year. In that final pre-war year, again, there were 96 distilleries at work there, compared with 95 the preceding season. A slight improvement, but only slight, and when we recall there were only 15 operative in 1933, we must also remember that the beginning of the century had seen 156 at work.

Coming more down to his own days, the late Mr Brodie Hepburn felt compelled to write, in January 1937, as a ripple of improvement might be suspected, that 'In the reports of the recent debates in Parliament on the economic problems of the Highlands and Islands of Scotland, no mention appears of the decline of the Highland distilling industry, due solely to the Government's continuance of the war-tax on their output. In 1914 there were 133 distilleries at work in Scotland, of which over 100 were situated in the Highlands . . . In 1935 the number of distilleries working in Scotland was 64, in the Highlands alone 52 . . . If distilling was an English industry, I do not believe that the exorbitant war-tax would have continued to this day. There is no excuse whatever for the present Government taxing a Scots and Highland industry to the extent of nearly £30,000,000 per year as in 1936.'

Yet a Highland correspondent was able to report that the year just gone was 'the busiest that Highland distillers have experienced since the war. Production has everywhere been speeded up to an amazing degree, and it is apparent already that the "boom" now on is likely to continue.' Similarly Southard & Co. Ltd were able to say in a circular of about the same date that 'The whisky market has provided the most sensational feature of the years . . . Prices of single whiskies quoted in the market are considerably above prices of blends being offered in overseas markets by certain regular exporters.'

Or, as *The Scotsman* put it in summary fashion in February 1938, commenting on the pre-war boom, 'The course of production over the past fifty years has been characterised by a time of strong demand and high production alternating with low demand and restricted make. Thus the distiller finds it difficult to forecast requirements and regulate his production. Moreover, he has to reckon with a lapse of three years before he can market it. That storage requirement is attended, of course, with the need for a certain expenditure . . . Not long ago, whisky of age could be bought at the price of new.'

In 1930, as we have seen, stocks of whisky in Scotland amounted to 137·2 million gallons. Thereafter they diminished with reduced production to reach only 121·9 million in 1934. They then gradually mended by small quantities to attain 123·9 million in 1936. The boom set in: they became 127 million the next year, moved up to 134·9 million in 1938, and on the eve of war stood at 144·25 million gallons.

With wartime restrictions on distilling, they of course sank heavily during the conflict and the post-war years, reaching their nadir in 1947 when they were only 79·8 million gallons. Today they are well in excess of 700 million gallons.

We cannot here pursue all the vicissitudes of whisky in war on the home market, and the stages by which it reached the position it holds today, when the home market takes less than twenty per cent of releases from bond. This meant that the position has effectively reversed since 1900: the home market now takes little more than was then exported, and the exports now exceed what was then drunk in the British Isles.

But in that war whisky came early to the taxman's block, in September 1939, not towards its end as in World War I, and again in the spring of 1940 the excise axe was unleashed against it. As in the previous war, the industry did not bemoan its fate: too much, it was realised, was at stake. In April 1942, and again in April 1943, the duty was increased, bringing it in all to 157s. 6d. a proof gallon, or more than ten times as much as it had been throughout most of the earlier war, and more than five times as much as it had been when that war had ended. It was further increased in the immediate post-war years and was thought to be incapable of further enlargement in April 1948 when Stafford Cripps lifted the duty to 210s. 10d. There it remained until the Tory Chancellor of the Exchequer Selwyn Lloyd began the oppression of the sixties in July 1961, with a near-unconstitutional device of his 'regulator' device giving him the power ahead of parliamentary ratification, as needed with all budget increases, to increase duties by ten per cent. Again, from 1964–9 the tax on whisky has been multiplied for the twofold reason that politicians can think of no other means to satisfy governmental extravagance than to punish the individual whisky consumer, and that the hidden power of the prohibitionist party is still of account, and not to be dismissed lightly.

But beginning with wartime, the other damaging element of the taxation of spirits has come increasingly to the fore: that unconstitutional power assumed by McKenna in the autumn of 1915 of restricting persons and firms from withdrawing their own property from bond in a move intended to anticipate heavy losses to their own estates. That power grabbed by McKenna was increasingly acted upon in the war and post-war budgets and was finally given an air of legality, if not equity, in the Act consolidating Customs and Excise powers, etc., in 1952.

That same Act gave the first statutory expression to the findings of the 1908–9 royal commission, with which we began, on the matter of Scotch whisky by adopting the definition proposed by the commission with the addition of Lloyd George's three-year statutory minimum age, and runs: 'Spirits described as Scotch whisky shall not be deemed to correspond to that description unless they have been obtained by distillation in Scotland from a mash of cereal grain saccharified by the diastase of malt and have been matured in warehouse in cask for a period of at least three years.' [Customs and Excise Act, 1952, Clause 243 (I) (b).] That definition had been preluded in the Finance Act of 1933. The 1969 Finance Act redefined Scotch whisky with a wealth of technical detail.

We cannot here pursue the tortuous path by which these restrictions, both physical and financial were imposed. Suffice it to say that they are logical developments of those earlier years when were shaped the age, habits and industries in which we live.

Some of the lessons learned by the industry in World War I were quickly applied by the industry itself in its successor. Anticipating governmental intervention which had fixed home releases in 1917 at fifty per cent of the 1916 quantities, the Scotch Whisky Association as early as February 1940, introduced its own scheme of rationing for the home market. The percentage was gradually reduced, what with the industry's own emphasis on exports, the need to conserve stocks – taught especially by the closing years of World War I, the early post-war years and sheer business aptitude – and the restrictions on distilling, so early imposed in the second world conflict. (There was restricted production from 1940–2 inclusive, none at all from 1942–4, and very tightly controlled output thereafter.)

From the spring of 1947 until the end of 1953, an arrangement had to be made annually between the Scotch Whisky Association, the Ministry of Food, and the Board of Trade setting forth an export objective, a home market allocation and making an allowance of cereals for distilling. One thing, for instance, it meant was that from May 1947 the home market was to get only twenty-five per cent of what it had got in the 'standard' year, from March 1939, to February 1940, a poor year in any case, as we have seen, for home consumption of Scotch whisky. A year later, as from May 1948, that percentage was moved even lower, to twenty per cent. Even when governmental rationing for the home market was lifted, from the beginning of 1954, the individual firms of the industry still found it incumbent on themselves to retain some form of quota system, or rationing, for the home market because of the problems posed by all the years when their output was restricted.

In line with that restriction on output ran parallel another restriction, that on price. Warned by experience in World War I and just after, as noted above, the Whisky Association, as we have seen earlier, itself imposed a maximum and minimum price structure on its product for the home market. Although first aimed at preventing exploitation of the market place by overcharging on the beverage, it later became a weapon in the hands of individual firms – its effectiveness as an association matter was destroyed in the mid-fifties – to maintain prices at a standard level adjusted to producer, wholesaler and retailer. Early in 1965 with the coming into effect of the Resale Prices Act that structure was removed, and just as fifty or sixty years ago brands have to find their own sales and levels on the home market. The clock has come full cycle. But the main difference today is that little room is given for manœuvre because of the continuance of that principle initiated by Lloyd George in 1909 of taxing whisky with a duty increase then equal to more than one-third of the original duty: an increase of 3*s*. 9*d*. on the basic duty of 11*s*. Today, the home market must endure a duty of 321*s*. 377*s*. per proof gallon as compared with that of March 1900, when 6*d*. a gallon was added to make it the 11*s*. that Lloyd George found and exploited in 1909. Prohibition will adopt any means towards its end.

28

The beginning of mergers

TIME, WE KNOW, is like an ever-rolling stream, which also makes it possible to ascend the stream in the direction of its source. Thus about the middle of the last century we find the first tentative signs of the trend, which has persisted to this day, away from *laissez-faire*: towards combination in all forms of economic enterprise, towards its complement of collective self-help among the wage-earners of the nation, towards regulation by the state in the economic and social fields. The drift since then towards greater organisation among men, both as specialised groups and as total communities, has been virtually continuous and in more modern times the momentum has increased continually. Especially, in the last century, it was with the generation after 1870 that the drift was so much accelerated and that society encountered the forms and attitudes taking clear shape in the form in which they exist today. The organisation of industry itself and the conditions of work within it were becoming ever more and more complex; industrial and other forms of enterprise inevitably responded to the growing complexity of the day.

Most of the industrial, commercial and financial expansion of earlier generations had been carried out in simpler social and technical conditions by the family firm or the small partnership, with unlimited liability for all partners and unlimited freedom for the master. Although the joint-stock enterprise with limited liability was on the way to its present dominating position, even by 1900 the family business and the small firm predominated in every country: even in Great Britain four-fifths of the 62,762 active joint-stock companies registered in 1914 were private companies, family firms and private partnerships in a new guise. Again, although limited liability was ultimately to be a new means of raising capital for industry through the stock exchange, it was not until after 1890 that it began to be used to any great extent for this purpose. But increasingly after 1870, however, we find that the small firm was being replaced by the large limited liability company which now for the first time entered the producing, commercial and financial fields. By 1900 Great Britain, like other industrialised countries, had a dual economy – a large traditional sector hardly touched by organisational change and a limited but economically dominant modern sector comprising the major industries and a large part of the financial and commercial enterprise, the typical unit of which was a limited liability undertaking on a considerable scale.

This had arisen in two manners: either from the growth in size and capital of larger firms, or from the amalgamation of firms. The processes were supplemented by the formation of associations of firms for agreements on prices, the creation of trusts and the establishment of cartels by which firms in one industry sought to control sections of subsidiary and associated industries on which they depended. We need not here pursue the details of these developments; it is sufficient to recall, for instance, the names of Krupps, Nobel, Rockefeller, J. & P. Coats (a virtual world monopoly in cotton thread), and Rockefeller's phrase, 'The day of combination is here to stay. Individualism has gone, never to return.'

Further, it must be noted that alongside every firm that expanded in size or set out to amalgamate others, there were more than one that, failing to expand or to survive the new, often international, competition, became ripe for amalgamation. For every firm bent on association and monopoly so as to expand the markets and profits, there was another led in the same direction by its need to conserve them, by the greater concern for security resulting from needing larger and larger amounts of capital in conditions of increasing competition. Incidentally, we may note that the movement towards amalgamation and association was not limited to producers and employers: it was as evident among wage-earners and consumers.

It came to this, that the increasing competition of the latter part of the last century – it became unfettered in the generally prosperous third quarter of the century – was altogether too bracing an air for British (and other) businessmen and by the 1880's they everywhere sought shelter not only behind protective tariffs but in addition behind agreements to restrict what was called 'cut-throat competition'. These agreements were of two types: those aimed at maintaining the sovereign independence of the firms which entered into the voluntary contract to restrict competition; and those which aimed at creating a larger business unit by submerging the identity of existing businesses in that of a larger business. The former method has been given many names – cartel, pool conference, syndicate, *comptoir* – but it generally portended similar policies: members would agree not to sell below a certain price; they might come to an agreement to divide the market, whether by geographic area or by quota. This might even culminate in some sort of central marketing agency, and especially in Great Britain out of such arrangements would emerge a fully-fledged new amalgamated firm. Indeed, it is true to say that British industry in search of stability went by preference for the more permanent type of association. So fluctuations in sales and profits brought about, to begin with, amalgamations that were principally of the 'horizontal' type, that is, between firms which made and sold the same, or very similar products. Simultaneously technology brought with it amalgamations of the 'vertical' kind. As the child of its age, in as concrete historical setting as any other British industry, the whole distilling industry of the United Kingdom was subject to just those forces here sketched in brief. The Scottish end of that industry is here our main concern, though the English and Irish distilling activities enter into it also, and it is to the reactions of those trends and tendencies as manifested in Scotland that we must now turn our attention.

After a fitful eighteen years of utilising the still patented by Coffey in 1831, and introduced to Glasgow in 1838, some half-dozen patent still distillers in Scotland in 1856 found competition so keen that they entered 'into a Trade Arrangement for one year', having for its object the approportionment of the trade amongst them in certain defined proportions. It lasted only the year, to be followed by a period of very keen competition again, so keen indeed that more than one of them reached the verge of bankruptcy. One such Scottish distiller went so far as to have circulars printed calling a meeting of creditors when the suggestion of making another trade arrangement reached him, so causing him to hold his hand. That was in 1865, and on 17 May of that year a second Trade Arrangement was entered into, dated from the 10th of that month, to last until 10 July of the year following, by which the quantity of spirits to be delivered by each member house was regulated by the proportions of 28·66, 28·00, 19·80, 9·75, 7·64 and 6·15 per cent.

At the second meeting of the Association, proposals were made to bring about an arrangement with the London and Irish grain distillers, and later in the year a Liverpool distiller was accepted into the Association. In August of that year, the first mention is made of the price of spirits: as the London distillers had raised their price, the Scotch Association increased the price in Scotland, to 1s. 7d. per proof gallon. A few weeks later, the Association was extended in length of time 'in order to enable the Association to enter into a Trade Arrangement with the Irish distillers. With the Liverpool distiller definitely in, the percentage points were redistributed and five Irish grain distillers agreed 'to enter into a Trade Arrangement with the Scotch Association for one year, on the footing that the home market should be supplied during that period in the proportion of 7,000,000 gallons for the Scotch Association and 1,400,000 gallons for the Irish Houses'. On the same day the price of grain spirits was raised to 1s. 8d. the proof gallon, net cash. In the ensuing month as the London distillers had raised their price to 2s. the proof gallon, it was agreed to raise the Scotch price to 1s. 9d.

London distillers were always a thorn in the side of the Scottish ones, but in June 1866 agreement was reached between them both by which the Scotch Association members were to restrict their spirits shipments to London while the London distillers were to keep up their price. This meant also the increasing of the Scotch price to 1s. 10d. per gallon immediately. Moreover, before the agreement expired in October 1866, it was agreed to continue it for two more years with an amended percentage distribution between the eight members. The agreement with the Irish distillers was renewed, with modifications, for two years, but a Glasgow member was dissatisfied with his quota percentage and withdrew from the Association.

In the second half of 1868 negotiations were begun again to perpetuate the Association on the expiry of its two years' life, and, ignoring minutiae, it was carried on and the agreement with the Irish distillers was renewed for three years. Other special arrangements with distillers outside the Scotch Association were also made, and before the agreement ended it was resolved to renew it 'for an indefinite period' but subject to termination by any member on giving three months' notice. Later, some took advantage of this condition of membership and in December 1872 the remaining six Scotch Association members formed themselves into a new Association on similar lines to the old one, but this time to run for one year only and with a reallocation of points, or shares of the home market. It is of interest, too, to note that as early as 1865 they had resolved to make a warehouse rent charge. It had not been regularly enforced but with the new Association a new scale of charges was introduced and applied, even by some distillers outside the Association. Actually, the scale was not varied until mid-1921.

The next two years, from 1874 to 1876, saw little of outstanding interest, but only minor variations. This means that the days of tentative fumbling were approaching their end; the first phase of reaction to the changing years was nearly over. Negotiations were, in fact, proceeding for a form of closer, more stable union. The Scottish grain, or patent still distillers were fitting into the pattern of historic events and trends outlined above. It is not possible to say who originally propounded the scheme for amalgamation, but the memorandum outlining it was drawn up by Mr Alexander Moore, C.A., of Glasgow, who was auditor to a member firm. As the memorandum put it: 'A suggestion has been made that the principal firms engaged in the grain distillery business should form themselves into one Company under the Limited Liabilities Act. The suggestion originated in the fact that these firms are already associated for the protection of their common interests, and from the idea that their amalgamation into a Company would both extend and confirm the advantages derived from that Association, whilst it would afford other and important benefits which the Association cannot give. Such a Company would differ entirely from any Limited Company hitherto formed, inasmuch as it would not require to appeal to the public for subscriptions to its Capital, and it would be entirely under the direction of men practically acquainted with the business. The Capital of the Company could be fixed at the sum equal to the Capital ascertained to be in the firms amalgamating, with such additions as may be agreed upon for future extensions, and the Stock

393

of the Company would be allocated to the parties as the consideration for the transfer made of their respective businesses.'

We cannot enter into a detailed report of the memorandum, but as typical and representative of the times and the economic and intellectual milieu we may make these excerpts: 'In the working of the business the Company would have all the benefit of combined action – economy could be secured in the purchase of the necessaries for the distilleries, as such could be under the direct control of a properly qualified party taking his instructions from the Board of Directors and being responsible to them. The disposal of the produce of all the distilleries in the same way could be conducted through the same agencies, and with a saving of expense a much greater control could be exercised over the credit to be given to purchasers. The annoyance of undue competition would also be avoided, and the possible interference with the trade from new sources would not be so likely . . . The regulation of supply for the demand would at all times be more under their control than it can be under present arrangements.'

The first 'Meeting of Promotors of a Limited Liability Company to take over the distilleries of the Promotors and to carry on the business of Distillers' was held in Edinburgh in November 1876. Messrs Menzies & Co., of Caledonian grain distillery, also of Edinburgh, withdrew, but otherwise matters progressed, Menzies himself assisting the promotion and writing that he would 'enter into a trade arrangement with the Company, when formed, for a period of years' on the principle of sharing the market.

In the upshot, and after feelers were put out in various directions, six firms joined the company: M. Macfarlane & Co., of Port Dundas distillery; John Bald & Co., of Carsebridge distillery; John Haig & Co., of Cameron Bridge distillery; McNab Bros. & Co., of Glenochil distillery; Robert Moubray, of Cambus distillery; Stewart & Co., of Kirkliston distillery. The nominal capital of the company was fixed at £2 million, divided into 40,000 shares of £50 each, but it was agreed to issue meantime only 12,000 shares in part payment of the purchase price to be divided amongst the member firms in proportion to the points upon which the former Trade Arrangement had been based, while the balance of the purchase price was to be satisfied by the issue of five per cent mortgage and ordinary debentures repayable at certain fixed periods. The company was finally registered on 24 April 1877 and at the first meeting of directors, held the next day, it was agreed the company should take over the various distilleries and begin business on 1 May. Thus was born The Distillers Co. Ltd.

It was agreed that each vendor should, for the most part, continue as manager of his distillery while also being represented on the board. Ross, later to become managing director and ultimately chairman of the company, wrote long after the original amalgamation, and with a wealth of personal experience of the company from its very early days: 'While as a temporary measure, to allow of the several businesses being properly consolidated, the arrangement was no doubt beneficial, it had this distinct disadvantage that each manager was inclined to regard the distillery under his charge as still his own and to shape his policy as if the other distilleries were still his competitors. Strange as it may seem, it was many years before this feeling was overcome, and it was only after the removal of the original vendors from the direct management and the placing of the control under one head with a staff of well-qualified officials under him that the real benefits of amalgamation were realised.'

At a staff dinner in 1898, Mr W. S. Fraser, who had known well all these original partners in the amalgamation, summarised them as 'the determined Haig', 'the politic Bald', 'the impetuous Macfarlane', 'the subtle Moubray', 'the anxious Stewart', and 'the cautious McNab'. By then also Menzies & Co. had joined the amalgamation and earned the phrase of 'the bold Menzies'. It is also of interest to note some production figures. In 1877, the year of the amalgamation there were made in Scotland 11,381,000 gallons of grain whisky by means of the patent still. This compares with 5,410,000 in 1857, the year following the first Trade Agreement, and with 5,325,000 in 1867, ten years before the final move in the game. Ten years after the amalgamation, in 1887, grain whisky was made to the extent of 9,396,000 gallons, and in line with the booming nineties the total for 1897 was 17,300,000 gallons. With the recession in the early years of this century it slipped back in 1907 to 14,340,000 gallons. In short, one of the benefits of amalgamation: the ability to speed up or equally to reduce production promptly, and by means of an overall, centralised control.

Chapelizod distillery, Dublin, renamed Phoenix Park, was not an amalgamation, but an investment, a purchase by the newly formed D.C.L. in 1878, a purchase which brought the issue capital of the company to the nominal value of £650,000. At the time of writing the authorised capital is £200,000,000. As Lord Forteviot put it in 1927: 'This company has been a series of amalgamations. Its birth was the result of an amalgamation, and the company has gone on amalgamating ever since . . . We have closed down something like twenty distilleries in the last twenty years without very much hardship to anybody. That could not have been done without amalgamation. They would have been closed down, no doubt, but somebody would have suffered very severely.' Just one of the benefits of the world-wide drive to combination.

While the Dublin deal was going on, attempts were made to form a larger association to embrace the whole of the grain spirit distillers of the United Kingdom outside London. The agreement was finally signed at the beginning of the distilling year, 1 October 1878, and was to have lasted five years. At the end of that time, in 1883, the U.K. Distillers Association was renewed and partnered also by supplementary agreements of varying length of time with some distillers not members of the Association.

But personal factors may intervene in the course of history, however logical seems its flow. Towards the end of November 1880, Graham Menzies, of Menzies & Co., of Caledonian distillery, died and early in the eighties the partners of Menzies & Co. proposed they should now be taken into the D.C.L. on the basis originally arranged, the only condition made, and a significant one in light of subsequent events, was that there should also be taken over the rectifying business carried on by Menzies, Dr ̧sdale & Co. at Tooley Street, London. The agreement was concluded and a further issue of shares was made and new debentures created. Amalgamation was in the air, and Jas Stewart & Co. proposed the D.C.L. should take over their grain and malt whisky distillery at Saucel, Paisley. The directors of the D.C.L. rejected the scheme.

But the Caledonian distillery takeover produced its own reaction in the whisky industry. In the summer of 1885 it became known that the blenders were feeling that with the Caledonian joining the combine there was a danger of monopoly and the only thing to do was to set up their own grain whisky distillery at Edinburgh. The event that triggered off the new grain distillery plans was the refusal of the U.K. Distillers Association to reduce their price as the London distillers had done. By the end of the year, the promoters of the new distillery, the

North British distillery, decided to go ahead; talks between the dealers and blenders and the D.C.L. had broken down. The anti-monopolists went into action and within a couple of years the trend to amalgamation had resulted in its opposite, a new and proudly in-dependent grain distillery. But, curiously, and so strong were the tendencies of the age as outlined at the beginning of this chapter, the North British directors agreed from the start that they had no other intention than to work alongside the D.C.L. and others in a friendly spirit. They did not become members of the U.K. Distillers Associ-ation, but they agreed to regulate their prices and conditions of sale in accordance with the Association rules. In any case, members of that Association were falling foul of each other, and it was dissolved in September 1886.

The new competitor, the North British distillery, had one side-effect of remarkable portent to recuperate for the expected loss of markets, the D.C.L. decided to enter the export trade. An anonymous correspondent writing from Scotland at the end of 1887 put it thus: 'The new departure of the Distillers Co. Ltd in the colonies, has caused some talk in Scotland, and the comments are not altogether of a laudatory nature. The D.C.L., not manufacturing anything but cheap Scotch whisky, it is presumed that they have become blenders of Highland and other makes, and so entered into competition with those who have used their products as a basis and to cheapen the more expensive malts. In fact, this move may be looked upon as a counter one to the building of a Grain Distillery at Gorgie . . . One thing is certain, and that is, that the more Grain Spirit the Colonists consume as whisky, the better will this great Grain-producing Company like it and naturally the chief exporters to the Antipodes have done their best to use as little "Malt" Whisky as could be managed compatibly with covering up the characteristics of the "Grain". Whether this tendency has been for the good of Scotch whisky, we leave to wiser heads than ours, but at all events it has played the game most suitable to the D.C.L., and it remains to be seen how they will prosper in taking up the running.'

But another warning about combinations was given about this time, in the shape of the failure of Kidd, Eunson & Co., an old-established Leith firm. Their failure can be attributed to the very large stock of whisky they had been 'carrying': they had been the centre of what was known as the 'whisky-ring' in Leith and Edinburgh. Their extensive dealings probably consisted largely of mysterious 'crossings', which may show a profit on paper, but the actual profit of which depends on the full realisation of the bills belonging to them. It served to underline again the prior need of extensive capital in any combine attempting to be of a large and extensive character, a lesson more fundamental than ever to the industry today.

In the summer of the same year as their spectacular failure, 1887, there came another amalgamation, that of malt whisky distilleries, an amalgamation which has today grown to very great proportions. In June was formed the Highland Distilleries Co., amalgamating Bunnahabhain distillery, Islay, the property of the Islay Distillery Co. Ltd, and Glen Rothes-Glenlivet distillery of William Grant & Co.

The other major side-effect on the D.C.L. of the new grain distillery by Edinburgh was, luckily for the nation, to drive the company more vigorously into the production of yeast, a step which saved the nation's food supplies in World War I and led to an amalgamation of its own: the agency for the sale of the yeast made at the company's distilleries was taken into the company's own hands and to make sure of the yeast's outlets as well as increase the market for their increasing output, the proposal was made to the principal buying agents in England for yeast to combine their businesses into a limited liability company in which the D.C.L. would have the controlling interest. So was born the United Yeast Co., registered in December 1899 and so was assured an outlet for more than eighty per cent of the entire yeast output of the D.C.L.

A curious side-kick of the 1877 amalgamation was felt in 1893-4. Messrs John Haig & Co., the original owners of Cameron Bridge grain distillery, had moved their dealers' business to Markinch when the amalgamation took place, and carried on their Markinch activities quite separately from amalgamation. With the whisky boom of the nineties, they needed more malt whisky and planned to build a distillery of their own in the Highlands. But when the two businesses were detached at the time of the D.C.L. amalgamation, it was stipulated that so long as any partner of John Haig & Co. continued to be a manager or director of a D.C.L. distillery, Haig was bound to draw its whole supplies of whisky from the D.C.L. This condition could not be met with in so far as the demand for Highland malt whisky was made in Haig's boom years of the nineties. Thus the D.C.L. board

398

decided to build a Highland malt whisky distillery rather than let Haig's build one for themselves, and so came about the first entry of the D.C.L. into Highland malt distilling, an industry in which today they have a dominant position. All because of the articles of amalgamation and the boom in Haig whisky. The distillery, Knockdhu, was a year or more in the building and came on stream in November 1894. After the Pattison crash of 1898, the peak of British whisky consumption around the turn of the century and the gradual recession of home demand in the opening years of the twentieth century, there came a spate of amalgamations in the D.C.L. field. Particularly in the grain whisky province there was a feeling that too much grain whisky was being produced. Towards the end of the nineties, the owners of Dundashill pot still distillery added a patent still; a new grain distillery was built at Gartloch, near Glasgow, which added to the stream pouring forth while Ardgowan distillery, near Greenock, was yearly increasing its output. None of them was a financial success, but negotiations were nevertheless begun as to purchase. By the middle of 1902, the D.C.L. acquired two distilleries, the Loch Katrine distillery, Adelphi, Glasgow, and the Ardgowan distillery, Greenock. Because of an existing contract the latter had to be run separately for some years and was only finally amalgamated into the D.C.L. in 1907. The Loch Katrine acquisition meant, luckily, that Mr Archibald Walker joined the D.C.L. board, where he was particularly valuable in the mighty national effort the company put up in World War I, as seen earlier.

Times seemed hard in those early years of the century, and amalgamation seemed the cure for all ills. So three other distilleries came to the company with proposals of amalgamation: the Dundashill distillery, Glasgow, Gartloch distillery, near Glasgow, and the Lea Valley distillery, London. All proposals were declined. Though across the water, in Ireland, a minor burst of amalgamations held sway: the Connswater and Avoniel distilleries in Belfast, and the Derry distillery in Londonderry amalgamated to form the United Distilleries Ltd.

The two combines, the D.C.L. and the U.D.L., began talks to bring about a working arrangement for the betterment of the trade, but as these languished for a time, the D.C.L. put into operation the whole basis of the combine idea: to cut back over-production in Scotland, they closed Ardgowan temporarily. Dundashill had ceased making, and fresh dealings resulted in the D.C.L. acquiring the whole of the share capital of J. & R. Harvey & Co. Ltd, owners of Dundashill, which was at once closed down, permanently, though use was made of the buildings and the firm's blending and export business were perpetuated.

Meantime, the Fife Distillery Co. Ltd had set up a malt whisky distillery near Cameron Bridge distillery; it never succeeded, and finally was purchased by the D.C.L. for £6,000 – a third of its cost – and closed down, though the buildings continued to be used.

The Irish in these years were being peculiarly Irish-difficult. There were attempts to form another U.K. Distillers Association – to control grain spirit output – but they always flopped because of Irish obstructionism, with the usual result that both sides hated each other more than before. In this case, after the U.K. Association talks had petered out, in a blaze of fury, active and open warfare broke out between the U.D.L. and the D.C.L.'s Phoenix Park distillery. Grain whisky prices in Ireland, as a result, fell below Scottish and English prices. The U.D.L. then bought a bankrupt brewery in Edinburgh to convert into a grain distillery – for competition against the D.C.L. on its own doorstep. There could have been chaos. Luckily, some sense came on the scene.

It took a momentous form, as will be seen later, in the guise of an exchange of shares: the D.C.L. acquired one-half of all the shares issued in the U.D.L., paying in ordinary shares of the D.C.L. on the basis of one D.C.L. share of £10 being equal to two shares of £10 each in the U.D.L. An agreement was also made providing for the division of the trade between the Irish distilleries of the two companies in defined proportions. Also, two representatives of each company were to join the board of the other. This linkage with U.D.L. was to result in international complications and the further extension of the D.C.L. in Ireland and England, as will later be seen.

A curious attempt at amalgamation was caused about the same time by the event of a personal death, as has so often occurred in the history of the industry this century. Saucel distillery had been left by his father to Robert Stewart Menzies – the same family as Caledonian distillery, the late-entrant to the original amalgamation – and on his death it came into the possession of Graham Menzies, chairman of the D.C.L. up to the time of the big amalgamation in 1925. Graham Menzies offered to sell the distillery to the company and although the offer was refused, the deal took the form of the D.C.L. becoming responsible for selling the existing stocks of Saucel malt and grain whiskies while Menzies agreed to close down and dismantle the distillery. Even had the proposed amalgamation taken place, that, no doubt, was what would have ensued.

When the company acquired the Adelphi distillery from Archibald Walker & Co. in 1902, it had been considered whether or not to take over also the same company's Vauxhall distillery at Liverpool. In the event, a working arrangement was concluded. After five years' trial of this arrangement it was decided the Vauxhall distillery and associated works could be operated better under the direct control of the D.C.L. So in July 1907 was acquired Vauxhall distillery and its subsidiary businesses. Out of this completed amalgamation sprang a fresh lease of life to a tentative manner of working of the D.C.L. Let Graham Menzies tell it, as he informed shareholders at the time: 'In some respects the business is different from that carried on at most of our Scotch distilleries – for example, a large business is carried on there in the manufacture and preparation of spirits for industrial purposes. That is a business which we think has a good future before it, and as the principal market for this spirit is in England, we believe that the trade can be developed better from an important centre like Liverpool than from any of our Scotch distilleries.' Thus the entry of the major grain potable spirit group into industrial spirit production may be seen as a result of the use of amalgamation to curtail grain whisky output in the years of home trade recession.

That theme of over-production was also to be heard in the malt whisky side of the industry. Then came the 'What Is Whisky?' case, the Lloyd George budget and its crisis from 1909–10, continuing and deepening depression in the home trade, failures and crashes. The Scottish malt distillers were taken to task for not amalgamating: 'It is doubtful whether it would ever be possible to combine the malt distilleries in so comparatively few hands as would put that section of the trade on all fours with the grain section as far as ease in guiding is concerned. It has to be admitted that the merging of interests would eliminate the smaller distillers altogether. But that is just what is happening now, and it would be the wiser policy to save something while it is possible than be wiped out by adverse conditions . . . As far as hitting the taste of the market is concerned, everyone is pretty well agreed that this is being done; but the internal troubles of the distilling industry are still acute, and it is these which have to be remedied. Mr Lloyd

George's budget was the last straw; but even supposing that malevolent attack upon the trade had never been delivered, the course of the disease would not have been arrested. So long as there was no serious diminution in the huge aggregation of stocks, the breakdown could only have been a matter of time, and this breakdown was hastened by the unreasonably large output in the distilling year 1908–9. After all, the whisky market is not without limits, and although these are constantly extended, it would be some years before any material impression would be made upon the stocks now piled up in the Highlands . . . If the distillers had during the last ten years or so studied the trend of the consuming market, alike as regards its capacity and actual demands, instead of concentrating their thoughts upon the making and selling of their products to the trade, they would have had a clearer grasp of the situation, and, in all probability, would be largely free from the stock incubus which weighs so heavily upon them today.'

A few months later, the proposed amalgamation of the Highland Distilleries Co. and the Dailuaine-Talisker Distilleries Co. got as far as the courts. The disaster was that it was not pursued, though before the coming war was over, Dailuaine-Talisker had successfully amalgamated, after the death of the chief proprietor.

Rumours came thick and fast of the formation of a syndicate to corner all the malt and grain whisky stocks made since 1902, *The Times*, by the middle of 1911, bringing it down to such a combine to corner malt whiskies only. There had been much unobtrusive buying going on; blenders, it was considered, were on to a good thing – they were faced with the constant bettering of the stocks and were able to buy dirt-cheap, at little more than cost price. Some of the malt distilleries were facing bankruptcy and forced closure. The time was ripe for malt whisky amalgamations. It happened, and shortly before the outbreak of war in 1914 came the first salvation of the malt distillers.

29

Mergers continue

BUT BEFORE we venture on an examination of that first major merger of malt whisky distilleries, their temporary salvation, we must reascend the ever-rolling stream for a moment. We have noted the acquisition by the D.C.L. of the Vauxhall distillery, at Liverpool, of Messrs Archibald Walker & Co. This takeover was the means of removing a difficulty in coming to an arrangement with the other English distillers as regards the control and sale of spirits for methylating and industrial purposes. The negotiations then resulted in the formation of the Industrial Spirit Supply Co. Ltd, registered in October 1907, not with the object of making a profit on its capital – the nominal capital was £100 – but so to control the sales of spirit for industrial purposes as to eliminate the worse form of competition: all sales were to be made through one centre, under the charge of Honeywill Bros. as agents, with Ross, managing director of the D.C.L., as chairman.

A few months later the directors of Hammersmith distillery approached the D.C.L. with suggestions of a takeover. As with Ardgowan distillery the deal was done by paying partly in preference shares in the D.C.L. and partly in ordinary shares, 1,990 of the latter and 8,700 of the former. At the time of the deal, in February 1910, there were only three distillers, as distinct, too, from rectifiers, in London: Hammersmith, Three Mills (J. & W. Nicholson & Co. Ltd) and Wandsworth distillery (John Watney & Co. Ltd), and the Hammersmith acquisition had this important effect on the D.C.L. development: the Tooley Street, London, rectifying distillery, incorporated as a result of Menzies's Caledonian distillery joining the group in 1884, had drawn its raw spirit from its Caledonian parent, as in the time when Menzies owned both, and there was a frequent surplus of Scotch grain spirit. This not only involved heavy transport expenses from Leith to London, but as raw spirits in London were generally cheaper than in Scotland and with the late nineteenth-century boom in 'Scotch' all the grain spirit made at the Caledonian was needed to meet demand, it meant that with the Hammersmith acquisition Tooley Street was able to draw on that London distillery for its supplies, and so free Edinburgh of the incubus of supplying precious grain whisky to be turned into gin and cordials.

But more significantly, and with this we may leave the industrial spirit amalgamations of the D.C.L., Hammersmith distillery was also the largest supplier of spirits for industrial purposes of those in the Industrial Spirit Supply Co. Ltd. So what with the Vauxhall acquisition, the long-term result of Walker's amalgamation of Adelphi distillery in 1902, and Hammersmith, the D.C.L., the product of defensive amalgamation of grain distillers, became the preponderating influence of the industrial spirit trade.

In March 1911, the company further spread its influence in the south by 'taking an interest' in the old-established Bloomsbury, London, liqueur distillers, Messrs Humphrey Taylor & Co. Ltd. It was only in the last year of World War I that the D.C.L. bought the balance of the shares and debentures in Humphrey Taylor, and that they closed down the Tooley Street rectifying plant, the business being amalgamated with J. & J. Vickers & Co., another D.C.L. acquisition, at Fulham, London.

In the same year as the Humphrey Taylor 'interest', in 1911, the deal being confirmed by the board of the D.C.L. in January 1912, there came to a head another classic example of an acquisition by the D.C.L. to maintain prices. The Irish grain distillers were a thorn in the side of the London distillers, frequently unloading their spirit, primarily the result of yeast production, more cheaply than the London distillers themselves could make it. The main offender was the Dundalk distillery, who threatened to continue their London dumpings, with increased output, but also to do the same to the industrial spirit market. Mr Richard Nicholson tried to talk Mr Malcolm Murray, of Dundalk, into sense, with no result. Proposals for Murray to sell Dundalk to the U.D.L. fell through: U.D.L. wished to pay in shares; Dundalk wanted cash. Ross stepped in and saved the day by paying cash, £160,000, to Dundalk. Before closing the deal, Ross came to an arrangement with the other distillers for securing a recognised share of the industrial spirit trade for Dundalk on the basis of not competing with this distillery's spirits in the London and other home markets. Dundalk was finally closed down in 1923 after the 'troubles' leading to Irish home rule in 1922.

We need not reascend the stream of history too far or in too great detail in the nineteenth century as concerns amalgamations in the malt whisky distilling world beyond noticing the acquisition of the Edinburgh distillery, formerly Glen Sciennes Lowland malt distillery, by Andrew Usher in 1860, the same Usher who was chairman later of the dealers' and blenders' co-operative distillery, the North British grain distillery, and to take brief notice of the malt distillery amalgamations of the closing years of the century. The distinctive feature of those acquisitions was that whereas the amalgamation of the leading grain distillers to form the D.C.L. was a defensive move in face of a tenuous and uncertain market, by the eighties and nineties the reverse was the case: the amalgamations with malt distilleries were undertaken in a spirit of confidence and an atmosphere of booming sales. The motive was to ensure supplies of basic material, to guarantee adequate and fairly priced supplies of malt whisky, particularly Highland malt whisky.

One, for example we have noted: how in 1887, Highland Distilleries Co. was formed to amalgamate Bunnahabhain, Islay, and Glen Rothes-Glenlivet. It was about the same time that Mr Wm Sanderson, a blender of Leith, and first managing director of the North British grain distillery, took a partnership in Glengarioch Highland malt distillery: he was ensuring his supplies of both malt and grain whiskies. This partnership was soon to become Mr Sanderson's sole partnership; he amalgamated the distillery into his other Scotch whisky activities. It was in similar vein of booming sales at home and the beginning of overseas sales of any volume that other firms stepped in to amalgamate units of the distilling section of the industry into their own distributive organisations. To instance but a few: to Glentauchers Highland malt distillery they built in 1897, James Buchanan & Co. acquired Bankier in 1903, and Convalmore acceded to them in 1906; their later amalgamations and purchases will be noted in due course. In 1890, John

Dewar & Sons Ltd acquired on a long lease from the Duke of Atholl for the distillery at Tullymet, near Ballinluig. Later they found ground and built another near Aberfeldy. In 1903, John Haig & Co. added Glen Cawdor to their malt-distilling activities. John Walker & Sons, in 1893, as the boom gained momentum, acquired Cardow distillery, at Knockando, on the Spey, from Mrs Elizabeth Cumming, part of the transaction being that Mr J. F. Cumming, who had managed it for his mother, was appointed a director of the Walker company and was to continue in control at the distillery. The firm we know today as White Horse Distillers, then named Mackie & Co. were, *inter alia*, distillers at Lagavulin, Islay, and on the completion of Craigellachie Highland malt distillery, Mackie controlled its output.

But in the years preceding World War I, the conditions leading to amalgamations and takeovers were completely different: they were accomplished under duress, a lack of confidence in whisky by the investing public, a recession in the home market and hesitant sales abroad. Lacking the strict tightness of control of the grain whisky-producing section of the industry, the malt-distilling world was experiencing a period of depression and failure. Early in 1912 there came another spate of rumours of a syndicate being formed to buy up large quantities of old whisky, several members of the syndicate being connected with the blending business. In this case, as was pointed out, they would be running up prices against their own firms, to the detriment, no doubt, of their own shareholders of the blending firms.

Then came the bombshell: the old-established business of A. & J. Dawson Ltd, of St Magdalene distillery, Linlithgow, a Lowland malt whisky firm, had to put its affairs into the hands of a liquidator. As was now becoming customary in the industry, the D.C.L. was approached: would it buy the firm, either by itself or in partnership with others? At first, the board would have none of it. They were not Lowland malt distillers. In October, with the new season beginning, the Lowland malt distillers met at Glasgow and increased their price by 2*d.* per proof gallon. The board of the D.C.L. gave their managing director, Ross, authority to make an offer for St Magdalene distillery and on 1 November he reported that he had acquired it on the basis of the company's assuming all the liabilities and acquiring all the assets and of paying over in cash to the liquidator a sum of £14,000 which would enable him to pay the preference holders 10*s.* in the pound. A new company was formed at once under the same name with a nominal capital of £60,000 divided into 40,000 ordinary of £1 each and 20,000 preference, also of £1 each. At this point came one of the clearest indications to date of the trend to amalgamation: the whole of the preference shares were taken up by Mr J. A. Ramage Dawson, the managing director of the old company, while the ordinary were subscribed for by the D.C.L., Mr Dawson, Messrs John Walker & Sons, and others.

The effect was magical. 'After the Linlithgow purchase by the D.C.L. becoming known,' it was said at the time, 'there was what may be termed a bit of a scramble among some of our blending houses to secure Lowland malts. This was owing to the fact that large quantities of Linlithgow hanging on the market were being offered at a very moderate price; and to the knowledge that now this whisky has fallen to the D.C.L., it will at any rate not be thrown on the market at whatever price it may fetch. This has consequently had the effect of firming the price of all Lowland malts.'

The year 1913 opened with renewed speculation concerning a distillery combine, especially as so many in the Highlands could be 'picked up cheap'. The whole matter was gone about very quietly; tentative takeover arrangements were made. Then a company already running several distilleries came into the picture, almost accidentally, the question then assuming a more serious aspect: Is the proposal of the nature of a combine, it was asked, and if so, what distillery firms is it proposed to include? Generally, the suggestion was, not to combine firms themselves but the distilleries not already owned by blending houses. The syndicate was even credited with the idea of buying up anything between forty and fifty malt distilleries, and then, in classic manner, closing half of them to restore prices by reduced output and control of stocks.

It was known that some of London's leading financiers were behind some of the Scottish concerns in holding stocks for them at about bank rates. The latter, in turn, did the holding for the blending houses. Thus, it was considered, the formation of the syndicate would simplify the fundamental problem of financing stocks. For *The Scotsman* newspaper observed about the same time that 'the whole industry is hampered by want of capital'. The confidence reviving after the Pattison crash was damped down by the 1909–10 Lloyd George budget and falling home sales. By the middle of 1913 the 'so-called big distillery combine' was alleged to have £1,250,000 behind it in the form of the assets of English and French wine and spirit interests and to have offered to purchase at once or to control the output of various Highland distilleries, the buildings and plant to remain in the hands of the distillery owners. But the business did not mature: the syndicate found they were dealing with people who were not giving anything away and the latter simply rejected the idea of dual ownership.

Across the water took place an amalgamation of which we have already heard in its later activities and its deep effect on the whisky industry in Scotland, the formation, also in 1913 of the Distillers Finance Corporation. The company was formed of eight of the leading Irish distillers and a number of the principal blending houses in Belfast and Dublin to acquire a half-interest in the U.D.L. and the blending businesses of Mitchell & Co. of Belfast Ltd, Kirker Greer & Co. Ltd, Young King & Co. Ltd, Brown, Corbett & Co. Ltd, all of Belfast, and Mitchell Bros. Ltd, of Glasgow. It caused intense friction between the D.C.L. and the U.D.L. as the latter acted in the matter without referring it to the D.C.L. although Distillers had members on the U.D.L. board. To anticipate events, the fixing of a minimum age of whisky in 1915 brought the D.F.C. begging to be taken over by the D.C.L., an event which was postponed by disagreement at the time and, as we shall see, only eventuated in 1922.

To revert to distilling in Scotland, it was just about the time that D.C.L. went shares in the St Magdalene distillery, Linlithgow, that the affairs of the Leith whisky firm of James Ainslie & Co. got so involved they had to be placed in the hands of a trustee. Among the Ainslie assets was a half-interest in Clynelish distillery, Sutherland, the other half belonging to Mr John Risk, formerly of Bankier distillery. By arrangement, Mr Risk bought up Ainslie's share and by a somewhat complicated transaction sold half of the shares in the new company controlling Clynelish to the D.C.L.

Meantime James Gray, of Glenkinchie Lowland malt whisky distillery, among other interests, had been trying to amalgamate the bulk, if not all, of the Lowland malt plants. Negotiations tended to peter out, but with D.C.L. interested in St Magdalene things improved and five distilleries decided to join forces against the sea of troubles facing the distilling world. Valuations of the five were reduced allowing the capital of the company to be fixed at £300,000, divided into 220,000 five per cent preference and 80,000 ordinary shares, both of £1 each. The company was registered on 1 August 1914 under the title of Scottish Malt Distillers Ltd, and the board was made up of representatives of each of the five amalgamating distilleries under the chairmanship of Mr Wm Ross, of the D.C.L. The five distilleries were: Glenkinchie distillery, of Pencaitland; Rosebank, of Falkirk; St Magdalene, of Linlithgow; Grange, of Burntisland; and Clydesdale, of Wishaw.

As was commented on the eve of the registration, 'It is anticipated that the amalgamation will result in considerable economies. The cost of manufacturing will be reduced by concentrating production, as far as possible, at certain distilleries. Raw materials will also be obtained at lower cost through the large quantities bought. In addition, there will be the substantial advantage of the experience at all of the distilleries being placed at the disposal of each individual concern, while there should be a saving in administrative costs. At the same time, it is intended to preserve the various staffs intact as far as possible, at least for the present, but no doubt in due time considerable economies will be effected through the concentration of administrative work.'

We have recorded the Buchanan-Dewar merger and the same year saw a further joint distillery acquisition by the D.C.L. and John Walker & Sons Ltd. In November 1915 the D.C.L. secured for £5,000 the Coleburn-Glenlivet Highland distillery, John Walker & Co. having agreed to take a half-share in the deal. Later it was arranged for Coleburn to be merged with the Clynelish Distillery Co. Ltd, that company increasing its capital by £10,000, to be subscribed for by Walker, who thus got a one-third interest in it, the other two-thirds being held by the D.C.L. and Mr Risk, as above.

What with the war, governmental interference in the industry, the Immature Spirits Act of 1915, violent changes were taking place in the industry. As Ross put it in 1927, 'The company at first avoided any important association with the pot still industry, or with the blending side of the Trade, which it properly regarded as outside its sphere, but during the war we were more or less forced into the position of having to take up stocks and carry on businesses then in existence, or be left behind in the race for the premier position in the Trade. From that time onwards the acquisition of malt distilleries and blending businesses came fast and furious.'

The year 1916 saw this 'fast and furious' movement reach a peak. In March that year, the D.C.L. took over John Begg & Co. Ltd with its lease of Royal Lochnagar distillery which lasted until Whitsunday, 1923, when it passed to another firm, one with which the D.C.L. has since amalgamated. Also in that March, the company took over John Hopkins & Co. Ltd with its Tobermory distillery on the island of Mull. The toll was mounting. The proposed and attempted amalgamation of some of the more important Highland distilleries of the summer of 1915, as we saw, came to nothing, despite the efforts of Mr Ross as chairman of the seven or eight distillers involved. In the following spring Mr Ross was again approached by one of the most important of the group of Highland distillers, Dailuaine-Talisker Distilleries Ltd, which controlled three distilleries. In the upshot, and forecasting the shape of things to come, Dailuaine-Talisker was taken over by the D.C.L. and three large distiller-blender firms, John Walker & Sons Ltd, John Dewar & Sons Ltd and W. P. Lowrie & Co. (seven-eighths owned by James Buchanan & Co. Ltd). The new board consisted of one representative of each of the four takeover firms, Mr Ross being chairman.

The outstanding merger of 1917 was undoubtedly that of Messrs J. & G. Stewart Ltd into the D.C.L. But war conditions and co-operative working stimulated distillery fusions, so that early in 1918 the D.C.L. took over the Bristol distillery along with its allied rectifying business of J. & J. Vickers & Co. Ltd, of Fulham, London, a deal concluded by means of D.C.L. shares and cash as payment. A few months later the company acquired the bulk of the shares of the Yoker distillery company, one half of the shares purchased being offered to John Dewar & Sons Ltd, W. P. Lowrie & Co. and John Walker & Sons Ltd, the same firms as had been involved in the Dailuaine-Talisker deal. Walker turned the offer down, so the other two went halves in the fifty per cent option. About the end of 1920 the D.C.L. offered to buy back all outside shares and this being practically effected, the distillery was closed down.

As the war ended and in the first year or so of peace (of a sort), rumours multiplied of syndicates and combines. In point of fact what was happening was more of the nature of a very close working association between the leading firms, then generally accepted as the D.C.L., Buchanan (alone or through Lowrie), Dewar, Haig, and Walker. The 1919 acquisition of Haig by the D.C.L. is reviewed hereafter, but it was in the same year that Scottish Malt Distillers Ltd, formed on the eve of war, gave a foretaste of things to come by acquiring its first Highland distillery, Glenlossie-Glenlivet, and at the end of the year it took over the Edinburgh Lowland malt distillery of Andrew Usher & Co. Ltd, which also meant the closing down of Clydesdale distillery, a foundation member of Scottish Malt Distillers and its transference to D.C.L. who put it to other uses. The non-whisky distillery acquisitions about this time of Preston's Liverpool Distillery Co. Ltd and the Derby distillery of King, Howmann & Co. Ltd need not distract us here.

Towards the end of 1917 the death occurred of James Calder who began off about 1860 as a brewer in Alloa, but about 1891 got Bo'ness malt distillery, converting it three years later into a grain distillery, one most productive too in the field of yeast. So much so, in fact, that during World War I yeast meant the D.C.L. and Calder. For some time after his death, talks were carried on by the D.C.L. with James Calder & Co. with a view to talking over the company's two distilleries, Bo'ness and Gartloch, with the main object of curtailing production. The talks continued some time, and it was only in the summer of 1921 that the merger was completed. The plants were duly closed, and also in line with reducing output the D.C.L. closed down its Phoenix Park distillery, in Dublin, at about the same time, the summer of 1921. Similarly, Camlachie distillery was acquired by the company, and closed down as a distillery, the buildings being put to other uses. On the closing down of Bo'ness and Gartloch, the D.C.L. issued a circular putting the whole position so clearly as to demand reproduction here: 'The danger of over-production of whisky has become a serious menace, and it is hoped that the amalgamation now arranged will assist in the general regulation of production, and do something towards mitigating the evil. Such action has been characterised as an attempt to secure a monopoly of the grain distilling industry, but we hope to show that any benefit to be derived from such amalgamation will, as in the past, be shared with our customers.' In short, the wheel had turned full circle: amalgamations were back where they started from; they were no longer the result of boom conditions but of conditions similar to those prevailing at the time of the primary amalgamation which led to the formation of the D.C.L. in 1877.

In the following March, that of 1922, occurred another important and decisive death, that of R. C. W. Currie, managing director of Tanqueray, Gordon & Co. Ltd. He was himself an amalgamator. Beginning his business career at the age of eighteen at the Four Mills Distillery, at Bromley-by-Bow, London, in 1892 he took over the old-established gin business of Gordon & Co., amalgamating it six years later with Tanqueray's, of Vine Street, and continuing it at 132 Goswell Road, London, as Tanqueray, Gordon & Co. Ltd. He was also a director of the D.F.C., of which we have spoken above. The end result was that the D.C.L. took over the D.F.C.

The yeast and international repercussions of the takeover have been discussed, and other aspects of it are examined below, but for the moment it is sufficient to observe that by it the D.C.L. acquired a firmer foothold in the industrial spirit market, and in London gin distilling as well as in distilleries in Scotland. Now the D.F.C. controlled, in Ireland, the Avoniel Distillery Ltd, the Irish Distillery Ltd, David Watt & Co. Ltd, Brown, Corbett & Co. Ltd, Young, King & Co. Ltd, Mitchell & Co. of Belfast, Ltd, and in Scotland the Ferintosh Distillery Co. Ltd, near Dingwall, Mitchell Bros. Ltd, of Glasgow, and in London, Tanqueray, Gordon & Co. Ltd. The acquisition of the latter brought to the D.C.L. not only a sure outlet of spirit for rectification, but a stage nearer the fulfilment of the old dream of so amalgamating all the U.K. spirit producers as to create a safe and stable spirit industry, at the least on its production side. And also in 1922 may be mentioned two distillery acquisitions by Scottish Malt Distillers, Dean distillery, at Edinburgh, its production activities being stopped, and North Port distillery, Brechin.

But it was in 1923 that a concerted action involving a set of distilleries came to fruition. The old Dundee firm of James Watson & Co. Ltd in May approached the D.C.L. with an offer to be taken over. But the D.C.L. withdrew over the question of stocks about which there was an understanding they should be shared by Buchanan-Dewar and Walker, and 'Watson's No. 10 Whisky' which it was suggested should be dropped, an attitude not shared by the D.C.L. In the event, then, the three blending companies went ahead, split up the eight million gallons of whisky stock and shared out the distilleries. In this way Dewar, for

instance, incorporated three of Watson's distilleries – Ord, Parkmore
and Pulteney – and with Aultmore which they acquired about the same
time they then controlled seven in all. Buchanan, who had purchased
Lochruan and Port Ellen, Islay, after the war, concentrated on stocks,
having the previous year, 1922, acquired Benrinnes-Glenlivet distillery
along with Dewar by means of the subsidiary Lowrie. And it was
in 1923 that Walker incorporated Mortlach Highland malt distillery
into its structure. In the summer of the same year, Buchanan-Dewar
entered into a provisional arrangement to take over Mackie & Co.,
known today as White Horse Distillers Ltd, which deal, had it gone
through, would have added still further distilleries to the two blending houses.

Nor was the D.C.L. inactive on the gin front. It had begun on that
side of the industry with the 1884 amalgamation with Caledonian
distillery and its London rectifying plant at Tooley Street. With the
taking over of Bristol Distillery and its gin connection, J. & J. Vickers &
Co. Ltd, of Fulham, the two businesses were merged into one and
Tooley Street was disposed of. Then in 1922 the company acquired
Tanqueray, Gordon & Co. by the D.F.C. deal. Now for some time
feelers had been put out – the trade was in a bad way with the 1918–20
increases in duty and the recession at home – with the object of
amalgamating the whole of the English gin businesses into one organisation. Some were in favour; some equally opposed. But about the end
of 1923, the D.C.L. was approached by Sutton, Carden & Co. Ltd and
it was arranged for the D.C.L. to take them over by means of a cash-
and-shares deal. That transaction was completed early in 1924, and
within a month negotiations were opened with two other gin firms who
were amalgamated promptly into the D.C.L. – Messrs Boord & Son,
of Tooley Street, and Sir Robert Burnett & Co., of Vauxhall distillery,
London. The prices were, in each case, partly cash, partly shares in the
D.C.L.

More particularly in Scotland, where business had never been so bad
all the century, the leading firms were acting more and more in co-
operation, even to the point, as has been shown, of purchasing distilleries in common. In the end there occurred 'the big amalgamation' of the
D.C.L., Buchanan-Dewar – themselves amalgamated, as we have seen,
since 1915 – and Walker. The enlarged board had its first meeting in
Edinburgh on 19 June 1925, and one of the first consequences of the

amalgamation was the curtailment of malt distilling activities as already prevailed in the D.C.L.-dominated grain whisky distilling side of the industry.

Each of the four firms owned malt distilleries and as a first step to planned restriction of output, the D.C.L. acquired the whole balance of the preference and ordinary shares in Scottish Malt Distillers not already possessed by them, the preference being paid in cash at par, and the ordinary exchanged for an equal number of D.C.L. shares. The result of this absorption, in addition to the considerable interest the D.C.L. now held in Highland malt distilleries, was that an arrangement was arrived at with other malt distillers to reduce malt whisky production by at least twenty-five per cent along with a similar grain whisky reduction arrangement curtailing production by the same percentage. Mr John Risk, it will be remembered, held a one-third interest in the Clynelish Distillery Co. He was bought out and in November 1925, it was announced that the whole of the Clynelish shares were held by the parent and associated companies. Also towards the close of 1925, the D.C.L. acquired the business, including malt distilleries, of Macdonald, Greenlees & Williams Ltd, whose chairman Sir James C. Calder had had amalgamation dealings with the D.C.L. over Bo'ness and Gartloch distilleries.

Obviously, with the rationalising genius of Ross in charge – he became chairman of the D.C.L. at the time of 'the big amalgamation' – it was not long before all the malt distilleries in the now greatly enlarged firm, a giant made the bigger by the addition of White Horse Distillers Ltd in 1927 with its distilleries in the Highlands, Islay and Campbeltown, were themselves amalgamated into an enlarged Scottish Malt Distillers. By the opening in October 1930, of the distilling season the scheme was completed of incorporating into the wholly-owned Scottish Malt Distillers the 42 malt distilleries of the group. Of the total number, eight represented Scottish Malt Distillers' own, twenty-eight were acquired from various blending companies in the group and six had been owned by separate distillery companies which were wound up and the assets conveyed to Scottish Malt Distillers. The aim and result of this amalgamation of malt distilling interests were greater economy in working generally which it was considered would lower production costs. The geographic breakdown was into thirty-three Highland malt distilleries, eight Lowland, five Islay and five Campbeltown distilleries, making fifty-one in all more; shortly afterwards several more were added.

Let Ross have the last word on the subject of distillery amalgamations, the main framework of which has just been outlined, although the process has continued ever since and is still going ahead today. He was speaking at the Edinburgh and London 'Jubilee Celebrations' of the D.C.L. in 1927. In Edinburgh, he explained that, including the original six distilleries, the company had acquired to the date of speaking twenty-four patent still distilleries, in England, Scotland and Ireland, of which only ten were in active operation at the time of the celebrations: two had been converted into yeast factories and twelve, or half that number had been either temporarily or permanently closed. He continued that the company then controlled forty-seven pot still distilleries, forty-four of which were in Scotland and three in Ireland. 'Of these,' he added, 'only twenty-seven have operated during the past season, and the remainder have been closed down either temporarily or permanently – standing monuments to the success which has attended governmental action in strangling a home industry by over-taxation.'

He repeated the same figures in London and added what is not only the fact of the matter but its best defence and illumination: 'The D.C.L. first went into malt whisky distilling and blending particularly for the home market during the war, especially about the period 1915 when so many small firms were going to the wall. The D.C.L. had to do this if only to save their grain distilling interests because there was a possibility of all these distilleries and the other blending firms and their stocks falling into the hands of their rivals who might then be able to dominate or dictate to the D.C.L. As far as the small blender and distiller was concerned the D.C.L. was his salvation. The D.C.L. was in a much better position to bear the loss of closing down an uneconomical or unworkable distillery than the small man whose entire capital it was. If the D.C.L. had not bought him up he would have been ruined, whereas he got a fair price and was able to invest his money elsewhere, and the D.C.L. could carry the loss; or he was amalgamated into the D.C.L.'

It must not be thought that the above distillery amalgamations were the only ones of the formative years. Booth's Distilleries, for instance, acquired three Highland distilleries before they were themselves amalgamated, in 1937, into the D.C.L. Again, the Perth firm of

Arthur Bell & Sons Ltd incorporated in the inter-war years three Highland malt distilleries to add to their foundation holding in the North British grain distillery founded as a 'defensive' mechanism against what was feared, as has been seen, to be the monopolistic possibilities of the D.C.L. Later, firms from across the Atlantic have, as noticed earlier, incorporated into their own structure on setting up in Scotland both Lowland and Highland distilleries. The process continues; history never stands still.

30

Further acquisitions

THE NATION-WIDE, indeed, world-wide, prevailing trend to amalgamation was particularly accelerated in the case of the Scotch whisky industry by both World War I and its consequent increased governmental intervention under the dominating, if not domineering guidance of the man who became Prime Minister half-way through the war, Lloyd George. Not only had his pre-war budget of 1909–10 set the economic conditions in the industry for an accentuated diversion to crises and mergers – best exemplified by the merger known as Scottish Malts Ltd – but his action in introducing a three-year minimum age for whisky in 1915 again underlined and emphasised the need to merge, if only on a capital basis. The merger about the same time of Messrs James Buchanan & Co. Ltd. and John Dewar & Sons Ltd, later to be known as Buchanan-Dewar Ltd, but highlights the prevailing trends. On the other hand, and as we have seen, it provided both the opportunity and necessity for many smaller men and firms to get out of the industry or to merge. Instances have been noted along the way, and the further governmental – indeed, bureaucratic – interference over such matters as the maximum strength at which whisky was to be retailed in the United Kingdom, the interference with distilling itself, the rationing of home market supplies, the curtailment of exports, the tight price structure for the home market, and finally the three budgets of 1918, 1919 and 1920 all increasing the duty and price to the customer, with ordered prices at every level, again induced many to get out of the industry. The curtain was rapidly descending on an age of free enterprise – and rising on another, the age of state intervention in every walk of life, every aspect of business activity.

What with the cessation of distilling and the other factors mentioned earlier, as the war entered its last year there was an acute shortage of current and anticipated supplies of matured whisky. It was in this atmosphere that in December 1917 it was reported to the board of the D.C.L., now firmly embedded in both the export and domestic trade of blended whiskies, that the purchase had been effected of the business and, more important, the stocks of whisky belonging to Messrs J. & G. Stewart, an old-established firm of Edinburgh and Leith. The following month, the *Record* put its finger on the real point of issue: 'What all this portends it is difficult to forecast with whispers of other deals of a similar nature' in mind, 'but obviously these developments are of far-reaching importance to the Trade as a whole. The tendency to concentrate the diminishing stocks in few hands must be fraught with incalculable consequences of the ever-tightening control of officialdom, whether through the media of the Central Control Board or the Food Controller. All the same, we cannot help feeling that the big interests who are increasing their stake in the Trade so substantially know what they are doing, and that they will use their giant's strength in no tyrannical fashion.'

That was but one of the many purchases, investments and amalgamations made over the period, and in addition to those already noticed it is possible in the ensuing pages to pick out only the more important and formative of the industry as a whole, and the inevitable reaction and counter-reaction they induced.

For the air of the deceasing individualist world was dark with rumours of the imposition of a combine, monopoly, control such as had induced its antagonists in the previous century to form their own grain distillery by Edinburgh, the North British Distillery. As Ross put it concerning these late-war and post-war years when he was managing director of the D.C.L.: 'The close relationship with other distillers brought about by war conditions was responsible for the frequent fusions which took place within the next few years.' But in the last spring of World War I, were summarised some of the fears relative to the impending formation of a mighty combine formed of the major powers in the whisky industry. The lay press, it was noted, was crowded with rumours of 50 million sterling combines while the technical press admitted a degree of co-operation and concerted action which was common knowledge in the trade. The co-operation did not leave the distilleries out of account, if only because of the financial interest they represented of the distributors. But there was a growing hostility to the industry itself on the part of certain well-placed public men who did not consider that the carrying through of financial combinations of this sort was 'directly conducive to the more effective prosecution of the war'. Some big interests, who were buying up all the stocks of whisky they could, seemed to give the lie to any suggestion of merger, but it was also quite feasible that these stocks could later be pooled.

The 1918 budget, already discussed, with its increased bureaucratic control over prices and quotas, forced many more out of the trade and industry while driving more and more stocks and plants into the hands of the remainder. Disregarding the lesser absorptions, the next major such, the greatest and most impressive since the amalgamation of Buchanan and Dewar early in the war, took place in the March following it with the absorption of Messrs. John Haig & Co. Ltd by the D.C.L.

Again as Ross put it in his memoirs: 'The year 1919 was to see considerable extensions of the Company's business. First and foremost came the purchase of the whole of the ordinary shares in the old-established dealer's business of John Haig & Co. Ltd, Markinch. This was effected for a consideration of £124,000 in cash and the issue of 6,000 new D.C.L. shares of £10 each at par ... This business was originally carried on in conjunction with the Cameron Bridge Distillery, and when that last-mentioned property was taken over by the D.C.L. the dealers' business was removed to its present headquarters at Markinch.' Or as Mr James Laver expressed it, with our amalgamation inquiry in mind: 'After the Armistice, restrictions on the manufacture and sale of whisky were gradually relaxed and amalgamation became the order of the day. It was by this time evident to the Haig directors that large amounts of capital were required to develop the business and as a result of lengthy negotiations the directors, in March 1919, agreed to accept an offer by the Distillers Company, based partly on cash and partly on an issue of Distillers Company shares.' All the directors but one retired, though later Field-Marshal Earl Haig rejoined the board and ultimately became chairman. The Field-Marshal's membership of the board is itself in line with the amalgamating tendency of the period. In 1921 he succeeded in uniting the various organisations of ex-service-men which had been created to deal with their grievances into one body, the British Legion, of which he became the first president. He also became chairman of the United Services Fund, created to adminis-ter for the benefit of ex-servicemen and their dependants the large profits made by canteens during the war. Together, the United Services Fund and the British Legion formed the largest benevolent organisation ever created in Great Britain. He was then both a formator as well as a creature of his times, and the D.C.L. was to take on the same pattern to become the greatest distilling organisation not only in Great Britain but in the world, as a result of amalgamations skilfully carried through by Mr Wm Ross and other directors.

The Haig acquisition was succeeded by others and in two months' time the company's share capital was increased to £2,500,000. That same month came a question in the House on the matter of amalgama-tions, when Colonel Wm Thorne asked the Food Controller if he was aware that at least a dozen firms of distillers were forming themselves into a big whisky combine; if he was aware that the objects were to proceed by easy stages to develop a monopoly in the supply of whisky; was he aware that if such a combine were formed many of the mana-gers and travellers would be sacked who had been working for the various distillers for periods ranging from ten to twenty-five years. The Food Controller had, of course, no information as to such a combine.

The matter, however, was felt to be of sufficient urgency to merit a long passage in the statement made by the chairman of the D.C.L., Graham Menzies, at the May extraordinary general meeting when he said: 'Rumours have gained currency in the press recently as to a scheme being on foot to amalgamate about a dozen of the largest whisky firms in the country, and in which this company's name was associated . . . No formulated scheme for such a combine has ever been before this board, and while any such proposal would undoubtedly receive full and fair consideration, this is not a matter which your directors would ever dream of carrying through without putting the whole position before the shareholders for their approval. What your directors have in view at present is something much less ambitious' – the acquisition of the whole of the share capital of Preston's Liverpool

Distillery Co. Ltd. He then put the Haig acquisition in perspective: 'Your directors were also approached some considerable time ago with the view to taking an interest in the old-established firm of John Haig & Co. Ltd. These negotiations have only now been consummated on terms satisfactory to this company.' By way of explanation, the chairman added that the successors of the Haigs of the original D.C.L. formation-amalgamation 'are now anxious to be freed from their (Markinch) responsibilities and considered this company was the natural outlet through which to dispose of their interests'. That was in May and only cursory reference was made at the annual general meeting in July.

Lesser and more peripheral acquisitions were made by various firms and by autumn the air was once more thick with talk of 'developments of a more or less sensational character in the Scotch whisky trade.' There was talk of a merger of one well-known Edinburgh blending house with another, of a possible new combination of Highland malt whisky distillers, of more than one direct negotiation to acquire malt distilleries.

Then at the annual meeting of Scottish Malt Distillers, it was announced that as the fine old firm of Andrew Usher & Co. - to whom Edinburgh owes its Usher Hall - was closing its accounts: the Scottish Malt Distillers had purchased Usher's Edinburgh distillery, bought by the firm's founder in 1860 as he pioneered the blending of malt and grain whiskies. The withdrawal of Usher's from the market was also an event in the sense, too, that not only had they pioneered blending but had provided the first chairman for the anti-monopoly North British grain distillery. The prime independent, then, was now contributing to the feared-monopolistic company.

As Ross put it in his own words: 'Another of the old-established firms who agreed to seize the favourable opportunity of liquidating their business was Andrew Usher & Co., Edinburgh ... Having disposed of their distillery property, Messrs Andrew Usher & Co. set about liquidating some of their whisky stocks, part of which came into the company's hands through the medium of a third party. Eventually, however, they approached the company direct to take over the balance of their stocks, together with their offices ... and their bonded stores ... This ... was carried through on behalf of J. & G. Stewart Ltd, the business being merged into that company.'

By December the industry was once more in the House: Mr Ben Tillet asked the Food Controller if he was aware that 'The whole of the bonded stocks of whisky in the United Kingdom were in the hands of three distillery combines or companies known as the Whisky Trust; and seeing that these trusts, now that the restrictions on clearances from bond were removed, were refusing to supply the licensed traders and distributors . . .' No information was the expected reply to the first part and the assurance that large holders of whisky were 'doing their utmost' to meet requirements. To break the alleged Trust, Tillet proposed that the three-year minimum age should be reduced to one. Austen Chamberlain would have none of that; he was 'not aware' of any withholding of supplies and matured stocks were 'sufficient to supply a reasonable demand'. (As that demand had been slashed in the 1919 budget and was to be yet again in the 1920 budget no wonder the Chancellor could describe stocks in those terms.)

By the year's end the D.C.L. had itself been dubbed in common trade parlance 'the Combine' – and animosity, jealousy and resentment were growing apace. But sanity prevailed with some and a correspondent wrote that 'The Combine is now a large producer of malt whisky, and is bound to play an increasingly important part in the affairs of the pot still branches of the industry. If there is a branch of the Scotch whisky Trade that has displayed that pre-eminently present-day business quality "vision" it is the patent still. What is dubbed the Combine . . . [is] one of the strongest and most efficient business organisations in the country.'

The Combine continued to make acquisitions; others followed suit, and a note of warning was issued: 'Even the biggest blending houses regard with something akin to dismay the disappearance of so many well-established firms from the Scotch whisky Trade. This inevitably means that at least a proportion of the old firms' trade falls to the lot of the biggest distributors, who, although they have spent lavishly in building up a new worldwide trade, are in no mood to see the demand indefinitely extended at the present juncture. Their stocks of single whiskies . . . are no more than sufficient to see them through until such times as production has made good wartime ravages on their stocks.

'In these circumstances the rumours that one hears as to the possibility of other important Scotch whisky blending houses changing hands are disquieting. The developments of the next few months may fall little short of sensational. For one thing, it may be taken for granted that the producing and distributing ends are to be brought into even closer association than hitherto. Distribution is not unlikely to be ultimately controlled as closely as production by one set of interests and that the same set of interests. The absorptions of the past year or two have been gradually paving the way for some such development.

'And now one hears whispers – much too credible to be ignored – of certain important distributors being approached by the leading producing interests with the view of further absorptions. The decision of Bulloch, Lade & Co. Ltd to realise and quit has given some of their erstwhile competitors the opportunity of picking up a little much-needed stock, and only seems to have whetted their appetite for more . . . One of the results of recent and prospective realisation is to bring to the market an unusually large number of distilleries. Already six or seven could be named as for sale . . . No doubt the surviving distributing houses . . . might be possible buyers . . . but as a rule they already own distilleries from which at a pinch they could draw a bigger proportion of their requirements. Then, doubtless, the Combine, which is credited with practically controlling production through one or other of its branches, would in the ultimate result be buyers, but that would probably be more with a view to obtaining control of existing plant than as a matter of dire necessity, and consequently its offer is not likely to err on the side of generosity. In short, while distilleries are by no means such white elephants as they were a few years ago, they are at the moment somewhat of a drug on the market, and to sell require to be offered cheap.'

The Times, reviewing the year in which such important and so many exchanges had taken place, wrote: 'The tendency appears to be in the direction of ever larger concerns and the swallowing up of the smaller companies,' a move not expected by that newspaper to have 'a detrimental effect on the industry as a whole'. It was believed that 'the large combines will be an added source of strength. The reason why so many firms are going out of the trade appears to be that the amount of capital required to carry on business on the lines now necessary is much larger than formerly. Stocks have to be purchased and kept in bond for long periods, while at the same time the cost of production has risen so enormously, so that it is only concerns with large capital which can carry on the industry successfully.'

423

Later that year, the D.C.L. was to illustrate that truth by raising its capital from £2,500,000 to £4 million, and other leading firms went to the market for capital just around this time. At the extraordinary meeting sanctioning this increase in D.C.L. capital, Ross explained the need as follows: 'Not only have the values of raw materials and stocks of all kinds increased enormously, but it must be borne in mind that the directors have acquired during the past few years several valuable businesses, the prices of which were paid for in cash. This has caused a drain on our finances in two directions. Not only had the original price to be found, but extra capital is now required to carry on these businesses, all of which falls upon the parent company. It is satisfactory to know that these recent purchases have all shown, and I hope will continue to show, an excellent return upon the investment.'

While similar acquisitions went ahead, the first sign of financial and organisational opposition appeared towards the end of the year, 1920: a company was registered with a nominal capital of £150,000, having been formed 'with a view to creating an organisation of brewers and merchants and others interested in the whisky trade for assuring supplies of Scotch malt whisky, and also for securing manufacturers' profits.' The new company thus acquired, from J. P. O'Brien & Co. Ltd which had attempted its own series of amalgamations, including that of Bulloch, Lade & Co. Ltd, and was now in voluntary liquidation, four malt distilleries. The motive of its formation is at once apparent: it was proposed to allocate the annual output of whisky to subscribers in proportion to the shares subscribed by them respectively, and it was estimated that each subscriber for 1,000 shares of £1 each would receive an allocation of approximately 3,000 gallons of malt whisky per annum. Any unwanted allocation could be sold; any member not taking up or selling his allocation, or part of it, could revert it to the company for the benefit of other members. In effect, as the ring of concentrated ownership was closing around them, these men and firms were fighting it off, and trying to preserve their own freedom of action by establishing a rival concentration of ownership.

In the ensuing year, 1921, acquisition and amalgamation went on apace, some of them having been recorded already in previous chapters. Stagnation and recession were now settling into the whisky industry, as to others in Britain with the end of the post-war boom. As was noted on the eve of that year's budget: 'The whisky trade is feeling the general stagnation prevalent all over the country . . . [There is] a general desire on the part of tired traders and holders to get out of the trade altogether . . . Much whisky is likely to come on the market. This naturally means a fall in prices. The number of buyers is very much reduced owing to the number of retirals . . . There is bound to be a fall in prices in bond, and if the public demand falls off, the shortage of stocks would not be felt so much.' As but one instance: in April that year the old-established business of J. G. Thomson & Co., of Leith, sold their stocks to the D.C.L., while retaining their wine connection and reserving the right to re-enter the whisky trade at any time. Again, Thos F. Kennedy, a whisky broker of Glasgow with a well-balanced stock sold it all to the D.C.L., W. P. Lowrie & Co. Ltd, John Walker & Sons Ltd, and James Watson & Co. Ltd, the latter firm to be swallowed up in turn in a couple of years. Thirdly, Taylor & Ferguson Ltd, also of Glasgow, went into voluntary liquidation after selling their stock to W. H. Holt & Sons Ltd, of Aberlour distillery and Chorlton-cum-Hardy, and in the company registered, as noted above, in the December of the previous year. One side-effect is apparent of all this takeover activity: holders for the trade, an ancient institution, were being squeezed out or just plain getting out.

Before examining the major amalgamation of 1922, that of the D.C.L. and D.F.C., of which we have earlier written much, especially in connection with the international standing of the whisky industry and the projected Scotch-American yeast production war and terms, we must first turn for illumination of the period and personalities to the D.C.L. quinquennial dinner held in May 1922. After the usual initiatory toasts, Sir Alexander Walker proposed the D.C.L., saying: 'Its appetite still seems voracious, in spite of the gargantuan feast it has indulged in. Its appetite seems to grow with eating, and it is apparently able to absorb, digest and assimilate all it swallows. Nothing seems to escape the Company. My experience in the war showed me that, contrary to the policy of a great many multiple businesses, the D.C.L. has concentrated their energies on their original and principal business. I am quite satisfied that so long as the present board of directors and the managing director continue in their present position the Company will make progress.' Speaking of his thirty-five years' experience of the company, Sir Alexander said 'they had constantly improved their standards of manufacture and the economic factor in their operations

... His experience in the Ministry of Munitions was that the D.C.L. was one of the few exceptions that did not require to be taught how to turn out their goods to meet the requirements of wartime ... From the first day and always (the D.C.L.) were able to supply everything that was demanded of them without a single change in personnel, equipment or machinery. That was a magnificent record.'

Replying, Ross, general manager of the company, took up the monopoly issue, saying: 'I have no wish to emphasise the fact that the Company has acquired several blending businesses in the last decade. It might disturb the equanimity of Lord Dewar and Sir Peter Mackie ... Any acquisitions of this nature have been in the direction of consolidating the Company's interests, and not with the view of creating a monopoly, real or assumed. Personally, I have never felt that the growth of the Company on the lines which it has assumed makes us less dependent on the friendly feelings of our customers ... The fact that the Company is the best example extant of the ways of the octopus ... Power has at all events never been abused. I have been quietly told, "My good fellow, that is all right as long as W. H. Ross is in charge of affairs, but after all you are only mortal, and when you go we shall be at the mercy of any autocrat who takes your place." ... It by no means follows, however, that any autocrat will take my place.'

In that summer came news that the D.C.L. had signed a provisional agreement to buy ordinary shares in the D.F.C. for approximately £3 million, the real reasons being in the complex conditions, some of them outlined earlier, in the yeast and industrial spirit industries. Ross gave details at the annual general meeting that July (1922) and no words can better his on that occasion: 'With the desire to consolidate still further the production of spirit in this country, your directors have had under consideration during the past month proposals to acquire the remaining shares in the United Distilleries Ltd, of Belfast, of which we already own practically the one-half. The other half of these shares which carry with them control of that company are held by the Distillers' Finance Corporation Ltd which also owns or controls various other important blending and distributing businesses in the north of Ireland, Glasgow and London. Within the past week we have concluded a provisional agreement with the directors of the Finance Corporation whereby we agree to buy and they agree to recommend to their shareholders to sell the whole of the ordinary shares of the Finance Corporation at a price which works out at rather under £3 million. This, you will no doubt feel, is a very large sum to pay for a concern whose businesses are to a great extent situated in Ireland. It will, therefore, be a relief for you to know that of the surplus assets over liabilities shown in said businesses there is represented in actual cash in bank about £1·2 million while as part consideration of the price, your directors are proposing to issue to the shareholders of the Finance Corporation about 53,000 of new shares in this company at a premium of £10 per share, thereby reducing the purchase figure by roughly £530,000. This will then leave only about £740,000 to finance temporarily until some of the other assets can be realised. Thereafter the permanent burden left upon this company will be the £530,000 of additional capital . . .

'The transaction will be concluded on or about August 31st next [1922]. This may involve the holding of special meetings of shareholders to authorise increased borrowing powers to be left in the hands of the directors. I shall not attempt to estimate the value of this amalgamation to you as shareholders and also to the whole industry . . . It will be the duty of your directors to see that the business of the two companies is conducted in such a way as to secure the greatest economy in working. It will also give your directors power to regulate the production of spirits in accordance with the demand, and thus avoid the bogy of over-production from which most industries periodically suffer.'

This was the most brilliant piece of work accomplished to that date by Ross; the D.C.L. financing was accomplished, as a contemporary said, 'with consummate skill'. At the extraordinary meeting in August the necessary resolutions to raise the limit of the company's borrowing power were passed, the needed cash was loaned by the bank – it was repaid within the year – and the following year the company's authorised capital was raised from £4 million to £6 million.

The concerns controlled by the D.F.C. were: Avoniel Distillery Ltd, The Irish Distillery Ltd, David Watt & Co. Ltd, the Ferintosh Distillery Co. Ltd near Dingwall, Brown, Corbett & Co. Ltd, Young, King & Co. Ltd, Mitchell Bros. Ltd of Glasgow, Mitchell & Co. of Belfast Ltd, and Tanqueray, Gordon & Co., gin rectifiers, of London.

That latter in particular caused some consternation in the trade. As we have seen, the D.C.L. already had spirit and gin interests in both London and England, as well as Scotland and Ireland. One result of the last-named acquisition by the D.C.L. was to stir Booth's Distillery Ltd to take over the London grain spirit distillery at Wandsworth of Messrs John Watney & Co. Ltd the following year, 1923. As Lord Lurgan, the then chairman of Booth's, said at the annual meeting of the company in June 1928: 'Wandsworth has distinctly turned the corner, and we are working at a profit which, I am glad to say, is steadily increasing. I would remind you that the Wandsworth distillery was purchased primarily for the purpose of insuring us against our being cornered at any time for our very large supplies of distilled spirit, and at first showed certain losses . . .' The reference to 'insurance' is obvious: the fear of being cornered by the D.C.L.

On the financial acumen shown in the deal, Mr Ross enlarged at the annual general meeting of 1923, expatiating: 'The price actually paid for the shares in question [in the D.F.C.] amounted to £2,996,623 5s. 10d., which was partly met by an issue of 52,901 D.C.L. £10 ordinary shares at a premium of £10 each, this premium being deducted from the price, thus reducing the figure to £2,467,613 5s. 10d. Shortly before the settlement of the purchase price a final dividend was paid by the Finance Corporation amounting to £157,186 8s. 7d., which, having been largely earned prior to the purchase, was not regarded as a revenue item, but was treated as capital, and therefore deducted from the purchase price, bringing the figure previously mentioned down to £2,310,426 17s. 3d. Although your directors have no reason to be dissatisfied with the bargain they made, they decided to make the investment thoroughly safe . . . and have written off a further sum of £110,426 17s. 4d., which leaves the value of the investment standing in our books at the nett figure of £2·2 million.'

On the question of thus writing off such large sums, Ross explained that 'the great drop of our national beverage, due to the present monstrous duty and other causes, forces a curtailment of production. A reduction of production means a closing down of certain of our works, and the consequent necessity for keeping these properties well written down in our books . . . We think it is a prudent policy.'

Towards the end of the year of the D.F.C. transaction, 1922, another important transaction took place when the large stocks of whisky held by Robertson & Baxter Ltd, of Glasgow, were acquired jointly by the Buchanan, Dewar and Walker companies in conjunction

with the D.C.L. The further importance lay in the fact that Robertson
& Baxter controlled – had since October 1906 – Haig & Haig Ltd, and
it was a condition of the purchase that the goodwill of the latter, of
Haig & Haig Ltd, should in future be vested in the purchasers of the
stock. For the time being the Haig & Haig brand – 'Pinch' – was withdrawn from the market and the four purchasing companies shared the
stocks equally. By arrangement, John Haig & Co. Ltd paid the purchase price and on the advice of their lawyers registered in Scotland on
8 May 1925, another company under the title of Haig & Haig Ltd. But
the more significant element in the deal is the close co-operation of the
four giants – the D.C.L., Buchanan, Dewar and Walker. They were
shortly to shake Scotland – and beyond.

31

The great amalgamation

As THE fateful year of 1922 closed, came news of the impending purchase of one of the largest stocks of single whiskies in the country by a combination of four or five distributing houses. The owners, a private limited company, were said to hold 'several million gallons' and to possess several malt whisky distilleries as well, of course, as their own brands. It was another case of getting out in a diminishing market and letting the giants grow larger still. At the same time, Dean distillery, on the Water of Leith, was going into voluntary liquidation and the distillery and 'substantial stocks of whisky' were passing to the Scottish Malt Distillers. The distillery, in line with curtailed production, was dismantled and converted into bonded warehouses, while the stocks were passed on by the company to its member companies and sold.

When in March John Walker & Sons Ltd offered £2 million six per cent first mortgage debenture stock at a price of ninety-nine per cent and 1,499,993 seven per cent cumulative preference shares of £1 each at par, the lists opened at 9.30 a.m. and closed an hour later. A week earlier it had registered as a public company and obviously there was something in the wind, while a couple of months later Buchanan-Dewar announced a dividend on ordinary shares of thirty per cent free of tax.

Minor amalgamations and outright purchases had been taking place when came the stunning news of the passing of James Watson & Co. Ltd, of Dundee. Watson had sold their assets to Buchanan-Dewar and to Walker and gone into voluntary liquidation. The very manner of that passing is worth examination and forecast the shape of things to come. In May of that year James Watson & Co. Ltd, founded in 1815, converted into a limited liability company in 1896 with a nominal capital of £500,000, equally divided between ordinary and preference shares, was offered to the D.C.L. But as the stock was very large, about 8 million gallons, and there was 'an understanding' that any such stocks should be shared in by the other three giants – Buchanan, Dewar and Walker – permission was gained from Watson to bring the proposal to the notice of the other three. The D.C.L. thought it would be a mistake to allow the business with its own brand of 'Watson's No. 10 Whisky' to be dropped, and, therefore, that if the stocks of whiskies were bought it ought to be run on the understanding that the four companies would continue to run the business as a joint concern. The others did not agree; the D.C.L. withdrew from the deal and the other three carried it through. It was not only stocks that were shared out, but, as noticed earlier, distilleries as well, to be followed up by the formation of the Tay Bonding Co. of Dundee and separate acquisitions of the other members of the trio.

Reporting the takeover, the *Record* joined with the D.C.L. in its reservations concerning it and said: 'The intention of the purchasers, who want the whisky for their own requirements, is to wind up the business and suppress the Watson brands (even the popular No. 10), which from many points is, we think, to be greatly deplored. The more eggs that are put into one basket, the more easy it will be for the Government to take control of that basket when it chooses to do so.' For it must be remembered that the movement initiated by Lloyd George in World War I to take over the distilling industry was by no means dead in the minds of many, any more than in the minds of others was the idea of prohibiting it altogether.

But at the annual general meeting of the D.C.L. that July the chairman, Graham Menzies, put the questions of governmental interference and over-taxation in their correct perspective as occasioning mergers and purchases. They had pleaded with the Chancellor, he said, for a reduction in the spirit duty, 'not so much in the interests of the large firms in the Trade who were fortunate in possessing stocks of whisky bought and paid for before the war, but in the interests of the smaller, although still important, firms who in many cases were obliged to buy their supplies of old whisky on the market at high prices with which to carry on their businesses, or do as so many have been forced to do – liquidate their wholly inadequate stocks and go out of business altogether ... The fact is, that with a duty of 72*s*. 6*d*. per gallon, the capital required to finance a good going business tends to drive the Trade more and more into the hands of the few who can command the extra capital.'

Shortly after that meeting came a proposed amalgamation which indeed showed how clearly the words of Menzies were no mere fancy: Buchanan-Dewar entered into a provisional agreement to acquire the whole of the ordinary shares of Mackie & Co. (Distillers) Ltd, known to us today as White Horse Distillers Ltd. In the event the deal did not take place, though a few years later White Horse was to join Buchanan-Dewar and others in their setting as part of the D.C.L. group. In any case the pace of amalgamations and takeovers by the leading four firms – the Combine and Buchanan, Dewar and Walker – did not slacken and in February 1924 Buchanan-Dewar doubled their ordinary share capital by the issue of 2 million fully paid bonus shares of £1 each to existing shareholders; the annual meeting of the D.C.L. in July revealed the acquisition of a London rectifying business and the negotiations proceeding for that of two others. The old-established Aberdeen firm of Black & Ferguson (established 1797), holders of the largest and oldest stocks of whisky in the north of Scotland, representing nearly all the best-known distilleries, sold their entire stock – about 300,000 proof gallons – to Buchanan-Dewar. As was remarked, it was but 'the latest of similar deals – holders of big stocks prefer to accept prices than face future uncertainties created by the prohibitive spirit duty which has reduced consumption so considerably'.

As the year closed, it was noted that 'distillery shares are to the fore because of rumours of amalgamations. The largest whisky enterprise is Buchanan-Dewar, itself a fusion of two of the most prominent producers with an issued share capital of slightly over eight and three-quarter million. Next in point of capitalisation is the Distillers Co. Ltd, whose issued shares, preference or ordinary, aggregate over five and a half million, thirdly comes John Walker & Sons, whose issued share and debenture capital slightly exceeds four and three-quarter million. It is obvious,' continued the report, 'that the capital of any company formed to effect a consolidation of interests would have to be very large, the combined capital of the three undertakings approaching twenty million. Moreover, each company's ordinary shares, on which dividends of seventeen and a half, ten and twenty per cent respectively have been paid for the last financial year, are all quoted at high premiums so that a capitalisation much more generous than that of the three independent companies would be justified. Early this year, ordinary shareholders of Buchanan-Dewar received one hundred per cent scrip bonus out of reserves. The highest price of the old shares was 107*s*. 6*d*., while the new shares now stand at 65*s*. 6*d*., or the equivalent of 131*s*. for the old, at which price the yield on the basis of the last dividend of seventeen and a half per cent is a little over five and a quarter per cent. Distillers £1 shares are quoted at 46*s*., and on the basis of the last dividend of ten per cent give a return of almost four and three-eighths per cent. Walker's shares at 62*s*. 3*d*. yield six and three-eighths per cent on the basis of twenty per cent dividend for 1923–24, and are thus the cheapest security of the group, especially as the company's reserves have not yet been capitalised.'

As the year closed, it was announced that Buchanan-Dewar had arranged to buy the stocks and distilleries of Peter Dawson Ltd, and, significantly, it was the first such deal announced on the B.B.C. Interest was growing and broadening.

With the possibility, if not probability, of further amalgamations growing, so too grew the opposition to them. As a Glasgow correspondent wrote: 'The air is rife with rumours about amalgamations, etc., but no one has any definite information. These amalgamations, in whisky circles, are not looked upon with too much favour, because these, as a rule, aim at monopoly which is not too good for trade generally. It must be said that the public do not regard these huge syndicates with too favourable an eye, as it destroys, to some extent, private enterprise and competition.'

By the end of January 1925 rumours became certainties with the announcement that the trio we have noticed so often were to merge with the D.C.L. That company declared that they would acquire the ordinary shares of John Walker & Sons Ltd and of Buchanan-Dewar Ltd by the issue of five D.C.L. shares (ranking *pari passu* with the existing ordinary shares) for every four ordinary shares of the other two companies. The D.C.L. would thus become in part a holding company, but the three companies were to retain their individuality from the joint stock point of view and for all trading purposes. The D.C.L. had then an issued ordinary capital of £3,685,000 in £1 shares, while John Walker's ordinary was £1,260,000 and that of Buchanan-Dewar was £4 million. Hence the D.C.L. would be required to issue £6,575,000 of new ordinary capital to acquire the whole of the ordinary on the terms mentioned. The D.C.L. dividend was ten per cent for the year ending the previous 15 May, while Buchanan-Dewar paid ten per cent final dividend on its capital – which had been increased by a bonus of one hundred per cent in shares the previous October – the interim having been fifteen per cent – and both interim and final having been tax free. John Walker & Sons Ltd had only been in existence long enough in its then form as a public company to present one balance sheet with a profit and loss account for the period from 31 December 1922 to 31 May 1924, and for this period it paid twenty per cent free of income tax after writing off nearly as much as the cost of the dividend in preliminary expenses.

The comment of the *Record* on the announcement was succinct and to the point: 'The reason for the merger which will form one of the biggest industrial combines in Great Britain, lies presumably in the position of the industry with regard to stocks of matured spirit, and this amalgamation puts the old Edinburgh company in the strongest possible position as masters of the disposal of whisky throughout the world in every outlet of the Trade. It will inspire the confidence of the whole Trade to know that Mr W. H. Ross will be chairman of the new concern.' The Glasgow correspondent withdrew his previous strictures and confessed that the D.C.L. 'has always aimed at a policy of live and let live'.

To know how it came about, we must turn to the recollections of Ross and the accounts of the extraordinary meeting together with the annual general meeting of the company. He observed how they had been working together for years, both by absorbing large stocks which came on the market and by co-operating in joint ownership of distilleries themselves. As the three companies grew, said Ross, it became more and more necessary for them to assure themselves of their sources of supply of single whiskies. 'This was a comparatively simple matter in the case of the main constituent of their blends,' he wrote, 'viz, malt whisky, as the number and variety of the distilleries supplying this product rendered any possible scarcity most unlikely. It was different in the case of grain whisky, which may be regarded as an equally essential element in all popular brands of whisky. These grain distilleries in recent years had become concentrated in fewer and still fewer hands, and although no complaint has ever been made that the remaining distillers had ever abused the power so possessed, it naturally became a matter of graver concern and importance to these three big firms since their businesses had assumed such colossal dimensions. Obviously there were three courses open to the firms referred to, viz., to trust the distillers to act fairly by them . . . to build a distillery or distilleries of their own; or to attempt to bring about an amalgamation with their main suppliers.'

He then recalled the D.C.L. position, 'that when the North British Distillery was built the directors of the D.C.L. looked upon this action as a direct attack by certain blenders on their province as distillers, and, partly from necessity to secure another outlet and partly as a reply to what at the time was regarded as an unfriendly act, they resolved to enter the export trade as competitors in blended whisky . . . Matters continued in this half-hearted position until war broke out, when the need for conserving stocks became imperative. The opportunity then presented itself of acquiring other businesses, the stocks of which, although secured primarily for supplementing our export supplies, had eventually to be partially utilised in supplying the quota to home customers.'

The alternatives, as above, were clear, but the first left something to be desired; the second seemed so destructive in its final effects that all accepted the third, amalgamation, as the most attractive. The position was further complicated for the D.C.L. in that, being mainly distillers, they had to consider their other customers who were not likely to look favourably on the D.C.L.'s linking up with competitors of the blender-customers. One suggestion was that the grain whisky manufacturing side of their business should be separated entirely from the blending side and the latter only should enter into amalgamation. That, incidentally, was one reason for the formation, as we have seen, of the Distillers Agency Ltd at the beginning of 1924. Another proposal was to link up all the D.C.L. blending subsidiaries into one company, an idea rejected by the other parties to the ultimate merger. Further, as the D.C.L. had business of a more varied nature than the others, there was 'a greater sense of security pertaining to their goodwill than to a business which was solely dependent for its success on the continuance of the present social habits of the people'. The D.C.L. thus claimed that if the whole business was to be merged they were entitled to more consideration than anything fixed just on past profits only. A formula was impossible to obtain.

But at a meeting towards the end of 1924 to discuss the future of the Haig & Haig brand, Lord Stevenson said that the recurring difficulties might be removed if the larger issue of amalgamation were seriously tackled. Mr Ross suggested that they might as well take the public's estimation of the value of the shares as the basis of exchange. At that time, the D.C.L. shares were quoted at 42s. to 43s., and the shares of the other two companies at 10s. to 12s. more, so that the relative values were roughly five D.C.L. shares for four in either of the other two. The idea caught on; a proposal of making the basis of fusion on the average of profits over the two preceding years was made and turned down – the D.C.L. had acquired so many companies in the time that no true estimate of profits was possible. Joint auditors inspected the balance sheets and profit and loss accounts of all participants and their report satisfied three of the four parties that the terms suggested were 'fair and reasonable'. The fourth party had difficulties because of special agreements then in existence, but these were adjusted and that party also agreed on the common line. It was also agreed that the D.C.L. should be the holding company – and not Buchanan-Dewar as also suggested – and so the D.C.L. took steps to increase its authorised capital from £6 million to £15 million, so allowing a margin for future extension beyond what was needed for the main amalgamation.

At an extraordinary meeting of the D.C.L. held in Edinburgh on 30 April agreement was secured to all the proposals, the amalgamation, the increased capital and the new articles of association. In the case of Buchanan-Dewar over ninety-nine per cent acceptances were secured; in the case of John Walker & Sons Ltd it was over ninety-one per cent, the lower percentage being because of a large trust estate who were precluded from holding shares in anything else than John Walker & Sons Ltd. It was later declared in the D.C.L. accounts for the year that they had up to then allotted 6,460,859 new ordinary shares of £1 each, fully paid, in respect of the acceptances, and including the 50,000 shares agreed to be allotted as capital compensation for loss of office to certain directors of John Walker & Sons Ltd. At the May board meeting, Mr Ross had been elected chairman.

A new board had to be constituted for the greatly enlarged company. Under the chairmanship of Ross, the other members elected, after a reshuffle of old members and to represent the newcomers to the company were: eight new directors as nominees of Buchanan-Dewar, Lords Woolavington, Forteviot, and Dewar, the Hon. John Dewar, and Messrs A. J. Cameron, P. M. Dewar, W. Harrison and W. Morrison; plus three new directors as nominees of John Walker & Sons Ltd, Sir Alexander Walker, Lord Stevenson, and Mr A. J. Hogarth. This made a total board of twenty-one members after readjustments among the old D.C.L. directorate and personnel.

At the annual meeting of John Walker & Sons Ltd in the same July as all these changes, the chairman, Sir Alexander Walker, reiterated that 'The change which has taken place in the ownership of the ordinary shares of the company will make no difference to the conduct of the business. We shall continue to carry on the old firm on the traditions and policy of the past ... We have every reason to believe that our association with the Distillers Co. Ltd will be advantageous to all concerned.'

At the annual meeting of the D.C.L. the same month, the new chairman, Ross, outlined the structure of the company: 'In carrying out this amalgamation we have increased our Ordinary share capital by over one hundred and seventy per cent, bringing the total issue of ordinary shares to 10,289,812 shares, which, added to the preference capital, makes a total issued capital of nearly $12\frac{1}{4}$ million, against an authorised issue of £15 million.' The incorporation into the D.C.L. of the companies just amalgamated raised, as Ross stated, the question of the presentation of accounts. The next year would include the purchases and then, he went on, 'A question for consideration whether some fuller information should be supplied, so as to give a clearer indication of the nature of the securities held. The question as to whether a company such as ours, which is both a trading and a holding company, should furnish something in the nature of a consolidated balance sheet is one on which accountants differ, and personally I am not sure whether it is in the best interests of the shareholders that too detailed information should be given, so long as the auditors can certify that the investments are safely valued and are producing sufficient return.'

The monopoly accusation rankled, and, he knew, was close to the thinking of many in the trade and industry. At the time of the extra-ordinary meeting in March, Ross had given a firm assurance on the matter, but doubts still remained. At the March meeting he had said: 'When proposals for a fusion of interests such as that contemplated are brought forward I suppose it is only natural that a feeling of apprehension should arise in the minds of some of our customers lest the change involved may lead to somewhat different treatment being meted out to them than they have received in the past. To all such I wish to give the assurance that this fusion if ultimately carried through will make no difference whatever to the policy hitherto exercised by the Distillers Company. I can the more readily give this assurance, seeing that the control of that policy is still to be left in my hands. It has been my proud boast in the past that our smallest customer has received the same measure of justice as our most important buyers, and it will be my constant aim to perpetuate such a policy.'

Now, with that fusion accomplished, he returned to the charge of the 'taunt which is sometimes applied to us, that this company has become a monopoly, a trust or a combine, all I would say is that we are at least in good company. When I see banks, insurance companies, railways, industrial companies of every description, and even churches amalgamating, there must be something more in the movement than mere greed of gain. In no industry at present is there more need of closer co-operation – nay, even amalgamation, if necessary – than in that of distilling and its allied trades. It is not a question of placing oneself in a position to make huge profits, but it is an act of self-preservation. Where we have so many enemies without the gates it behoves those within to close their ranks. Take the case of production. It is obvious to everyone ... there is a very considerable over-production of whisky taking place, and if this is not checked it will mean a débâcle in the Trade which only the strongest may survive ... [This] must be tackled by the whole distilling trade.' Some of the action on that score we have noticed already in the closure of distilleries and the reduction of output.

Further amalgamations continued to take place, as, for example, at the end of that year which resulted in the D.C.L.'s acquiring from Sir James Calder the whole of the stocks and some of the properties of Macdonald, Greenlees & Williams Ltd, with the distilleries being mostly closed down in pursuance of the policy announced that summer.

Disregarding the many fusions of a minor nature taking place, we

come to 1927, the year when the fiftieth anniversary of the birth of
D.C.L. was celebrated, and Ross felt it necessary to return to the 'combine' charge, of which these words formed part: 'Personally, I am not
ashamed to be regarded as one of a combine. I go further and say, that
if Britain is to retain its prestige in the trade of the world, the more our
industries of a similar nature can co-operate or combine together in
order to effect economies, the more likely will they be to retain if not
increase our share of international trade. In mentioning the term
"combine", however, I do not suggest a monopoly formed for the
purpose of cornering a commodity to the detriment of the public at
large. I refer to a combine whose purpose it is to produce and distribute
an article at a reasonable price consistent with giving the best quality
and service, and where the benefits to be derived from such combination are divided fairly amongst consumers, the workers, and the shareholders.' (A nice order of priorities.)

Well aware of antagonisms prevailing, he went further, saying:
'Further, my conception of a combine is that it should be strong
enough to withstand the temptation to crush a weaker competitor who
is striving by legitimate means to make an honest livelihood, and at the
same time strong enough to keep in check unscrupulous competitors,
whose sole aim is to trade on the reputation of others and who delight
to make themselves objectionable in the hope that they will be bought
out at a reasonable premium.'

That same month of May 1927, Mr G. Mackie Campbell, chairman
of White Horse Distillers Ltd – Sir Peter Mackie, Bt, had died in late
1924 – told shareholders of the stress of competition and certain disposals of property, including a distillery, they had made. At the annual
general meeting of the D.C.L. the following July Ross in turn informed shareholders that 'The inclusion of malt whisky distilling in
their field of operation was but a further step by the directors towards
paving the way for a fusion with the most important distributors of
whisky throughout the world – a fusion which has been made more
complete within the last few days by the purchase of a controlling
interest in the "White Horse" brand of Scotch whisky . . . the offer of
this business . . . has been accepted by practically the whole of their
ordinary shareholders, and while the business will continue to be
carried on as a separate entity and by practically the same management,
it will, I hope, form a valuable addition to that section of the company's

business. It will be the aim of your directors so to guide the affairs of the entire company that, while looking after the interests of the shareholders we may, at the same time, see that full justice is done to our customers, and that they may eventually share in any benefits arising from a more comprehensive system of distribution which may now be possible.'

So much for the framework of the amalgamations of the industry, a tendency which still continues and may be expected to last as long as man. As Lord Forteviot said at that 1927 dinner, the company was born 'as the result of an amalgamation, and the company has gone on amalgamating ever since'. Today, of course, restrictive legislation and legal processes hinder the full continuation of that trend, but it still exists.

Also remaining active and vocal is the strain of opposition to amalgamation, combine, monopoly which Ross took such pains to dissolve, thereby proving the reality of its existence and the virulence of its nature. Shortly after the White Horse acquisition, for instance, Wm Teacher & Sons Ltd carried an advertisement, saying in part,

Combine or Non-Combine
. . . Press recently of the latest important absorption by the Combine which is threatening to control the Scotch Whisky Trade.
Ours is the leading FREE or independent brand on the market
. . . Prevent the creation of an absolute monopoly.

In January of the following year, 1928, there was registered in Edinburgh the Scottish Independent Distillers Co. Ltd, with the object: 'To amalgamate, take over, or enter into a working agreement with other Scotch whisky houses carrying on similar businesses of distillers, blenders, bottlers, vine growers, brewers, etc.', obviously a defensively directed move to the end that those who in difficult days wished to amalgamate would be provided with an alternative to the D.C.L., 'the Combine'. One of the two directors was Mr J. Barclay, of 55 West Regent St, Glasgow, the other Mr A. P. Hill, of Montreal, Canada.

By the end of that same year an alternative, non-combine grain whisky distillery was opened in Glasgow by the Scottish Grain Distilling Co. Ltd and at the following lunch, the chairman, Mr J. C. Duffus, said: 'This scheme was fostered not with any object of fighting any combine, but with the sole object of protecting ourselves and our friends against any control or monopoly of a branch of our Trade that has been free since its inception, and which you will agree with me is so highly essential.' To this, Mr Wilfrid Hiscox, the managing director, added: '... the reason for this company. This, I repeat, was to ensure our independence and to put us on an equal basis with our principal competitors ... When my colleagues and I decided to seek co-operation in our plans, the enthusiastic and powerful support we at once received was ample justification for my view that others, like ourselves, could not feel content while depending on any monopoly for their essential supplies.'

Ten years later, at the opening in September 1938 of the Hiram Walker & Sons (Scotland) Ltd grain distillery at Dumbarton, Mr Harry C. Hatch, president of the Hiram Walker organisation, acclaimed it as 'the largest and most modern distillery in the whole world' and went on to say that they had become 'increasingly conscious of the scarcity of grain whisky in Scotland. In fact, there were times when we could not secure from the then available sources sufficient for our estimated requirements ... If there appears to be a note of confidence in these remarks please do not mistake it for belligerence. The competition we bring to these Isles will be a competition based on quality, efficiency and service ... [we do not wish] the D.C.L. to imagine that it will regard our operations here as anything other than a development which corrects a situation in the industry which in the long run we believe could not have been for its ultimate benefit.'

War intervened, with its fresh rash of amalgamations, particularly with the D.C.L., and after that war there developed conflict about the export of immature whisky and related matters. Some of the active feelings aroused by the subject triggered off feelings that had lain dormant some time, particularly about the position and undoubted influence of 'the Combine', found expression in the formation in February 1952, of the Independent Scotch Whisky Association, the imputation being, as we have seen too in earlier years, that the association was not independent of its major members. The late Mr J. W. Hobbs, distiller, of Inverlochy Castle, Fort William, was elected chairman of the new body, and after the meetings, of forty-nine persons representing thirty-four firms, a statement was issued saying that the purpose of the new association was 'to act on behalf of independent traders whose businesses are being affected by monopolistic practices. It was the strong opinion of every member at the meeting that the existing associations were unduly influenced by a particular group or cartel whose aim was to drive the independent out of business and to capture all markets – both at home and abroad. Consequently, with no dissentients, an association in favour of free and fair trading practices was formed.'

Mr W. Graham, a solicitor of Glasgow, was made secretary of the new association, and brought the issue to more specific terms in these words: 'We believe that when the regulation about "young" whisky was made, the Board of Trade were wrongly informed that only one association represented the whole Trade, and they did not consult the independent traders. The new association are a combination of people who up to now have never combined.'

It would not be wise or of sufficient historic interest to bring nearer today the undoubted difference of opinion that still prevails within the industry on the subject of 'the Combine', amalgamations, purchases, and the like. It is accepted that this process is endemic to the Scotch whisky as to any other form of business activity, and particularly since the last war the whole picture has become increasingly variegated with the injection of large amounts of foreign capital and overseas owner-ship within the industry bringing with them their own varieties of amalgamation.

32

Scotch pioneers (i)

'THE PROPER study of mankind is man,' we were assured by Alexander Pope, so let us turn to examine briefly a few of the more outstanding men who paved the way so successfully through crisis and obstruction for Scotch whisky to assume its present position of world pre-eminence. A convenient personage to start off the quest is the late James Barclay who died as recently as January 1963, at the age of seventy-seven. In the previous October whisky men from all over the world had arrived in Glasgow for the presentation to him of his portrait on the sixtieth anniversary of his life in the whisky trade. Mr Tom Scott, of Hiram Walker & Sons (Scotland), was in the chair and a preliminary résumé of Jimmy Barclay's career was given by Mr Stanley Holt, whose private firm had the largest inventory of Scotch whisky in England and probably the largest such anywhere held by a private firm. As Holt put it, Barclay began in whisky in 1902, arrived in Glasgow in 1909 to become employed by Mackie & Co., headed by the man who was later to become Sir Peter Mackie. Those early years were further enlarged upon by banker Sir John Maxwell Erskine, who said: 'Our guest this evening, a son of the soil in the north of Scotland, in an area where everything combines to produce Scotch at its best, started work sixty years ago at 2s. 6d. per week as an office boy in Benrinnes-Glenlivet distillery ... In seven years Jimmy was in Glasgow when he joined Mackie & Co. Distillers Ltd, the proprietors of White Horse, and worked under Peter Mackie, later Sir Peter Mackie, and in a short time was in charge of home trade, bonded warehouses and distilleries.

After only nine years he was appointed director of Hazelburn distillery, Campbeltown, where at that time there were twenty-two distilleries; now there are only two.'

A convenient point to let Jimmy Barclay tell his tale as he did that night in Glasgow. Speaking of those years, Barclay said that 'they were all individual distillers then – not like today. Everyone was separate and there was big business doing. Working conditions were different, too; as a boy at Benrinnes I was refused permission to stop work at one o'clock on a Saturday afternoon to go off to the Highland Games and had to remain until the usual hour of six. My next boss, Sir Peter Mackie, generally known as "Restless Peter", was equally characteristic of the times. His office was decorated with a big sign, "Take nothing for granted" and, on the other side, "Honesty is the best policy".'

Later on Barclay set up on his own account as a whisky merchant and broker by acquiring James & George Stodart Ltd and also later became a director of Chivas Bros Ltd, the former having since passed into the ownership of the Canadian-controlled firm of Hiram Walker & Sons, and the latter now a subsidiary of Seagram Distillers Ltd, basically, also Canadian controlled but with the widest American ramifications. At that Glasgow dinner, heavily represented by the transatlantic element in today's Scotch whisky trade, there were attempts to draw Barclay on his American days, back through repeal to prohibition times, but all he would say was, 'I travelled all over. I have no regrets, though I have had some narrow squeaks I may tell you.'

Some slight enlargement of Barclay's American activities – which we have in the course of this work had occasion to notice – was provided in 1966 by Mr Lester Pearson, president of the Barton Distilling Co., based on Chicago, who said in Glasgow: 'I, and thus Barton, was really introduced into the Scotch trade and to Littlemill distillery through the good offices of the well-known James Barclay. Jimmy Barclay, as he was affectionately known, was literally raised in a distillery. He had an important part in bringing Scotch whisky to the attentions of the Americans and his benevolent, farsighted influence extends over the industry here and in the United States even to this day. He has been credited with having been the guiding light to many of the most prominent foreign interests who have become important entities in the Scotch whisky distilling industry. The very largest international distillers have consulted him and relied on his advice and have

444

acquired important brands which he originated. The House of Stuart brand, which is Barton's leading brand of Scotch, was owned by his company known as the House of Stuart Bonding Company, and which Barton acquired from him. Actually Jimmy Barclay introduced me to Mr Duncan G. Thomas, and this introduction led to the invitation to Barton's joining forces with Littlemill distillery. And so the benevolent influence of the famous and beloved Jimmy Barclay still pervades this newest Scotch development at Loch Lomond distillery.'

At the time of his death, Barclay was chairman and managing director of the Glasgow firm of whisky blenders and exporters T. & A. McClelland Ltd, a hotel owner in both Scotland and the Bahamas, and the owner of several farms in Scotland where he also maintained a pedigree herd of Aberdeen-Angus cattle. And as was put at the time of his decease, 'For a son of the soil in the north of Scotland, he had made his name as famous in the world of Scotch whisky as that of Haig, Dewar, Buchanan, Mackie or Walker in the last sixty years, but to a different audience. The public knew not his name, but the Trade the world over did.' Apart from what he had earlier distributed, Barclay left in his will £751,145.

So much for Jimmy Barclay whose career, restricted to whisky, summarises Scotch in the period: from a bleak Highland malt distillery that could pay no dividends for years before World War I, through the fame and power of 'Restless Peter' Mackie, the turbulence of American prohibition, to the present international fame and American penetration of the industry. Others were not so restricted, but typify the incursion of the wine and spirit world into whisky proper, such men, for instance, as Sir Walter Gilbey, Bt., who died in November 1914 at the age of eighty-three. Of old country stock, Walter and brother Alfred, after Army service in the Crimean War, set themselves up in London as modest wine merchants and were later joined by another brother, Henry. Their business flourished and the grocer with the off-licence became their agent in every town, and in almost every village in England. In an incredibly short time the brothers found themselves at the head of a gigantic business. Scotch, as we have seen, began its upward boom in the 1880s and in 1887 the firm bought Glen Spey Highland malt whisky distillery to assure themselves of supplies. Scotch went on booming, and in 1895, shortly after, for instance, John Walker & Sons Ltd bought Cardow distillery to ensure supplies, Gilbey bought another, Strathmill, at Keith, Banffshire. Although the early years of this century saw somewhat of a Scotch recession, Gilbey went ahead and in 1904 bought yet another Highland malt distillery, Knockando. Despite this plenitude of malt whisky it was only in 1905 that Gilbey acceded to common practice and began the blending of both malt and grain whiskies as we know today, and which shortly after his adherence to the blending practice came up for court action and scrutiny by the royal commission on whisky and other potable spirits, as we have seen earlier.

Gilbey was made a baronet in 1893 through the influence of Glad-stone – Sir Walter was a strong, outspoken Liberal to the end of his days – and when he died was not only a whisky producer, blender and distributor, but also one of the leading agriculturists and horse breeders in the country, a jam and lavender water manufacturer on top of the continuing wine and other spirit interests of the firm he had helped found. As token of his success and particularly Scotch success, he left unsettled property of the gross value of £425,156 of which the net personalty amounted to £320,383.

Another example of the incursion of the wine merchant into the whisky trade is provided us by James Mackinlay who died in May, 1926, in his eighty-fourth year. Coming of a Leith, Edinburgh, wine firm, James went to London at the age of eighteen or nineteen to Sherry shippers Hauris & Nephews in order to get outside experience of the mysteries of the wine trade. On his return two years later to Leith, he was taken into partnership by his father, one time Bailie Mackinlay. It was only as the seventies drew to a close that brands of Scotch whisky began to become well known, and his Leith firm then held agencies for various wines and for Macfarlane's whisky, later to become known as 'Port Dundas' whisky, and later to be merged into the D.C.L. With the whisky boom in England of the 1890s well under way, James Mackinlay and his brother C. W. Mackinlay and Mr Birnie, of Inverness, erected Glen Mhor distillery at Inverness and so established the firm of Mackinlay & Birnie. On its incorporation as a limited company it acquired near-by Glen Albyn distillery, and James Mackinlay remained a director of both companies until his death. With his wine origins he did not restrict himself to whisky, but took a keen interest in all licensed trade affairs, though his whisky interest was given particular notoriety and expression by the evidence he gave at the royal 'What Is Whisky?' commission with which we began. His broader trade interest led him to act for years as honorary secretary of the Edinburgh and Leith Wholesale Wine and Spirit Trade Association, while his interests beyond the trade were many and varied: he was at different times an assistant of the Edinburgh Company of Merchants, a director of the Leith Hospital, a life member of the Edinburgh Chamber of Commerce, of the Honorary Company of Edinburgh Golfers, Old Luffness, an original member of the New Luffness Golfing Club, and a member of the Edinburgh Burgess Golfing Society, the Dunbar Club, the New Club, North Berwick, while as a keen shot he was always out on 12 August. When he died in 1926 he left £130,897 gross and his son Lieut.-Col. Charles Mackinlay succeeded him as senior partner of the firm Charles Mackinlay & Co. Ltd, while also being a director of the blenders' North British grain distillery we have noticed and of Mackinlay-Birnie Ltd. He joined the company in January 1890, and it is typical of the incipient world growth of Scotch that he then travelled practically every country in the world on its behalf. His war injuries hastened his death – practically all his life he was associated with Army service – and he died at the end of 1934 at the comparatively early age of sixty-three. He left a personal estate of £92,212.

Similarly George Crabbie, who died in January 1929 at the age of eighty, was another example of the Leith wine merchant venturing wholeheartedly into whisky. Until a year before his death he was a vigorous chairman of the family firm of Messrs John Crabbie & Co. Ltd, still with us but a fairly recent member of the D.C.L. group. George Crabbie never ventured, as did Gilbey and Mackinlay into distillery ownership – some of the reasons for that have become apparent already – but he had many commercial interests in Scotland and was connected with a number of well-known firms in Leith and Edinburgh. Like many, as we shall see, in the industry, George Crabbie took a keen and active interest in local affairs: he was for years a member of the Perthshire County Council – being succeeded by his son J. E. Crabbie – was a justice of the peace for the county, a member of the Royal Scottish Archers, the King's bodyguard in Scotland, and as well as collecting engravings and prints was a specialist cultivator of trees and shrubs. His personal estate in Great Britain, on his death, amounted to £551,232.

One more example of the incursion of the wine and spirit world into

447

direct production and distribution of Scotch must suffice, this time in the person of James Robertson who died in January 1944. Born in 1864, the eldest son of Alexander Robertson, of Sandhills, Monkton, Ayrshire, after his education at Glasgow Academy he entered his father's business of wine and spirit merchants, Robertson & Baxter. As we have noted along the way on occasion, their interests widened out to include the then initially booming Scotch so that by the time of his decease, Robertson was chairman not only of the family firm of Robertson and Baxter, but also of the Highland Distilleries Co. Ltd and the blenders' North British Distillery Co. Ltd. He became vice-president of the Whisky Association, later the Scotch Whisky Association, and as a wine and spirit man with whisky production facilities was at one time president of the North of Scotland Malt Distillers Association. Typical of those in whisky he was active in his business until just before his death, and outside business was a well-known sportsman: he was at one time captain of Prestwick Golf Club; a member of the Royal and Ancient, Troon and Moray Golf Clubs; and of the Royal Burgess Golfing Society of Edinburgh. In this field he was also a keen angler and a shot. At the time of his death his personal estate in Great Britain was £187,130.

A distiller with whom Robertson was closely associated was James Grant, J.P., until his death in December 1927 at the age of eighty-eight, senior partner of Highland Park distillery, Orkney, which had been established in 1798. This James Grant was a veteran distiller, and Highland Park distillery, now a subsidiary of Highland Distilleries Co. Ltd which owns in all five malt whisky distilleries, incorporates practices and principles Grant brought with him from his birthplace Glenlivet, almost of the nature of a Mecca to whisky connoisseurs. His father was distiller and manager at the Glenlivet distillery, and in 1888, as Scotch was entering its boom, James Grant became managing partner at Highland Park, and soon afterwards became sole partner there. As befitted a distiller in the ancient tradition, James Grant's principal hobby was farming and in addition to his Orkney properties he had expanded his vision to the Argentine where he had considerable interests and to which country he made frequent visits to inspect his estates. In his younger days a keen sportsman, he was never a man absorbed by public affairs though he took his share in the affairs of his adopted county as a justice of the peace, a county councillor, and as

chairman of the Parish School Board. Although Grant's former distillery is now amalgamated into the Highland Distilleries Co. Ltd
which we have noted in connection with James Robertson, it still
preserves its separate identity under the style of James Grant & Co.
(Highland Park Distillery) Ltd, a silent reminder of the many mergers,
purchases and acquisitions we have noted along the way. Mr James
Grant's estate was valued at his death at £45,047.

Such were a few instances of the urban wine and spirit merchant
enlarging his sphere of operations to invade the whisky world. One of
the best examples of the Highland distiller enlarging his operations to
become a blender and distributor is provided for us by Major William
Grant whose firm now make malt whisky not only in the Highlands
but also in the Lowlands of Scotland and in furtherance of their
blending and distributing activities now produce their own grain
whisky as well. A fascinating, almost romantic story is that of Major
Grant.

When he died at Dufftown in January 1923, he was in his eighty-
fourth year, had been ill for some years and, latterly, blind. The son of
William Grant of Dufftown who had fought at the battle of Waterloo,
and consequently known locally as 'Old Waterloo', Major Grant, as
he became, was educated at Mortlach parish school, after which he was
apprenticed to shoemaking. Before long Mr Findlater, factor to the
Duke of Fife, engaged him as manager of Kininver Lime Quarries in
1863. Grant was there some three years, returning in September 1866
to Dufftown to become clerk to Gordon & Cowie at their Mortlach
distillery. He was there twenty years, until the autumn of 1886 when
he acquired, together with his eldest son John the lease for the Glenfiddich distillery.

He had saved some money over the years and managed to buy for
£120 the second-hand distillery equipment which came on the market.
William and his six sons then literally set about building the distillery,
named after the burn which passed by it Glenfiddich. His daughters
themselves cut the peat needed for drying the malt in the kiln their
father and brothers erected. The work began late in 1886 and on
Christmas Day of the following year they ran their first whisky. Five
years later he built his second, and neighbouring distillery in the
recently acquired Balvenie Castle, which he bought for £200, along
with twelve acres of land.

449

Scotch was in its boom decade and William, as we have seen, took immediate advantage of it to the extent that the initial exports to the Lowlands and England were succeeded by family-managed exports overseas. We cannot here relate all the experiences and expansion of the company, first formed shortly after the Balvenie acquisition as a private limited company – which it still is – of which founder William was managing director until his death, when his estate was valued at £65,153.

In himself, William Grant was an enthusiastic volunteer and as early as 1868 enlisted as a private. He gradually rose, becoming a major, and as well as being most active in local affairs was an equally enthusiastic freemason. So delightfully impressive a character was he that he figures in *Oor Ain Folk* and the strain must have run in the family for two of the nephews of his great-grandfather figure as the Cheeryble brothers in Charles Dickens's *Nicholas Nickleby*. It is of interest that of the three sons who survived the Major, one, Captain Charles Grant, was not only a member of the family firm but also owned Glendronach Highland malt distillery. The fifth son of his father, he served as a midshipman for a time before becoming manager at Glenfiddich distillery and later at Balvenie. When Wm Grant & Sons was formed into a private limited company, Charles went to Glasgow to attend to the company's expanding interests there and in World War I served with the 6th Gordon Highlanders. With them he served in France and there can be no doubt that his severe injuries at the battle of Neuve Chapelle hastened his death at the early age of fifty-four in August 1926. He also, like his father before him, undertook his full share of public work and was also president of the local Unionist Association. After he bought Glendronach in 1920, he also resembled his father in his distilling ability and the changes and improvements he carried out at Glendronach were such as to draw the comment that he had 'almost remodelled the whole of the buildings'. In addition to real estate, Captain Charles Grant left personal estate in Great Britain of £45,313.

His brother John, the eldest son of the Major, an active distiller member of the family company, died at Dufftown about the beginning of 1933. In 1881 he had graduated in arts at Aberdeen University – one of the five brothers who graduated there – and was for some years a schoolmaster at Ythanwells School. With the death of his father in

1923 he withdrew from schoolmastering and became chairman and managing director of the family company until his own death. Personally, he was a skilled musician, was for years the enthusiastic president of the Dufftown Choral Union and under his presidency the society performed many of the best oratories to gain a most creditable place in musical festivals. He began the local Boy Scouts and for years was its esteemed and able scoutmaster, a role which brought him correspondence from all over the world as his former scouts emigrated. He, too, was a member of various public bodies, a keen sportsman who got his blue ribbon of the Banffshire Volunteers in rifle shooting at the age of seventeen.

A glance at a Highland malt distiller representative of many of his calling, Captain John Fleetwood Cumming, of Cardow distillery at Knockando, Strathspey. It had been in the hands of the Cumming family since it was set up following the rationalisation of distilling laws in 1823. With the 1890s quest by the blenders of distilleries to guarantee their sources of supply it was purchased in 1893 from widowed Mrs Elizabeth Cumming by Alexander Walker, jun., on behalf of John Walker & Co., Ltd., and John F. Cumming who had managed it for his mother was appointed a director of Johnnie Walker to continue in control of the distillery. So he lived through the boom years of Scotch, its recession, its improvements and depressions until his death in January 1933, when he died at the age of sixty-nine years. Like so many of his sort, he was active in local affairs and for over forty years he represented his native parish of Knockando on Moray County Council. In 1920 his abilities were given full recognition and he was appointed convener, being also deputy lieutenant for the county of Moray. He retired from his position with John Walker & Sons Ltd when the firm was converted to a limited company and so was free to devote more time to his agricultural interests: he carried on farms at Cardow and Kinloss and was the tenant of a sheep farm on Kellas estate. During World War I his public services were further extended by becoming recruiting officer for Morayshire, with the rank of captain, and was later awarded the O.B.E. for his services. Being a distilling-farming Scot he was also a keen golfer and was for some time the captain of the Moray Golf Club. He was survived by his widow, his third son, Ronald S. Cumming (now Sir), for some years chairman of the D.C.L. and of the Scotch Whisky Association, and by a married daughter, Mrs Miller Stirling. Captain John F. Cumming, O.B.E., D.L., left personal estate of £137,410.

Let us turn to some of the most prominent Merchant Adventurers of the industry who not only guided the fortunes of Scotch through its troublous and formative years but themselves fashioned those years and formulated the industry in the shape we know it today. First, James Buchanan, who died in August 1935 as Lord Woolavington, G.C.V.O. Born at Brockville, West Canada, in August 1849 he was the youngest son of Alexander Buchanan, of Bankhill, Stirlingshire, but, delicate, as throughout his life, he was brought back to Scotland at the age of one year, to be cared for and educated privately. He began his business career in London in November 1879 as representing the Leith whisky firm of Charles Mackinlay & Co. Ltd. He was handicapped, he recalled, by being 'an entire stranger' and had only two friends in the whole of the city. 'That I should fail to do so [succeed] never entered my head,' he said. In 1885, reading the signs of public taste aright and being possessed of outstanding business and administrative ability, he decided to set up in business for himself at 61 Basinghall Street, London, E.C. Such whisky as was then sold was mainly of the self whisky – unblended – variety, and, said Buchanan, 'What I made up my mind to do was to find a blend sufficiently light and old to please the palate of the user. This I fortunately was able to do, and I made rapid headway. I need hardly say that I was on the quest for business night and day, getting introductions and getting to know people wherever I could.'

We cannot here follow all that rapid headway, but suffice it to say that early on he secured the contract for the supply of Scotch whisky – 'Buchanan's Blend' – to the House of Commons and the following year he moved to 20 Bucklersbury, E.C. By the time of the 1887 Jubilee 'Buchanan's Blend' was on sale in most public houses. His lifelong interest in horses was already becoming apparent: he drove around the city with a striking black pony and red-wheeled buggy, with behind him a spruce, dapper 'tiger', or page, of perfect poise and deportment.

The year 1898 saw the city's acknowledgment of Buchanan's ability: he bought the 'Black Swan Distillery' in Holborn for £87,000 within twenty-four hours of hearing that it was coming on the market. With his name and escalating reputation, Buchanan was able to raise more capital than was needed. Shortly afterwards, to illustrate another trait in his character came the incident of the Pattison failure. He was asked by a syndicate to value Pattison's stocks; he replied he was too busy. He was then told that none of the Scottish bankers would accept any other name than his, and if he should refuse the scheme would fall through. He was told to charge whatever he liked. He undertook the task on the understanding that if they wished to give anything for his services they could send a cheque for £50 to the Wine and Spirit Benevolent Association. Throughout his life James Buchanan was most generous in his gifts to charitable and public causes. Indeed, both he and his wife were renowned for their generosity and it cost her her life.

In 1892, while on one of his health trips, Buchanan married a nurse, Anne, the daughter of Mr Thomas Pounder, and she died in 1918 due to her overwork in nursing the war-wounded. Ten years later, in 1928, Buchanan, or Woolavington, as he then was, gave £125,000 to Middlesex Hospital for the provision of middle-class paying wards in memory of his wife, while at the same time he put £50,000 at the disposal of King George V for the restoration of the nave of St George's Chapel, Windsor.

Indeed, the considerable wealth he accumulated as a result of his business genius was very largely devoted to charity and public causes. To mention only the most outstanding such gifts, in addition to those already listed: £5,000 for the log book of the *Victory* to be then deposited in the British Museum; Will Longstaff's 'Menin Gate at Midnight' he bought and gave to the Australian Government in memory of the Australian forces killed in World War I; when an appeal was made for £4,000 to fit out the old *Implacable* as a training ship he sent a cheque for the entire sum; the Tariff Reform League, of which he was vice-president, received lavish support from him; in 1926 he gave £10,000 to Edinburgh University to endow the Animal Breeding Research Department; about a year before his death he gave £10,000 to the London Hospital to defray the cost of a department for beds for paying patients of moderate means; in the same year he gave £2,500 each to the Licensed Victuallers' School and the Licensed Victuallers' Benevolent Institution; shortly before his death he presented a similar sum to the Royal Chest Hospital, London. His generosity in such causes persisted after his death: his many bequests in his will included £15,000 for the Licensed Victuallers' School, and a like sum for the

Benevolent Institution, and should no children result from the marriage of his only child, Catherine, to Captain Reginald N. Macdonald, Scots Guard, retd., the ultimate residue was to go 'for the promotion of the cure and treatment of cancer'.

Something of his sheer business brilliance we have noticed in the earlier story, but not only was Buchanan acutely aware of the sort of Scotch the public wanted, he was equally aware of the amalgamation tendencies of his age. These have been discussed in sufficient detail; they are mentioned here as expressions of his many-sided genius and acumen which brought him from comparative obscurity to a position of world pre-eminence in the potable spirit world.

Another facet of that many-sided personality we have briefly glanced at: his love of horses. Early in his career, while on a health trip he visited Argentina where a Mr Kincaid lent him horses for riding and driving while there. He returned home with the trainer Alvarez and the jockey Gomez and in 1889 began racing under the name of 'Mr Kincaid'. A year or two later he dropped the pseudonym and began using his own name. The first classic he won was the St Leger, with his Hurry On, bought as a yearling for 500 guineas. As a three-year-old it ran in six races and won all and sired Buchanan's two Derby winners, Captain Cuttle, 1922, and Coronach, 1926, the latter also winning the Eclipse Stakes and the St Leger. Both of these were bred by Buchanan who acquired in his lifetime a considerable reputation as a notable bloodstock breeder.

Parallel to this turf activity was Buchanan's general business interest in horses: we have seen his early pony and buggy equipment and being an excellent judge of horses himself he decided early on to have outstanding horses and vans. The coachmen and trouncers (van guards) were dressed after the style of the famous coachman James Selby; the horses were of the old coaching type, many of them over 17 hands high; they were worked in pairs and could draw a load of three tons, additional to the van, at a smart trot. He held an unbeaten record for his van horses, and in 1904 inaugurated the London Van Horse Society's annual parade in Regent's Park, now, alas, discontinued from lack of entrants.

With the withdrawal of the Buchanan van horses – due to traffic problems – *The Times* published in May 1936 a leader on them, 'No More Heeltaps'; 'A former Buchanan horse, or even a former

454

Buchanan pair, may be seen, perhaps, here and there, but to recognise them would be like meeting an old friend in reduced circumstances. Without their own gleaming carts and glittering chains, without the grey top-hats and smart liveries of the drivers and the men whom it seems only proper to call the guards, the horses will not be their old selves ... They were beautiful creatures, beautifully turned out. And they were ours to enjoy all the year round ... For forty years the Buchanan horses have always been there, and as gay, as beautiful a sight as any coach or carriage could have offered in the now antiquated era of the horse.'

As early as 1908 James Buchanan was known to own, in partnership with Lord Aberdeen, 20,000 acres in British Columbia where he grew fruit and crops and raised cattle 'to great profit'. At the time of his death he not only owned property in British Columbia, but in addition to Lavington Park, Petworth, Sussex, where he bred cattle, sheep and thoroughbred horses, he had properties in British East Africa and the Argentine. Distilleries, blending and bottling plants in Scotland need not be listed; they were, of course, the basis of his business.

With his home at Lavington Park, as above, Buchanan was made high sheriff of Sussex in 1910; was later made an Hon. LL.D. of Edinburgh University; was created a baronet in 1920; raised to the peerage as James, Baron Woolavington in 1922; and in 1931 was appointed G.C.V.O. When he died at Lavington Park, in August 1935, in his eighty-sixth year, he left an estate of the gross value of £7,150,000 'so far as can at present be ascertained', reported *The Times* later, with net personalty £7 million on which estate duty of £3,510,828 19s. 5d. had been paid by the time of the newspaper's account.

In all the wealth of his personality, his complex personality, three features stand out as marking James Buchanan, Baron Woolavington: his brilliance in the Scotch whisky world as a pioneer of the spirit on the English and world markets; his sportsmanship and love of horses; finally, his unbounded generosity to hospitals, charitable institutions and public causes.

The many Haigs have already been remarked upon during the narrative.

33

Scotch pioneers (ii)

CONTINUING OUR proper study of mankind among the princely Merchant Adventurers of the Scotch whisky industry who helped make the industry what it is today and firmly placed it where it is, we come to the brothers Dewar, John the elder and his younger brother Thomas, eventually to become Lord Forteviot and Lord Dewar respectively.

To appreciate the magnitude of the achievement of these two brothers, we must first briefly examine their antecedents. They were true sons of the Scottish soil and give us yet another example of young Scottish manhood in the last century and this making the world their oyster with their native spirit. The founder of the firm, John Dewar, after a couple of years as a joiner at Aberfeldy, where his sons were later to establish a malt whisky distillery, joined his Perth city wine and spirit merchant uncle James Alexander in 1828, was taken into partnership in 1837 and in 1846, at the age of forty, set himself up as a wholesale wine and spirit merchant in Perth. His business was practically confined to Perthshire to begin with, and gradually scattered itself over most of Scotland. In 1879, the year James Buchanan went to London, John Alexander, the second surviving son of John Dewar, was admitted into partnership with his father, and in the following January the father died, aged seventy-four, leaving John Alexander in control at the age of twenty-three.

John Alexander Dewar, later Lord Forteviot, had previously spent some time with a Leith firm, equipping himself with the latest in the then whisky metropolis of Scotland. His younger brother, Thomas

Robert, also spent some time in Leith and with the firm we have noticed, Robertson & Baxter, of Glasgow, and in 1881 entered the business with John Alexander, being admitted to the partnership in 1885. Thomas Robert was then aged twenty-one.

Now the firm, restyled John Dewar & Sons, had for a brief space had English agents in London and Manchester, and with Thomas now a partner it was decided, in 1885, to tackle the market as only a Dewar could. Thomas came to London that year. He spent his first two years preparing the soil and that initial wooing of the London market took, in the words of Mr John L. Anderson, who recorded the firm's earlier progress, 'seven strenuous years of march and counter-march, of hopes and fears, of victory and failure. Mr Dewar spent his first two years . . . in distributing samples of his wares broadcast, in persuading and generally casting his bread upon the waters in the hope that it would return after many days.'

Two years after his arrival Thomas opened their first London office at 6 Warwick Street, Pall Mall, and was so little known then that he had to find security for the rent before he was allowed to move in. Tentative orders for their whisky in bulk, in octaves and quarters, began to come in from well-known houses and presently the orders began to arrive more frequently. Their bottled goods were also being asked for by hotel saloon bars and West End restaurants; in 1888, after much intense competition, Dewar's was chosen by Spiers & Pond for the sole supply to their numerous catering houses. This brought the whisky into some measure of prominence and larger and more important orders began to flow in.

But all that meant hard, continuous work for both ends of the firm: for Perth under John Alexander and London under Thomas. Their own abilities were far and away above average, but they had also this advantage that they were not afraid of work itself.

The marches and counter-marches, the steady expansion of the business, both in supplying, in erecting their own distilleries and later buying others, and in distributing, first in London and across England, then abroad to British colonies and settlements, cannot be allowed to detain us here.

To turn to John Alexander who, it may be said, was in command in the fashioning of the firm to make it a household word the world around, as early as 1883 he evinced practical interest in his native city and was elected a member of the Perth town council at the age of twenty-seven. While still a young man he was made city treasurer five years later, and in 1893 he was unanimously elected Lord Provost, a position he held for six years. In those years of unstinted work for the city and council of Perth his efforts were most valuable in the interests of all concerned, so that when he stood for Parliament as the member for Inverness-shire in the Liberal interest he won the seat and held it till 1916. Half-way through that tenure of office he was made a baronet in 1907, in recognition of his many and valuable services and three years later he bought Dupplin and other property from the Earl of Kinnoull. Of Dupplin he made a model estate; nothing that could be done for the happiness and comfort of those who served with him was left undone, while the estate was also known as 'one of the best stock-breeding grounds in the country'. He was created Lord Forteviot of Dupplin in January 1917, which title expresses his intense feeling as a true son of the soil of Scotland: the historic village on the Dupplin estate was the last Pictish capital in Scotland and was long the royal residence, while Forteviot was the first Scots capital. Lord Forteviot was deputy lieutenant of Perthshire, and both Perth itself and Perth-shire will long remember him for his philanthropy. Among his gifts, were £16,000 towards the restoration of St John's parish church as a war memorial for the county; £15,000 to build and equip a maternity ward at the Perth Royal Infirmary; £13,000 to build a model lodging house in the city.

As we have noticed previously, the brothers Dewar were abreast not only of public taste and preference in offering them the whiskies of their choice; they were abreast, too, of the major tendencies of the age, so that if their initial proposal of an amalgamation between Buchanan, Dewar and Walker came to naught at the time, the amalgamation of Buchanan and Dewar was achieved shortly after the outbreak of World War I, to be followed, as we have seen, by other purchases and mergers culminating in the big amalgamation of 1925. Again, as with all the Merchant Adventurers of Scotch whisky the clarity of mind, the organising ability, the power of correct decision were uppermost in the person of John Alexander Dewar, and when he died in November 1929 at the age of seventy-three years, his estate amounted to £4,405,977, on which the duty was £1,722,885. Lord Forteviot was twice married, unlike his brother Thomas who remained single.

We cannot leave Lord Forteviot without a glance at a close working partner who became a director of Dewar's and, after the amalgamation, of the D.C.L., Alexander John Cameron. A native of Ross-shire, he joined the Dewars in 1890 and early displayed a remarkable bent for blending old Scotch whiskies. He experimented in many directions and introduced some revolutionary changes in the method of selecting and vatting various grain and malt whiskies, changes since adopted by the rest of the trade, and, in brief, consisting of blending and marrying the grain whiskies and the malts separately in advance of a final blending and marrying of the blended malts and blended grains. Alexander Cameron died a little in advance of Lord Forteviot, in August 1928, and the inventory of his estate amounted to £211,886.

To revert to Thomas Dewar, born at Perth in January 1864, and the firm's pioneer in London, and early in the 1890s he set out on a world-wide tour, lasting two years, to search out and appoint representatives in the leading colonial and foreign markets. Such was his restless, but effective, energy that he appointed on that trip thirty-two first-class responsible agents, visited twenty-six different countries, and arranged for opening shipments on consignment to all the great commercial ports and cities of the two hemispheres. This was the foundation on which ten years later Mr P. M. Dewar was to build the enduring super-structure of the company's world-wide business which lasts to today.

Thomas also played his part in local and national politics: from 1892–5 he was on the London County Council as representing West Marylebone; from 1897–8 he was Sheriff of the City of London, later becoming a Lieutenant of the City; as a Unionist, as distinct from his Liberal brother John, Thomas was member of Parliament for St George's, Tower Hamlets, from 1900–6, the latter year being the pro-Liberal, anti-Conservative landslide. In 1902 Thomas was knighted and in 1917 created a baronet. He did not attempt to re-enter Parliament after the Tory débâcle of 1906, but concentrated on his increasing business interest, his other occupations and hobbies. In 1919 he was created Baron Dewar of Homestall, reflecting his home at The Homestall, East Grinstead, Sussex. His elder brother Arthur, formerly solicitor general for Scotland was made a judge of the Court of Session with the title of Lord Dewar, but the latter had died in 1917.

Thomas was one of the earliest pioneers of motoring and gave the Dewar Trophy for the most meritorious motor-car performance of the year. In 1897 he first registered his colours as a racehorse owner and in 1927, the same year as Lord Woolavington, he was elected a member of the Jockey Club. He had original ideas about horsebreeding and was a very valuable owner in the sense that he was thoroughly independent and had only the best interests of horseracing at heart. Coursing also interested him and he won the Waterloo Cup in 1915 with Winning Number, which he had bought for 280 guineas. In addition, he was a great pigeon and poultry fancier, probably winning more prizes than any other fancier of his day, his greatest triumph coming in 1928.

As a raconteur and after-dinner speaker he was so famous internationally that he published a book on the subject, *Toasts and Maxims and Wisdom Compressed*. His other writings included: *A Ramble round the Globe*; *Prohibition in the U.S., Canada and New Zealand*; *Experiences of the Gothenburg System*. Lord Dewar tried his hand at painting, and once said, addressing the Royal Institute of Painters in Water Colours: 'I can claim to be an amateur artist, although I may not look like one. When I look at my work I often think of the other amateur artist who asked a friend to give him an opinion, the subject being a cow in a meadow. The friend said, "The ship seems all right, but I think you have made the sea just a little bit too green."' We have space for but few of his epigrams and sayings, such as: 'Competition is the life of trade, but the death of profits'; 'If you persistently advertise a good article, the public will make a beaten track to your door. If you advertise a bad article, you may cast your bread upon the waters, and you will be very lucky if you ever see it again.' 'It's the constant advertiser who gets the trade'; 'A man's reputation is known by the things which are not found out about him and a man would be following the funeral of his reputation if they were found out'; 'A Scotsman is never at home except when he's abroad'; 'Man reaps what he sows – unless he is an amateur gardener.' And many more of the same breed too manifold for reproduction here.

When Lord (Tommy) Dewar died suddenly at his home in April 1930, less than six months after the death of his brother Lord Forteviot, his peerage became extinct, as he had never married, and when probate was granted to his estate it was proved at £5,000,000 'so far as can be at present ascertained'. His chief beneficiary was his nephew John A. Dewar, but his various and many bequests included named members of the staff and group with ten years' or more service.

Scotch pioneers (ii)

Thus we come to 'Restless Peter', Sir Peter Jeffrey Mackie, practical formulator of the firm we know today as White Horse Distillers Ltd. The business activities of the predecessors of White Horse Distillers can be traced back to 1801, and the Mackies themselves were a very old Stirlingshire family holding lands there along with properties in Edinburgh – the White Horse Inn, for example. Peter Jeffrey Mackie joined the firm, then run by his uncle James Logan, in 1878, and first underwent some practical distillation training at their Islay distillery of Lagavulin. With the boom of the 1890s their whisky trade, both for home and export, grew rapidly and under, no doubt the impetus of Peter Jeffrey bursting with youthful activity, the style of the firm was changed to Mackie & Co., his uncle retiring soon afterwards. By degrees, they conquered a growing market and it may be said that it was the forceful energy of Peter Jeffrey Mackie himself who was responsible for their gradual penetration of the English and then over-seas markets.

As we have seen in the case of Jimmy Barclay, who received his initial Glasgow training from 'Restless Peter' Mackie, employees had to apply themselves full out, or every member of the staff – such was the nature of Peter Mackie – from the highest to the lowest, had to interest himself in every activity of the company. Mackie drove himself as hard: he was a leading trade speaker up and down the country, particularly in the days of the Lloyd George budget crisis; he took a passionate interest in political affairs, and was president of the Scottish Unionist Association; he was also vice-president of the Glasgow Unionist Association. He wrote on tariff reform and imperial federation both before and after World War I.

During those pre-war years the hard and long work of Peter Mackie and others on the staff, including repeated visits to overseas markets, resulted in outstanding progress everywhere, and the chairman's only son, Captain James Logan Mackie, was just completing a world tour to learn the export trade when war broke out and he hurried home to join up. Unhappily, he was killed outside Jerusalem in 1917.

But with his customary motto, 'Nothing is impossible', Mackie forged ahead. He himself travelled extensively, and with that restless bent to which Jimmy Barclay has drawn our attention his interest in exploration prompted him to finance an expedition which threw great light on a people previously unknown: 'The Mackie Ethnological

461

Expedition' to East Africa was conducted by one of the foremost anthropologists of the day, Canon Roscoe, who carried out researches on the border of the then Uganda Protectorate from May 1919 to November 1920. Canon Roscoe had the advantage of being the only white man to mix with the Bakitara, and finding their traditions of centuries uncorrupted was able to get most valuable information on their customs, laws and languages, later made available to scholars the world over in two volumes.

During World War I Mackie was very vigorously identified with various charities and national appeals and in 1915, for instance, presented the Lord Provost of Glasgow with an eighteenth-century document of civic interest, now in the city archives, a goodly sum having been realised by its auction at the time for the War Relief Fund. His vigour and liveliness carried him far beyond his whisky distilling – he had large interests in Islay, Kintyre and on Speyside – blending and bottling interests in Glasgow to find expression in his collection of old silver, old china, antique furniture, paintings, his estates at Lavagulin, Islay; Corraith, Symington, Ayrshire; and Glenreasdell, Tarbert; in his being a justice of the peace for Argyll, Ayr and Lanark; in his Fellowship of the Royal Society of the Arts; in cricket and golf, of which he was a generous patron.

Made a baronet in 1920, when he died in September 1924, his only son having been killed in the Ayrshire Yeomanry in 1917, he left two daughters, both of whom were married so that his sons-in-law, Captain G. Mackie-Campbell and Captain G. F. Boyle, were among the pall-bearers at his funeral at St Ninian's Episcopal church at Troon, in which is a rich stained-glass window commemorating the only son killed in Palestine.

Sir Peter Mackie left, in addition to considerable real estate, personal estate of the total value of £528,753, of which his interests in White Horse Distillers Ltd amounted to £311,486, and his holdings in war loans, etc., to £120,582. The amount of estate duty payable on the personal estate as declared was computed at approximately £137,476.

Alexander Walker, who died as recently as May 1950 as Sir Alexander Walker, K.B.E., at the age of eighty-one years is the next of our Merchant Adventurers in Scotch. The original John Walker, after whom the firm is named, came of small farmers of Ayrshire stock and in 1820 established himself in Kilmarnock in an Italian warehouse, grocery and wine and spirit business. After the flood disaster of 1852 his son Alexander became increasingly active in business and in the then current manner of exporting Scotch by means of a system of 'Adventure Merchant Business' brought the firm into its first contact with overseas markets and openings. It is not too much to say that these first export activities of Alexander Walker, senr., built up an overseas connection which formed the basis of their present export business. When he died in 1889, his three sons George Paterson, John, and Alexander continued the business, the latter having joined it, at the age of nineteen, only the previous year, after a legal training with one of the best firms in Ayrshire and a technical grounding in wines and spirits with Robertson & Baxter, of Glasgow.

Applying himself to the technical and commercial problems of distilling, blending and bottling – his powers of concentration were proverbial – in 1890 he was made a director, and in 1893 was instrumental in purchasing, as noticed, the Cummings's Cardow malt distillery. That was, in short, but the beginning of his takeovers in the whisky world which continued even after the big amalgamation with the D.C.L. and others in 1925.

But to revert to the man himself, after his marriage in 1895 he made his home at Troon, of which town, along with Kilmarnock, he was a very great benefactor, dispensing sums amounting to £200,000, in return and acknowledgment of which he received the freedom of Troon. In 1899, in line with the dominant trend to amalgamation of his day, the firm acquired under his guidance an interest in the business of Slater, Rodger & Co. Ltd, of Glasgow, a firm they were to absorb completely in time. But we cannot here follow through the detailed history of the firm itself. Suffice it to say that Alexander Walker, jun., was equally alive to the approaching advertising age, and it is to him that is owed the figure of his ancestor Johnnie Walker. In 1908 the company was registered as a private limited liability company in terms of the new Companies Act of 1907, and the same year saw the emergence of the Johnnie Walker figure. Alexander Walker, jun., had under consideration the introduction of a portrait of the original John Walker into the firm's advertising and he summoned up the famous artist Tom Brown who in a small, rapidly executed sketch portrayed the original Johnnie Walker as the man the world now knows so well. So clearly did he embody the features and the form of the founder of the firm that the sketch was immediately adopted and has gone on ever since. A fine sidelight, in fact, on the ability and awareness of Alexander.

As we have seen there took place about this time abortive discussions concerning an amalgamation with Buchanan and Dewar. They came to nothing at the time, though were later realised after many years spent in co-operating with the other firms. The 1909–10 negotiations were allowed to drop as Alexander Walker, and the other parties to the discussions, came to the conclusion that the time was not quite ripe. But the fact that they took place at all presents us with a fine testimony to the clarity of their vision, particularly that of Alexander Walker.

World War I intervened, and like so many in the industry Alexander was unequalled in his national efforts: his aid was enlisted by the Government for assistance to the Ministry of Munitions and other departments and after the war he played a prominent part in the disposal of Government surplus, particularly of spirit, whose course we have traced earlier. Indeed, from 1918 to 1920 he placed himself entirely at the service of the Ministry of Munitions and the Munitions Disposal Board, for which wholehearted public service he was granted a knighthood.

Still most active in the whisky world – when the public company of John Walker & Sons Ltd was formed in 1913 he became joint managing director and later chairman and he continued all the inescapable labours whose general course has been outlined in earlier chapters – Sir Alexander nevertheless engaged wholeheartedly on several occasions in important undertakings on behalf of the Government. For years Sir Alexander was an active member of the Ayrshire Electricity Board, and was largely responsible for the board's rapid development and the efficient distribution of electricity throughout Ayrshire; from 1929 the area gas supply committee was under his chairmanship, and he was also chairman of the Board of Trade committee inquiring into the possibility of a gas grid in the west of Scotland.

More locally, in addition to the large gifts he made to Kilmarnock and Troon, Sir Alexander was chairman of the board of governors of the college at Troon and he made constant endeavours to promote higher education along with schemes for the health and recreation of the community. He made generous gifts of building land for sites on the South Beach to add to the attractions of the burgh of Troon as a holiday resort and was the most active individual sponsoring the swimming pool at Troon. In 1944 he presented the town council with £10,000 and a substantial amount of heritable property adjoining the municipal buildings in connection with the establishment in Troon of a health centre for the treatment of rheumatism and kindred ailments. No wonder that he was given, in 1946, the Freedom of Troon, and it speaks volumes for both parties that he was the first man ever to receive the honour. Indeed, he was then the only survivor of the nine commissioners appointed to govern the burgh of Troon when it was formed in 1896. Apart from Johnnie Walker, the world-famous Scotch, Sir Alexander's best monument, at least in Troon, lies in his control of the Marr Trust and the erection there of the Marr College.

After a funeral service at St Ninian's Episcopal church at Troon, as in the case of Sir Peter Mackie, as we have seen, Sir Alexander was buried at Troon cemetery. His wife had died in 1948, and he was survived by two sons and two daughters. Passing away in his eighty-second year after a lifetime of service and experience, and warned by prevailing death duties, no doubt, Sir Alexander's estate, amounting to £568,599, was comparatively modest.

A close associate of Sir Alexander's was Mr James – later Lord – Stevenson who joined the firm at Kilmarnock as a youth, later opened up their Birmingham office in 1897, transferred to London and was made a director in 1908. Later he was to become joint managing director, and in that commanding position he became a great influence in the trade. Still Mr Stevenson, on the outbreak of World War I, he placed, as we have seen, his services entirely at the disposal of the Government on the understanding that whatever his work it was on a purely honorary basis. His work with Lloyd George and in the national effort we have to some extent already noticed, and it is pertinent here to recall his post-war speech in which he recalled Lloyd George's Budget of 1915 which was scrapped in its original form as the minimum age of whisky and certain other spirits was introduced. Said Stevenson about that occasion: 'I am the real author of the Immature Restrictions Bill. It was I who suggested to the present Prime Minister'– Lloyd George – 'when he was Chancellor of the Exchequer, that "All spirits should be kept in bond for three years." Mr Lloyd George has done many fine things for his country ... By no means the least of his achievements was the placing on the Statute Book "That all spirits shall be kept in bond for three years".'

In 1917 for his remarkable war services Stevenson was made a baronet and became vice-chairman of the Ministry of Munitions Advisory Committee. Among other responsible positions he held were: surveyor-general of supply at the War Office, 1919–21; member of the Army Council, 1919; of the Air Council, 1919–21; vice-chairman of the Advisory Committee on Civil Aviation; commercial adviser to the Secretary of State for the Colonies, where he again assumed national importance as chairman of the British Rubber Investigation Committee, the result of their investigation being the saving of the rubber planting industry.

In 1922 there was conferred upon him the honour of K.C.M.G. and in 1923 he had to accept at the Government's insistence the chairmanship of the new Board of Management of the British Empire Exhibition at Wembley and when the exhibition was opened in April 1924 he was raised to the peerage as James, Baron Stevenson of Holmbury, in Surrey. He died at the age of fifty-three in June 1926, worn out before his time. As Mr Winston Churchill said of him, at the close of a long tribute: 'It is the language of bald truth to say that in ten years' public service for honour alone he wore out and consumed the whole exceptional strength of his mind and body. Barely fifty, he had exhausted in the service of the State the vital forces by which an easier and less disinterested career might have been carried to a long old age. He ranks with the good soldiers who died of the injuries and strains they received when giving all that was in them to the national cause. He leaves behind him an example of public spirit, of rectitude, and of flexible originative capacity, which those who aspire to be leaders of British industry may well emulate, and a memory which those who were his friends will never let die.'

As there were no children of his marriage, the barony is extinct and he left an estate of £313,706 gross, the net personalty being £250,547.

A brief glance at another Walker, Archibald Walker whose name has occurred in these pages particularly in connection with the contribution the patent still distillers of Scotland made to the war effort in World War I. Born in Glasgow in 1858, Archibald Walker was the eldest son of Archibald Walker of Loch Katrine, Vauxhall and Limerick distilleries. He had not quite finished college when his father died in 1880 and he had soon to join the firm. When Loch Katrine distillery was absorbed by the D.C.L. he joined the board of the company and five years later the Vauxhall distillery, as we have seen, was also incorporated. Now Archibald Walker had taken an M.A. with first-class honours in natural science at Trinity College, Oxford, and because of his technical knowledge during World War I was appointed to superintend on behalf of the Government the introduction of the manufacture of acetone for munitions, of which we have taken note above. In addition, and he succeeded, in so far as he was allowed the raw material, in producing alcohol for munitions from potatoes, at Ardgowan.

Walker retired from the D.C.L. board in 1934, but the breadth of his interests can be seen from the fact that he played Rugby for Oxford and Scotland, rowed for his college eight, was a member of the Royal Company of Archers, was a Fellow of the Institute of Chemistry, deputy chairman of the Clydesdale Bank, a director of the old Glasgow & South-Western Railway Co., was for a time vice-chairman of the Ayrshire Territorial Army Association, for years hunted with the Lanarkshire and Renfrewshire Hounds, engaged in many charitable and philanthropic activities and was most lavish in his private bene-factions. He was pre-deceased by his wife, and when he died in June 1945 he left one son and one daughter, and was himself aged eighty-six years. His personal estate in Great Britain amounted to £828,960.

34

Scotch pioneers (iii)

THERE REMAIN for us to consider but two giants among the Merchant
Adventurers of the Scotch whisky industry who oversaw and assisted
in its fashioning into the form which we know today – William
Dudgeon Graham Menzies and William Henry Ross.

First, Graham Menzies, born in 1857 of an old Edinburgh distilling
family who had installed a Coffey still in the 1840s under the personal
supervision of John Dore, Coffey's own assistant who later took over
his master's business. Menzies was educated at Rugby and during those
years the arrangements were made between the patent still distillers
which we have earlier recounted, arrangements which led to the
formation of the D.C.L. in 1877.

The year previous to that, 1876, Menzies left his school to join the
family distilling firm, Menzies & Co., of Caledonian distillery, Edinburgh. He continued a partner until it was absorbed by the D.C.L. in
1884, and the following year he was elected to the board of that company. That is, his first years in active business were dominated by the
then prevailing trend to amalgamation, a trend prominent, as we have
seen in all British – indeed, in world – industry and business. His mind,
then, was set on those lines from the start and in combination with
William Ross he was to perform the great amalgamations of the
potable spirit world in Britain, to begin with, and then around the
globe until the D.C.L. became in his day the biggest such distiller in
the world. One result, as already noted, of Caledonian's joining the
D.C.L. was the formation of the North British Distillery Co. Ltd and

its blenders' grain whisky co-operative distillery. Menzies was gaining early and impressive evidence of the need for and dangers of amalgamation. He was an amalgamator all his life; he never ceased to believe in its virtues and necessity, but was never so short-sighted as to imagine that it solved all problems without raising others in their place.

In May 1897 the first fixed chairman of the D.C.L., Mr Andrew Drysdale, died and in June Menzies was elected as chairman, at the age of forty, while at the same meeting Ross was offered – and accepted – the post of General Manager and Secretary to the company: a fine amalgamation of two amalgamators!

There is no need here to recapitulate every event in the history of the company and the industry in which he took part; that has been touched upon in brief earlier, but a few more remarks on the man himself are not out of place. First, in the years before Caledonian's absorption by the D.C.L. and after leaving school, Menzies travelled extensively around the world. It was a premonition, a foreshadowing of the lines on which the company into which he was later to be amalgamated was to develop. He saw much of Australia, the scene of the first overseas investment of the D.C.L. He visited India, for long, especially with British Forces well entrenched there, a most lucrative overseas market for all whisky firms when bitten by the export bug. Significantly, he saw much of both North and South America and the British West Indies, all most productive and profitable areas for the D.C.L. and other whisky firms. Menzies had, then, from his earliest days a double dose of the compulsive need for both amalgamation and export.

A few personal notes before moving on to some aspects of his handling of affairs. In 1890 he married the youngest daughter of Sir George Wombwell, Bt, by whom he had three sons, the eldest of whom adopted a military career and was killed in the first year of World War I. He was the principal landowner in the parish of Kettins, Forfarshire; he was most active in local affairs, serving as a member of the County Council of Angus, as chairman of his parish council and as justice of the peace for the county of Angus. In addition to the posts which accompanied his chairmanship of the D.C.L. he was an extraordinary director of the Royal Bank of Scotland, and a director of Flemington Coal Company. On his death in October 1944, in his eighty-seventh year, he left personal estate in Great Britain to the value of £1,446,813.

We can now turn to glance at some of his own sayings and contemporaries' opinions to illustrate what the story to date has unfolded. For instance, indicative of the cautious attitude of mind which dominated his financial conservatism in handling the company's affairs is this passage from his report to the annual meeting in July 1912: 'The stocks are now virtually what they were previous to the 1909 budget . . . We have no wish to repeat the mistake which was made twelve years ago and which led to such an overproduction as to make it unprofitable for any ordinary buyers to hold a stock.'

In his first report after the outbreak of World War I, he made mention of the newly passed Immature Spirits Act in his address to shareholders in July 1915: 'So far as this company is concerned we have never opposed a measure of compulsory bonding, although your directors think that ample time ought to have been allowed for the members of the Trade to adapt themselves to the new conditions.' He went on to discuss company policy in general, saying, 'For the last thirty years' – he had been a director and/or chairman for just that period, so the passage is self-revelatory – 'it has been the policy of this company to spread its risks so that failure in any one direction should not unduly affect the profits earned. Following out this policy, we have built up a large industry in yeast . . . Another branch of business which we have cultivated, and which is likely to extend as time goes on, is the supply of strong spirits for industrial purposes. At the moment . . . alcohol is playing a very important part in the production of high explosives, and the demands made upon us for this spirit at the present time are very heavy. Although the price obtained for this spirit is less than what we receive for potable spirit, we consider it so essential in the country's interest to keep this trade fully supplied that we may still find it necessary to curtail the quantities we had already allocated for whisky purposes.'

His amalgamating instincts had been given full rein by the time he made his July 1916 report against a background of discontent in the trade, a discontent to grow and reminiscent of the 1884–5 period: 'I would not have it supposed that we have been exacting an undue toll out of our customers. Prices have had to be raised, of course – raised in proportion to the advance in the cost of raw materials, wages, etc., but had we wished to exact the full advance obtainable in the market for our various products, we might easily have doubled our profits. Your directors have taken a longer view of the position. This company is not in business for today only ... Our policy has been to conserve the future and act in the best interests of the whole Trade.'

As the war progressed and drew to its end, Menzies contented himself with less pronouncement on general affairs of the company and industry, leaving that for the managing director, William Ross, to handle, but at the July meeting in 1921 when the double effect of steeply increased duties, in 1918, 1919 and 1920, plus the recession were being felt he made a statement which could be issued today: 'The consumption of liquor in this country is being rapidly killed except amongst those customers who can afford to pay the present high prices and those who, while not able to afford it, are yet willing to spend their last sixpence to get what they want, no matter at what cost. Between these two sections lie the great mass of the population who neither can afford to pay the present exorbitant prices nor who desire to drink to excess, but yet feel the want of their usual stimulant. Do the Government really think that they are studying the best interests of the country by compelling abstinence of liquor through high duties and diverting into other channels the money which but for these high duties would be used for the legitimate enjoyment and sustenance of the body?' Menzies had not become so remote from the public as to overlook or forget the effects of daily life on the consumers of his product.

That theme was resumed in another direction in his last statement to shareholders as chairman in July 1924. Of industrial strife, then beginning to tear the country and emerge as the General Strike of 1926, Menzies was able to report that 'We have been particularly free', continuing, 'Where any question of wages has arisen, we have been able to meet our workmen's representatives and adjust matters with them to our mutual satisfaction.' Later he resumed the nightmare of over-production in a falling market which had haunted his first years as chairman and the Pattison failure: 'Production,' he reported, had been 'well controlled – with the object of preventing, if possible, that glut on the market which overproduction inevitably brings about. Our difficulty, however, in so regulating the production is to forecast what the consumption of spirits is likely to be three years hence, when the present production is set free for home use.'

In May 1925 Ross was elected, as the big amalgamation came to a head, the chairman of the company and Menzies retired from that post, though not from the board. He had been chairman, then, twenty-eight years and with his further years on the board, to July 1931, he served on it in all forty-eight years. At the annual meeting in July 1925, Ross, the new chairman, acknowledged the great honour paid to himself and proposed to Menzies 'our grateful thanks for the great services which he has rendered to the company during his tenure of the chair. Mr Menzies has been a director of the company for over forty years, and has served as chairman for the long period of twenty-eight years. It was felt by him that the present was an appropriate time to retire from the chair ... an ordinary member of the board.' Menzies withdrew from the chair, that is, when the two dominant themes of his young manhood reached fulfilment: the greatest amalgamation in whisky history after a series of potable spirits and related amalgamations, and the firm establishment of whisky distribution around the globe despite prohibition in the United States, against which obstacle Scotch was, however, making inroads such as would prove the most solid of post-repeal foundations.

Two months before Menzies died in October 1944, at the age of eighty-six, there died in Edinburgh his long business subordinate, associate and chief, William Henry Ross at the age of eighty-two years. Together they made the D.C.L. and the industry what it is still today, with the emphasis going to Ross's share. As the *Record* said at the time of his decease, 'Mr Ross was undoubtedly one of the most outstanding figures in the Scotch whisky industry in the three decades commencing with the opening of the century. It can be said that the building up of the vast business known as the Distillers Co. Ltd – the rationalisation of the Scotch whisky trade – is due in no small measure to his foresight, amounting to genius.'

A handy summary of a person who still stands out well above his contemporaries, as they themselves acknowledged, leads to this conclusion: that the best thing that ever happened to the Scotch whisky industry was the failure in 1878 of the City of Glasgow Bank.

It happened in this way. In June 1862 there was born to a farmer in the parish of Carluke a son, christened as William Henry. A year later the father, Mr Ross, left Carluke to take up a lease of the farm of Westfield on the Dundas estate, near South Queensferry, on the Firth of Forth. The boy Ross had his early education at the local school, and

went later to George Watson's College in Edinburgh which he left at
the age of fifteen to take up a junior appointment at the Grassmarket,
Edinburgh, branch of the City of Glasgow Bank. A year later the
bank failed and the sixteen-year-old lad within twelve days had
obtained an appointment as a junior clerk with the D.C.L., which had
only been formed, as we have seen, by an amalgamation, in May 1877.
His promotion was rapid: in 1884, at the age of twenty-two, he was
accountant and cashier; in 1889, at the age of twenty-seven, he succeeded Mr E. F. Dudgeon as Secretary; in 1897, at the age of thirty-five,
when Menzies succeeded to the chairmanship, he became general
manager and secretary. In 1900 he joined the board as managing
director, at the age of thirty-eight. It was, as we have seen, after this
latter appointment and with like-thinking Graham Menzies in the
chair, that the main extension of the company's business took place.
Indeed, when he joined the company and it first went public, its
authorised capital was just under £1 million; when he assumed the
chair, it had been increased to £15 million.

There lie a couple of clues to this extraordinary man's character. His
position with the D.C.L. was due to a financial failure, due, basically
to faulty, extravagant behaviour. Just before he became managing
director, and just after his dual post assumption as general manager and
secretary, there occurred the Pattison failure, as we have seen. Now
that was the close of the decade when 'everyone wanted to be in
whisky'. The two events, allied with his sharing of the conviction
of his age that the future lay in amalgamation, shaped his whole
being and made him, if possible, an even more fervent believer in the
benefits, nay, necessity of amalgamation. Many of those mergers
we have seen in the course of this story, and they may be said to owe
themselves not only and simply to the economic trends of the day,
the passing circumstance, but to the determination of Ross to
rationalise the whole potable spirit industry, and that determination
was reinforced, made determined by that double experience of his
younger days: the failure of the City of Glasgow Bank and the Pattison
crash.

So deep an impression did the latter make upon him that more than
twenty years after it happened he wrote: 'Their extravagance in conducting business, including the somewhat palatial premises they erected,
was the talk of the Trade, but so large were their transactions and so

473

wide their ramifications that they infused into the Trade a reckless disregard of the most elementary rules of sound business. Encouraged by the ease with which financial assistance could be obtained from the Scotch banks of the day, investors and speculators of the worst kind were drawn into the vortex and vied with each other in their race for riches. The unhealthy demand thus created induced many malt distilleries to double or treble their output, while the shares of new companies formed to acquire existing distilleries or to build new ones were eagerly subscribed for by a confiding public. Such was the over-production of Scotch whisky during that period that even until recent years' – Ross was writing in early 1924– 'the result was still felt . . . The boom which was then at its height completely collapsed, the banks withdrew their credits, and many firms were obliged to ask protection from their creditors, while others were hopelessly crippled in their future business . . . One of the largest assets was a fine range of Excise-bonded warehouses situated at Bonnington, Leith, which, it was stated, had cost Pattisons, Limited, over £60,000. These were exposed to auction . . . and were bought on behalf of the Distillers Company, Limited, at £25,000.'

There you have Ross and the first expression of what were to become his guiding principles in a career of unexampled and unrivalled success. It was that sort of behaviour and experience, allied with the trend of the day towards mergers, which led him to declare war his whole life on 'senseless competition' and attempt to bring about an amalgamation, at least an arrangement, between all the potable spirit producers of the United Kingdom. In this he did not entirely succeed – and it was before the days of Monopoly Commissions and Restrictive Practices Acts – but he might have been hailed by the Marxists as embodying their master's dictum that 'Capitalism leads to monopoly in preparation for the final monopoly – State ownership.' With Lloyd George's hare-brained schemes in World War I for nationalising the 'drink traffic' in that war, and including even at one time the whisky distilling industry, Ross was faced with that proposition in practical terms.

This is not the place to trace in detail his many transactions and moves towards achieving rationalisation in the distilling trade. We have told the outstanding points of that story, and of some of his other related activities – such as helping to win World War I by harnessing the patent still distillers to the national effort – in earlier chapters. But some more personal elements of the story may here be recalled with advantage.

Of course as those mergers and purchases proceeded Ross assumed many other positions of responsibility, such as chairman of the new acquisition, but these are too many to detail and show us little of the man as he was in himself. Now as early as 1895 he was elected a member of the old Edinburgh Merchant Company; he was also a member of the Edinburgh Chamber of Commerce, and for two terms of three years each was a director of the same while also serving a term of three years as the Chamber's representative on the Leith Dock Commission. This was also an expression of his early belief in the advantages and benefits of export, a belief deepened in his conviction by the early response of the blenders to what they feared was the growth of monopoly after the D.C.L. acquisition of Menzies's Caledonian distillery by building their own grain whisky distillery and so forcing the D.C.L. to explore the export market, and to concentrate on yeast production and amalgamation, the United Yeast Company, which also helped save the nation in World War I, being one of Ross's favourite achievements. During that war he acted, as we have seen, as intermediary between the Government and the distillers for the supply of alcohol for munition purposes – and received the O.B.E. for his services. (That award was valued and regarded somewhat more highly than it is today. Even so, it was disproportionately small for the magnitude of effort which Ross put into the job.)

Now Ross possessed truly wonderful qualities of absorption and organisation; he was, in that age of clear-sighted giants, in a class of his own. But he had many other sterling qualities, lacking in many of his and our contemporaries, and the obituary published in the company's gazette is one of the most succinct summaries of the qualities and attributes which put Ross where he was for ten years, the most important man in the world in potable spirits: 'One can put these down,' says the obituary of his qualities, 'as courage, foresight, a first-class accounting brain, a splendid memory, straight thinking, with prompt and sound decision on matters at issue, a blend of "sauviter in modo" and "fortiter in re" in negotiating, a great capacity for hard work, a full share of Scots caution, and above all, a very high code of commercial morality. It was realised the world over that his word was his bond, and every emissary of the company benefited by the atmosphere so created when outside concerns appreciated that in the hands of the Distillers Company Limited they were certain of a straight deal. His clear brain enabled him to grasp the essential features of a case promptly and to "cut the cackle" and arrive at decisions which seldom had to be reversed.' That ability was early seen not only in the first amalgamations which he achieved this century, but his clear and concise action in the 'What Is Whisky?' case with which we opened: without his decision then to undertake the case at Islington and follow it through to the royal commission, Scotch whisky as we and the world know it today would not be in existence.

It can be seen at many of the stages recorded in our foregoing story. He was probably the prime mover in the formation of the Whisky Association in World War I; he helped form the Scottish branch of that association, becoming its first chairman, and in 1924 was unanimously elected chairman of the London Council in order to rationalise and co-ordinate the activities, etc., of the association. That association, too, as well as the D.C.L., may be taken as a Ross memorial.

But to come to the opinions of the men who know him best and worked closest with him. At the quinquennial dinner of the D.C.L. in Edinburgh, in 1922, Sir Alexander Walker said of him that he was 'a great silent man, and reminded him of the wise old owl that sat in the oak, and the more he thought the less he spoke, and the less he spoke the more he heard ...'

Indeed, some even called him 'The Abraham Lincoln of the Trade' – his care and attention went far beyond the production of malt and grain whiskies: it took in the whole of the licensed trade, particularly in Scotland with its threats of local prohibition, the inequitable working of the local veto system, the repulse of the 'drys', just as his wide interests and alertness led to his being made a member of the Council of the (then) Federation of British Industries and many related committees.

With the accession of Ross to the chairmanship of the D.C.L. in May 1925, on the completion of the big amalgamation – Ross's greatest monument – and its promulgation at the annual meeting in July, Lord (Tommy) Dewar gave this assurance and paid this tribute: 'The complex and competitive interests of the past are now happily under the wholesome influence of unity. The competition that we have experienced from those we are amalgamating with is but a memory of the past ... It will be unnecessary for us in the future to go to any

476

extreme means to get business and our hope and desire will be to endeavour to raise the standard of ethics in the industry.' Going on to their new chairman he said: 'Unaided by outside influence, but entirely due to his individual genius, initiative and imagination, Mr Ross has reached the apex and the most important position that the company could offer. We now look upon him as our new Moses to take us out of the wilderness of strenuous competition and lead them into the land flowing with respectable dividends.'

Ross's own reaction to talk and fear of the Combine and monopoly we have already recounted: it was but part of the sanity and experience of the man which led him to assure all of the fairness with which all would be treated while at the same time insisting on the necessity for amalgamations in the then (and present) state of the British economy.

He was seriously injured in Glasgow near the beginning of 1917 when a lorry ran over him making compound fractures in one leg and seriously damaging the other. But that was as nothing to the misfortune which overtook him a few years before his retirement from the D.C.L. chair and related positions in 1935: because of a shipboard mishap while on a business trip to the firm's investments in Australia he was blinded in both eyes. With his usual courage in adversity, he persevered in his work, and only resigned in 1935. That resignation was deferred to the October of that year when it became effective. And at the annual meeting in July when the matter was discussed, Ross then said: 'Fifty-one years have been spent in positions of trust and responsibility, and therefore I have had a good deal to do with the promotion of new ideas and in framing the policy of the company during those years. I have also been the chief official of the company for not less than thirty-five years, and in 1925, when the big amalgamation took place, I was honoured in being asked to take the chair, which I have occupied since that time.'

It was then that Mr W. H. Fraser, W.S., said about the subject of our consideration, in moving this resolution, 'That this meeting offers to Mr Ross the grateful thanks of the stockholders of the D.C.L. for the valued services rendered by him to the company for a period of fifty-seven years, and assures him that their best wishes will follow him into his retirement from active duty,' that Mr Ross 'had all the qualities which would lead any man to the top of the tree in any line of life he had chosen for his own. He had great tenacity of purpose combined

477

with caution and clear vision and ability to convey his views. This infinite capacity for work, high sense of duty, and charm of manner which endeared him to all, had enabled him to convert opponents to allies, and to cement friendships.'

When Ross died in his eighty-fourth year in August 1944, he was survived by two sons and a daughter – one son has since become Sir Henry Ross, and was before retirement chairman of both the D.C.L. and the Scotch Whisky Association. Among his benefactions may be mentioned a gift of £5,000 to the Edinburgh City Corporation for a bandstand in Prince's Street Gardens; £8,000 to Edinburgh Royal Infirmary Extension Fund; and £40,000 to set up the W. H. Ross Foundation, its purpose defined as being 'investigating the origin and causes of blindness and utilising the results of such investigation towards its prevention and cure'. His estate was valued for probate at £246,000.

APPENDIX

The primacy in blending

WE BEGAN with the blenders and it is appropriate to close with them. Interest is constantly arising as to who began blending Scotch whiskies when. A close examination of the question serves to underpin the position of primacy formerly granted to Andrew Usher on general grounds, the Usher to whom, incidentally, we owe the Usher Hall in Edinburgh. The only other possible claimant to the honour and distinction of initiating the practice of blending the traditional pot still whisky of Scotland and the 'new-fangled' grain whisky from patent stills is W. P. Lowrie who died in 1916 and who was accorded a brief obituary in which the claim was made that he began it all. His case will be examined later.

But first, Andrew Usher, jun. He was the son of Andrew Usher, sen., who was in turn, the son of James Usher of Toftfield, adjoining Abbotsford, renamed Huntlyburn when Sir Walter Scott purchased Abbotsford. Andrew, sen., was born at Totfield in 1782, later moved to Edinburgh, set up business in Meadow Place, south of the Meadows, and after various peregrinations settled in 1823 at the then 24 (now 34) West Nicolson Street, in a house formerly belonging to Lady Nicholson. There was born in January 1826, a son Andrew, the subject of our inquiry.

There were in all born four sons: Andrew, John, James and Thomas. The latter two moved into brewing, and laid the foundations of what later came to be known as the Park Brewery. Andrew, jun., and John joined their father as 'distillers'. That description is open to question as

479

a strictly accurate description of their function. It was then a term frequently and indiscriminately used throughout the last century. Witness, even as late as the Edinburgh Exhibition of 1886, of which it was reported by a correspondent: 'The astonishment we experienced at the amount of unknown "distillers" represented! There are many figuring under this title of whom we have never previously heard as owners of distilleries.' That was, of course as the last-century boom in blended Scotch whiskies was about to enter on its climax of the nineties: everyone had to be a distiller, to be 'in whisky'. It was, in effect, simply the perpetuation of the earlier indiscriminate use of the term as applying to anyone 'in spirits'.

Moreover, their earliest activity as Andrew Usher & Co. was not confined to whisky: it embraced the blending and bottling of wines and spirits and the production of British wines, which latter activity was only abandoned in 1892 because of the predominance of Scotch whisky.

Now the date 1853 has been suggested as the date when Andrew, jun., began blending whiskies. But blending at that date was frequently practised and then meant, as far as can be ascertained, simply the mixing together of various single malt whiskies as made in the traditional pot still process, blending as originally understood. The abolition of the corn laws in 1846 had allowed the economic use of imported maize in the production of patent still, or grain, whisky. But, even so, grain whisky, or patent still spirit, made from (mostly) maize did not 'take on' easily. The first such distillery was set up at Port Dundas, Glasgow, and many there were after that date who soon fell by the wayside. By the mid-fifties the majority of the patent still distillers remaining entered into a trade arrangement for a year to allocate the trade amongst themselves. The arrangement was renewed from time to time, as recalled earlier, until in 1877 six patent still distillers amalgamated to form the D.C.L. Neither Andrew Usher nor W. P. Lowrie was amongst them. Nevertheless, in that twenty years of arrangements, patent still distilling was in a parlous state – the major reason for their amalgamating – and it was not, in fact, until 1864–5, according to company records that maize was used by any of them, when it was used at Cambus and Cameron Bridge distilleries. It is, of course, possible that it may have been used earlier but no record kept.

To revert to the year of 1853 when Andrew Usher, jun., is thought by some to have begun blending in the modern sense. That year is of other, and relevant significance: Gladstone that year abolished the malt tax as it applied to distillers, raised the duty on Scotch from 3*s*. 8*d*. per proof gallon to 4*s*. 8*d*. and made the spirit safe, through which emerges under lock and key the newly condensed distillate, compulsory at all distilleries.

Some of the condition of the whisky industry in Scotland then is revealed by the fact that in 1852 there were 139 malt, or pot still distilleries at work there; they fell next year to 122, and continued to do so until in 1860 they numbered only 108. That decade of the fifties saw a continuing rise in spirit duties which effectively discouraged both distillers and drinkers.

In 1854 the duty payable on Scotch spirits was raised to 6*s*. the proof gallon; in 1855 it was brought into line with the rate prevailing in England, 8*s*. the proof gallon. In 1858 the Irish spirit level of duty was equated to that of England and Scotland and in 1860 there was a twofold increase, applicable to all parts of the United Kingdom, first to 8*s*. 1*d*. then to 10*s*. It stayed there for a quarter of a century.

But the consternation and depression prevailing with that double increase of 1860 was most profound and intense and widespread. It was thought the end had come. To quote only a fragment of a letter from a Scotch distiller to Disraeli written about that time: 'But in 1860 Mr Gladstone raised the duty in the three kingdoms to ten shillings per gallon. The injurious effects of this policy were at once apparent. At the termination of the year, although the increase had only been in operation six months, the consumption had fallen to 21,800,000 gallons. Six months' experience of a ten shillings duty accounted for the non-appearance of two and a quarter millions of gallons. The depletive process continued steadily. In 1861 the consumption was only 20,045,000 gallons; in 1862 it was 19,700,250 gallons; and in the year ending 31st March 1863, it was 18,788,000 gallons ...

'The eight shillings duty had severely stretched the sinews, if it had not altogether exceeded the strength of the trade. But when the duty was finally raised to ten shillings, the consumption again and more seriously fell away; it continued to fall away by year, and it is at this moment still decreasing. This continued depression furnished the best proof of the repressive or prohibitory character of the present high rate of duty ... Ever since the duty was raised to ten shillings the consumption has steadily decreased ... (the duty is) clearly beyond its power of endurance.'

Such was the climate of the industry when Andrew, jun., purchased a distillery, a Lowland malt whisky pot still distillery close to Edinburgh, so close indeed that it was named the Edinburgh distillery. Many thought the trade was doomed and were getting out of it while they could. Not so Andrew Usher. He acquired it from Messrs Duncanson & Co., and it was carried on as a separate venture under John Duncanson, a member of the former family of owners, and on his death he was succeeded in charge by his son John E. Duncanson.

That purchase by Andrew Usher reveals considerable courage and foresight on his part. But he was encouraged, maybe inspired, in the venture by an Act of that year which, in effect, laid the foundations of blending malt and grain whiskies as we know it today. To appreciate the Act we must again return to the monumental year of 1853.

In that latter year provision was made to cover losses in store or in the distillery in respect of wash, the raw material to be distilled into spirit. Then came the 1853 Act (16 and 17 Vict. c. 37) which permitted British plain spirits – i.e. such spirits as whisky – to be warehoused in nine-gallon casks and permitted, on payment of duty, their racking in the warehouse, provided that not less than ten gallons were racked into one cask. The ten gallons figure was fixed on as being the minimum quantity allowed to be delivered from a store for home consumption.

But the most important feature of the Act was the actual establishment of distillers' warehouses, a move profoundly affecting Andrew Usher. Section 23 of the Act reads: 'No distiller shall have or use any warehouse for the warehousing of spirits without payment of duty situated at any other place than his own entered premises, not until such warehouse has been approved by the Commissioners of Inland Revenue; providing that any distiller may warehouse spirits in any general warehouse appointed by the Commissioners of Inland Revenue and for which security by bond shall have been given as directed by the Acts in force in that behalf.'

That concessionary Act accompanied, in effect, the duty increase of that year and the enforcement of the spirit safe whereby the newly made distillate was put under lock and key. The 1860 increase in duty of two shillings was also accompanied by a major concession, that of the Spirits Act 1860 (23 and 24 Vict. c. 114). This Act gave the distiller the privilege of using any materials he thought proper, provided that the gravity of the wort – the liquid to be fermented – could be ascertained by the saccharometer. The Act also permitted warehousing not only in casks, but, most significantly, in vats. Above all, its most important provision, it permitted vatting, blending or racking within the warehouse with a deficiency allowance of one half of one per cent. Previously, blending could only be performed with spirits on which duty had already been paid, a duty regarded at the time, 1860, as crippling, destructive and excessive. The twofold allowance of vats in warehouses and duty-free blending within them combined to allow the initiation of large-scale blending. This was further encouraged by the patent still distillers, only too anxious to find any outlet for their spirit, grain whisky, in the hard times they were then experiencing, as noted above.

The further benefit of the combined events of duty-free blending in warehouses and the patent still distillers' search for outlets was that the falling market for whisky could only be restored to health by blending the more expensive malt whisky from the pot stills, as made, for instance, at Andrew Usher's Edinburgh distillery, or at the premier Highland malt whisky distillery, the Glenlivet, for which Andrew Usher acted as sole agent, with the less expensive grain whisky, made at the patent still distilleries close to Edinburgh and Glasgow. Indeed, even within Edinburgh where Andrew Usher was to be prime mover in setting up what was the largest and most productive patent still distillery in Europe until the eve of World War II, the North British distillery of which we have spoken earlier.

As Arthur John Tedder, later knighted, put it at the 'What Is Whisky?' inquiry in 1908: 'The tendency in blending was to reduce the cost, because each spirit comprising the blend would have a different monetary value ... There were two classes of blends – blends of pot still spirits made from different distilleries, and blends of pot still and patent still spirits. The latter class largely preponderates. Where pot still spirits are blended, very often spirits produced from quite a large number of distilleries would be mixed so as to give a proper flavour.

The proportion of pot still to patent still spirits in the blending varies very much.'

Ross, then managing director of the D.C.L., said, more precisely: 'Before 1860, the very little blending carried on had to be done after the spirits had paid duty. Irish whiskey at this time was predominant in the market, chiefly on account of its uniformity in style, whereas in Scotland, even amongst pot still whiskies, they were vastly dissimilar. When a man asked for Scotch whisky or spirits, he never knew whether he would get the high flavoured North Country, Islay or Campbeltown whisky, or the less flavoured Lowland Malt whisky, or the pure grain whisky (patent still). This was the blender's opportunity, and he soon began to mix the various grades of Scotch whisky together, and produced a fairly uniform type of whisky, with none of the pronounced flavours of any one of the individual parts. The public at once took to this new style of whisky ... The popularity of Scotch whisky in England is due entirely to blended whisky, which is much better suited to those living a sedentary life.'

No one was named, unfortunately, as pioneering that blending, but for the moment it is more relevant to glance at some production figures. In 1857 pot still malt whisky made in the traditional manner was produced to the amount of 5,469,000 proof gallons, and patent still whisky to a little less, to 5,410,000 gallons. That was, of course, prior to the 1860 Act allowing duty free blending and before blending as practised by Andrew Usher began. Ten years later, in 1867, pot still whisky production had dropped to 4,767,000 gallons, in line with the tales of woe described above, while patent still spirit, a little in recession, managed a total of 5,325,000 gallons. In 1877, the year of the D.C.L. amalgamation, both recovered: the pot still score was 7,162,000 and the patent still score was 11,381,000 gallons. Their blended combination was beginning its upward march, a march uninterrupted until the turn of the century. Actually, in 1897 the totals were: pot still whisky produced, 13,979,000 gallons; patent still whisky, 17,300,000 gallons.

Andrew Usher was personally very much concerned in that increased output, especially of patent still spirit. Times had been hard for the patent still distillers and when six of them amalgamated in 1877, it was a case of 'marry or die'. A few years later, the largest grain distiller in Scotland, Menzies, of Caledonian distillery in Edinburgh, 'married'

into the D.C.L. combination of 1877. The blenders, such as Andrew
Usher and William Sanderson, mainly bought their whiskies on the
market. Many had no distillery ownership at all. The blenders
now feared a monopoly on the part of the patent still distillers, a
monopoly of grain whisky. Further to exacerbate their feelings (and
pockets) was the fact that the London distillers had reduced their price
for spirits, but the U.K. Distillers Association 'did not see their way' to
make a similar reduction of prices in other parts of the United
Kingdom.

In August 1885 the rumour gained currency that some of the blenders were planning their own co-operative patent still distillery. The
D.C.L. attempted negotiations; they failed; the blenders went ahead to
form the North British Distillery Co. Ltd to manage their own patent
still distillery in the Gorgie district of western Edinburgh. It came on
stream about September–October, 1887.

The prime mover in the whole affair was none other than Andrew
Usher. The choice was obvious: as an initiator of blending malt and
grain whiskies, with a fine practical and organising intelligence, with
a near-by Lowland malt whisky distillery and with having to lease
extra ground at St Leonard's station because of the expansion of his
distilling-blending operations, he was the only man to assume leadership.

So Andrew Usher became chairman of the North British Distillery
Co., and another rising distiller-blender, William Sanderson, of Leith,
its managing director. The other members of the board were: John M.
Crabbie, George Robertson, John Somerville, James McLennan, and
Alexander Murdoch.

Indeed, so successful was the blenders' co-operative distillery for
producing grain whisky, that the Northern Malt Distillers determined
'to test the question whether it is not "adulteration" to put grain spirit
into malt and dub the "blend" "Highland whisky". If such a decision
were obtained,' wrote a contemporary observer, 'it would fall like a
bombshell into the "grain" market, and with the "butterine" question
fresh in our memory, we do not put such a decision out of the region
of possibility.' And at the annual meeting in July of the North of
Scotland Malt Distillers Association held at Elgin, it was recorded that
'the attention of the Association was particularly directed against the
adulteration of whisky, and, in order to secure the public against that

practice, the meeting came to a resolution to apply to the Board to enforce the Adulteration Act.'

That enforcement, or its variant, did not come to a head for nearly twenty years, in the Islington-Clerkenwell prosecutions and the resultant royal commission, as we have already seen. But in 1890-1 a select committee of the House of Commons examined many aspects of whisky production and possible safeguards. Its report quoted 'certain distillers in Belfast and Scotland' that 'blends of pot still and patent still whiskey were in large demand by the consumers, who thus obtained a cheaper and milder whiskey containing a smaller quantity of fusel oil and other by-products'. The committee also found that blending whiskies had become 'a large trade. From thirteen to fourteen million gallons are operated upon in warehouses in this way ... Various blends are made, either by the mixture of pot still products, or by the addition of silent spirits from patent stills. In the latter case, cheapness is often the purpose of the blend, but it is also stated that it incorporates the mixture of several whiskies more efficiently. The blends, even when made from old spirits of various kinds, are frequently kept in bond for a considerable time ... Your committee do not recommend any increased restrictions on blending spirits. The trade has now assumed large proportions, and it is the object of blending to meet the tastes and wants of the public, both in regard to quality and price. The addition of patent still spirits ... may be viewed rather as a dilution than an adulteration, and, as in the case of the addition of water, is a legal act within the limits of strength regulating the sale of spirits.'

Vindicated and crowned with the success of his blending technique and of the grain distillery he had prompted, Andrew Usher, jun., died 1 November 1898, a respected and munificent patron of the city of Edinburgh, witness his £100,000 gift to build a public hall, the Usher Hall as we know it today, a striking monument to the brilliant idea of blending malt and grain whiskies. His son Sir Robert Usher, Bt, succeeded him and after the even division of the bench at Clerkenwell in the 'What Is Whisky?' cases, he was elected chairman of the dis-tillers-blenders deputation to wait upon John Burns, president of the Local Government Board. That alone is itself a valuable testimony to the primacy accorded by all in Scotland to the House of Usher in so far as related to blending. He was even elected chairman of the deputation in his absence from the initial meeting, an absence easily explained: he was very ill at the time. The result of the deputation was, of course, the 'What Is Whisky?' royal commission with which we opened this series of studies.

Some of Sir Robert's evidence at the commission is relevant to quote here. Asked about blending before 1860, he replied: 'I cannot answer that, but any little blending that may have been done prior to that date was done in duty paid stores, as it was not until the year 1860 that the Excise authorities, by 23 and 24 Vict., cc. 114, sec. 23, permitted blending in bond. The point is, that they allowed blending of pot and patent still whisky, but they did not permit the mixing of British and Foreign spirits.'

Before 1860, he continued, it was practically confined to Scotland: 'Very little indeed was sent to England or abroad. What business there was was in pot still, but it was sent to England in single casks, and really was dealt with in more as a curiosity.' But after 1860, said Sir Robert, 'the trade in Scotch whisky increased by leaps and bounds, the reason being, to my mind, that the blend is lighter and more easily digested, and thus more suited to the public taste. My personal opinion is that the pot still is improved and made more wholesome when blended with patent.'

Blending, he claimed, was already helping the export trade: 'Up to 1880,' he said, 'there was very little export business done. A small quantity of very high-flavoured pot still was sent to the United States, and it was mixed there with American spirit and sold as Scotch whisky. Since that time, owing to a certain extent to the failure of the brandy crop about that time, and also to the excellent quality sent abroad by the blenders, Scotch whisky has come into very great favour all over the world, and is now a trade of very great value to Scotland. My firm sends large quantities of blended whiskies to various parts of the world – America, India, Australia, South Africa, etc., where we have agents. We do not export much pure pot still whisky . . . Blending is really a business by itself which requires the greatest care, a fine sense of taste and smell, a large knowledge of the various whiskies, and, I may add, in most cases, a heavy outlay of capital.'

We have already examined the report of the commission, but suffice it to say that all the evidence indicates that Usher, particularly Andrew, jun., was the pioneer and patron of the modern blending technique. Yet in July 1916 there died in Glasgow one William Phaup

Lowrie, whose business, after years of close association was acquired by James Buchanan & Co. in 1906. At the time of his death, Lowrie was in his eighty-sixth year, having been born at Dalkeith in 1831. He served an apprenticeship with the Commercial Bank, Scotland, and in early manhood became associated with John Ramsay, of Kidalton, Islay, in the management of Port Ellen distillery on that island, and in Ramsay's numerous agencies. In the autumn of 1869 Lowrie started on his own account as a broker for Scotch whiskies and as a commission agent for selling them from an office in Ann Street, Glasgow. From there he moved, with improving circumstances, to end up in Washington Street.

In his abbreviated obituary notice – abbreviated because of war casualties – the claim was made that 'he initiated the present system of blending, and was the first to obtain an indulgence from the Excise to bottle in bond. This brought his firm in touch with the leading houses and paved the way for the "proprietary brands" now so common in the Trade.'

The assertion about Lowrie's being the first to obtain an indulgence to bottle in bond is questionable. In 1865 the warehousing of British compounded spirits for home consumption was authorised (28 and 29 Vict., c. 98) and about the same time, by 27 Vict., c. 12, provision was made for the reduction in strength of spirits with water in a specially approved warehouse. This was an indispensable step to bottling in bond: the reduction in strength from 100 proof or more to, say 80 or 85 proof. Then by 30 and 31 Vict., c. 27, provision was made for bottling spirits in a bonded warehouse for home consumption. This was an obvious corollary to their reduction in warehouse to bottling strength, and the dating of this Act – no question of an 'indulgence from the Excise to bottle in bond' arises – would well anticipate Lowrie's setting up for himself, and then as a broker and commission agent, which well preceded his bottling. In fact, he usually sold in bulk, in cask, and we can recall his expression to James Buchanan of the hope that bottled Scotch would not usurp bulk Scotches. Moreover, the 1860 Act, allowing blending duty free in bond, anticipated Lowrie's appearance on the scene by years.

The palm, then, in this contest as to priority in blending would seem indisputably to go to Andrew Usher, jun., to whom stands as memorial Usher Hall, Edinburgh, and the flourishing state of the Scotch whisky industry today. Some confirmation of Andrew's precedence may be found in the fact that the late Sir Oliver Riddell, who died in November 1918, only a few weeks after celebrating the sixtieth anniversary of his joining the firm of Andrew Usher & Co. was commemorated in obituary notices as 'one of the first, if not *the* first, Scotchmen to introduce blended Scotch whisky into England'.

Index

Aberdeen County Council, 21
Aberdeen grain distillery, 183
Aberfeldy distillery, 406, 456
Aberlour distillery, 425
Acetone, 212
Adelphi distillery, 143, 210, 399, 466
Adeney, W. E., on 1908 royal commission, 32
Advisory Committee of Alcohol Supplies, 210, 214–15
Agriculture and whisky production, 375 et seq.
Ainslie & Heilbron (Distillers) Ltd., 315
Ainslie, James & Co., 144, 408
Alberta, 303
Amalgamation, trend, 141–2; examples, 142 et seq., 394 et seq., 403 et seq., 417 et seq.; the great amalgamation, 430 et seq.
American interests in Scotland, 328–30, 380–2, 442, 444–5
American whiskey, 251, 264, 290, 291; off U.K. quota, 318, 357–8
Amulree, Lord, on 1930 royal commission, 226, 369
Anderson, J. L., of Dewar's, 121, 457
Anti-Cutting Association, 221
Aqua, 31–2
Archer, John, 236
Ardgowan distillery, 210, 214, 399
Armstrong, H., 73
Army and Navy Stores, 39
Ashley, Col. A., 288
Asquith, H. H., 117; and Edward VII, 119, 161, 214
Australia, 136; minimum age, 136; 149,

150, 151; best overseas market, 153; 157, 158, 273, 281, 325, 335, distilling investment in, 337 et seq.; 343–4
Avoniel distillery, 412, 427

Bagot, Major, 211
Bahamas, prohibition imports, 298–9; 335, 445
Bald, John & Co., 394, 395
Baldwin, S., 298, 326–7
Balfour, A. J., 102; Declaration of Palestine, 213
Balmoral, 185
Balvenie distillery, 449
Bankier distillery, 146, 405, 408
Barclay, J., 440; profile, 443–5, 461
Barton Distilling, Scotch interest, 382, 444
Bayne, S. C., 210
Beer, 1914 duty increase, 169
Begg, John, Ltd, 150, 184, 185, 277, 410
Belfast, 49, 408
Bell, Arthur & Sons Ltd, 416
Belloc, on 1909 budget, 109
Benrinnes-Glenlivet distillery, 132, 413, 443
Bermudas, 299
Billard, Rear Admiral F. C., U.S.N., 303–4
Birmingham, 258
Black & Ferguson, 432
Black Sea, 279
Blending, 1–2; Select Committee on, 4–5; on trial, 15 et seq.; 36, 41, 45, 58
Blending, primacy in, 479–89